Jazz Theory

Jazz Theory

Contemporary Improvisation, Transcription, and Composition

Ron Westray

FHB | FIRST HILL BOOKS

FIRST HILL BOOKS
An imprint of Wimbledon Publishing Company
www.anthempress.com

This edition first published in UK and USA 2024
by FIRST HILL BOOKS
75–76 Blackfriars Road, London SE1 8HA, UK
or PO Box 9779, London SW19 7ZG, UK
and
244 Madison Ave #116, New York, NY 10016, USA

British Library Cataloguing-in-Publication Data
A catalogue record for this book is available from the British Library.

Library of Congress Cataloging-in-Publication Data: 2023944415
A catalog record for this book has been requested.

ISBN-13: 978-1-83998-971-1 (Hbk)
ISBN-10: 1-83998-971-8 (Hbk)

ISBN-13: 978-1-83999-063-2 (Pbk)
ISBN-10: 1-83999-063-5 (Pbk)

Cover Credit: Ron Westray

This title is also available as an e-book.

CONTENTS

PREFACE

The stimulus for my research around jazz theory holds a direct relationship to my engagement in the Usonian musical system via Western Europe; and *this* volume represents a culmination of most of the theoretical-compositional skills that I set out to understand and master, as a student of music, over four decades ago. While I have had guidance from many teachers, much of the *real* work involved me learning in my own way and toiling to corroborate the theory of perceived sound in Western Art Music (of which "jazz" is a microcosm). Though I have been lauded for my prowess as an improvisor, the "data" has a chance to really flourish in the compositional *process* (which allows for contemplation and revision).

I am focused on demystifying traditional and contemporary conceptions (for myself) and "relaying" that information to the student that they may matriculate even faster. My teaching involves tools and references such as music transcription and chord/scale analysis that provide the student with historical and contemporary knowledge that is bolstered by discussions and explanations of (the) underlying harmonic implications and musical aesthetics—theory in practice.

To apply practical usage to conceptual and speculative ideas, my research explores and recalibrates the theoretical/artistic process of composed (sonic) gestures and musical expressions, including improvisation, related to a perceived harmonic landscape (i.e., the broad theoretical-sonic culture commonly, albeit imprecisely, referred to as "jazz") Albeit the common designation (jazz) could be more accurately perceived as "a" science of acoustic design (and auditory culture) dedicated to the process of overt theoretical application (and in support of the mastery of acoustic construction that captures and modifies, creates, and re-creates and reflects the "sound" that is clearly corroborated in the recorded history). In this volume, I have attempted to resolve certain disconnects between speculation, realization, and actualization—a complex-research *Meilleur.*

–Ron Westray

ACKNOWLEDGMENTS

I extend my heartfelt gratitude and acknowledgment to the following remarkable individuals and entities: Dr. Michael Coghlan, your sage advice and deep knowledge, coupled with the much-needed "jargon" regarding the subject matter, have been invaluable. Your guidance has significantly contributed to this volume, and for that, I am profoundly grateful. Tenor Saxophonist Kamil Qui: Your expertise in editing and transforming the Coltrane Solos has added a unique and masterful touch to this volume. Thank you for your dedication and talent. Stephen Smith, thank you for entrusting me with the care of your transcendent "Mao's Blues" transcription—a true pièce de résistance of the Y2K NYC piano style. I am honored to include it in this volume. Jisu Woo, my diligent and meticulous music copyeditor, your tireless efforts in transcribing and engraving the Coltrane drafts and the digital versions of my handwritten harmonic-graphs have been paramount in bringing this project to fruition. Thank you for your dedication and hard work. Tom McGill (PhD), thank you for the authoritative codification of my studio lectures with you (and for allowing me to use them within this volume). To my family, friends, allies, and associates, I express my deepest appreciation for your unwavering support throughout this journey. Your encouragement and belief in me have been a constant source of strength. Finally, my sincere gratitude to Anthem Press and the dedicated staff at Deanta Global. Thank you for believing in this project and for your invaluable contributions to it's success.

—Ron

INTRODUCTION

While jazz curricula have existed and evolved for over sixty years in the university setting, the consolidation of a unified didactic process in jazz pedagogy has not. As such, many misnomers and faulty practices have seeped into the teaching of the jazz art form. My teaching involves tools and references that provide the student with historical and contemporary knowledge. This volume represents a manual, method book, glossary, and compilation—a compendium. I have attempted to demystify the underlying theoretical constants that corroborate aural responses and theoretical structure. Though modes are discussed from a fundamental point of view, I am not (necessarily) a proponent of "modes of modes" as a (single) solution to jazz improvisation. With regard to scale-syllabus-subject-matter, there is some overlap. This is not mere redundancy. Mixed presentation of the material is crucial for serving aptitude and preference. I am delighted to present the papers of my former graduate student in composition, Tom McGill, PhD. Based on the thoroughness of his work, including his inventive diagrams, and his ability to objectively represent my taxonomy, I am utilizing Tom's Arranging Methods term paper (solely) as the chapter on composition—including many of his (studio) method-based arrangements—which serve as objective models (rather than my own compositions) of application *by* the student. Furthermore, I have included McGill's paper on Jazz Theory Methods—an impressive and efficient organization of *many* of the core jazz theories discussed in this volume, at large. I can't teach *how* I hear; but, having learned how to hear, I *can* teach *what* it is. By the same token, I realize that music, like Zen, needs no explanation. But framework is essential. After all, what is stuff without form; and what is form without stuff? Based on the size of this volume, the tendency *may* be to sift through the information. I offer that the reader should, or could, spend considerable time pondering the rules of even *one* line-item. While it may be said that more description was warranted for certain entries (e.g., the Graphs), I do not intend to explain *everything.* The Polymorphic Root System (PRS) offers the most creative and original techniques and concepts and forms the core strength and arguably presents the most valuable component of my work. The PRS employs chord symbol notation as a system of pitch class and set theory groupings—thereby enabling users not overly comfortable with the tradition of Western set theory or music notation (or even aware of these complex theoretical constructions) to easily embrace these compound structures. It is worth noting that this section contains the most detailed and explanatory texted material in support of the notated musical examples. In addition to perhaps not calling enough attention to the fact that in "jazz" we treat V^7(Mixolydian) as Tonic (I)—as corroborated by the fact that (based on root movement) the first-five bars (measures) of the (handy) "blues form" is (actually) a V-to-I resolution—an inverted-sonic-reality distorted by the rhythmic imperative of jazz. Within this "static" usage of a (typically) shifting-chord-quality is birthed a finite group of impositions referred to as alternates and extensions—matched by *specific* linear "paths" (scales). In fact, the "chord/scale" symbiosis is most prevalent in the Mixolydian (and Locrian) mode (other modes, not so much). Another Mixolydian "peeve" is the fact that composers and publishers are still writing and printing B^{b7} blues charts with "two-flats" in the starting key signature. In this case, the "key" is (theoretically) E^b Major. It's the same for the other two V^{7s} involved in the form: E^{b7} (4-flats) and F^7 (2-flats); students (and professionals) should stop "making up" things on "the blues" (V^7)—including (but not limited to) the imposition of the "blues scale" as a solution to fundamentally (yet figuratively) *changing* the key signatures *within* the form of the blues (just as you would if the key signatures were literal), which, they, kind of, are. Consequently, the teaching of Rhythm Changes is, also, completely remiss on information. For instance, the playing of relative minor (G^{m7}) on the VI chord is a moot point against B^b Major. Better stated (and corroborated) is the process of the VI7^{b9} > II7^{b9} > V7^{b9}—illuminating the power of inverted diminished and "altered" mixolydian functions. Furthermore, the tonic is better served in Ionian (i.e., Major$^{6/9}$) as heard in most of the landmark recordings of Rhythm Changes (I^7, not so much). The question comes to mind, "What can you [actually] teach about transcription?" I can show how it looks when it's done well. I don't mean the quality of the manuscript. I mean the metrical/melodic/harmonic accuracy (all the while retaining the "associated" nuances of the performer). This is why most of my energy has been dedicated to *some* of Coltrane's most manually/technically breathtaking solos on the Tenor and Soprano saxophones. Most importantly, my passion for decoding Coltrane is to point out the specificity of [t]his process—*the* process. Q: "How did I get started with the transcriptions?" A: Fundamentally, I knew the source recording(s) "by heart" (vocally) from listening to the "solo" for years before [even] starting. Q: "Well didn't Coltrane have other options during the solo?" A: Yes; but these are the choices that were made. Just as in life, we can't exercise *all* available options at once; we do what's appropriate (logical) for the contextualized environment. The Blues is a context. The Chord-Scale-Theory is a context. To say (or believe) that "solos" are constructed solely from the imagination is a wonderfully romantic notion; but it just doesn't "cut it" in the "real" arena of jazz improvisation. Western musical theory, composition, improvisation, and the chord/scale relationship are all highly structured and informed by a long history of development and analysis. While there's certainly a level of creativity and interpretation involved, it's not accurate to characterize these aspects as purely guesswork. Let's break down each component to clarify: **Musical Theory**: Western music theory is based on a systematic understanding of musical elements such as rhythm, harmony, melody, and form. It's grounded in centuries of academic study and analysis, providing a structured framework for understanding how musical elements relate to each other. **Composition**: Composition in Western music is guided by principles of harmony, melody, rhythm, and form. Composers draw upon established techniques and rules to create coherent and expressive musical works. While creativity and inspiration play a significant role, composers apply their understanding of musical theory to shape and structure their compositions. **Improvisation:** Even in improvisation, musicians draw upon their knowledge of scales, chords, rhythmic patterns, and musical styles. Improvisation is a creative act, but it's informed by a deep understanding of musical theory and stylistic conventions. Skilled improvisers use this knowledge to create spontaneous and cohesive musical expressions. **The Chord/Scale Relationship**: The relationship between chords and scales is a fundamental aspect of Western music theory. Different scales are associated with specific chords, and understanding these relationships is crucial for creating harmonically accurate compositional and improvisational choices. **The history of Jazz**: Like other genres in Western music, Jazz is continually documented and analyzed. Jazz has its own set of theories, improvisational practices, and stylistic conventions. Musicians and scholars have studied its evolution, styles, and notable figures to understand and appreciate its development. These aspects are built on a strong foundation of knowledge, analysis, and established principles (rather than guesswork). I am not proposing that "scales and hexachords" are what great solos, compositions, or theories are made of. I *am* saying that it takes this "data" to learn *how* to hear and *what* to think. **Transcription:** It is of utmost importance that we *demystify* the world of music and dispel myths to foster a deeper understanding and appreciation among both enthusiasts and professionals. By promoting and providing clear communication, collaborative learning environments, and evidence-based explanations (such as transcriptions), myths and misconceptions concerning music can be debunked. Freedom comes by way of structure. Finally, I offer this volume as a guide—a non-emotional-systematic-approach to musical expression and exploration.[1]

"There's no time for feelings when you're playing bebop."—R.W.

1 "[John] Coltrane's music can be considered as an example of what Deleuze refers to as 'a process of becoming,' whereby individual modes undergo a continual flux or transformation, resulting in the development of new potentialities" (Bishop, 2012).

MUSIC IS MATH: AN EFFECTIVE APPROACH TO TEACHING JAZZ IMPROVISATION

I believe that theory *is* composition, *is* improvisation—and that music *is* math.

You can view the chord-to-scale relationship in jazz improvisation as "data" that can be transposed throughout relative and absolute functions . Ultimately, translating music into math helps to demystify simple improvisation, and it levels the playing field for specialists (and non-specialists) to approach jazz theory, improvisation, transcription, and composition.

What is this knowledge?

A. Diatonicism
B. Bitonality
C. Polytonality

What are the elements that comprise it?

A. Mode Implications/Usage
B. Chord/Scale Relationships
C. Advanced Scale Usage
D. Rhythmic Conventions & Rhythmic Improvisation

How is this knowledge harvested?

A. Cognition (**C**omprehension, **A**pprehension, **R**easoning, **D**iscernment)
B. Ear Training
C. Memorization

The Process: "Using the math"

A. Conceptualization
   1. The Idea
   2. Patterns (conventional)
B. Formulation
   1. Translation
C. Articulation/Execution
   1. Technical Mastery (Virtuosity)
D. Context
   1. Aural Feedback (Performer's "Voice")
   2. Kinesthetic Feedback (The Musical Environment)
   3. Decisions, decisions…

At first, not even the legends of jazz could play.
They had to learn how to hear and what to think.
See with your ears; and *hear* with your eyes. —R.W.

Harangue III: The Perfect Pitch

Absolute pitch (AP), often called perfect pitch, is the rare ability to name or re-create a given musical note without the benefit of a visual reference.

The chord/scale relationship in jazz improvisation is corroborated by the recorded history of classic jazz. The difference in the "level" of two jazz-improvisors can ultimately be reduced to sheer memorization—not just hearing (as to position perfect pitch as "the solution" to jazz improvisation).

"That's like saying that someone who knows all the words in the dictionary is automatically a great writer."—R.W.

To the point, absent harmonic understanding, pitch-recognition has "zip" to do with jazz vocabulary. What's jazz vocabulary? Listen. It's "the sound" you expect to hear. It's there in the styles of all the great-harmonic-improvisors. It's a common thread in the "knitting and weaving" process. Imitation leads to stylization; and the transcription process must be converted into general, theoretical wherewithal. I would also propose that there is no such thing as hearing the note "before" you play it. I would say that one should "know" the note before they play it. Having completed many of the most complex Coltrane (sheets-of-sound) solos, I am confident that "Trane" is not hearing the sound prior to such expositions. It's all application and confirmation (post-note). In Western music (of which jazz is a microcosm), technique (including hearing) is established through the memorization and the repetition of scalar/linear values. Harmonic specificity and velocity (accuracy and precision) within jazz improvisation (not to be confused with blues "expression") are achieved through preparation (not by fiat).

Harangue IV: The Blues Scale Does Not Exist in Nature

The Blues scale is a six-note-minor-pentatonic-scale containing a #4 scale degree in relationship to the root-note of the scale. This scale is commonly used in the twelve-bar blues progression, Boogie-Woogie, Soul, RnB, Jazz, and Funk—to name a few.

It is a hybrid-scale—an alternative-fact assembled within a formerly burgeoning jazz-education-system; and, somewhere along the way, your well-meaning band-director told you to play "this on this" so that the adjudication/concert would go off without a hitch. It was the same when I matriculated. Now, it's time to stop using it as a short cut for teaching and playing the blues form (i.e., V^7 chords). It is an inaccurate-harmonic-solution (and a poor choice). Dominant chords (V^7) are supported by the Mixolydian scale producing a major-third (as per the chord-root). The blues scale (with its minor-third) does not describe the true-quality of the V^7 chord. Yeah, Yeah, "Coltrane 'walked the bar' in blues-bands down south." But I'm sure he was not "putting down" the blues scale, as such.

-Diatonic Studies (Prerequisites) **See Section 6.2 (The Root Progression System)**

Scale Quality/Type	**Related Chord Symbols (partial)**
Ionian/Augmented	maj7/maj7+5
Aeolian	m(b6), m7, m9, m11
Dorian	m6, m7, m9, m11
Major Lydian	maj7, maj7#11
Mixolydian	V7, V9, V13
Dominant Bebop	V7
Major6 Diminished Scale[2]	maj7+5
Whole Tone	V7, V7#5
Ionian/Aeolian	maj7, m7 (rel.)
Harmonic Minor	m(b6), m(maj7), m7b5
Blues Scale[3]	(V7*) Dorian, ii V7 (I)

2 The Major6 diminished scale is a major scale with an added flat-sixth scale degree (i.e., the Maj6 bebop and min6 bebop scales). The movement of the chord inversions degrees (the I chord, major or minor, and its respective diminished chord) are played like a scale and all the inversions of M6, m6, and dim7 can be utilized accordingly. Hence, the min6 diminished scale is a harmonic minor scale (ascending) with an added natural 6th scale degree.

3 Albeit a popular root-reference for V7*, this volume does not purport the use of the Blues scale as a superlative choice to the Mixolydian scale (and its exponents). Conversely, the Blues scale does have excellent utility in the Dorian mode (via tonic and

-Fundamental Applications (Prerequisites)

- All scale qualities and types, per scale degree (i.e., through the modes), in all twelve keys, ascending (and descending) to top and bottom of instrumental, technical range.
- Four qualities of triads (Major, Minor, Augmented, Diminished), through inversions, in all twelve keys, ascending (and descending) to top and bottom of instrumental/technical range.
- Diatonic Seventh Chords[4] for all scale qualities and types, per scale degree (mode), through inversions, in all twelve keys, ascending (and descending) to top and bottom of instrumental/technical range.

side-slipping POV's) and offers complex tension and release (alternate) note choices when super-imposed onto the common ii-V7-I progression—anticipating the resolution to tonic; from a comprehensive standpoint, it presents a needed (formulaic) challenge towards overall proficiency.

4 A four-note-tertian-chord per scale degrees: **1** (root), **3** (third), **5** (fifth), **7** (seventh), 2-4-6-8, 3-5-7-9, etc.

Chapter 1

ADVANCED SCALE STUDY

<u>Section 1) Forms of Dominant Scale</u>

1.1.1. Mixolydian

APPENDIX 1.1.1.
MIXOLYDIAN

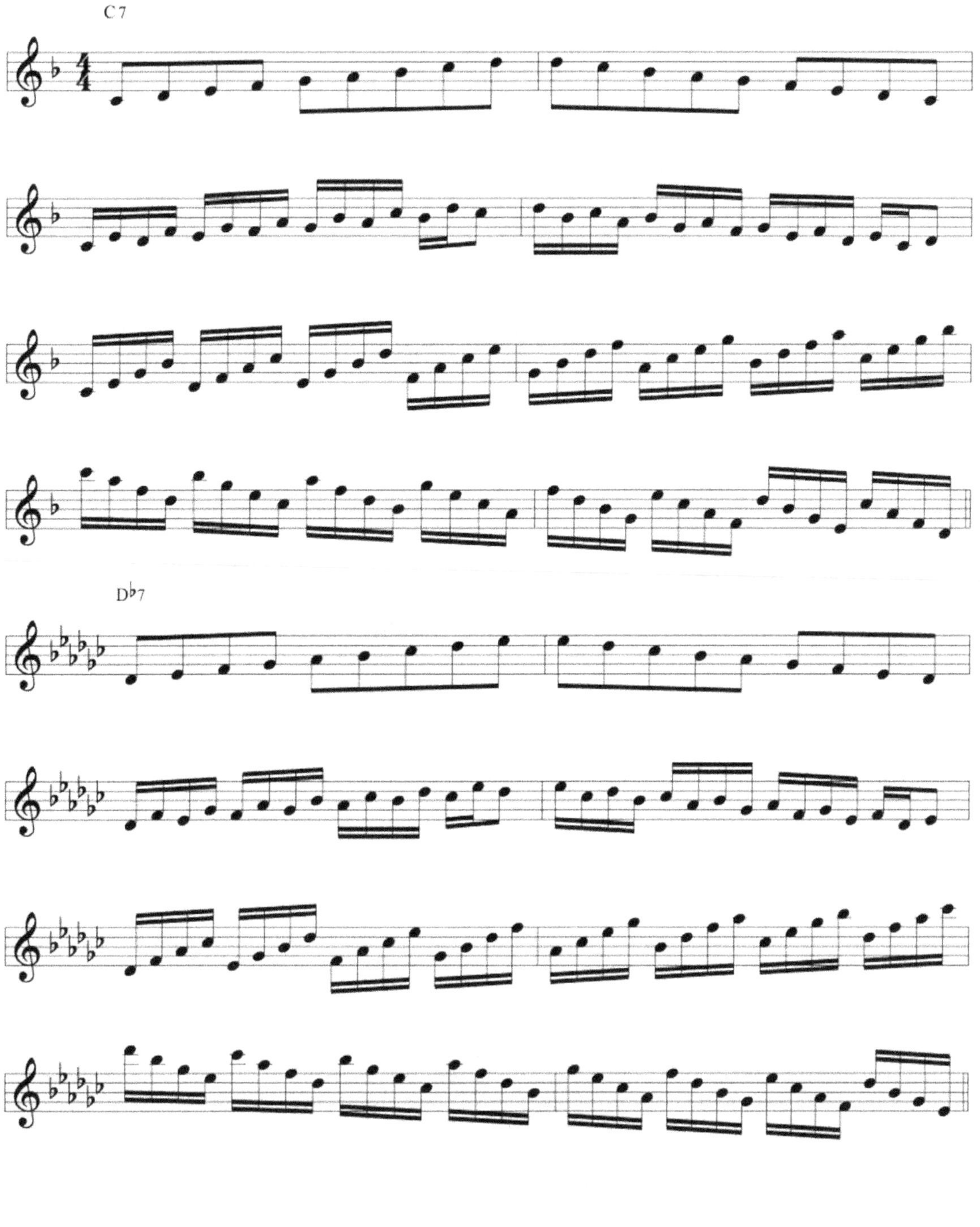

Appendix 1.1.1. Mixolydian

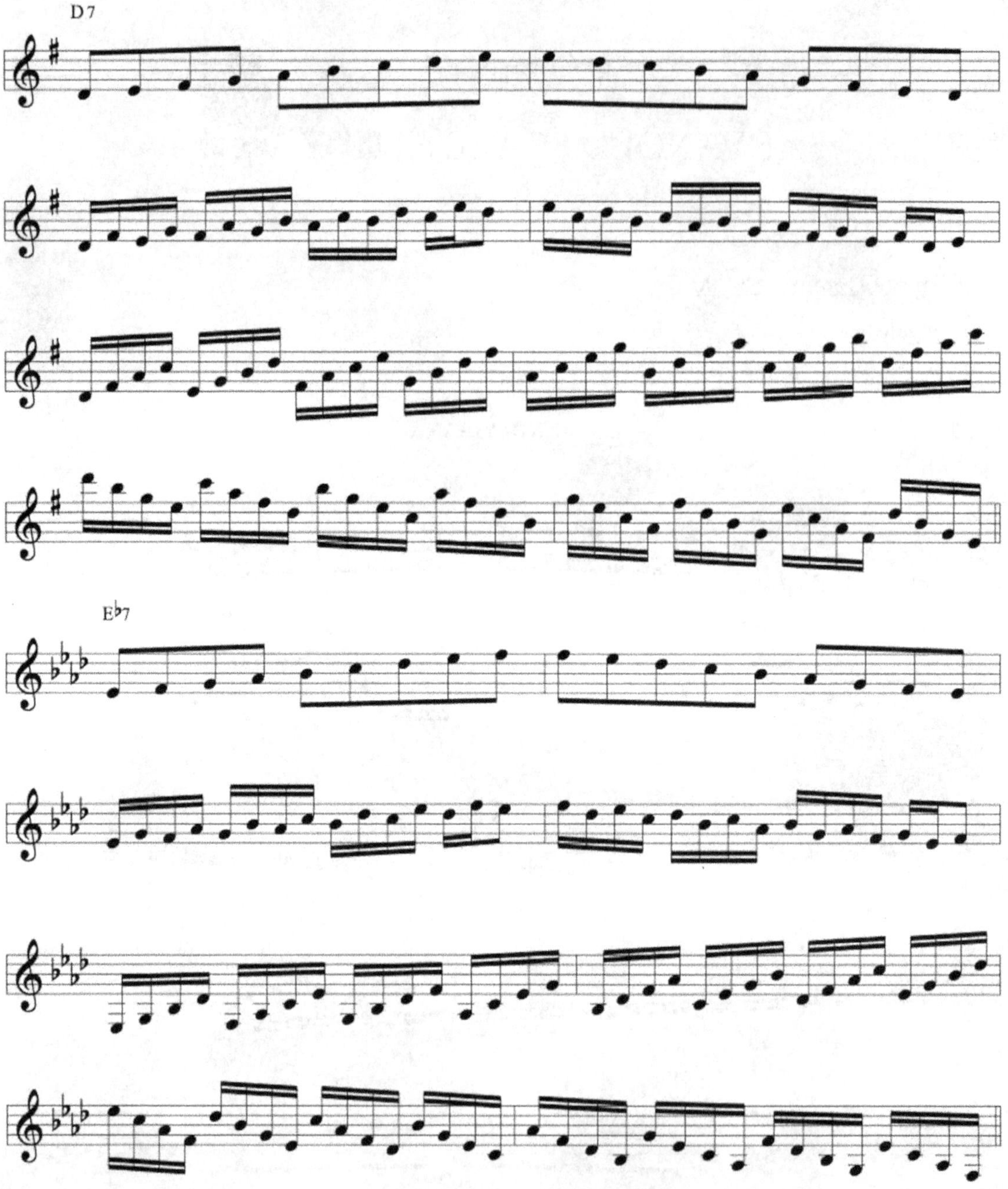

Appendix 1.1.1. Mixolydian

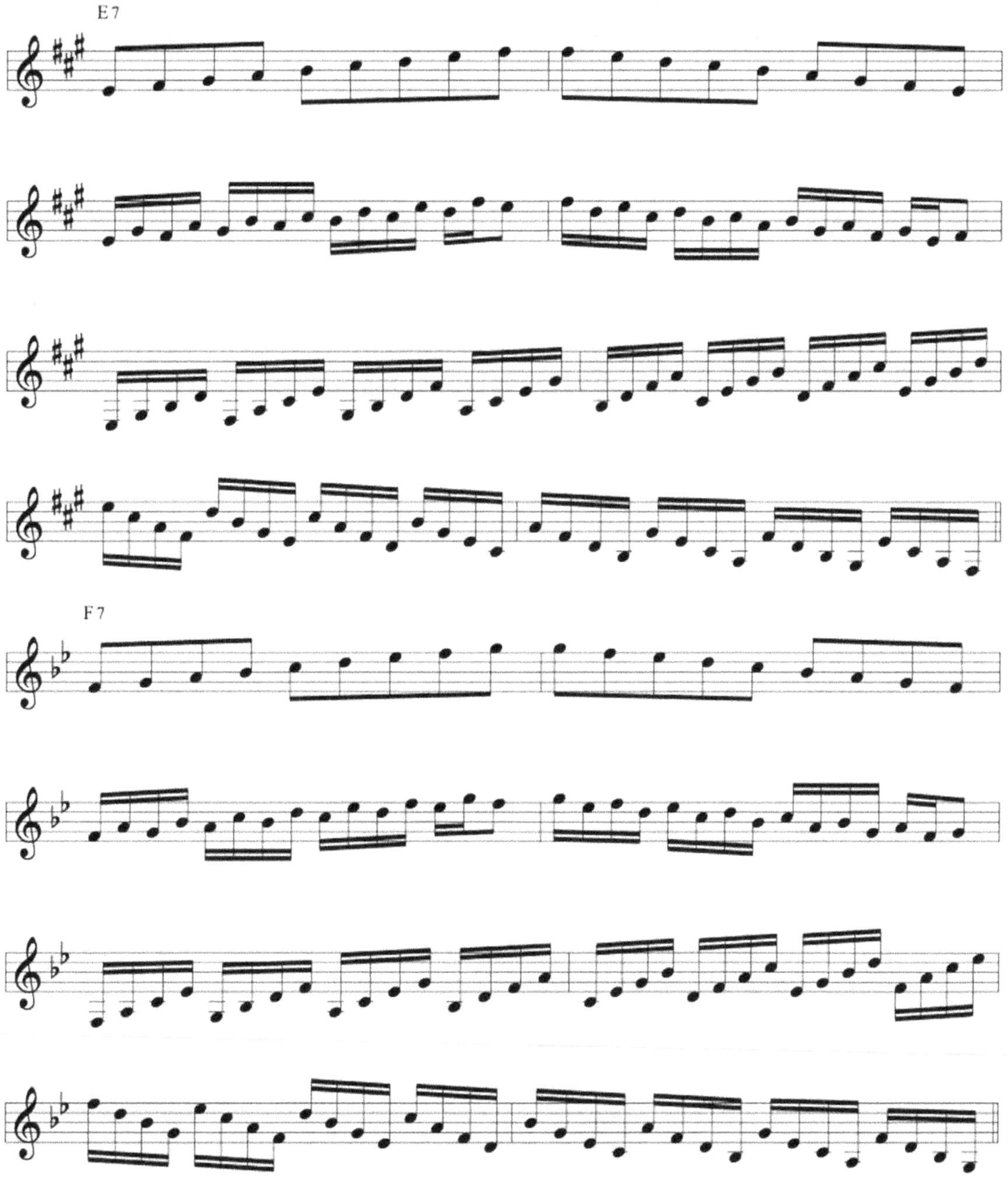

Appendix 1.1.1. Mixolydian

Appendix 1.1.1. Mixolydian

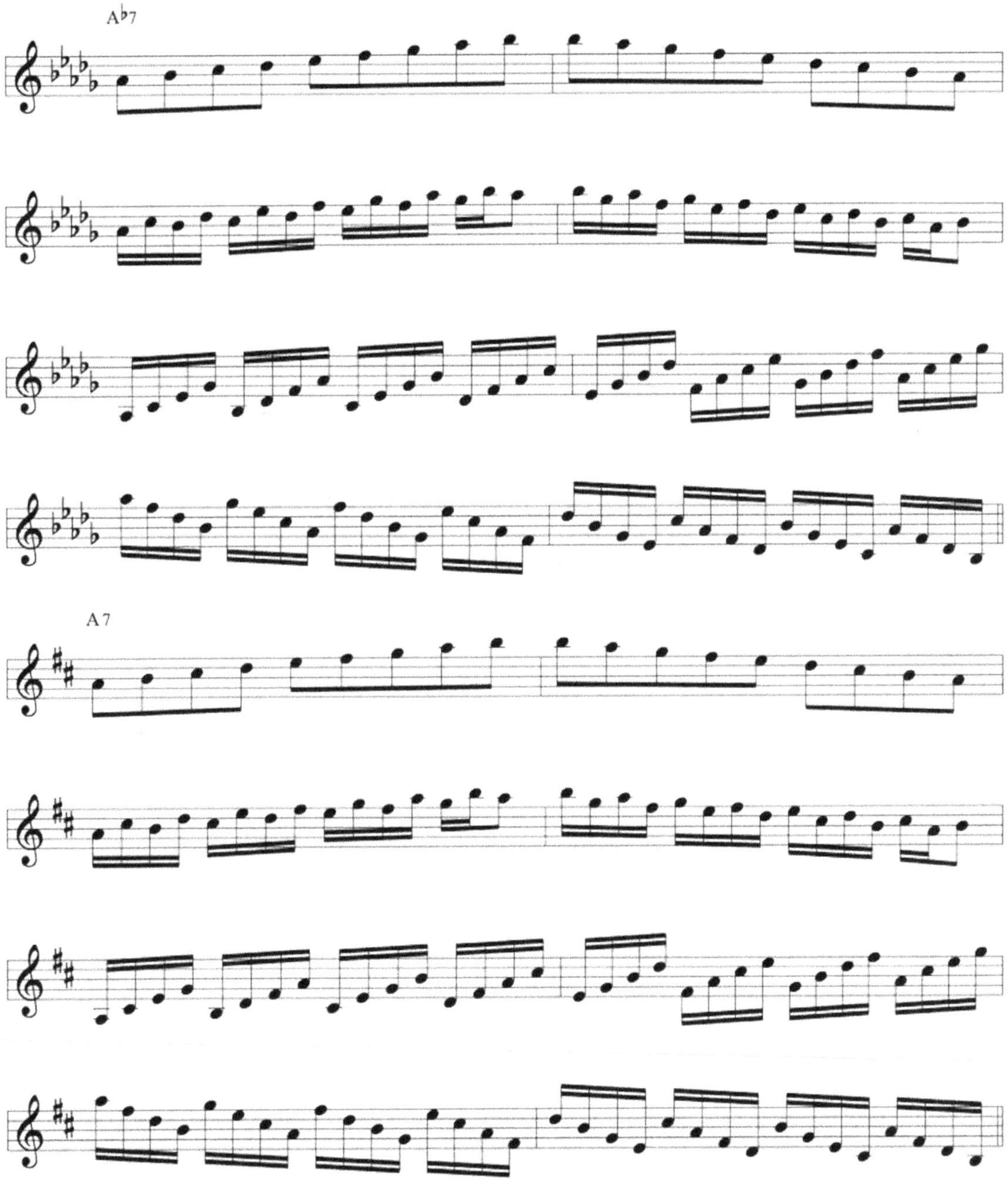

Appendix 1.1.1. Mixolydian

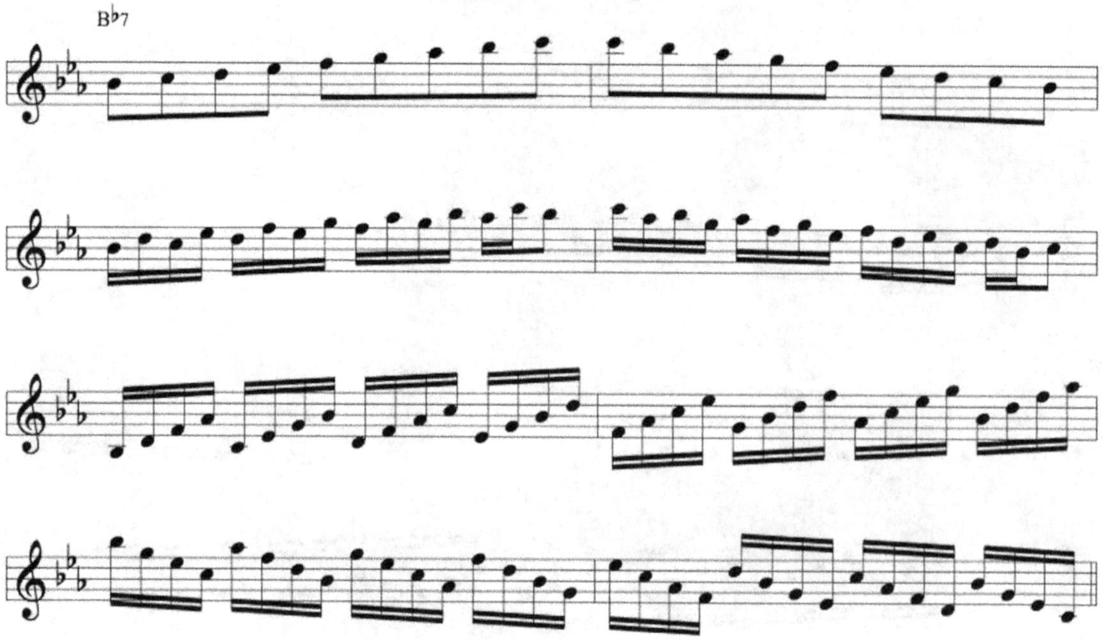

Section 1) Forms of Dominant Scale

1.1.2. Lydian Dominant
1.1.3. Melodic Minor Equivalent

Description: See Chapter 8.2

APPENDIX 1.1.2./1.1.3.
LYDIAN DOMINANT/MELODIC MINOR EQUIVALENT

1.1.2. C 7(♯11)

1.1.3. Gm(maj7)

Appendix 1.1.2./1.1.3. Lydian Dominant/Melodic Minor Equivalent

1.1.2. D♭7(♯11)

1.1.3. A♭m(maj7)

Appendix 1.1.2./1.1.3. Lydian Dominant/Melodic Minor Equivalent

1.1.2. D 7(♯11)

1.1.3. A m(maj7)

Appendix 1.1.2./1.1.3. Lydian Dominant/Melodic Minor Equivalent

1.1.2.

1.1.3.

Appendix 1.1.2./1.1.3. Lydian Dominant/Melodic Minor Equivalent

1.1.2.

1.1.3.

Appendix 1.1.2./1.1.3. Lydian Dominant/Melodic Minor Equivalent

1.1.2. F 7(♯11)

1.1.3. Cm(maj7)

Appendix 1.1.2./1.1.3. Lydian Dominant/Melodic Minor Equivalent

1.1.2. G♭7(♯11)

1.1.3. D♭m(maj7)

Appendix 1.1.2./1.1.3. Lydian Dominant/Melodic Minor Equivalent

1.1.2. G7(♯11)

1.1.3. Dm(maj7)

Appendix 1.1.2./1.1.3. Lydian Dominant/Melodic Minor Equivalent

1.1.2. A♭7(♯11)

1.1.3. E♭m(maj7)

Appendix 1.1.2./1.1.3. Lydian Dominant/Melodic Minor Equivalent

1.1.2. A 7(♯11)

1.1.3. Em(maj7)

Appendix 1.1.2./1.1.3. Lydian Dominant/Melodic Minor Equivalent

1.1.2.

1.1.3.

Section 1) Forms of Dominant Scale

1.1.4. Super Locrian

Description: See Chapter 8.2

APPENDIX 1.1.4.
SUPER LOCRIAN
(with hybrid key signatures)

Appendix 1.1.4. Super Locrian

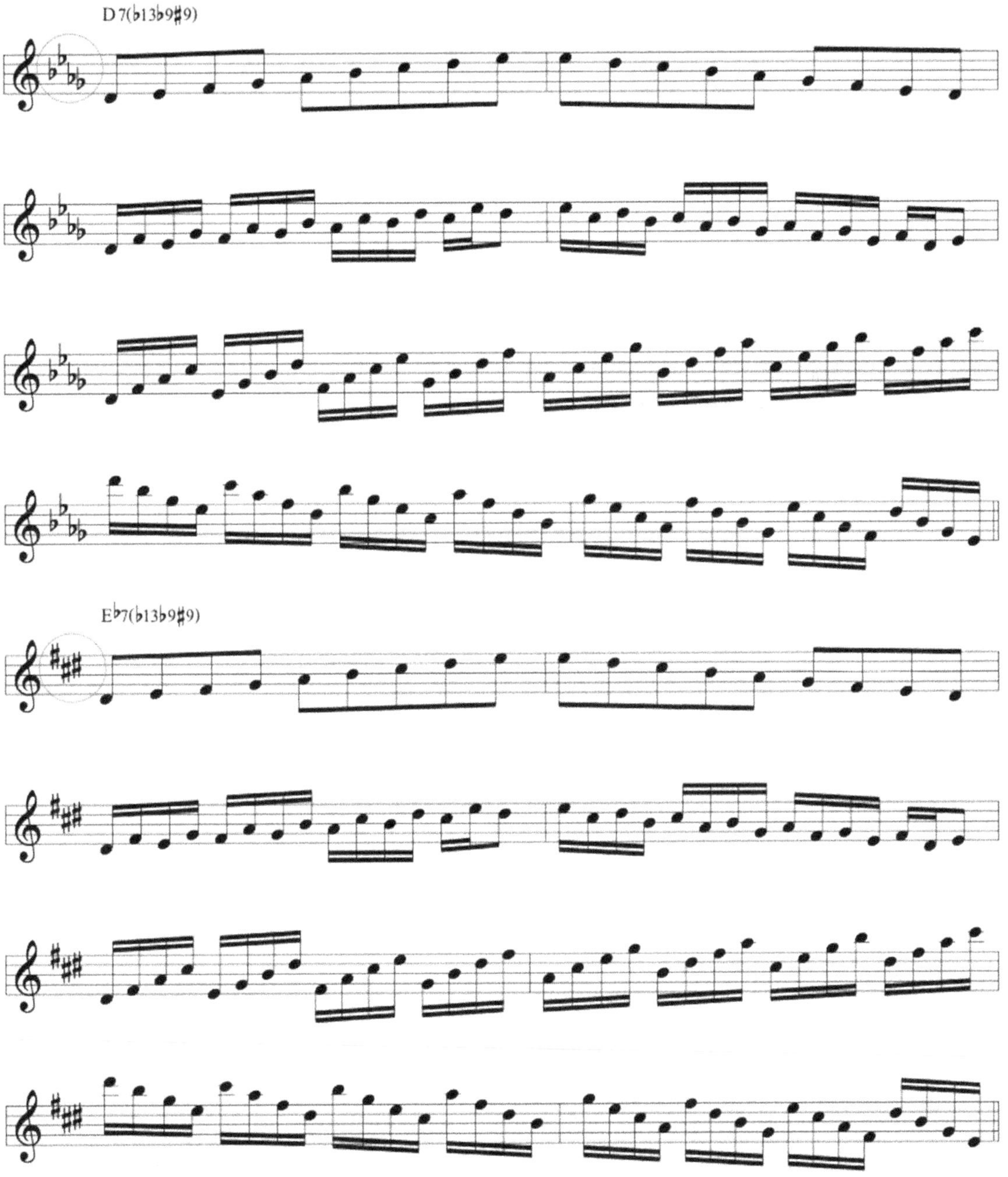

Appendix 1.1.4. Super Locrian

Appendix 1.1.4. Super Locrian

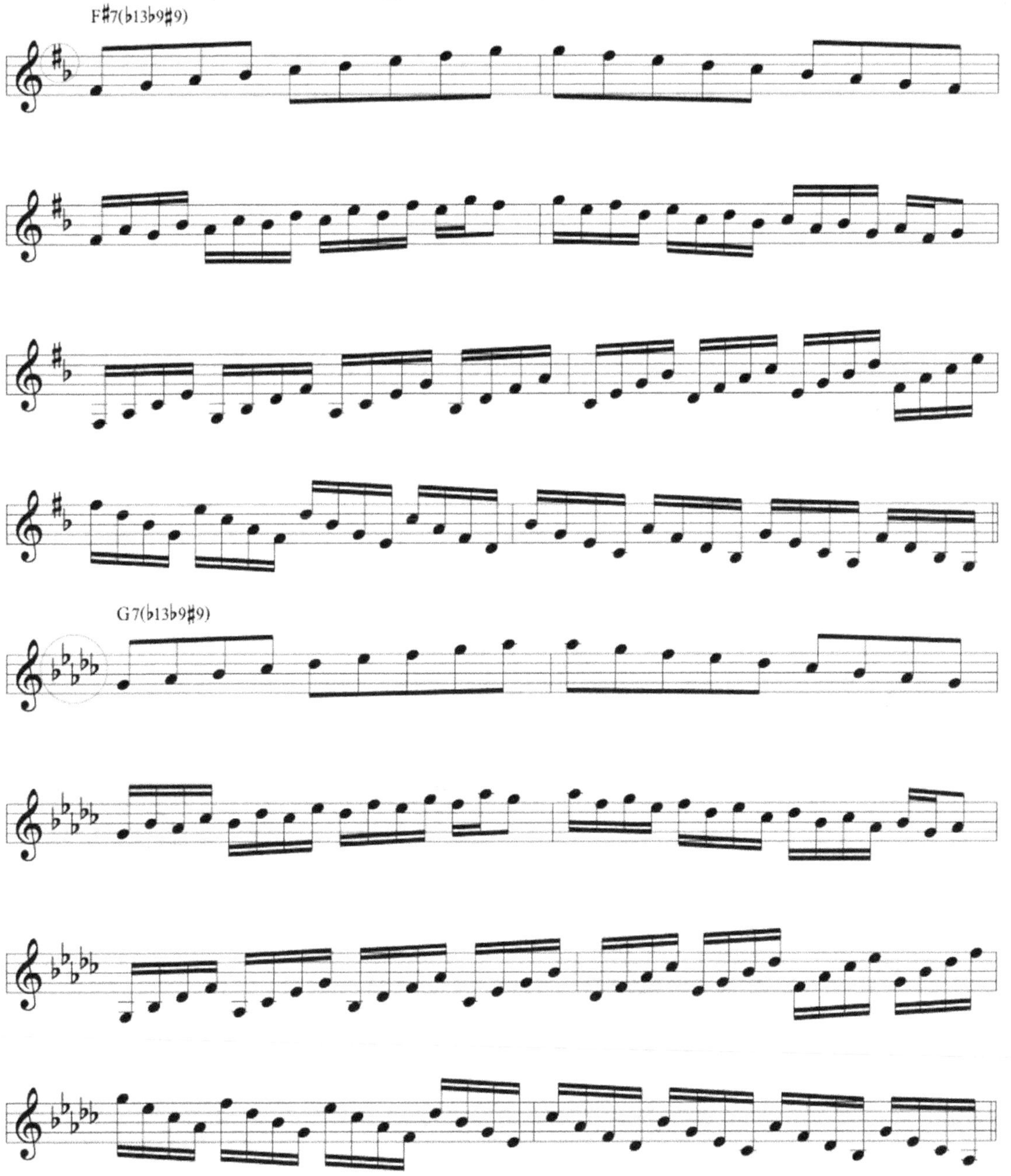

Appendix 1.1.4. Super Locrian

Appendix 1.1.4. Super Locrian

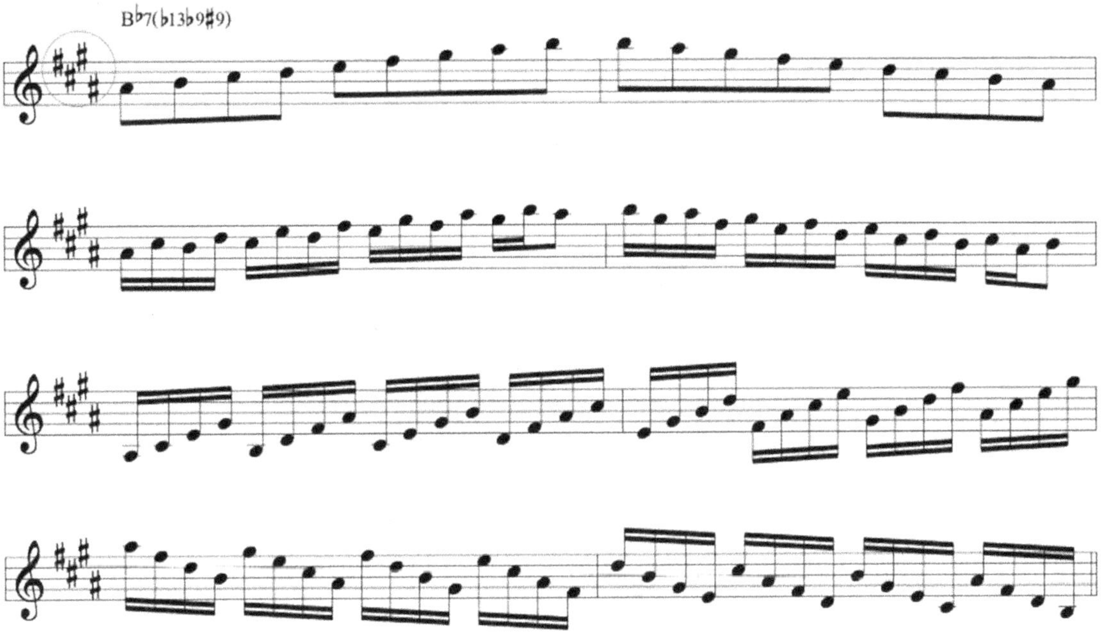

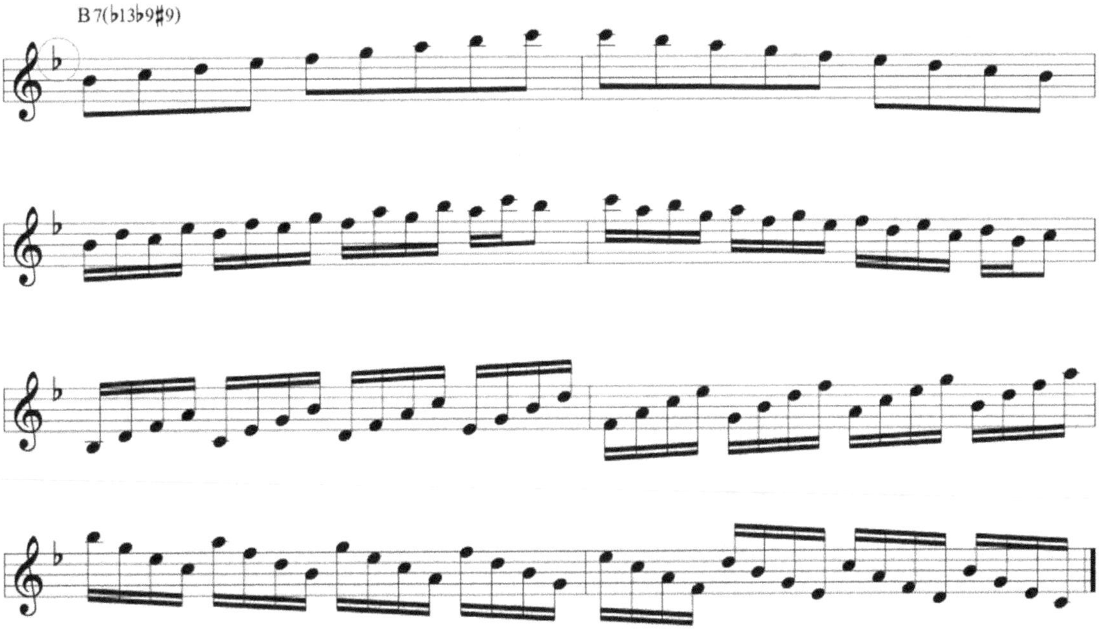

Section 1) Forms of Dominant Scale

1.1.5. Whole Tone Scale

1.1.5.1. Whole Tone (Scale/Thirds)

1.1.5.2. Augmented Triads (Per Degree)

Description: See Chapter 8.2

APPENDIX 1.1.5.1./1.1.5.2.
WHOLE TONE SCALE, THIRDS/AUGMENTED TRIADS PER DEGREE

1.1.5.1. C+7

1.1.5.2. C+7

1.1.5.1. D♭+7

1.1.5.2. D♭+7

Appendix 1.1.5.1./1.1.5.2. Whole Tone Scale, Thirds/Augmented Triads Per Degree

1.1.5.1. D+7

1.1.5.2. D+7

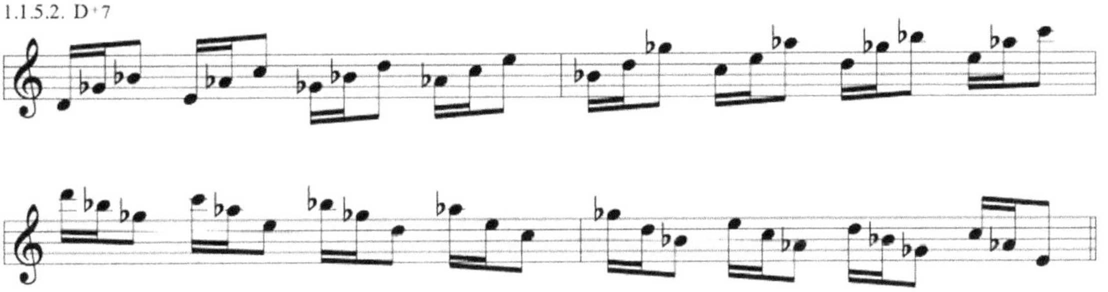

1.1.5.1. E♭+7

1.1.5.2. E♭+7

Appendix 1.1.5.1./1.1.5.2. Whole Tone Scale, Thirds/Augmented Triads Per Degree

1.1.5.1. E+7

1.1.5.2. E+7

1.1.5.1. F+7

1.1.5.2. F+7

Appendix 1.1.5.1./1.1.5.2. Whole Tone Scale, Thirds/Augmented Triads Per Degree

1.1.5.1. G♭+7

1.1.5.2. G♭+7

1.1.5.1. G+7

1.1.5.2. G+7

Appendix 1.1.5.1./1.1.5.2. Whole Tone Scale, Thirds/Augmented Triads Per Degree

1.1.5.1. A♭+7

1.1.5.2. A♭+7

1.1.5.1. A+7

1.1.5.2. A+7

Appendix 1.1.5.1./1.1.5.2. Whole Tone Scale, Thirds/Augmented Triads Per Degree

1.1.5.1. B♭+7

1.1.5.2. B♭+7

1.1.5.1. B+7

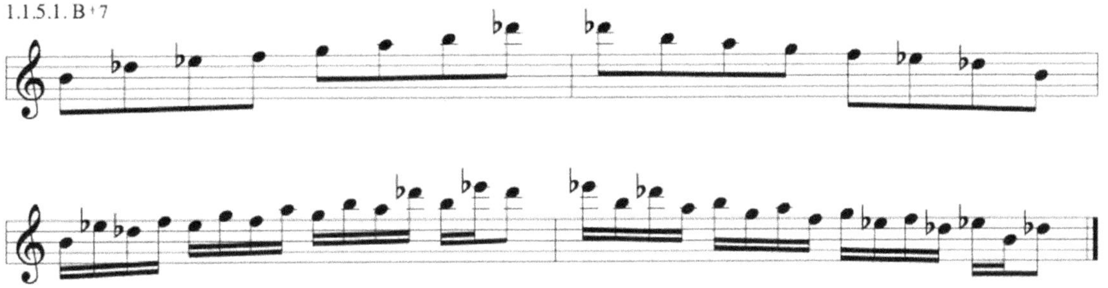

1.1.5.2. B+7

Section 1) Forms of Dominant Scale

1.1.5.3. Augmented Triads Weaving Per Degree

Description: See Chapter 8.2

APPENDIX 1.1.5.3.
AUGMENTED TRIAD WEAVING PER DEGREE

Appendix 1.1.5.3. Augmented Triad Weaving Per Degree

Appendix 1.1.5.3. Augmented Triad Weaving Per Degree

<u>Section 2) Augmented Scale/Melodic Minor Equivalent</u>

1.2.1. Augmented Scale

1.2.2. Melodic Minor Equivalent

Description: See Chapter 8.2

APPENDIX 1.2.1./1.2.2.
Augmented Scale/Melodic Minor Equivalent

Appendix 1.2.1./1.2.2. Augmented Scale/Melodic Minor Equivalent

1.2.1. D maj7(♯5)

1.2.2. D maj7(♯5)

1.2.1. E♭maj7(♯5)

1.2.2. E♭maj7(♯5)

Appendix 1.2.1./1.2.2. Augmented Scale/Melodic Minor Equivalent

1.2.1. E maj7(♯5)

1.2.2. E maj7(♯5)

1.2.1. F maj7(♯5)

1.2.2. F maj7(♯5)

Appendix 1.2.1./1.2.2. Augmented Scale/Melodic Minor Equivalent

1.2.1. G♭maj7(♯5)

1.2.2. G♭maj7(♯5)

1.2.1. G maj7(♯5)

1.2.2. G maj7(♯5)

Appendix 1.2.1./1.2.2. Augmented Scale/Melodic Minor Equivalent

1.2.1. A♭maj7(♯5)

1.2.2. A♭maj7(♯5)

1.2.1. A maj7(♯5)

1.2.2. A maj7(♯5)

Appendix 1.2.1./1.2.2. Augmented Scale/Melodic Minor Equivalent

1.2.1. B♭maj7(♯5)

1.2.2. B♭maj7(♯5)

1.2.1. B maj7(♯5)

1.2.2. B maj7(♯5)

Section 3a) Diminished and Inverted Diminished Scales

1.3.1. Diminished Scale/Thirds

APPENDIX 1.3.1.
DIMINISHED SCALE, THIRDS

Appendix 1.3.1. Diminished Scale, Thirds

Appendix 1.3.1. Diminished Scale, Thirds

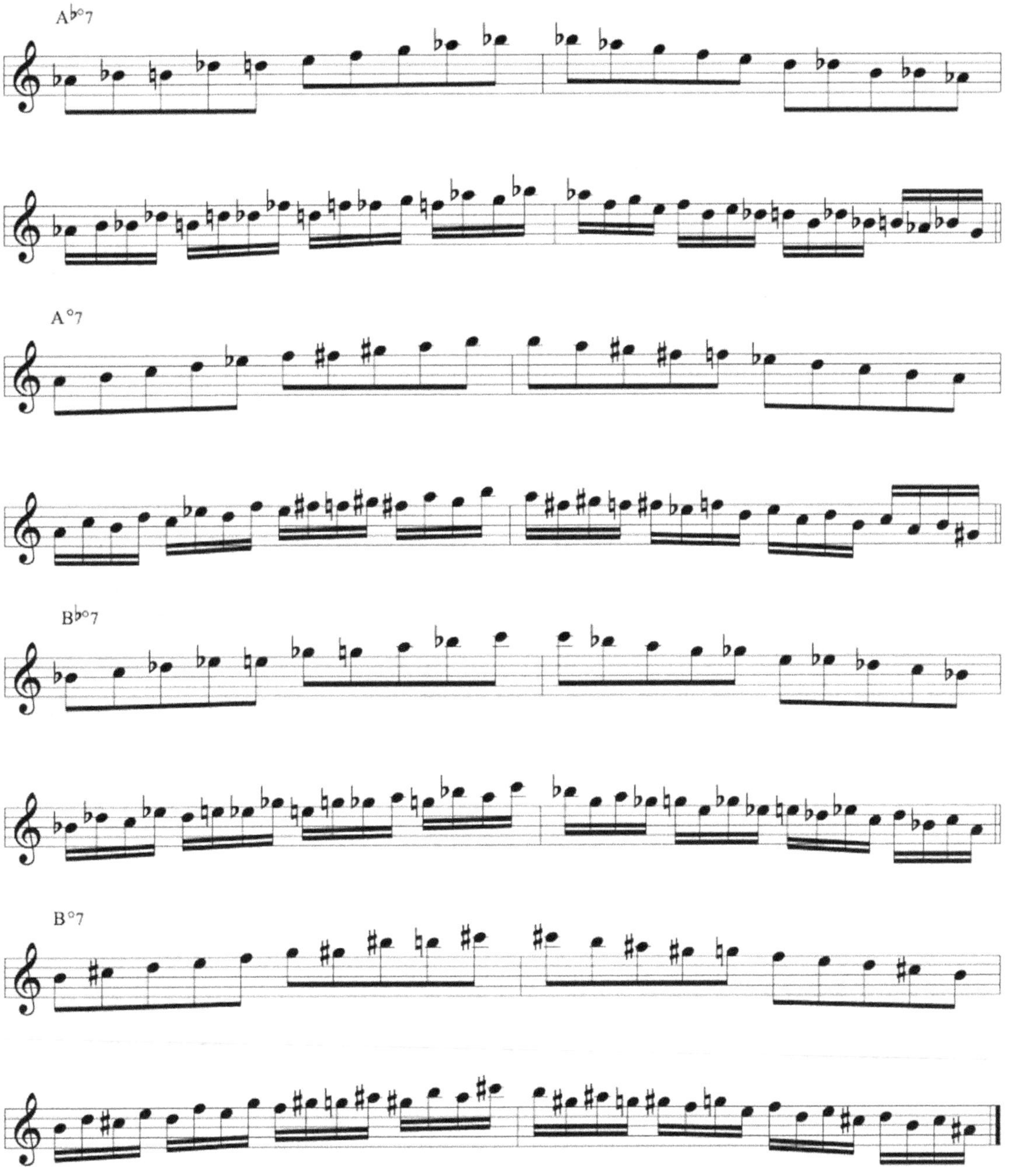

Section 3a) Diminished and Inverted Diminished Scales

1.3.2. Diminished Scale 7th Chords Per Degree

Description: See Chapter 8.2

APPENDIX 1.3.2.
DIMINISHED SCALE 7TH CHORDS PER DEGREE

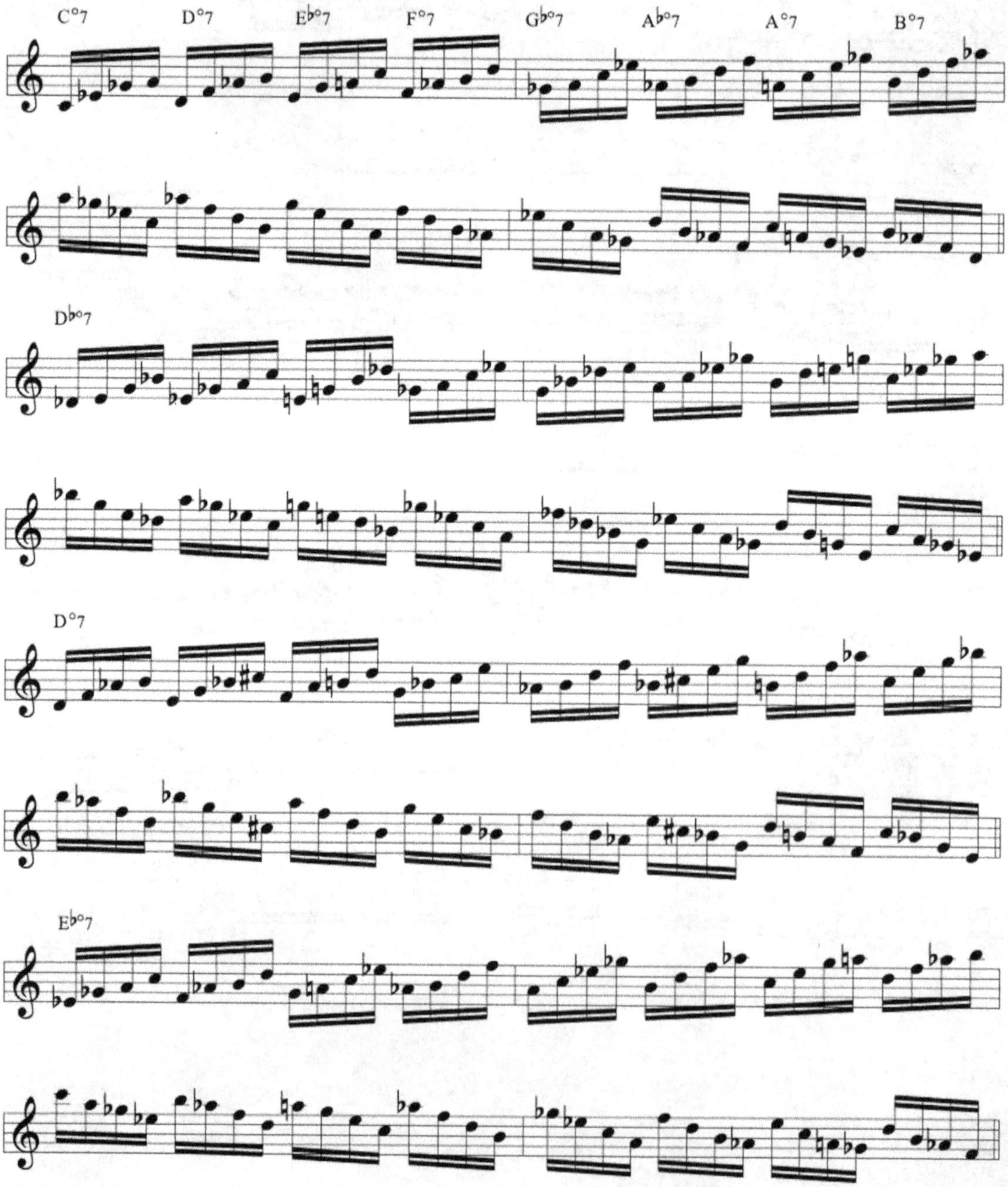

Appendix 1.3.2. Diminished Scale 7th Chords Per Degree

E°7

F°7

G♭°7

G°7

Appendix 1.3.2. Diminished Scale 7th Chords Per Degree

A♭°7

A°7

B♭°7

B°7

Section 3a) Diminished and Inverted Diminished Scales

1.3.3. Diminished Scale 7th Chords Weaving Per Degree

Description: See Chapter 8.2

APPENDIX 1.3.3.
DIMINISHED SCALE 7TH CHORDS WEAVING PER DEGREE

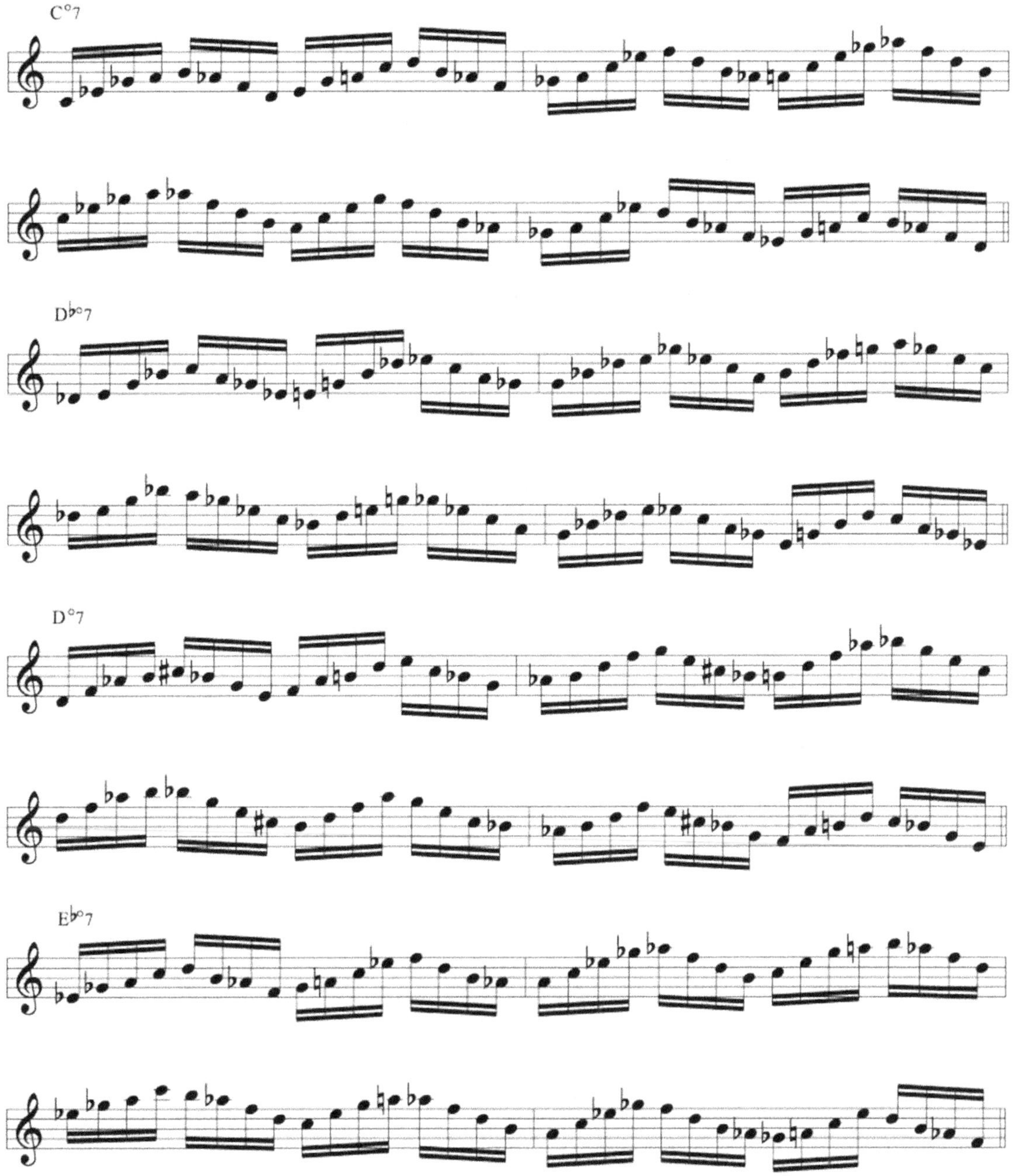

Appendix 1.3.3. Diminished Scale 7th Chords Weaving Per Degree

Appendix 1.3.3. Diminished Scale 7th Chords Weaving Per Degree

Section 3a) Diminished and Inverted Diminished Scales

1.3.4. Inverted Diminished Scale/Inverted Diminished Scale in Thirds

Description: The half/whole scale as per the V^7root (Inverted Diminished) The minor third relationship within Inverted Diminished just three points of departure before repeating. $V7^{b9\ 13}$ imply the point of departure for inverted diminished.

APPENDIX 1.3.4.
INVERTED DIMINISHED SCALE, THIRDS

Appendix 1.3.4. Inverted Diminished Scale, Thirds

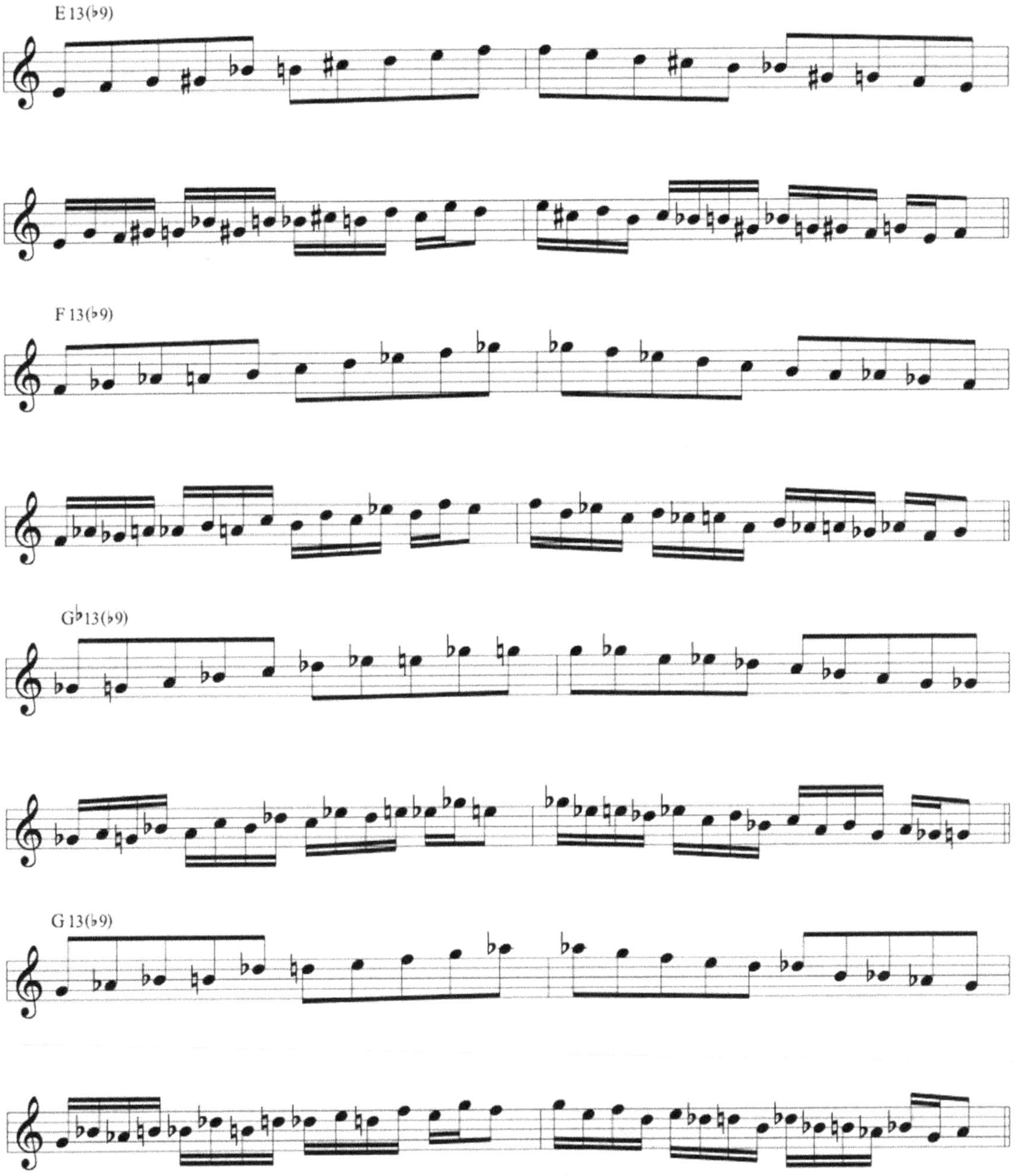

Appendix 1.3.4. Inverted Diminished Scale, Thirds

Section 3a) Diminished and Inverted Diminished Scales

1.3.5. Inverted Diminished Scale 7th Chords Per Degree

Description: See Chapter 8.2

APPENDIX 1.3.5.
INVERTED DIMINISHED SCALE 7TH CHORDS PER DEGREE

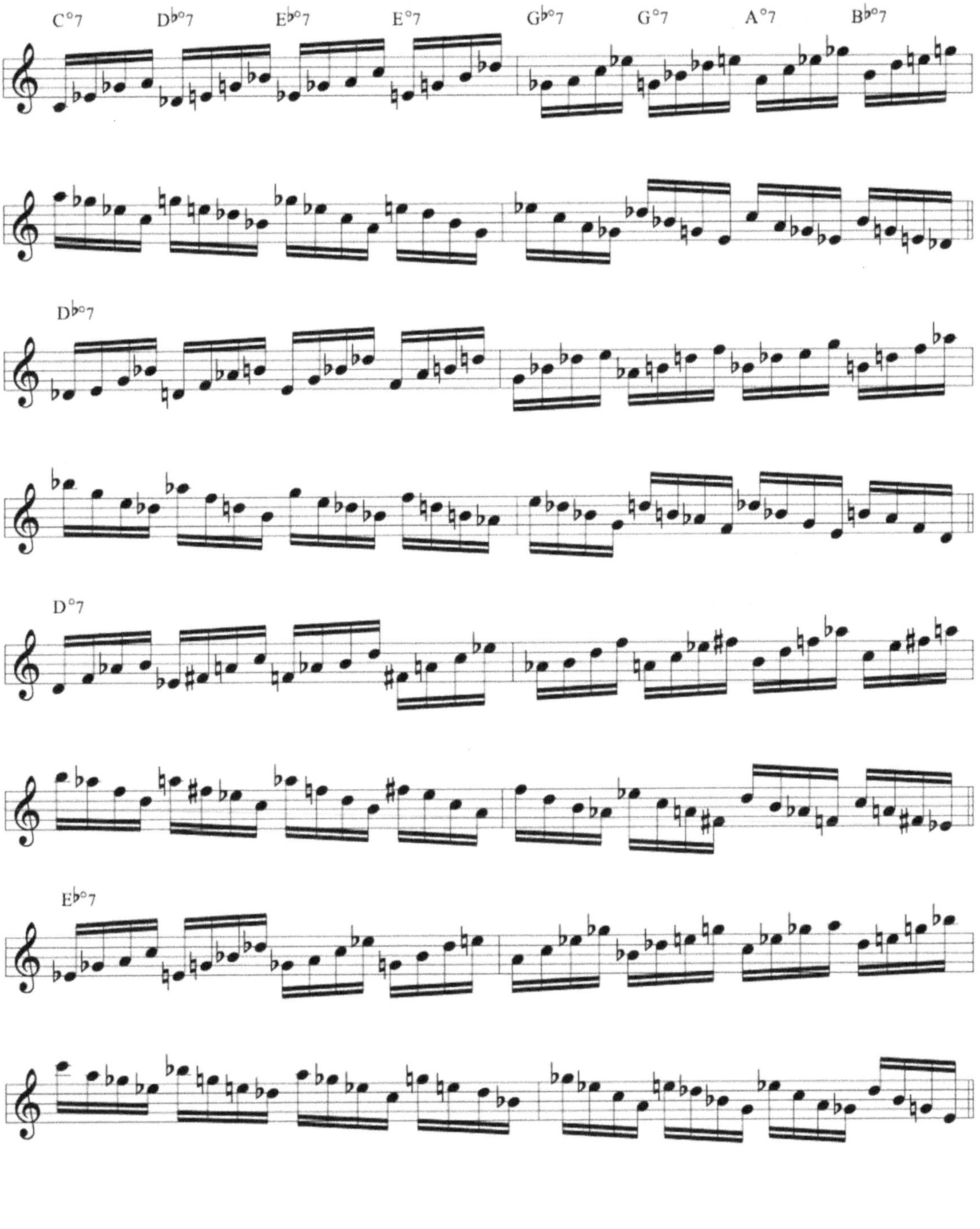

Appendix 1.3.5. Inverted Diminished Scale 7th Chords Per Degree

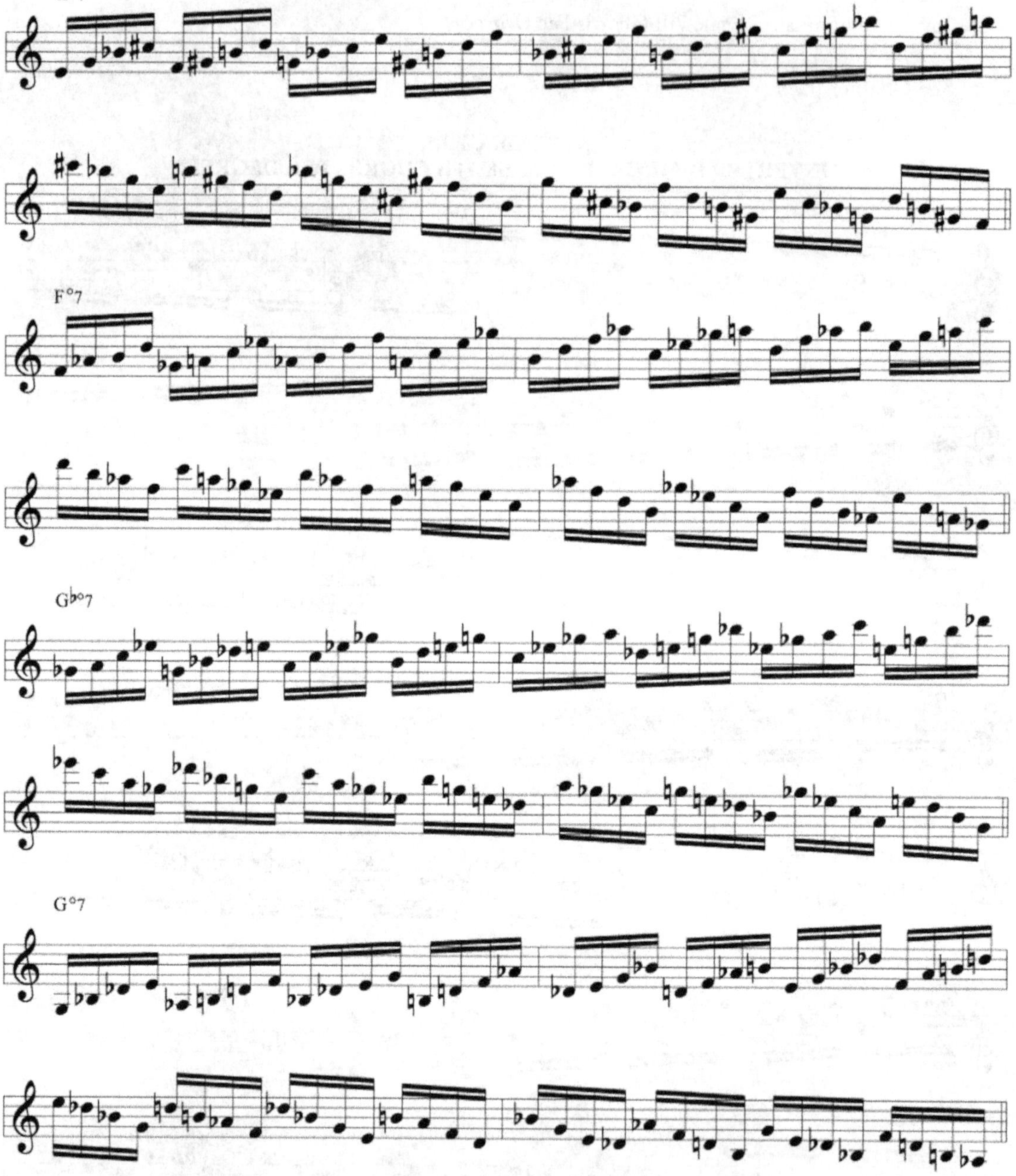

Appendix 1.3.5. Inverted Diminished Scale 7th Chords Per Degree

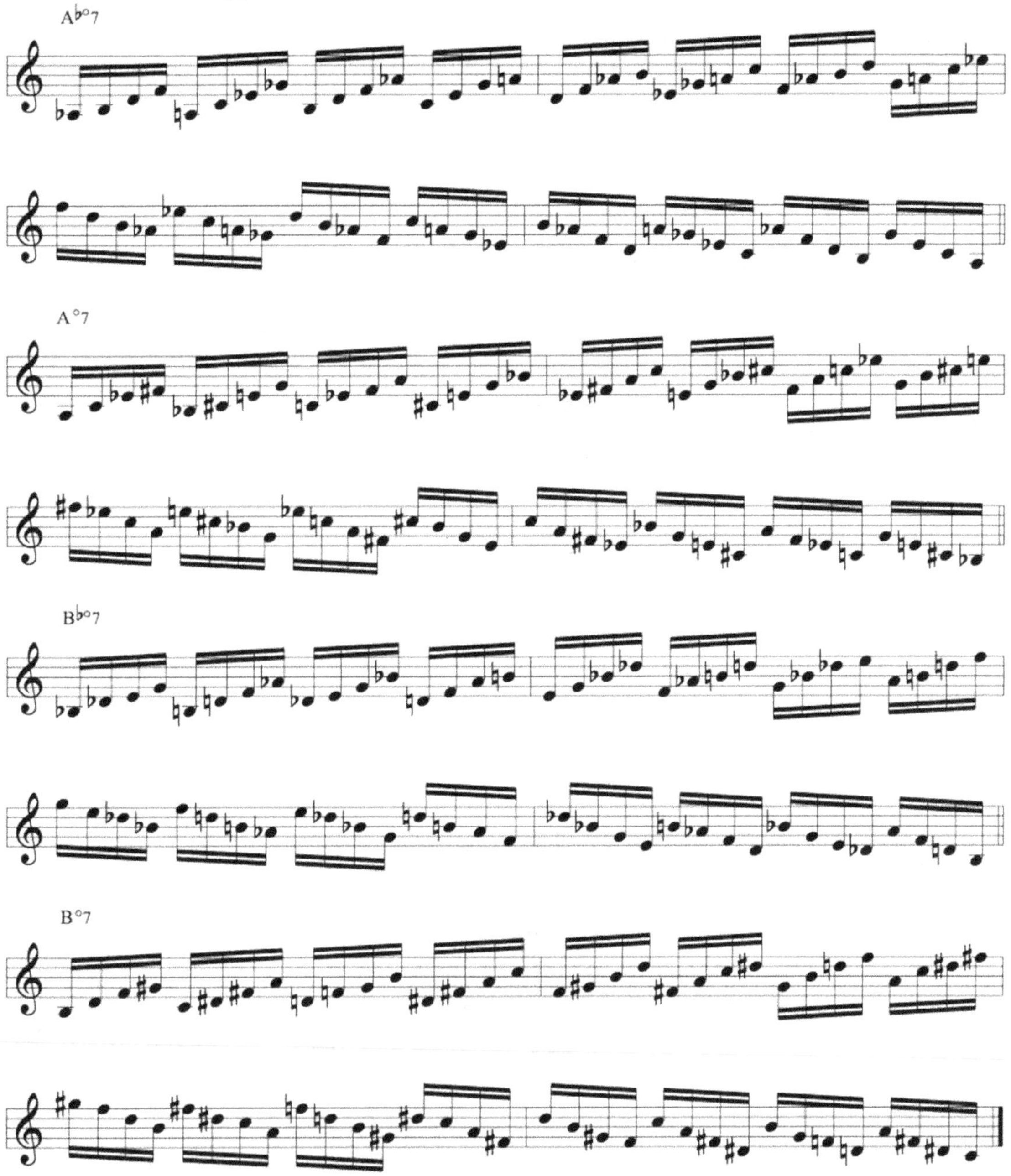

Section 3a) Diminished and Inverted Diminished Scales

1.3.6. Inverted Diminished Scale 7th Chords Weaving Per Degree

Description: See Chapter 8.2

APPENDIX 1.3.6.
INVERTED DIMINISHED SCALE 7TH CHORDS WEAVING PER DEGREE

Appendix 1.3.6. Inverted Diminished Scale 7th Chords Weaving Per Degree

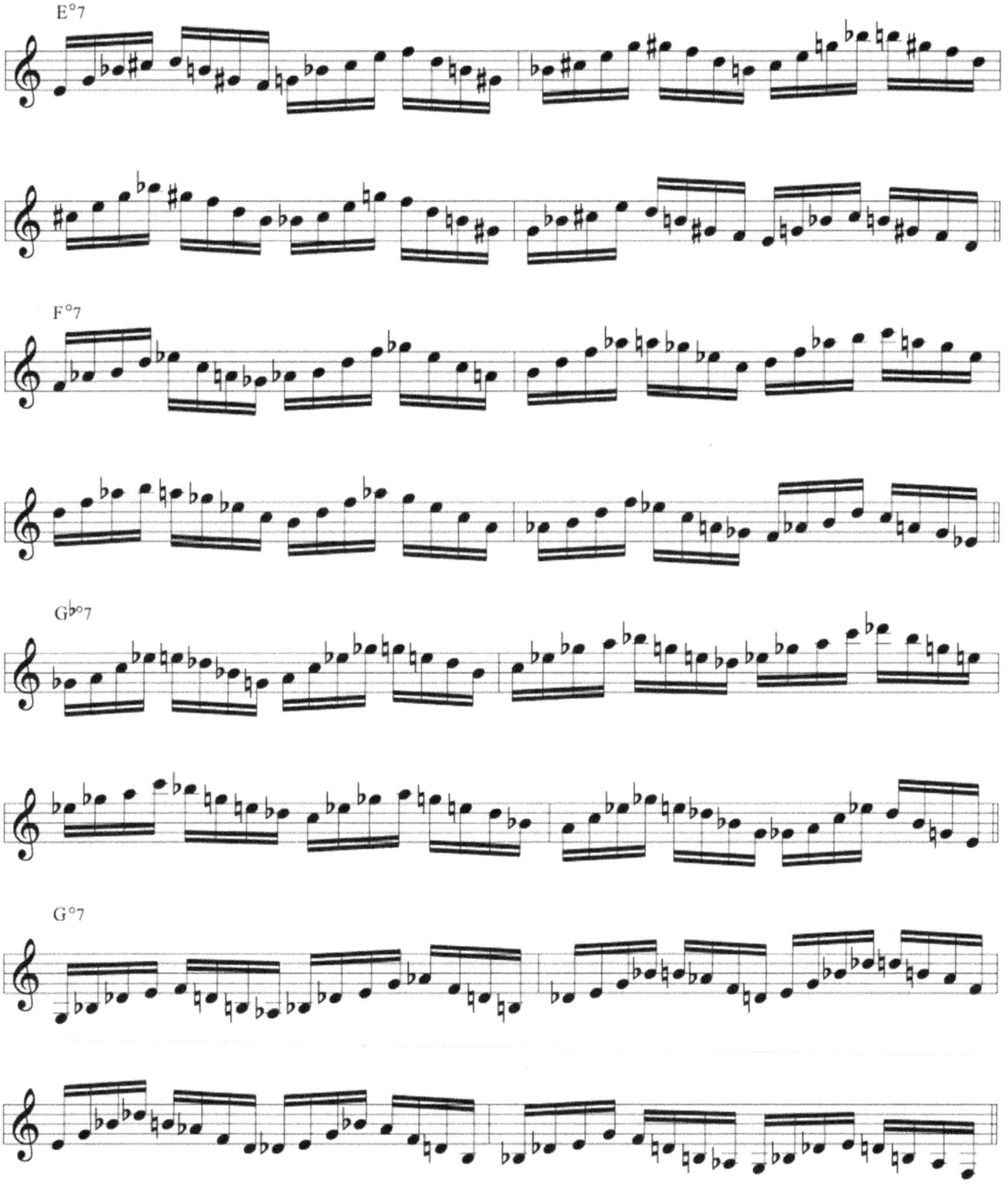

Appendix 1.3.6. Inverted Diminished Scale 7th Chords Weaving Per Degree

<u>Section 3a) Diminished and Inverted Diminished Scales</u>

1.3.7. Diminished Scales Ascending and Descending in Half Steps

Description: See Chapter 8.2

APPENDIX 1.3.7.
DIMINISHED SCALES ASCENDING AND DESCENDING IN ½ STEPS

Section 3a) Diminished and Inverted Diminished Scales

1.3.8. Inverted Diminished Scales Ascending and Descending in Half Steps

Description: See Chapter 8.2

APPENDIX 1.3.8.
INVERTED DIMINISHED SCALES ASCENDING AND DESCENDING IN ½ STEPS

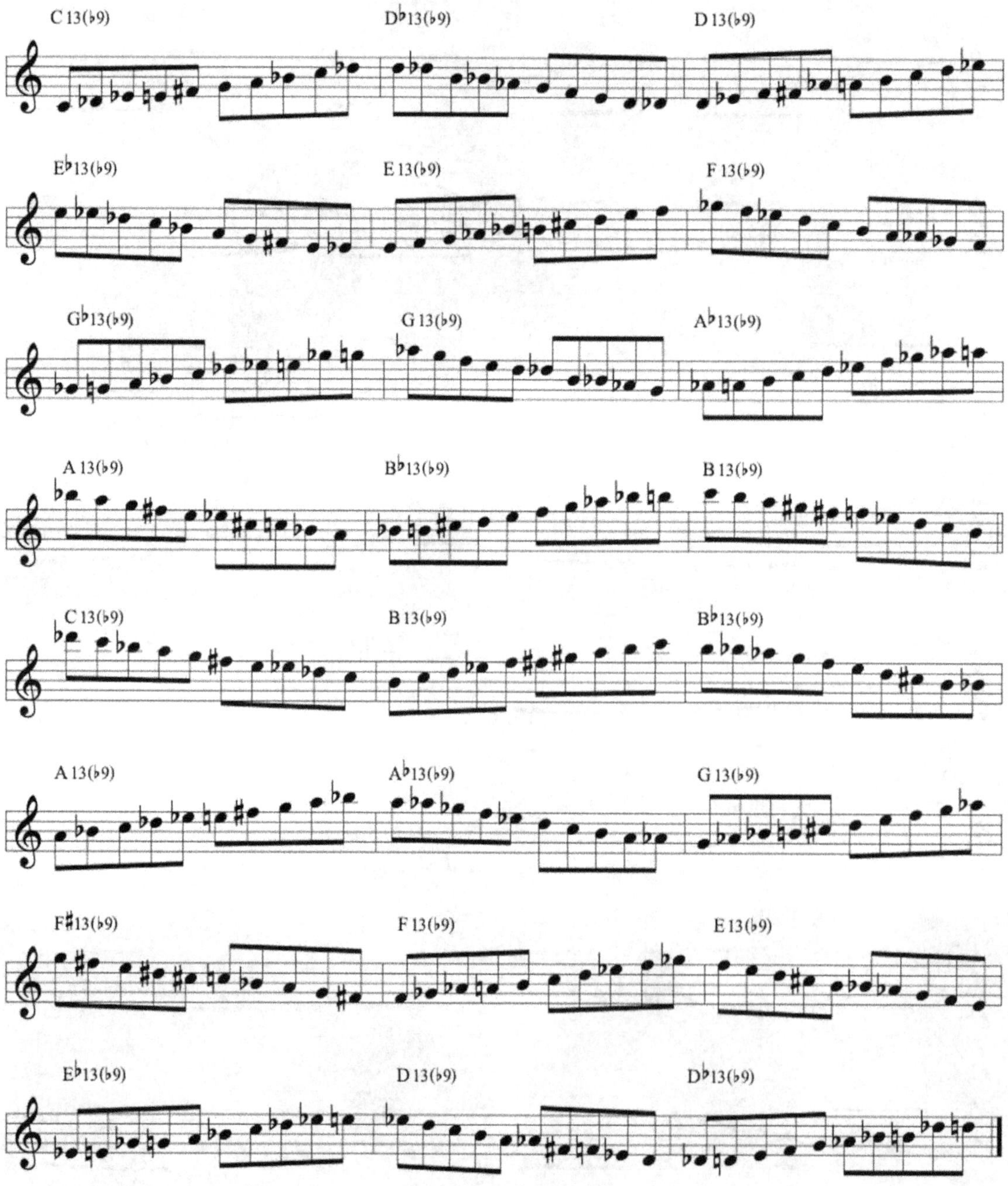

Section 3a) Diminished and Inverted Diminished Scales

1.3.9. Diminished Scale Ascending/Inverted Diminished Scale Descending

1.3.10. Inverted Diminished Scale Ascending/Diminished Scale Descending

Description: See Chapter 8.2

APPENDIX 1.3.9./1.3.10.
D.S. ASCENDING, I.D.S. DESCENDING/I.D.S. ASCENDING, D.S. DESCENDING

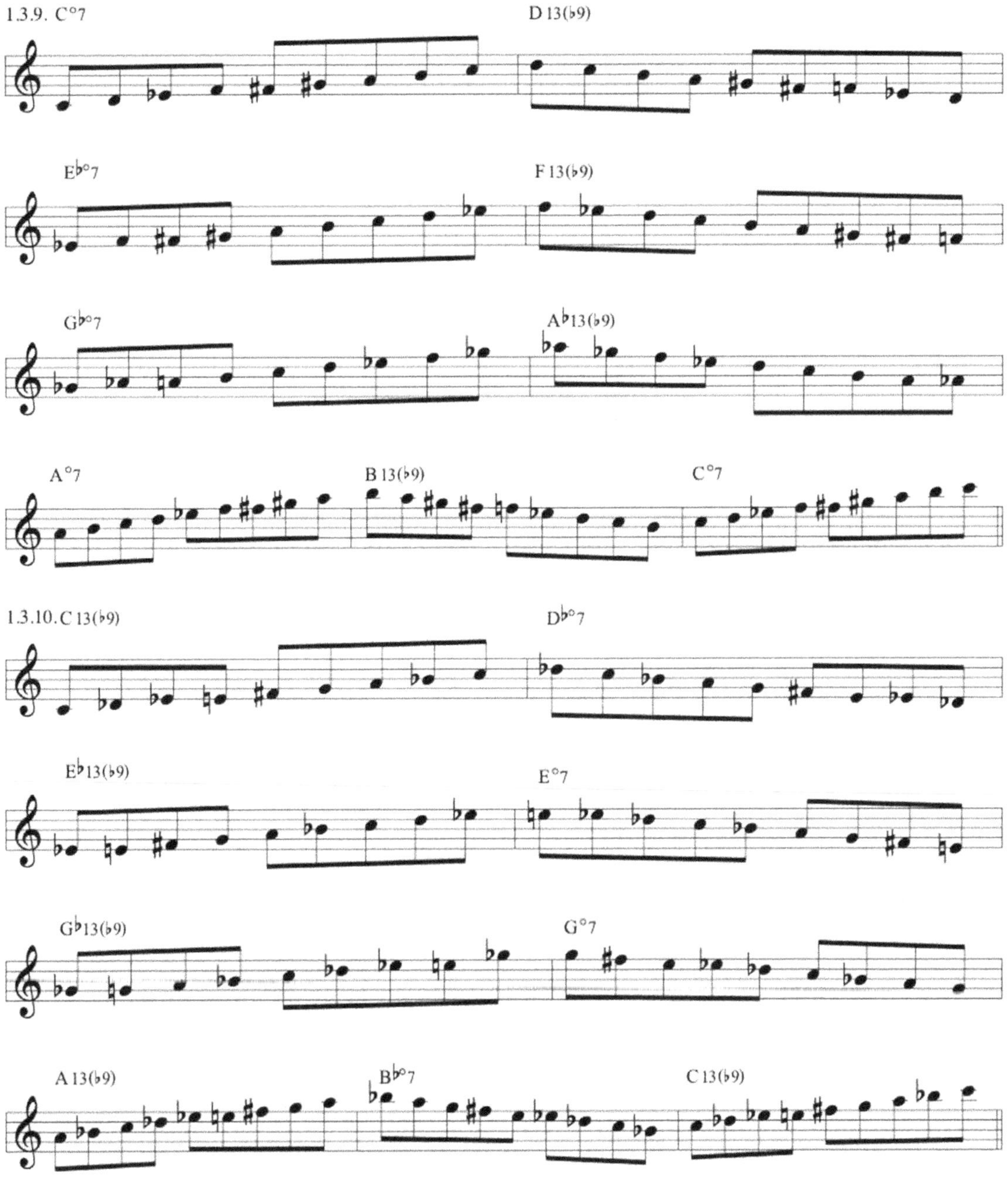

Appendix 1.3.9./1.3.10. D.S. Ascending, I.D.S. Descending/I.D.S. Ascending, D.S. Descending

1.3.9.

1.3.10.

Appendix 1.3.9./1.3.10. D.S. Ascending, I.D.S. Descending/I.D.S. Ascending, D.S. Descending

1.3.9.

1.3.10.

1.3.11. Alternating Diminished Scale and Inverted Diminished Scale Weaving in Half Steps

APPENDIX 1.3.11.
ALTERNATING D.S AND I.D.S. SCALE WEAVING IN ½ STEPS

Appendix 1.3.11. Alternating D.S and I.D.S. Scale Weaving In ½ Steps

Appendix 1.3.11. Alternating D.S and I.D.S. Scale Weaving In ½ Steps

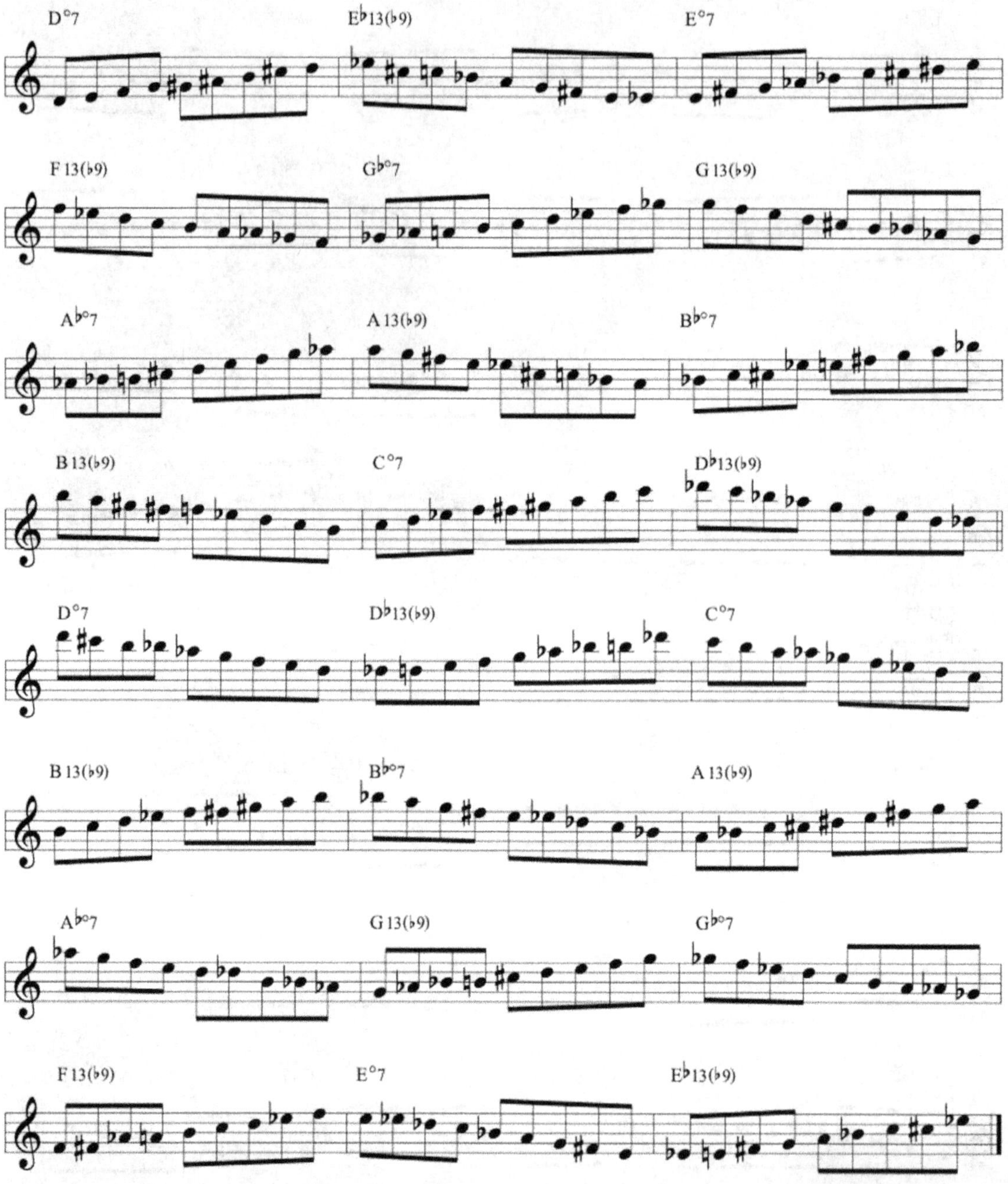

Section 3a) Diminished and Inverted Diminished Scales

1.3.12. Diminished 7th Chord Weaving via Whole Steps

Description: See Chapter 8.2

APPENDIX 1.3.12.
Diminished 7th Chord Weaving via Whole Steps

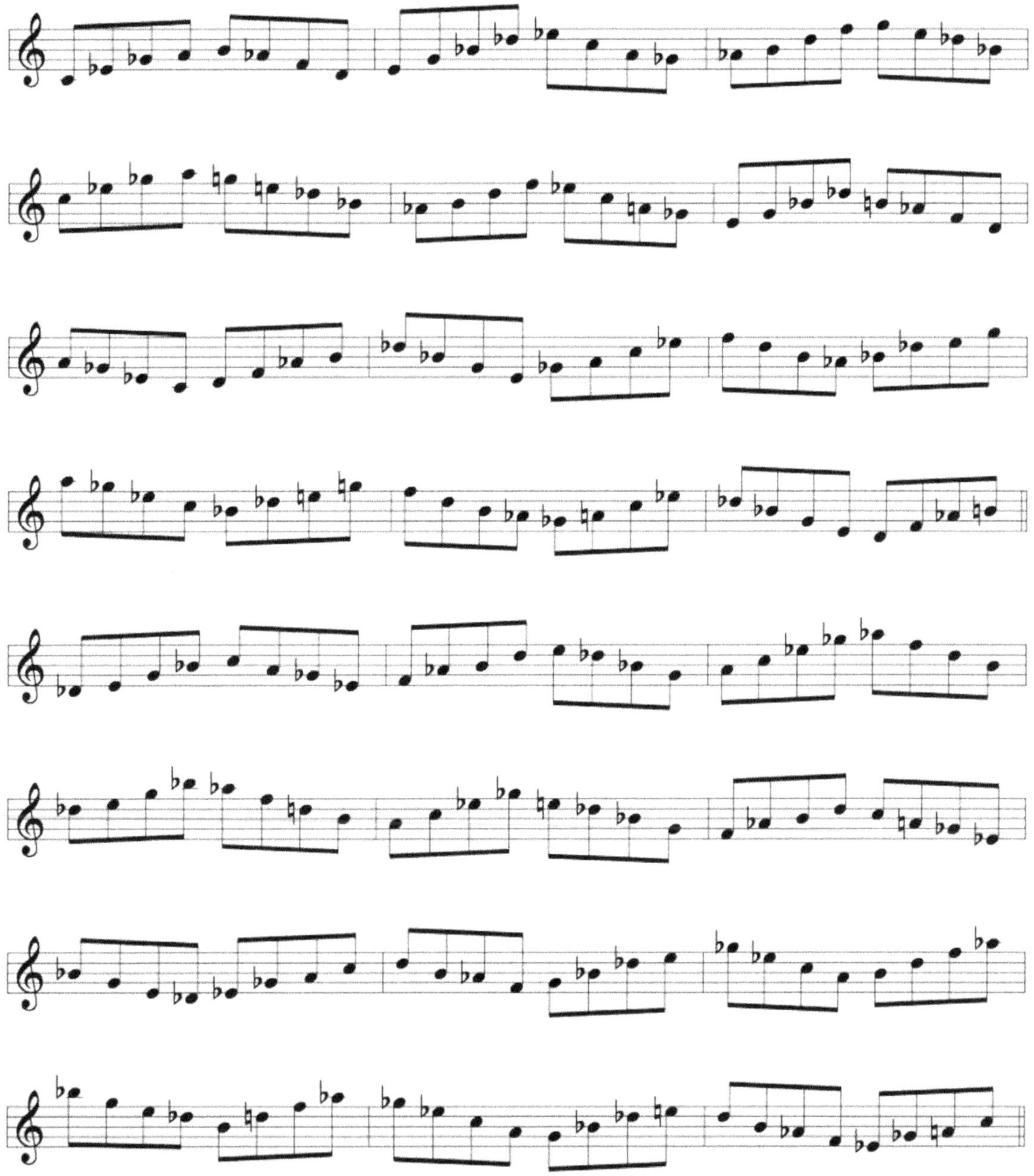

Appendix 1.3.12. Diminished 7th Chord Weaving via Whole Steps

Section 3a) Diminished and Inverted Diminished Scales

1.3.13. Diminished 7th Chord Weaving via Half-Steps

Description: See Chapter 8.2

APPENDIX 1.3.13.
Diminished 7th Chord Weaving via ½ Steps

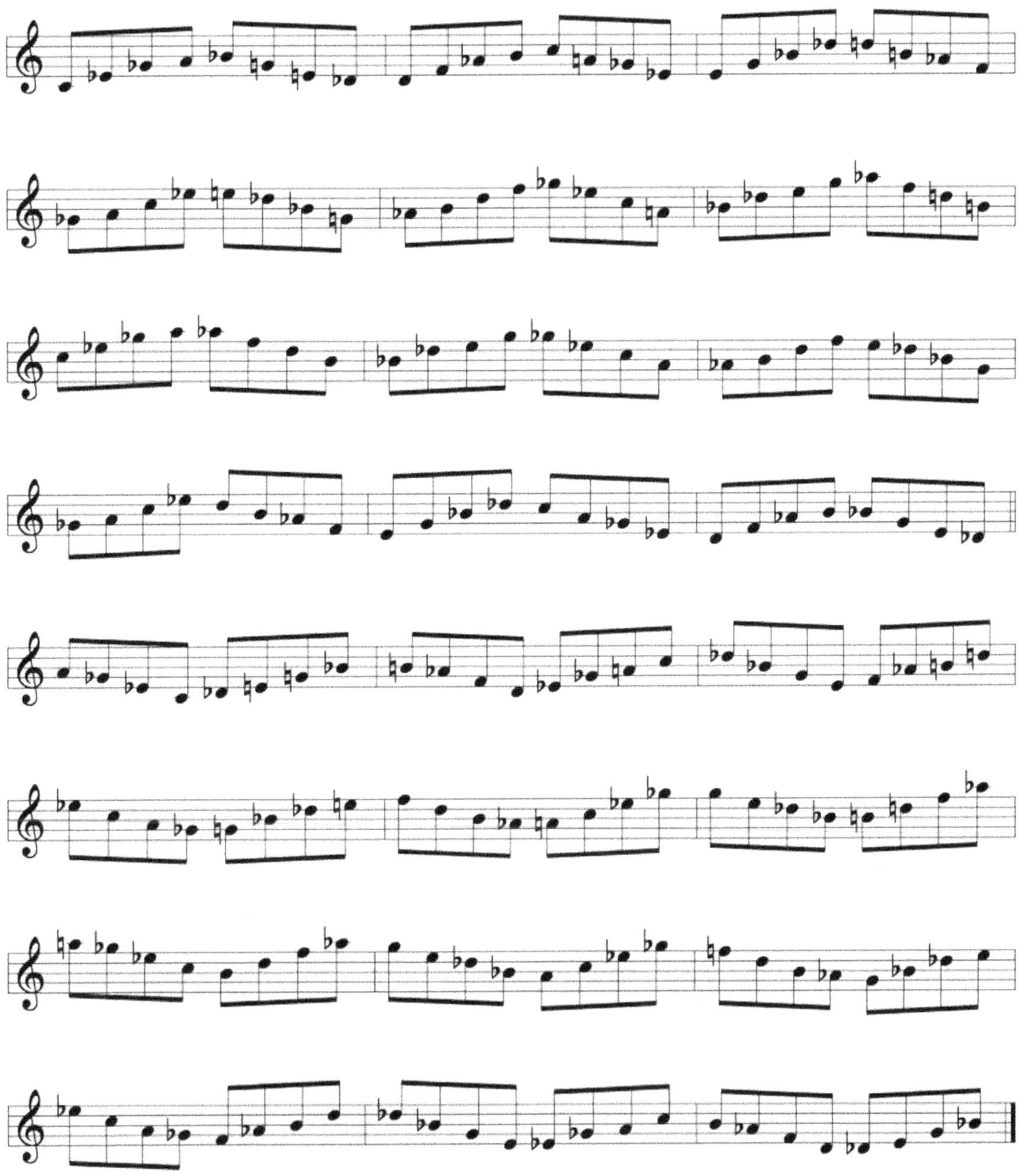

1.3.14. Graph: Inverted Diminished Exponents

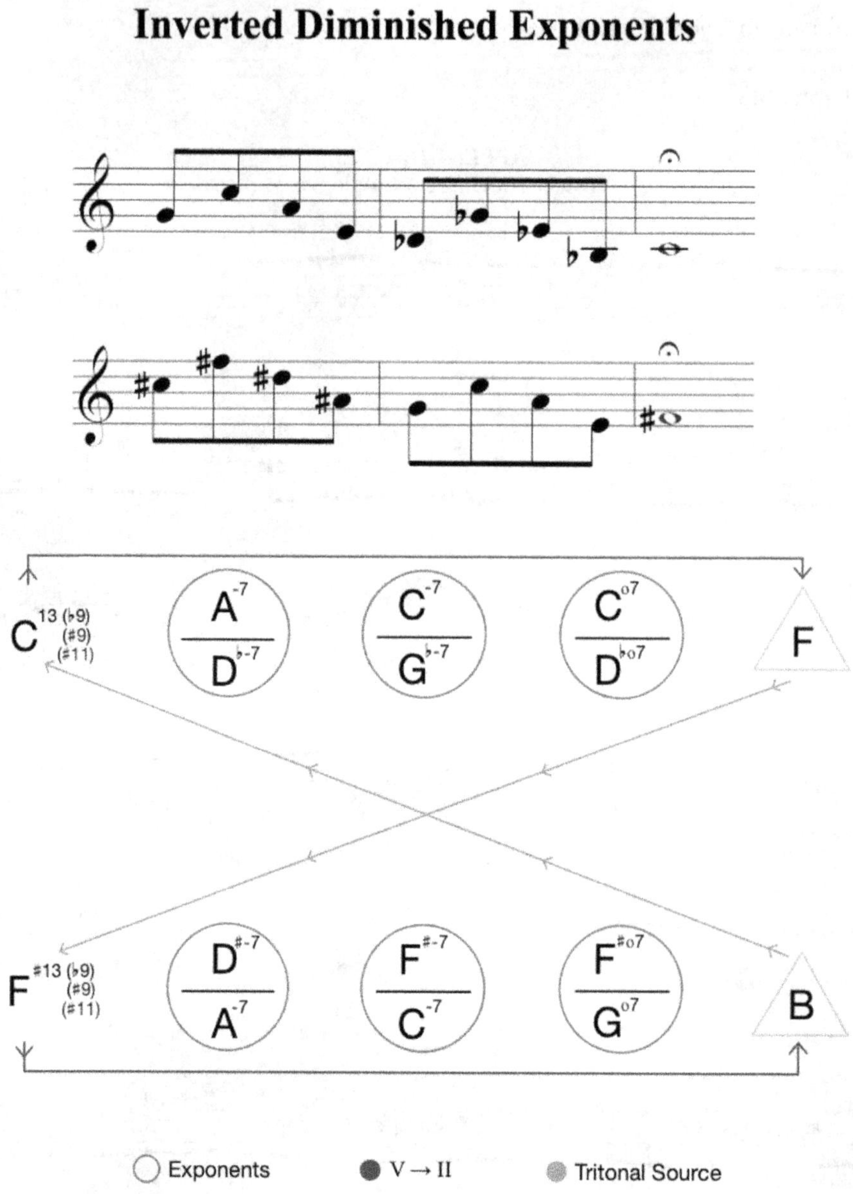
Inverted Diminished Exponents
C13 (♭9) (♯9) (♯11)
A-7
D♭-7
C-7
G♭-7
Co7
D♭o7
F
F♯13 (♭9) (♯9) (♯11)
D♯-7
A-7
F♯-7
C-7
F♯o7
Go7
B
Exponents
V → II
Tritonal Source

Section 3b) Two-In-One

1.3.15. Major 7 Disparities in the "Two-in-One"

Description: There are two fully diminished triads imbedded in the Inverted Diminished Scale V7b9 combines the two FULLY DIMINISHED chords—forming a Major 7th disparity.

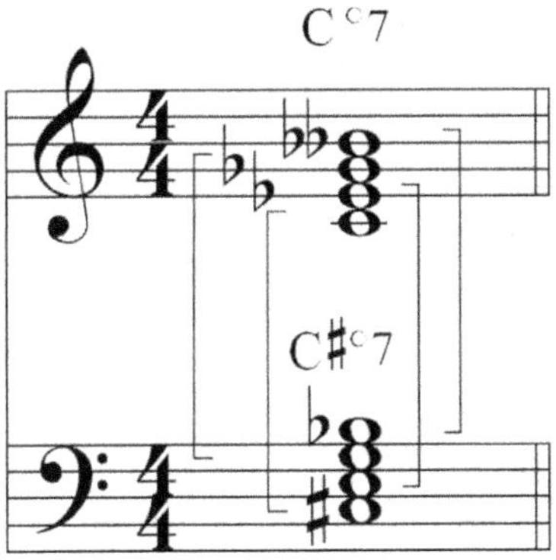

Section 3b) Two-In-One

1.3.16. Two-in-One

Description: The FullyDiminshed **chords can be** inverted via the modes of the Octatonic scale (i.e., half/whole, inverted diminished) to create a series of passing notes/chords.

APPENDIX 1.3.15.
TWO-IN-ONE

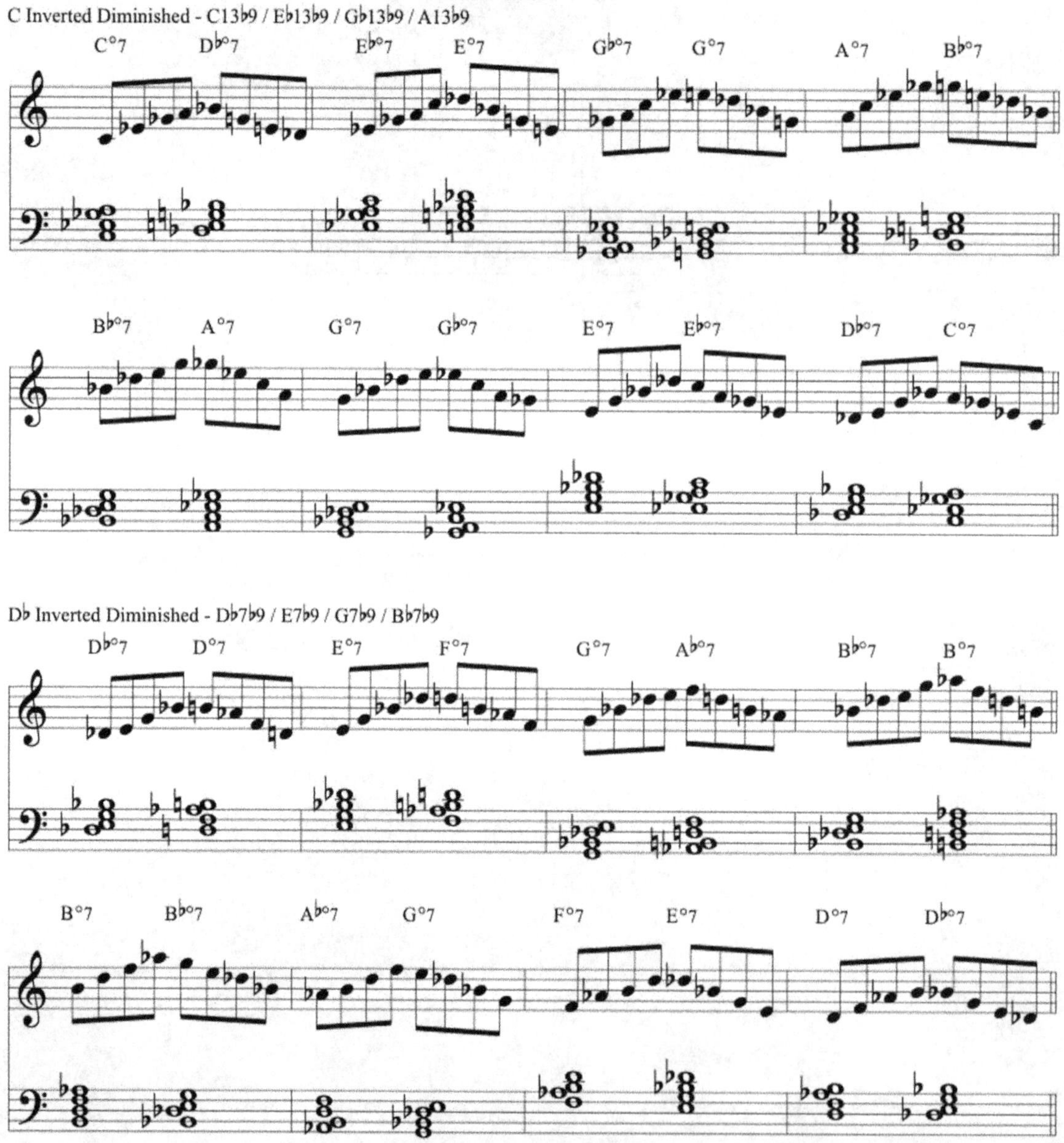

Appendix 1.3.15. Two-In-One

D Inverted Diminished - D7♭9 / F7♭9 / A♭7♭9 / B7♭9

Section 3b) Two-In-One

1.3.17. Two-in-One via Major 7th

Description: See Chapter 8.2

APPENDIX 1.3.16.
TWO-IN-ONE VIA M7

Section 3b) Two-In-One

1.3.18. Two-in-One via Ascending Minor 3rds

Description: See Chapter 8.2

Section 3b) Two-In-One

1.3.19. Double Diminished

Description: See Chapter 8.2

APPENDIX 1.3.18.
DOUBLE DIMINISHED

Chapter 2

CHORD SCALE SOLUTIONS

2.1. Chord Syllabus

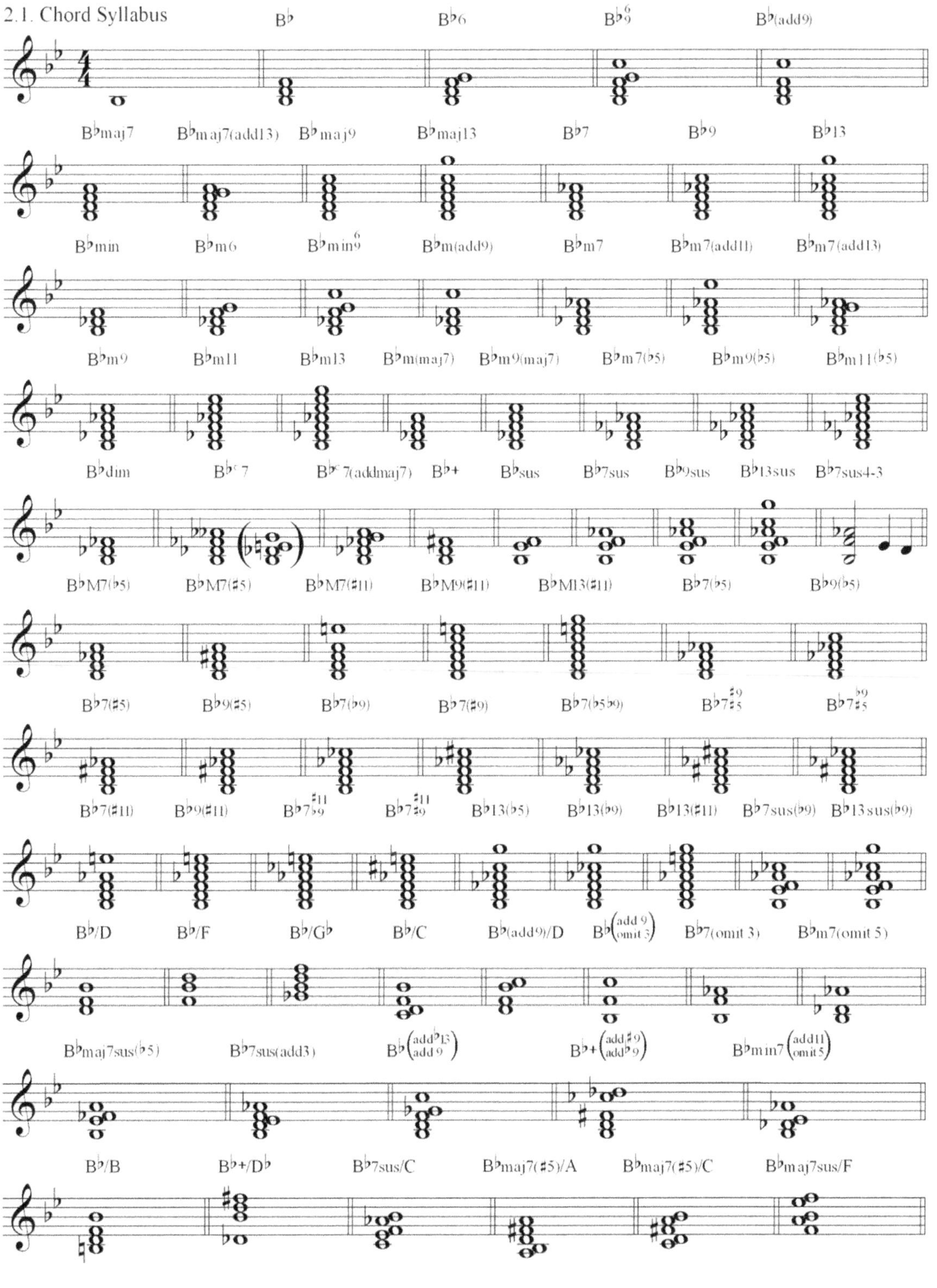

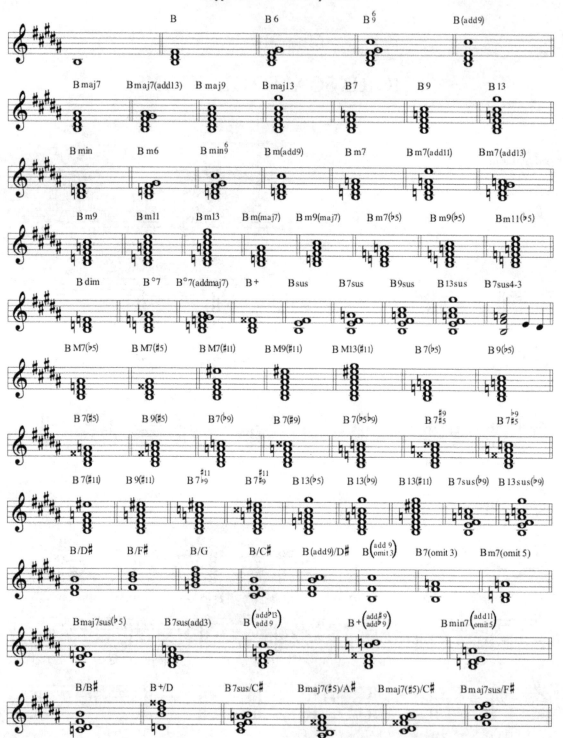

Appendix 2.1. Chord Syllabus

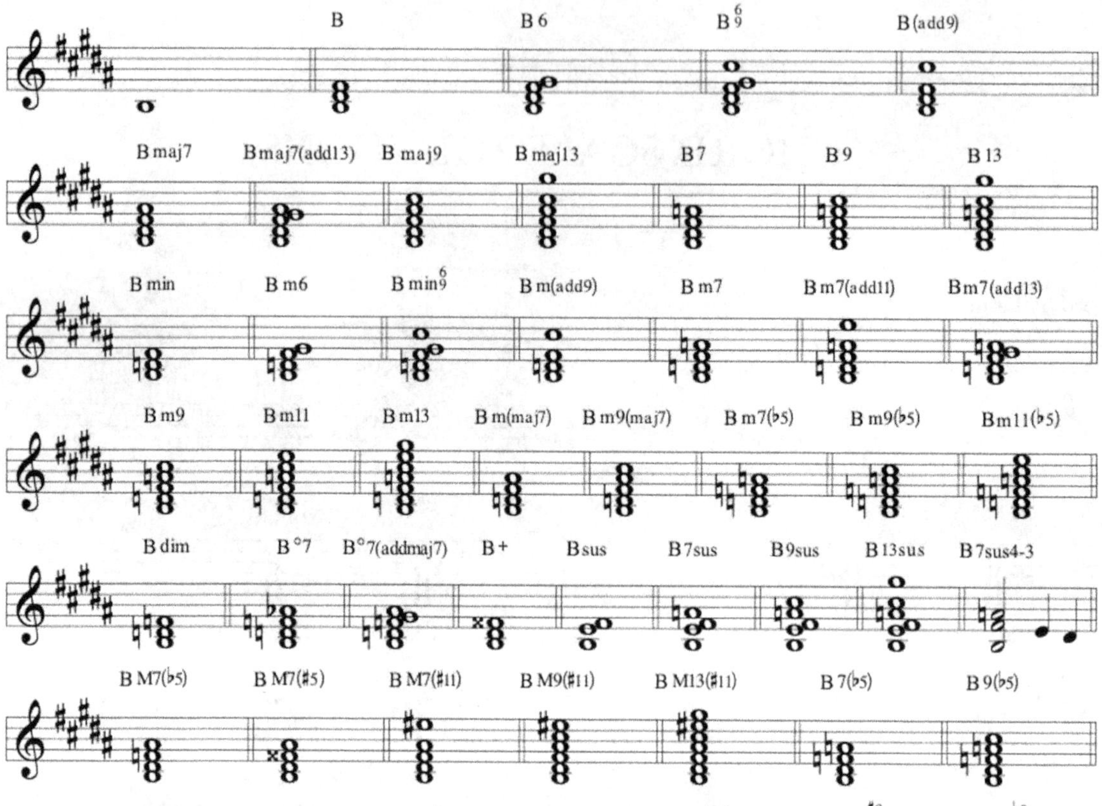

Appendix 2.1. Chord Syllabus

C
C 6
C 6 9
C(add9)
Cmaj7
Cmaj7(add13)
C maj9
C maj13
C7
C9
C13
C min
C m6
C min 6 9
C m(add9)
C m7
C m7(add11)
Cm7(add13)
C m9
C m11
C m13
C m(maj7)
C m9(maj7)
C m7(♭5)
C m9(♭5)
C m11(♭5)
C dim
C°7
C°7(addmaj7)
C+
C sus
C 7sus
C 9sus
C 13sus
C 7sus4-3
C M7(♭5)
C M7(♯5)
C M7(♯11)
C M9(♯11)
C M13(♯11)
C 7(♭5)
C 9(♭5)
C 7(♯5)
C 9(♯5)
C7(♭9)
C 7(♯9)
C 7(♭5♭9)
C 7 ♯9 ♯5
C 7 ♭9 ♯5
C 7(♯11)
C 9(♯11)
C 7 ♯11 ♭9
C 7 ♯11 ♯9
C 13(♭5)
C 13(♭9)
C 13(♯11)
C 7sus(♭9)
C 13sus(♭9)
C/E
C/G
C/A♭
C/D
C(add9)/E
C(add 9 omit 3)
C 7(omit 3)
Cm7(omit 5)
Cmaj7sus(♭5)
C 7sus(add3)
C(add♭13 add 9)
C+(add♯9 add♭9)
C min7(add11 omit 5)
C/C♯
C+/E♭
C 7sus/D
Cmaj7(♯5)/B
Cmaj7(♯5)/D
Cmaj7sus/G

Appendix 2.1. Chord Syllabus

Appendix 2.1. Chord Syllabus

Appendix 2.1. Chord Syllabus

Appendix 2.1. Chord Syllabus

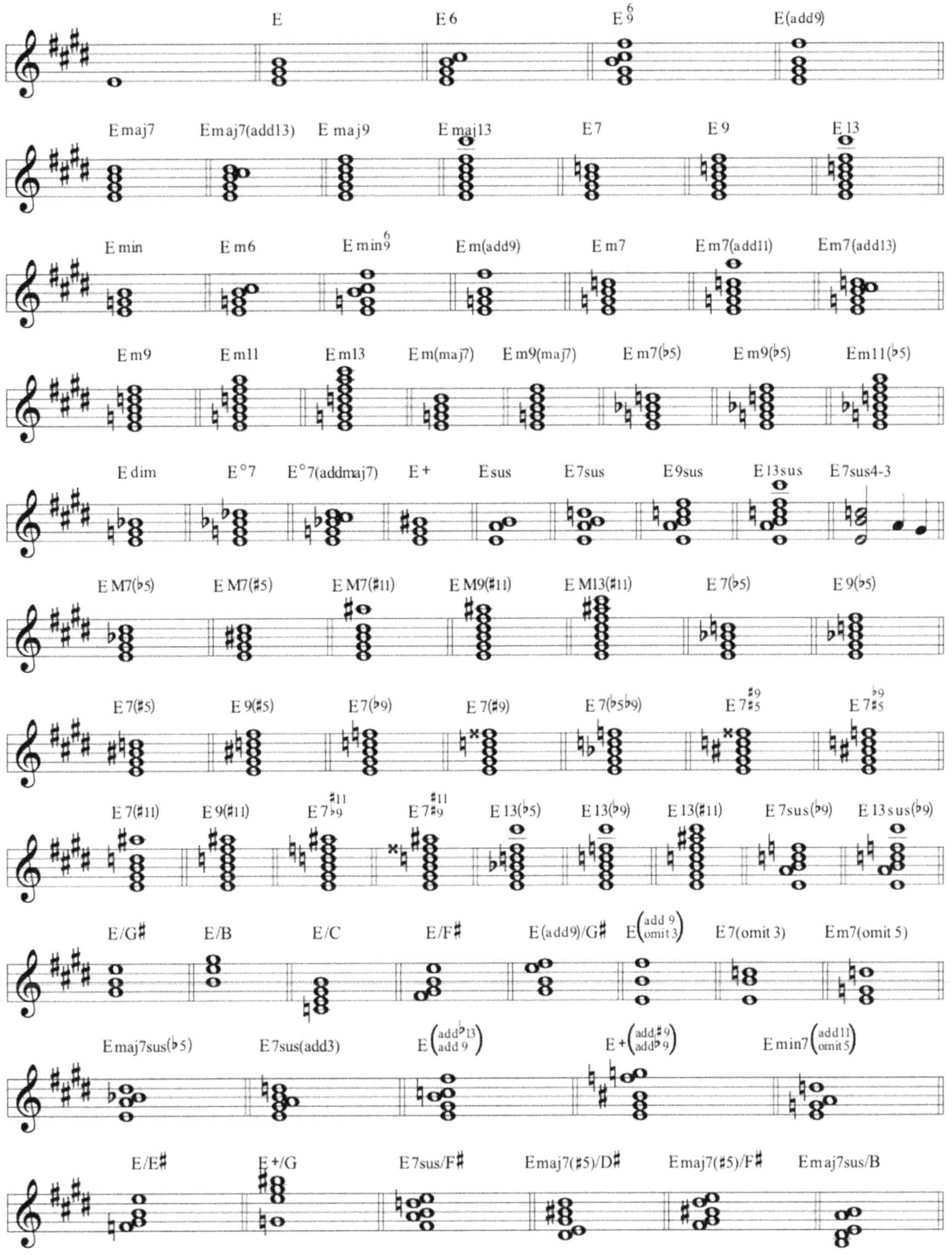

Appendix 2.1. Chord Syllabus

Appendix 2.1. Chord Syllabus

Appendix 2.1. Chord Syllabus

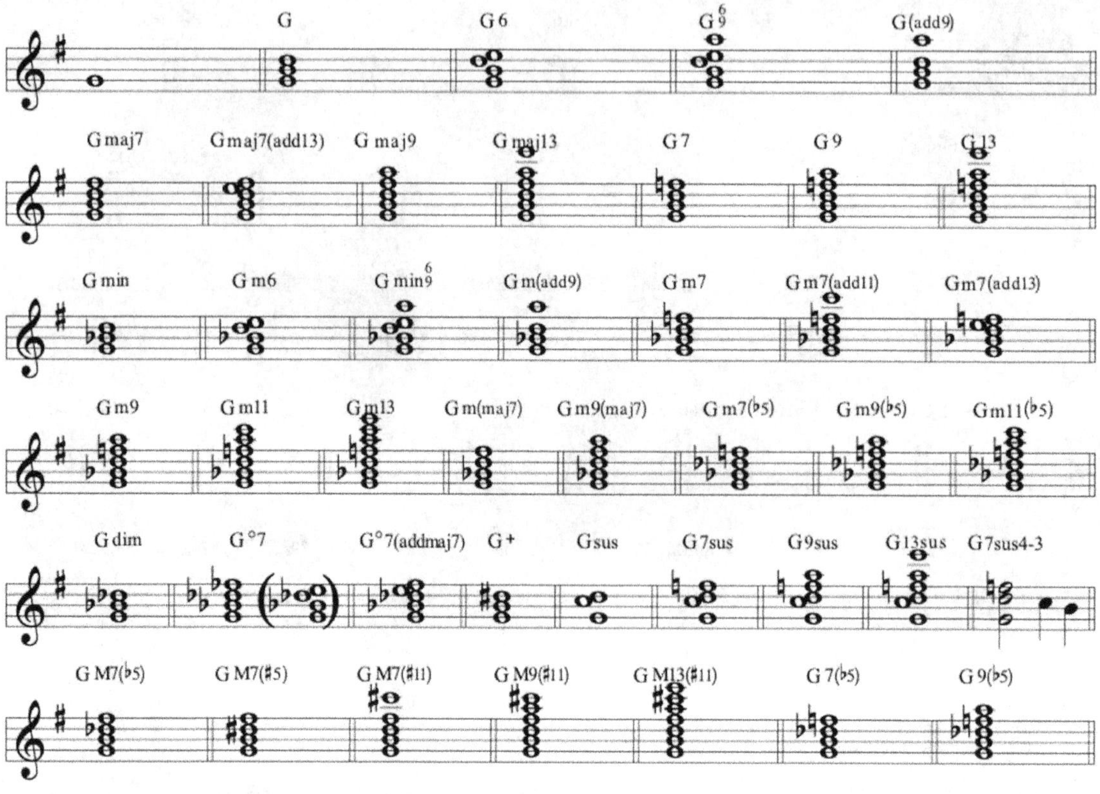
G G6 G6/9 G(add9)
Gmaj7 Gmaj7(add13) G maj9 G maj13 G7 G9 G13
G min G m6 G min6/9 G m(add9) G m7 G m7(add11) Gm7(add13)
G m9 G m11 G m13 G m(maj7) G m9(maj7) G m7(♭5) G m9(♭5) G m11(♭5)
G dim G°7 G°7(addmaj7) G+ Gsus G7sus G9sus G13sus G7sus4-3
G M7(♭5) G M7(♯5) G M7(♯11) G M9(♯11) G M13(♯11) G 7(♭5) G 9(♭5)
G 7(♯5) G 9(♯5) G 7(♭9) G 7(♯9) G 7(♭5♭9) G 7♯9/♯5 G 7♭9/♯5
G 7(♯11) G 9(♯11) G 7♯11/♭9 G 7♯11/♯9 G 13(♭5) G 13(♭9) G 13(♯11) G 7sus(♭9) G 13sus(♭9)
G/B G/D G/E♭ G/A G(add9)/B G(add 9 / omit 3) G 7(omit 3) G m7(omit 5)
Gmaj7sus(♭5) G7sus(add3) G(add♭13 / add 9) G+(add♯9 / add♭9) Gmin7(add11 / omit5)
G/A♭ G+/B♭ G7sus/A Gmaj7(♯5)/F♯ Gmaj7(♯5)/A Gmaj7sus/D

Appendix 2.1. Chord Syllabus

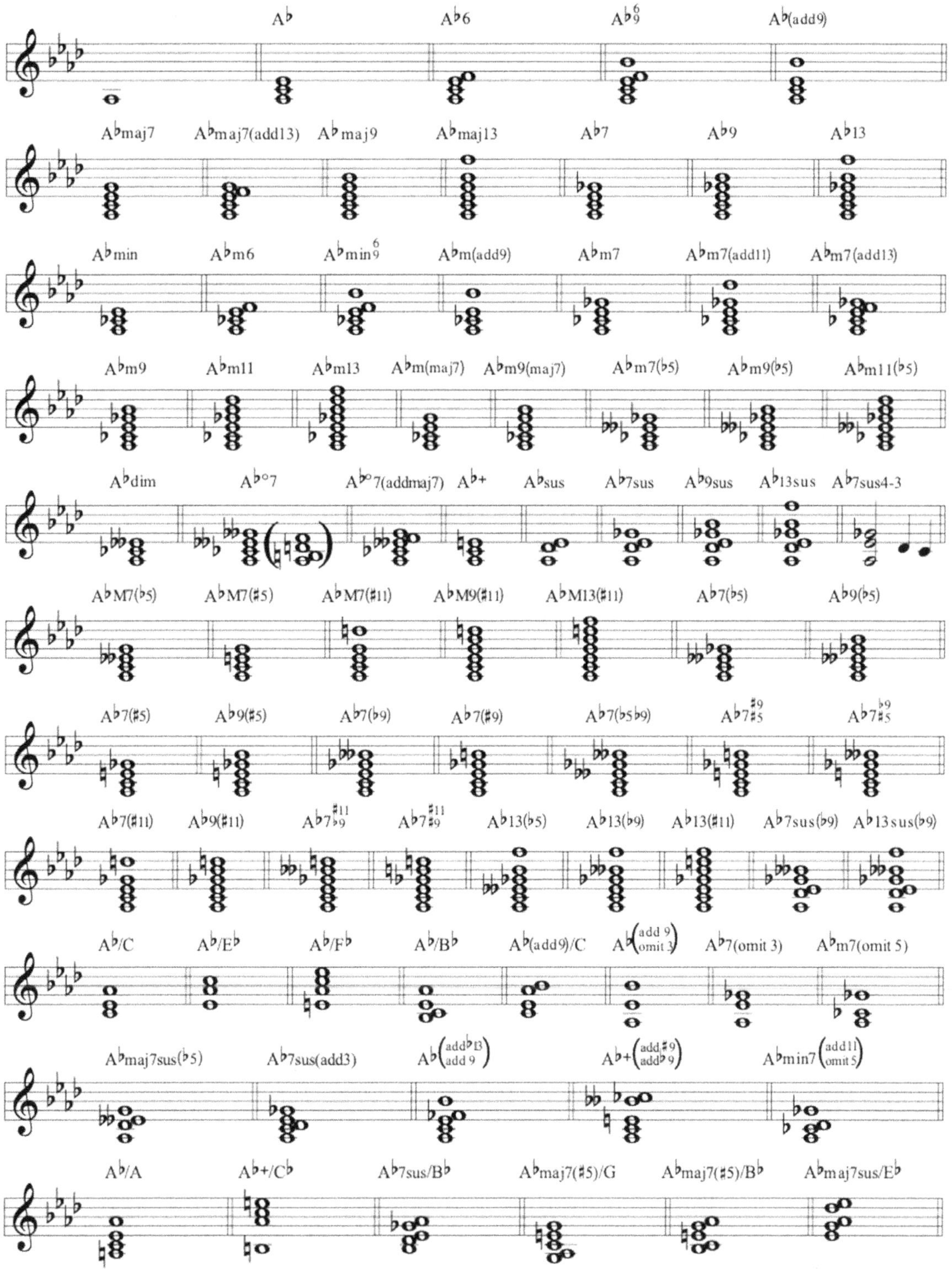

Appendix 2.1. Chord Syllabus

2.2. Chord Scale Solutions for Ionian/Dorian/Phrygian

Description: See Chapter 8.2

APPENDIX 2.2
CHORD SCALE SOULTIONS FOR IONIAN, DORIAN AND PHYRGIAN

Appendix 2.2. Chord Scale Solutions for Ionian, Dorian, Phrygian

2.3. Chord Scale Solutions for Major Lydian

Description: See Chapter 8.2

APPENDIX 2.3.
Chord Scale Solutions for Major Lydian

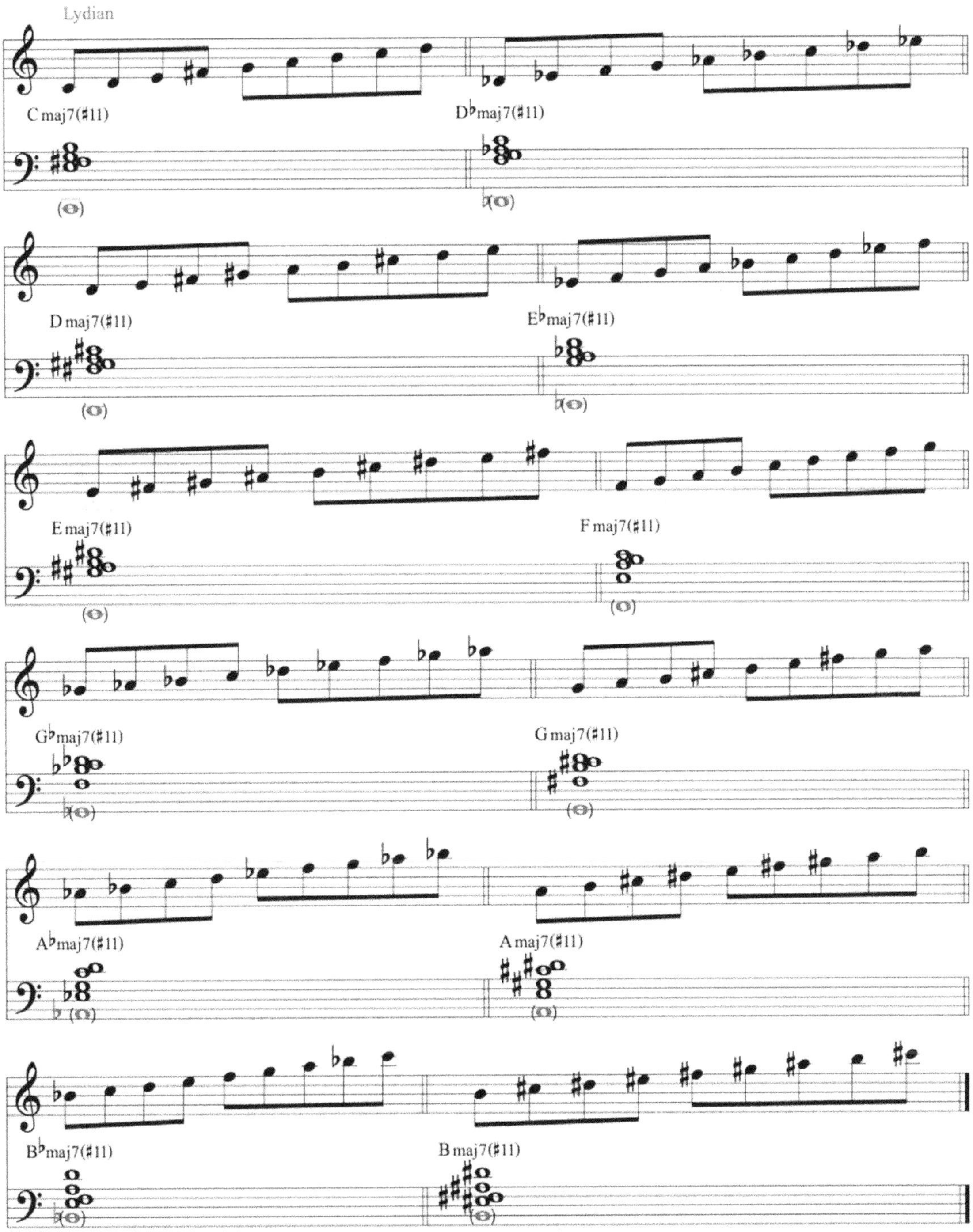

2.4. Chord Scale Solutions for Maj7(#5)

Description: See Chapter 8.2

APPENDIX 2.4.
CHORD SCALE SOLUTIONS FOR MAJ7(#5)

2.5. Chord Scale Solutions in Dominant

Description: See Chapter 8.2

APPENDIX 2.5.
CHORD SCALE SOLUTIONS IN DOMINANT

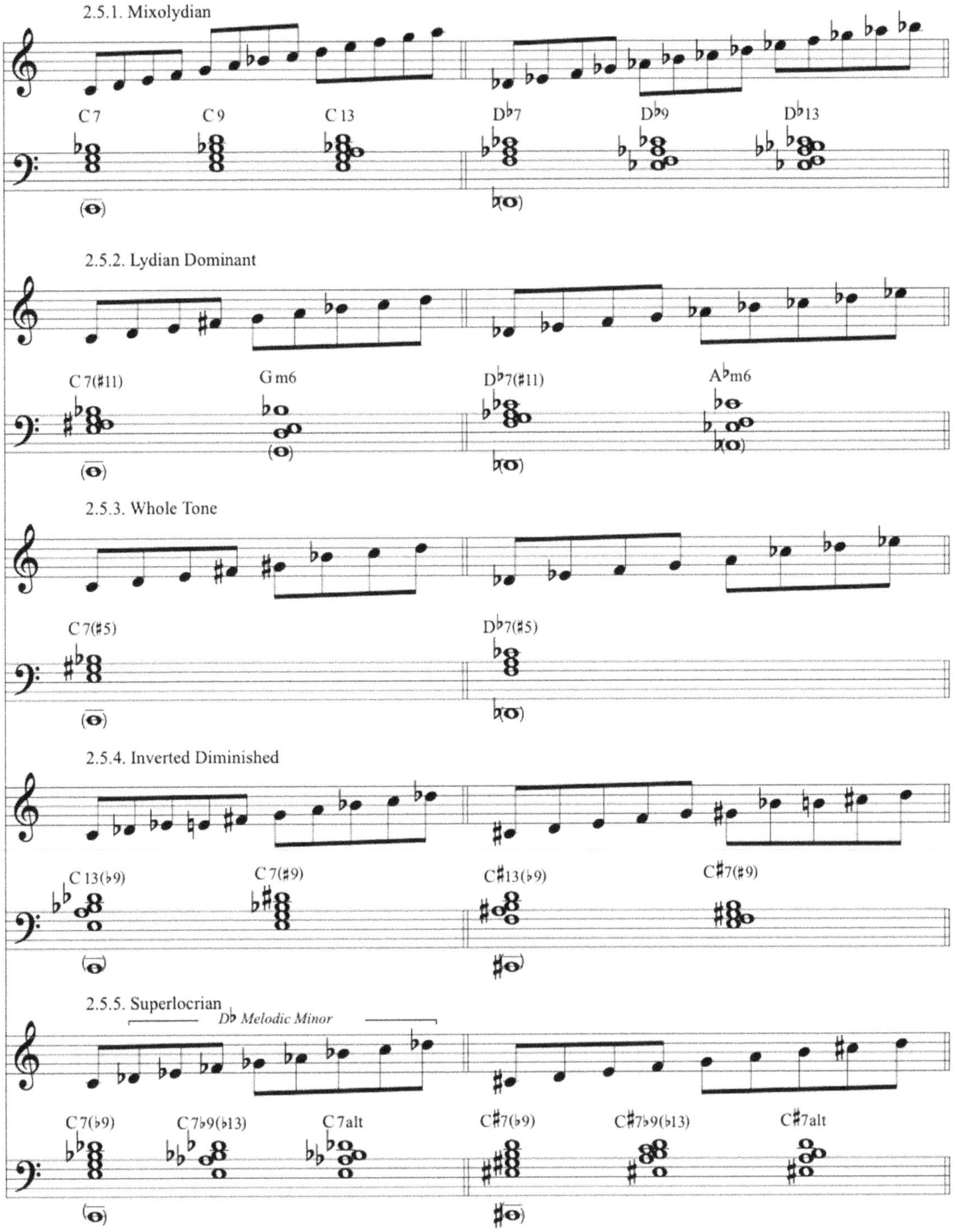

Appendix 2.5. Chord Scale Solutions In Dominant

2.5.1. Mixolydian

2.5.2. Lydian Dominant

2.5.3. Whole Tone

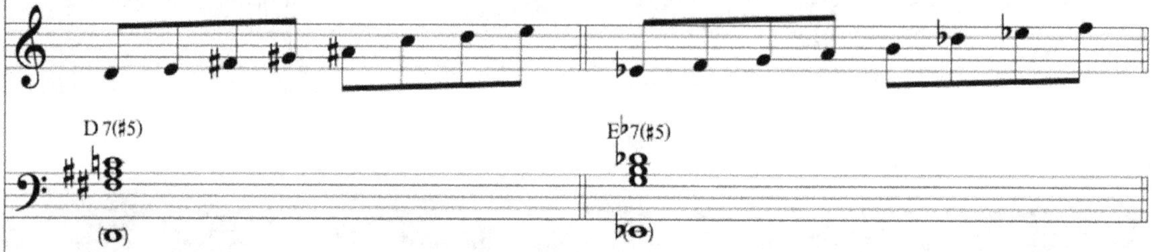

2.5.4. Inverted Diminished

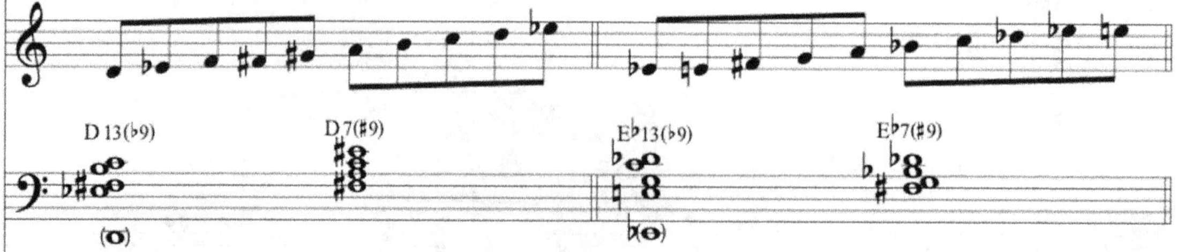

2.5.5. Superlocrian

Appendix 2.5. Chord Scale Solutions In Dominant

2.5.1. Mixolydian

2.5.2. Lydian Dominant

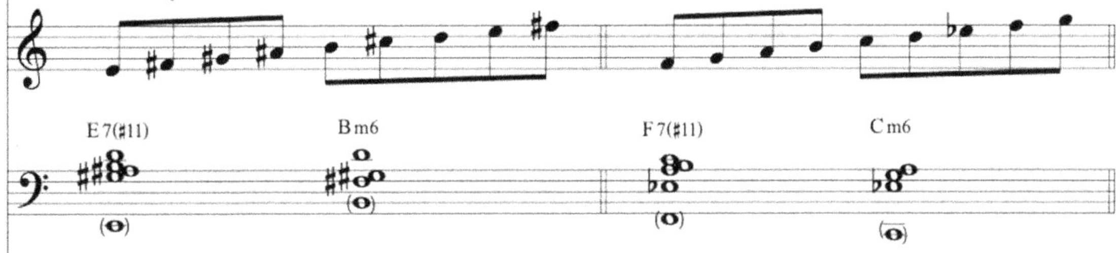

2.5.3. Whole Tone

2.5.4. Inverted Diminished

2.5.5. Superlocrian

Appendix 2.5. Chord Scale Solutions In Dominant

2.5.1. Mixolydian
G♭7
G♭9
G♭13
G 7
G 9
G 13
2.5.2. Lydian Dominant
G♭7(♯11)
D♭m6
G 7(♯11)
D m6
2.5.3. Whole Tone
G♭7(♯5)
G 7(♯5)
2.5.4. Inverted Diminished
G♭13(♭9)
G♭7(♯9)
G 13(♭9)
G 7(♯9)
2.5.5. Superlocrian
G♭7(♭9)
G♭7♭9(♭13)
G♭7alt
G 7(♭9)
G 7♭9(♭13)
G 7alt

Appendix 2.5. Chord Scale Solutions In Dominant

2.5.1. Mixolydian
A♭7
A♭9
A♭13
A7
A9
A13
2.5.2. Lydian Dominant
A♭7(♯11)
E♭m6
A7(♯11)
Em6
2.5.3. Whole Tone
A♭7(♯5)
A7(♯5)
2.5.4. Inverted Diminished
A♭13(♭9)
A♭7(♯9)
A13(♭9)
A7(♯9)
2.5.5. Superlocrian
A♭7(♭9)
A♭7♭9(♭13)
A♭7alt
A7(♭9)
A7♭9(♭13)
A7alt

Appendix 2.5. Chord Scale Solutions In Dominant

2.5.1. Mixolydian
B♭7
B♭9
B♭13
B 7
B 9
B 13
2.5.2. Lydian Dominant
B♭7(♯11)
F m6
B 7(♯11)
F♯m6
2.5.3. Whole Tone
B♭7(♯5)
B 7(♯5)
2.5.4. Inverted Diminished
B♭13(♭9)
B♭7(♯9)
B 13(♭9)
B 7(♯9)
2.5.5. Superlocrian
B♭7(♭9)
B♭7♭9(♭13)
B♭7alt
B 7(♭9)
B 7♭9(♭13)
B 7alt

2.6. Chord Scale Solutions for Aeolian

Description: See Chapter 8.2

APPENDIX 2.6.
CHORD SCALE SOLUTIONS FOR AEOLIAN

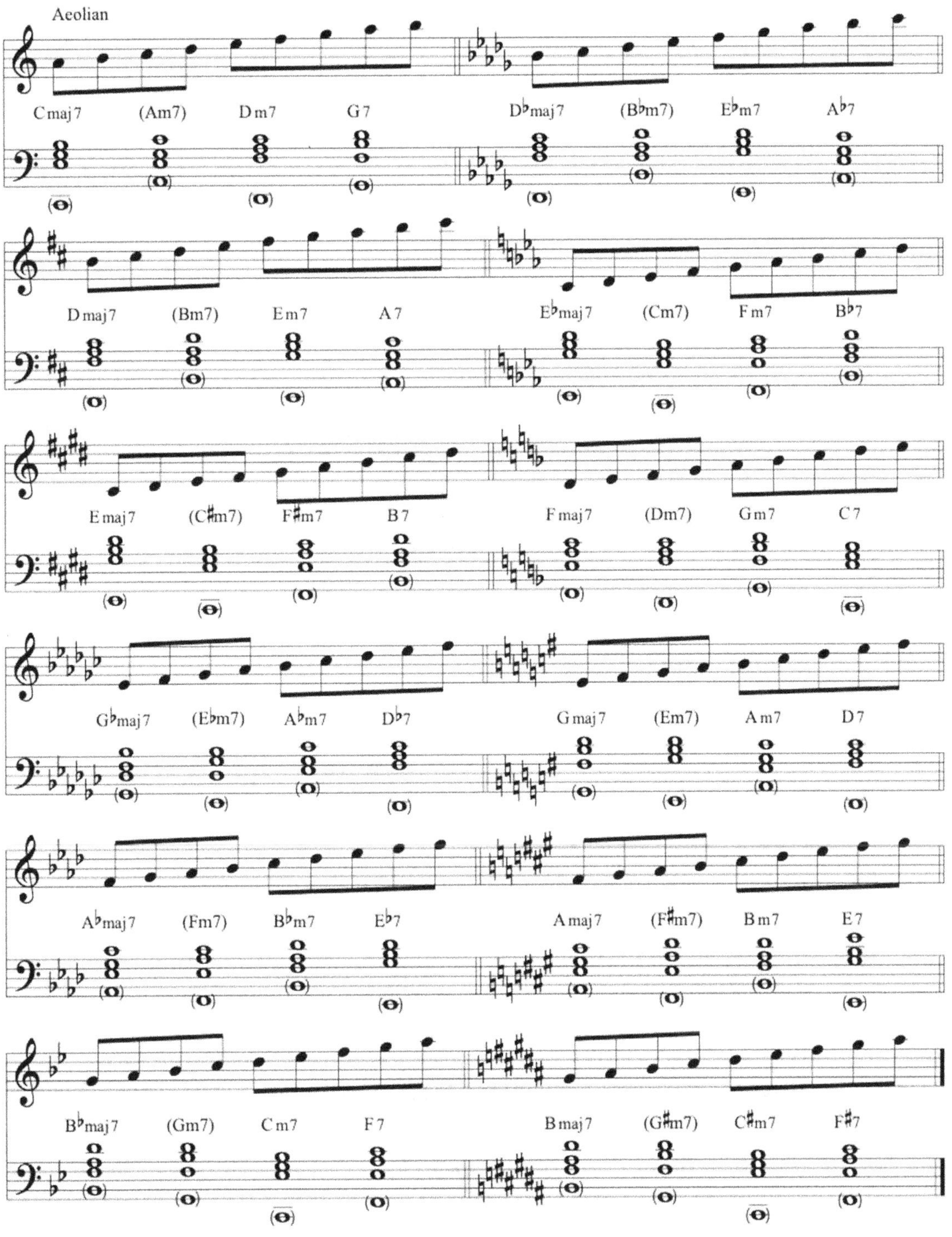

2.7. Chord Scale Solutions for Minor 6th/Minor (Ma7th)

Description: See Chapter 8.2

APPENDIX 2.7.
CHORD SCALE SOLUTIONS FOR MIN6, MINMAJ7

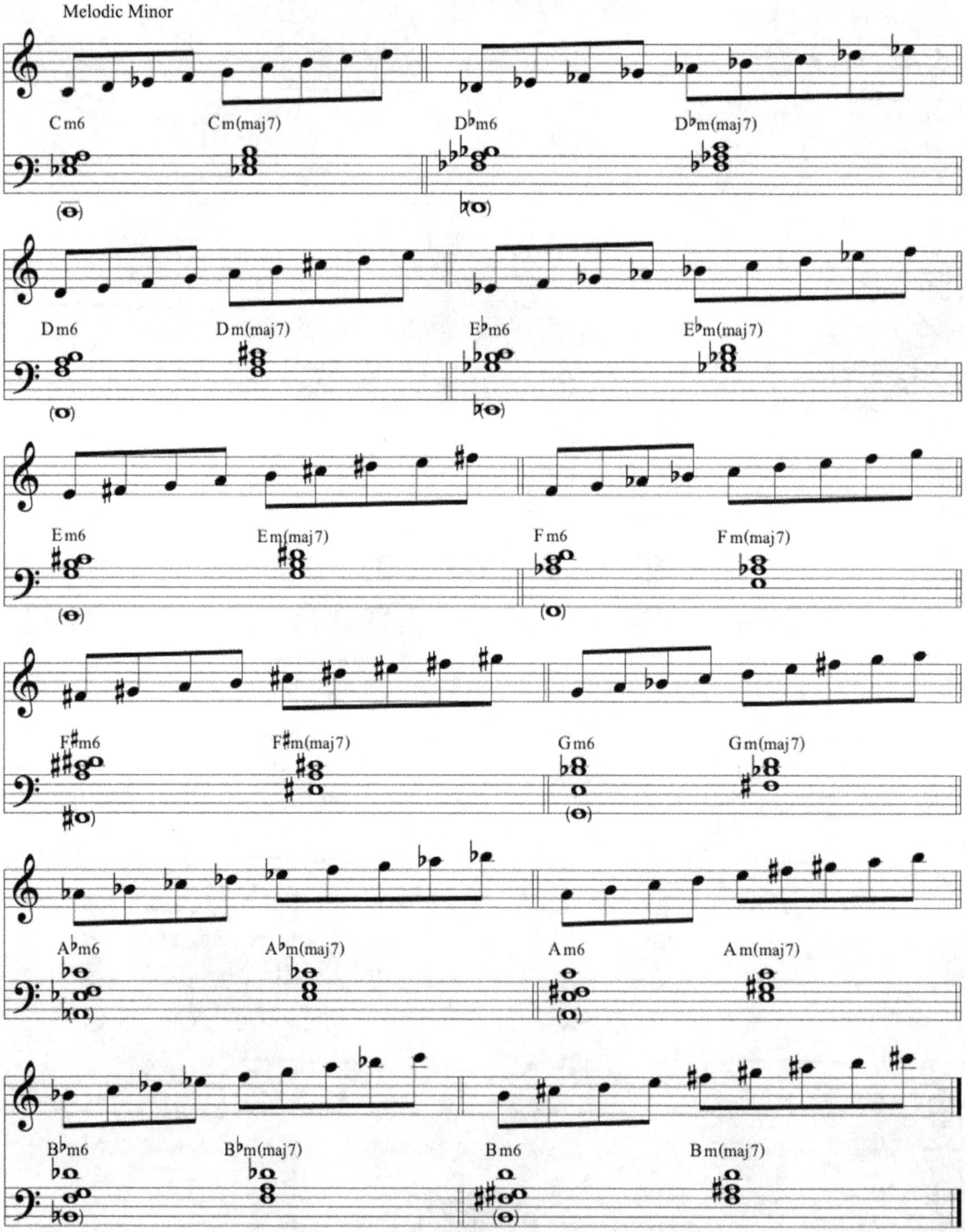

2.8. Melodic Minor Equivalents

Description: See Chapter 8.2

Appendix 2.8. Melodic Minor Equivalents

2.9. Chord Scale Solutions in Half-Diminished 7th

Description: See Chapter 8.2

APPENDIX 2.9.
Chord Scale Solutions in Half-Diminished 7th

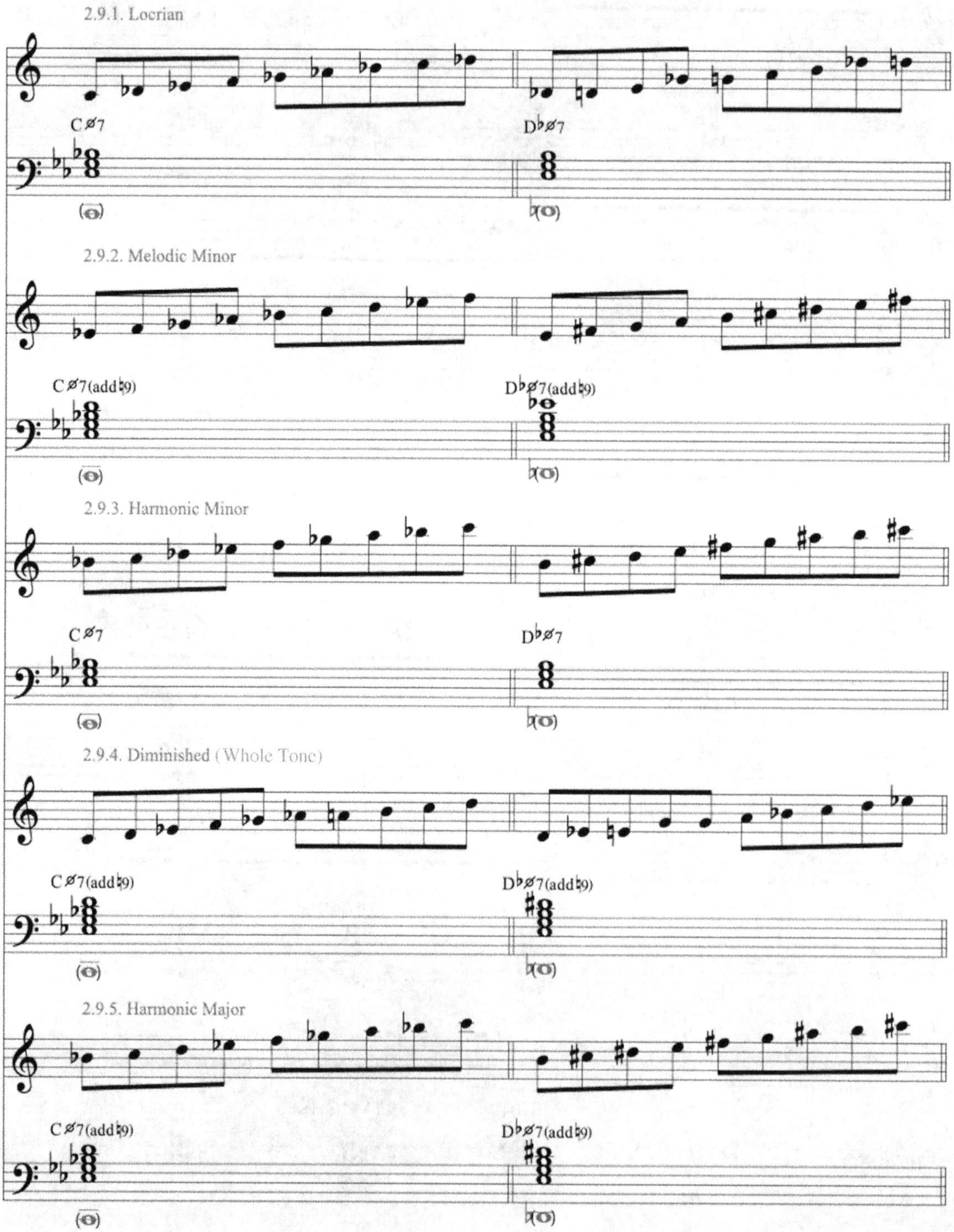

Appendix 2.9. Chord Scale Solutions in Half-Diminished 7th

2.9.1. Locrian

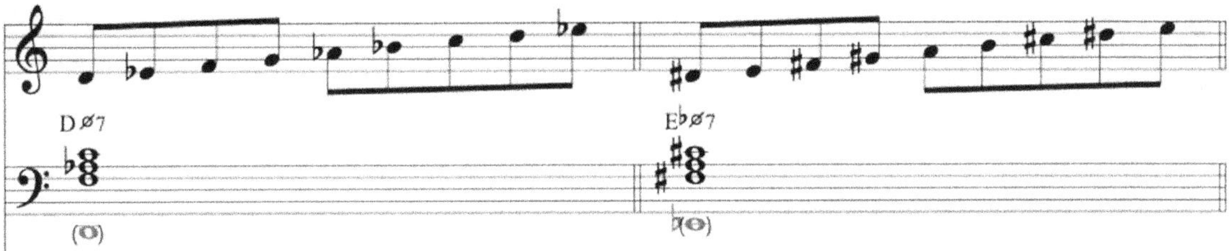

2.9.2. Melodic Minor

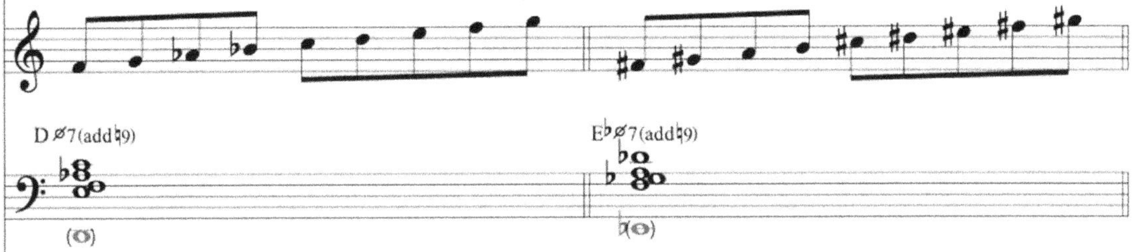

2.9.3. Harmonic Minor

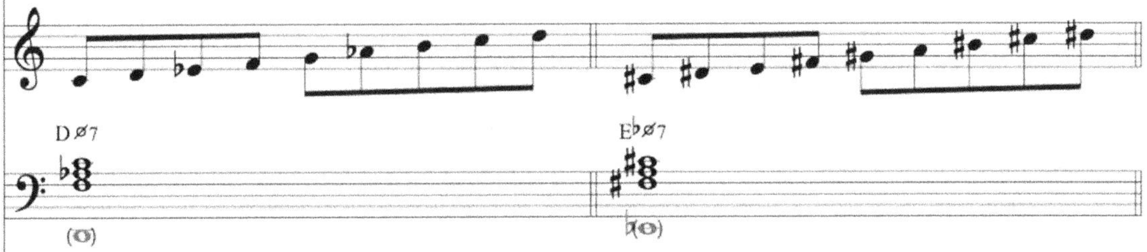

2.9.4. Diminished (Whole Tone)

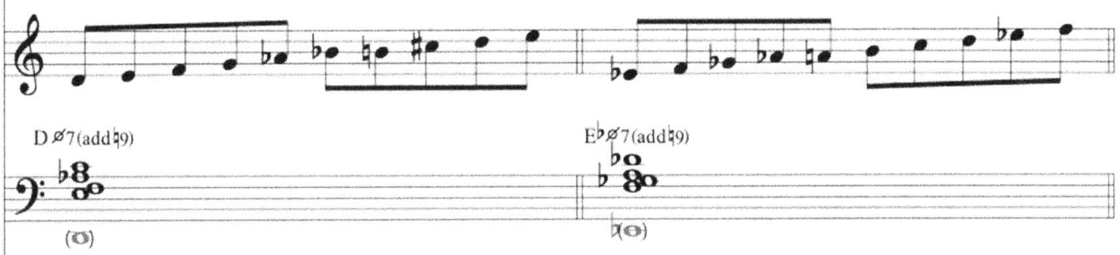

2.9.5. Harmonic Major

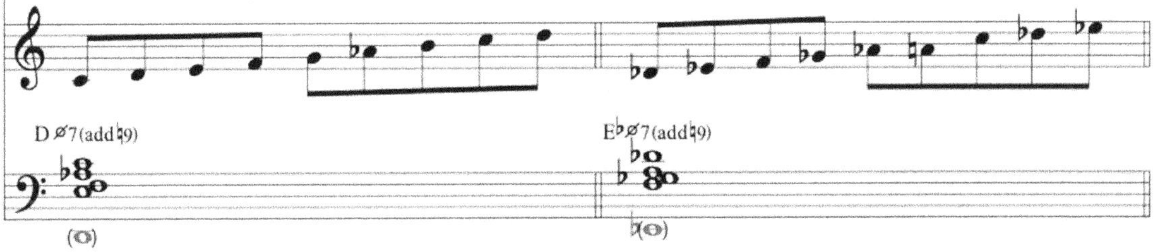

Appendix 2.9. CChord Scale Solutions in Half-Diminished 7th

2.9.1. Locrian

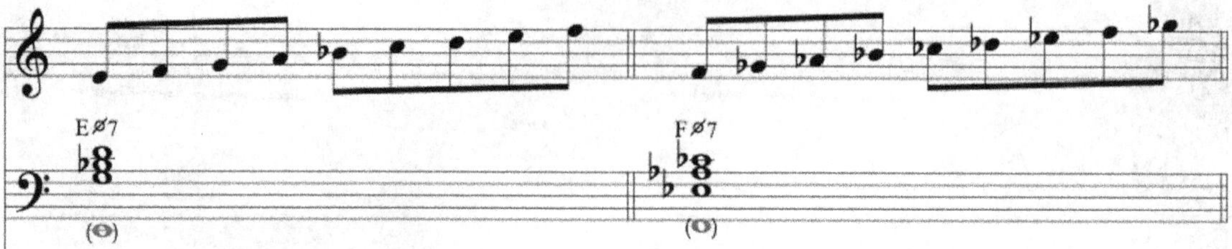

2.9.2. Melodic Minor

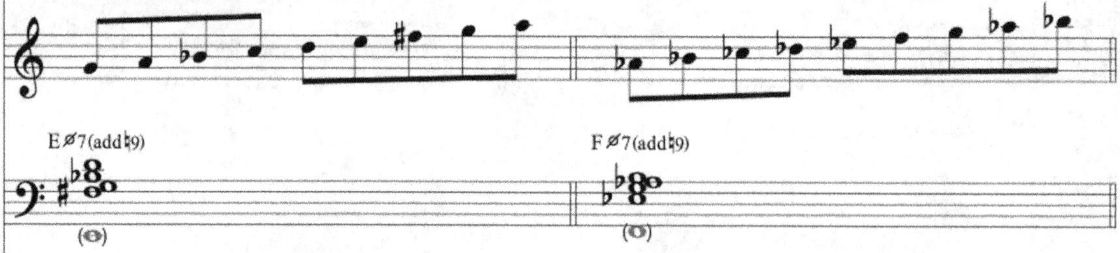

2.9.3. Harmonic Minor

2.9.4. Diminished (Whole Tone)

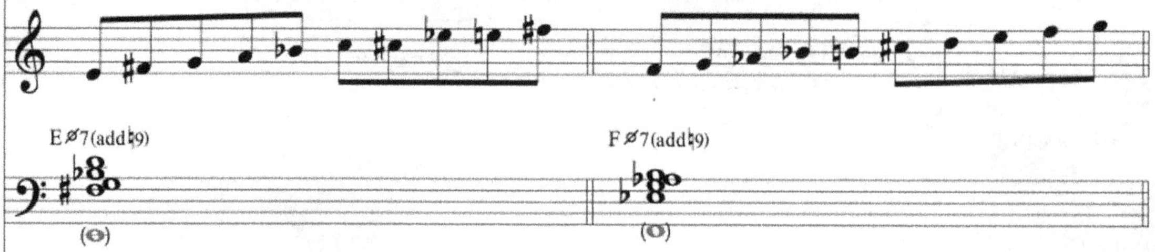

2.9.5. Harmonic Major

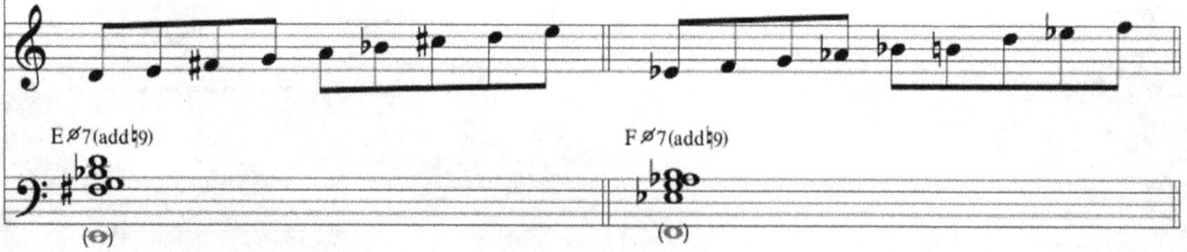

Appendix 2.9. Chord Scale Solutions in Half-Diminished 7th

2.9.1. Locrian

2.9.2. Melodic Minor

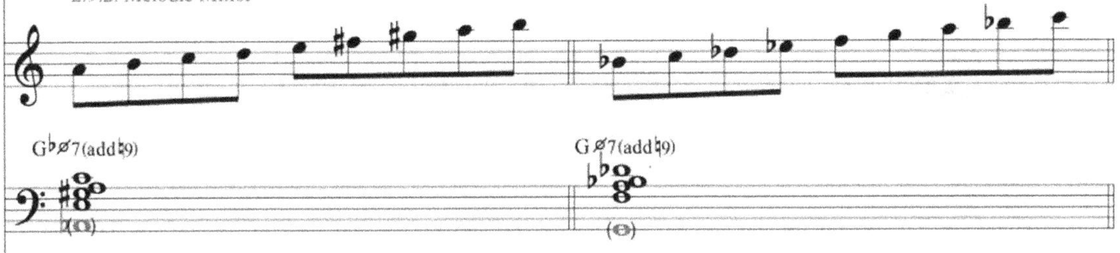

2.9.3. Harmonic Minor

2.9.4. Diminished (Whole Tone)

2.9.5. Harmonic Major

Appendix 2.9. Chord Scale Solutions in Half-Diminished 7th

2.9.1. Locrian

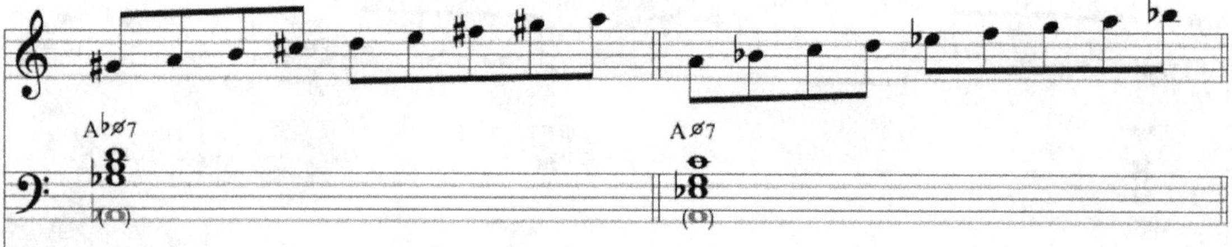

2.9.2. Melodic Minor

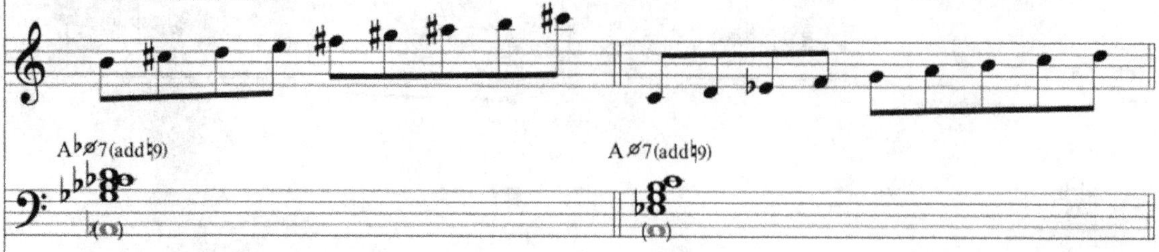

2.9.3. Harmonic Minor

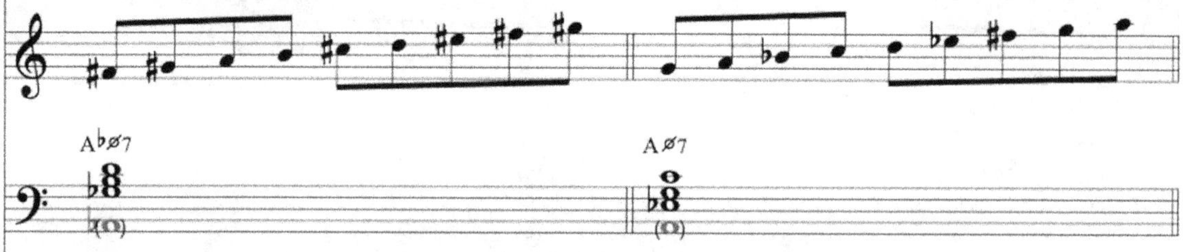

2.9.4. Diminished (Whole Tone)

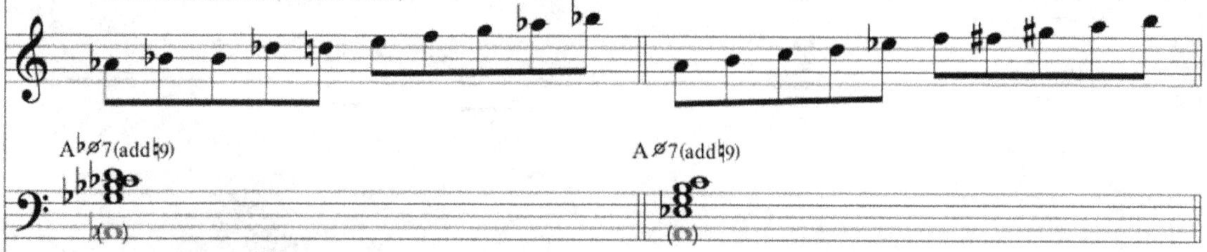

2.9.5. Harmonic Major

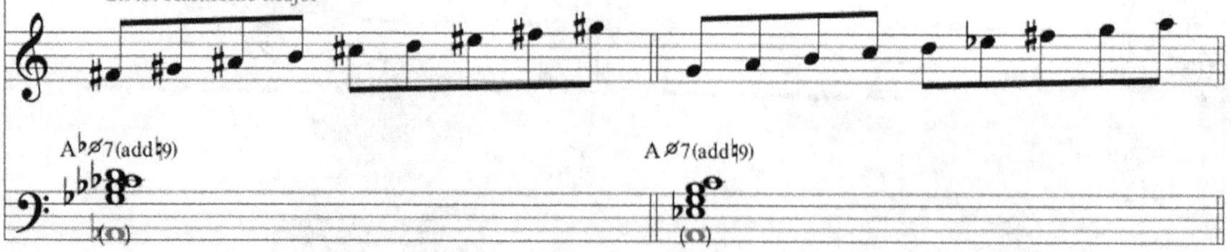

Appendix 2.9. Chord Scale Solutions in Half-Diminished 7th

2.9.1. Locrian

2.9.2. Melodic Minor

2.9.3. Harmonic Minor

2.9.4. Diminished (Whole Tone)

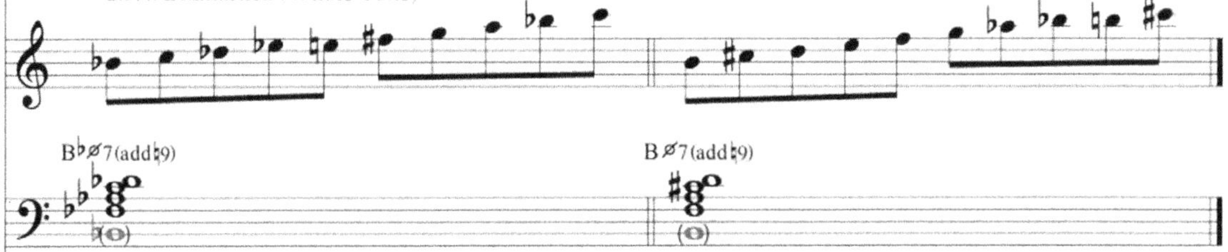

2.9.5. Harmonic Major

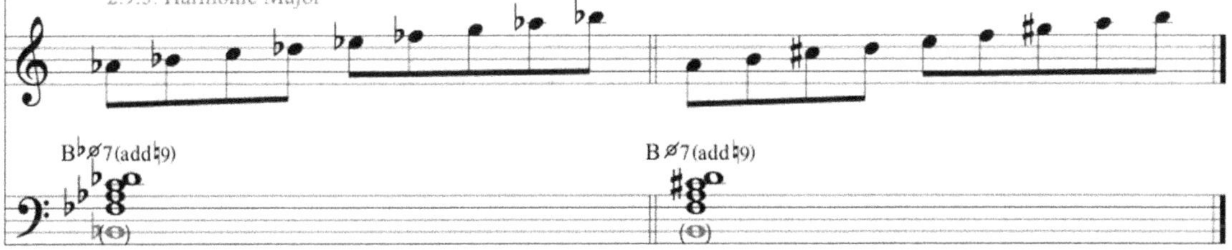

2.10. Chord Scale Solutions for Fully Diminished 7th

Description: See Chapter 8.2

APPENDIX 2.10.
Chord Scale Solutions for Fully Diminished 7th

2.10.1. Graph: Correlation via 2-5-1

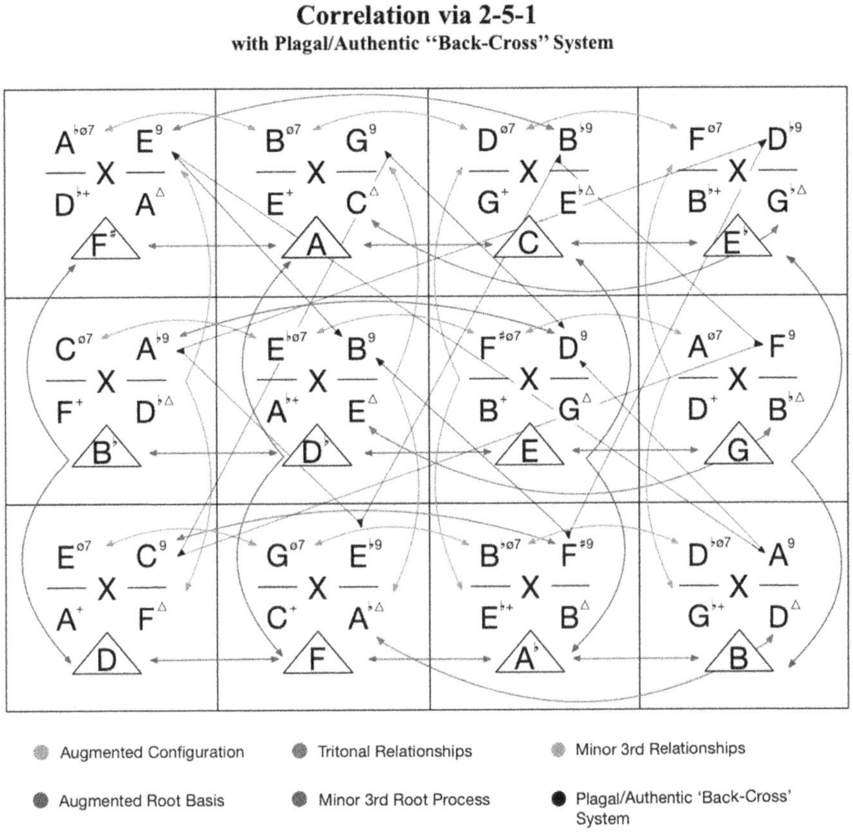
Correlation via 2-5-1
with Plagal/Authentic "Back-Cross" System
A♭ø7 X E9
D♭+ A△
F♯
Bø7 X G9
E+ C△
A
Dø7 X B♭9
G+ E♭△
C
Fø7 X D♭9
B♭+ G♭△
E♭
Cø7 X A♭9
F+ D♭△
B♭
E♭ø7 X B9
A♭+ E△
D♭
F♯ø7 X D9
B+ G△
E
Aø7 X F9
D+ B♭△
G
Eø7 X C9
A+ F△
D
Gø7 X E♭9
C+ A♭△
F
B♭ø7 X F♯9
E♭+ B△
A♭
D♭ø7 X A9
G♭+ D△
B
Augmented Configuration
Tritonal Relationships
Minor 3rd Relationships
Augmented Root Basis
Minor 3rd Root Process
Plagal/Authentic 'Back-Cross' System

Chapter 3

ALTERNATE SOLUTIONS IN DOMINANT

3.1. The X-Configuration

Description: See Section 8.2 for examples

3.1.1. The X-Configuration, Dorian-V7 (Solution A)

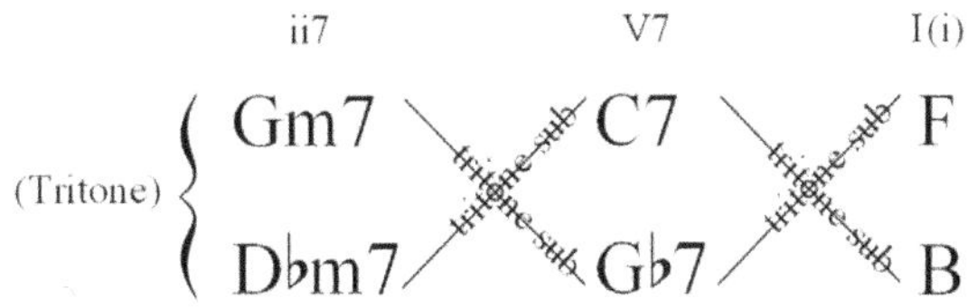

3.1.2. The X-Configuration, V7-Lydian, Super Locrian (Solution B)

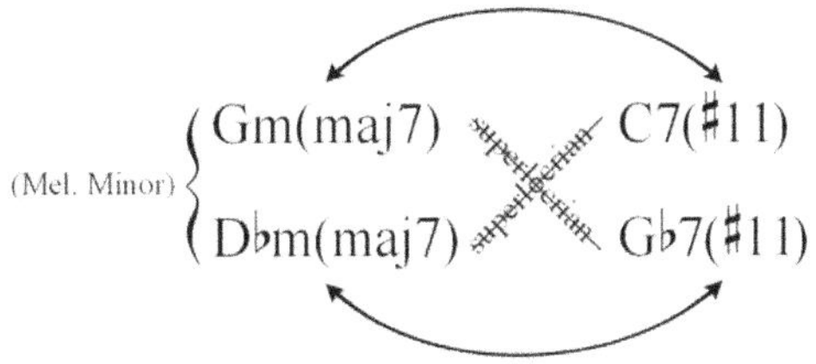

3.1.3. The X-Configuration (Solution C)

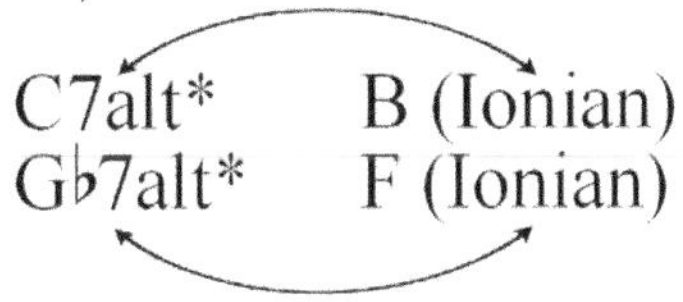

* Denotes the presence of the Major 7th passing tone against the V^7 root, much like the Major 7th in the Dominant Bebop scale.

3.1.4. The X-Configuration, Locrian V7 (Solution D)

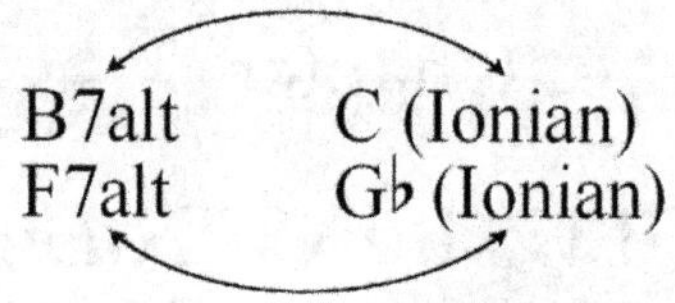

3.1.5. Graph: Augmented Conversions via 2-5-1 with Tritone Subs and Melodic Minor Equivalents

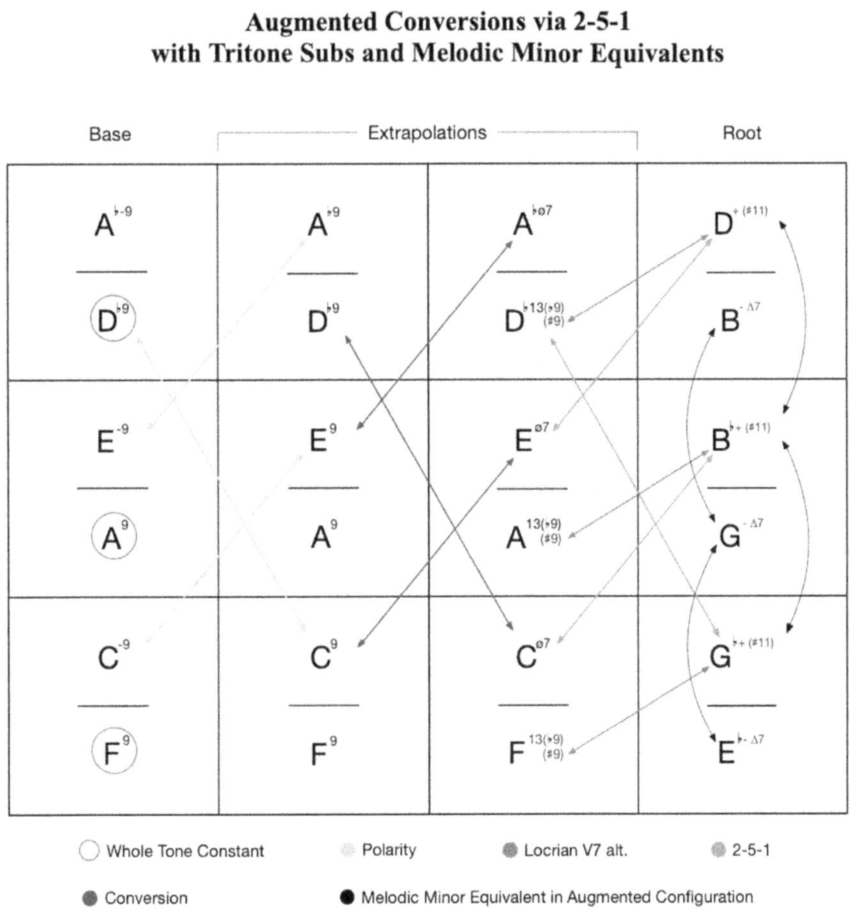

3.2. Alternate Solutions in Dominant

Description: See Section 8.2 for examples

APPENDIX 3.2.
ALTERNATE SOLUTIONS IN DOMINANT

Appendix 3.2. Alternate Soultions In Dominant

3.2.1 Major Pentatonic Tritone Sub 3.2.2. V7 Tritone Sub Parent Scale 3.2.3. V7 Locrian

Chapter 4

THE II-V PROGRESSION AND TRITONE SUBSTITUTION

Section 1) The ii-V

4.1.1. ii-V Patterns

APPENDIX 4.1.1.
ii-V PATTERNS

Appendix 4.1.1. ii-V Patterns

E7 A7 D Em7 A7 D
Em7 Am7 Dm Em7(♭5) A7(♭9) D
E7 A7 D Em7 A7 D
Em7 Am7 Dm Em7(♭5) A7(♭9) D
F7 B♭7 E♭ Fm7 B♭7 E♭
Fm7 B♭m7 E♭m Fm7(♭5) B♭7(♭9) E♭
F7 B♭7 E♭ Fm7 B♭7 E♭
Fm7 B♭m7 E♭m Fm7(♭5) B♭7(♭9) E♭

Appendix 4.1.1. ii-V Patterns

F♯7 B7 E F♯m7 B7 E
F♯m7 Bm7 Em F♯m7(♭5) B7(♭9) E
F♯7 B7 E F♯m7 B7 E
F♯m7 Bm7 Em F♯m7(♭5) B7(♭9) E
G7 C7 F Gm7 C7 F
Gm7 Cm7 Fm Gm7(♭5) C7(♭9) F
G7 C7 F Gm7 C7 F
Gm7 Cm7 Fm Gm7(♭5) C7(♭9) F

Appendix 4.1.1. ii-V Patterns

A♭7 D♭7 G♭ A♭m7 D♭7 G♭
A♭m7 D♭m7 G♭m A♭m7(♭5) D♭7(♭9) G♭
A♭7 D♭7 G♭ A♭m7 D♭7 G♭
A♭m7 D♭m7 G♭m A♭m7(♭5) D♭7(♭9) G♭
A7 D7 G Am7 D7 G
Am7 Dm7 Gm Am7(♭5) D7(♭9) G
A7 D7 G Am7 D7 G
Am7 Dm7 Gm Am7(♭5) D7(♭9) G

Appendix 4.1.1. ii-V Patterns

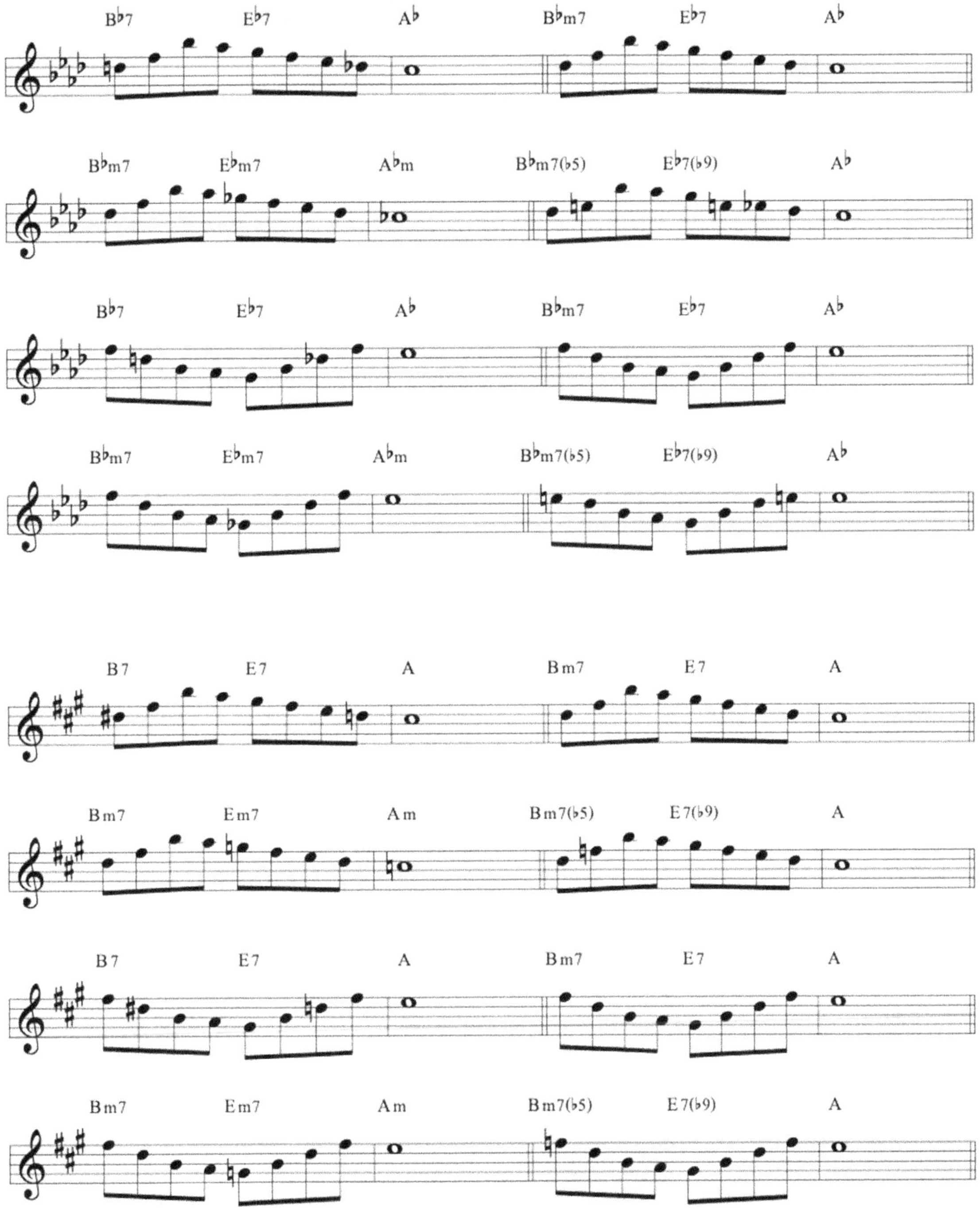
B♭7 E♭7 A♭ B♭m7 E♭7 A♭
B♭m7 E♭m7 A♭m B♭m7(♭5) E♭7(♭9) A♭
B♭7 E♭7 A♭ B♭m7 E♭7 A♭
B♭m7 E♭m7 A♭m B♭m7(♭5) E♭7(♭9) A♭
B7 E7 A Bm7 E7 A
Bm7 Em7 Am Bm7(♭5) E7(♭9) A
B7 E7 A Bm7 E7 A
Bm7 Em7 Am Bm7(♭5) E7(♭9) A

Appendix 4.1.1. ii-V Patterns

C7 F7 B♭ Cm7 F7 B♭
Cm7 Fm7 B♭m Cm7(♭5) F7(♭9) B♭
C7 F7 B♭ Cm7 F7 B♭
Cm7 Fm7 B♭m Cm7(♭5) F7(♭9) B♭
C♯7 F♯7 B C♯m7 F♯7 B
C♯m7 F♯m7 Bm C♯m7(♭5) F♯7(♭9) B
C♯7 F♯7 B C♯m7 F♯7 B
C♯m7 F♯m7 Bm C♯m7(♭5) F♯7(♭9) B

Section 1) The ii-V

4.1.2. Inner Motion of ii-V

Description: See Chapter 8.2

APPENDIX 4.1.2.
INNER MOTION OF ii-V

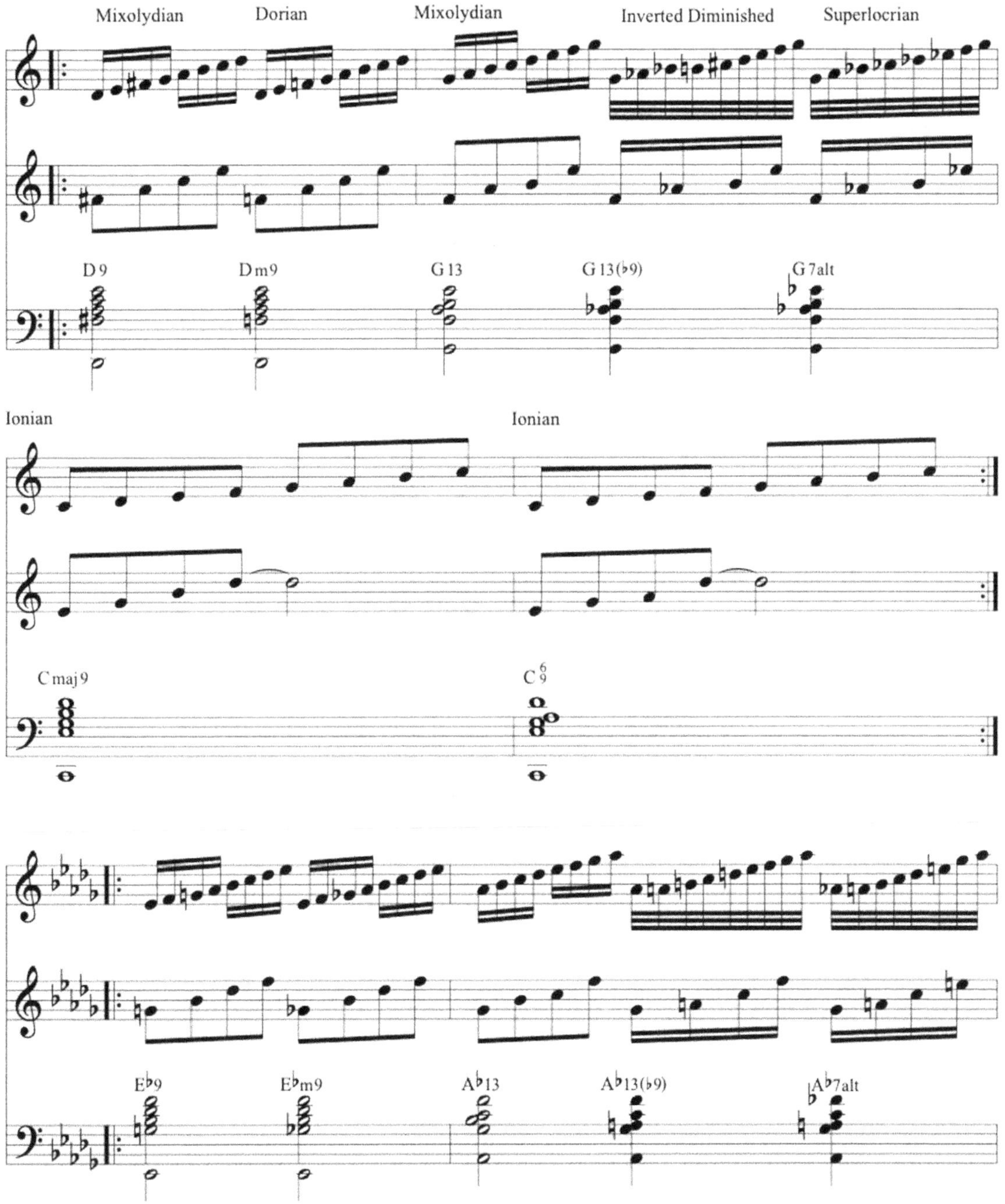

Appendix 4.1.2. Inner Motion of ii-V

D♭maj9
D♭6/9
E9
Em9
A13
A13(♭9)
A7alt
Dmaj9
D6/9

Appendix 4.1.2. Inner Motion of ii-V

F9
Fm9
B♭13
B♭13(♭9)
B♭7alt
E♭maj9
E♭6/9
F♯9
F♯m9
B 13
B 13(♭9)
B 7alt

Appendix 4.1.2. Inner Motion of ii-V

Emaj9
E6/9
G9
Gm9
C13
C13(♭9)
C7alt
Fmaj9
F6/9

Appendix 4.1.2. Inner Motion of ii-V

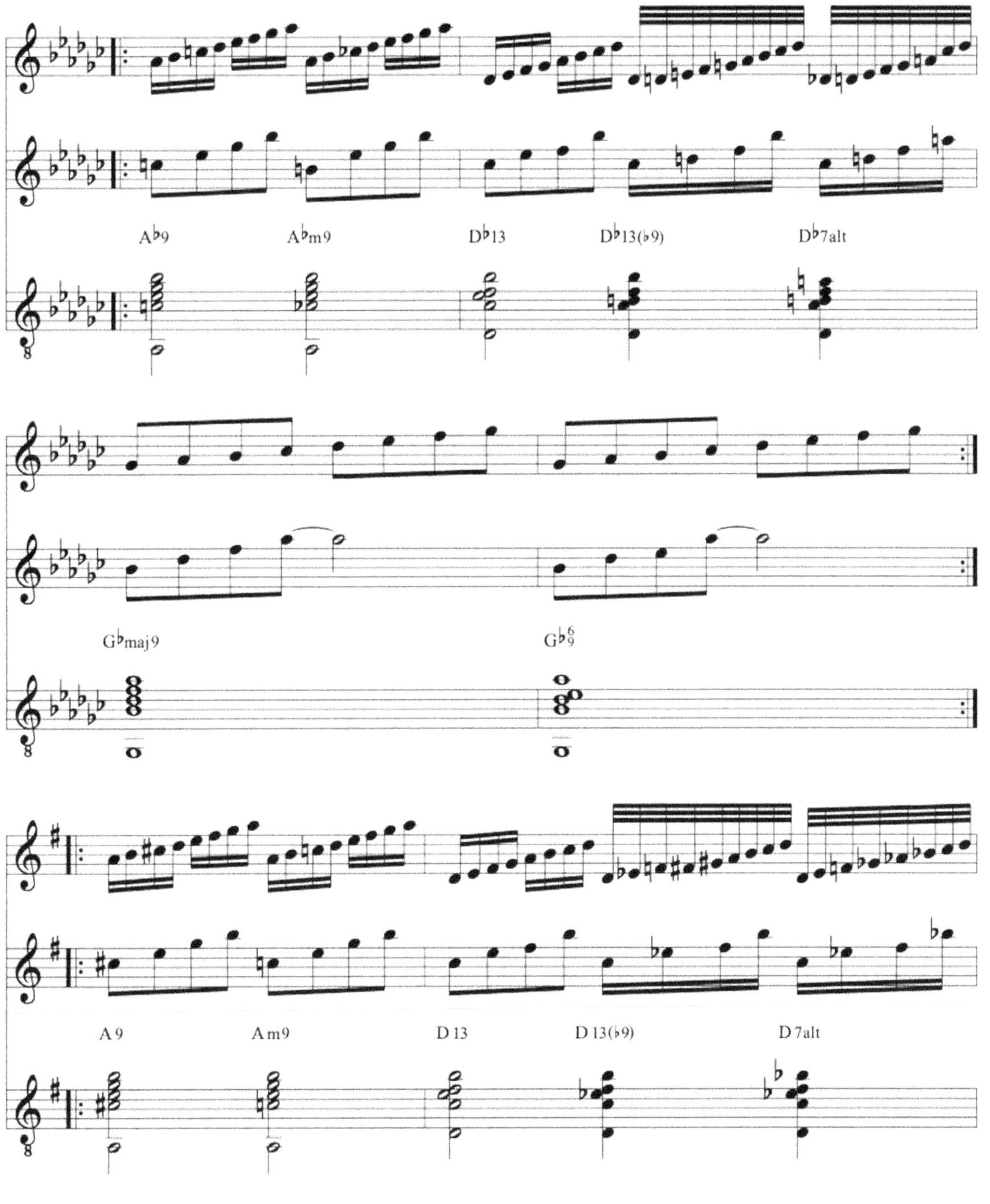
A♭9
A♭m9
D♭13
D♭13(♭9)
D♭7alt
G♭maj9
G♭6/9
A 9
A m9
D 13
D 13(♭9)
D 7alt

Appendix 4.1.2. Inner Motion of ii-V

Gmaj9
G6/9
B♭9
B♭m9
E♭13
E♭13(♭9)
E♭7alt
A♭maj9
A♭6/9

Appendix 4.1.2. Inner Motion of ii-V

B9
Bm9
E13
E13(♭9)
E7alt
Amaj9
A 6/9
C9
Cm9
F13
F13(♭9)
F7alt

Appendix 4.1.2. Inner Motion of ii-V

B♭maj9
B♭6/9
C♯9
C♯m9
F♯13
F♯13(♭9)
F♯7alt
B maj9
B 6/9

Section 1) The ii-V

4.1.3. False ii-V

Description: See Chapter 8.2

APPENDIX 4.1.3.
False ii-V

2 Appendix 4.1.3. False ii-V

A♭m7 D♭7 G♭maj7 Bm7 E7 G♭maj7 Dm7 G7 G♭maj7 Fm7(♭5) B♭7(♭9) G♭maj7 (E♭m7)
Am7 D7 Gmaj7 Cm7 F7 Gmaj7 E♭m7 A♭7 Gmaj7 F♯m7(♭5) B7(♭9) Gmaj7 (Em7)
B♭m7 E♭7 A♭maj7 D♭m7 G♭7 A♭maj7 Em7 A7 A♭maj7 Gm7(♭5) C7(♭9) A♭maj7 (Fm7)
Bm7 E7 Amaj7 Dm7 G7 Amaj7 Fm7 B♭7 Amaj7 A♭m7(♭5) D♭7(♭9) Amaj7 (F♯m7)
5
Cm7 F7 B♭maj7 E♭m7 A♭7 B♭maj7 F♯m7 B7 B♭maj7 Am7(♭5) D7(♭9) B♭maj7 (Gm7)
9
C♯m7 F♯7 Bmaj7 Em7 A7 Bmaj7 Gm7 C7 Bmaj7 B♭m7(♭5) E♭7(♭9) Bmaj7 (A♭m7)

Section 1) The ii-V

4.1.4. Tritone ii-V

Description: See Chapter 8.2.

APPENDIX 4.1.4.
TRITONE ii-V

Appendix 4.1.4. Tritone ii-V

Bm7
E7
E#m7
B♭7
Amaj7
Cm7
F7
F#m7
B7
B♭maj7
C#m7
F#7
F×m7
B#7
Bmaj7
Dm7
G7
A♭m7
D♭7
Cmaj7
E♭m7
A♭7
Am7
D7
D♭maj7
Em7
A7
B♭m7
E♭7
Dmaj7

4.1.4.1. Semi-Tri-Tonal Relationship in Dorian

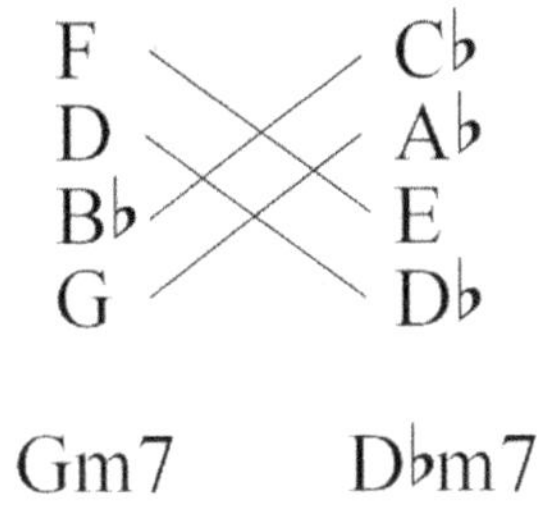

4.1.4.2. Semi-Tri-Tonal Relationship in Dominant

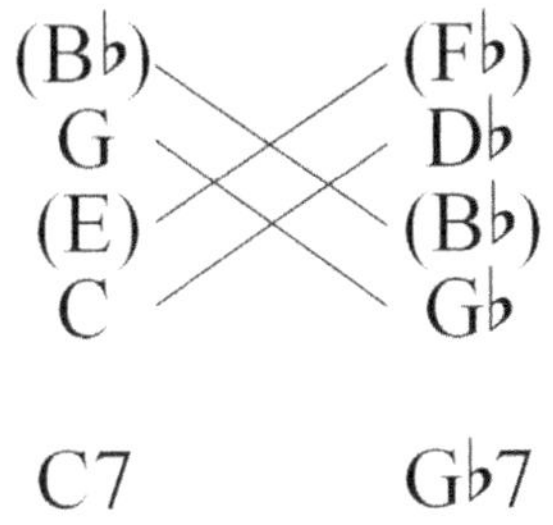

4.1.4.3. Tritone ii-V (Linear/Vertical)

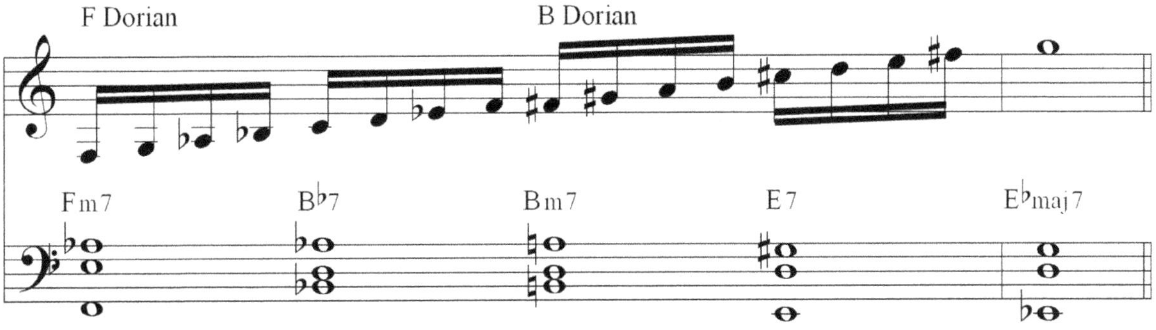

4.1.4.4. Graph: 2-5-1 and Substitutions

2-5-1 and Substitutions

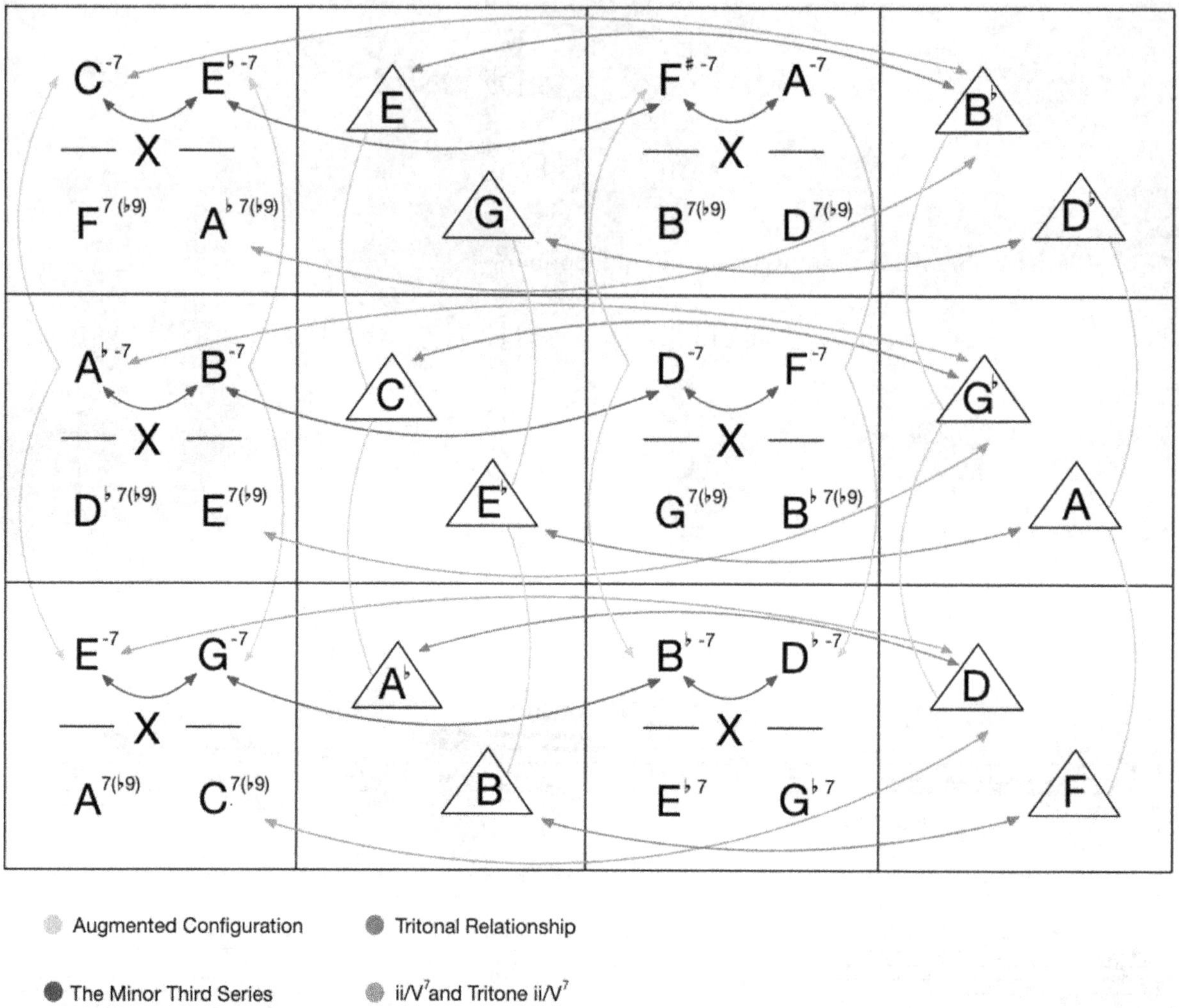

Section 2) 1625, 3625, and 2536

4.2.1. 1625, 3625, and 2536

Description: Progressions that move in fourths, V^7 exponents descend in half-steps, and ascend in whole- steps (substituting the tritone [root] for every other semi-tone)

APPENDIX 4.2.1.
1625, 3625 & 2536

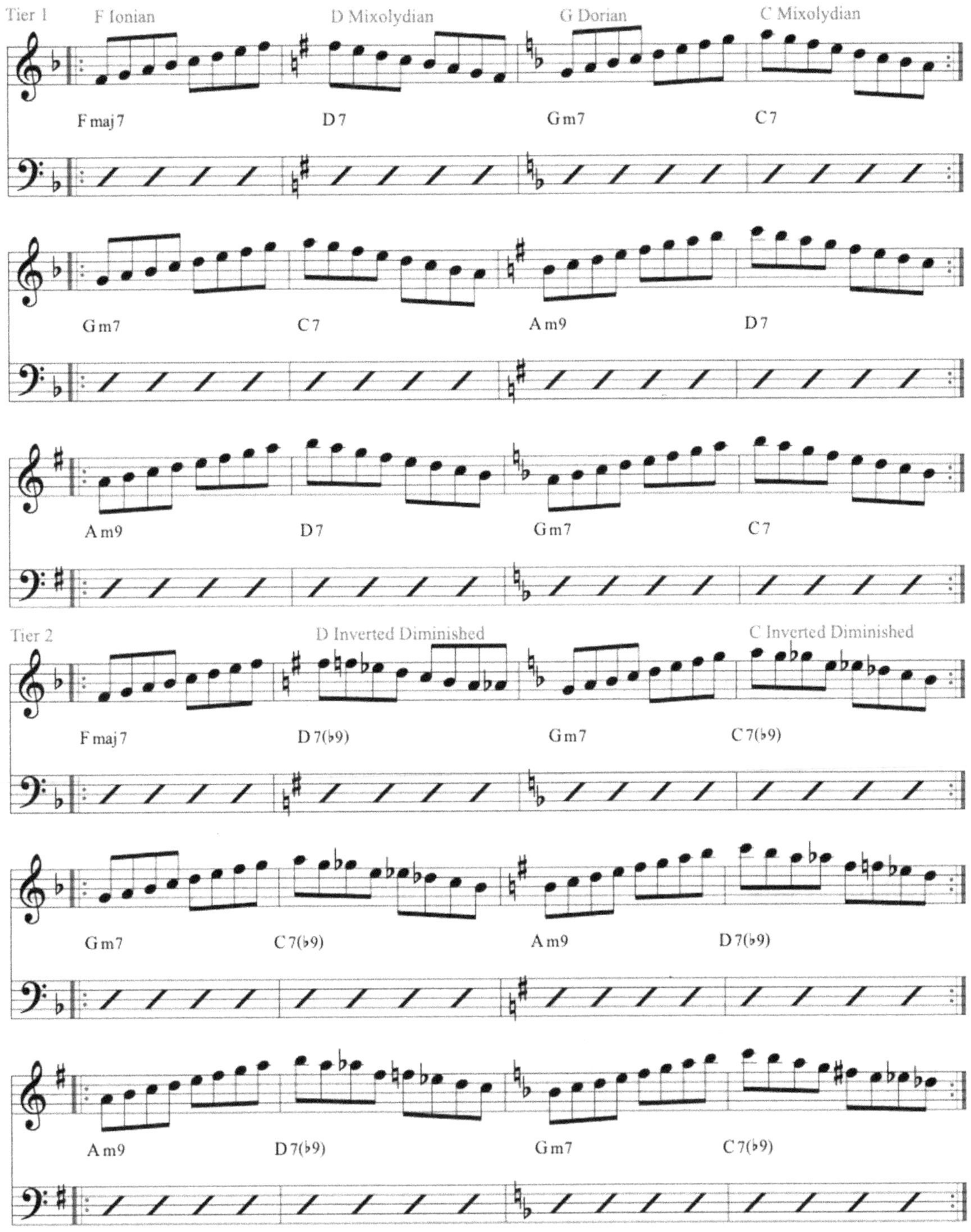

Appendix 4.2.1. 1625, 3625 & 2536

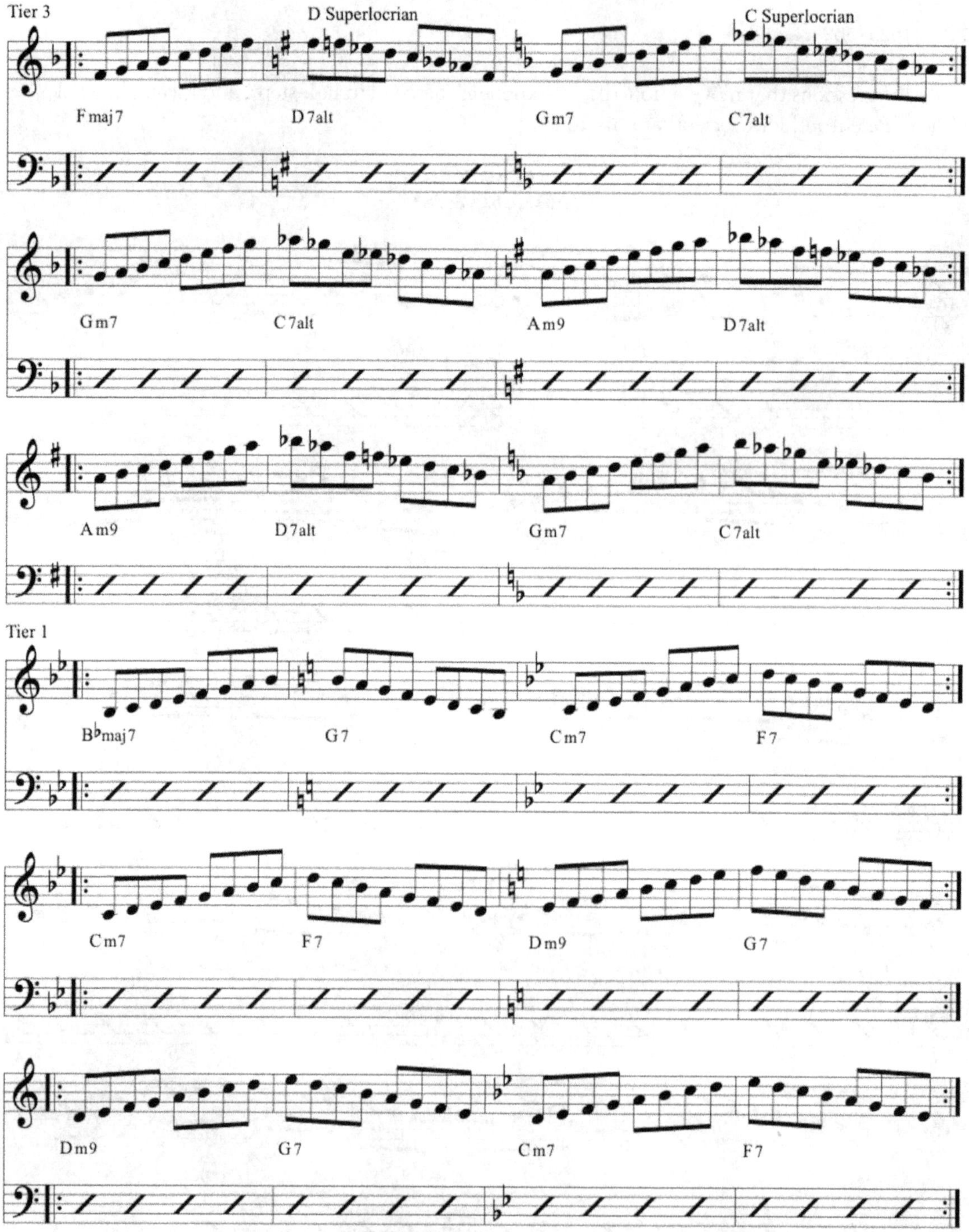
Tier 3
D Superlocrian
C Superlocrian
Fmaj7
D7alt
Gm7
C7alt
Gm7
C7alt
Am9
D7alt
Am9
D7alt
Gm7
C7alt
Tier 1
B♭maj7
G7
Cm7
F7
Cm7
F7
Dm9
G7
Dm9
G7
Cm7
F7

Appendix 4.2.1. 1625, 3625 & 2536

Tier 2

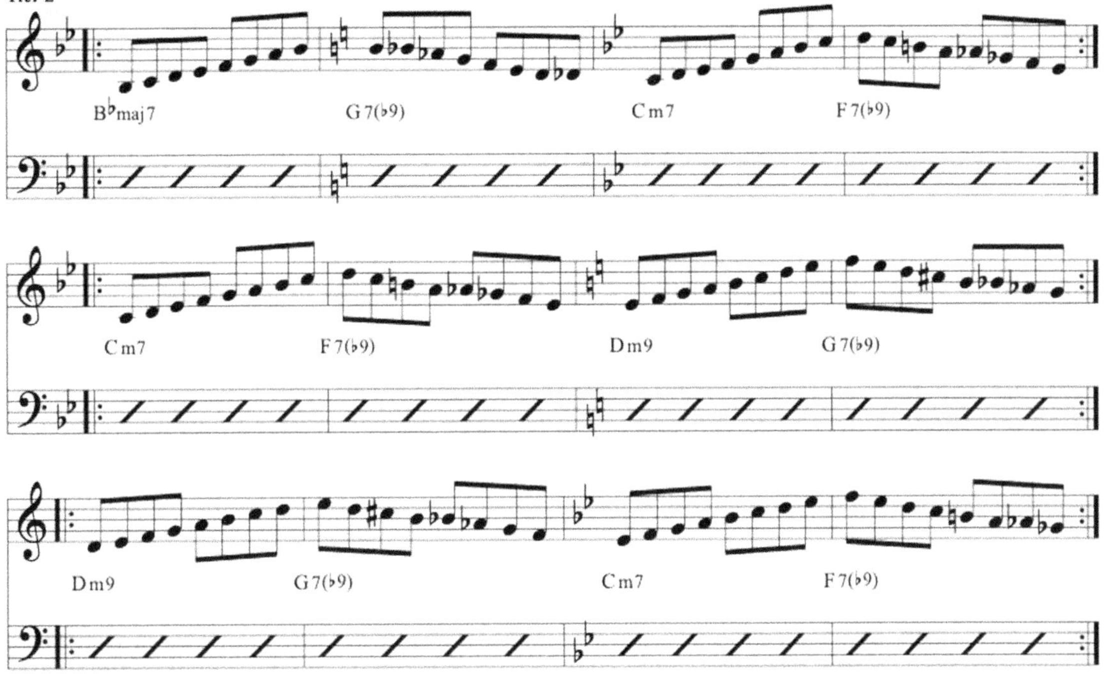
B♭maj7
G7(♭9)
Cm7
F7(♭9)
Cm7
F7(♭9)
Dm9
G7(♭9)
Dm9
G7(♭9)
Cm7
F7(♭9)

Tier 3

B♭maj7
G7alt
Cm7
F7alt
Cm7
F7alt
Dm9
G7alt
Dm9
G7alt
Cm7
F7alt

Appendix 4.2.1. 1625, 3625 & 2536

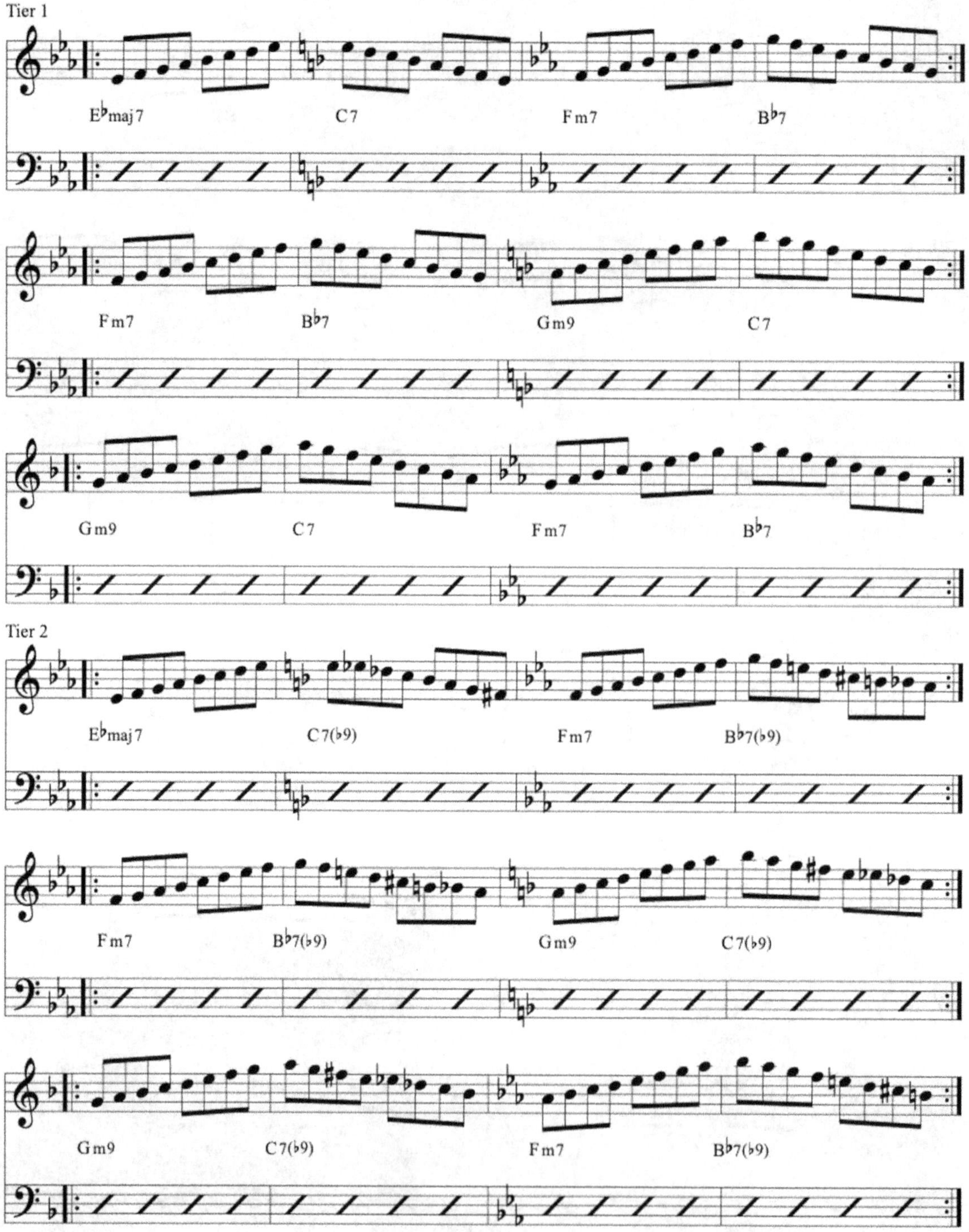
Tier 1
E♭maj7 C7 Fm7 B♭7
Fm7 B♭7 Gm9 C7
Gm9 C7 Fm7 B♭7
Tier 2
E♭maj7 C7(♭9) Fm7 B♭7(♭9)
Fm7 B♭7(♭9) Gm9 C7(♭9)
Gm9 C7(♭9) Fm7 B♭7(♭9)

Appendix 4.2.1. 1625, 3625 & 2536

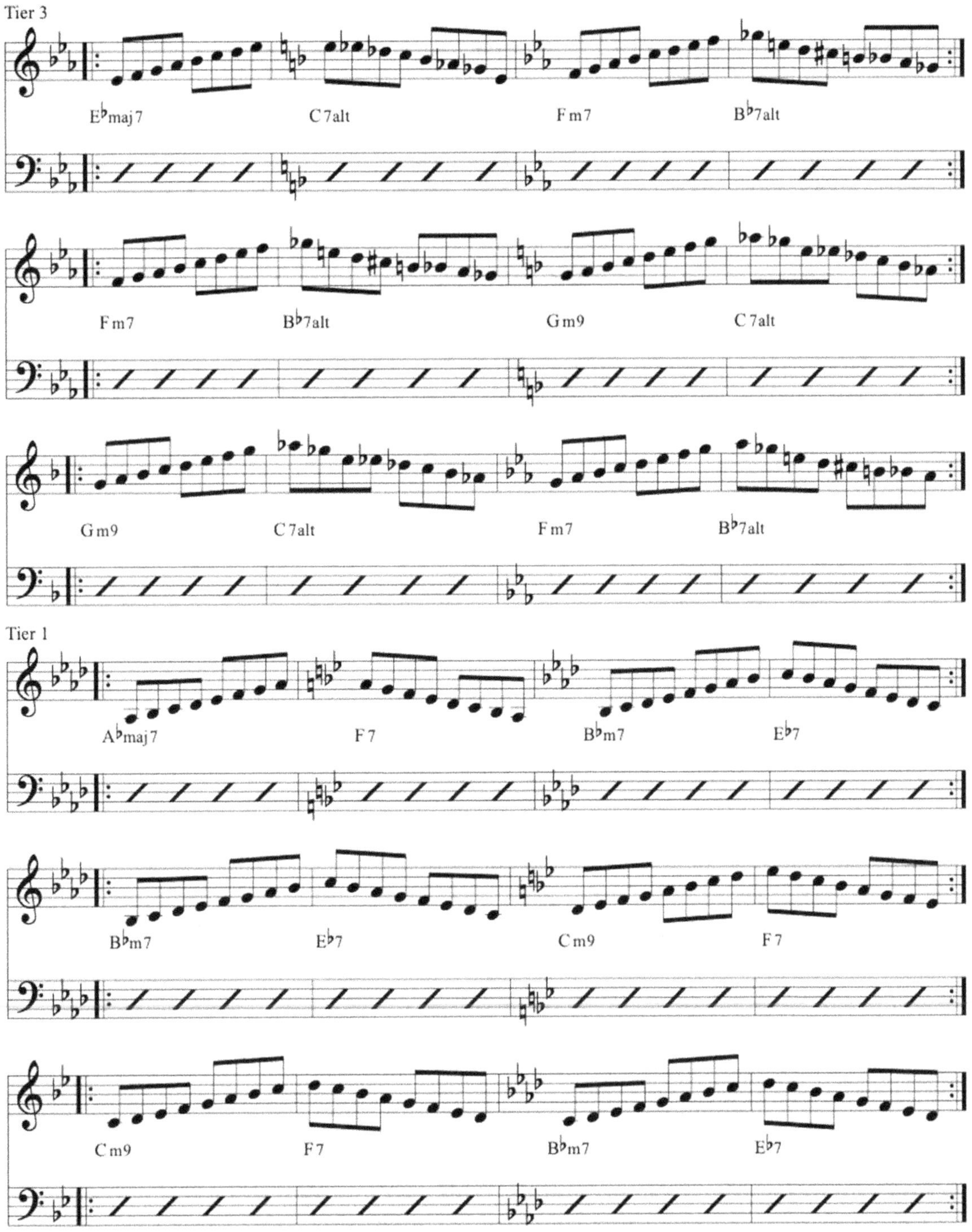
Tier 3
E♭maj7
C7alt
Fm7
B♭7alt
Fm7
B♭7alt
Gm9
C7alt
Gm9
C7alt
Fm7
B♭7alt
Tier 1
A♭maj7
F7
B♭m7
E♭7
B♭m7
E♭7
Cm9
F7
Cm9
F7
B♭m7
E♭7

Appendix 4.2.1. 1625, 3625 & 2536

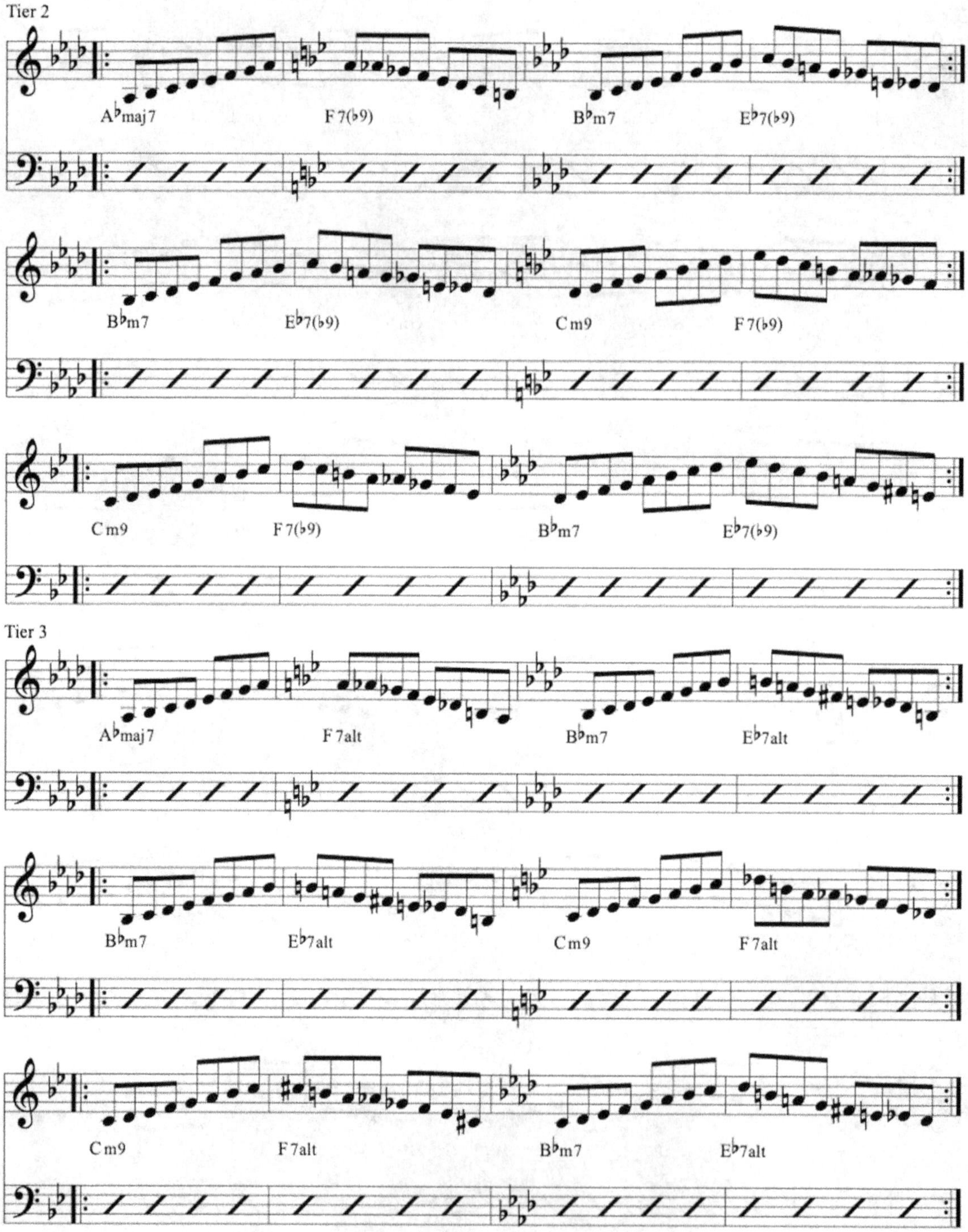
Tier 2
A♭maj7
F7(♭9)
B♭m7
E♭7(♭9)
B♭m7
E♭7(♭9)
Cm9
F7(♭9)
Cm9
F7(♭9)
B♭m7
E♭7(♭9)
Tier 3
A♭maj7
F7alt
B♭m7
E♭7alt
B♭m7
E♭7alt
Cm9
F7alt
Cm9
F7alt
B♭m7
E♭7alt

Appendix 4.2.1. 1625, 3625 & 2536

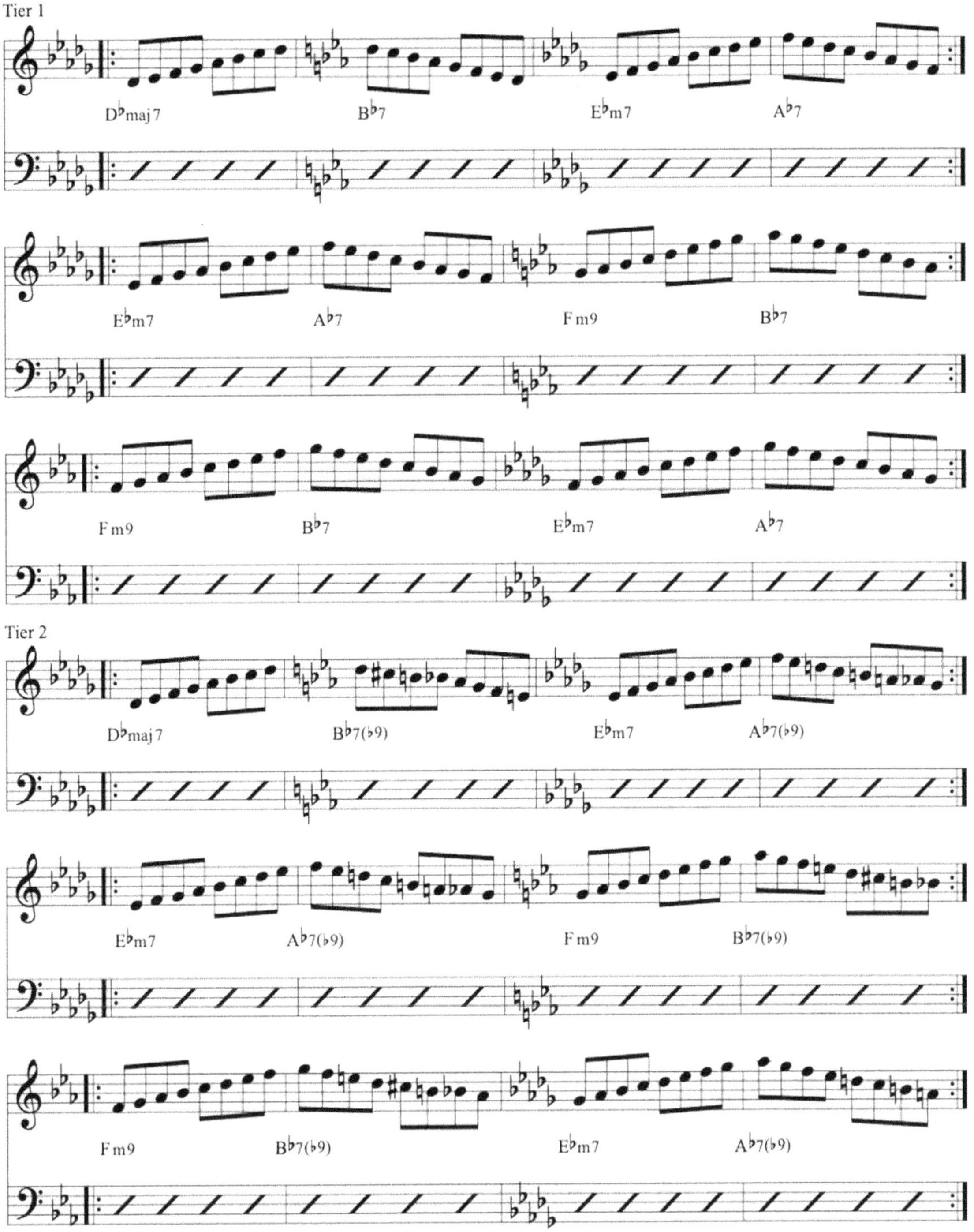
Tier 1
D♭maj7
B♭7
E♭m7
A♭7
E♭m7
A♭7
F m9
B♭7
F m9
B♭7
E♭m7
A♭7
Tier 2
D♭maj7
B♭7(♭9)
E♭m7
A♭7(♭9)
E♭m7
A♭7(♭9)
F m9
B♭7(♭9)
F m9
B♭7(♭9)
E♭m7
A♭7(♭9)

Appendix 4.2.1. 1625, 3625 & 2536

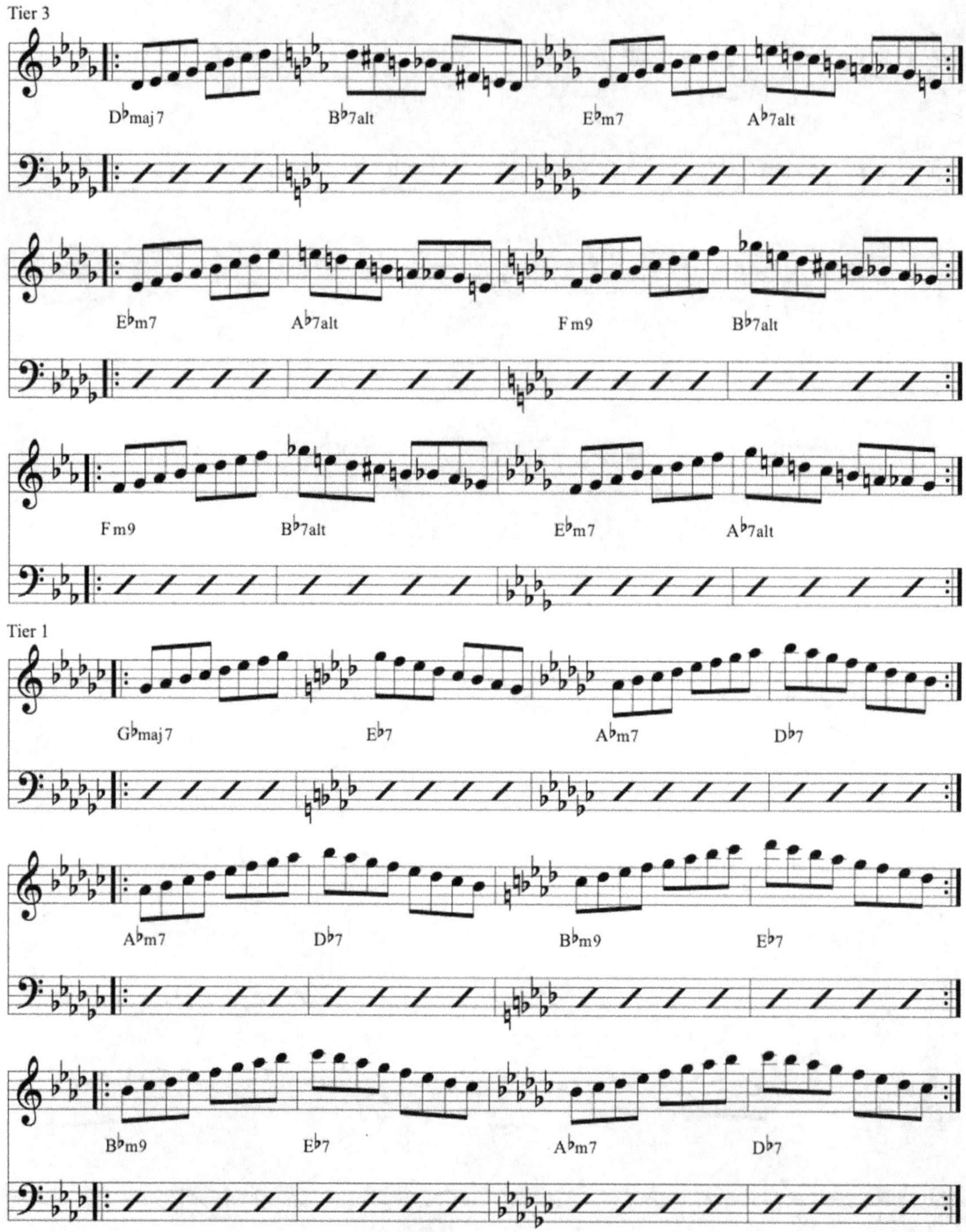
Tier 3
D♭maj7
B♭7alt
E♭m7
A♭7alt
E♭m7
A♭7alt
F m9
B♭7alt
F m9
B♭7alt
E♭m7
A♭7alt
Tier 1
G♭maj7
E♭7
A♭m7
D♭7
A♭m7
D♭7
B♭m9
E♭7
B♭m9
E♭7
A♭m7
D♭7

Appendix 4.2.1. 1625, 3625 & 2536

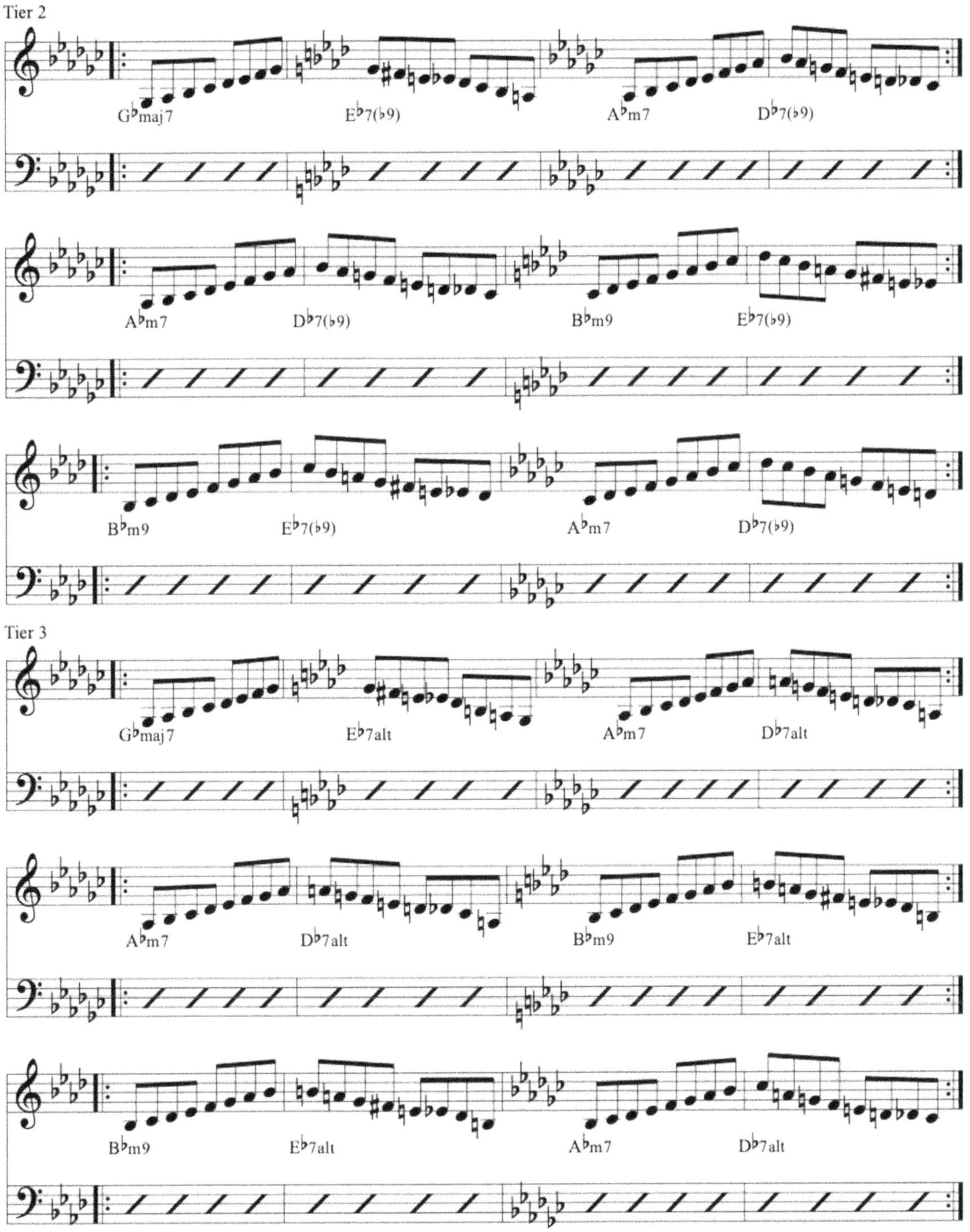
Tier 2
G♭maj7
E♭7(♭9)
A♭m7
D♭7(♭9)
A♭m7
D♭7(♭9)
B♭m9
E♭7(♭9)
B♭m9
E♭7(♭9)
A♭m7
D♭7(♭9)
Tier 3
G♭maj7
E♭7alt
A♭m7
D♭7alt
A♭m7
D♭7alt
B♭m9
E♭7alt
B♭m9
E♭7alt
A♭m7
D♭7alt

Appendix 4.2.1. 1625, 3625 & 2536

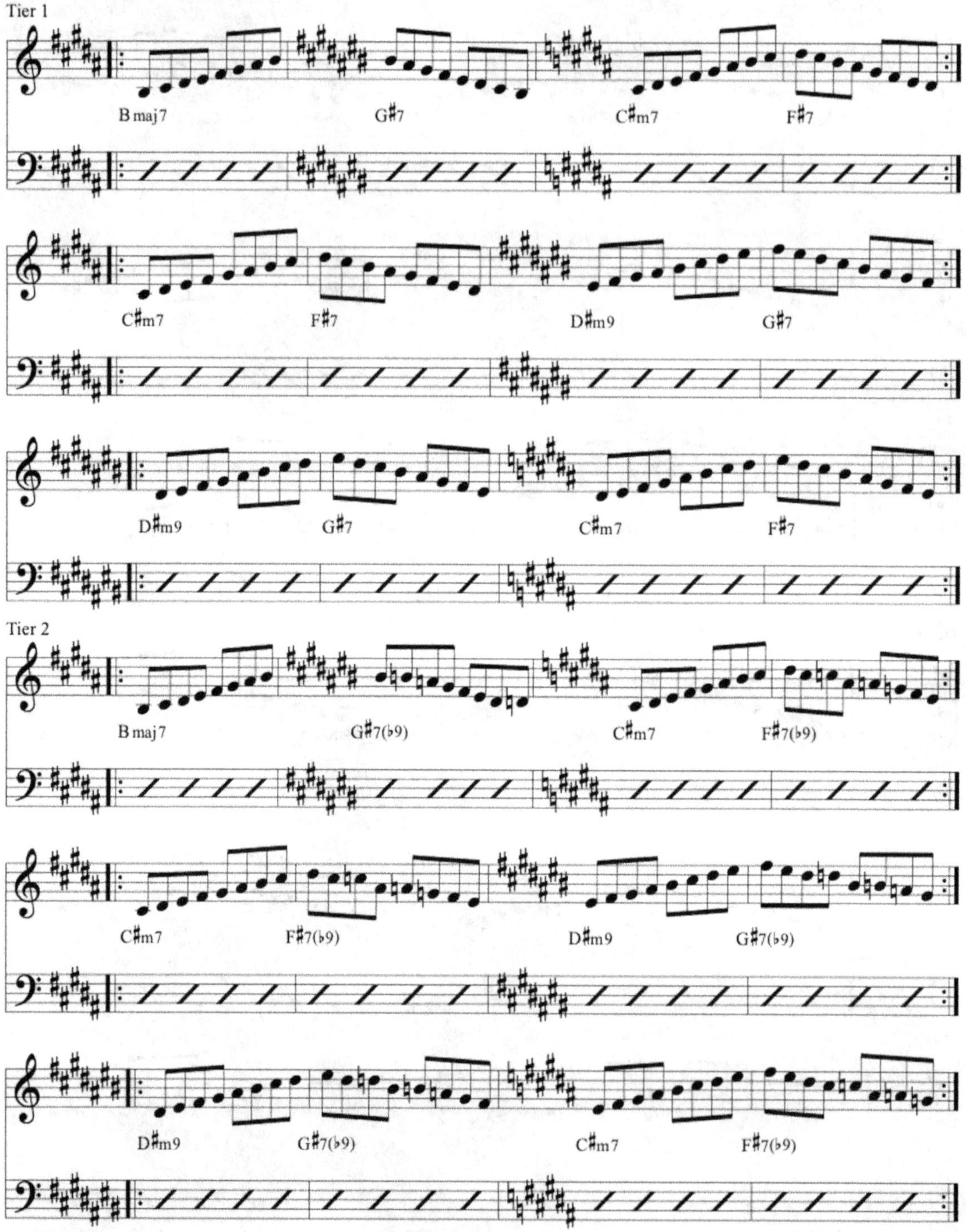
Tier 1
B maj7
G♯7
C♯m7
F♯7
C♯m7
F♯7
D♯m9
G♯7
D♯m9
G♯7
C♯m7
F♯7
Tier 2
B maj7
G♯7(♭9)
C♯m7
F♯7(♭9)
C♯m7
F♯7(♭9)
D♯m9
G♯7(♭9)
D♯m9
G♯7(♭9)
C♯m7
F♯7(♭9)

Appendix 4.2.1. 1625, 3625 & 2536

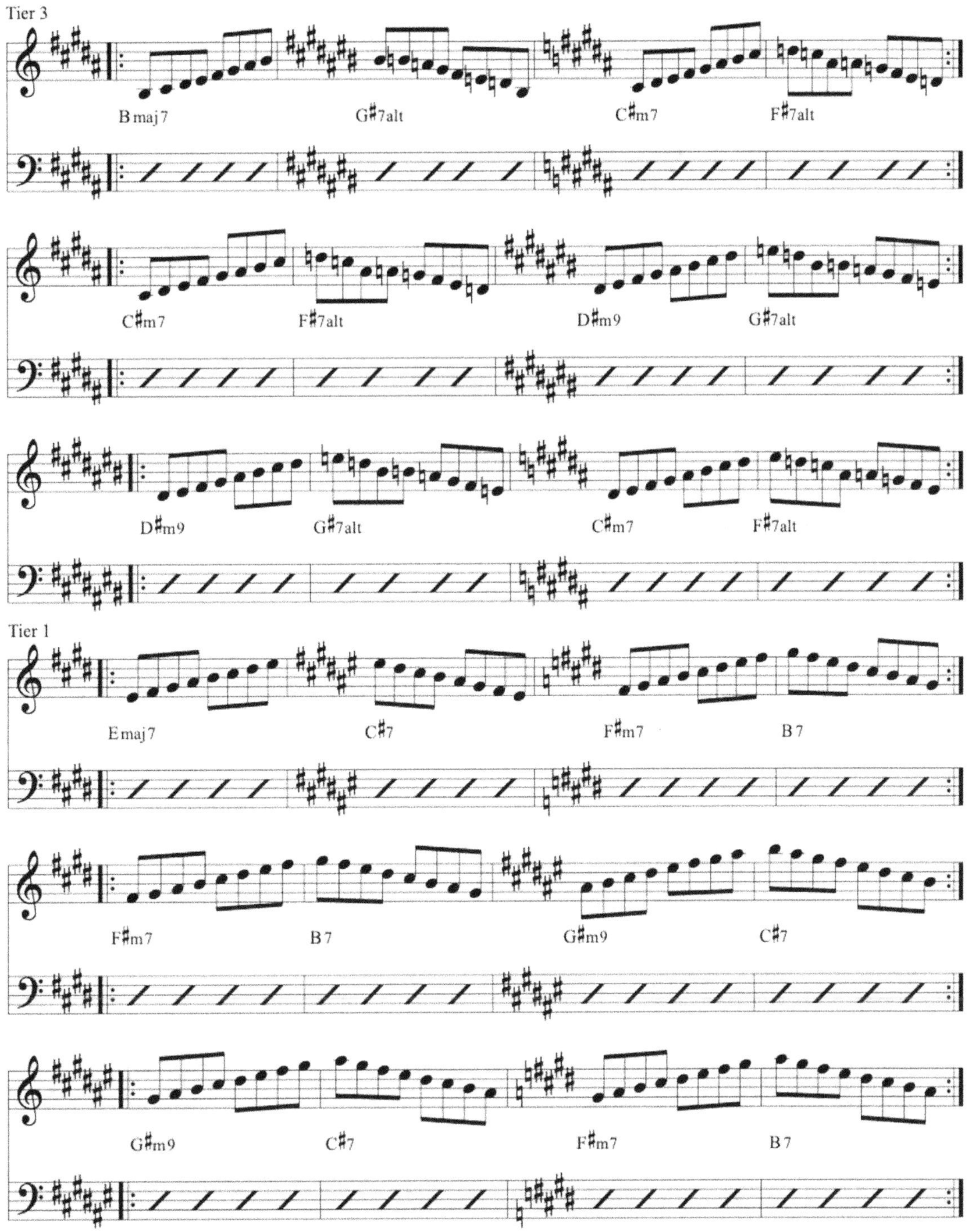
Tier 3
Bmaj7
G♯7alt
C♯m7
F♯7alt
C♯m7
F♯7alt
D♯m9
G♯7alt
D♯m9
G♯7alt
C♯m7
F♯7alt
Tier 1
Emaj7
C♯7
F♯m7
B7
F♯m7
B7
G♯m9
C♯7
G♯m9
C♯7
F♯m7
B7

Appendix 4.2.1. 1625, 3625 & 2536

Tier 2

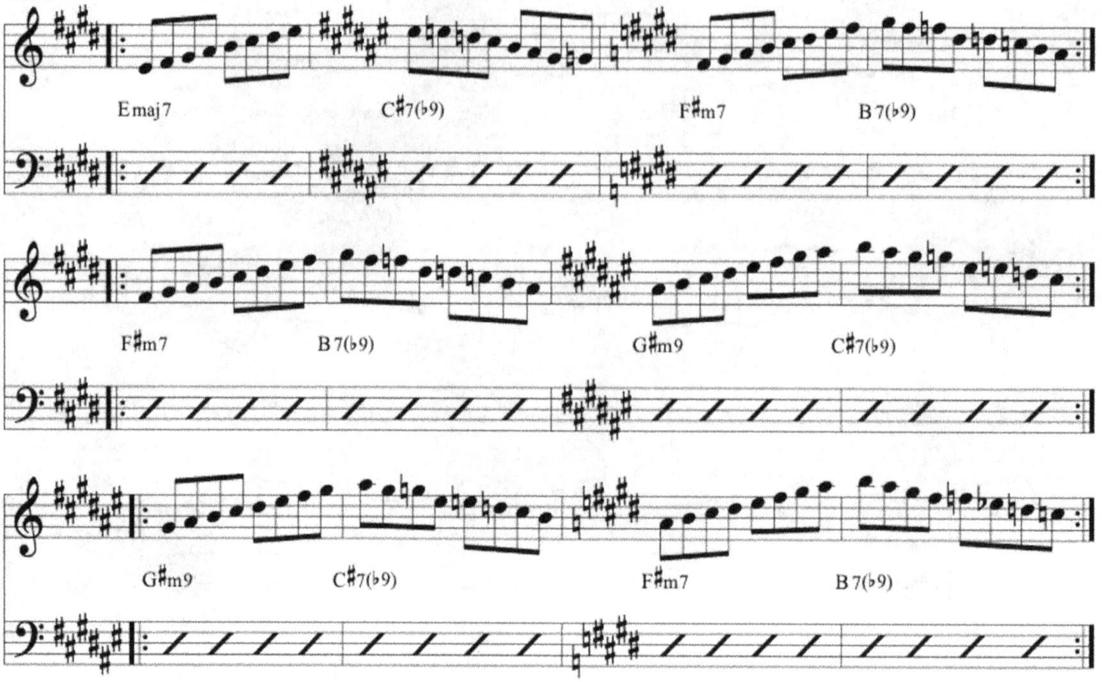
Emaj7
C♯7(♭9)
F♯m7
B7(♭9)
F♯m7
B7(♭9)
G♯m9
C♯7(♭9)
G♯m9
C♯7(♭9)
F♯m7
B7(♭9)

Tier 3

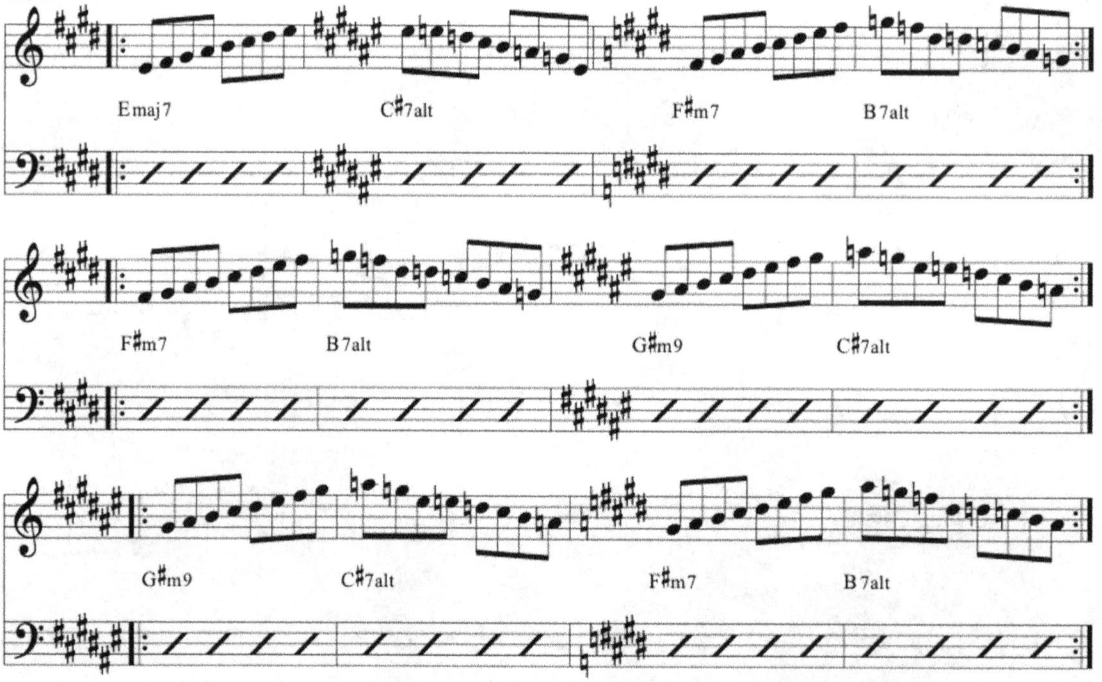
Emaj7
C♯7alt
F♯m7
B7alt
F♯m7
B7alt
G♯m9
C♯7alt
G♯m9
C♯7alt
F♯m7
B7alt

Appendix 4.2.1. 1625, 3625 & 2536

Tier 1

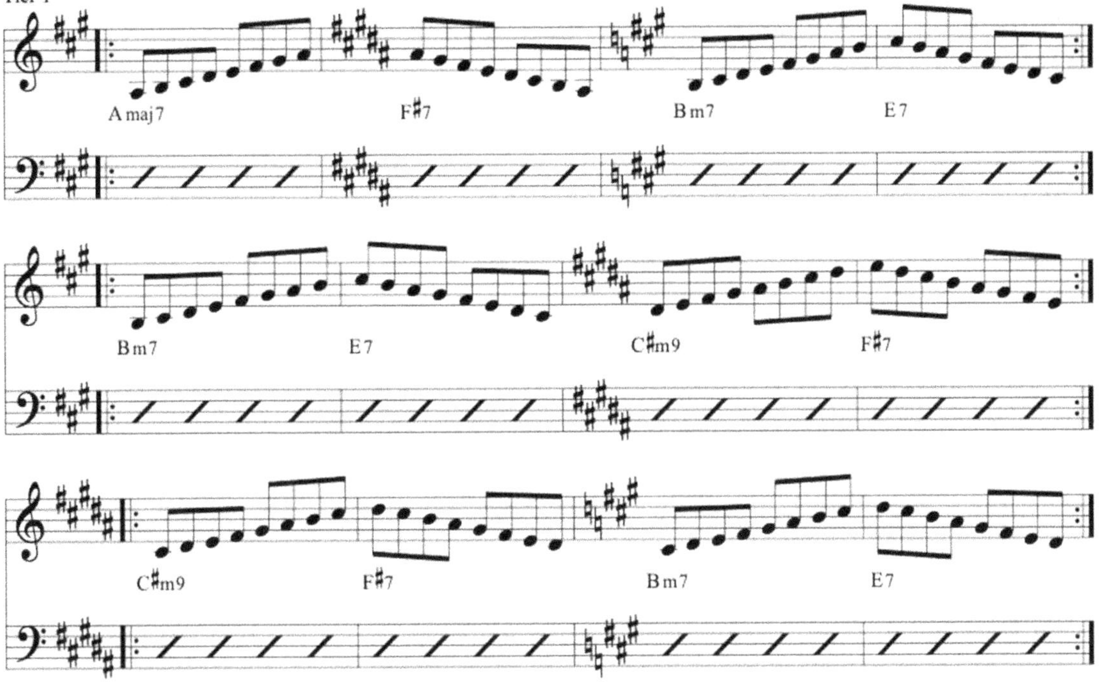
A maj7
F♯7
Bm7
E7
Bm7
E7
C♯m9
F♯7
C♯m9
F♯7
Bm7
E7

Tier 2

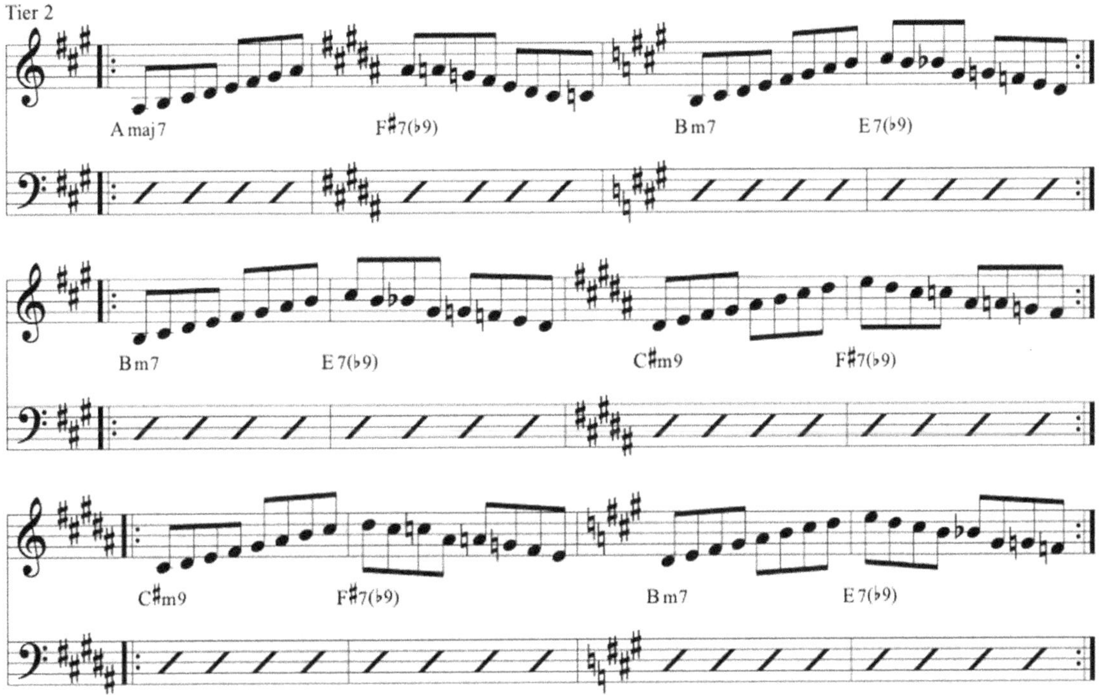
A maj7
F♯7(♭9)
Bm7
E7(♭9)
Bm7
E7(♭9)
C♯m9
F♯7(♭9)
C♯m9
F♯7(♭9)
Bm7
E7(♭9)

Appendix 4.2.1. 1625, 3625 & 2536

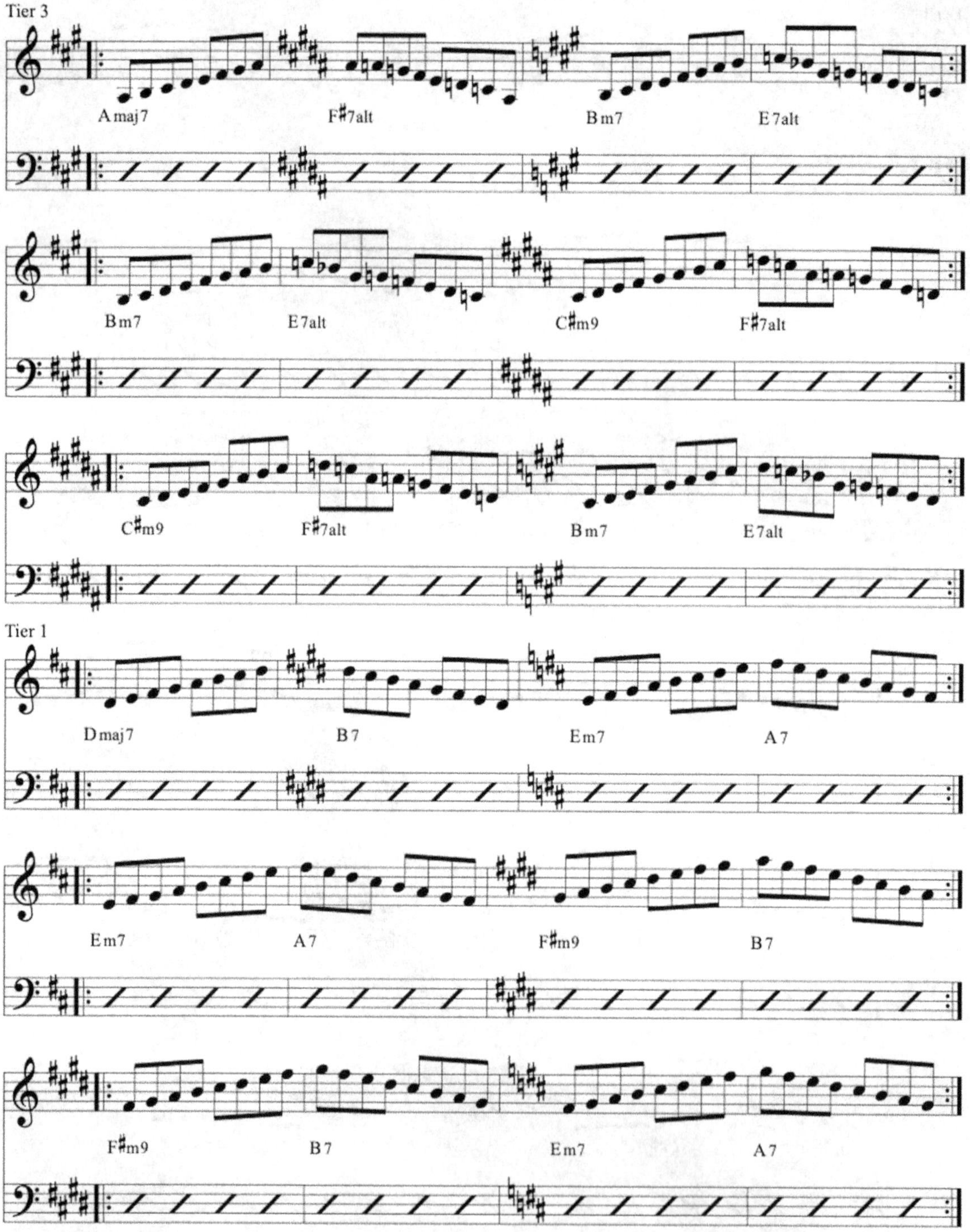
Tier 3
Amaj7
F#7alt
Bm7
E7alt
Bm7
E7alt
C#m9
F#7alt
C#m9
F#7alt
Bm7
E7alt
Tier 1
Dmaj7
B7
Em7
A7
Em7
A7
F#m9
B7
F#m9
B7
Em7
A7

Appendix 4.2.1. 1625, 3625 & 2536

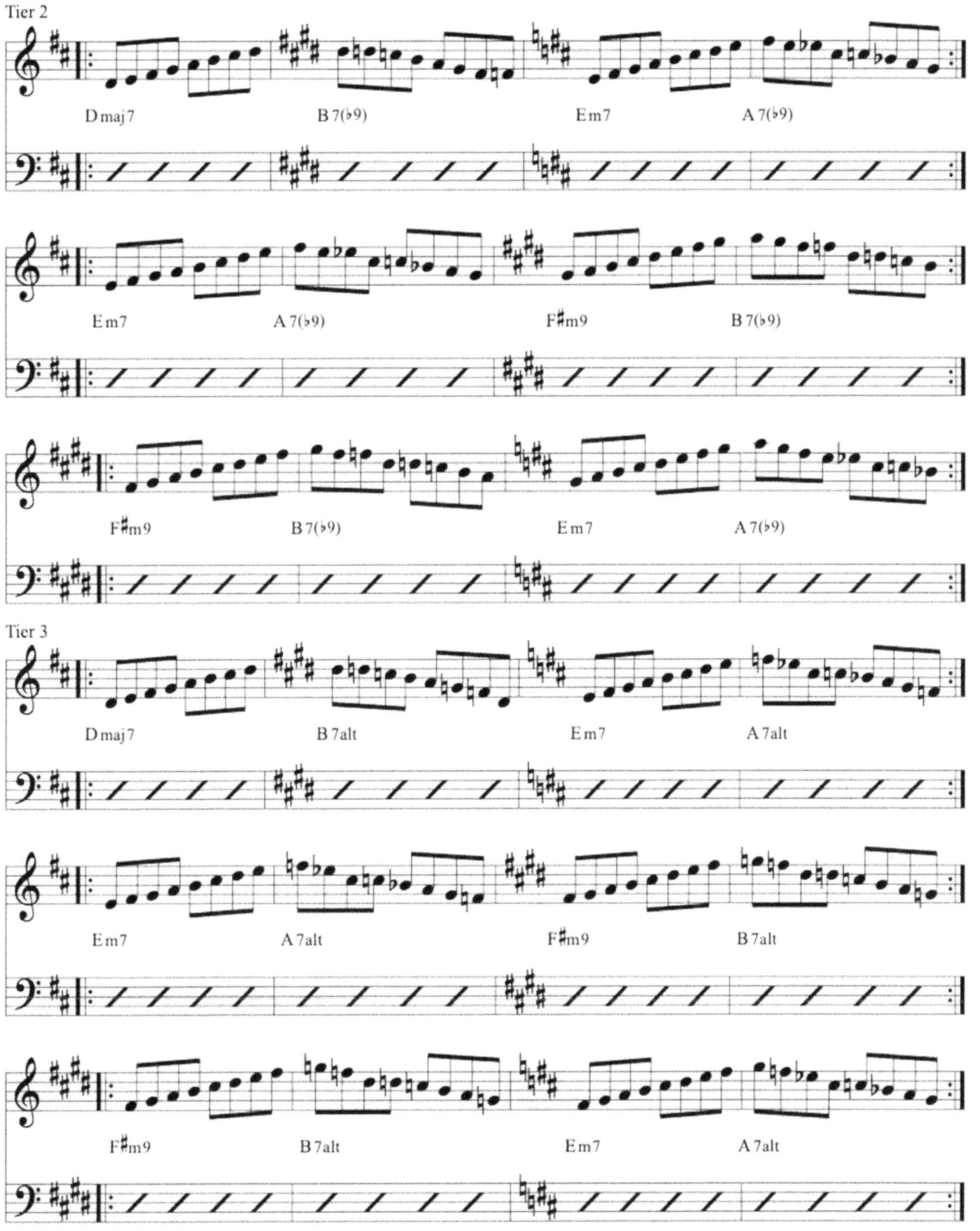
Tier 2
Dmaj7
B7(♭9)
Em7
A7(♭9)
Em7
A7(♭9)
F♯m9
B7(♭9)
F♯m9
B7(♭9)
Em7
A7(♭9)
Tier 3
Dmaj7
B7alt
Em7
A7alt
Em7
A7alt
F♯m9
B7alt
F♯m9
B7alt
Em7
A7alt

Appendix 4.2.1. 1625, 3625 & 2536

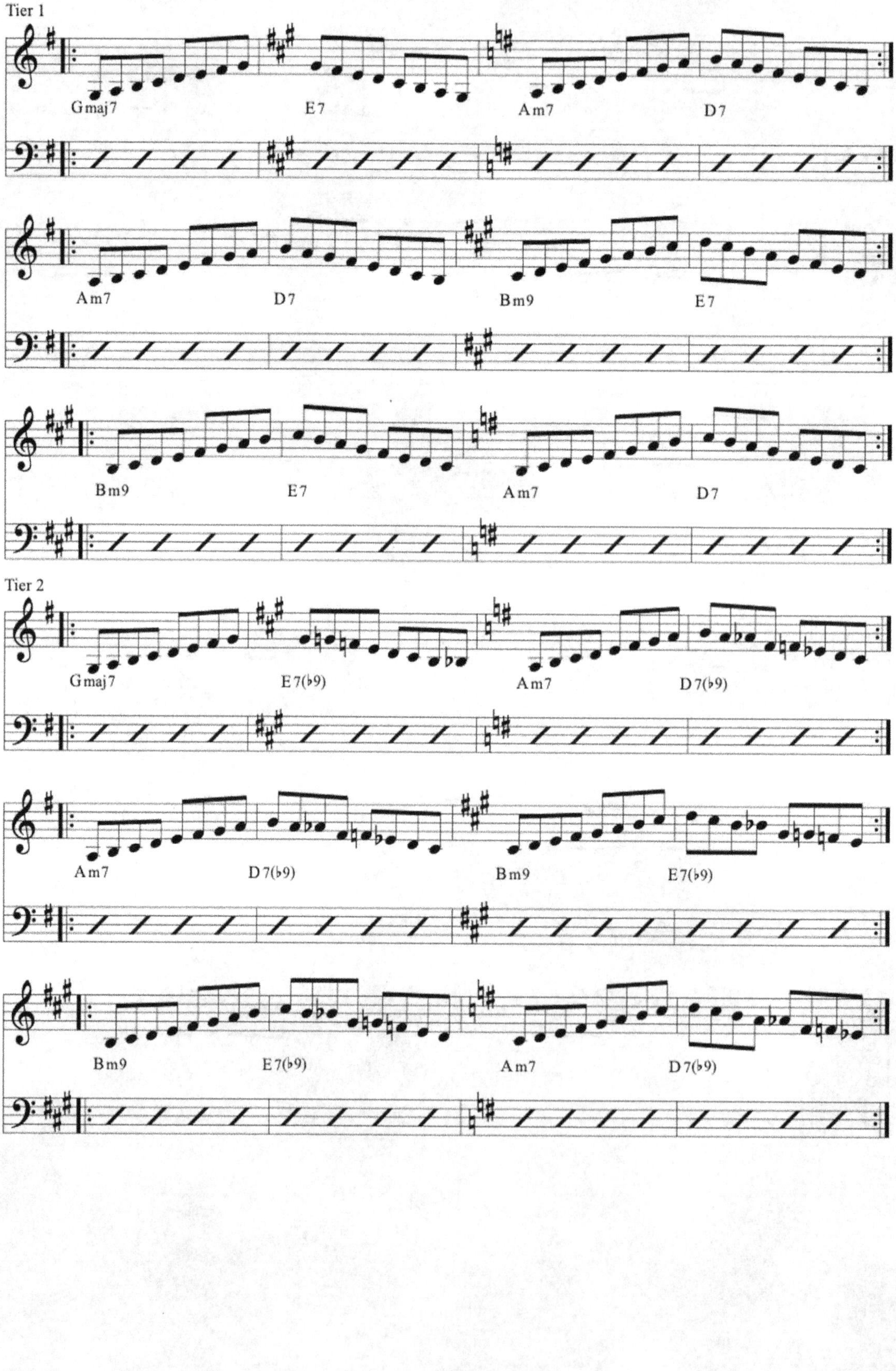
Tier 1
Gmaj7
E7
Am7
D7
Am7
D7
Bm9
E7
Bm9
E7
Am7
D7
Tier 2
Gmaj7
E7(♭9)
Am7
D7(♭9)
Am7
D7(♭9)
Bm9
E7(♭9)
Bm9
E7(♭9)
Am7
D7(♭9)

Appendix 4.2.1. 1625, 3625 & 2536

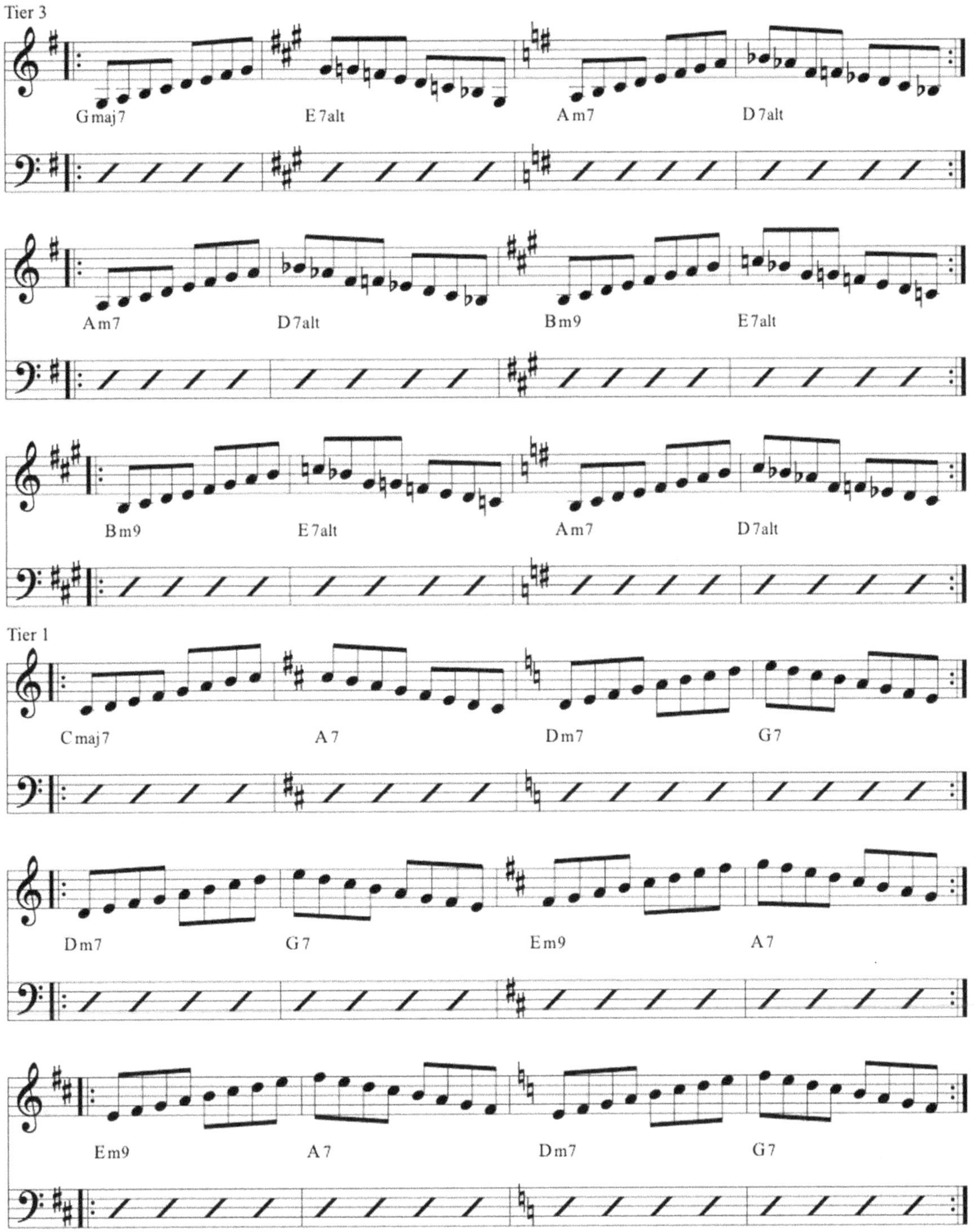
Tier 3
Gmaj7
E7alt
Am7
D7alt
Am7
D7alt
Bm9
E7alt
Bm9
E7alt
Am7
D7alt
Tier 1
Cmaj7
A7
Dm7
G7
Dm7
G7
Em9
A7
Em9
A7
Dm7
G7

Appendix 4.2.1. 1625, 3625 & 2536

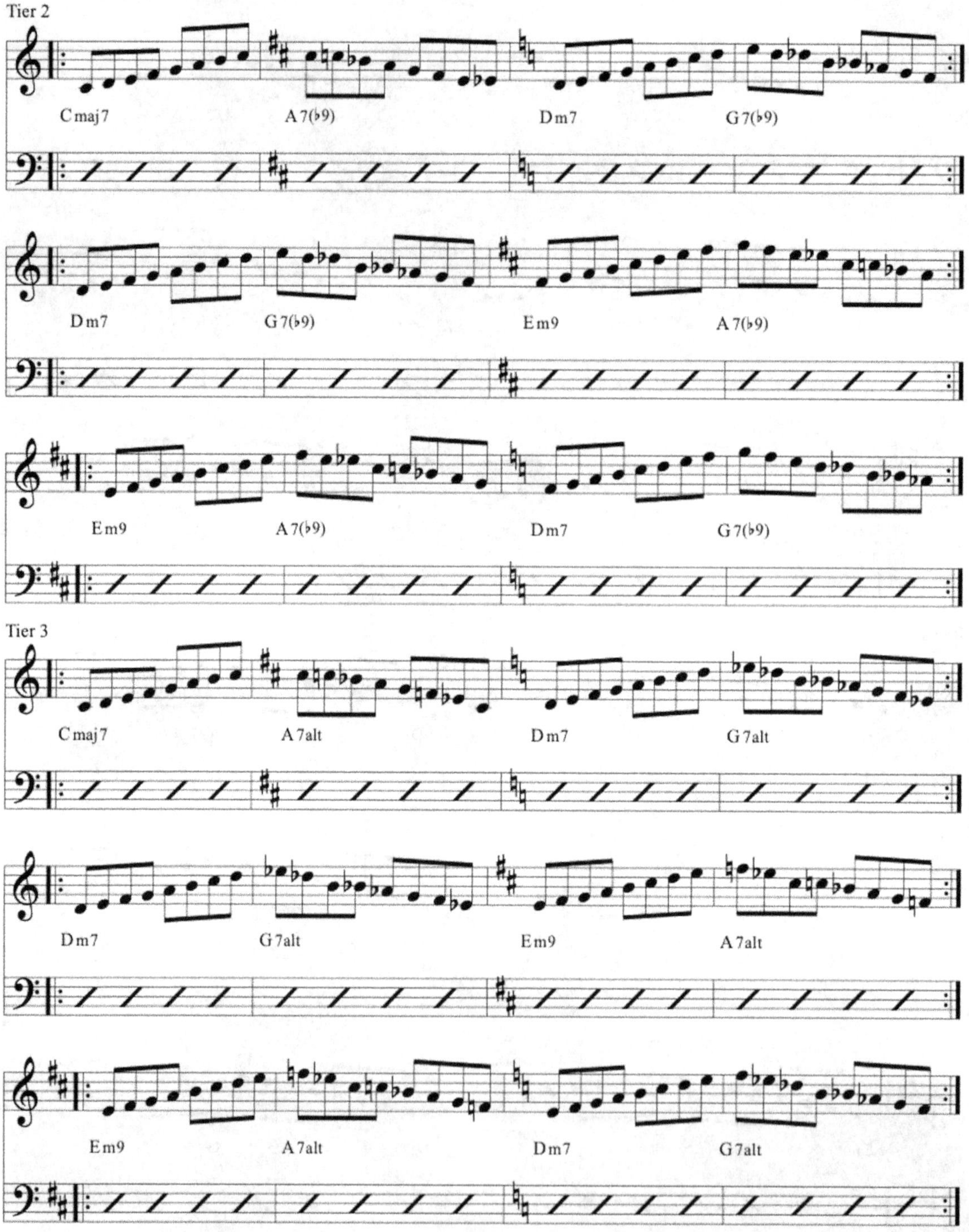
Tier 2
Cmaj7
A7(♭9)
Dm7
G7(♭9)
Dm7
G7(♭9)
Em9
A7(♭9)
Em9
A7(♭9)
Dm7
G7(♭9)
Tier 3
Cmaj7
A7alt
Dm7
G7alt
Dm7
G7alt
Em9
A7alt
Em9
A7alt
Dm7
G7alt

4.2.2. 2536, 3625 with Tritone Sub

APPENDIX 4.2.2.
2536, 3625 WITH TRITONE SUB

4.2.2.1. 2536, Ascending

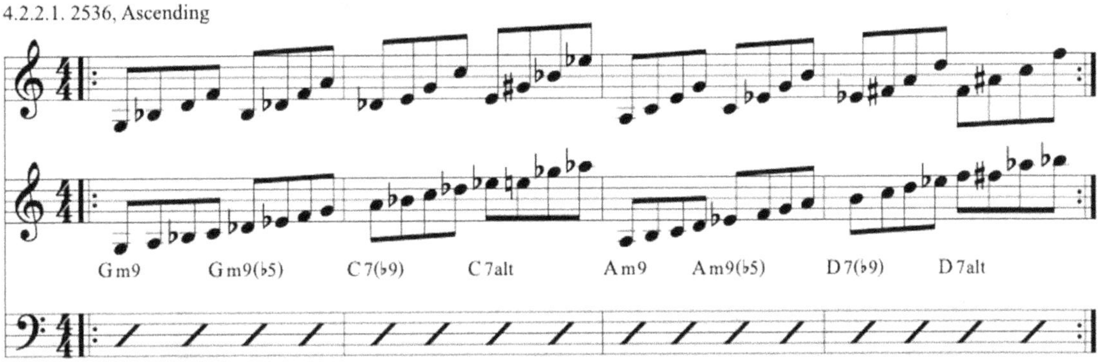

4.2.2.2. 2536 with Tritone Sub, Ascending

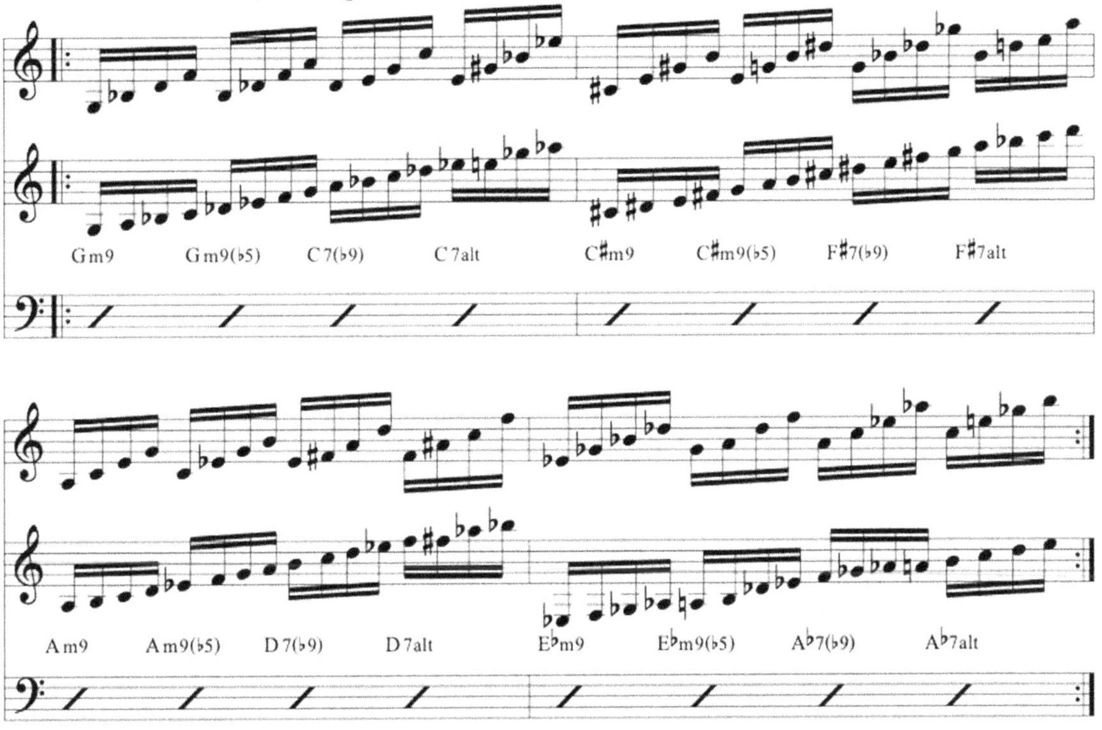

Appendix 4.2.2. 2536, 3625 with Tritone Sub

4.2.2.3. 2536, Ascending Retrograde

4.2.2.4. 2536 with Tritone Sub, Ascending Retrograde

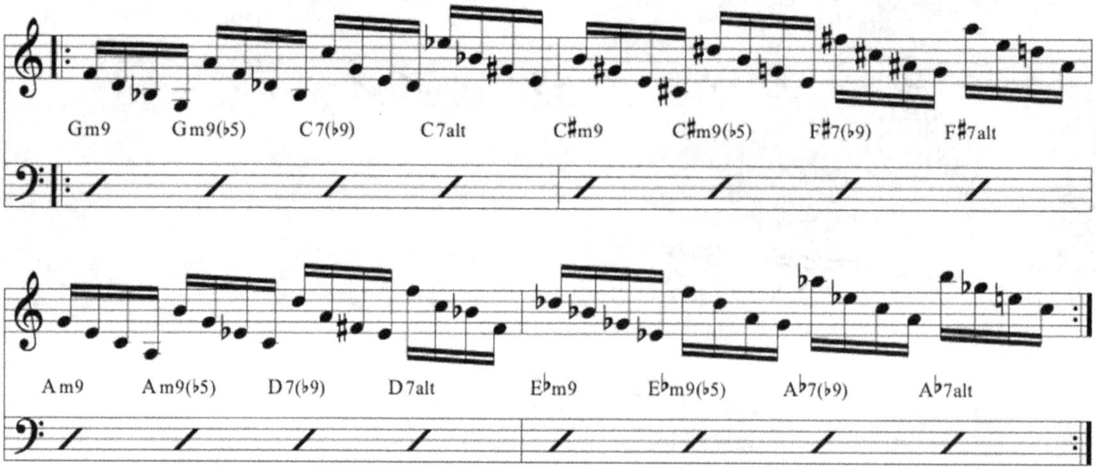

4.2.2.5. 2536, Retrograde

4.2.2.6. 2536 with Tritone Sub, Retrograde

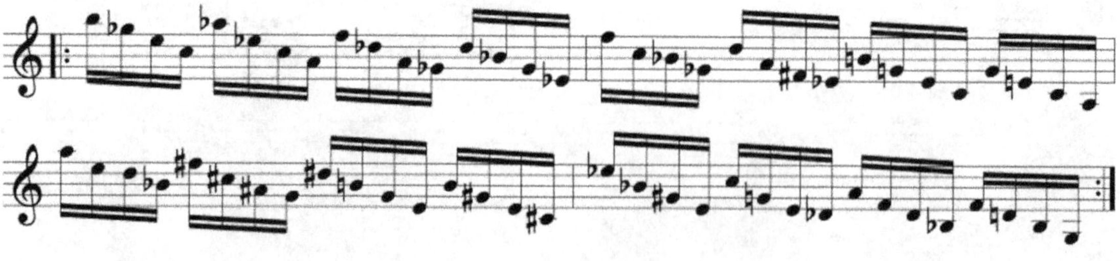

Appendix 4.2.2. 2536, 3625 with Tritone Sub

4.2.2.7. 3625, Ascending

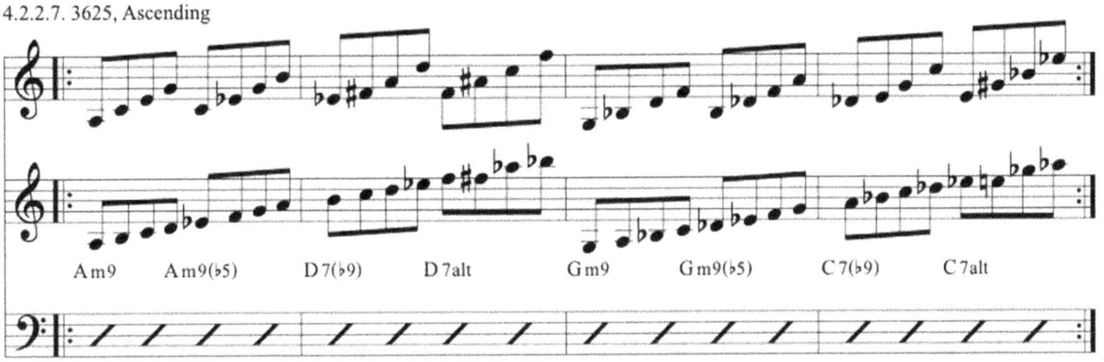

4.2.2.8. 3625 with Tritone Sub, Ascending

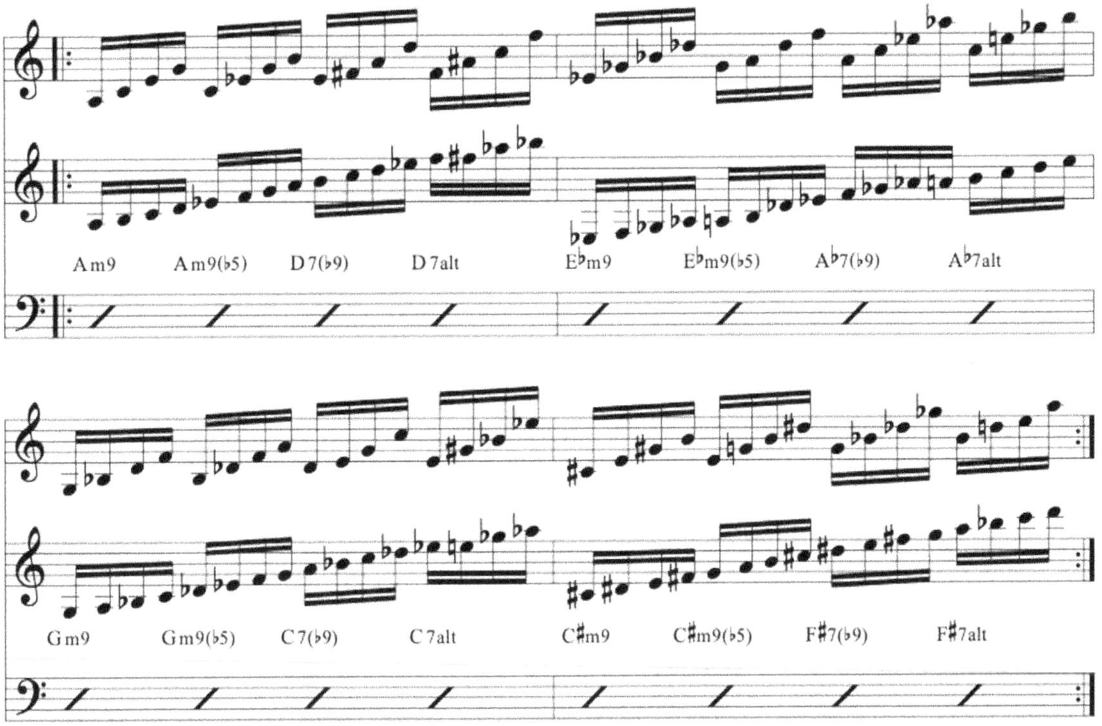

Appendix 4.2.2. 2536, 3625 with Tritone Sub

4.2.2.9. 3625, Ascending Retrograde

4.2.2.10. 3625 with Tritone Sub, Ascending Retrograde

4.2.2.11. 3625, Retrograde

4.2.2.12. 3625 with Tritone Sub, Retrograde

Appendix 4.2.2. 2536, 3625 with Tritone Sub

4.2.2.1.

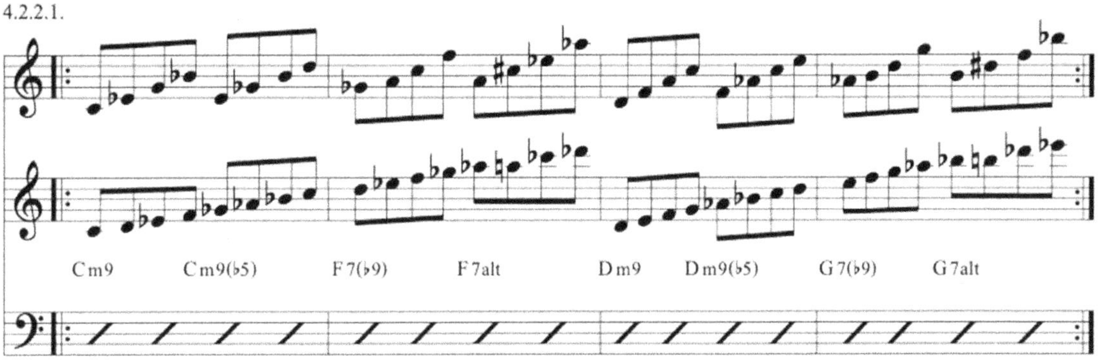

4.2.2.2.

Appendix 4.2.2. 2536, 3625 with Tritone Sub

4.2.2.3.

4.2.2.4.

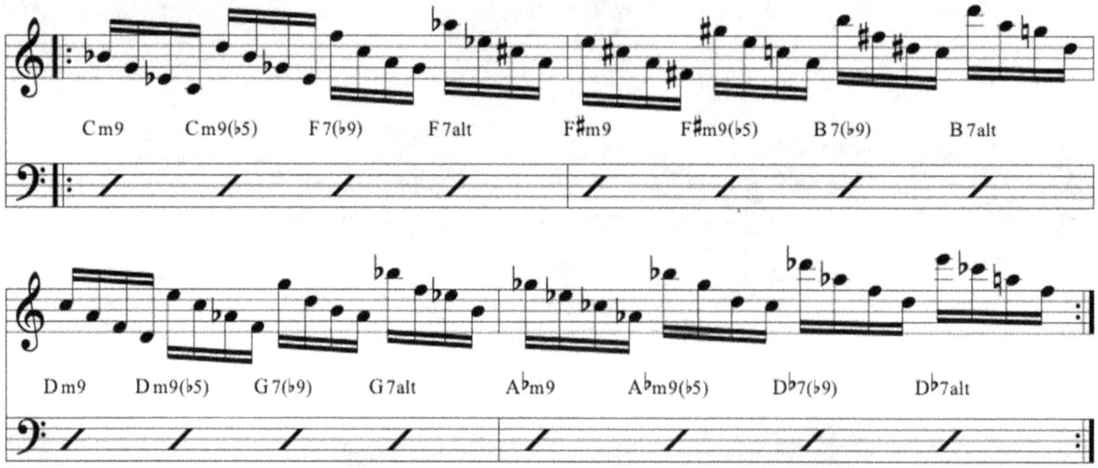

4.2.2.5.

4.2.2.6.

Appendix 4.2.2. 2536, 3625 with Tritone Sub

4.2.2.7.

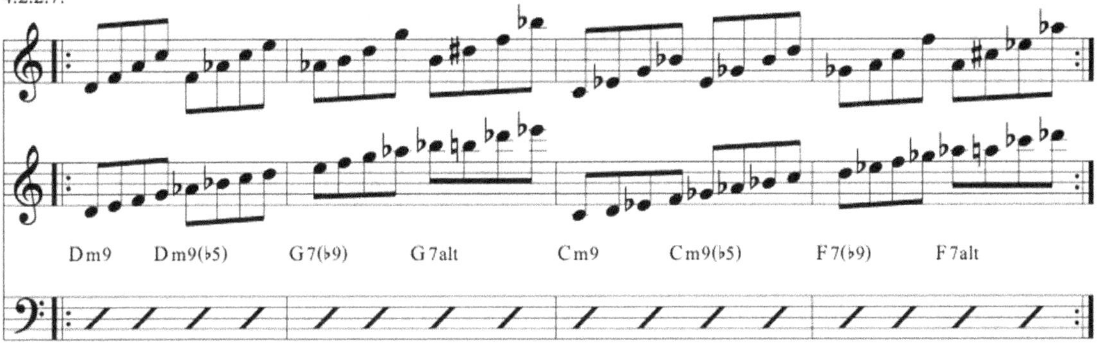

4.2.2.8.

Appendix 4.2.2. 2536, 3625 with Tritone Sub

4.2.2.9.

4.2.2.10.

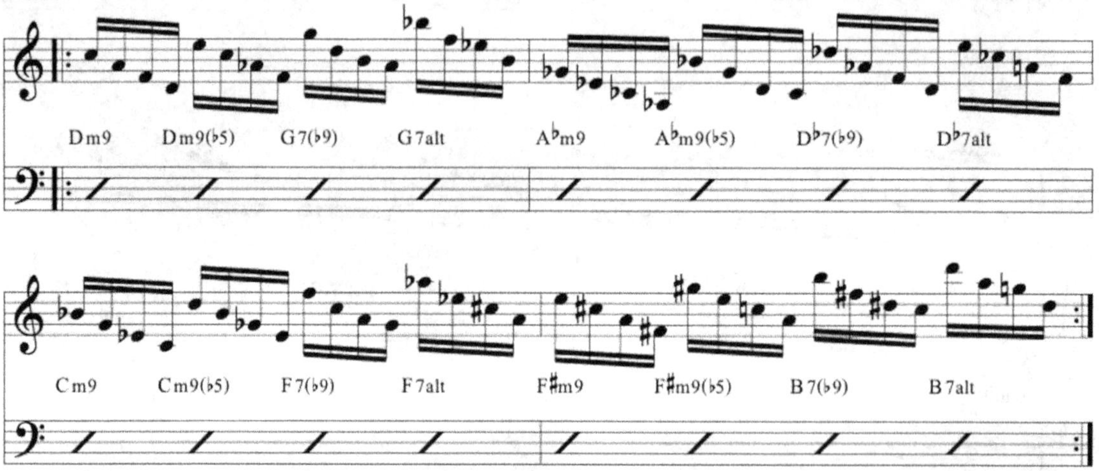

4.2.2.11.

4.2.2.12.

Appendix 4.2.2. 2536, 3625 with Tritone Sub

4.2.2.1.

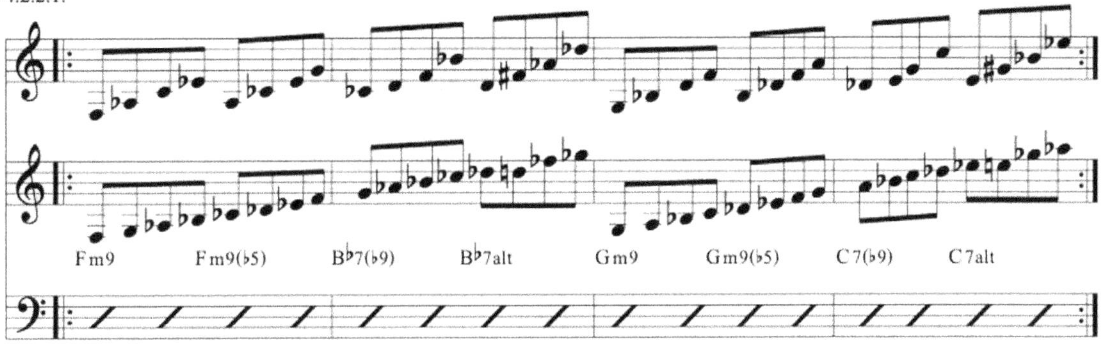

4.2.2.2.

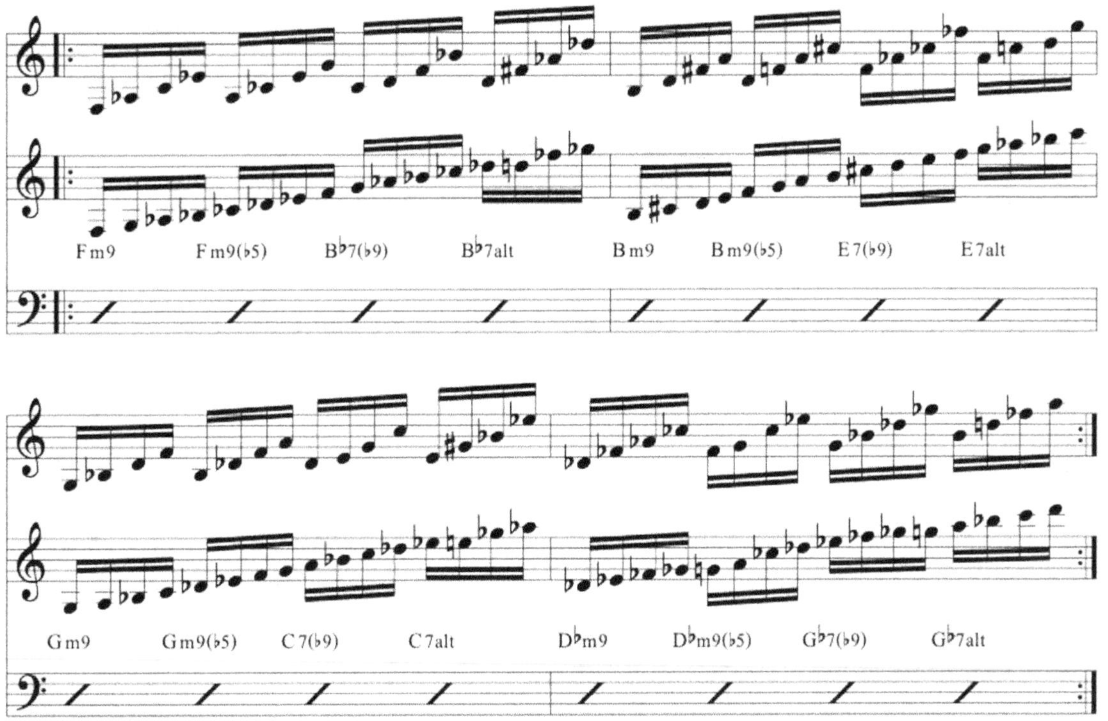

Appendix 4.2.2. 2536, 3625 with Tritone Sub

4.2.2.3.

4.2.2.4.

4.2.2.5.

4.2.2.6.

Appendix 4.2.2. 2536, 3625 with Tritone Sub

4.2.2.7.

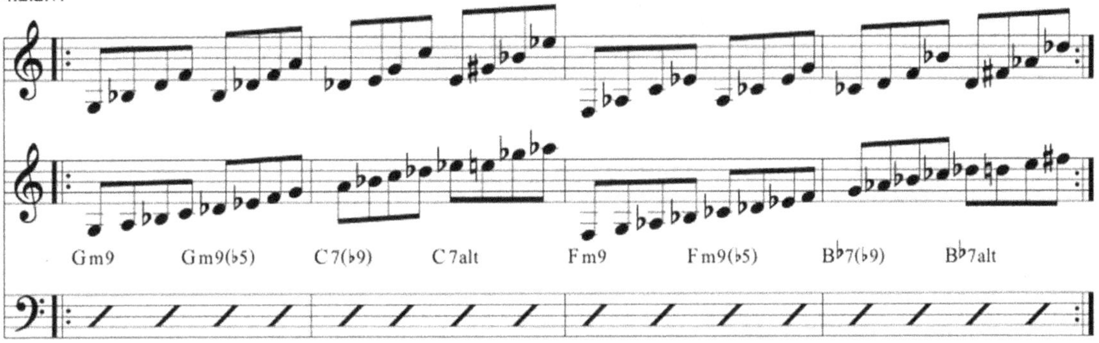

4.2.2.8.

Appendix 4.2.2. 2536, 3625 with Tritone Sub

4.2.2.9.

4.2.2.10.

4.2.2.11.

4.2.2.12.

Appendix 4.2.2. 2536, 3625 with Tritone Sub

4.2.2.1.

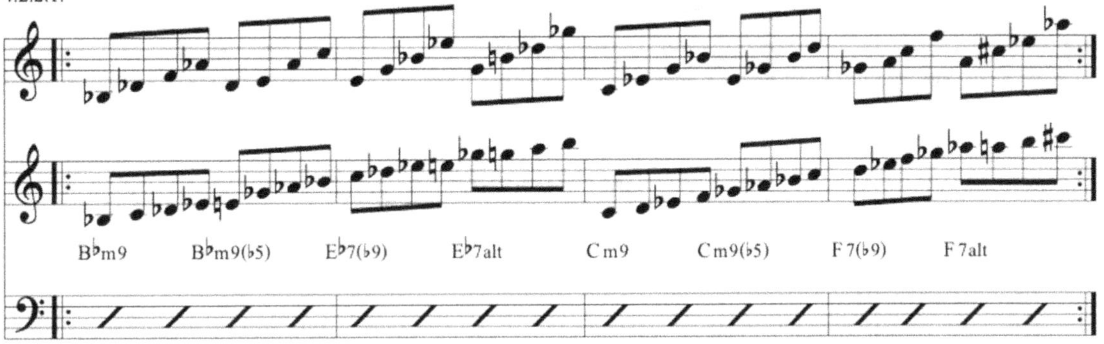

4.2.2.2.

Appendix 4.2.2. 2536, 3625 with Tritone Sub

4.2.2.3.

4.2.2.4.

4.2.2.5.

4.2.2.6.

Appendix 4.2.2. 2536, 3625 with Tritone Sub

4.2.2.7.

4.2.2.8.

Appendix 4.2.2. 2536, 3625 with Tritone Sub

4.2.2.9.

4.2.2.10.

4.2.2.11.

4.2.2.12.

Appendix 4.2.2. 2536, 3625 with Tritone Sub

4.2.2.1.

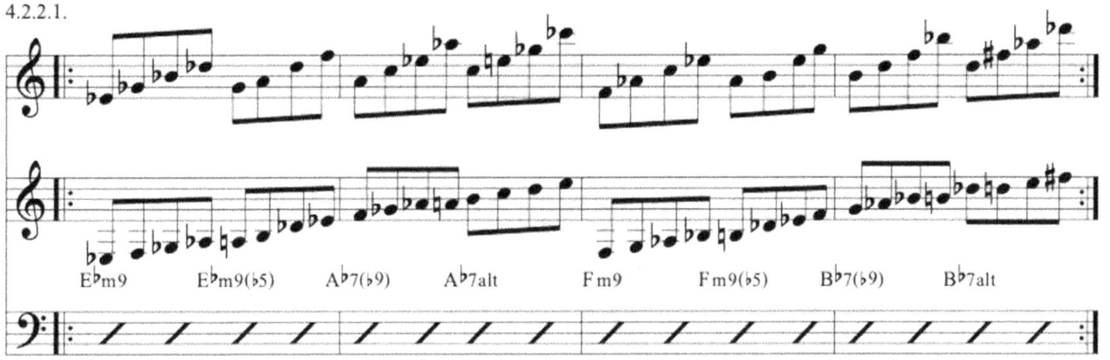

4.2.2.2.

Appendix 4.2.2. 2536, 3625 with Tritone Sub

4.2.2.3.

4.2.2.4.

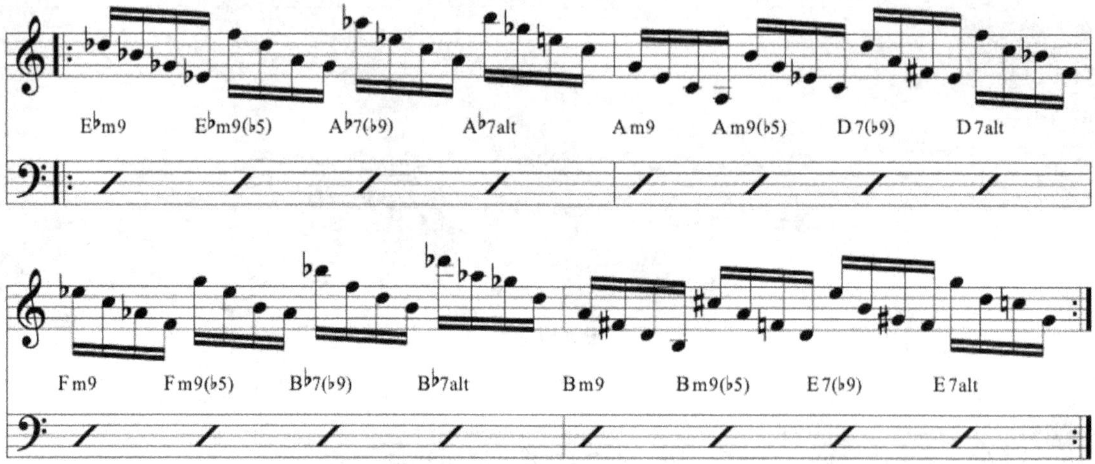

4.2.2.5.

4.2.2.6.

Appendix 4.2.2. 2536, 3625 with Tritone Sub

4.2.2.7.

4.2.2.8.

Appendix 4.2.2. 2536, 3625 with Tritone Sub

4.2.2.9.

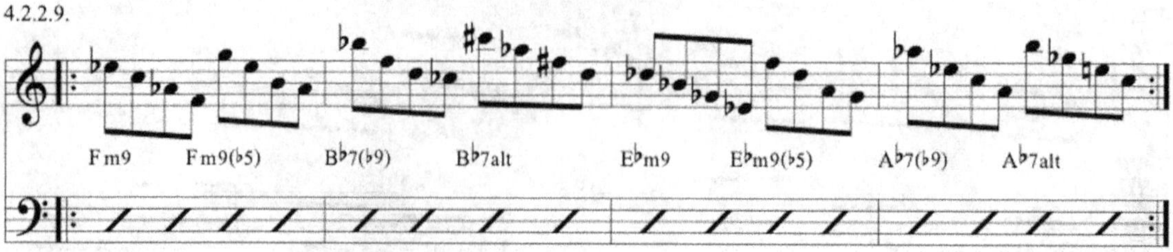

4.2.2.10.

4.2.2.11.

4.2.2.12.

Appendix 4.2.2. 2536, 3625 with Tritone Sub

4.2.2.1.

4.2.2.2.

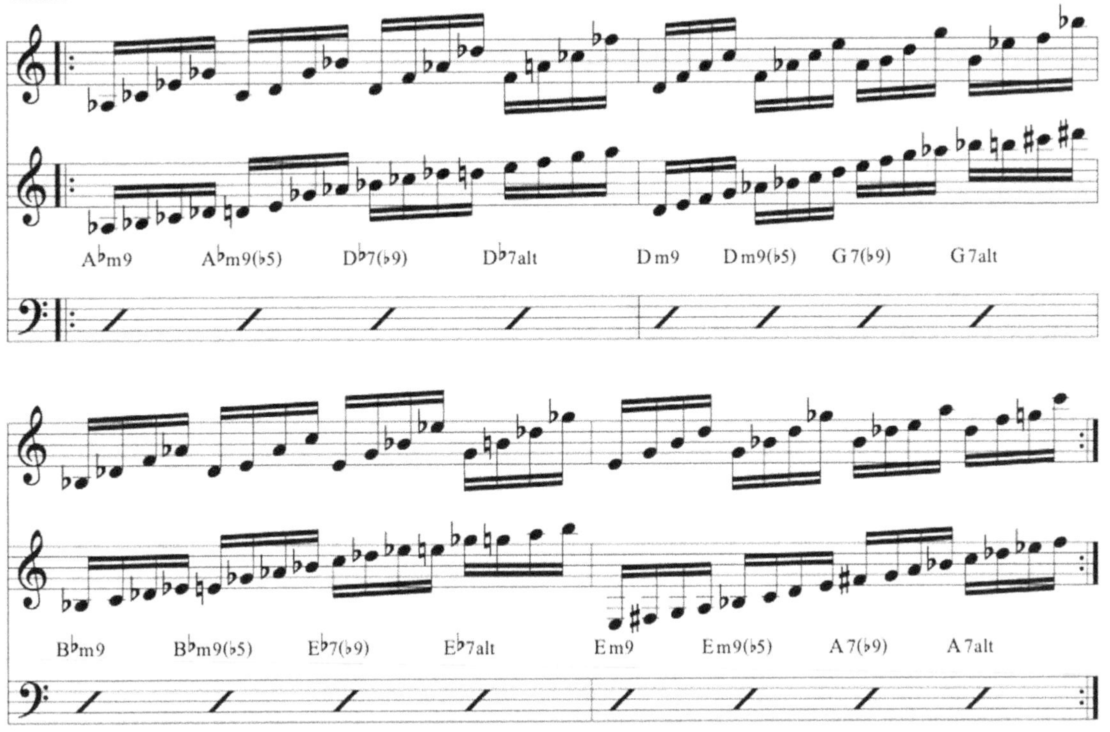

Appendix 4.2.2. 2536, 3625 with Tritone Sub

4.2.2.3.

4.2.2.4.

4.2.2.5.

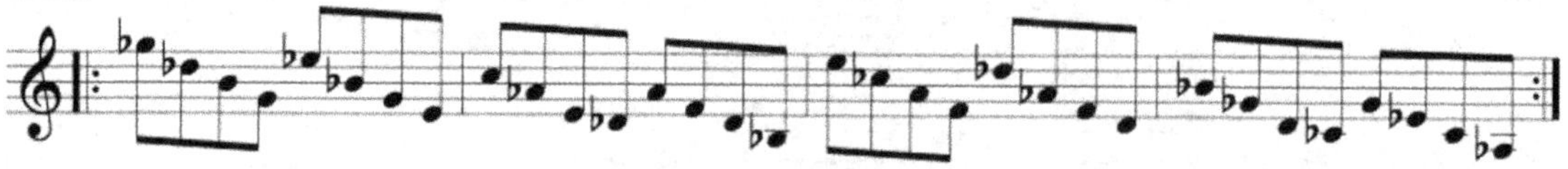

4.2.2.6.

Appendix 4.2.2. 2536, 3625 with Tritone Sub

4.2.2.7.

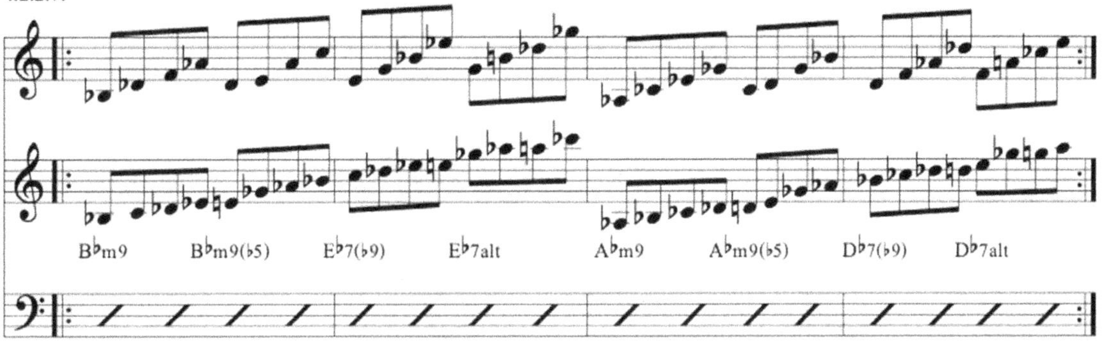

4.2.2.8.

Appendix 4.2.2. 2536, 3625 with Tritone Sub

4.2.2.9.

4.2.2.10.

4.2.2.11.

4.2.2.12.

Appendix 4.2.2. 2536, 3625 with Tritone Sub

4.2.2.1.

4.2.2.2.

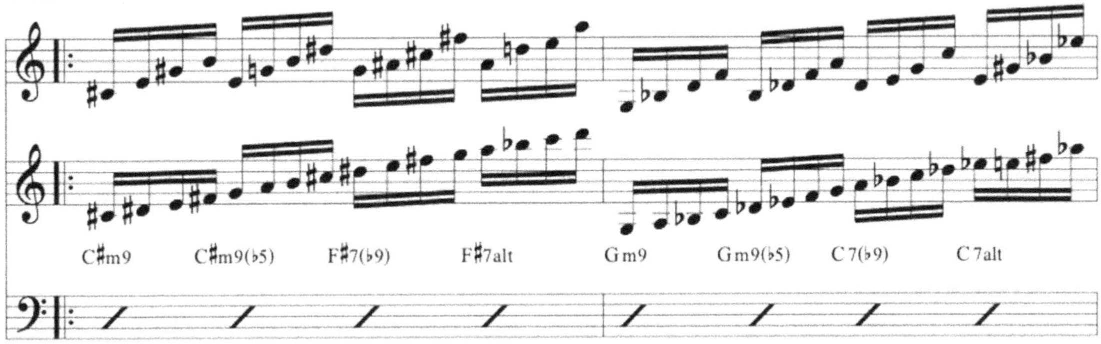

Appendix 4.2.2. 2536, 3625 with Tritone Sub

4.2.2.3.

4.2.2.4.

4.2.2.5.

4.2.2.6.

Appendix 4.2.2. 2536, 3625 with Tritone Sub

4.2.2.7.

4.2.2.8.

Appendix 4.2.2. 2536, 3625 with Tritone Sub

4.2.2.9.

4.2.2.10.

4.2.2.11.

4.2.2.12.

Appendix 4.2.2. 2536, 3625 with Tritone Sub

4.2.2.1.

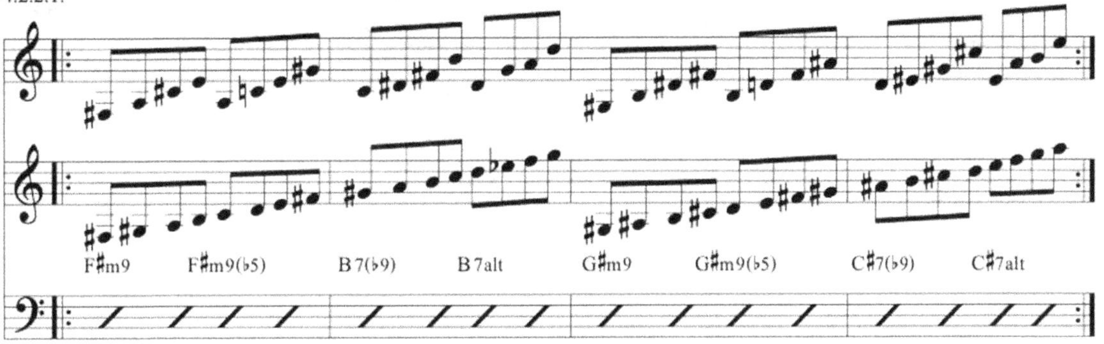

4.2.2.2.

Appendix 4.2.2. 2536, 3625 with Tritone Sub

4.2.2.3.

4.2.2.4.

4.2.2.5.

4.2.2.6.

Appendix 4.2.2. 2536, 3625 with Tritone Sub

4.2.2.7.

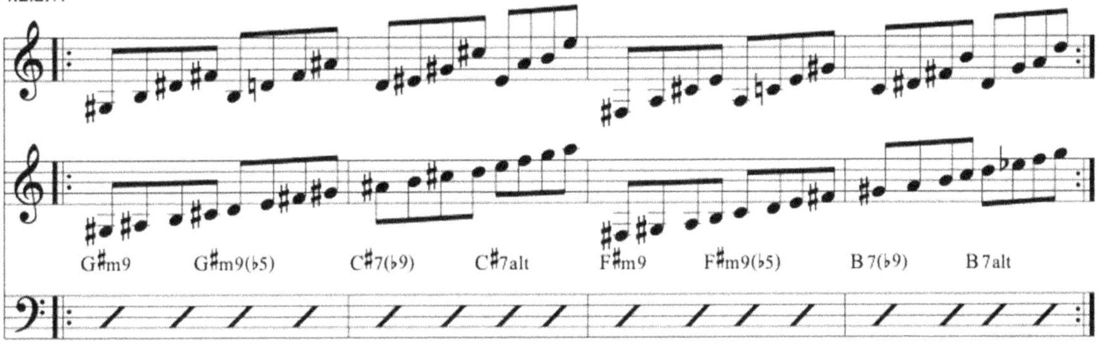

4.2.2.8.

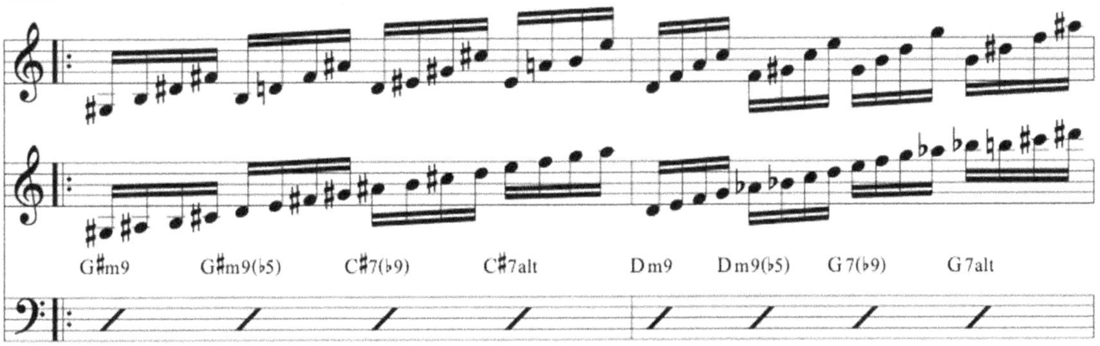

Appendix 4.2.2. 2536, 3625 with Tritone Sub

4.2.2.9.

4.2.2.10.

4.2.2.11.

4.2.2.12.

Appendix 4.2.2. 2536, 3625 with Tritone Sub

4.2.2.1.

4.2.2.2.

Appendix 4.2.2. 2536, 3625 with Tritone Sub

4.2.2.3.

4.2.2.4.

4.2.2.5.

4.2.2.6.

Appendix 4.2.2. 2536, 3625 with Tritone Sub

4.2.2.7.

4.2.2.8.

Appendix 4.2.2. 2536, 3625 with Tritone Sub

4.2.2.9.

4.2.2.10.

4.2.2.11.

4.2.2.12.

Appendix 4.2.2. 2536, 3625 with Tritone Sub

4.2.2.1.

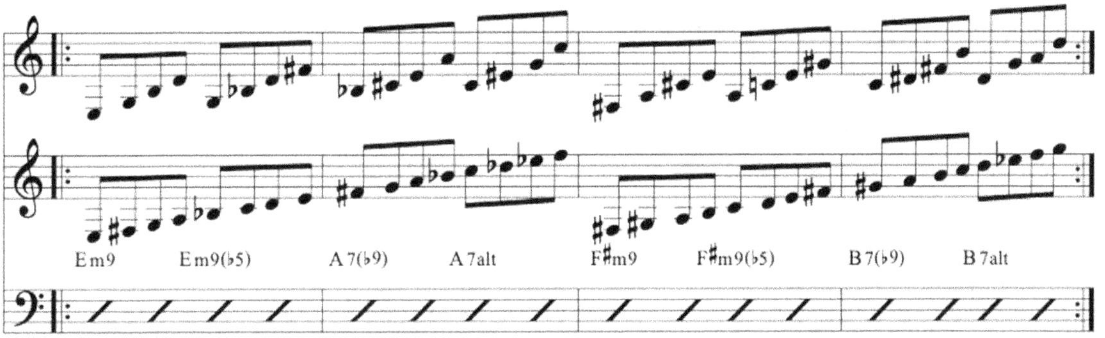

4.2.2.2.

Appendix 4.2.2. 2536, 3625 with Tritone Sub

4.2.2.3.

4.2.2.4.

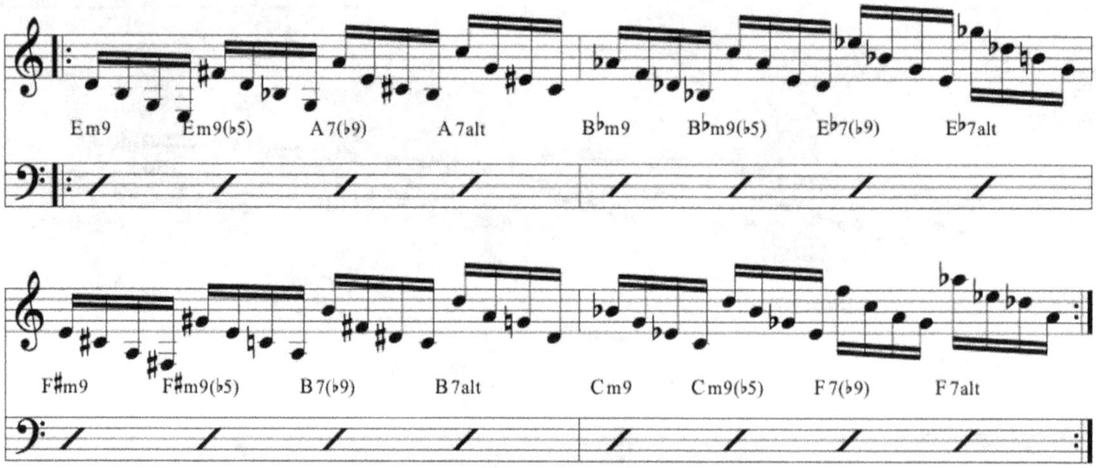

4.2.2.5.

4.2.2.6.

Appendix 4.2.2. 2536, 3625 with Tritone Sub

4.2.2.7.

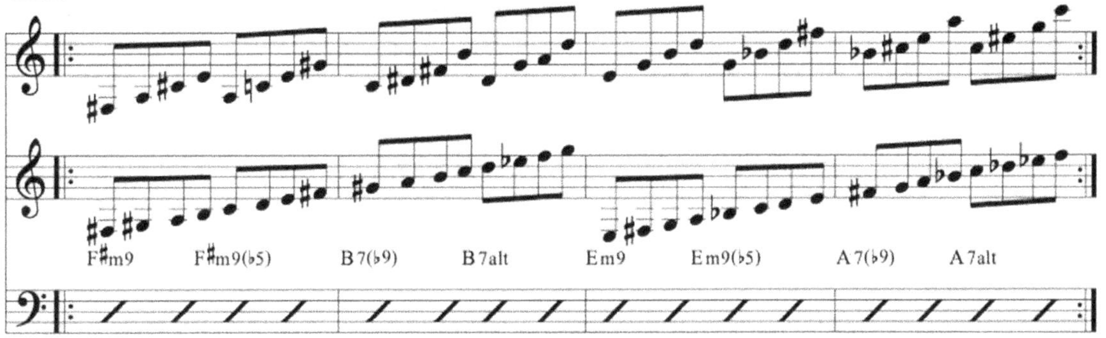

4.2.2.8.

Appendix 4.2.2. 2536, 3625 with Tritone Sub

4.2.2.9.

4.2.2.10.

4.2.2.11.

4.2.2.12.

Appendix 4.2.2. 2536, 3625 with Tritone Sub

4.2.2.1.

4.2.2.2.

Appendix 4.2.2. 2536, 3625 with Tritone Sub

4.2.2.3.

4.2.2.4.

4.2.2.5.

4.2.2.6.

Appendix 4.2.2. 2536, 3625 with Tritone Sub

4.2.2.7.

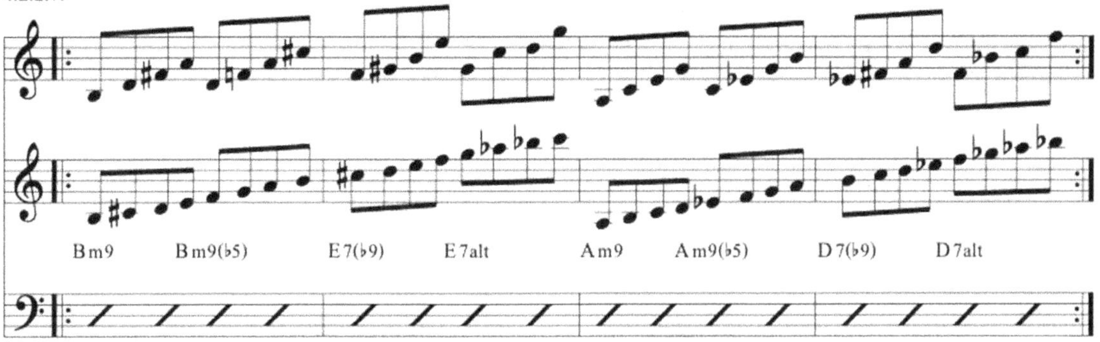

4.2.2.8.

Appendix 4.2.2. 2536, 3625 with Tritone Sub

4.2.2.9.

4.2.2.10.

4.2.2.11.

4.2.2.12.

Appendix 4.2.2. 2536, 3625 with Tritone Sub

4.2.2.1.

4.2.2.2.

Appendix 4.2.2. 2536, 3625 with Tritone Sub

4.2.2.3.

4.2.2.4.

4.2.2.5.

4.2.2.6.

Appendix 4.2.2. 2536, 3625 with Tritone Sub

4.2.2.7.

4.2.2.8.

Appendix 4.2.2. 2536, 3625 with Tritone Sub

4.2.2.9.

4.2.2.10.

4.2.2.11.

4.2.2.12.

4.2.3. 2536, 3625 with Tritone Sub Compressed

APPENDIX 4.2.3.
2536, 3625 WITH TRITONE SUB COMPRESSED

4.2.3.1. 2536 Compressed, Ascending

4.2.3.2. 2536 Compressed with Tritone Sub, Ascending

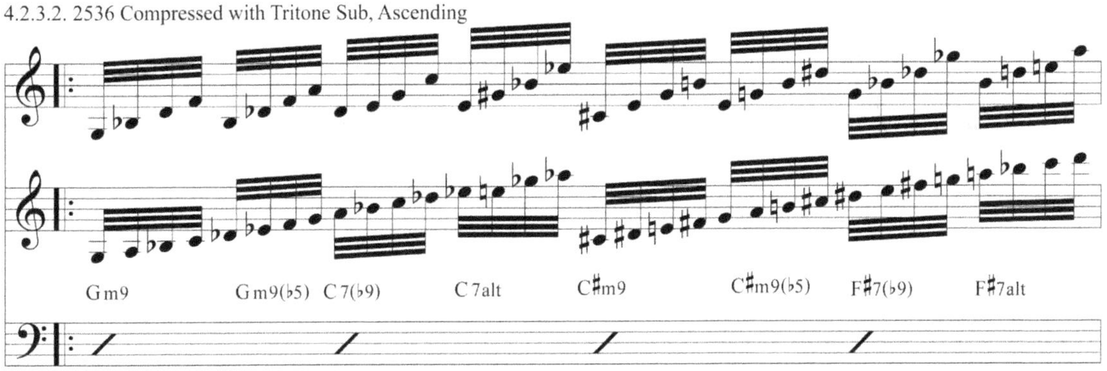

Appendix 4.2.3. 2536, 3625 with Tritone Sub Compressed

4.2.3.3. 2536 Compressed, Ascending Retrograde

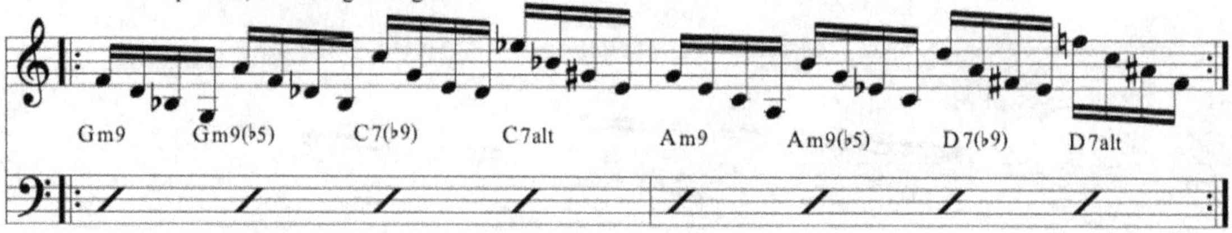

4.2.3.4. 2536 Compressed with Tritone Sub, Ascending Retrograde

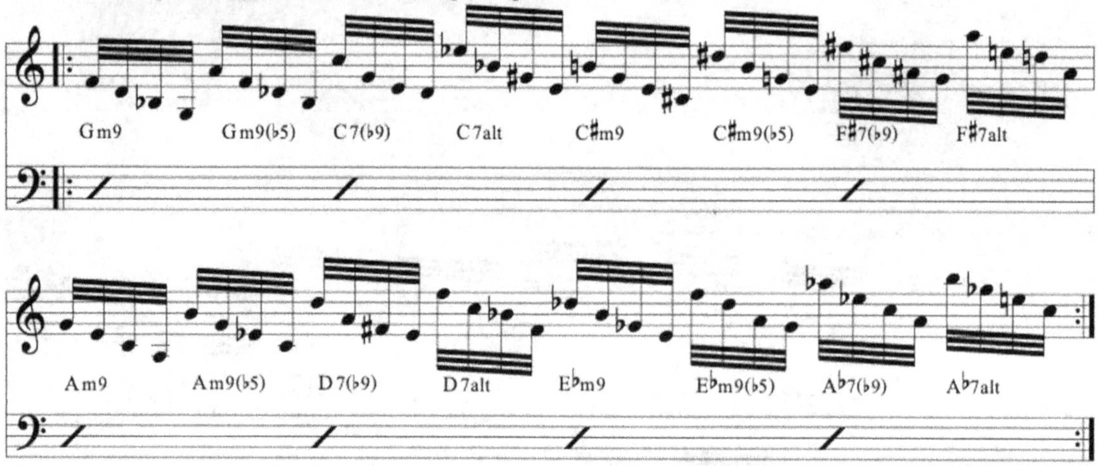

4.2.3.5. 2536 Compressed, Retrograde

4.2.3.6. 2536 Compressed with Tritone Sub, Retrograde

Appendix 4.2.3. 2536, 3625 with Tritone Sub Compressed

4.2.3.7. 3625 Compressed, Ascending

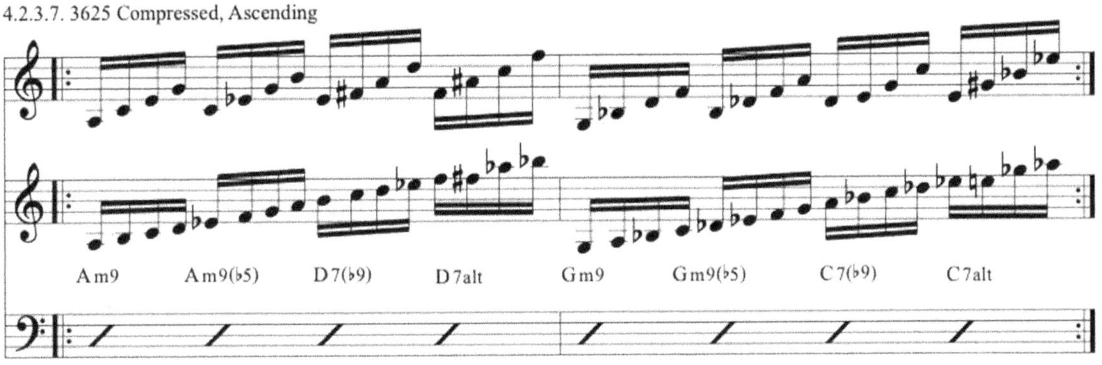

4.2.3.8. 3625 Compressed with Tritone Sub, Ascending

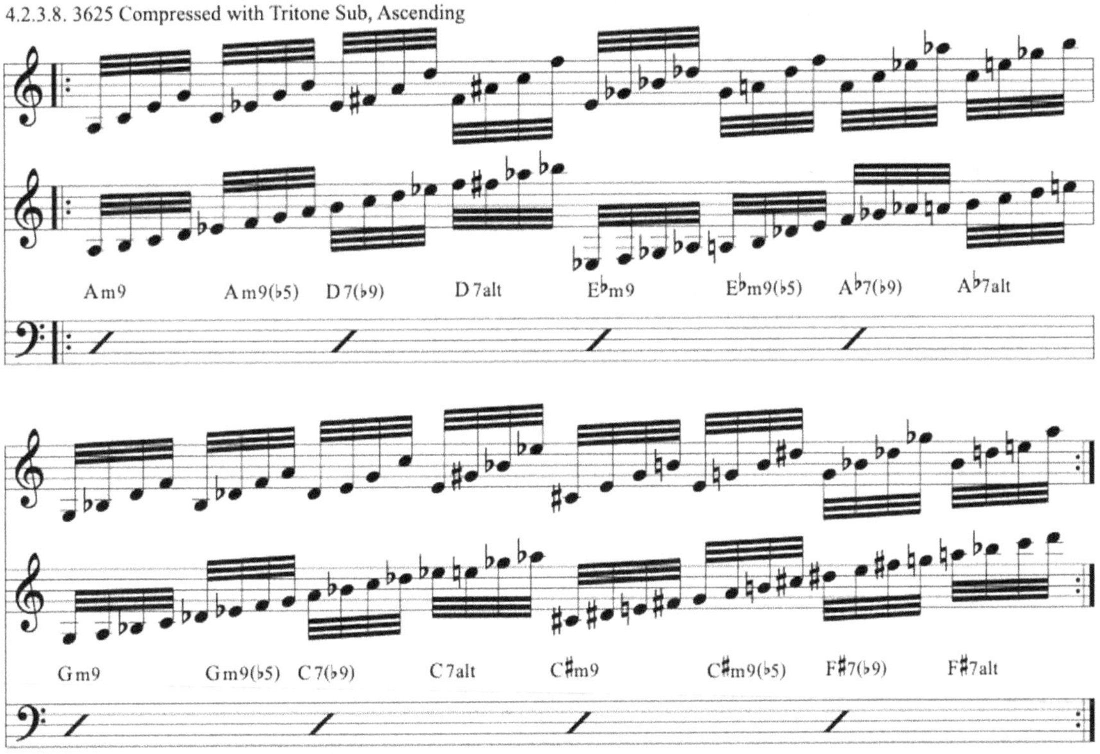

Appendix 4.2.3. 2536, 3625 with Tritone Sub Compressed

4.2.3.9. 3625 Compressed, Ascending Retrograde

4.2.3.10. 3625 Compressed with Tritone Sub, Ascending Retrograde

4.2.3.11. 3625 Compressed, Retrograde

4.2.3.12. 3625 Compressed with Tritone Sub, Retrograde

Section 3) Rhythm Changes and Progression Substitutions

The Rhythm Changes form follows a **||:** $I^{6/9}$-$VI7^{b9}$-$II7^{b9}$-$V7^{b9}$ progression in measures 1-2 with median substitution III^{-7}-VI^{7}-II^{7}-V^{7} structure in measures 3-4. Measure 5 represents I^{7} (Tonic) and/or substitute qualities, followed by IV in measure 6, culminating in the 2nd median substitute III^{m7}-$VI7^{b9}$-$II7^{b9}$-$V7^{b9}$ in measures 7-8 **:||**[**]

The **B Section**/ "The Channel" (mm. 9-16) is designated by Dominant chords, starting with III^{7} moving in (the cycle of) fourths every two measures, leading up to the $V^{7\,(mm.15\text{-}16)}$, transitioning to the last eight measures, resembling the first eight[**]

Furthermore, this section will discuss the values of the Alternate Functions in V^{7} (Inverted Diminished / Super Locrian) ascending in whole steps, descending in half-steps amid the cycle of fourths bass movement. Progressions move in fourths, harmonic info moves down in descending half-steps, except for the substitution of the tritone. Conversely, alternate "data" that is descending in half-steps is ascending in whole steps.

4.3.1. Rhythm Changes and Progression Substitutions

4.3.1.1. Rhythm Changes and Progression Substitutions, Tier 1: V7♭9

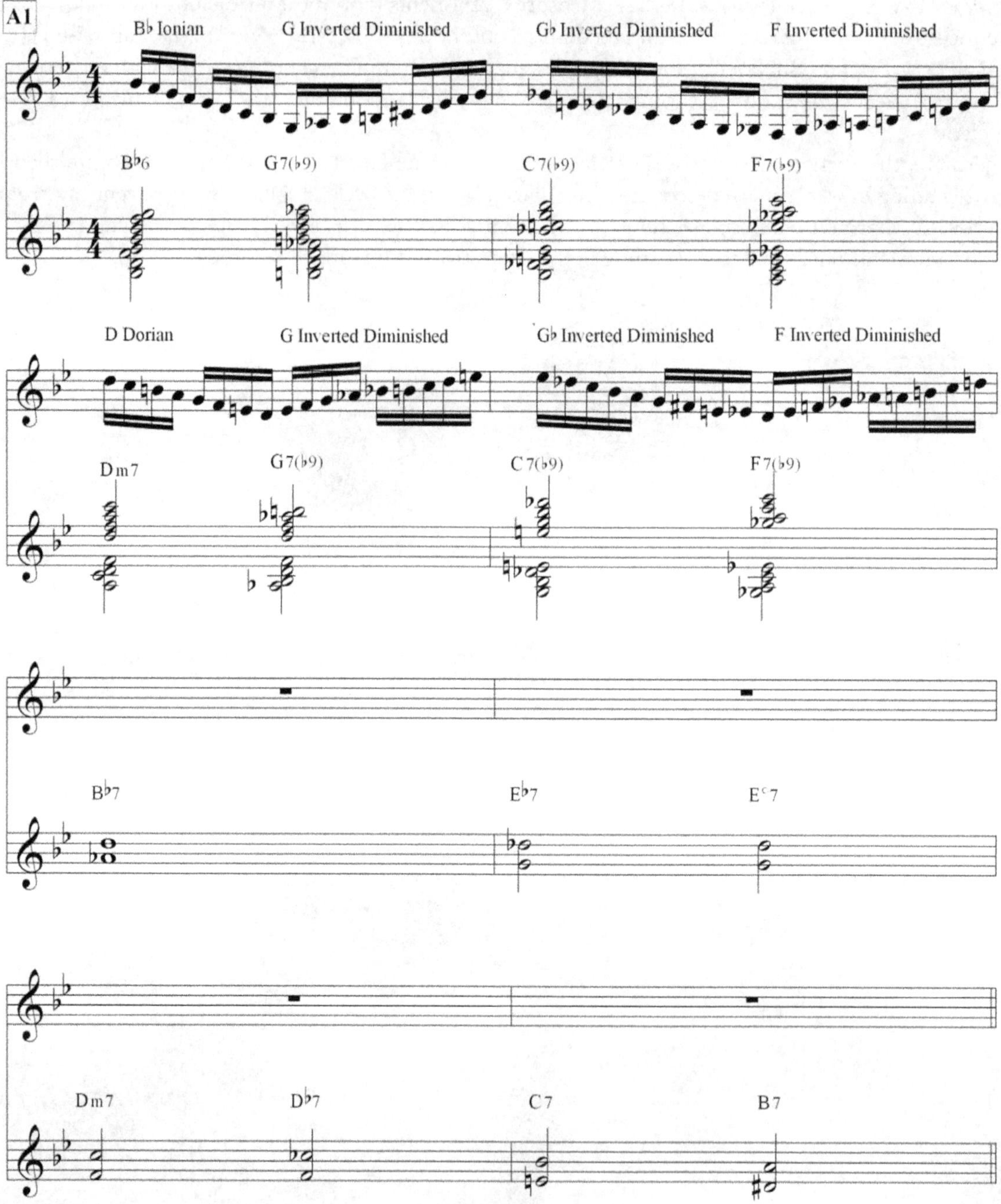

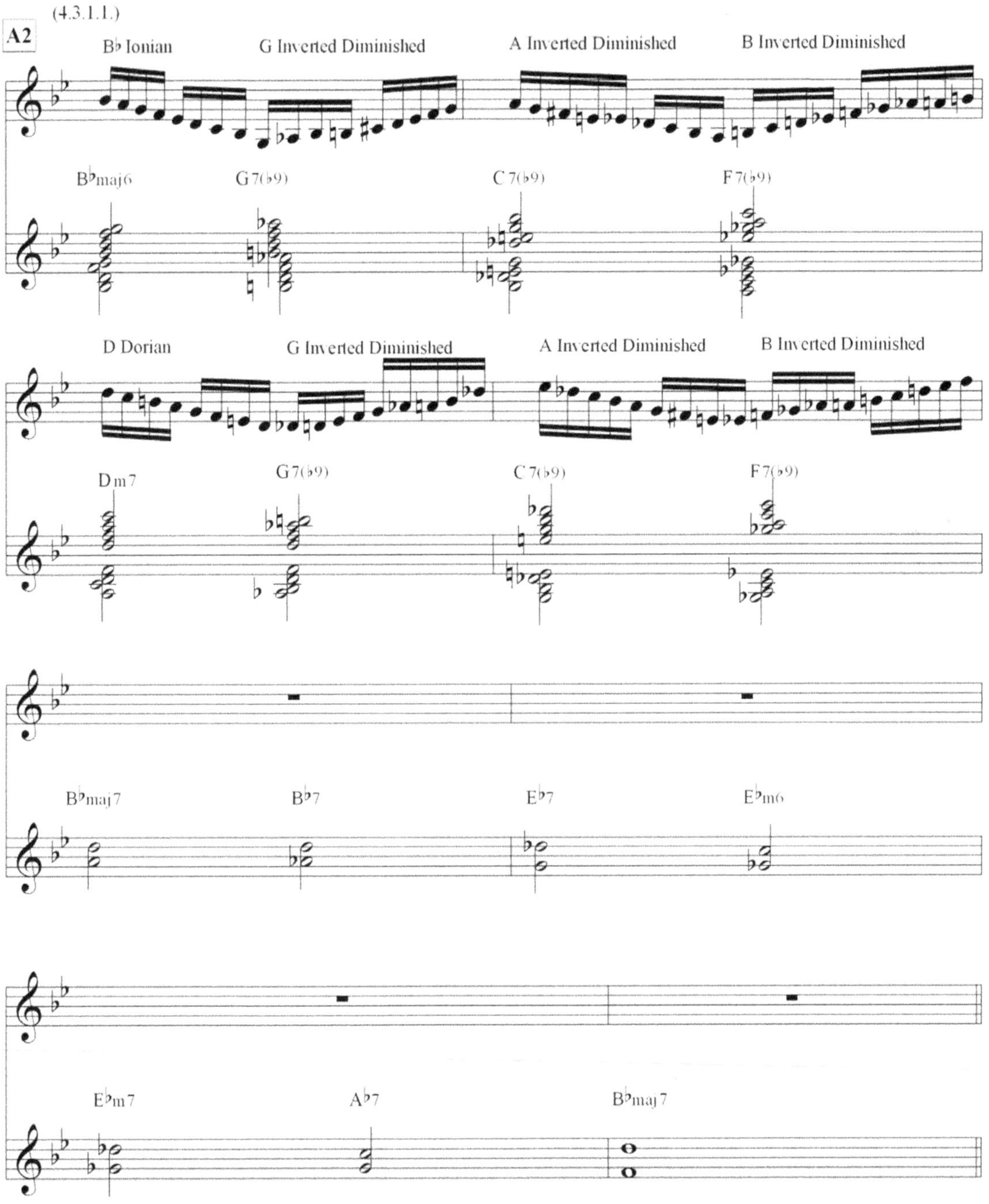
(4.3.1.1.)
A2
B♭ Ionian
G Inverted Diminished
A Inverted Diminished
B Inverted Diminished
B♭maj6
G7(♭9)
C7(♭9)
F7(♭9)
D Dorian
G Inverted Diminished
A Inverted Diminished
B Inverted Diminished
Dm7
G7(♭9)
C7(♭9)
F7(♭9)
B♭maj7
B♭7
E♭7
E♭m6
E♭m7
A♭7
B♭maj7

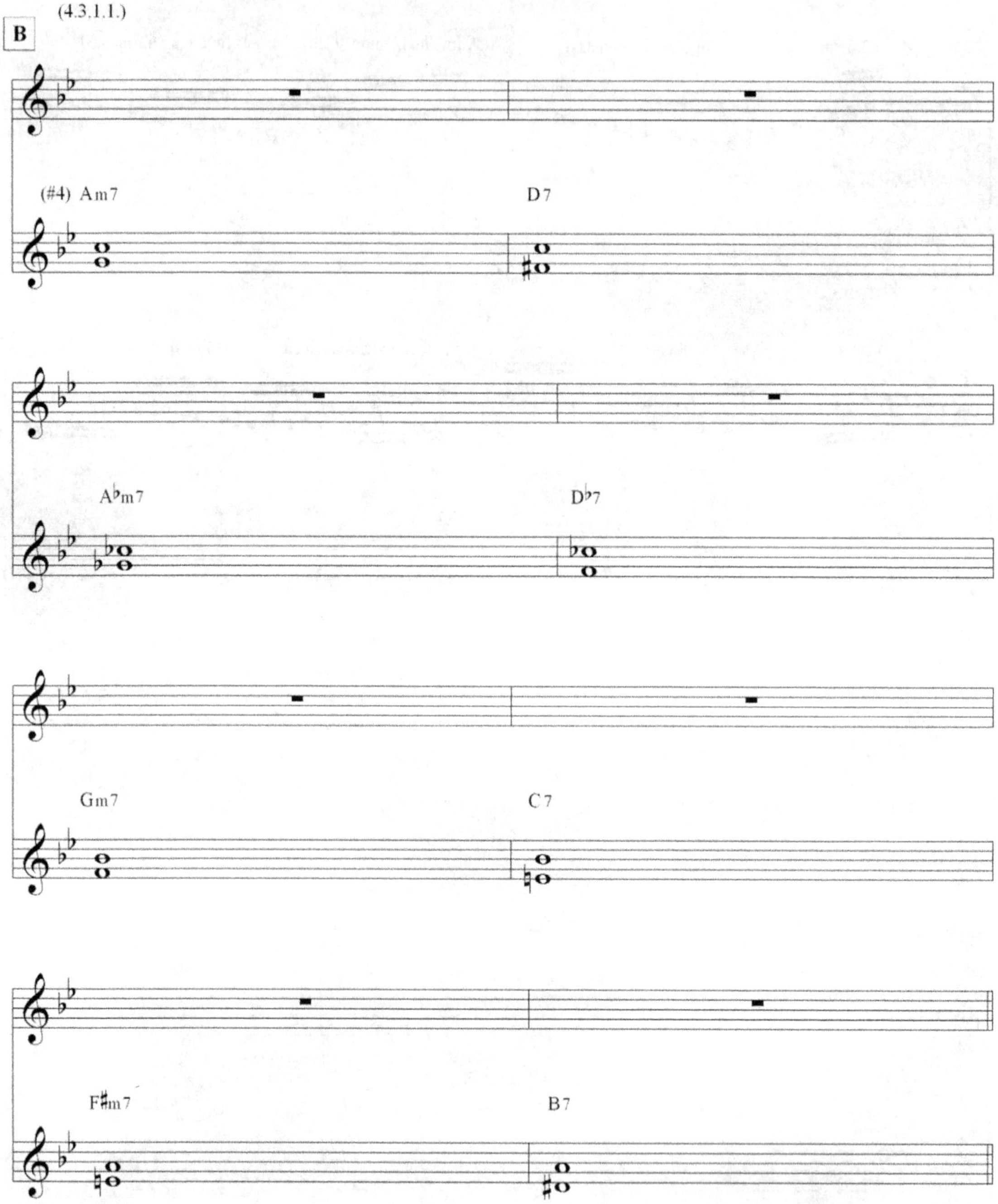
(4.3.1.1.)
B
(#4) Am7
D7
A♭m7
D♭7
Gm7
C7
F♯m7
B7

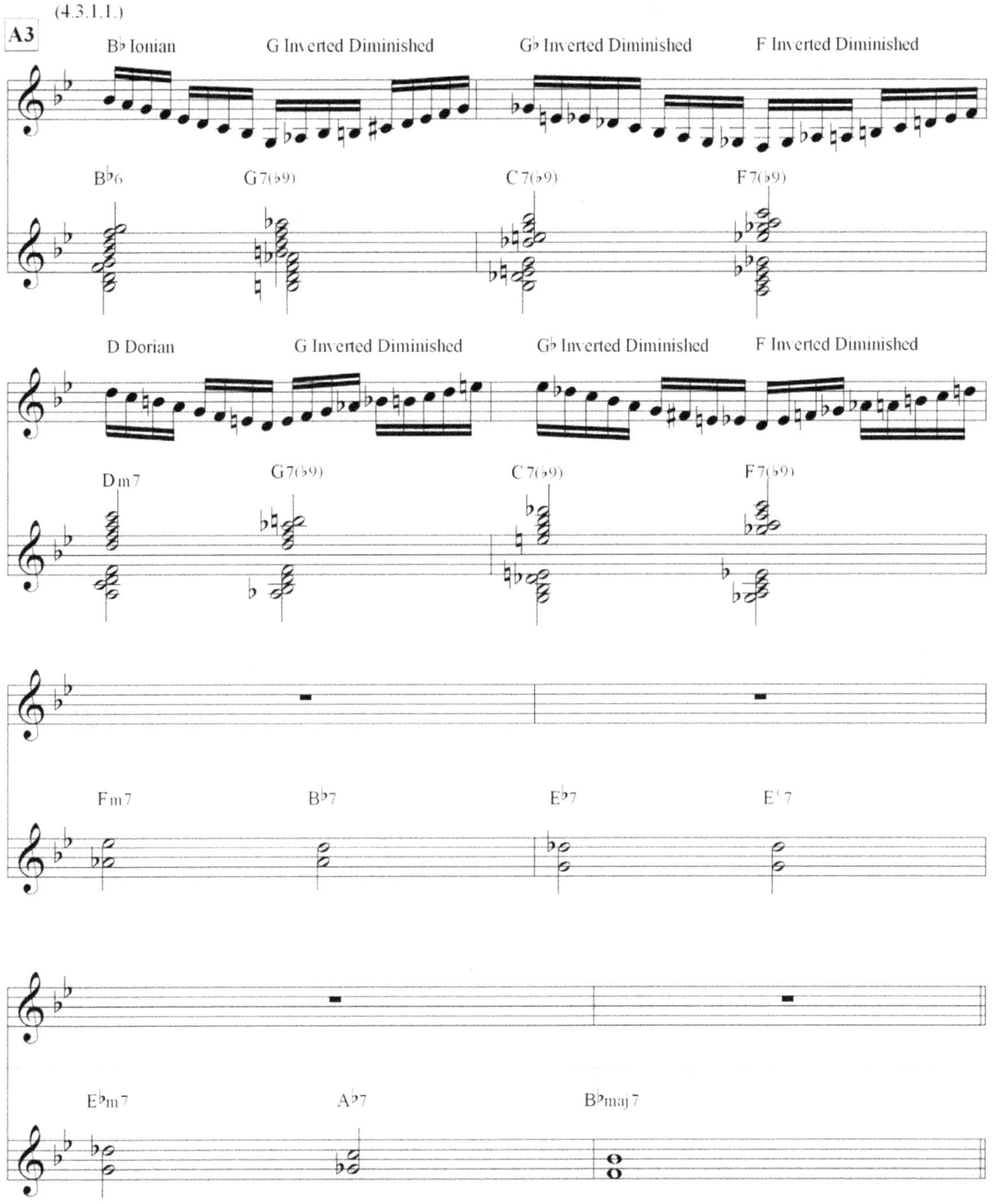
(4.3.1.1.)
A3
B♭ Ionian
G Inverted Diminished
G♭ Inverted Diminished
F Inverted Diminished
B♭6
G7(♭9)
C7(♭9)
F7(♭9)
D Dorian
G Inverted Diminished
G♭ Inverted Diminished
F Inverted Diminished
Dm7
G7(♭9)
C7(♭9)
F7(♭9)
Fm7
B♭7
E♭7
E♭m7
A♭7
B♭maj7

4.3.1.2. Tier 2: V7b9#11#9

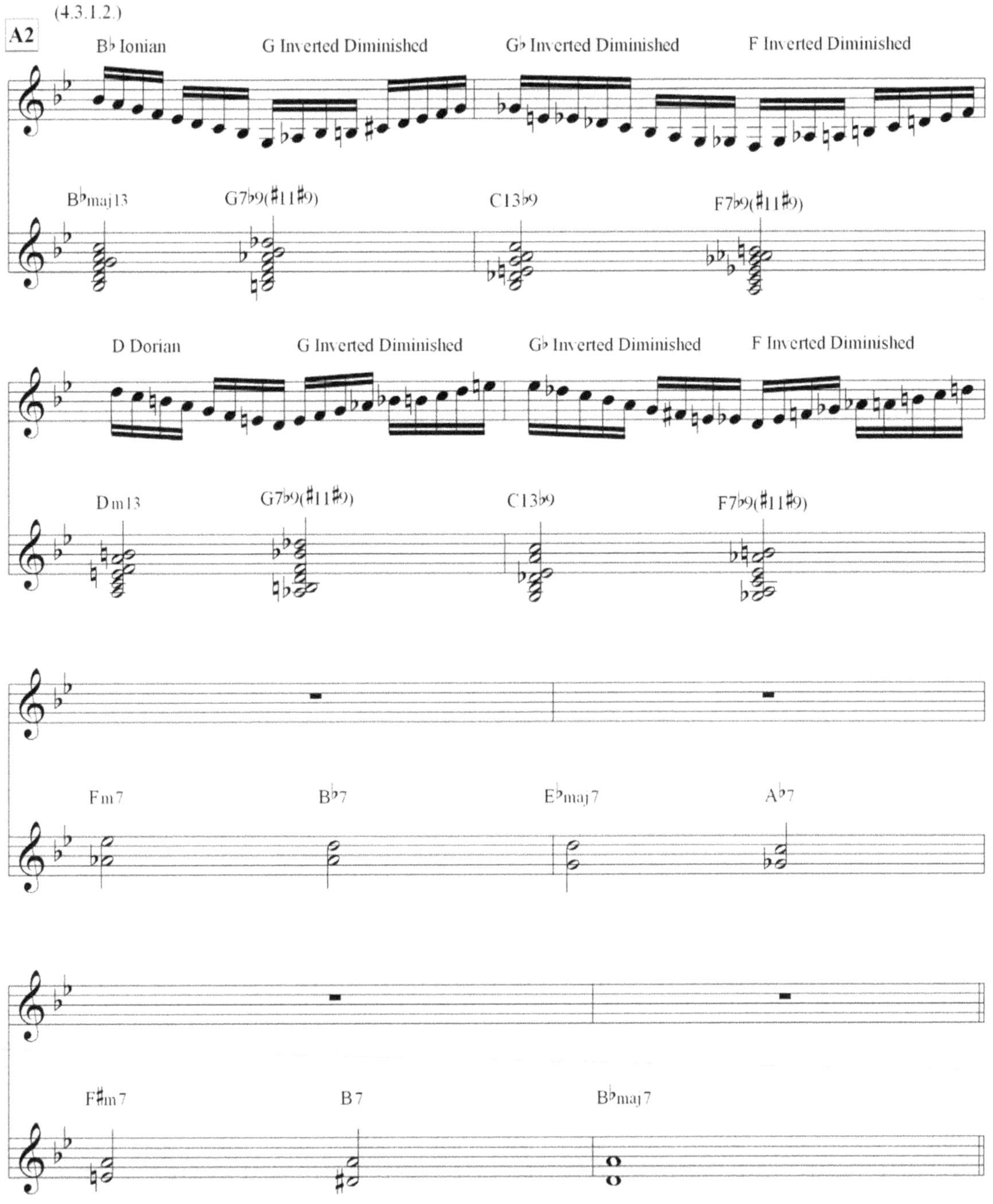
(4.3.1.2.)
A2
B♭ Ionian
G Inverted Diminished
G♭ Inverted Diminished
F Inverted Diminished
B♭maj13
G7♭9(♯11♯9)
C13♭9
F7♭9(♯11♯9)
D Dorian
G Inverted Diminished
G♭ Inverted Diminished
F Inverted Diminished
Dm13
G7♭9(♯11♯9)
C13♭9
F7♭9(♯11♯9)
Fm7
B♭7
E♭maj7
A♭7
F♯m7
B7
B♭maj7

(4.3.1.2.)
B
(#20) E♭m7
A♭7
Dm7
G7
D♭m7
G♭7
Cm7
F7

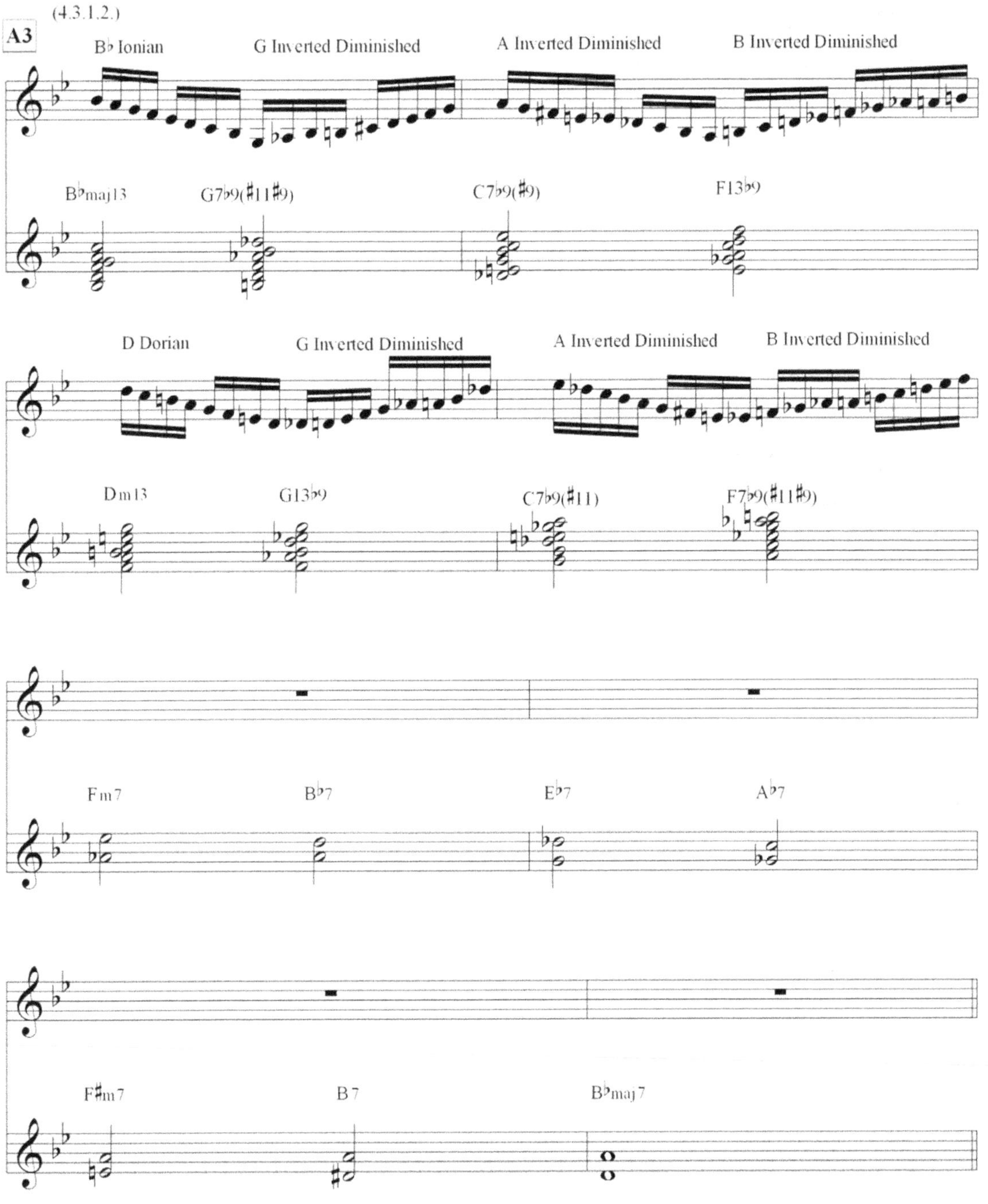
(4.3.1.2.)
A3
B♭ Ionian
G Inverted Diminished
A Inverted Diminished
B Inverted Diminished
B♭maj13
G7♭9(♯11♯9)
C7♭9(♯9)
F13♭9
D Dorian
G Inverted Diminished
A Inverted Diminished
B Inverted Diminished
Dm13
G13♭9
C7♭9(♯11)
F7♭9(♯11♯9)
Fm7
B♭7
E♭7
A♭7
F♯m7
B7
B♭maj7

4.3.1.3. Tier 3: V7alt

4.3.1.3. Rhythm Changes and Progression Substitutions, Tier 3: Altered

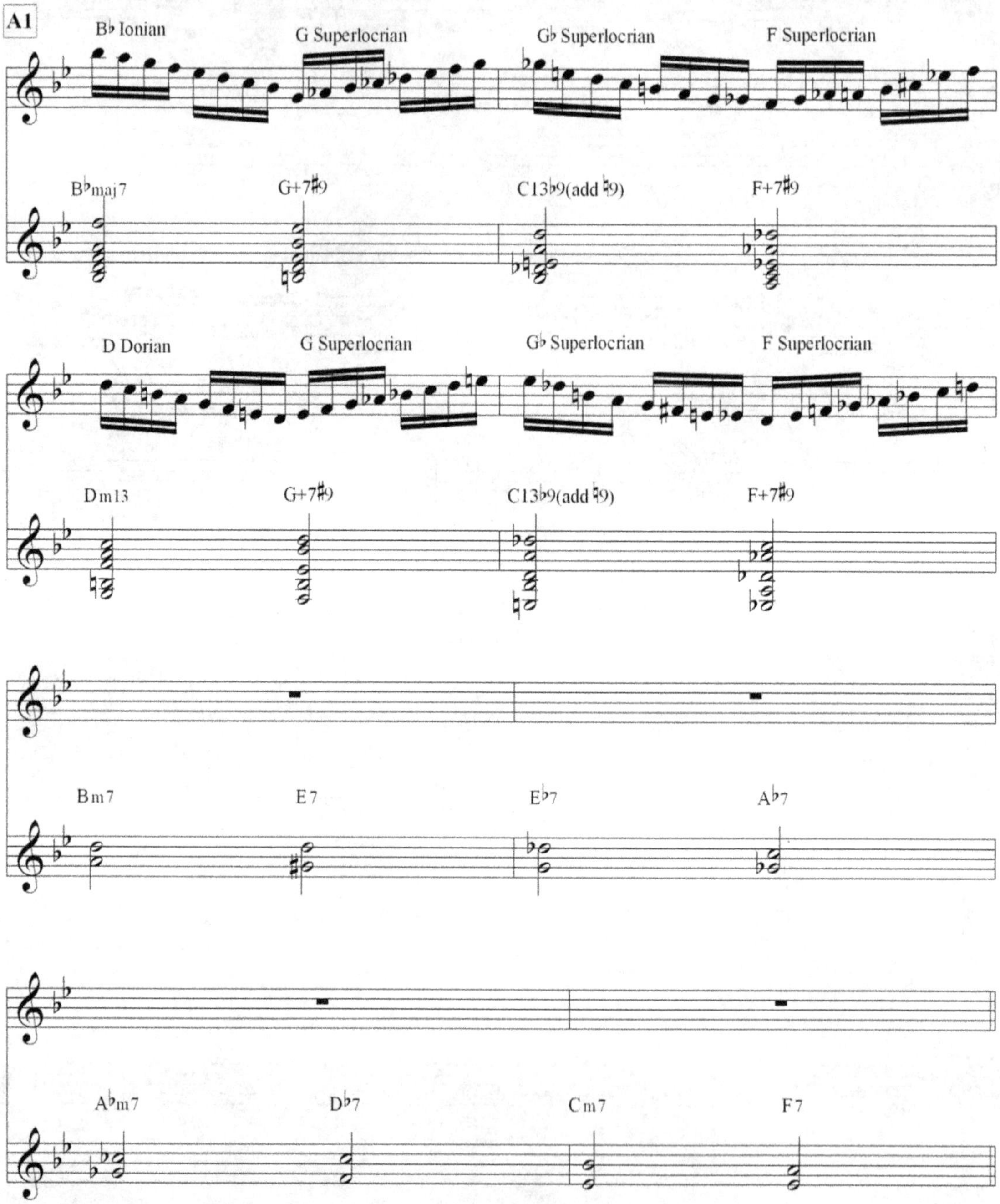

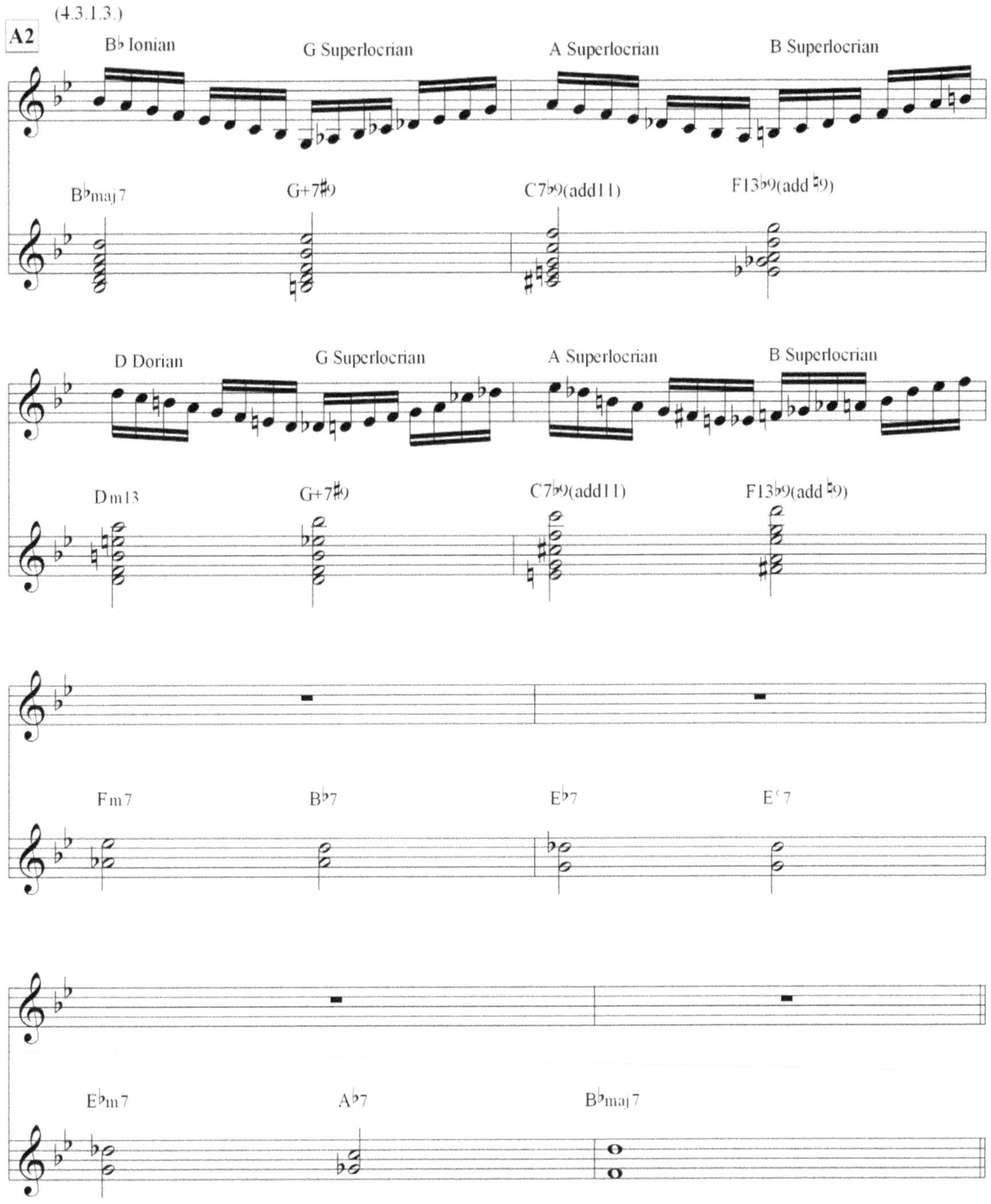
(4.3.1.3.)
A2
B♭ Ionian
G Superlocrian
A Superlocrian
B Superlocrian
B♭maj7
G+7♯9
C7♭9(add11)
F13♭9(add ♮9)
D Dorian
G Superlocrian
A Superlocrian
B Superlocrian
Dm13
G+7♯9
C7♭9(add11)
F13♭9(add ♮9)
Fm7
B♭7
E♭7
E♭7
E♭m7
A♭7
B♭maj7

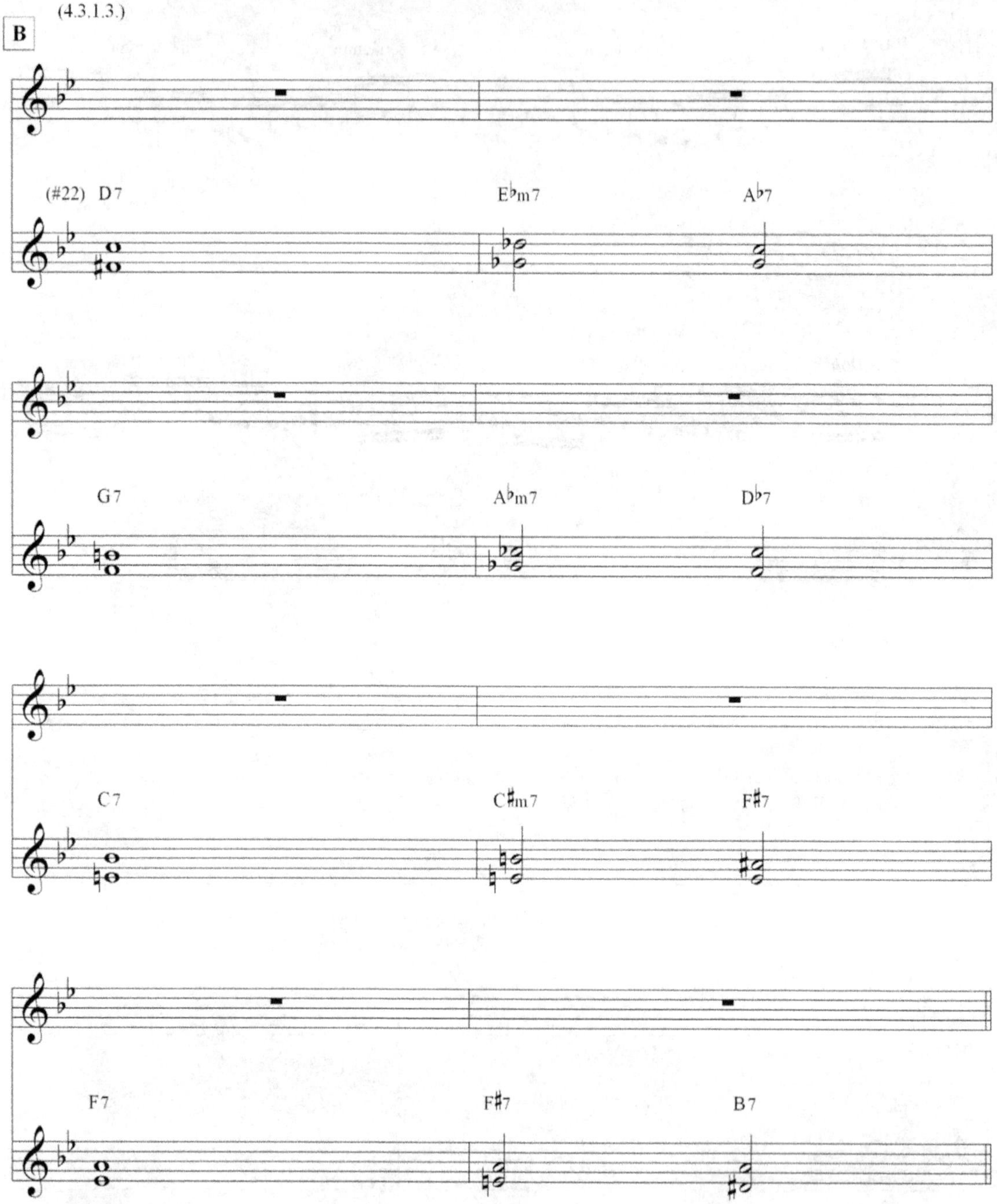
(4.3.1.3.)
B
(#22) D7
E♭m7
A♭7
G7
A♭m7
D♭7
C7
C♯m7
F♯7
F7
F♯7
B7

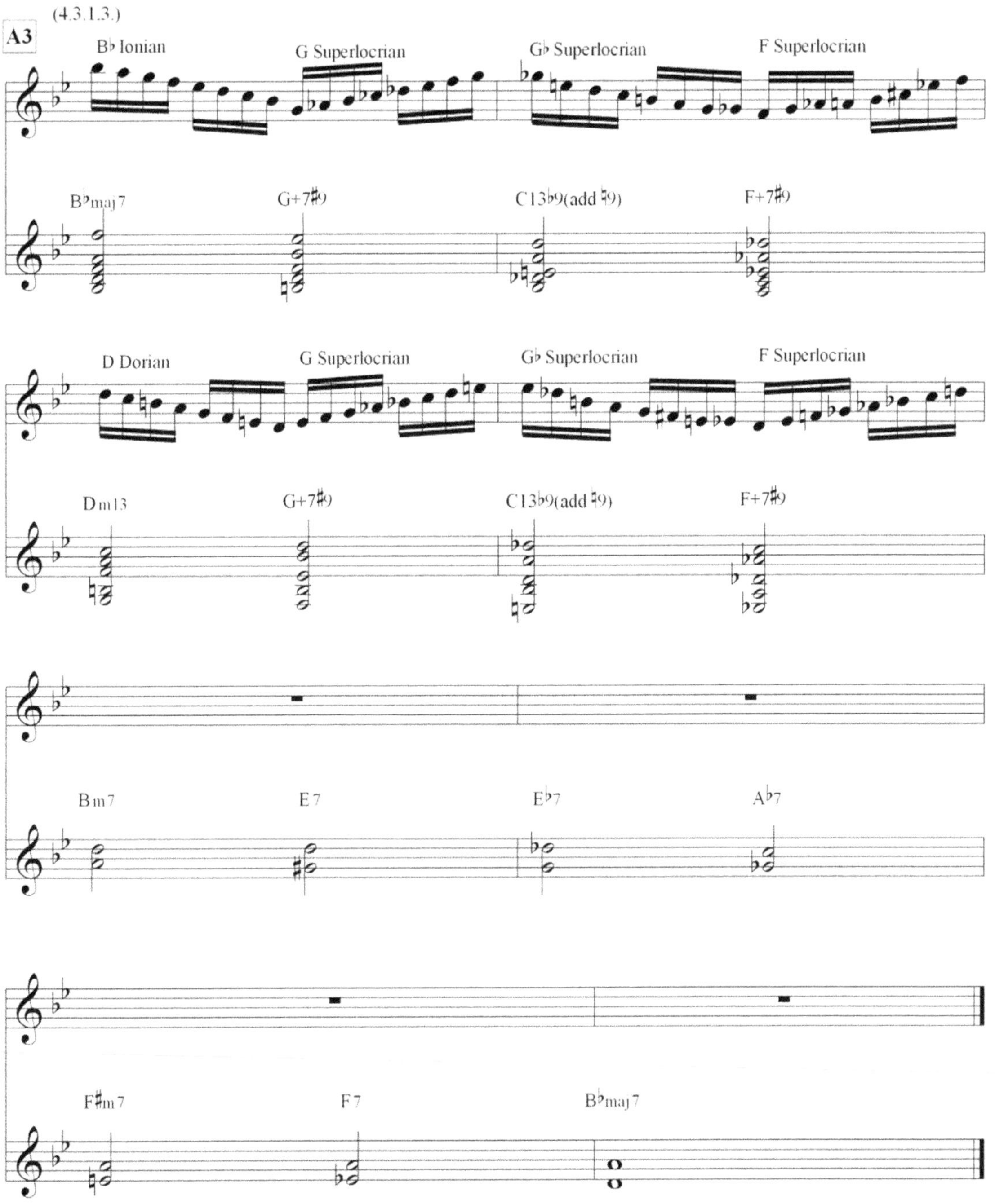
(4.3.1.3.)
A3
B♭ Ionian
G Superlocrian
G♭ Superlocrian
F Superlocrian
B♭maj7
G+7♯9
C13♭9(add ♮9)
F+7♯9
D Dorian
G Superlocrian
G♭ Superlocrian
F Superlocrian
Dm13
G+7♯9
C13♭9(add ♮9)
F+7♯9
Bm7
E7
E♭7
A♭7
F♯m7
F7
B♭maj7

4.3.2. Monk's Rhythm Changes (A Sections)

- Monk's version of first 8 bars of Rhythm Changes (in the key of Bb):
- Start b6 away from the root, moving in 4ths

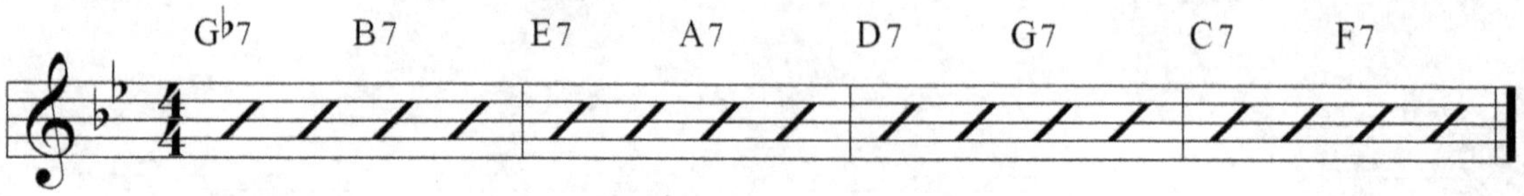

4.3.3. Sideslipping (Authentic and Plagal)

- Approaching the "alternating chords" (mm.2,4,6,8) from a <u>semi-tone above</u> (creates an Authentic cadence (in Tritone)
- Approaching the chords from a <u>semi-tone below</u> creates a Plagal cadence (in Tritone)

	1	**2**	**3**	**4**	**2**	**2**	**3**	**4**
A1)	**Db^7**	*(B^7)*	**Bb^7**	(E^7)	**Eb^7**	(A^7)	**Ab^7**	(D^7)
	Db^7	(A^7)	**Bb^7**	(D^7)	**Eb^7**	(G^7)	**Ab^7**	(C^7)
mm.5	**Db^6**	(D^7)	**Db^7**	(G^7)	**Gb^{maj7}**	(C^7)	**B^7**	(Gb^7)
	F^7	(B^7)	**Bb^7**	(E^7)	**Eb^7**	(A^7)	**Ab^7**	(D^7)
A2)	**Db^7**	(Gb^7)	**G^7**	(B^7)	**C^7**	(E^7)	**F^7**	(C^7)
	Db^7	(Ab^7)	**G^7**	(Db^7)	**C^7**	(Gb^7)	**F^7**	(D^7)
mm.5	**Db^6**	(C^7)	**Db^7**	(F^7)	**Gb^{maj7}**	(Bb^7)	**B^7**	(D^7)
	Eb^7	(G^7)	**Ab^7**	(C^7)	**Db^6**			
B)	F^7 (C^{min7}		F7$^{(alt)}$		(A^7) (E^{m7} (F#^{m7}		A7$^{(alt)}$) B7$^{(alt)}$)	
	Bb^7 (F^{min7}		Bb7$^{(alt)}$		(D^7) (A^{m7} (B^{m7}		D7$^{(alt)}$) E7$^{(alt)}$)	
mm.5	Eb^7 (Bb^{min7}		Eb7$^{(alt)}$		(G^7) (D^{m7} (E^{m7}		G7$^{(alt)}$) A7$^{(alt)}$)	
	Ab^7 (Eb^{min7}		Ab7$^{(alt)}$		(C^7)(G^{m7} (A^{m7}		C7$^{(alt)}$) D7$^{(alt)}$)	
A3)	**Db^7**	*(F^7)*	**E^7**	(Bb^7)	**A^7**	(Eb^7)	**D^7**	(D^7)
	Db^7	(Eb^7)	**E^7**	(Ab^7)	**A^7**	(Db^7)	**D^7**	(C^7)
mm.5	**Db^6**	(D^7)	**Db^7**	(G^7)	**Gb^{maj7}**	(C^7)	**B^7**	(E^7)
	Eb^7	(A^7)	**Ab^7**	(D^7)	**Db^6**			

4.3.3. Sideslipping (Authentic and Plagal Cadences)

4.3.4. Rhythm Changes: B Section Variations (partial)

		1	2	3	4	5	6	7	8
	1	D^7	D^7	G^7	G^7	C^7	C^7	F^7	F^7
	2	A$^-$	D^7	G^7	G^7	C^7	C^7	F^7	F^7
B	3	A$^-$	D^7	D$^-$	G^7	G$^-$	C^7	C$^-$	F^7
	4	A$^-$	D^7	Ab$^-$	Db^7	G$^-$	C^7	F#$^-$	B^7
S	5	Ab^7	Ab^7	B^7	B^7	D^7	D^7	F^7	F^7
e	6	Eb$^-$	Ab^7	F#$^-$	B^7	A$^-$	D^7	C$^-$	F^7
c	7	Ab^7	Ab^7	G^7	G^7	Gb^7	Gb^7	F^7	F^7
t	8	Eb$^-$	Ab^7	D$^-$	G^7	Db$^-$	Gb^7	C$^-$	F^7
i	9	A$^-$ D^7	Eb$^-$ Ab^7	D$^-$ G^7	Ab$^-$ Db^7	G$^-$ C^7	Db$^-$ Gb^7	C$^-$ F^7	F#$^-$ B^7
o	10	D^7	Eb- Ab^7	G^7	Ab$^-$ Db^7	C^7	C#$^-$ F#^{7}	F^7	F#$^-$ B^7
n	11	D^7	D^{7+9}	G^7	G^{7+9}	C^7	C^{7+9}	F^7	F^{7+9}
	12	A$^-$	D^{7+9}	D$^-$	G^{7+9}	G$^-$	C^{7+9}	C$^-$	F^{7+9}
	13	D^7 C^7	Bb^7 Ab^7	G^7 F^7	Eb^7 Db^7	C^7 Bb^7	Ab^7 Gb^7	F^7 Eb^7	Db^7 B^7

4.3.5. Graph: Cross Median Progressions

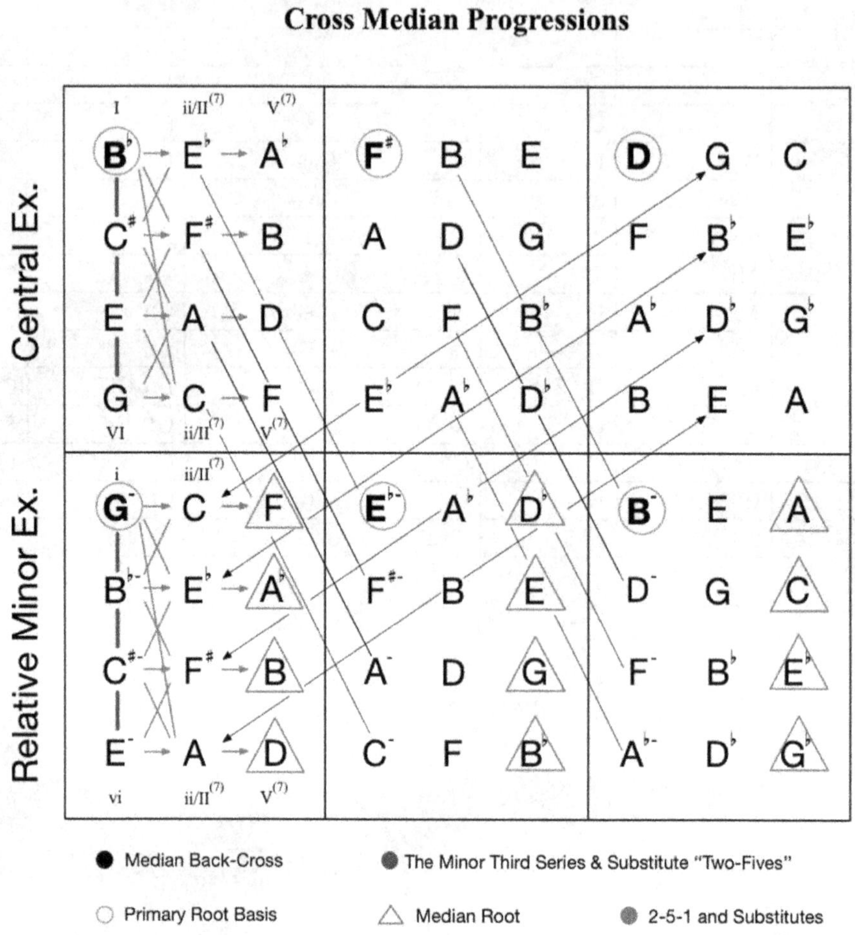
Cross Median Progressions
Central Ex.
Relative Minor Ex.
I
ii/II(7)
V(7)
VI
i
vi
Median Back-Cross
The Minor Third Series & Substitute "Two-Fives"
Primary Root Basis
Median Root
2-5-1 and Substitutes

Section 3a) Blues Progression Table

	1	2	3	4	5	6	7	8	9	10	11	12
1	F^{7}	F^{maj7}	F^{7}	F^{7}	Bb^{7}	Bb^{7}	F^{7}	F^{7}	C^{7}	C^{7}	F^{7}	F^{7}
2	F^{7}	F^{maj7}	F^{7}	F^{7}	Bb^{7}	Bb^{7}	F^{7}	F^{7}	C^{7}	Bb^{7}	F^{7}	C^{7}
3	F^{7}	Bb^{7}	F^{7}	F^{7}	Bb^{7}	Bb^{7}	F^{7}	F^{7}	G^{7}	C^{7}	F^{7}	C^{7}
4	F^{7}	Bb^{7}	F^{7}	F^{7}	Bb^{7}	Bb^{7}	F^{7}	D^{7}	G^{7}	C^{7}	F^{7}	C^{7}
5	F^{7}	Bb^{7}	F^{7}	F^{7}	Bb^{7}	Bb^{7}	F^{7}	D^{7}	G^{m7}	C^{7}	F^{7}	G^{m7} C^{7}
6	F^{7}	Bb^{7}	F^{7}	F^{7}	Bb^{7}	Eb^{7}	F^{7}	D^{7}	Db^{7}	C^{7}	F^{7}	Db^{7} C^{7}
7	F^{7}	Bb^{7}	F^{7}	C^{m7} F^{7}	Bb^{7}	Eb^{7}	F^{7}	A^{m7} D^{7}	G^{m7}	C^{7}	A^{m7} D^{7}	Gm^{7} G^{7}
8	F^{7}	Bb^{7}	F^{7}	C^{m7} F^{7}	Bb^{7}	Eb^{7}	A^{m7}	D^{7}	G^{m7}	C^{7}	A^{m7} D^{7}	G^{m7} C^{7}
9	F^{7}	Bb^{7}	F^{7}	C^{m7} F^{7}	Bb^{7}	B^{m7} E^{7}	F^{7} E^{7}	Eb^{7} D^{7}	G^{m7}	C^{7} Bb^{7}	A^{m7} D^{7}	Gm7 C7
10	F^{maj7}	E^{m7} A^{7}	D^{m7} G^{7}	C^{m7} F^{7}	Bb^{7}	Bo^{7}	A^{m7} D^{7}	Ab^{m7} Db^{7}	G^{m7} C^{7}	Db^{m7} Gb^{7}	F^{7} D^{7}	G^{m7} C^{7}
11	F^{maj7}	E^{m7} Eb^{m7}	D^{m7} Db^{m7}	C^{m7} Cb^{7}	Bb^{maj7}	Bb^{m7}	A^{m7}	Ab^{m7}	G^{m7}	C^{7}	A^{m7} Ab^{m7}	G^{m7} Gb^{7}
12	F^{maj7}	Bb^{maj7}	A^{m7} G^{m7}	Gb^{m7} Cb^{7}	Bb^{maj7}	Bb^{m7}	A^{m7}	Ab^{m7}	G^{m7}	Gb^{7}	F^{maj7} Ab^{m7}	G^{m7} Gb^{7}
13	F^{maj7}	Bb^{maj7}	A^{m7} G^{m7}	Gb^{m7} Cb^{7}	Bb^{maj7}	Bb^{m7}	Ab^{maj7}	Ab^{m7} Db^{7}	G^{m7}	G^{m7} C^{7}	A^{m7} D^{7}	Db^{m7} Gb^{7}
14	F^{maj7}	E^{m7} A^{7}	D^{m7} G^{7}	C^{m7} F^{7}	Bb^{maj7}	Bb^{m7}	A^{m7}	Ab^{m7} Db^{7}	G^{m7}	C^{7}	A^{m7} D^{7}	G^{m7} C^{7}
15	F^{maj7}	E^{m7} A^{7}	D^{m7} G^{7}	Gb^{m7} Cb^{7}	Bb^{maj7}	B^{m7}	A^{m7}	Ab^{m7} Db^{7}	G^{m7}	C^{7} Bb^{7}	A^{m7} D^{7}	G^{m7} C^{7}
16	F#^{m7} B^{7}	E^{m7} A^{7}	D^{m7} G^{7}	C^{m7} F^{7}	Bb^{maj7}	Bb^{m7} Eb^{7}	Ab^{maj7}	Ab^{m7} Db^{7}	Gb^{maj7}	G^{m7} C^{7}	A^{m7} D^{7}	G^{m7} C^{7}
17	F^{maj7}	F#^{m7} B^{7}	E^{maj7} Eb^{maj7}	Db^{maj7} B^{maj7}	Bb^{maj7}	B^{m7} E^{7}	A^{maj7}	A^{m7} D^{7}	G^{maj7}	Gb^{maj7}	F^{maj7} Ab^{maj7}	G^{maj7} Gb^{7}

Aebersold, Jamey. 1982. "Variations on Blues," in *Jazz Aids Handbook*. Jamey Aebersold: New Albany, IN.

Section 4) Coltrane

4.4.1. Trane's Substitution on Blues with Extensions

Description: Base progression in bold. Coltrane progression in parentheses. Hybrid progressions in brackets See Chapter 8.2

F^{7} (Gb^{7} B^{7})	**Bb^{7} Eb^{7}** (E^{7} A^{7})	**F^{7}** (D^{7} G^{7})	**F#^{7} B^{7}** (C^{7} F^{7})
Bb^{7} [E^{7}]	**Eb^{7}** [A^{7}]	**F^{7}** [D^{7} G^{7}]	**D^{7}** [C^{7} F^{7}]
G^{7} ^{C7} (Db^{7} Gb^{7}) [E^{7} A^{7}] [Bb^{7} Eb^{7}]	**F^{7} Bb^{7}** (B^{7} E^{7}) [D^{7} G^{7}] [Ab^{7} Db^{7}]	**F^{7}** (A^{7} D^{7}) [C^{7} Eb^{7}] [F#^{7} B^{7}]	**Bb^{7} Eb^{7}** (G^{7} C^{7}) [E^{7} A^{7}] [Db^{7} Gb^{7}]

4.4.2. Trane's Blues Turnaround

Description:

F^{7}	**Bb^{7} Eb^{7}**	**F^{7}**	**F#^{7} B^{7}**
Bb^{7}	**Eb^{7}**	**F^{7}**	**D^{7}**
G^{7} C^{7} (E^{m7} A^{7})	**F^{7} Bb^{7}** (Eb^{m7} Ab^{7})	**F^{7}** (D^{m7} G^{7})	**Bb^{7} Eb^{7}** (Db^{m7} Gb^{7})

4.4.3. Coltrane's Extended ii-V-I

4.4.3.1. Countdown ii-V w/ Countdown Extended I (a)

Description: see Chapter 8.2

Countdown ii-V				Extended I (a)			
E^{m7} F^{7}	Bb^{maj7} Db^{7}	Gb^{maj7} A7	D^{maj7}	D^{maj7} C^{7}	F^{maj7} B^{7}	Bb^{7} A^{7}	D^{maj7}
(Common ii-V)				*(Tonic)*			
E^{m7}	*A^{7}*	*D^{maj7}*	*D^{maj7}*	*D^{maj7}*	*D^{maj7}*	*D^{maj7}*	*D^{maj7}*

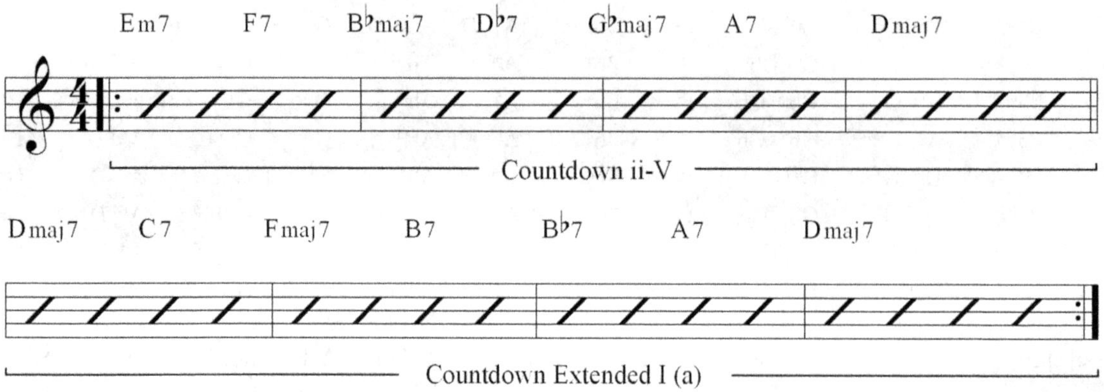

4.4.3.2. Giant Steps ii-V w/ Countdown Extended I (b)

Giant Steps ii-V			Extended I (b)					
B^{maj7} D^7	G^{maj7} Bb^7	Eb^{maj7}	Eb^{maj7} Gb^7	B^{maj7} D^7	G^{maj7} Bb^7	Eb^{maj7}	Eb^{maj7}	
(Common ii-V)			*(Tonic)*					
F^{m7}	*Bb^7*	*Eb^{maj7}*	*Eb^{maj7}*	*Eb^{maj7}*	*Eb^{maj7}*	*Eb^{maj7}*	*Eb^{maj7}*	

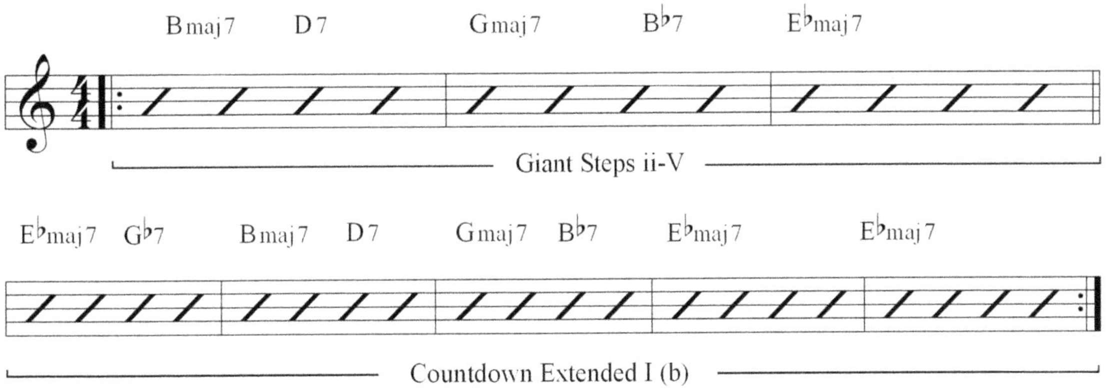

4.4.4. Giant Steps in Relative Minor

'Giant Steps'

Chord Progression (in Relative Minor)

Note that the original Giant Steps melody will still fit the new changes

4.4.5. Linear Construction via Coltrane's Modified ii-V and Extended Resolution to I

4.4.5.1. Countdown ii-V-I

Description: * Triple Augmented in Dominant, ^ Triple Augmented in Major

4.4.5.2. Giant Steps ii-V-I

4.4.5.3. Giant Steps ii-V-I (Extended)

4.4.5.4. Countdown Extended I (a)

Description: See Chapter 8.2

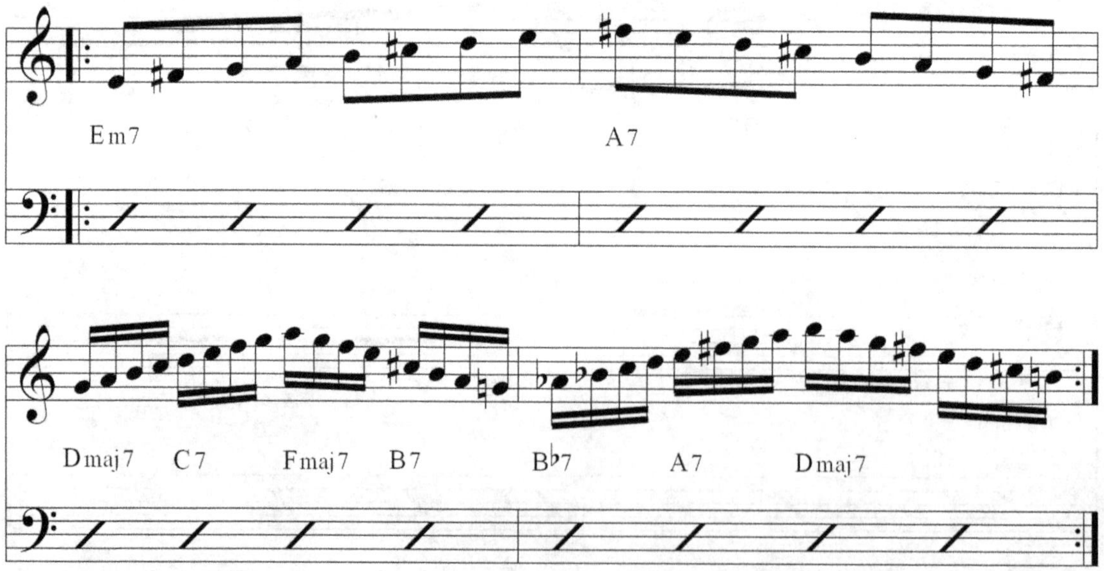

4.4.5.5. Countdown Extended I (b)

Description: See Chapter 8.2

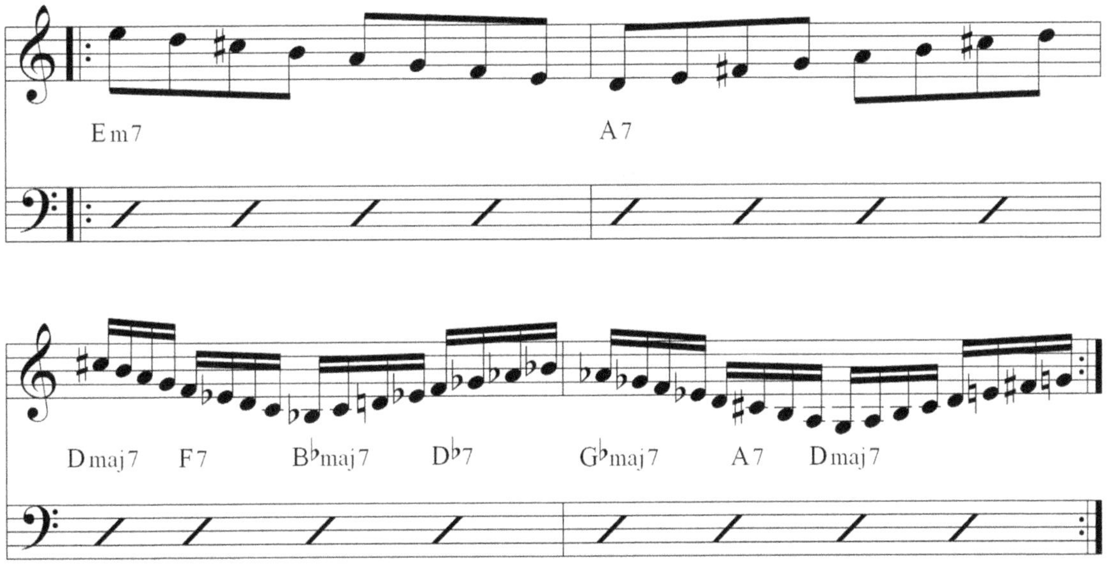

Section 5) Quartal/Quintal Chords

4.5.1. Quartal Voicings – Dorian

Description: Voicings spread out in 4ths over the quality of the chord. See Chapter 8.2

APPENDIX 4.5.1.
QUARTAL VOICINGS - DORIAN

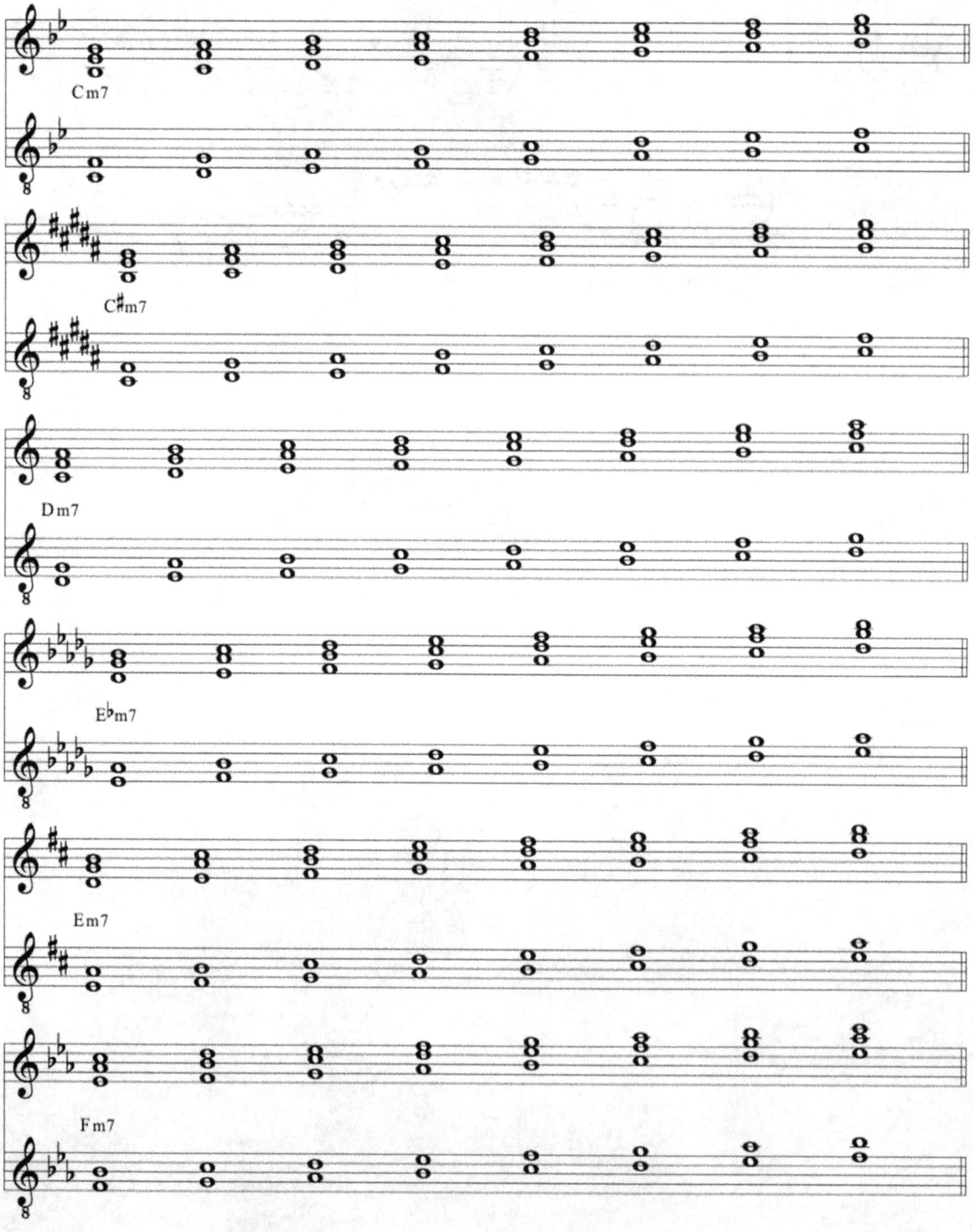

Appendix 4.5.1. Quartal Voicings - Dorian

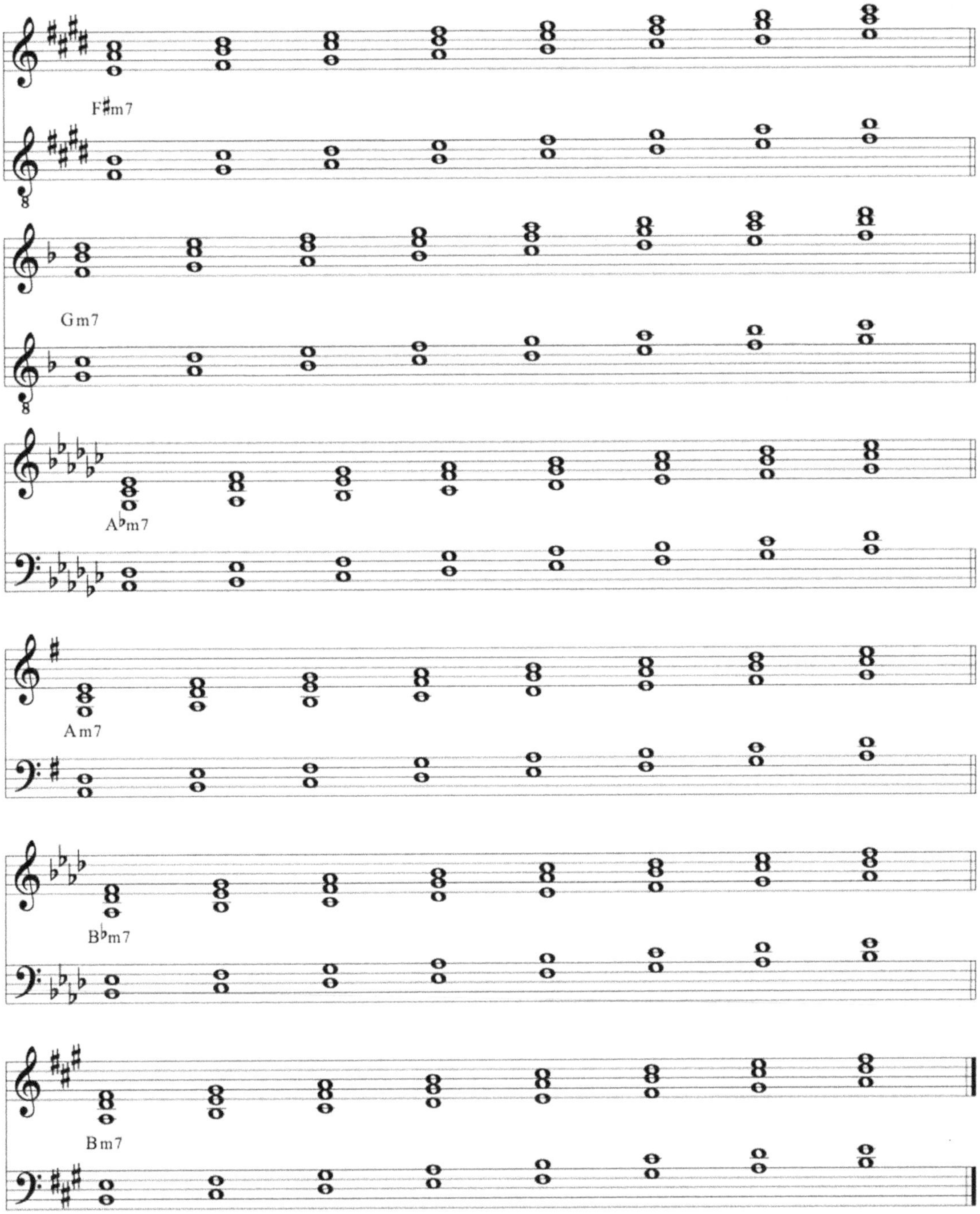

4.5.2. Quartal Voicings – Lydian Inversions

If we **raise the Fourth degree**, the Major 5-note Quartal ex. can be configured from a variety of **acceptable points of departure** (tonic, M6, #4, 9) and, pretty much, any degree of the scale, with this # alteration of the fourth degree.

APPENDIX 4.5.2
QUARTAL VOICINGS - LYDIAN INVERSIONS

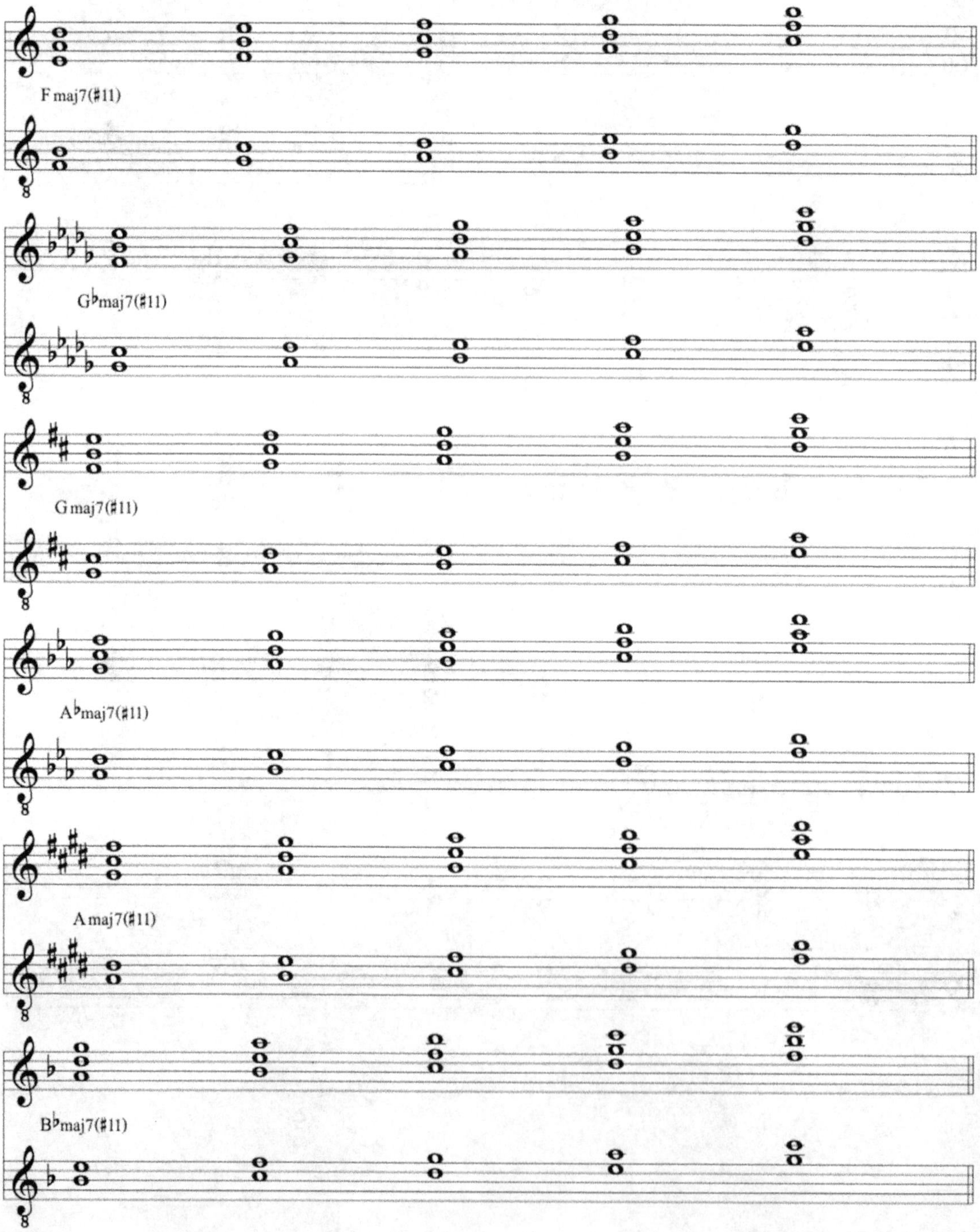

Appendix 4.5.2. Quartal Voicings - Lydian Inversions

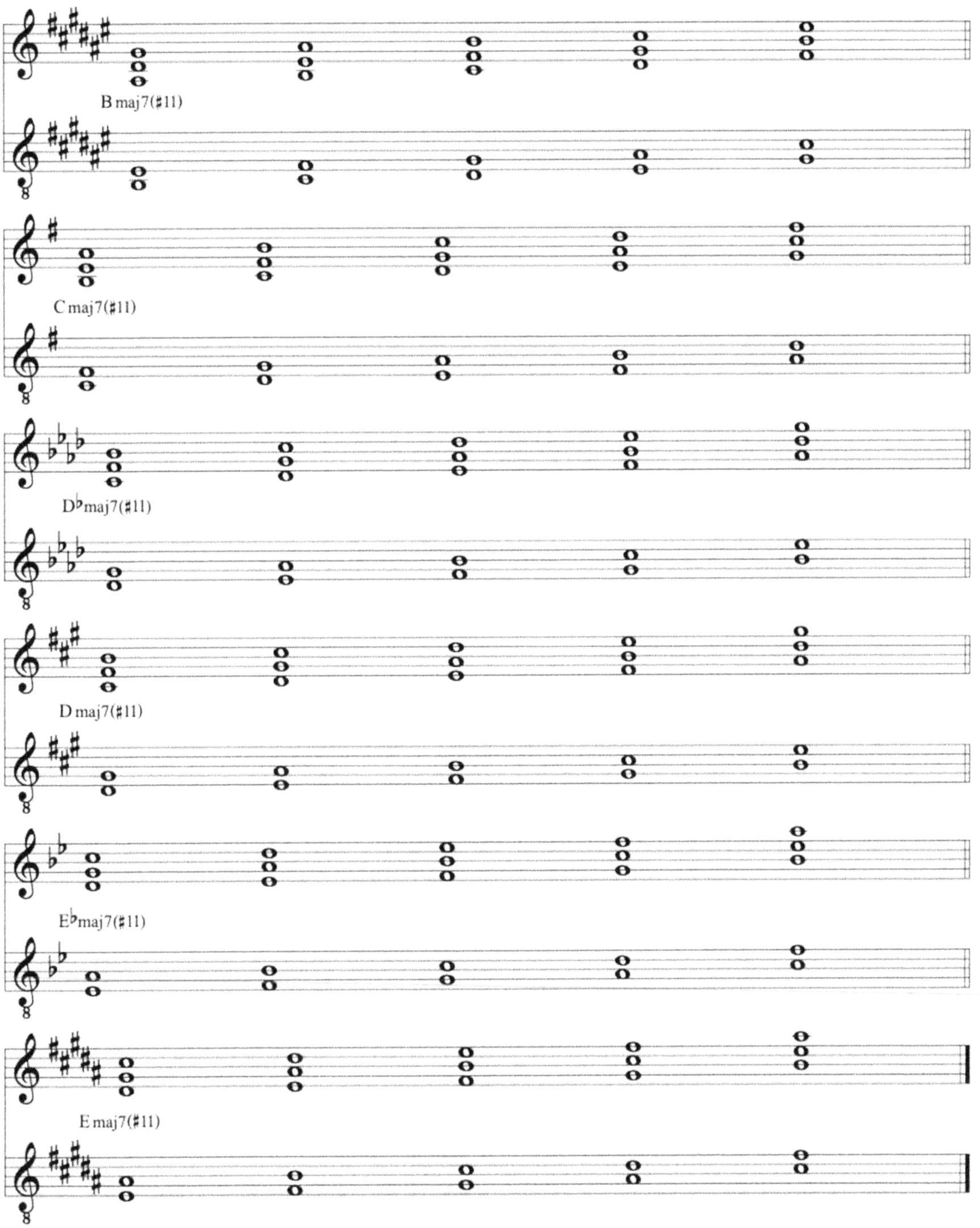

4.5.3. Quartal Voicings – Dominant

Description: See Chapter 8.2

APPENDIX 4.5.3.
QUARTAL VOICINGS - DOMINANT

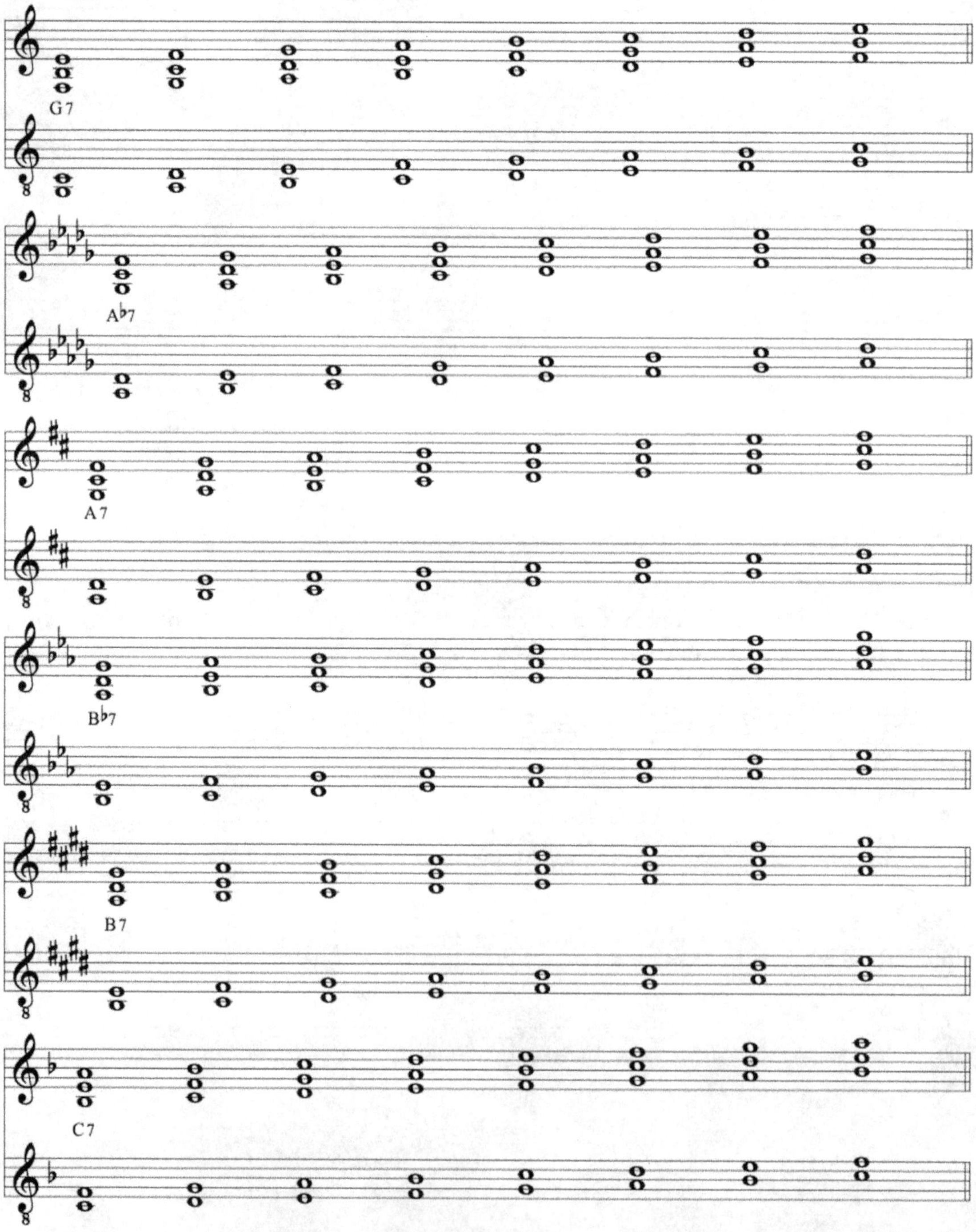

Appendix 4.5.3. Quartal Voicings - Dominant

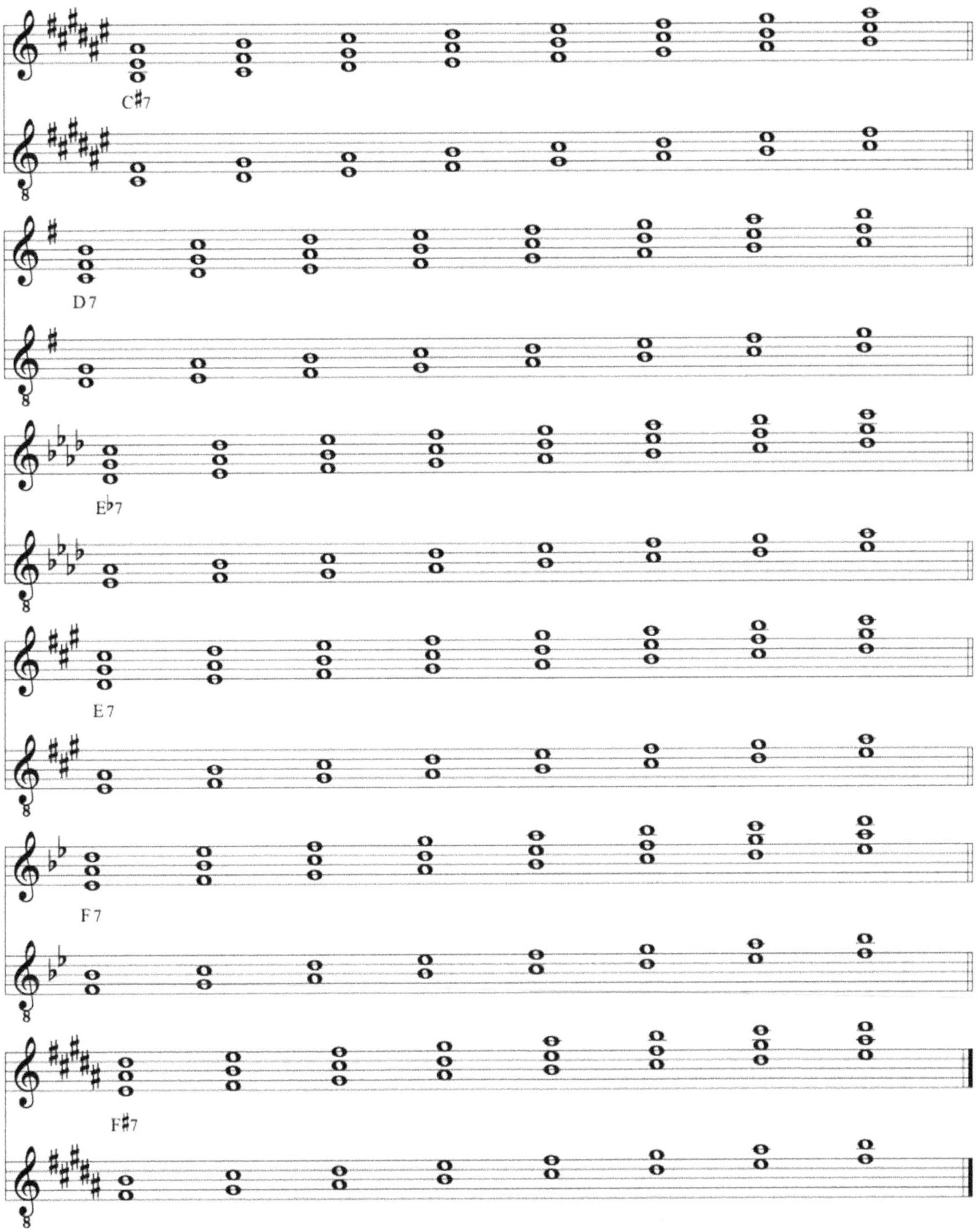

4.5.4. Quartal Voicings – Lydian Dominant

Description: See Chapter 8.2

APPENDIX 4.5.4.
QUARTAL VOICINGS - LYDIAN DOMINANT

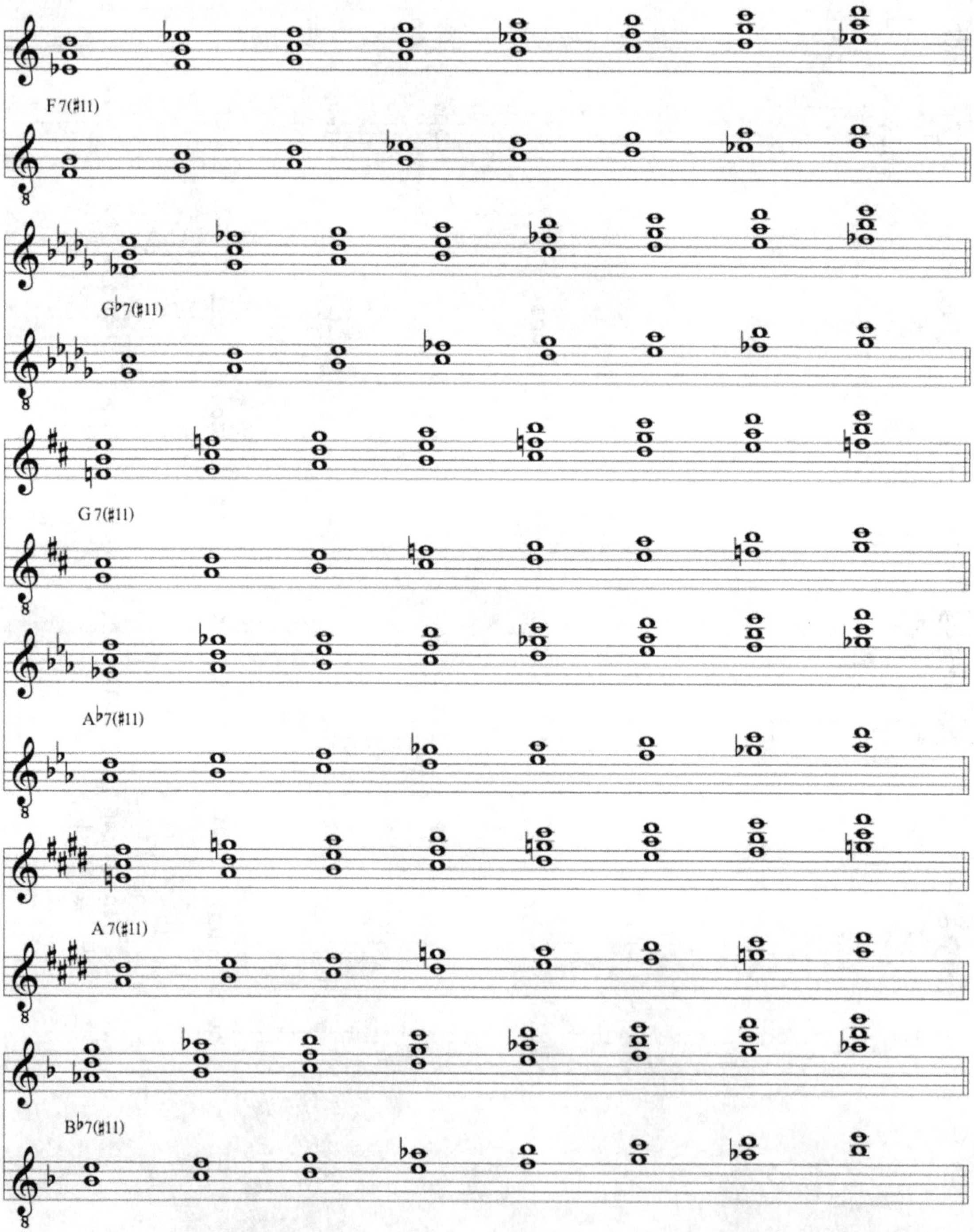

Appendix 4.5.4. Quartal Voicings - Lydian Dominant

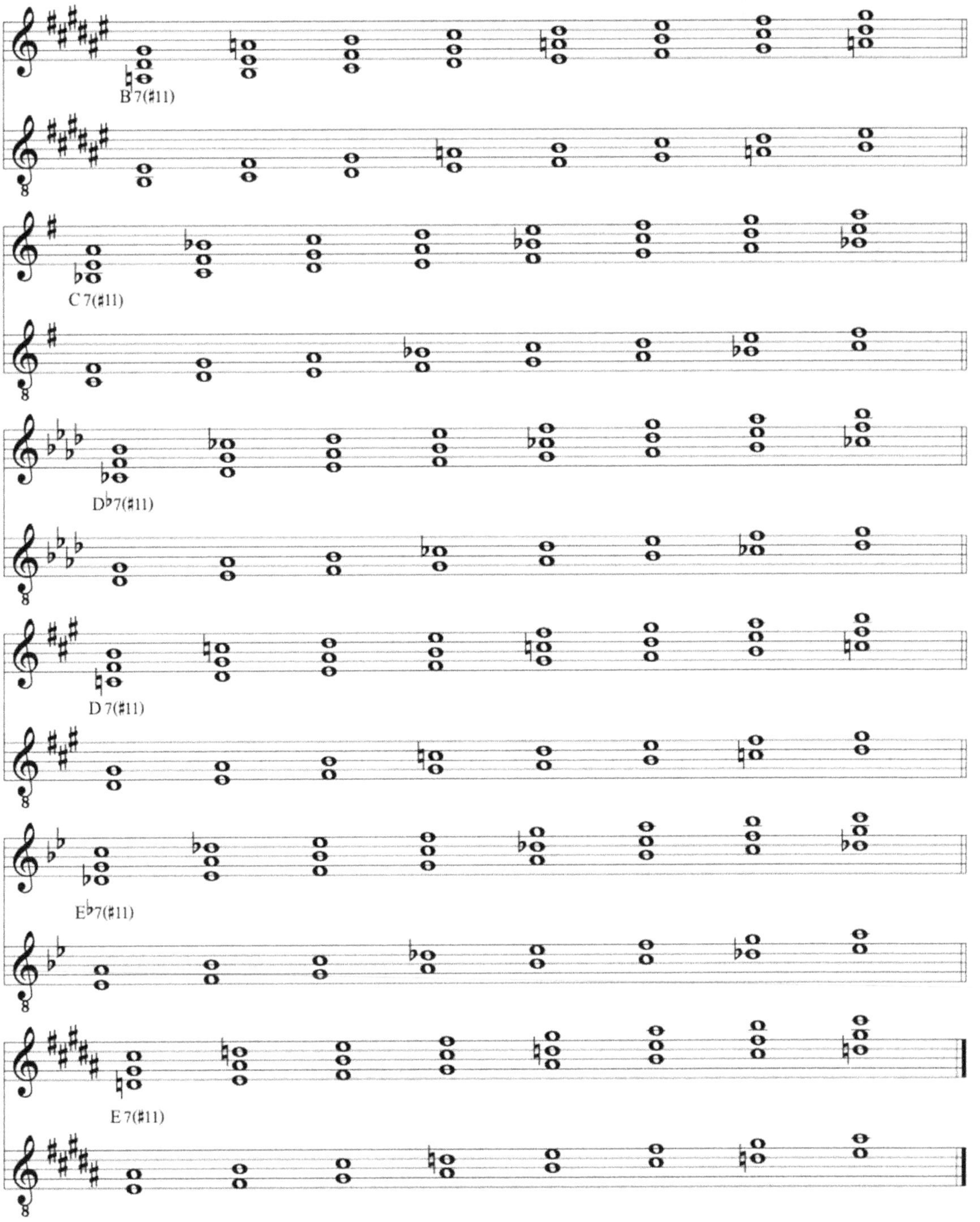

4.5.5. Chromatic Planing – Dorian

4.5.6. Whole Tone Planing (A Love Supreme)

4.5.6.1. Whole Tone Planing – Minor, System 1/2

4.5.6.2. Whole Tone Planing – Minor, System 2/2

APPENDIX 4.5.5./4.5.6.
CHROMATIC PLANING/WHOLE TONE PLANING

4.5.5. Chromatic Planing - Dorian

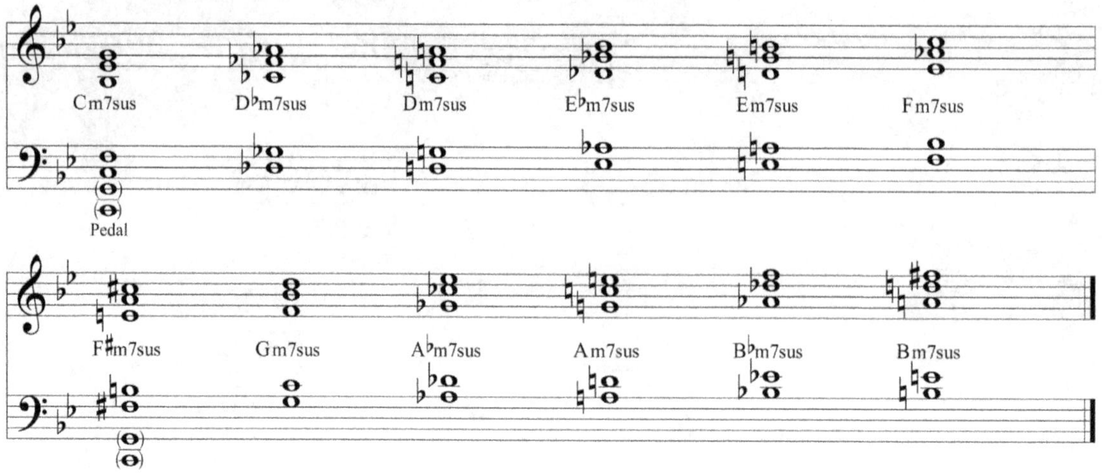

4.5.6. Whole Tone Planing (A Love Supreme)

4.5.6.1. Whole Tone Planing - Minor, System 1/2

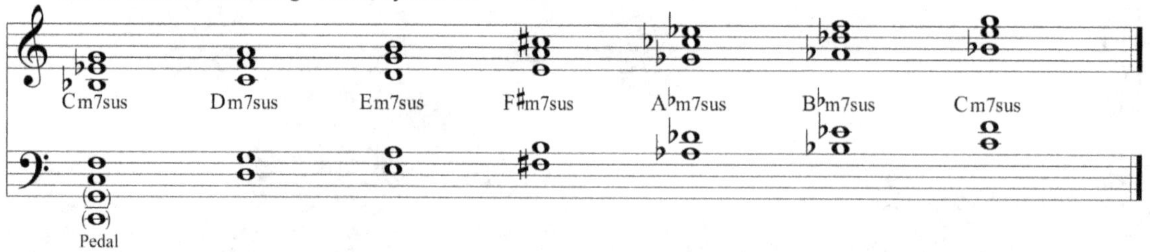

4.5.6.2. Whole Tone Planing - Minor, System 2/2

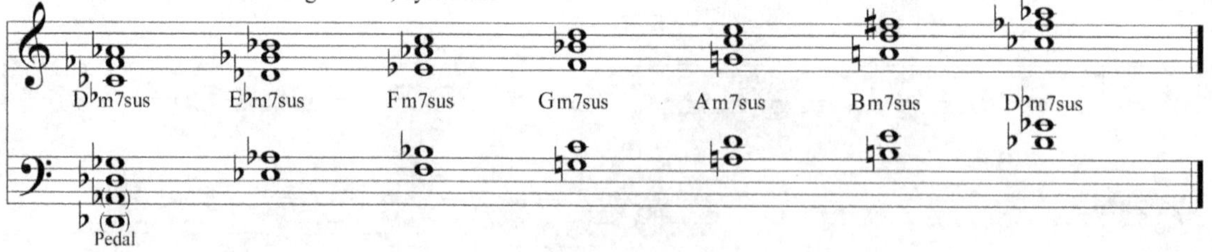

4.5.7. Quartal ii-V
- 4.5.7.1. Quartal ii-V – Root Position
- 4.5.7.2. Quartal ii-V – 1st Inversion
- 4.5.7.3. Quartal ii-V – 2nd Inversion (a)
- 4.5.7.4. Quartal ii-V – 2nd Inversion (b)

APPENDIX 4.5.7.
QUARTAL ii-V

Appendix 4.5.7. Quartal ii-V

4.5.7.1.
Fm7sus
B♭13sus
4.5.7.2.
Fm$^6_9$
B♭13
4.5.7.3.
Fm7sus
B♭7sus
4.5.7.4.
Fm9sus
B♭7sus
4.5.7.1.
F♯m7sus
B 13sus
4.5.7.2.
F♯m$^6_9$
B 13
4.5.7.3.
F♯m7sus
B 7sus
4.5.7.4.
F♯m9sus
B 7sus
4.5.7.1.
Gm7sus
C 13sus
4.5.7.2.
Gm$^6_9$
C 13
4.5.7.3.
Gm7sus
C 7sus
4.5.7.4.
Gm9sus
C 7sus

Appendix 4.5.7. Quartal ii-V

4.5.7.1.
A♭m7sus
D♭13sus
4.5.7.2.
A♭m6/9
D♭13
4.5.7.3.
A♭m7sus
D♭7sus
4.5.7.4.
A♭m9sus
D♭7sus
4.5.7.1.
Am7sus
D13sus
4.5.7.2.
Am6/9
D13
4.5.7.3.
Am7sus
D7sus
4.5.7.4.
Am9sus
D7sus
4.5.7.1.
B♭m7sus
E♭13sus
4.5.7.2.
B♭m6/9
E♭13
4.5.7.3.
B♭m7sus
E♭7sus
4.5.7.4.
B♭m9sus
E♭7sus

Appendix 4.5.7. Quartal ii-V

4.5.7.1.
Bm7sus
E13sus
4.5.7.2.
Bm6/9
E13
4.5.7.3.
Bm7sus
E7sus
4.5.7.4.
Bm9sus
E7sus
4.5.7.1.
Cm7sus
F13sus
4.5.7.2.
Cm6/9
F13
4.5.7.3.
Cm7sus
F7sus
4.5.7.4.
Cm9sus
F7sus
4.5.7.1.
C♯m7sus
F♯13sus
4.5.7.2.
C♯m6/9
F♯13
4.5.7.3.
C♯m7sus
F♯7sus
4.5.7.4.
C♯m9sus
F♯7sus

4.5.8. Graph: Minor Quartile Modulation Grid

Minor Quartile Modulation Grid
(with Extrapolations in Major)

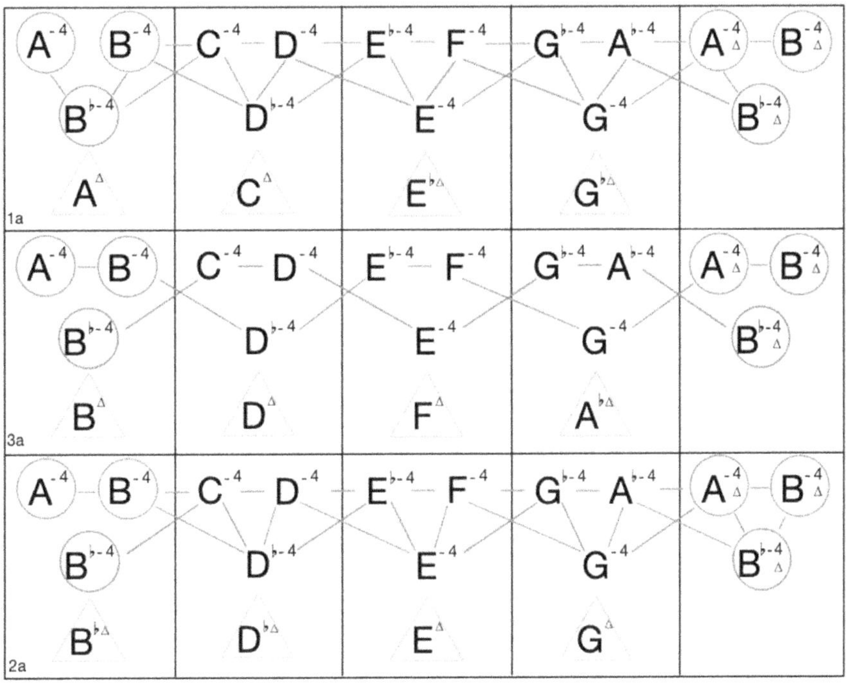

1a) Satellites in Inverted Diminished Sequence

Root Keys in Minor Third Sequence

3a) Satellites in Whole Tone Sequence

2a) Satellites in Fully Diminished Sequence

Chapter 5

TRANSCRIPTIONS (CHRONOLOGICAL)

Bud Powell   *Polka Dots and Moonbeams*   May 15, 1953

Bud Powell: Piano
Charles Mingus: Bass
Max Roach: Drums

Polka Dots and Moonbeams

Jazz at Massey Hall, Vol. 2
Original Jazz Classics - OJCCD-111-2
Recorded May 15, 1953

Jimmy Van Heusen, Johnny Burke
Transcribed by Ron Westray

2

Polka Dots and Moonbeams

Dm F6/9 A7(♭9) Dm6 E° E♭7 D13 D♭+7 B♭7 B7 C7 B♭7/B
Fmaj9 B♭maj7 Am9 Dm D♭7 F/C D7 Gm7 A+7 B♭maj7 Gm9/C A7/C♯
Dm7 D♭+M7 Fmaj7 B♭maj7 Am7 A♭m7
Gm7(♭5) C7(♭9) E♭7♯11♭9 G♭maj7(♯11) Fmaj7(♯11) Bm/E B♭7♯11

Polka Dots and Moonbeams 3

17
A maj 7
F♯9(b9)
B♭7/E
B m7
E 7(♭9)
19
C♯m7
F♯m7
B m7
E 7
21
A maj 7
F♯9(b9)
B♭7/E
B m7
E 7(♭9)
23
F♯m7
B 7
G msus/B♭
C 7(♭9)/G
(C13b9)

4 **Polka Dots and Moonbeams**

Fmaj9
Gm/C A7(♭9) Dm
E° E♭7 D13
D♭+7
B♭7 B7 C7
B♭7/B
Fmaj9
B♭maj7 Am9 Dm D♭7 F/C D7
Gm7
A+7 B♭maj7 Gm9/C A7/C♯
Dm7
D♭+M7
Fmaj7
B♭maj7 Am7 A♭m7
Gm7(♭5)
C7(♭9)
Gm7(♭5)
G♭maj7(♯11)
Fmaj7(♯11)
Bm/E B♭7♯11

Polka Dots and Moonbeams 5

Amaj7
F♯9(b9)
B♭7/E
Bm7
E7(♭9)
C♯m7
F♯m7
Bm7
E7
Amaj7
F♯9(b9)
B♭7/E
Bm7
E7(♭9)
F♯m7
B7
Gmsus/B♭
C7(♭9)/G
(C13b9)

6

Polka Dots and Moonbeams

Fmaj9 Gm/C A7(b9) Dm E° Eb7 D13 Db+7 Bb7 B7 C7 Bb7/B
Fmaj9 Bbmaj7 Am9 Dm Db7 F/C D7 Gm7 A+7 Bbmaj7 Gm9/C A7/C#
Dm7 Db+M7 Fmaj7 Bbmaj7 Am7 Abm7
Gm7(b5) C7(b9) Am7(b5) D7(b9)
Gm7(b5) C7(b9) Gbmaj7(#11) Fmaj7(#11) F+M7(b5)
Fine

Thelonious Monk *Work* September 22, 1954

Thelonious Monk: Piano
Percy Heath: Bass
Art Blakey: Drums

Work

Thelonious Monk - *Thelonious Monk and Sonny Rollins*
Prestige - OJCCD 59
Recorded September 22, 1954

Thelonious Monk

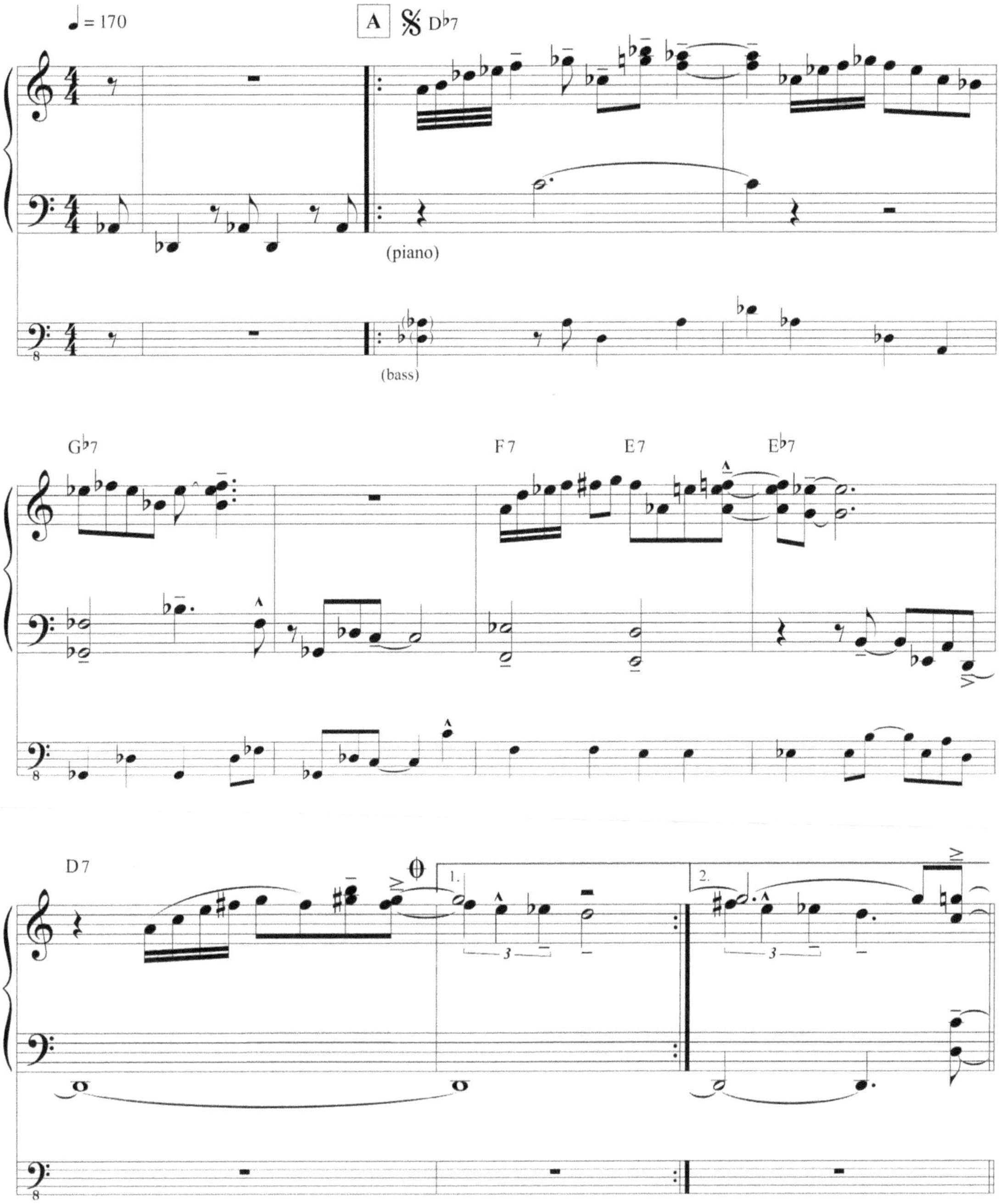

2

Work

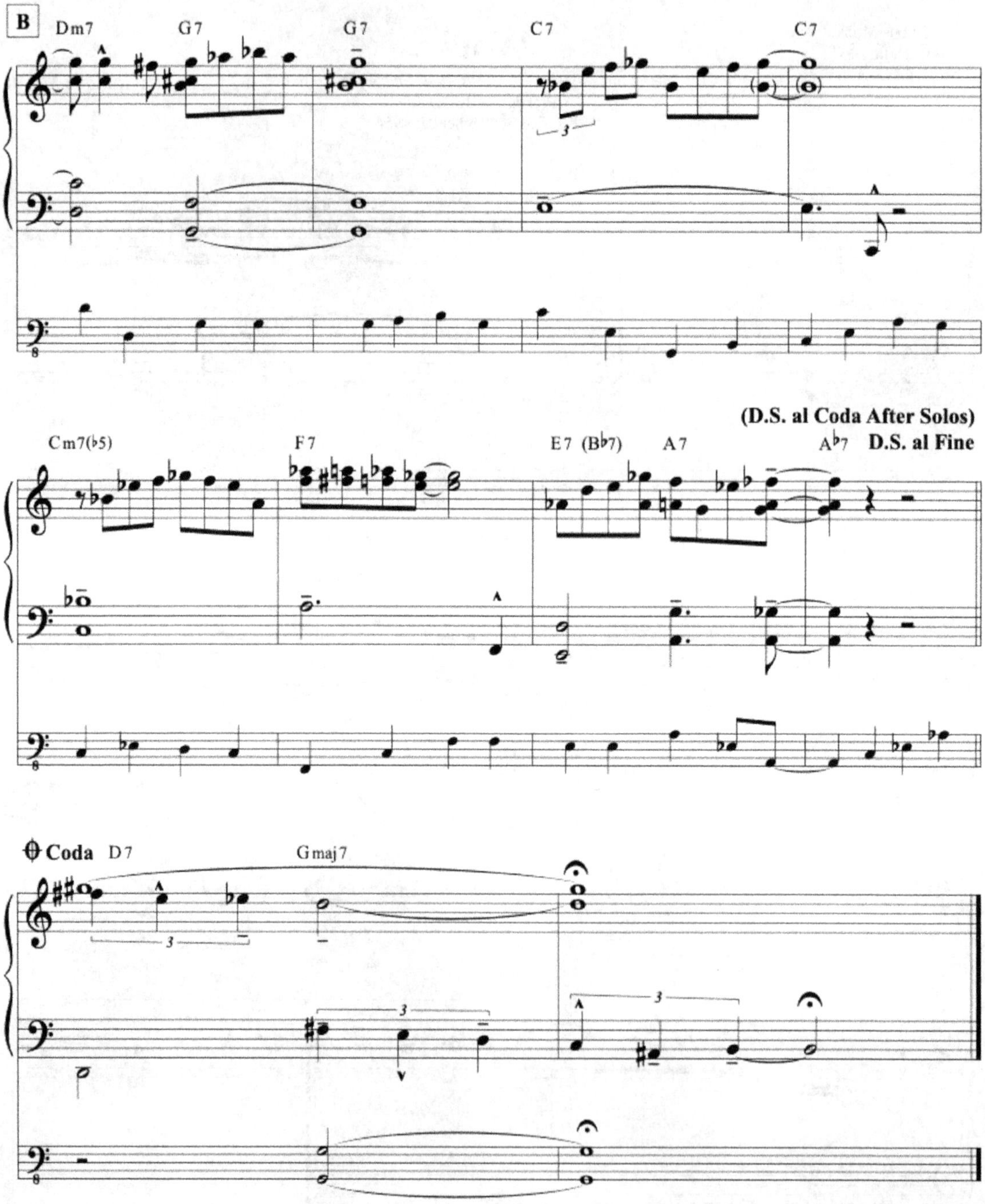
B
Dm7
G7
G7
C7
C7
(D.S. al Coda After Solos)
Cm7(♭5)
F7
E7 (B♭7)
A7
A♭7
D.S. al Fine
Coda
D7
Gmaj7

Clifford Brown | *Untitled Blues* | May 29, 1956

Clifford Brown: Trumpet
Sonny Rollins: Tenor Saxophone
Ritchie Powell: Piano
George Morrow: Bass
Max Roach: Drums

Untitled Blues

Clifford Brown - *At The Cotton Club 1956*
Rare Live Recordings - RLR 88624
Recorded May 29, 1956

Transcribed by Giovanni Ceccatell
Edited by Ron Westray

2 **Untitled Blues**

33
Cm7
F7
B♭7
Cm7
F7
D
B♭7
Fm7
B♭7
41
E♭7
B♭7
Dm7
G7
45
Cm7
F7
B♭7
Cm7
F7
E
B♭7
Fm7
B♭7
53
E♭7
B♭7
Dm7
G7
57
Cm7
F7
B♭7
Cm7
F7
F
B♭7
Fm7
B♭7

Untitled Blues 3

65
E♭7 B♭7 Dm7 G7
69
Cm7 F7 B♭7 Cm7 F7
G
B♭7 Fm7 B♭7
77
E♭7 B♭7 Dm7 G7
81
Cm7 F7 B♭7 Cm7 F7
H
B♭7 Fm7 B♭7
89
E♭7 B♭7 Dm7 G7
93
Cm7 F7 B♭7 Cm7 F7

4 **Untitled Blues**

I
B♭7
Fm7
B♭7
E♭7
B♭7
Dm7
G7
101
Cm7
F7
B♭7
Cm7
F7
105
J
B♭7
Fm7
B♭7
3
E♭7
B♭7
Dm7
G7
113
3
Cm7
F7
B♭7
Cm7
F7
117
3
K
B♭7
Fm7
B♭7
E♭7
B♭7
Dm7
G7
125

Untitled Blues 5

129
Cm7 F7 B♭7 Cm7 F7
L
B♭7 Fm7 B♭7
137
E♭7 B♭7 Dm7 G7
141
Cm7 F7 B♭7 Cm7 F7
M
B♭7 Fm7 B♭7
149
E♭7 B♭7 Dm7 G7
153
Cm7 F7 B♭7 Cm7 F7
N
B♭7 Fm7 B♭7
3
3

6

Untitled Blues

E♭7
B♭7
Dm7
G7
161
3
Cm7
F7
165
B♭7
Cm7
F7
167
O
B♭7
5
Fm7
B♭7
171
E♭7
B♭7
173
Dm7
G7
Cm7
F7
B♭7
Cm7
F7
176
P
B♭7
Fm7
B♭7

Untitled Blues 7

185
E♭7 B♭7 Dm7 G7
3
189
Cm7 F7 B♭7 Cm7 F7
Q
B♭7 Fm7 B♭7
197
E♭7 B♭7 Dm7 G7
201
Cm7 F7 B♭7 Cm7 F7
R
B♭7 Fm7 B♭7
209
E♭7 B♭7 Dm7 G7
213
Cm7 F7 B♭7 Cm7 F7

8 **Untitled Blues**

S
B♭7
Fm7
B♭7
221
E♭7
B♭7
Dm7
G7
225
Cm7
F7
B♭7
Cm7
F7
T
B♭7
Fm7
B♭7
233
E♭7
B♭7
Dm7
G7
237
Cm7
F7
B♭7
Cm7
F7
U
B♭7
Fm7
B♭7
245
E♭7
B♭7
Dm7
G7

Untitled Blues 9

249
Cm7 F7 B♭7 Cm7 F7
V
B♭7 Fm7 B♭7
257
E♭7 B♭7 Dm7 G7
261
Cm7 F7 B♭7 Cm7 F7
W
B♭7 Fm7 B♭7
269
E♭7 B♭7 Dm7 G7
273
Cm7 F7 B♭7 Cm7 F7
X
B♭7 Fm7 B♭7
3
3

10 **Untitled Blues**

281
E♭7 B♭7 Dm7 G7
3 3 3
285
Cm7 F7 B♭7 Cm7 F7
Y
B♭7 Fm7 B♭7
293
E♭7 B♭7 Dm7 G7
297
Cm7 F7 B♭7 Cm7 F7
Z
B♭7 Fm7 B♭7
305
E♭7 B♭7 Dm7 G7
309
Cm7 F7 B♭7 Cm7 F7
AA
B♭7

Duke Ellington *Such Sweet Thunder (Excerpt)* April 24, 1957

Five-Note Voicing Excerpt From Duke Ellington's

Such Sweet Thunder

(mm. 25-37)

Duke Ellington

Transcribed by Ron Westray

Thelonious Monk *Well You Needn't* June 26, 1957

Thelonious Monk: Piano
John Coltrane: Tenor Saxophone
Coleman Hawkins: Tenor Saxophone
Gigi Gryce: Alto Saxophone
Ray Copeland: Trumpet
Wilbur Ware: Bass
Art Blakey: Drums

Well You Needn't

Thelonious Monk - *Monk's Music*
Riverside - RLP 12-242
Recorded June 26, 1957

Thelonious Monk

2

Well You Needn't

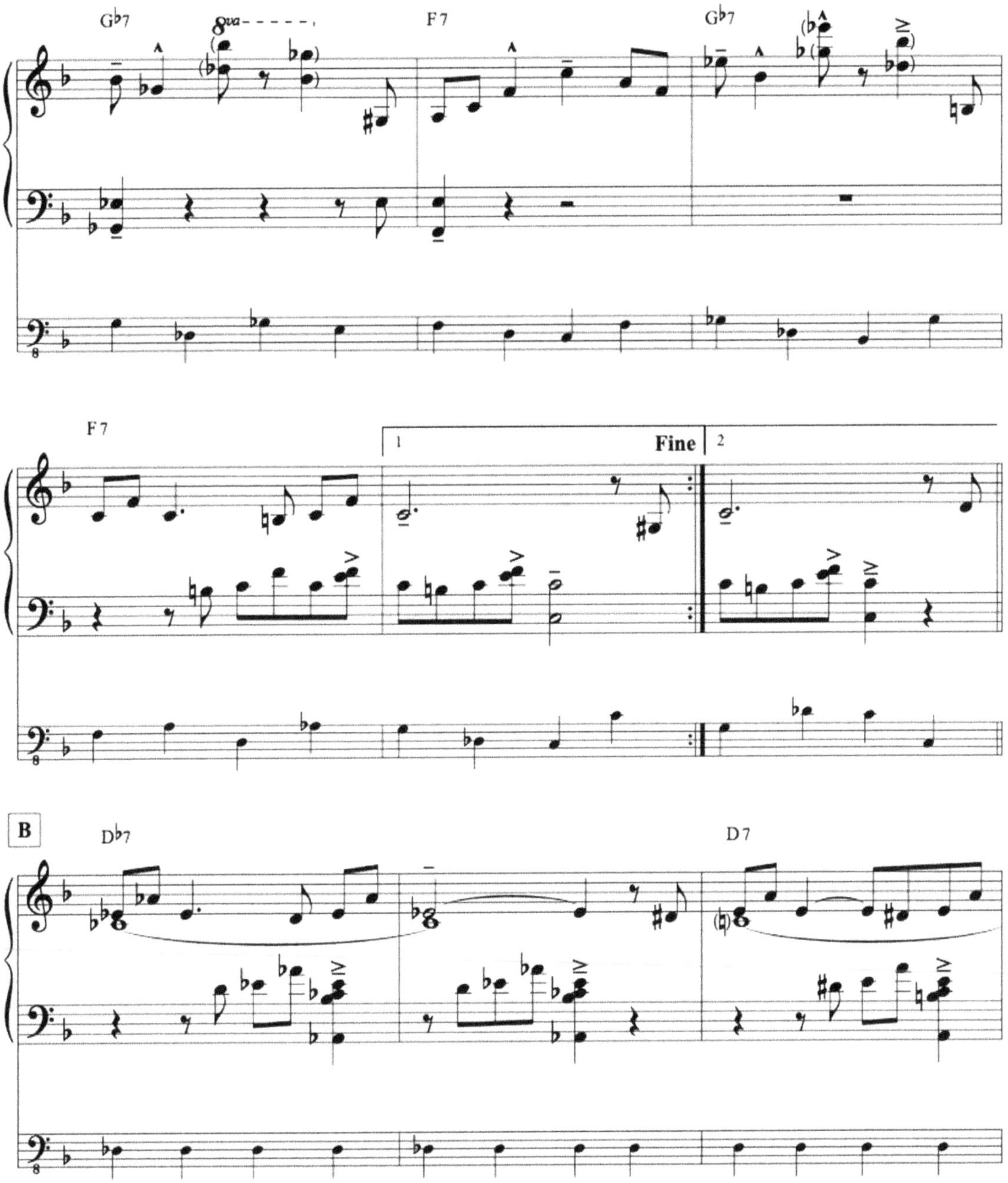
G♭7
8va
F7
G♭7
F7
1
Fine
2
B
D♭7
D7

Well You Needn't

3

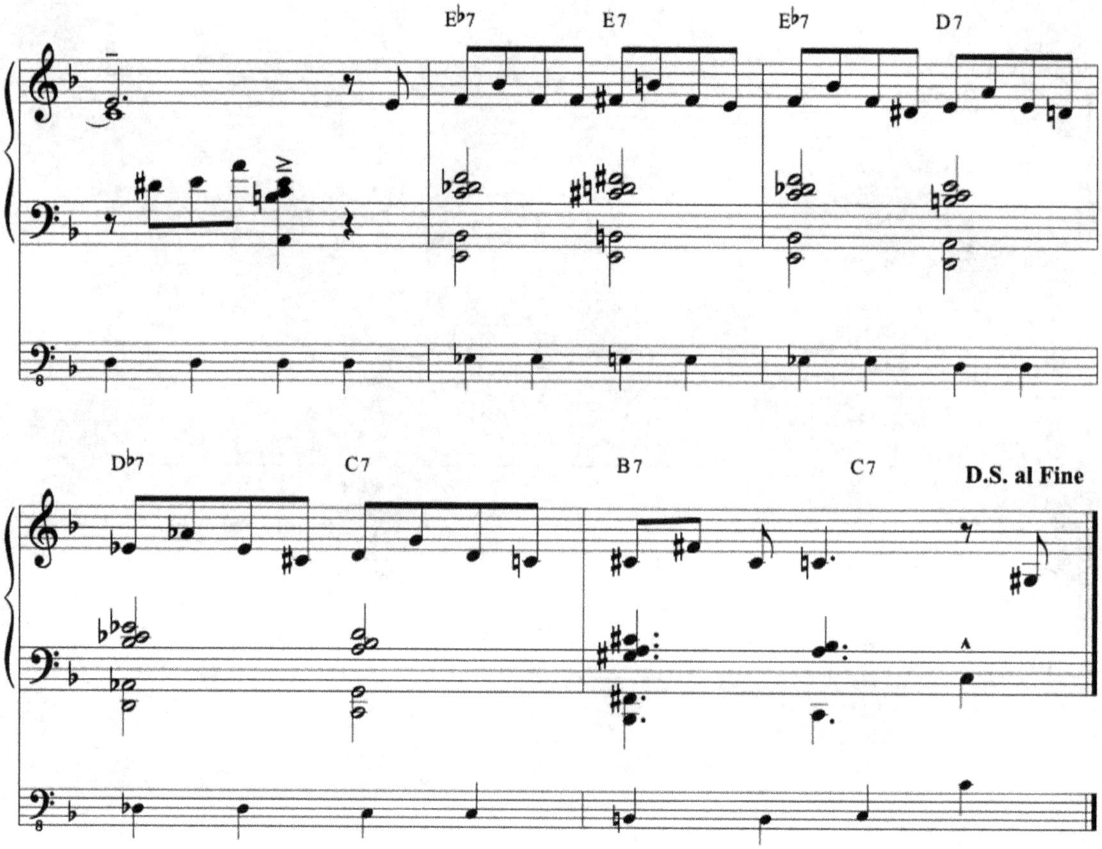

E♭7
E7
E♭7
D7
D♭7
C7
B7
C7
D.S. al Fine

Crepuscule With Nellie

Thelonious Monk: Piano
John Coltrane: Tenor Saxophone
Coleman Hawkins: Tenor Saxophone
Gigi Gryce: Alto Saxophone
Ray Copeland: Trumpet
Wilbur Ware: Bass
Art Blakey: Drums

Thelonious Monk - *Monk's Music*
Riverside - RLP 12-242
Recorded June 26, 1957

Thelonious Monk
Transcribed by Ron Westray

2 **Crepuscule With Nellie**

E♭7
E♭7 B♭m7 D♭ D E♭
3
F m7 C m7 B♭m7 E♭7 D7
D♭7 A♭6 D♭maj 7 D maj 7 E♭maj 7 E♭7 G♭6 G 6 A♭6 A B♭ B
D.S. al Coda
G♭7♯11 A♭maj 9 A
B♭ B C C 7

John Coltrane | *Evidence* | November 29, 1957

Evidence

John Coltrane Solo

Thelonious Monk Quartet with John Coltrane at Carnegie Hall
Blue Note - 35173
Recorded November 29, 1957

John Coltrane: Tenor Saxophone
Thelonious Monk: Piano
Ahmed Abdul-Malik: Bass
Shadow Wilson: Drums

Thelonious Monk
Transcribed by Ron Westray
Edited and Nomenclated by Kamil Qui

2

Evidence

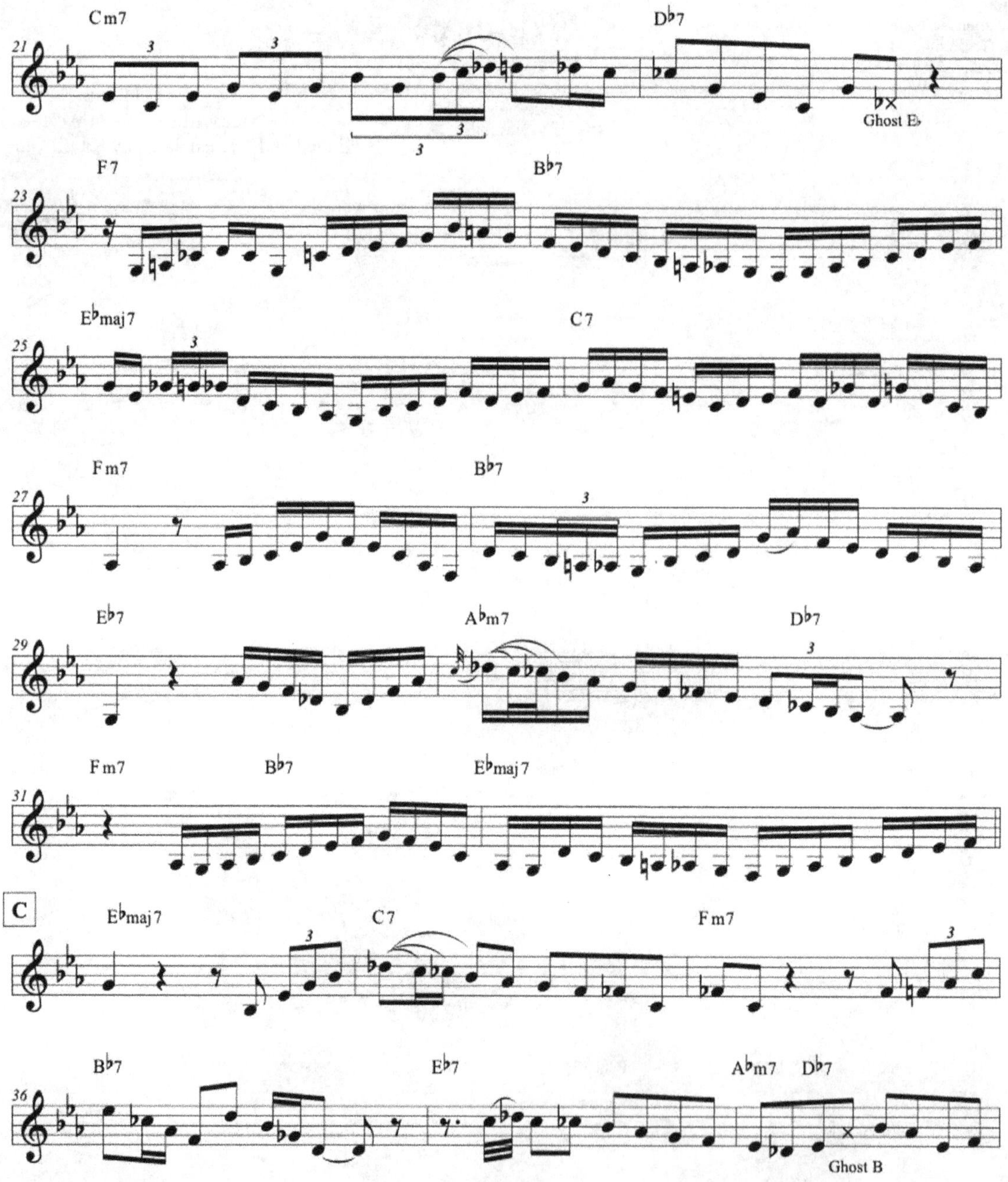
Cm7
D♭7
Ghost E♭
F7
B♭7
E♭maj7
C7
Fm7
B♭7
E♭7
A♭m7
D♭7
Fm7
B♭7
E♭maj7
C
E♭maj7
C7
Fm7
B♭7
E♭7
A♭m7
D♭7
Ghost B

Evidence 3

Fm7 B♭7 E♭maj7 E♭maj7
C7 Fm7 B♭7
E♭7 A♭m7 D♭7 Fm7 B♭7
E♭maj7 B♭m7 E♭7
A♭maj7 D♭7 Cm7
Ghost G
D♭7 F7 B♭7
E♭maj7 C7
Fm7 B♭7
Ghost G, A

4 Evidence

E♭7 A♭m7 D♭7 Fm7 B♭7 E♭maj7
D
E♭maj7 C7 Fm7
B♭7 E♭7 A♭m7 D♭7
Fm7 B♭7 E♭maj7
E♭maj7 C7
Fm7 B♭7
E♭7 A♭m7 D♭7
Fm7 B♭7 E♭maj7

Evidence 5

81
B♭m7
E♭7
3
83
A♭maj7
D♭7
3
3
85
Cm7
6
D♭7
3
87
F7
B♭7
89
E♭maj7
C7
3
Fm7
92
B♭7
E♭7
A♭m7
D♭7
95
Fm7
B♭7
E♭maj7
E

John Coltrane *Nutty* November 29, 1957

John Coltrane: Tenor Saxophone
Thelonious Monk: Piano
Ahmed Abdul-Malik: Bass
Shadow Wilson: Drums

Nutty

John Coltrane Solo

Thelonious Monk Quartet with John Coltrane at Carnegie Hall
Blue Note - 35173
Recorded November 29, 1957

Thelonious Monk
Transcribed by Ron Westray
Edited and Nomenclated by Kamil Qui

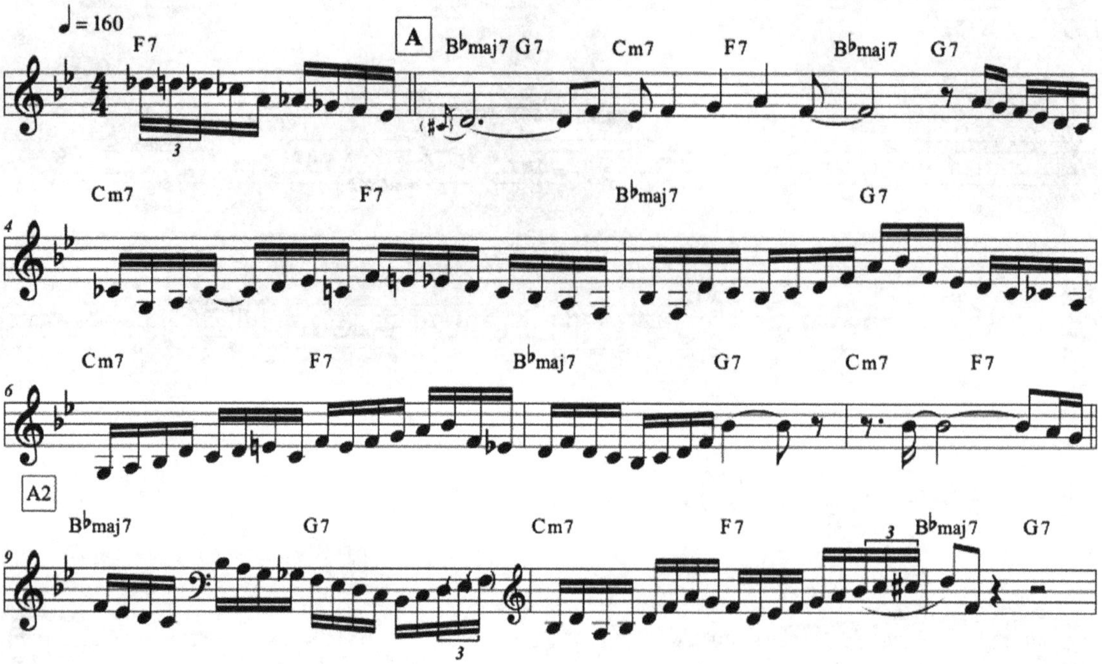

2 **Nutty**

Fm7 B♭7 E♭maj7
A3
Cm7 F7 B♭maj7 G7
Cm7 F7 B♭maj7 G7
Cm7 F7 F7 F7 G7
Cm7 F7 B♭maj7 G7 Cm7
A4
B♭maj7 G7 Cm7 F7
B♭maj7 G7 Cm7 F7
B♭maj7 G7 Cm7 F7

Nutty 3

39 B♭maj7 G7 Cm7 F7
41 B♭maj7 G7 Cm7 F7
A5
43 B♭maj7 G7 Cm7 F7
45 B♭maj7 G7 Cm7 F7
47 B♭maj7 G7 F7 B♭7
B2
49 E♭maj7 C7 Fm7 B♭7
51 E♭maj7 C7 Fm7 B♭7
53 E♭7 C7 Fm7 B♭7 E♭maj7

4 **Nutty**

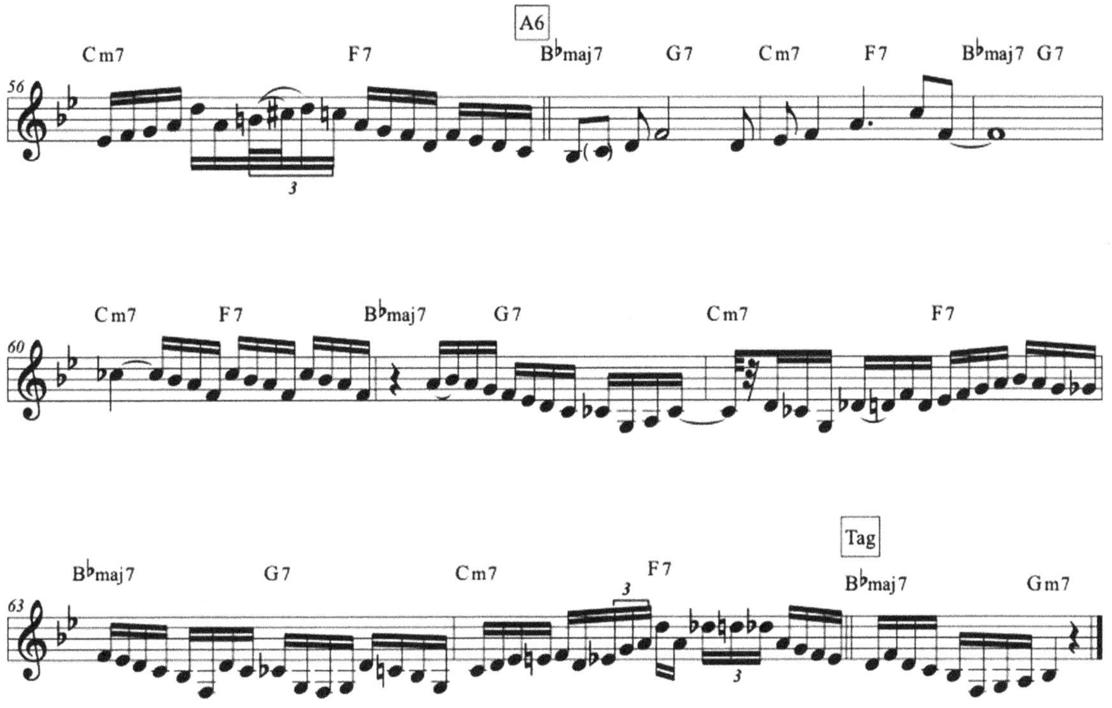
A6
Cm7
F7
B♭maj7
G7
Cm7
F7
B♭maj7 G7
56
Cm7
F7
B♭maj7
G7
Cm7
F7
60
Tag
B♭maj7
G7
Cm7
F7
B♭maj7
Gm7
63

John Coltrane *Billie's Bounce* December 13, 1957

John Coltrane: Tenor Saxophone
Red Garland: Piano
Donald Byrd: Trumpet
George Joyner: Bass
Art Taylor: Drums

Billie's Bounce

John Coltrane Solo

The Red Garland Quintet with John Coltrane - *Dig It!*
Prestige - PRLP 7229
Recorded December 13, 1957

Charlie Parker
Transcribed by Ron Westray

2

Billie's Bounce

21
Gm7
C7
23
F7
D7
Gm7
C7
E
F7
B♭7
B°7
27
F7
F7
29
B♭7
B♭7
31
F7
F7
33
G min7
C7
35
F7
D7
G min7
C7

Billie's Bounce 3

F
F7 B♭7 B°7
39
F7 F7
41
B♭7 B♭7
43
F7 F7
45
Gm7 C7
47
F7 D7 Gm7 C7
G
F7 B♭7 B°7
51
F7 F7 B♭7

4

Billie's Bounce

B♭7 F7 F7
Gm7 C7
F7 D7 Gm7 C7
H
F7 B♭7 B°7 F7
F7 B♭7 B♭7
F7 F7 Gm7
C7 F7 D7 Gm7 C7
I
F7 B♭7 B°7 F7

Billie's Bounce
5
F7
B♭7
76
B♭7
F7
78
6
F7
Gm7
80
3
3
C7
F7
D7
82
Gm7
C7
J
84

John Coltrane *Black Pearls* May 23, 1958

John Coltrane: Tenor Saxophone
Donald Byrd: Trumpet
Red Garland: Piano
Paul Chambers: Bass
Art Taylor: Drums

Black Pearls

John Coltrane Solo
Black Pearls
Prestige - PRLP 7316
Recorded May 23, 1958

John Coltrane
Transcribed by Ron Westray
Edited and Nomenclated by Kamil Qui

2

Black Pearls

B Gm7 C7b9 Fma7
Fma7 Fm7
Bb7b9 Ebma7
Dm7 G7b9 A Em7
A7b9 Dm7 G7b9
Em7 A7b9 Dm7(b5) G7b9
Cma7 C maj7
A 2nd Chorus
Em7 A7b9

Black Pearls

3

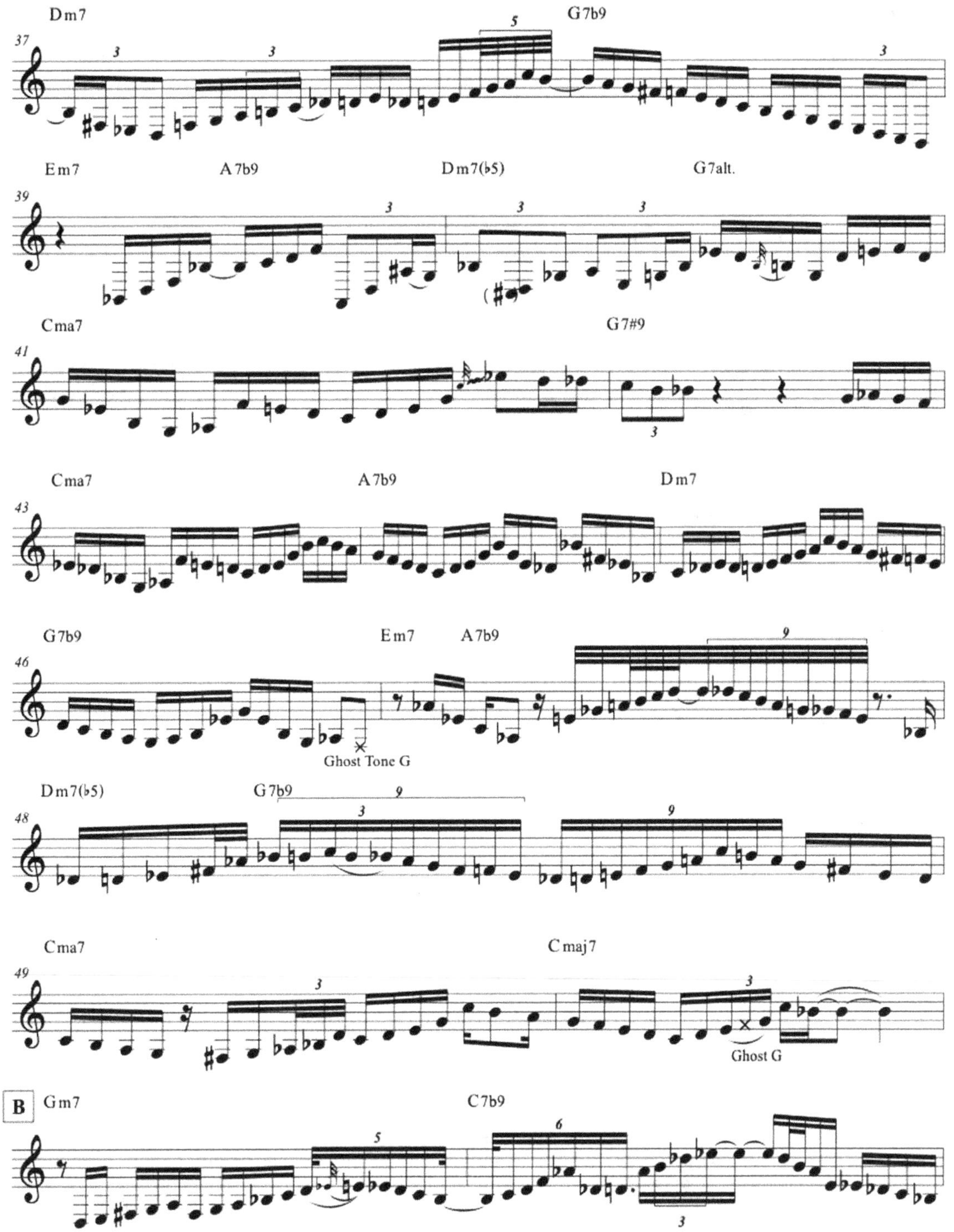
Dm7
G7b9
Em7
A7b9
Dm7(b5)
G7alt.
Cma7
G7#9
Cma7
A7b9
Dm7
G7b9
Em7
A7b9
Ghost Tone G
Dm7(b5)
G7b9
Cma7
Cmaj7
Ghost G
B
Gm7
C7b9

4

Black Pearls

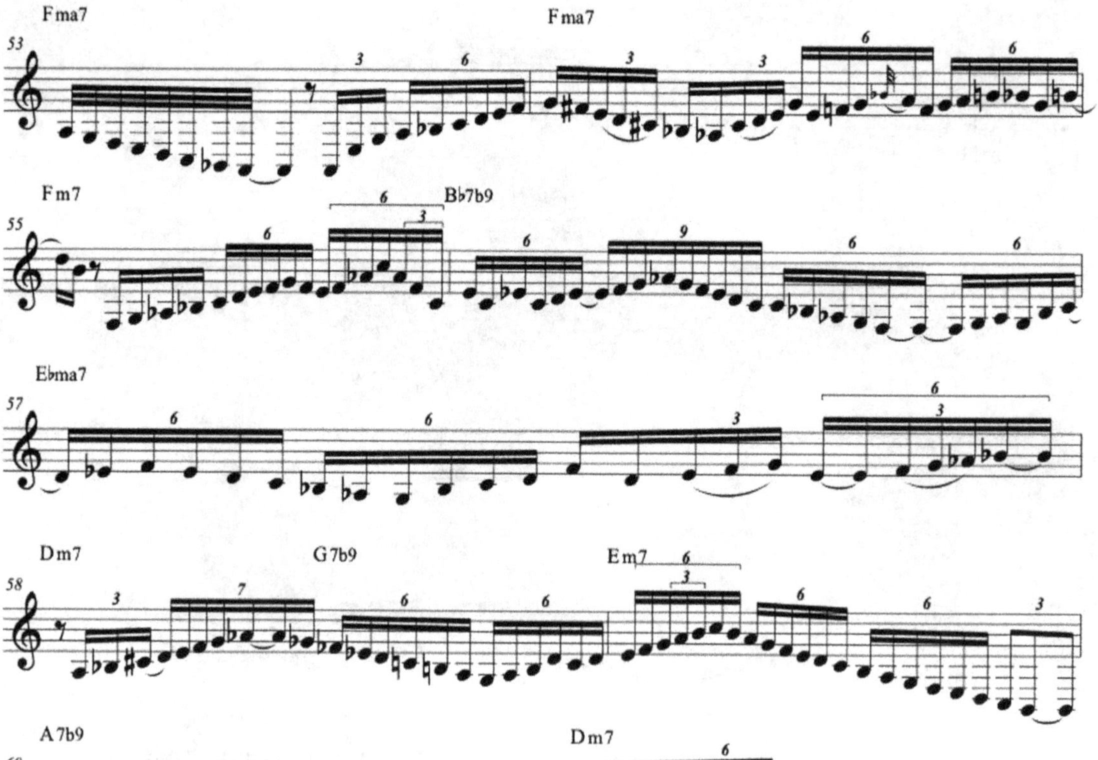
Fma7
Fma7
Fm7
B♭7b9
E♭ma7
Dm7
G7b9
Em7
A7b9
Dm7
Ghost C, D, E
G7b9
Em7
A7b9
Dm7(♭5)
G7b9
Cma7
Cmaj7
Em7
A7b9
Dm7

Black Pearls 5

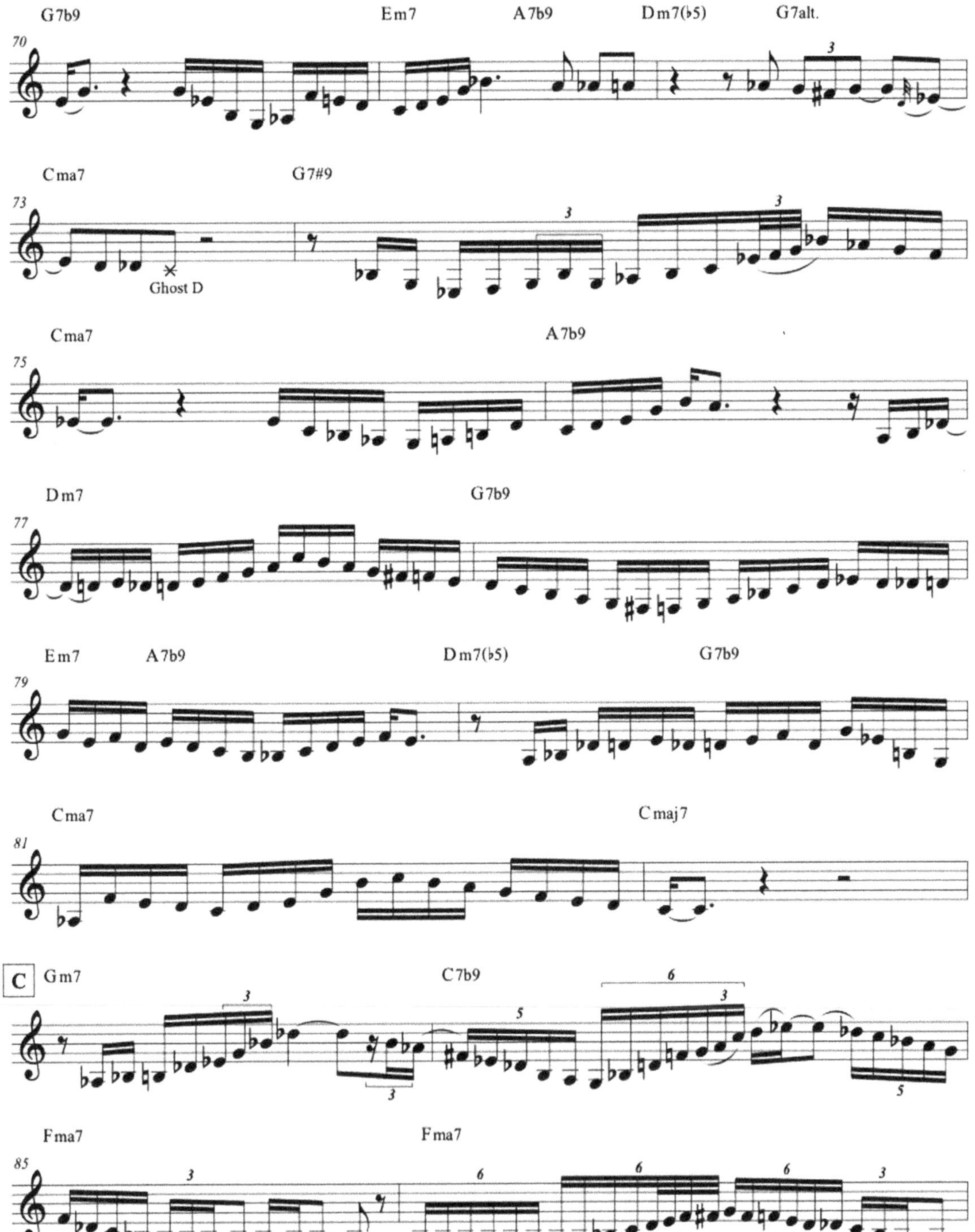
G7b9
Em7
A7b9
Dm7(b5)
G7alt.
Cma7
G7#9
Ghost D
Cma7
A7b9
Dm7
G7b9
Em7
A7b9
Dm7(b5)
G7b9
Cma7
Cmaj7
C
Gm7
C7b9
Fma7
Fma7

6

Black Pearls

Fm7
B♭7b9
E♭ma7
Dm7
G7b9
Em7
A7b9
Dm7
G7b9
Em7
A7b9
Dm7(♭5)
G7b9
Cma7
Cmaj7
D
Em7
A7b9
Dm7
G7b9
Em7
A7b9

Black Pearls

7

Dm7(♭5)
G7alt.
104
Cma7
G7#9
105
Cma7
A7b9
107
Dm7
G7b9
109
Em7
A7b9
Dm7(♭5)
G7b9
111
Cma7
Cmaj7
113
Ghost C, B
E
Gm7
C7b9
116

8 **Black Pearls**

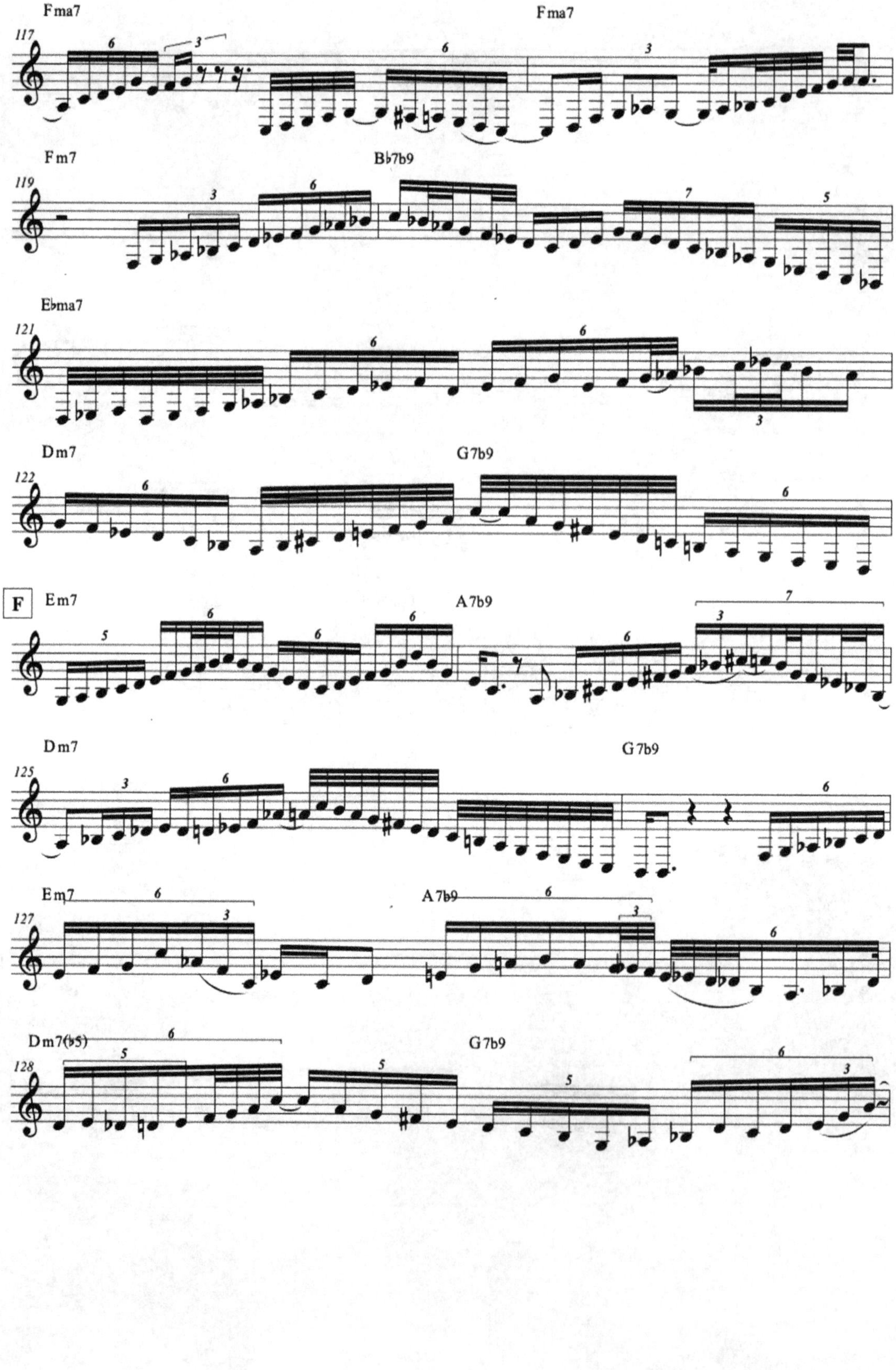

Fma7
Fma7
Fm7
B♭7b9
E♭ma7
Dm7
G7b9
F
Em7
A7b9
Dm7
G7b9
Em7
A7b9
Dm7(b5)
G7b9

Black Pearls 9

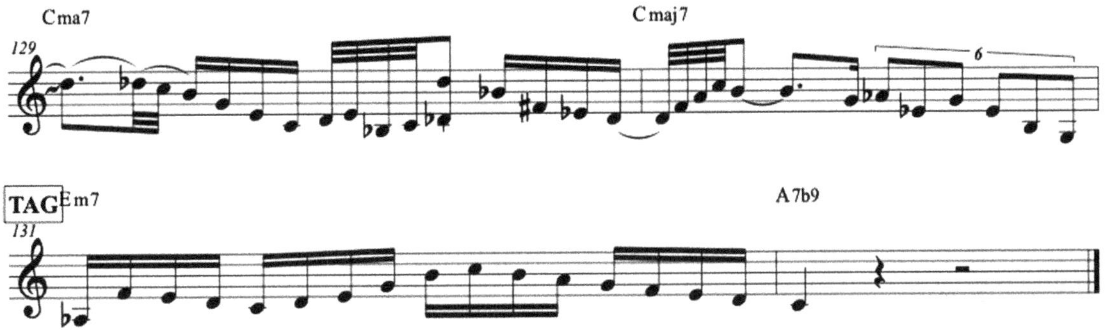
Cma7
129
Cmaj7
6
TAG
Em7
131
A7b9

John Coltrane | *Sweet Sapphire Blues* | May 23, 1958

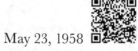

John Coltrane: Tenor Saxophone
Donald Byrd: Trumpet
Red Garland: Piano
Paul Chambers: Bass
Art Taylor: Drums

Sweet Sapphire Blues

John Coltrane Solo

Black Pearls
Prestige - PRLP 7316
Recorded May 23, 1958

Bob Weinstock
Transcribed by Ron Westray
Edited and Nomenclated by Kamil Qui

2

Sweet Sapphire Blues

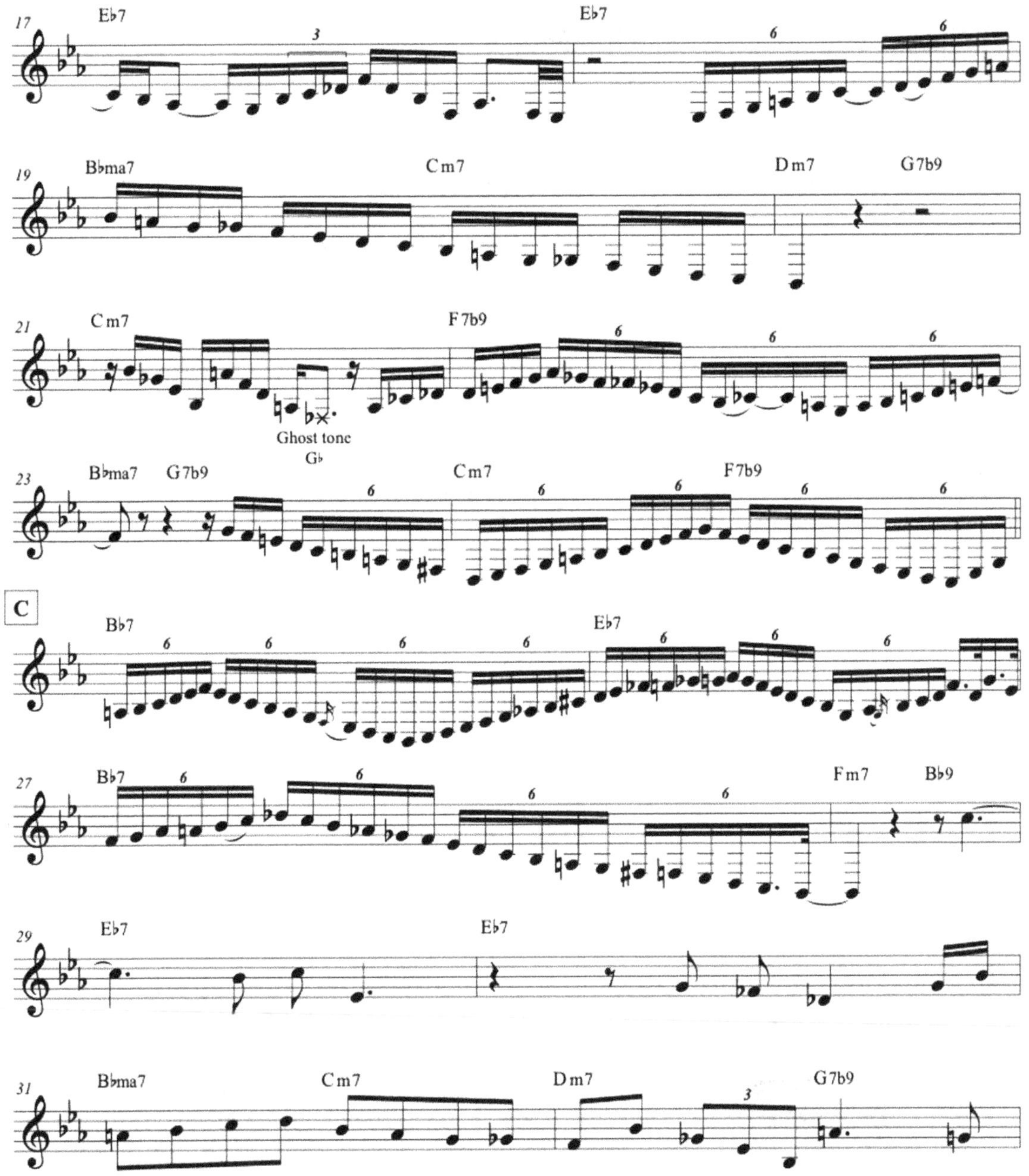

E♭7
E♭7
B♭ma7
Cm7
Dm7
G7b9
Cm7
F7b9
Ghost tone
G♭
B♭ma7
G7b9
Cm7
F7b9
C
B♭7
E♭7
B♭7
Fm7
B♭9
E♭7
E♭7
B♭ma7
Cm7
Dm7
G7b9

Sweet Sapphire Blues

3

33
Cm7
F7b9
35
B♭ma7
G7b9
Cm7
F7b9
D
B♭7
E♭7
39
B♭7
Fm7
B♭9
Ghost A
41
E♭7
E♭7
43
B♭ma7
Cm7
Dm7
G7b9
45
Cm7
F7b9
47
B♭ma7
G7b9
Cm7
F7b9

4

Sweet Sapphire Blues

E
B♭7
E♭7
51
B♭7
Fm7
B♭9
53
E♭7
E♭7
55
B♭ma7
Cm7
Dm7
G7b9
Ghost A
57
Cm7
F7b9
59
B♭ma7
G7b9
Cm7
F7b9
F
B♭7
E♭7
63
B♭7
Fm7
B♭9

Sweet Sapphire Blues

5

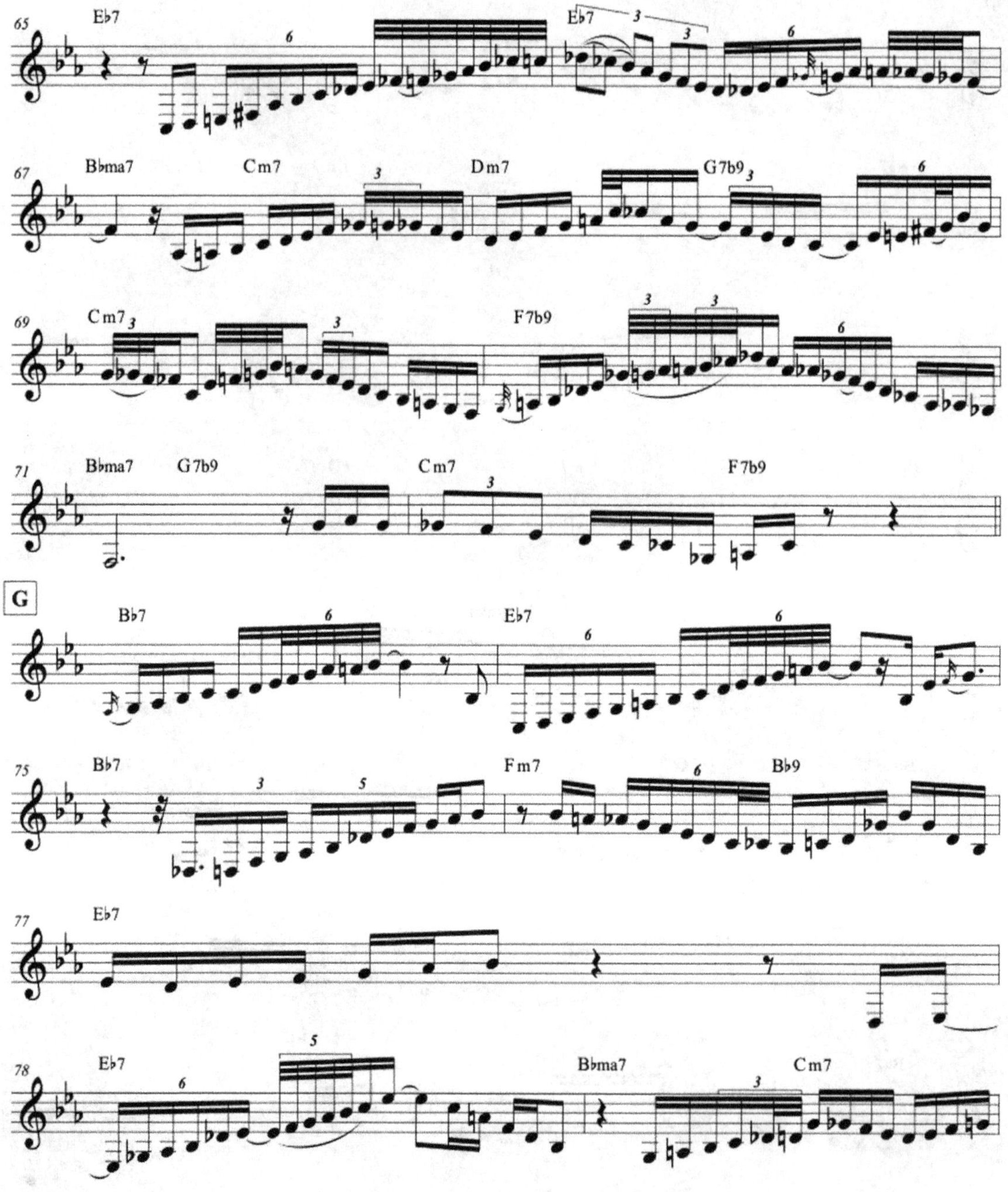

65
E♭7
E♭7
67
B♭ma7
Cm7
Dm7
G7b9
69
Cm7
F7b9
71
B♭ma7
G7b9
Cm7
F7b9
G
B♭7
E♭7
75
B♭7
Fm7
B♭9
77
E♭7
78
E♭7
B♭ma7
Cm7

6

Sweet Sapphire Blues

80 Dm7 G7b9 Cm7
82 F7b9 B♭ma7 G7b9
84 Cm7 F7b9 H B♭7
86 E♭7 B♭7
88 Fm7 B♭9 E♭7
Ghost E♭
90 E♭7 B♭ma7 Cm7
92 Dm7 G7b9 Cm7
94 F7b9 B♭ma7 G7b9 Cm7 F7b9

Sweet Sapphire Blues

7

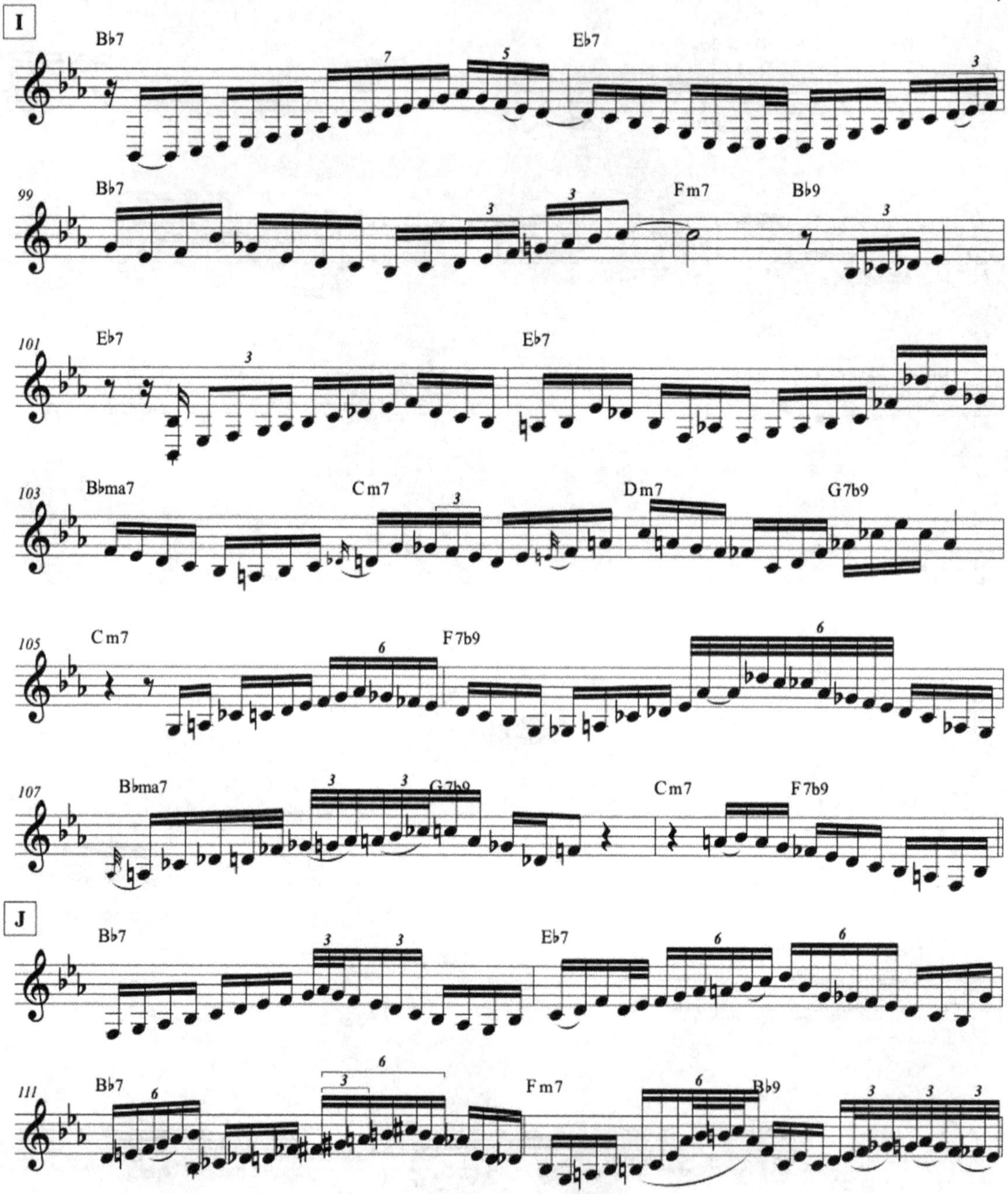
I
B♭7 E♭7
99 B♭7 Fm7 B♭9
101 E♭7 E♭7
103 B♭ma7 Cm7 Dm7 G7♭9
105 Cm7 F7♭9
107 B♭ma7 G7♭9 Cm7 F7♭9
J
B♭7 E♭7
111 B♭7 Fm7 B♭9

8

Sweet Sapphire Blues

113
E♭7
E♭7
115
B♭ma7
Cm7
Dm7
G7b9
117
Cm7
F7b9
119
B♭ma7
G7b9
Cm7
F7b9
K
B♭7
E♭7
123
B♭7
Fm7
B♭9
125
E♭7
E♭7
127
B♭ma7
Cm7
Dm7
G7b9

Sweet Sapphire Blues

9

129
Cm7
F7b9
131
B♭ma7
G7b9
Cm7
F7b9
L
B♭7
134
E♭7
135
B♭7
136
Fm7
B♭9
137
E♭7
Ghost A
E♭7
139
B♭ma7
Cm7
Dm7
G7b9

10

Sweet Sapphire Blues

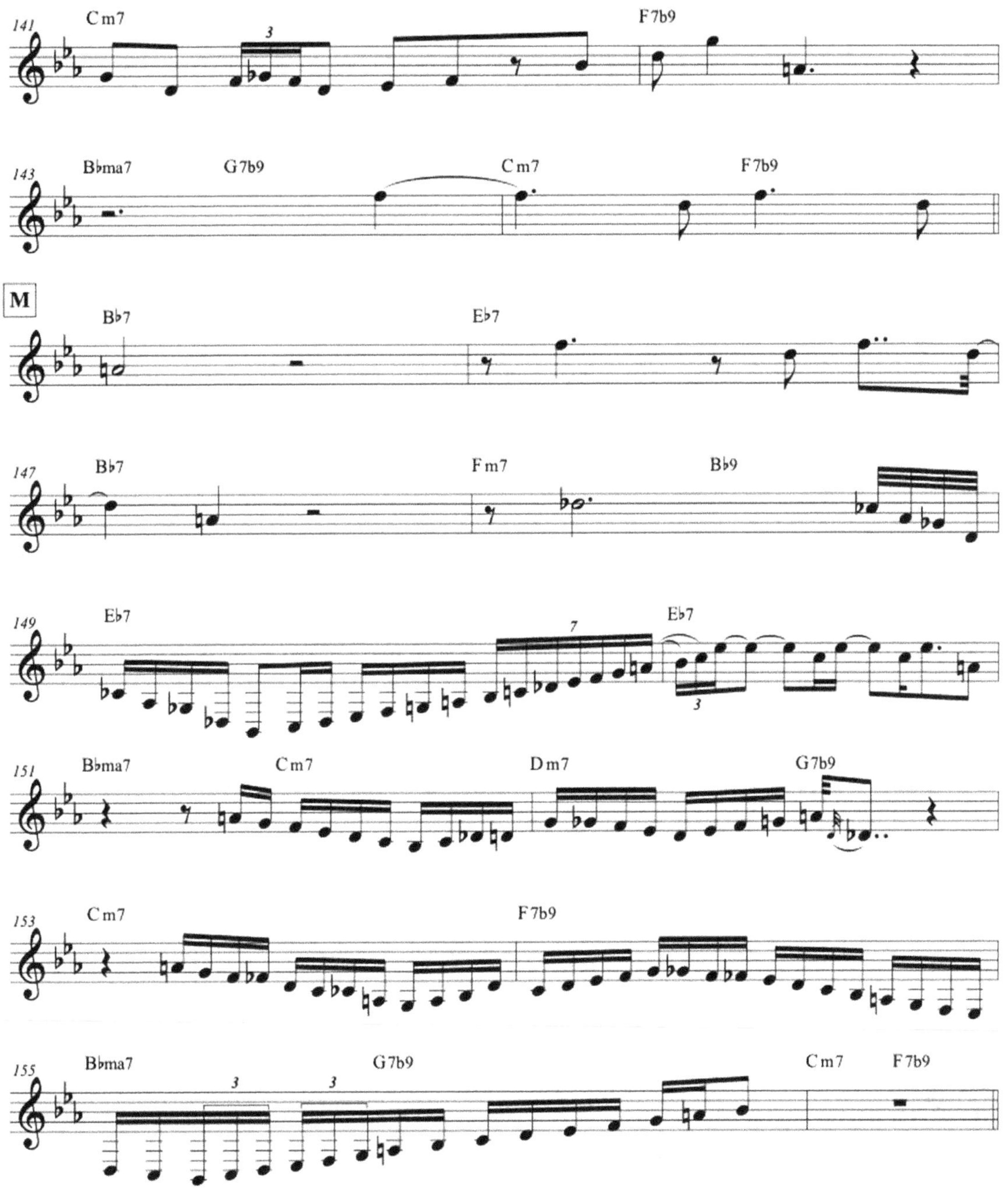
141 Cm7 F7b9
143 B♭ma7 G7b9 Cm7 F7b9
M
B♭7 E♭7
147 B♭7 Fm7 B♭9
149 E♭7 E♭7
151 B♭ma7 Cm7 Dm7 G7b9
153 Cm7 F7b9
155 B♭ma7 G7b9 Cm7 F7b9

Sweet Sapphire Blues
11
N
Bb7
Eb7
159
Bb7
Fm7
Bb9
161
Eb7
Eb7
163
Bbma7
Cm7
Dm7
G7b9
165
Cm7
F7b9
167
Bbma7
G7b9
Cm7
F7b9
O
Bb7
Eb7
171
Bb7
Fm7
Bb9

12

Sweet Sapphire Blues

173 E♭7 E♭7
175 B♭ma7 Cm7 Dm7 G7b9
177 Cm7 F7b9
179 B♭ma7 G7b9 Cm7 F7b9
P
B♭7 E♭7
183 B♭7 Fm7 B♭9
185 E♭7 E♭7 B♭ma7 Cm7 Dm7 G7b9
189 Cm7 F7b9
Q
191 B♭ma7 G7b9 Cm7 F7b9

Thelonious Monk *Light Blue* August 7, 1958

Thelonious Monk: Piano
Johnny Griffin: Ttenor Saxophone
Ahmed Abdul-Malik: Bass
Roy Haynes: Drums

Light Blue

Thelonious Monk - *Thelonious In Action*
Riverside - OJCCD 103
Recorded August 7, 1958

Thelonious Monk
Transcribed by Ron Westray

John Coltrane — *If I Were a Bell* — September 9, 1958

John Coltrane: Tenor Saxophone
Miles Davis: Trumpet
Cannonball Adderley: Alto Saxophone
Bill Evans: Piano
Paul Chambers: Bass
Jimmy Cobb: Drums

If I Were A Bell

John Coltrane Solo
Jazz At The Plaza, Vol. 1: Miles Davis Sextet
Columbia - C 32470
Recorded September 9, 1958

Frank Loesser
Transcribed by Ron Westray
Edited and Nomenclated by Kamil Qui

2

If I Were A Bell

Fmaj7 F7 B♭maj7 B°7
Fmaj7 B♭7 Am7(♭5) D7
Gm7 C7
Fmaj7 Am7 D7
B
G9 C7 Fmaj7 B♭m7 E♭7
Am7(♭5) D7 G7 Gm7 C7
Fmaj7 F7 B♭maj7 C7 Fmaj7 Em7(♭5) A7
Dm7 Bm7(♭5) E7 Am7 D°7 Gm7 C7
Ghost Tone
G or A♭

If I Were A Bell 3

G7
C7
Fmaj7
Am7(♭5)
D7(♭9)
G7
Gm7
C7
Fmaj7
F7
B♭maj7
B°7
Fmaj7
B♭7
Am7(♭5)
D7
Gm7
C7
Fmaj7
Am7
D7
C
G9
C7

4

If I Were A Bell

Fmaj7
Fmaj7
67
3
3
Am7(♭5)
D7
G7
Gm7
C7
69
Fmaj7
F7
B♭maj7
C7
Fmaj7
Em7(♭5)
A7
73
3
3
3
5
Dm7
Bm7(♭5)
E7
Am7
D°7
Gm7
C7
77
3
G7
C7
Fmaj7
B♭m7
E♭7
81
3
Am7(♭5)
D7(♭9)
G7
85
3
3
3
Gm7
C7
Fmaj7
F7
B♭maj7
B°7
88
3
3
3
3
3
Fmaj7
B♭7
Am7(♭5)
D7
Gm7
91

If I Were A Bell 5

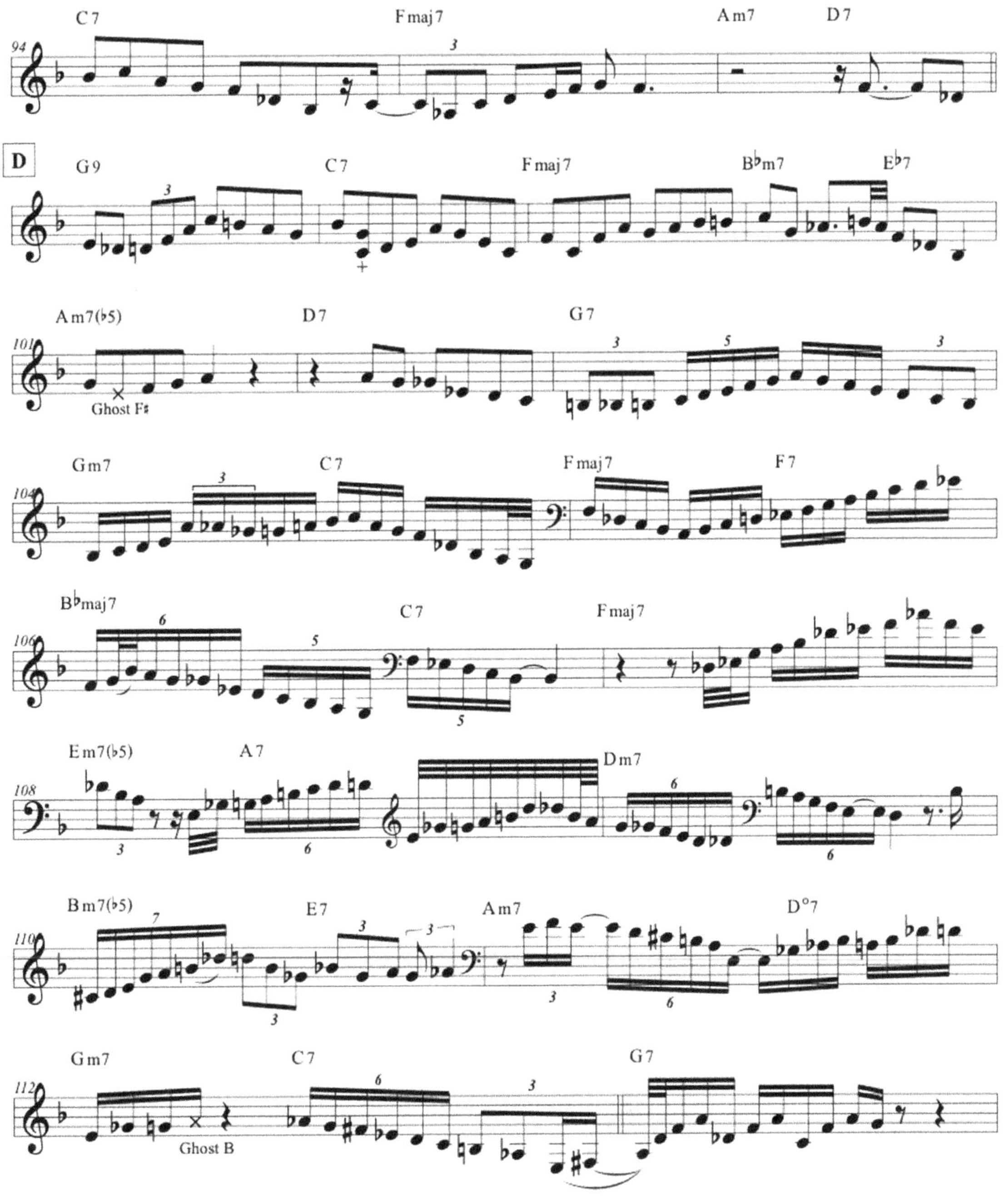
C7 Fmaj7 Am7 D7
94
D
G9 C7 Fmaj7 B♭m7 E♭7
Am7(♭5) D7 G7
101
Ghost F♯
Gm7 C7 Fmaj7 F7
104
B♭maj7 C7 Fmaj7
106
Em7(♭5) A7 Dm7
108
Bm7(♭5) E7 Am7 D°7
110
Gm7 C7 G7
112
Ghost B

6

If I Were A Bell

C7 Fmaj7
114
Am7(♭5)
116
D7(♭9) G7 Gm7 C7 Fmaj7 F7
118
Ghost E
B♭maj7 B°7 Fmaj7 B♭7 Am7(♭5) D7 Gm7
122
C7 Fmaj7 Am7 D7
126
E Vamp G-7 C7 A-7 D7
G-7 C7 A-7 D7 G-7
133
C7 A-7 A7
138

If I Were A Bell 7

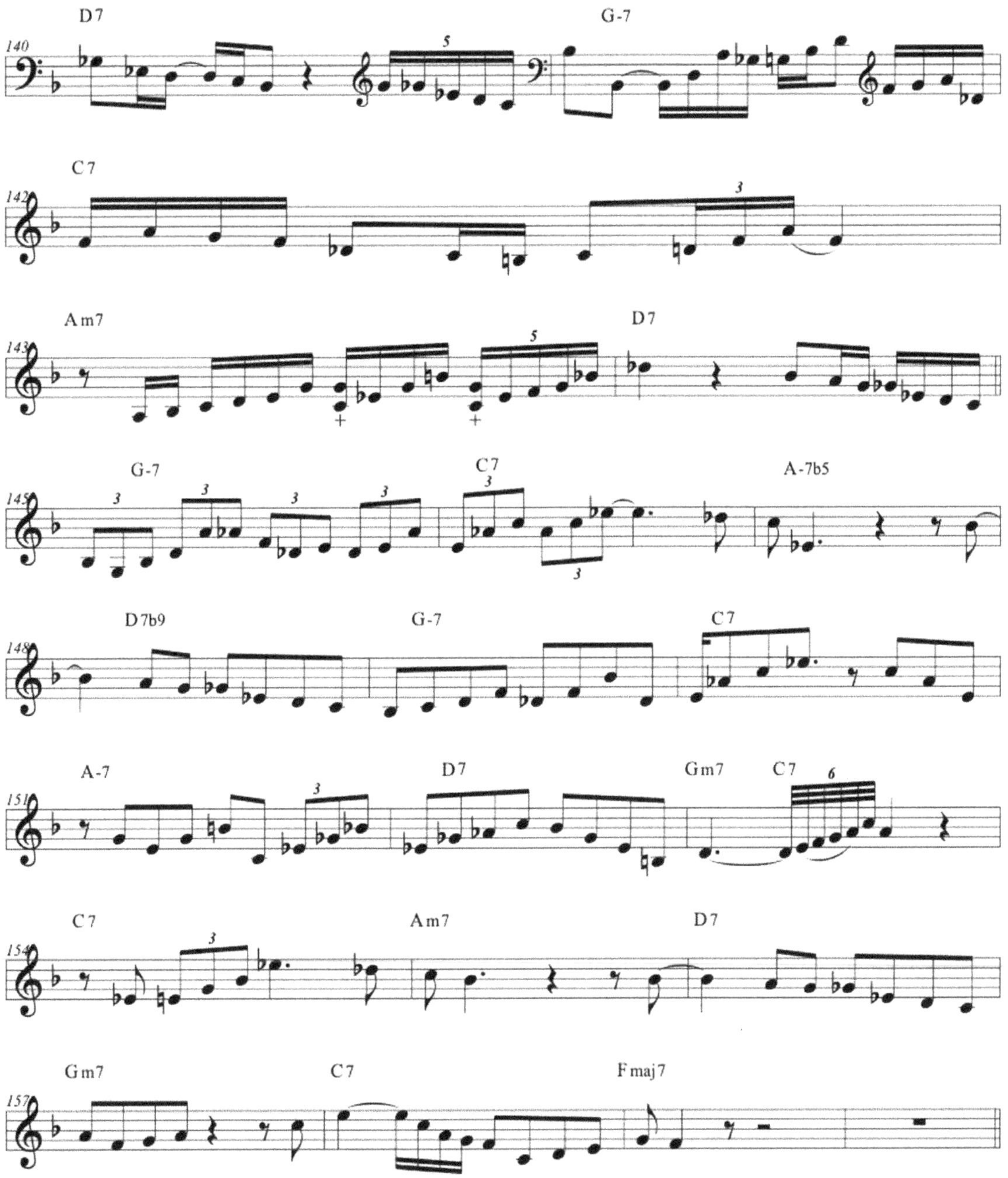
140 D7 G-7
142 C7
143 Am7 D7
145 G-7 C7 A-7b5
148 D7b9 G-7 C7
151 A-7 D7 Gm7 C7
154 C7 Am7 D7
157 Gm7 C7 Fmaj7

Thelonious Monk *Reflections* October 22, 1959

Thelonious Monk: Piano

Reflections

Thelonious Monk - *Thelonious Alone In San Francisco*
Riverside - OJC3284402
Recorded October 22, 1959

Thelonious Monk
Cross-Transcribed & Edited
by Ron Westray

2

Reflections

C7alt
Fm6
Fm7
B♭7(♭9)
Fm7
B♭7(♭9)
B♭m7
E♭7/A
D.S. al Coda
B♭m7
Em7
A7(♭9)
* Alternate Fill

John Coltrane *On Green Dolphin Street* March 22, 1960

John Coltrane: Tenor Saxophone
Miles Davis: Trumpet
Wynton Kelly: Piano
Paul Chambers: Bass
Jimmy Cobb: Drums

On Green Dolphin Street

John Coltrane Solo

Miles Davis & John Coltrane: Live In Stockholm, 1960
Dragon Records - DRLP 90/91
Recorded March 22, 1960

Bronislau Kaper
Ned Washington
Transcribed by Ron Westray
Edited and Nomenclated by Kamil Qui

2 **On Green Dolphin Street**

B
E♭maj7 E♭maj7 E♭m7 E♭m7
Ghost Tone
G
37
F9 E9 E♭maj7 Gm7 C7
41
Fm7 B♭7 E♭maj7 E♭7
Ghost A
Ghost A
45
A♭m7 D♭7 G♭maj7 Fm7 B♭7
49
E♭maj7 E♭maj7 E♭m7 E♭m7
53
F9 E9 E♭maj7 Gm7 C7
57
Fm7 Dm7(♭5) G7 Cm7 F7 F♯°7
Ghost B♮
61
Gm7 C7 Fm7 B♭7 E♭maj7 C7 Fm7 B♭7

On Green Dolphin Street 3

C
E♭maj7
E♭maj7
E♭m7
E♭m7
F9
E9
71
Gm7
C7
Fm7
Throat
(Ghost Tongue)
B♭7
75
E♭7
A♭m7
D♭7
79
G♭maj7
80
81
Over tone
85
Ghost F♯
87
Ghost F♮

4

On Green Dolphin Street

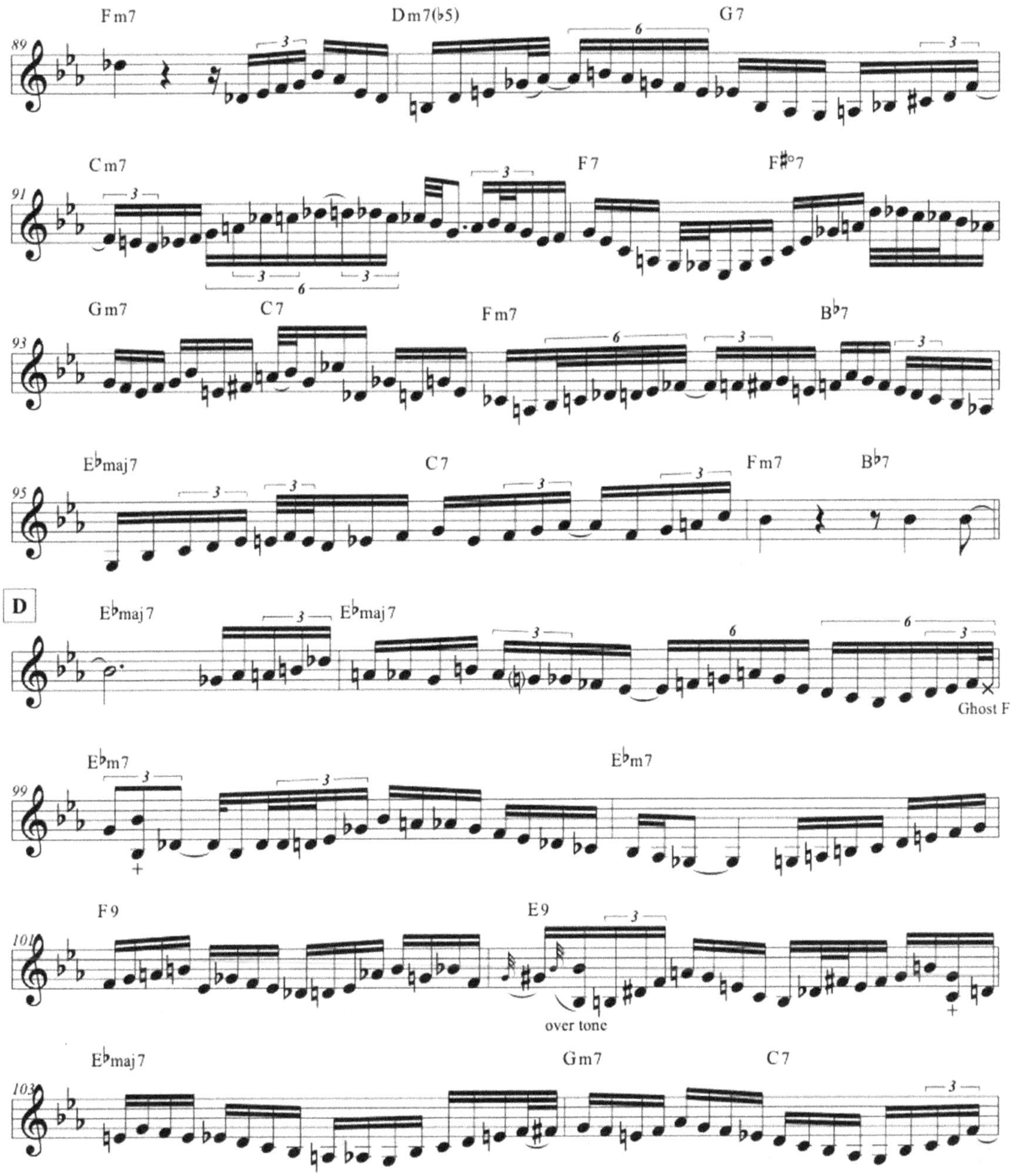
Fm7
Dm7(♭5)
G7
Cm7
F7
F♯°7
Gm7
C7
Fm7
B♭7
E♭maj7
C7
Fm7
B♭7
D
E♭maj7
E♭maj7
Ghost F
E♭m7
E♭m7
F9
E9
over tone
E♭maj7
Gm7
C7

On Green Dolphin Street 5

Fm7
B♭7
E♭maj7
E♭7
A♭m7
D♭7
G♭maj7
Fm7
B♭7
Ghost C
E♭maj7
E♭maj7
E♭m7
E♭m7
F9
E9
E♭maj7
Gm7
C7
Fm7

6 **On Green Dolphin Street**

Dm7(♭5) G7 Cm7 F7 F♯°7 Gm7 C7
122
Fm7 B♭7 E♭maj7 C7 Fm7 B♭7
126
E
E♭maj7 E♭maj7
E♭m7 E♭m7
131
F9 E9
133
E♭maj7 Gm7 C7
135
Fm7 B♭7
137
E♭maj7 E♭7
139

On Green Dolphin Street 7

A♭m7
D♭7
G♭maj7
Fm7
B♭7
E♭maj7
E♭maj7
E♭m7
E♭m7
F9
E9
E♭maj7
Gm7
C7
Fm7
Dm7(♭5)
G7
Cm7
F7
F♯°7
Gm7
C7

8 **On Green Dolphin Street**

158
Fm7
B♭7
E♭maj7
C7
Fm7
B♭7
F
E♭maj7
E♭maj7
E♭m7
E♭m7
165
F9
E9
E♭maj7
Gm7
C7
169
Fm7
B♭7
E♭maj7
E♭7
173
A♭m7
D♭7
G♭maj7
Ghost
Ab and C
Fm7
B♭7
177
E♭maj7
E♭maj7
E♭m7
E♭m7
181
F9
E9
E♭maj7
Gm7
C7
185
Fm7
Dm7(♭5)
G7
Cm7
F7
F♯°7

On Green Dolphin Street 9

Gm7 C7 Fm7 B♭7 E♭maj7 C7 Fm7 B♭7
Fork F
G
E♭maj7 E♭maj7 E♭m7 E♭m7
Ghost G
F9 E9 E♭maj7 Gm7 C7
Fm7 B♭7 E♭maj7 E♭7
A♭m7 D♭7
G♭maj7 Fm7 B♭7
E♭maj7 E♭maj7
Front F/
Fork F
E♭m7 E♭m7
Ghost G

10 **On Green Dolphin Street**

F9
E9
E♭maj7
Gm7
C7
213
Fm7
Dm7(♭5)
G7
Cm7
F7
F♯°7
217
Gm7
C7
Fm7
B♭7
E♭maj7
C7
Fm7
B♭7
221
H
E♭maj7
E♭maj7
E♭m7
E♭m7

John Coltrane *Walkin'* March 22, 1960

John Coltrane: Tenor Saxophone
Miles Davis: Trumpet
Wynton Kelly: Piano
Paul Chambers: Bass
Jimmy Cobb: Drums

Walkin'

John Coltrane Solo

Miles Davis & John Coltrane: Live In Stockholm, 1960
Dragon Record - DRLP 90/91
Recorded March 22, 1960

Richard Carpenter
Transcribed by Ron Westray
Edited and Nomenclated by Kamil Qui

2

Walkin'

Gm7 C7 F7 Gm7 C7
33
D
F7 B♭7 F7 F7
B♭7 B♭7 F7 F7
41
Gm7 C7 F7 Gm7 C7
45
Scoop
E
F7 B♭7 F7 F7
B♭7 B♭7 F7 F7
53
Gm7 C7 F7 Gm7 C7
57
F
F7 B♭7 F7 F7

Walkin' 3

B♭7 B♭7 F7 F7
65
Gm7 C7 F7 Gm7 C7
69
G
F7 B♭7 F7 F7
B♭7 B♭7 F7 F7
77
Gm7 C7 F7 Gm7 C7
81
H
F7 B♭7 F7 F7
B♭7 B♭7 F7 F7
89
Gm7 C7 F7 Gm7 C7
93
Palm D
Ghost C

4 ·

Walkin'

I
F7 B♭7 F7 F7
101
B♭7 B♭7 F7 F7
105
Gm7 C7 F7 Gm7 C7
J
F7 B♭7 F7 F7
113
B♭7 B♭7 F7 F7
117
Gm7 C7 F7 Gm7 C7
K
F7 B♭7 F7
124
F7 B♭7 B♭7

Walkin' 5

F7
Ghost Tongue
G.T
F7
Gm7
127
C7
F7
Gm7
C7
130
L
F7
B♭7
F7
F7
B♭7
B♭7
136
F7
F7
Gm7
139
C7
F7
Gm7
C7
142
M
F7
B♭7
F7
F7
B♭7
148

6 **Walkin'**

B♭7
F7
F7
150
Gm7
C7
153
B♭7
Gm7
C7
155
N
F7
B♭7
F7
F7
B♭7
160
B♭7
F7
162
F7
Gm7
C7
164
F7
Gm7
C7
167
Ghost F A

Walkin' 7

O
F7 B♭7 F7 F7 B♭7
174
B♭7 F7 F7 Gm7
178
C7 F7 Gm7 C7
P
F7 B♭7 F7 F7
Ghost G
185
B♭7 B♭7 F7 F7
189
Gm7 Ghost G C7 F7 Gm7 C7
Q
F7 B♭7 F7 F7
Ghost D
197
B♭7 B♭7

8 **Walkin'**

F7
199
F7
Gm7
201
C7
F7
203
Gm7
C7
R
F7
B♭7
F7
207
F7
B♭7
209
B♭7
F7
211
F7
Gm7
213
C7

Walkin'

9

215
F7
Gm7
C7
S
F7
B♭7
219
F7
F7
221
B♭7
B♭7
223
F7
F7
Gm7
(throat)
226
C7
F7
Gm7
C7
T
F7
B♭7
F7
F7
233
B♭7
B♭7
F7
F7

10 **Walkin'**

Gm7
C7
F7
Gm7
C7
237
Ghost G
U
F7
B♭7
F7
F7
B♭7
B♭7
F7
F7
246
Gm7
C7
F7
Gm7
C7
249
V
F7
B♭7
F7
F7
B♭7
B♭7
256
F7
F7
Gm7
259
C7
F7
Gm7
C7
262

Walkin'

11

W
F7 B♭7 F7 F7
269
B♭7 B♭7 F7 F7
273
Gm7 C7 F7 Gm7 C7
3
3
X
F7 B♭7 F7 F7
281
B♭7 B♭7 F7 F7
285
Gm7 C7 F7 Gm7 C7
Y
F7 B♭7 F7 F7

Thelonious Monk: Piano
Charlie Rouse: Tenor Saxophone
Harold Land: Tenor Saxophone
Joe Gordon: Trumpet
John Ore: Bass
Billy Higgins: Drums

San Francisco Holiday

(Worry Later)

Thelonious Monk - *At The Blackhawk*
Riverside - RLP 12-323/1171
Recorded April 29, 1960

Thelonious Monk
Cross-Transcribed & Edited
by Ron Westray

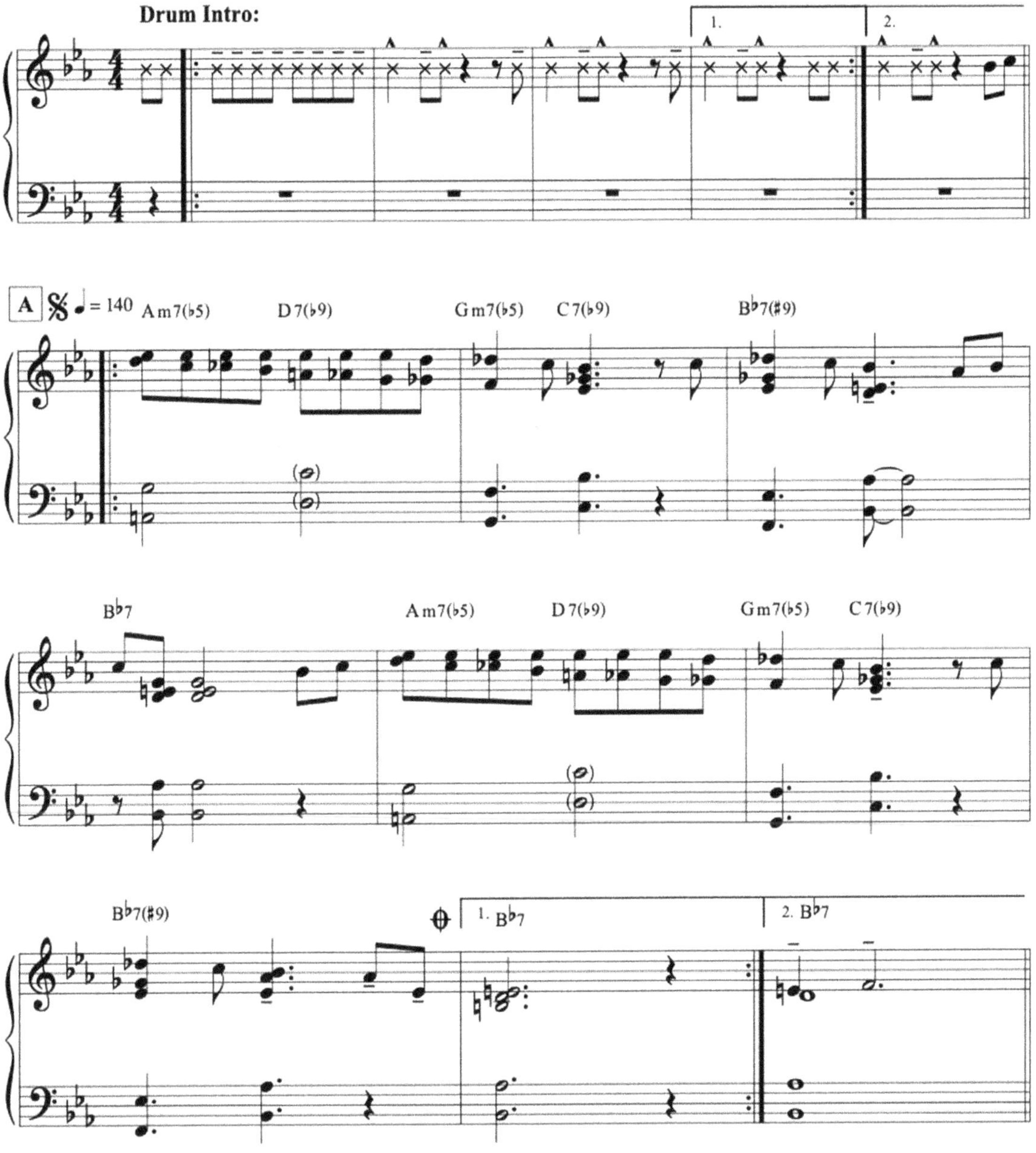

2

San Francisco Holiday

B
Cm7(♭5)
Cm7(♭5)
F7
Cm7(♭5)
F7
1. Cm7(♭5)
F7
2. Cm7(♭5)
F7
D.S. al Coda
Emaj6

John Coltrane *Take the Coltrane* September 26, 1962

John Coltrane: Tenor Saxophone
Duke Ellington: Piano
Jimmy Garrison: Bass
Elvin Jones: Drums

Take The Coltrane

John Coltrane Solo

Duke Ellington & John Coltrane
Impulse! - A-30
Recorded September 26, 1962

Duke Ellington
Transcribed by Ron Westray
Edited and Nomenclated by Kamil Qui

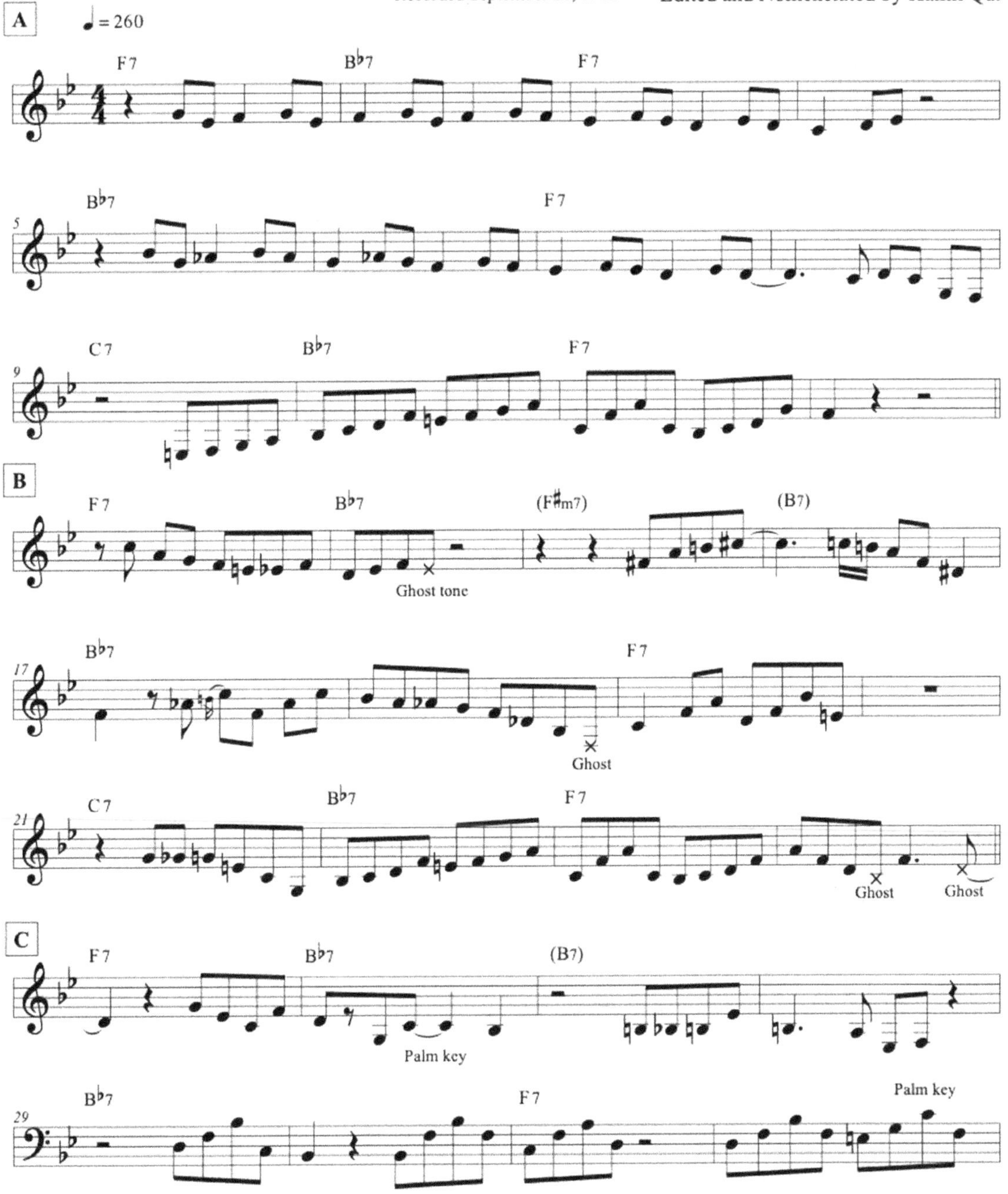

2

Take The Coltrane

C7
B♭7
F7
Palm key
D
F7
B♭7
(B7)
Ghost
B♭7
Ghost
F7
Ghost
C7
B♭7
F7
Ghost
Ghost
E
F7
B♭7
F7
B♭7
F7
C7
B♭7
F7
F
F7
B♭7
F7
Ghost
Ghost

Take The Coltrane 3

65
B♭7
F7
Ghost
Ghost
69
C7
B♭7
F7
Ghost
G
F7
B♭7
(F♯m7)
(B7)
Fake Fingering
77
B♭7
F7
Ghost
Ghost
81
C7
B♭7
F7
Ghost
H
F7
B♭7
F7
(B7)
89
B♭7
F7
93
C7
B♭7
F7
Ghost

4 **Take The Coltrane**

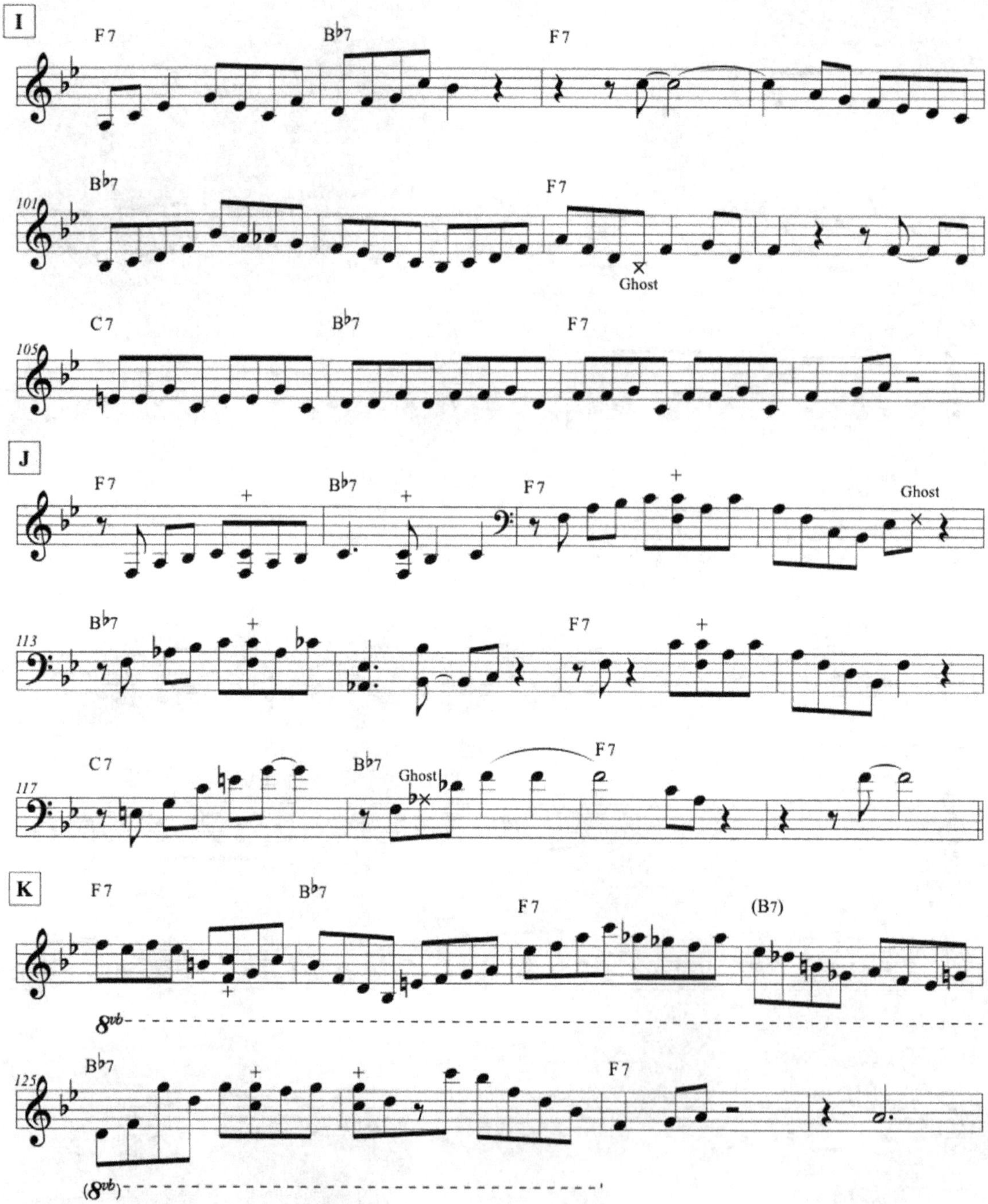
I
F7
B♭7
F7
101
B♭7
F7
Ghost
105
C7
B♭7
F7
J
F7
B♭7
F7
Ghost
113
B♭7
F7
117
C7
B♭7
Ghost
F7
K
F7
B♭7
F7
(B7)
8vb
125
B♭7
F7
(8vb)

Take The Coltrane 5

129
C7
B♭7
F7
Ghost
L
F7
Duke Ellington's Solo
M
F7
B♭7
137
F7
B♭7
141
F7
C7
B♭7
145
F7
F7
Ghost
N
B♭7
149
F7
(B7)
B♭7
153
F7
Ghost
G7
C7
Ghost
Ghost
Ghost
157
F7
Ghost
Ghost
F7
O
B♭7

6 **Take The Coltrane**

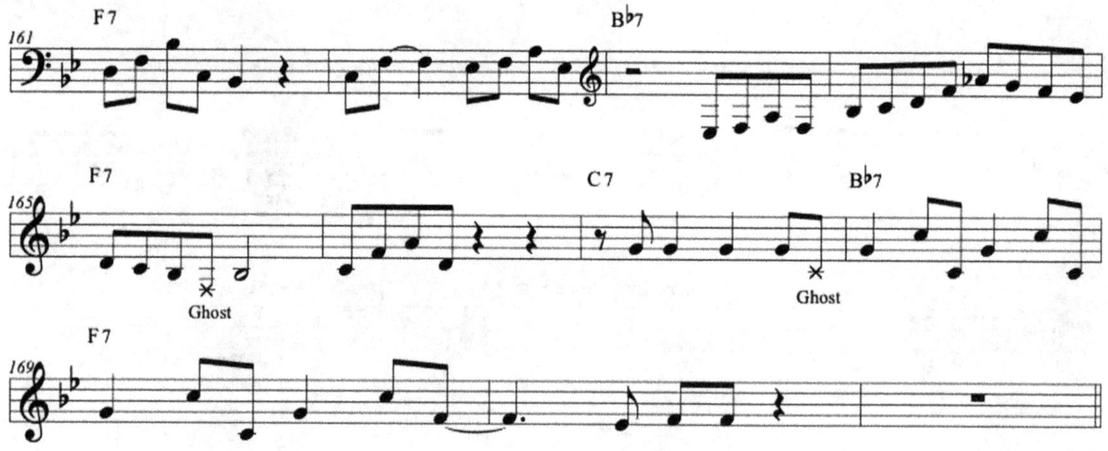
F7
B♭7
F7
C7
B♭7
Ghost
Ghost
F7

Thelonious Monk: Piano
Charlie Rouse: Tenor Saxophone
John Ore: Bass
Frankie Dunlop: Drums

Bright Mississippi

Thelonious Monk - *Monk's Dream*
Columbia - CS 8765
Recorded November 1, 1962

Thelonious Monk
Cross-Transcribed & Edited
by Ron Westray

2 **Bright Mississippi**

Bright Mississippi 3

4 **Bright Mississippi**

Bright Mississippi 5

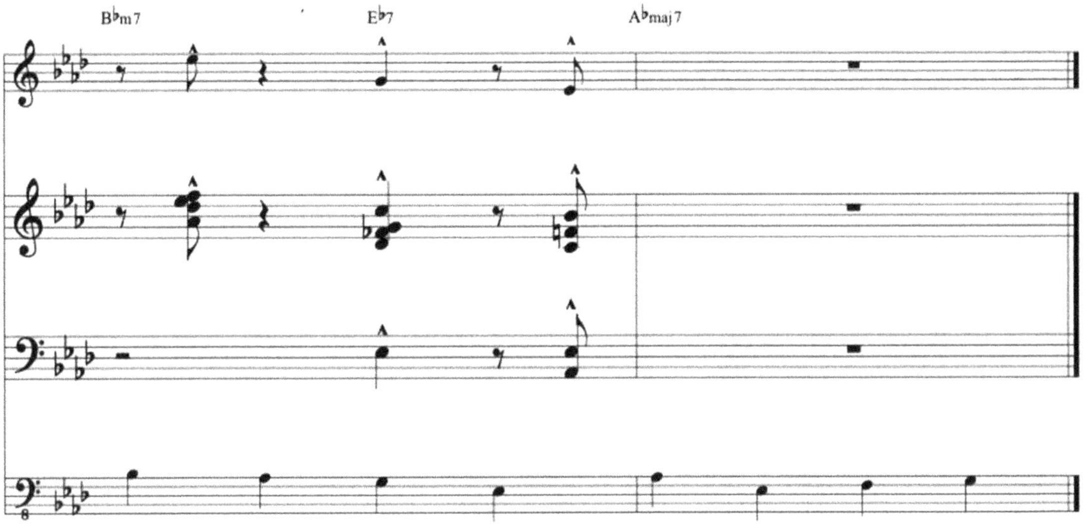
B♭m7
E♭7
A♭maj7

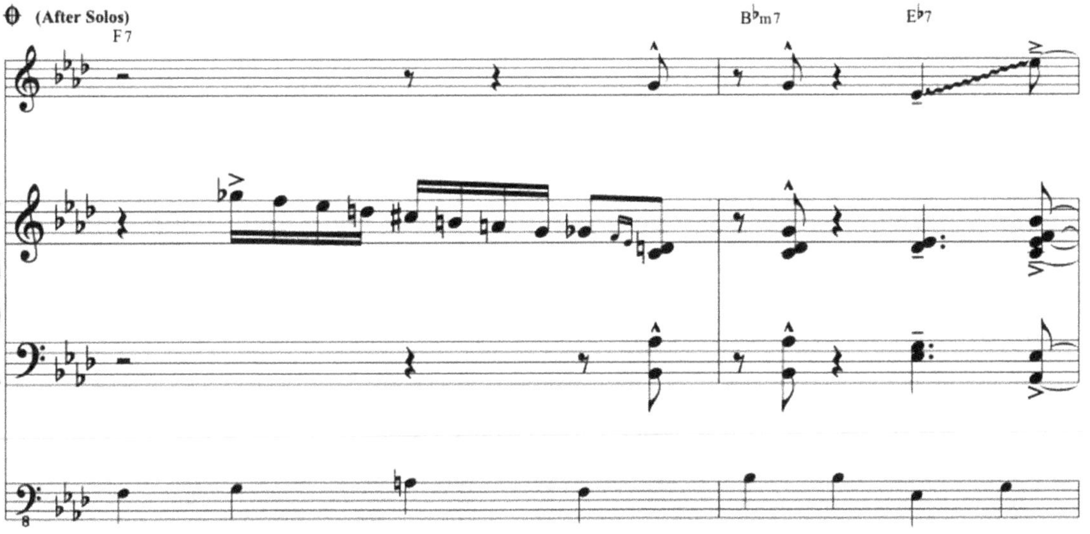
(After Solos)
F7
B♭m7
E♭7

6 **Bright Mississippi**

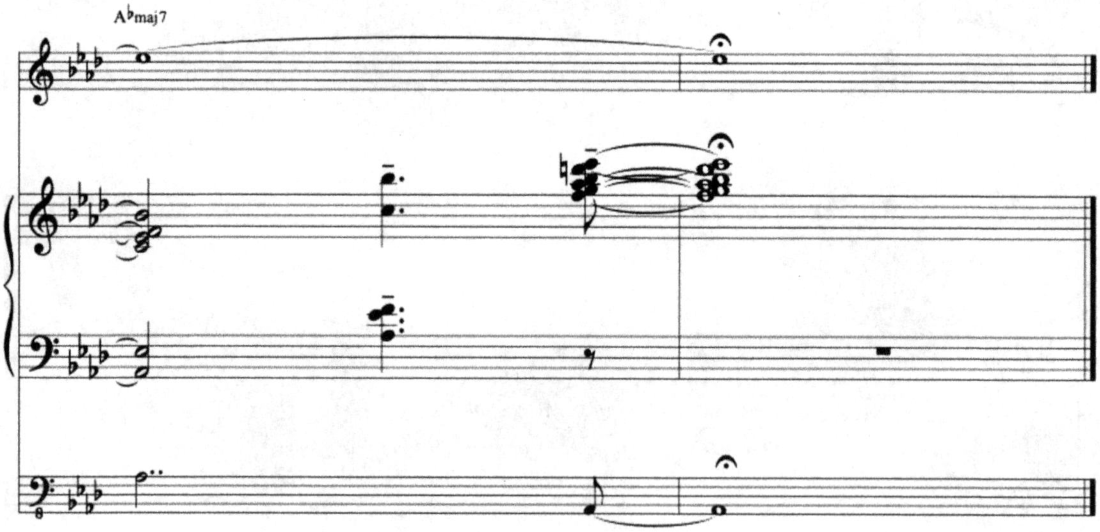

John Coltrane *Autumn Leaves* November 28, 1962

John Coltrane: Soprano Saxophone
McCoy Tyner: Piano
Jimmy Garrison: Bass
Elvin Jones: Drums

Autumn Leaves

John Coltrane Solo

'The Graz Concert, 1962

In Crowd Records - 996693

Recorded November 28, 1962

Transcribed by Ron Westray

Edited and Nomenclated by Kamil Qui

2
Autumn Leaves
B
Cm7 F7(♭9) B♭ma7 E♭ma7
37
Am7(♭5) D7(♭9) Gm6 G7(♭9)
41
Cm7 F7(♭9) B♭ma7 E♭ma7
45
Am7(♭5) D7(♭9) Gm6 Gm6
49
Am7(♭5) D7(♭9) Gm6 Gm6 (G7b9)
53
Cm7 F7(♭9) B♭ma7 B♭ma7
57
Am7(♭5) D7(♭9) Gm7 C7(♭9) FmᵀB♭7(♭9)
61
E♭ma7 Am7(♭5) D7(♭9) Gm6 Gm6 (G7b9)

Autumn Leaves
3
C
Cm7 F7(♭9) B♭ma7 E♭ma7
69
Am7(♭5) D7(♭9) Gm6 G7(♭9)
73
Cm7 F7(♭9) B♭ma7 E♭ma7
77
Am7(♭5) D7(♭9) Gm6 Gm6
81
Am7(♭5) D7(♭9) Gm6 Gm6 (G7b9)
85
Cm7 F7(♭9) B♭ma7 B♭ma7
89
Am7(♭5) D7(♭9) Gm7 C7(♭9) Fm7 B♭7(♭9)
93
E♭ma7 Am7(♭5) D7(♭9) Gm6 Gm6 (G7b9)

4
Autumn Leaves
D
Cm7 F7(♭9) B♭ma7 E♭ma7
3 3
Am7(♭5) D7(♭9) Gm6 G7(♭9)
101
3 3
Cm7 F7(♭9) B♭ma7 E♭ma7
105
Am7(♭5) D7(♭9) Gm6 Gm6
109
3
Am7(♭5) D7(♭9) Gm6 Gm6 (G7b9)
113
3 3
Cm7 F7(♭9) B♭ma7 B♭ma7
117
Am7(♭5) D7(♭9) Gm7 C7(♭9) Fm7 B♭7(♭9)
121
E♭ma7 Am7(♭5) D7(♭9) Gm6 Gm6 (G7b9)
125

Autumn Leaves
5
E
Cm7 F7(♭9) B♭ma7 E♭ma7
133 Am7(♭5) D7(♭9) Gm6 G7(♭9)
137 Cm7 F7(♭9) B♭ma7 E♭ma7
3
141 Am7(♭5) D7(♭9) Gm6 Gm6
145 Am7(♭5) D7(♭9) Gm6 Gm6 (G7b9)
149 Cm7 Ghost tone F7(♭9) B♭ma7 B♭ma7
153 Am7(♭5) D7(♭9) Gm7 C7(♭9) Fm7 B♭7(♭9)
157 E♭ma7 Am7(♭5) D7(♭9) Gm6 Gm6 (G7b9)

6

Autumn Leaves

F
Cm7 F7(♭9) B♭ma7 E♭ma7
Am7(♭5) D7(♭9) Gm6 G7(♭9)
165
Cm7 F7(♭9) B♭ma7 E♭ma7
169
Am7(♭5) D7(♭9) Gm6 Gm6
173
3
Am7(♭5) D7(♭9) Gm6 Gm6 (G7b9)
177
Cm7 F7(♭9) B♭ma7 B♭ma7
181
3
Am7(♭5) D7(♭9) Gm7 C7(♭9) Fm7 B♭7(♭9)
185
Ghost
E♭ma7 Am7(♭5) D7(♭9) Gm6 Gm6 (G7b9)
189
3

Autumn Leaves
7
G
Cm7 F7(b9) Bbma7 Ebma7
197
Am7(b5) D7(b9) Gm6 G7(b9)
201
Cm7 F7(b9) Bbma7 Ebma7
205
Am7(b5) D7(b9) Gm6 Gm6
Ghost
209
Am7(b5) D7(b9) Gm6 Gm6 (G7b9)
213
Cm7 F7(b9) Bbma7 Bbma7
217
Am7(b5) D7(b9) Gm7 C7(b9) FmBb7(b9)
221
Ebma7 Am7(b5) D7(b9) Gm6 Gm6 (G7b9)

8
Autumn Leaves
Cm7 F7(♭9) B♭ma7 E♭ma7
225
Am7(♭5) D7(♭9) Gm6 G7(♭9)
229
Cm7 F7(♭9) B♭ma7 E♭ma7
233
Am7(♭5) D7(♭9) Gm6 Gm6
237
Am7(♭5) D7(♭9) Gm6 Gm6 (G7b9)
241
Cm7 F7(♭9) B♭ma7 B♭ma7
245
Am7(♭5) D7(♭9) Gm7 C7(♭9) Fm7 B♭7(♭9)
249
E♭ma7 Am7(♭5) D7(♭9) Gm6 Gm6 (G7b9)
253

Autumn Leaves 9

257
Cm7 F7(♭9) B♭ma7 E♭ma7
261
Am7(♭5) D7(♭9) Gm6 G7(♭9)
265
Cm7 F7(♭9) B♭ma7 E♭ma7
269
Am7(♭5) D7(♭9) Gm6 Gm6
273
Am7(♭5) D7(♭9) Gm6 Gm6 (G7b9)
277
Cm7 F7(♭9) B♭ma7 B♭ma7
281
Am7(♭5) D7(♭9) Gm7 C7(♭9) Fm7 B♭7(♭9)
285
E♭ma7 Am7(♭5) D7(♭9) Gm6 Gm6 (G7b9)

10

Autumn Leaves

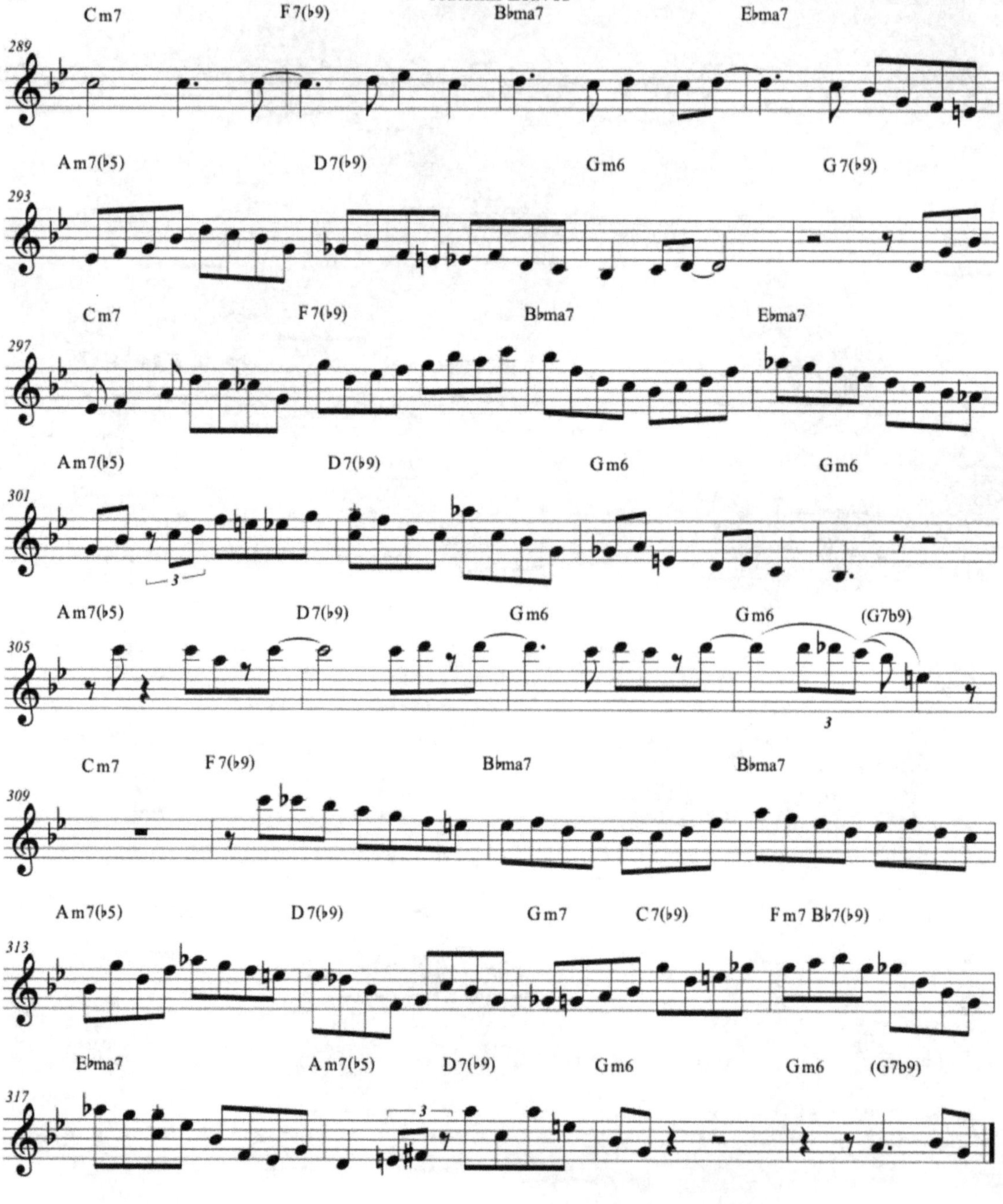
Cm7 F7(♭9) B♭ma7 E♭ma7
289
Am7(♭5) D7(♭9) Gm6 G7(♭9)
293
Cm7 F7(♭9) B♭ma7 E♭ma7
297
Am7(♭5) D7(♭9) Gm6 Gm6
301
Am7(♭5) D7(♭9) Gm6 Gm6 (G7b9)
305
Cm7 F7(♭9) B♭ma7 B♭ma7
309
Am7(♭5) D7(♭9) Gm7 C7(♭9) Fm7 B♭7(♭9)
313
E♭ma7 Am7(♭5) D7(♭9) Gm6 Gm6 (G7b9)
317

John Coltrane — *I Want to Talk About You* (Birdland ver.) — January 1, 1963

I Want To Talk About You

John Coltrane: Tenor Saxophone
McCoy Tyner: Piano
Jimmy Garrison: Bass
Elvin Jones: Drums

John Coltrane Solo
(Sans Cadenza)
℗ 1963 The Verve Music Group
Live at Birdland Jazzclub
Recorded, January 1, 1963

Billy Eckstine
Transcribed by Ron Westray

TWF 2019

I Want To Talk About You

2

Ebma7 Bbsus(b9)/F Bbsus(b9) Ebma7 (Fm7 F#m7 Gm7)
15
Bbm7 Eb7 Bbm7 Eb7
17
Bbm7 Eb7 Abma7
19
Dm7 G7b9 Cma7 Am7
21
Dm7 G7b9 Bb7 (E9) Fm7 Bb7(b9)
23
Ebma7 Bbm7 Eb7
25
Abma7 Abm7 Db7
27
Gm7 (Db7) C7b9 (E7) Fm7 Bb7alt.
29
Gm7 C7alt. Fm7 Bb7alt.
31

I Want To Talk About You

3

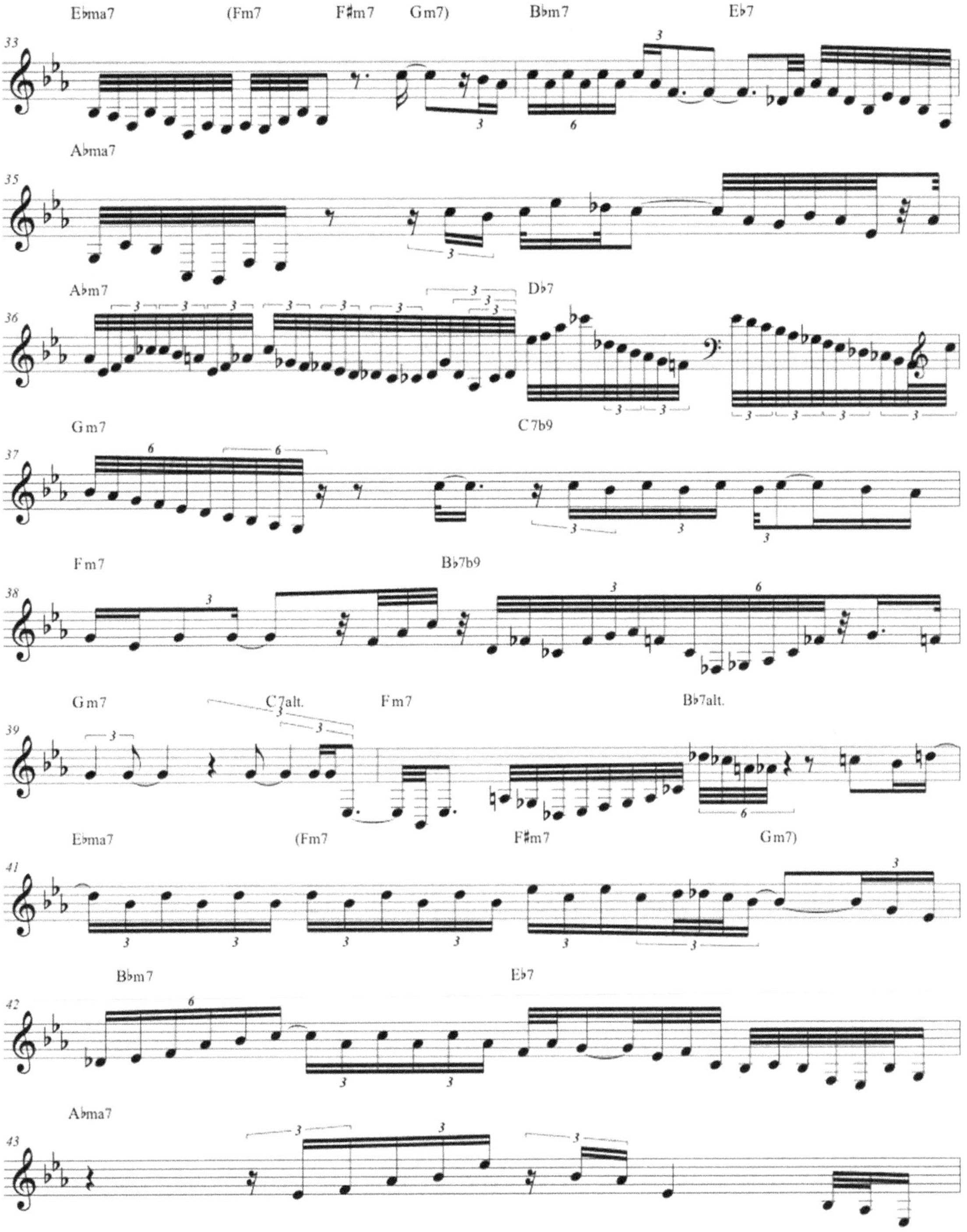
33
E♭ma7 (Fm7 F♯m7 Gm7) B♭m7 E♭7
35
A♭ma7
36
A♭m7 D♭7
37
Gm7 C7b9
38
Fm7 B♭7b9
39
Gm7 C7alt. Fm7 B♭7alt.
41
E♭ma7 (Fm7 F♯m7 Gm7)
42
B♭m7 E♭7
43
A♭ma7

I Want To Talk About You

4
A♭m7
D♭7
G m7
C 7b9
F m7
B♭7b9
E♭ma7
B♭sus(b9)/F
B♭sus(b9)
E♭ma7
(Fm7
F♯m7
Gm7)
B♭m7
E♭7
B♭m7
E♭7
B♭m7
E♭7
A♭ma7
D m7
G 7b9

I Want To Talk About You

5

54
Cma7
Am7
Dm7
G7b9
56
B♭7
(E9)
Fm7
B♭7(♭9)
57
E♭ma7
58
B♭m7
E♭7
A♭ma7
60
A♭m7
D♭7
61
Gm7
(Db7)
C7b9
(E7)
62
Fm7
B♭7alt.
Gm7
C7alt.
64
Fm7
B♭7alt.
B♭m7
E♭7
66
B♭m7
E♭7
B♭m7
E♭7

I Want To Talk About You

6

A♭ma7
Dm7
G7b9
Cma7
Am7
Dm7
G7b9
B♭7
(E9)
Fm7
B♭7(♭9)
E♭ma7
(Fm7 F♯m7 Gm7)
B♭m7
E♭7
A♭ma7
A♭m7
D♭7
Gm7(D♭7)
C7b9
(E7)
Fm7
Gm7
A♭m(M7)
E7
Gm7
C7
Fm7
Gm7
A♭m(M7)
E7
B♭13(♭9)
Fm7
Gm7
A♭m(M7)
E7
Gm7
C7
Fm7
Gm7
A♭m(M7)
E7
B♭13(♭9)

John Coltrane *Autumn Serenade* March 7, 1963

John Coltrane: Tenor Saxophone
Johnny Hartman: Vocals
McCoy Tyner: Piano
Jimmy Garrison: Bass
Elvin Jones: Drums

Autumn Serenade

John Coltrane Solo

John Coltrane and Johnny Hartman
Impulse! - A-40
Recorded March 7, 1963

Peter De Rose, Sammy Galop
Transcribed by Ron Westray
Edited and Nomenclated by Kamil Qui

2

Autumn Serenade

A♭7
Fm7
B♭7
E♭maj7
Cm7/G
Gm7(♭5)
C7alt
Fm7
B♭7
B
E♭m(maj7)
Ghost tongue
B♭7
E♭m(maj7)
Ghost/
Subtone-ish
A♭7
Fm7
Tongue
B♭7
Gm7
C7
Cm7
F7

Autumn Serenade 3

B 7
B♭7
E♭maj 7
B♭7
Ghost
Vamp
E♭maj 7
B♭7
E♭maj 7
B♭7
E♭maj 7
B♭7
E♭maj 7
B♭7
E♭maj 7
B♭7
E♭maj 7
B♭7
Subtone
Head Out
E♭m(maj7)
10
E 13(♯11)
softly
Vamp
E♭maj 7
E 13
soft
E♭maj 7
Subtone
E 13
E♭maj 7
E 13
E♭maj 7
E 13
E♭maj 7

John Coltrane *Lush Life* March 7, 1963

John Coltrane: Tenor Saxophone
Johnny Hartman: Vocals
McCoy Tyner: Piano
Jimmy Garrison: Bass
Elvin Jones: Drums

Lush Life

John Coltrane Solo

John Coltrane and Johnny Hartman
Impulse! - A-40
Recorded March 7, 1963

Billy Strayhorn
Transcribed by Ron Westray
Edited and Nomenclated by Kamil Qui

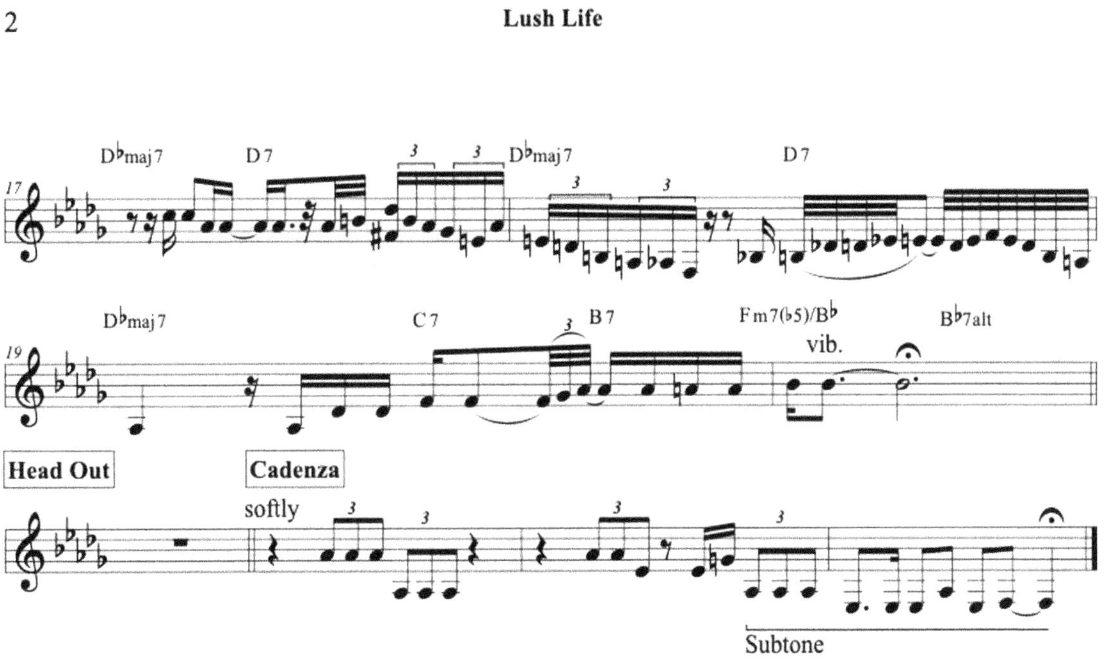
2
Lush Life
D♭maj7
D7
D♭maj7
D7
D♭maj7
C7
B7
Fm7(♭5)/B♭
B♭7alt
vib.
Head Out
Cadenza
softly
Subtone

John Coltrane *They Say It's Wonderful* March 7, 1963

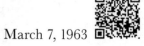

John Coltrane: Tenor Saxophone
Johnny Hartman: Vocals
McCoy Tyner: Piano
Jimmy Garrison: Bass
Elvin Jones: Drums

They Say It's Wonderful

John Coltrane Solo
John Coltrane and Johnny Hartman
Impulse! - A-40
Recorded March 7, 1963

Irving Berlin
Transcribed by Ron Westray
Edited and Nomenclated by Kamil Qui

2 **They Say It's Wonderful**

Fm7
Fm7(♭5)
B♭7(♭9)
Vib.
Palm D
Subtone
E♭maj7
Palm D
Gm7
C7
Fm7
pull back
Palm D
st.
Scoop
Palm D
Fm7(♭5)
B♭7(♭9)
E♭maj7
Gm7
G♭°7
Palm D
Fm7
Fm7(♭5)
B♭7(♭9)
Vib.
mf
B♭m7
Vib.
E♭7
f
A♭maj7
D♭7(♭9)
Palm D
Cm7
Gm7
Vib.
Am7
(D7)

They Say It's Wonderful 3

Gm7
Am7(♭5) D7(♭9)
58
Gm7
G♭m7
Palm D#
60
Fm7
Fm7(♭5)
B♭7(♭9)
62
Gm7
C7(♭9)
64
Fm7
B♭7
66
Scoop
Vib.
E♭maj7
68

John Coltrane — *Dear Old Stockholm* — April 23, 1963

Dear Old Stockholm

John Coltrane: Tenor Saxophone
McCoy Tyner: Piano
Jimmy Garrison: Bass
Roy Haynes: Drums

John Coltrane Solo
John Coltrane - *Dear Old Stockholm*
Impulse! - GRD-120
Recorded April 23, 1963

Varmeland
Transcribed by Ron Westray
Edited and Nomenclated by Kamil Qui

2

Dear Old Stockholm

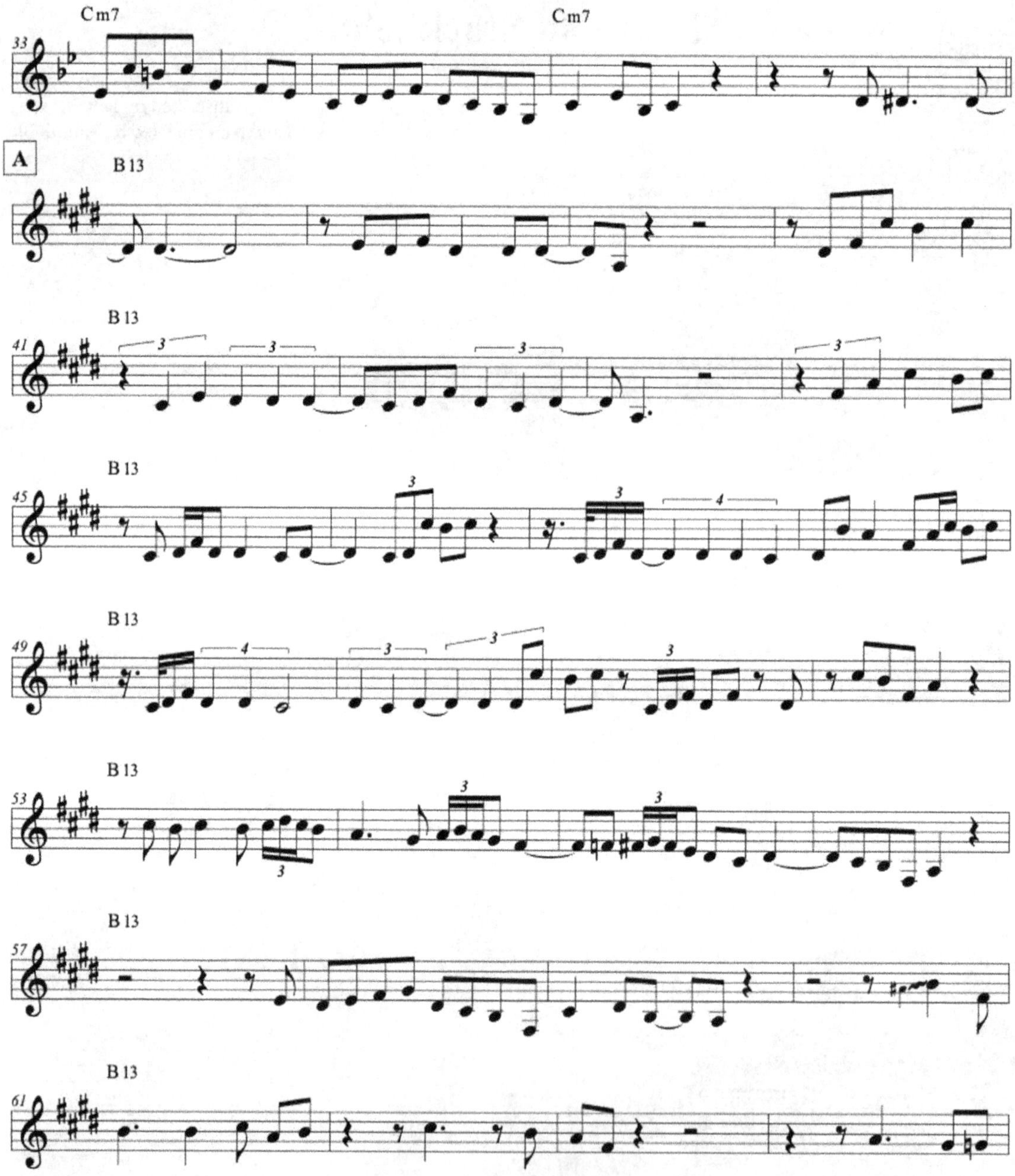
Cm7
Cm7
A
B13
B13
B13
B13
B13
B13
B13

Dear Old Stockholm 3

B 13
65
B 13
69
Ghost Tone
B 13
73
Ghost
Ghost
B 13
77
B 13
81
+
B 13
85
3
B 13
89
+
B 13
93
Ghost

4

Dear Old Stockholm

B 13
97
Ghost
B 13
101
B 13
105
B 13
109
B 13
113
B 13
117
B 13
121
B 13
125

Dear Old Stockholm 5

B 13
129
B 13
133
B 13
137
Ghost
Ghost
B
C m6/B
Ghost
C m6/B
145
Ghost
C m6/B
149
Fork F
Fork
C m6/B
153
Fork
Fork
C m6/B
157
6

6 **Dear Old Stockholm**

Cm6/B
161
C
Cm6/B
Cm6
Cm6
169
Fork
Cm6
173
Fork E
Fork
Cm6
177
Cm6
181
+
Cm6
185
Fork
Fork
+
Cm6
189
Ghost

Dear Old Stockholm 7

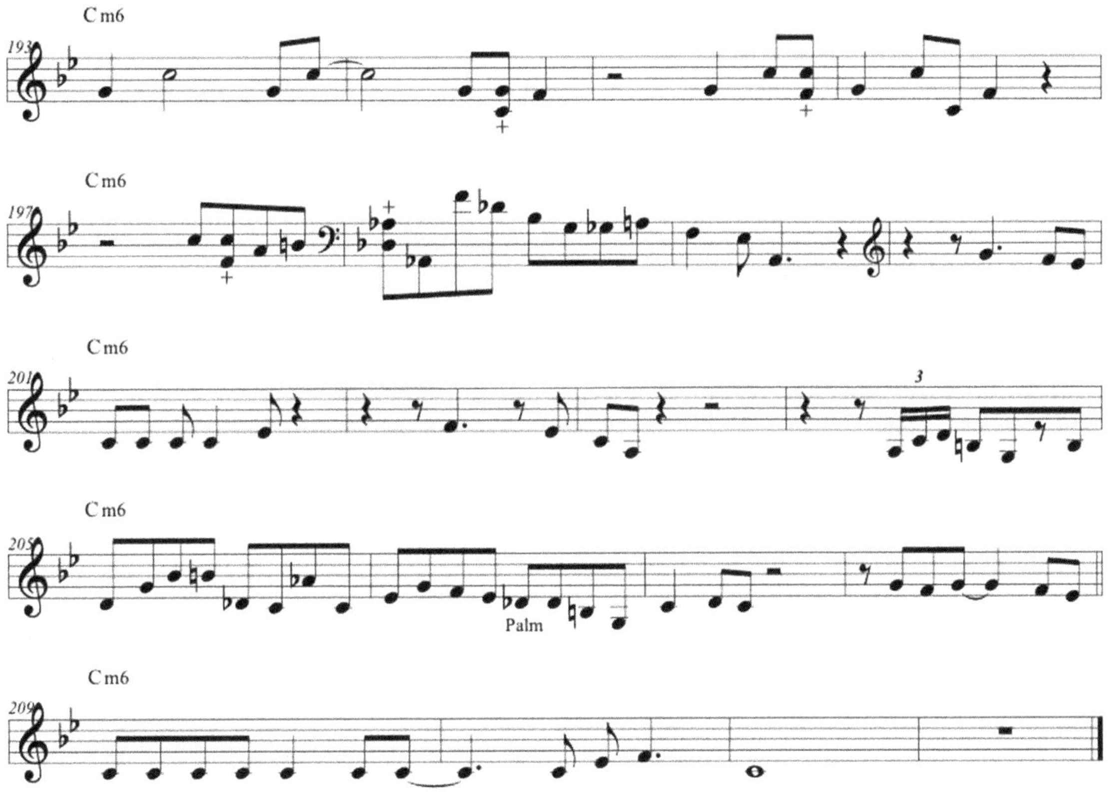
Cm6
Cm6
Cm6
Cm6
Palm
Cm6

John Coltrane *I Want to Talk About You* (Stockholm ver.) October 22, 1963

I Want To Talk About You

John Coltrane: Tenor Saxophone
McCoy Tyner: Piano
Jimmy Garrison: Bass
Elvin Jones: Drums

John Coltrane Solo
(Sans Cadenza)
℗ 1980 Pablo Records
Live in Stockholm, Sweden
Recorded, October 22, 1963

Billy Eckstine
Transcribed by Ron Westray
Edited and Nomenclated by Kamil Qui

2

I Want To Talk About You

Ebma7 Bbsus(b9)/F Bbsus(b9) Ebma7 (Fm7 F#m7 Gm7)
15
Bbm7 Eb7 Bbm7 Eb7
17
Bbm7 Eb7 Abma7
19
Dm7 G7b9 Cma7 Am7
21
Dm7 G7b9 Bb7 (E9) Fm7 Bb7(b9)
23
Ebma7 Bbm7 Eb7
25
Abma7 Abm7 Db7
27
Gm7 (Db7) C7b9 (E7) Fm7 Bb7alt.
29

I Want To Talk About You 3

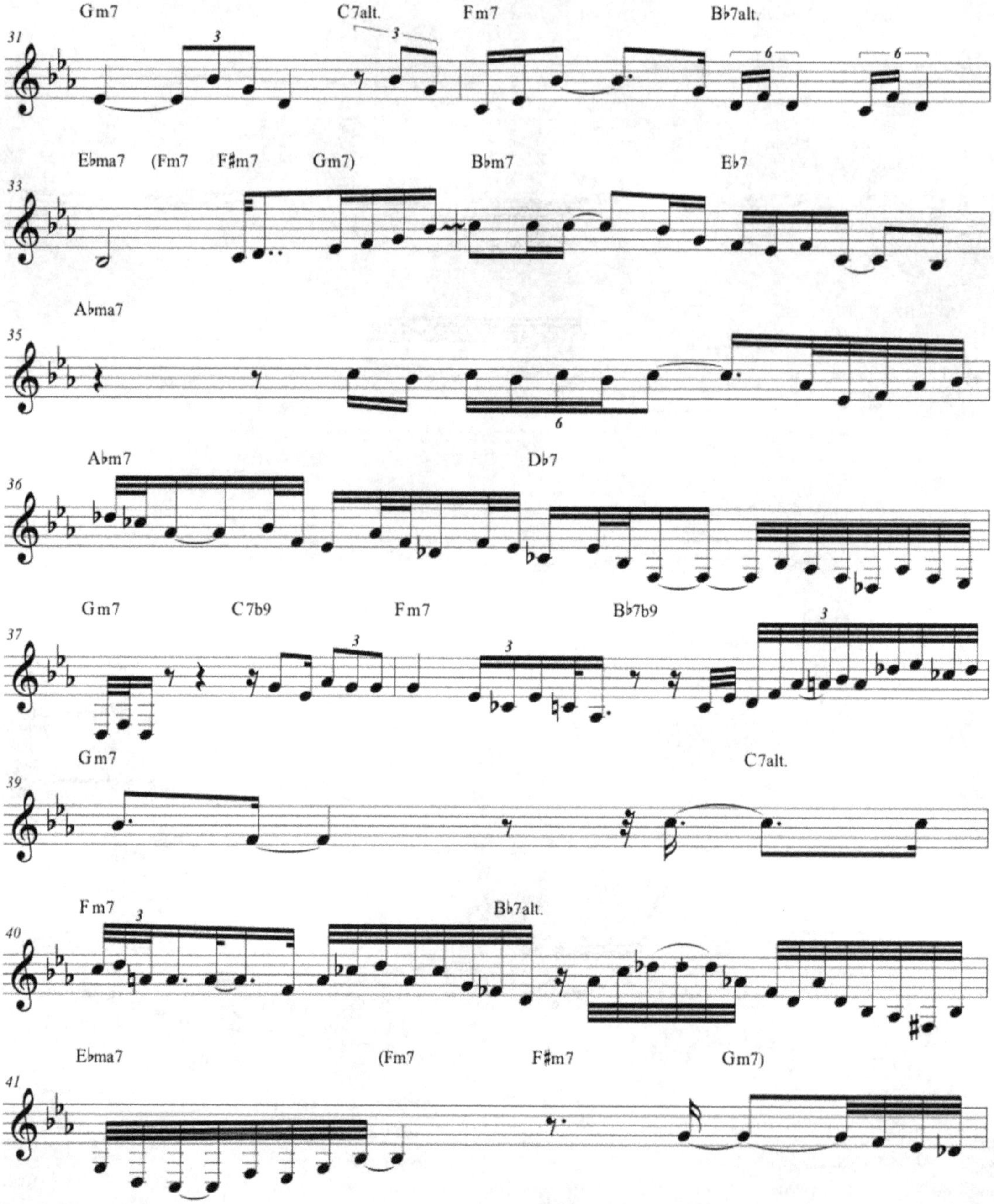
Gm7 C7alt. Fm7 B♭7alt.
31
3
3
6
6
E♭ma7 (Fm7 F♯m7 Gm7) B♭m7 E♭7
33
A♭ma7
35
6
A♭m7 D♭7
36
Gm7 C7♭9 Fm7 B♭7♭9
37
3
3
3
Gm7 C7alt.
39
Fm7 B♭7alt.
40
3
E♭ma7 (Fm7 F♯m7 Gm7)
41

4 I Want To Talk About You

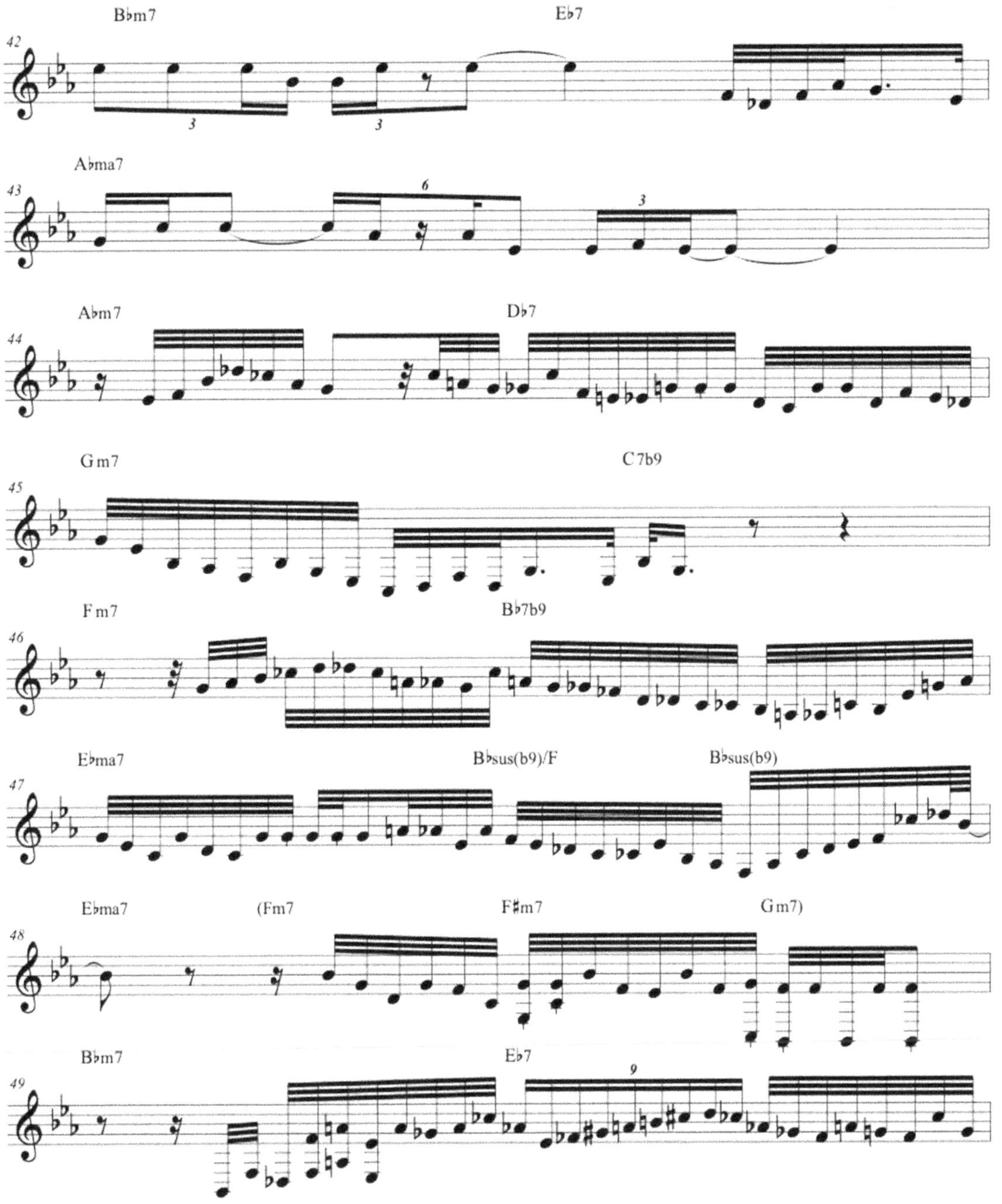

B♭m7
E♭7
A♭ma7
A♭m7
D♭7
G m7
C 7b9
F m7
B♭7b9
E♭ma7
B♭sus(b9)/F
B♭sus(b9)
E♭ma7
(Fm7
F♯m7
G m7)
B♭m7
E♭7

I Want To Talk About You 5

50
Bbm7
Eb7
51
Bbm7
Eb7
Abma7
Ghost
53
Dm7
G7b9
Cma7
Am7
9
55
Dm7
G7b9
56
Bb7
(E9)
Fm7
Bb7(b9)
57
Ebma7
Bbm7
Eb7
59
Abma7
Abm7
Db7
61
Gm7
(Db7)
C7b9
(E7)
Fm7
Bb7alt.
vib

6 I Want To Talk About You

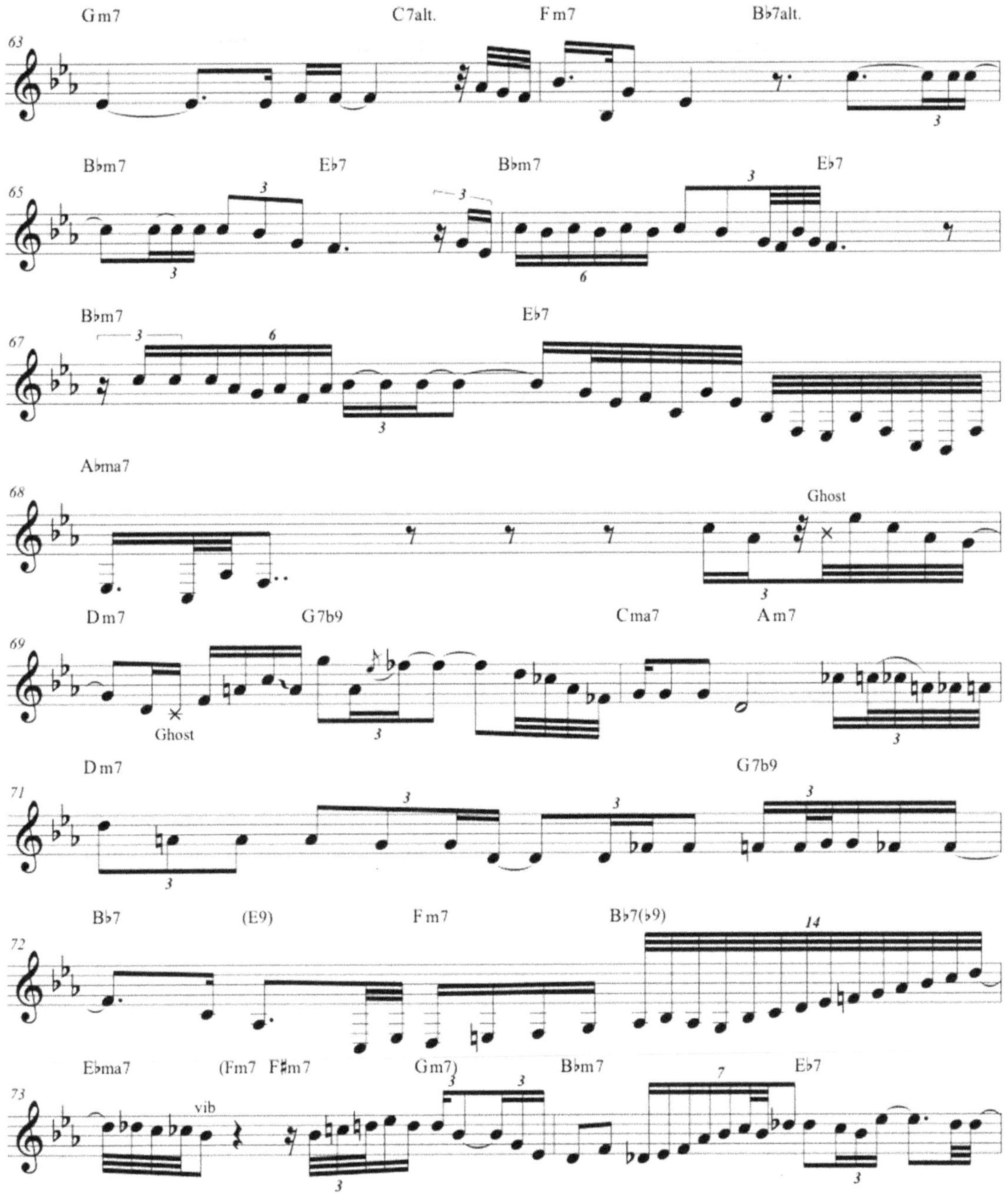
Gm7 C7alt. Fm7 B♭7alt.
B♭m7 E♭7 B♭m7 E♭7
B♭m7 E♭7
A♭ma7
Ghost
Dm7 G7b9 Cma7 Am7
Ghost
Dm7 G7b9
B♭7 (E9) Fm7 B♭7(♭9)
E♭ma7 (Fm7 F♯m7 Gm7) B♭m7 E♭7
vib

I Want To Talk About You
7
A♭ma7
A♭m7
D♭7
Gm7
(Db7)
C7b9
(E7)
Fm7
Gm7
A♭m(M7)
E7
Gm7
C7
Fm7
Gm7
A♭m(M7)
E7
B♭13(♭9)

Thelonious Monk *Oska T* December 30, 1963

Thelonious Monk: Piano
Charlie Rouse: Tenor Saxophone
Butch Warren: Bass
Frankie Dunlop: Drums
(With Big Band Accompaniment)

Oska T

Thelonious Monk - *Big Band and Quartet in Concert*
Columbia - CK 57636
Recorded December 30, 1963

Thelonious Monk
Cross-Transcribed & Edited
by Ron Westray

Thelonious Monk *Brake's Sake* February 10, 1964

Thelonious Monk: Piano
Charlie Rouse: Tenor Saxophone
Butch Warren: Bass
Ben Riley: Drums

Brake's Sake

Thelonious Monk - It's Monk's Time
Columbia - CK 63532
Recorded February 10, 1964

Thelonious Monk
Cross-Transcribed & Edited
by Ron Westray

2

Brake's Sake

Brake's Sake 3

B
G7
C7
D♭7
D.S. al Coda
Solos From 𝄋 Including Coda
A♭6
F♯7
B7
E♭7
A♭7(maj7)
A♭7

4

Brake's Sake

John Coltrane *Crescent* June 1, 1964

John Coltrane: Tenor Saxophone
McCoy Tyner: Piano
Jimmy Garrison: Bass
Elvin Jones: Drums

Crescent

John Coltrane Solo

John Coltrane - *Crescent*
Impulse! - A-66
Recorded June 1, 1964

John Coltrane
Cross-Transcribed & Edited by Ron Westray
Edited & Nomenclated by Kamil Qui

2

Crescent

B♭+7
E♭m7
A7
Dm 6 9
G7(♭9)
Cm 6 9
C
B♭7
E♭m7
E♭m7
A+7
Dm7
G7
Cm 6 9
Ghost tone
C or A

Crescent 3

D
B♭7alt
E♭m6/9
82
A+7
84
Dm7
G7alt
87
Cm6/9
89
E
B♭7alt
E♭m6/9
93
A7
A13(♭9)
95
Dm6/9

4

Crescent

98
Dm6/9
G7
Cm6/9
Vibrato
F
B♭7
E♭m6/9
107
A7
Dm6/9
111
G7
Cm6/9
114
G
B♭+7
117
E♭m6/9
A7
120
Dm(maj7)
122
G7alt

Crescent 5

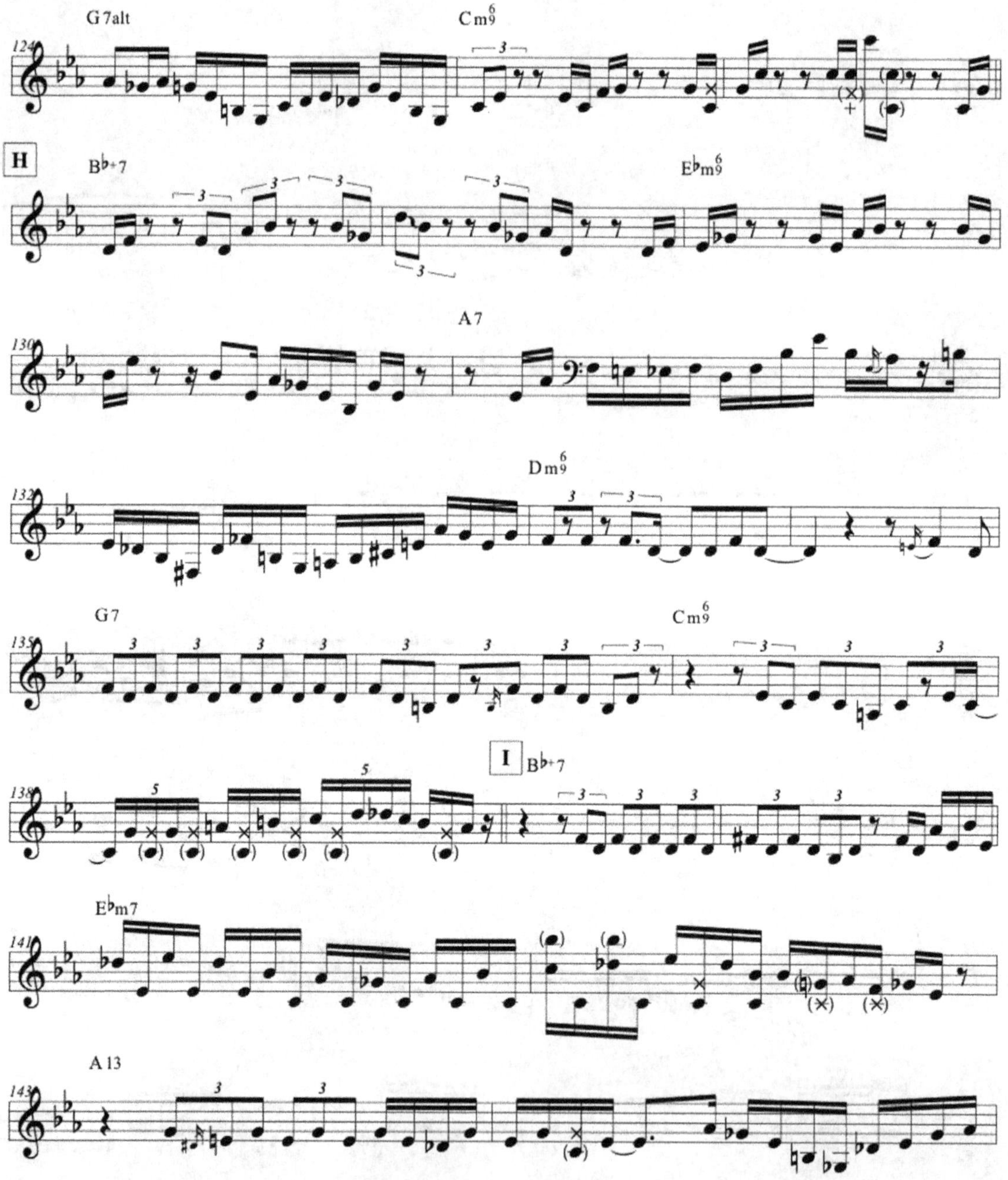
G7alt
Cm6/9
H
B♭+7
E♭m6/9
A7
Dm6/9
G7
Cm6/9
I
B♭+7
E♭m7
A13

6

Crescent

Dm(maj7)
G7
Cm6/9
J
B♭7
B♭+7
E♭m6/9
A+13(♯11)
A+7
Dm6/9
G+9
Cm6/9
K
B♭7alt
B♭7alt

Crescent 7

E♭m6/9
A7
Dm6/9
G9
vib.
Dm7
Head Out Rubato
A♭maj7(♯11)/G
E♭maj7(♯11)/D
In Time Em7(♭5)
A7
Dm6
G7sus
G7

8

Crescent

Cm7
B♭7sus
B♭7
E♭m7
A♭7
Em7
A+7
E♭maj7(♯11)/D
Em7(♭5)
A7
Dm7
G7sus
G7
Cm7
B♭7sus
B♭7
E♭maj7
A+7
Dm7(♭5)
G7
vib.
Out of Time
A♭maj7(♯11)/G
E♭maj7(♯11)/D

Thelonious Monk *Evidence* October 31, 1964

Thelonious Monk: Piano
Charlie Rouse: Tenor Saxophone
Larry Gales: Bass
Ben Reily: Drums

Evidence

Source Recording Unknown, Possibly From:
Thelonious Monk - *Live At The It Club*
Colmubia - CK 62588
Recorded October 31, 1964

Thelonious Monk
Cross-Transcribed & Edited
by Ron Westray

Evidence

E♭7
A♭m7
D♭7
B♭7
To Coda
1.
Fine
2.
B
B♭m7
E♭7
A♭maj7
A♭m7
E♭7
Gm7(♭5)
F7
B♭7
D.S. al Fine
(D.S. al Coda After Solos)

Evidence 3

Thelonious Monk *We See* January 10, 1967

Thelonious Monk: Piano
Charlie Rouse: Tenor Saxophone
Larry Gales: Bass
Ben Riley: Drums

We See

Thelonious Monk - *Straight, No Chaser*
Columbia - CK 64886
Recorded January 10, 1967

Thelonious Monk
Cross-Transcribed & Edited
by Ron Westray

2

We See

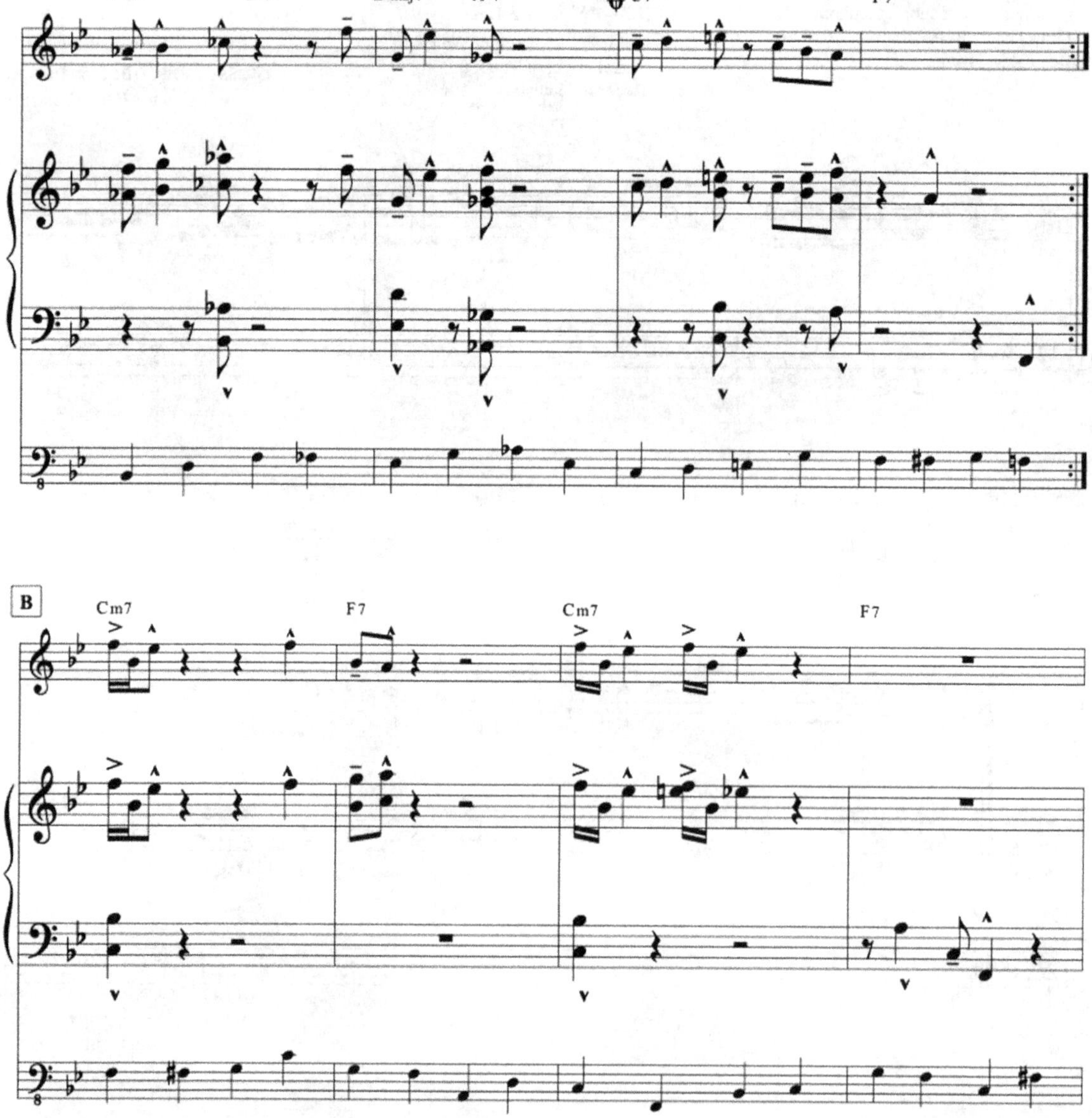
Fm7
B♭7
E♭maj7
A♭7
C7
F7
B
Cm7
F7
Cm7
F7

We See 3

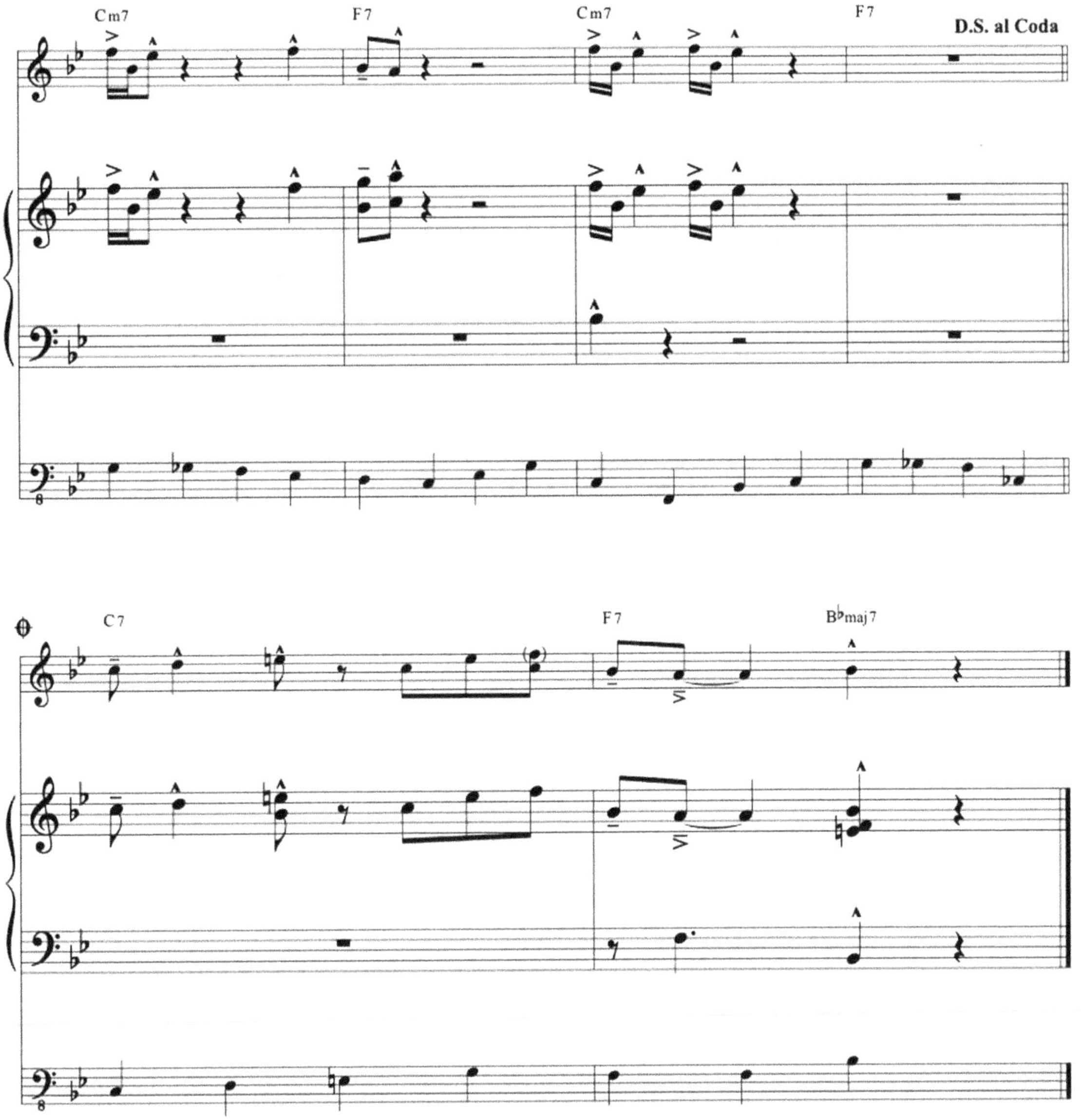
Cm7
F7
Cm7
F7
D.S. al Coda
C7
F7
B♭maj7

Thelonious Monk — *'Round Midnight* (Intro) — November 19, 1968

Thelonious Monk: Piano

'Round Midnight (Intro)

Thelonius Monk - *Monk Alone: The Complete Columbia Solo Studio Recordings: 1962-1968*
Columbia - CK 65495
Recorded November 19, 1968

T. Monk, Cootie Williams
Transcribed by Ron Westray

Wynton Marsalis *Blue Interlude* May 19, 1992

Wynton Marsalis: Trumpet, Composer
Herlin Riley: Drums
Marcus Roberts: Piano
Reginald Veal: Bass
Wes Anderson: Alto Saxophone
Todd Williams: Tenor Saxophone
Trombone: Wycliffe Gordon

Blue Interlude

Wynton Marsalis - Blue Interlude
Sony BMG Music Entertainment
Released May 5, 1992

Wynton Marsalis
Transcribed by Ron Westray

Blue Interlude
2
Eb7
Ab7
Db7
Db7
Db7
Gm7(b5)
C7b9
Fm6
Fm6
Band In
B
Cm13
Cm13
Gm13/C
Gm13/C
C13
C13
F13
F13
Abm7/Db
Abm7/Db
B2
Cm13
lay back
Cm13
Gm13/C
Gm13/C
1/2 valve----->
1/2 valve----->
C13
C13
F13
F13
Abm7/Db
Abm7/Db

Blue Interlude

B3
Cm13
Cm13
Gm13/C
3
3
57
Gm13/C
C13
C13
3
60
F13
F13
A♭m7/D♭
6
5
5
63
A♭m7/D♭
3
(cue)
Cm13
Cm13
66
Gm13/C
Gm13/C
C13
69
C13
F13
F13
72
A♭m7/D♭
lay back
A♭m7/D♭
3
75

Aaron Goldberg *Mao's Blues* February 2–3, 2000

Aaron Goldberg: Piano
Reuben Rogers: Bass
Eric Harland: Drums

Mao's Blues

Mao's Blues - *Unfolding*
J Curve Records - 1014
Recorded February 2-3, 2000

Aaron Goldberg
Transcribed by Steven Smith
Edited by Ron Westray

2

Mao's Blues

Gm7 C7 F7 A♭6 G7 G♭7
23
C
F7 B♭7 F7
B♭7 F7 D7alt
31
Gm7 C7 F7 A♭6 G7 G♭7
35
D
F7 B♭7 F7
B♭7 F7 D7alt
43
3

Mao's Blues 3

Gm7 C7 F7 A♭6 G7 G♭7
E
F7 B♭7 F7
B♭7 F7 D7alt
Gm7 C7 F7 A♭6 G7 G♭7
F
F7 B♭7 F7
8va
B♭7 F7 D7alt

4

Mao's Blues

Gm7 C7 F7 A♭6 G7 G♭7
71
G
F7 B♭7 F7
B♭7 F7 D7alt
79
Gm7 C7 F7 A♭6 G7 G♭7
83
H
F7 B♭7 F7
B♭7 F7 D7alt
91

Mao's Blues 5

95
Gm7 C7 F7 A♭6 G7 G♭7
I
F7 B♭7 F7
8va
(8va)
103
B♭7 F7 D7alt
107
Gm7 C7 F7 A♭6 G7 G♭7
J
F7 B♭7 F7

6 **Mao's Blues**

B♭7
115
F7
D7alt
Gm7
119
C7
F7
A♭6
G7
G♭7
K
F7
B♭7
F7
B♭7
127
F7
D7alt
Gm7
131
C7
F7
A♭6
G7
G♭7

Mao's Blues 7

L
F7
B♭7
F7
3
5
B♭7
8va
F7
D7alt
139
3
(8va)
Gm7
C7
F7
A♭6
G7
G♭7
143
M
(8va)
F7
B♭7
F7
(8va)
B♭7
F7
D7alt
151

8

Mao's Blues

(8va)
Gm7
C7
F7
A♭6
G7
G♭7
155
N
F7
B♭7
F7
163
B♭7
F7
D7alt
167
Gm7
C7
F7(♯9)
Fmaj7
A♭m7
Fm7sus

Mao's Blues
O
Trades With Drums
F7
A♭13
B13
8va
9
(B♭13)
175
6
6
F7
A♭6
G7
G♭7
183
F7
D13
B♭7
B13
B7(♭9)
(B♭13)
187
6
6
F7
D♭7sus
Dm7sus
E♭7sus
D.S. al Coda
195
Fm7
D♭7sus
Dm7
E♭7sus
Fm7
D♭7sus
Dm7sus
E♭m7
E5
F7(♭13)sus

Ron Westray *The Only Thing That's Wanting* (Excerpt) May 2–5, 2005

The Only Thing That's Wanting

Piano Excerpt (mm. 317-332)

Ron Westray

From *Chivalrous Misdemeanors: Select Tales from Don Quixote*
Performed by the Jazz at Lincoln Center Orchestra
May 2-5, 2005

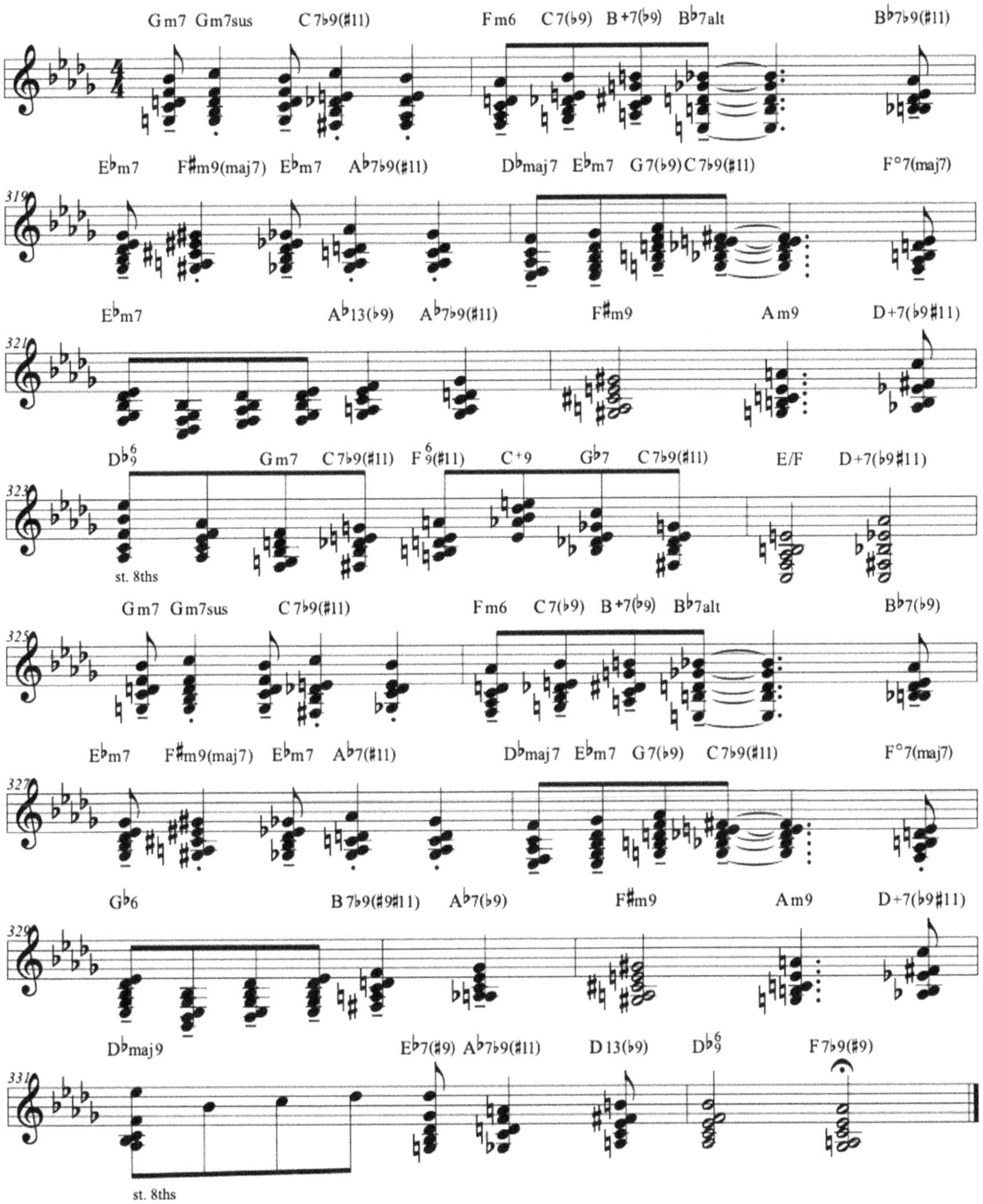

Chapter 6

ALTERNATIVE SYSTEMS

6.1. Triple Augmented

APPENDIX 6.1.1.
TRIPLE AUGMENTED IN MAJOR, DESCENDING

Appendix 6.1.1. Triple Augmented in Major, Descending

APPENDIX 6.1.2.
TRIPLE AUGMENTED IN MAJOR, ASCENDING

Appendix 6.1.2. Triple Augmented in Major, Ascending

APPENDIX 6.1.3.
TRIPLE AUGMENTED IN LYDIAN, DESCENDING

Appendix 6.1.3. Triple Augmented in Lydian, Descending

APPENDIX 6.1.4.
TRIPLE AUGMENTED IN LYDIAN, ASCENDING

Appendix 6.1.4. Triple Augmented in Lydian, Ascending

APPENDIX 6.1.5.
TRIPLE AUGMENTED IN DOMINANT, DESCENDING

Appendix 6.1.5. Triple Augmented in Dominant, Descending

- Again, the pattern may require resolution to a chord tone outside the pattern; however, being in Dominant the pattern provides the opportunity to resolve to more interesting chord tones such as the b9 and 13, though the resolution to the 4th (in the case of E) may not be ideal.

APPENDIX 6.1.6.
TRIPLE AUGMENTED IN DOMINANT, ASCENDING

Appendix 6.1.6. Triple Augmented in Dominant, Ascending

- In minor, the pattern is derived from the system starting on the leading tone of the root. Ex. Amin = Ab C E
- Ending the pattern on the root or third of one of the triads will yield a min[3], P[5], or maj[7].

APPENDIX 6.1.7.
TRIPLE AUGMENTED IN MINOR, DESCENDING

Appendix 6.1.7. Triple Augmented in Minor, Descending

APPENDIX 6.1.8.
TRIPLE AUGMENTED IN MINOR, ASCENDING

Appendix 6.1.8. Triple Augmented in Minor, Ascending

- The concept can also start on the ii-V to I and is just as powerful leading to I as when played over I
- Same pattern as used over a sustained major chord

APPENDIX 6.1.9.
TRIPLE AUGMENTED THROUGH COMMON ii-V-I, DESCENDING

Appendix 6.1.9. Triple Augmented Through Common ii-V-I, Descending

Appendix 6.1.9. Triple Augmented Through Common ii-V-I, Descending

Appendix 6.1.9. Triple Augmented Through Common ii-V-I, Descending

Appendix 6.1.9. Triple Augmented Through Common ii-V-I, Descending

Appendix 6.1.9. Triple Augmented Through Common ii-V-I, Descending

APPENDIX 6.1.10.
TRIPLE AUGMENTED THROUGH COMMON ii-V-I, ASCENDING

Appendix 6.1.10. Triple Augmented Through Common ii-V-I, Ascending

Appendix 6.1.10. Triple Augmented Through Common ii-V-I, Ascending

Appendix 6.1.10. Triple Augmented Through Common ii-V-I, Ascending

Appendix 6.1.10. Triple Augmented Through Common ii-V-I, Ascending

Appendix 6.1.10. Triple Augmented Through Common ii-V-I, Ascending

- The major pattern can also be used over the common ii-V that resolves to a minor i chord. The resolution at the downbeat will be a m3, P5 or M7.

APPENDIX 6.1.11.
TRIPLE AUGMENTED THROUGH COMMON ii-V RESOLVING TO MINOR i

Appendix 6.1.11. Triple Augmented Through Common ii-V Resolving to Minor i

- Use the major triple augmented pattern over the ii-V; however, at the i chord, reverse direction and use the appropriate system for the minor chord.
- Pay attention to how the two systems are connected.

APPENDIX 6.1.12.
MAJOR TRIPLE AUGMENTED TO MINOR TRIPLE AUGMENTED

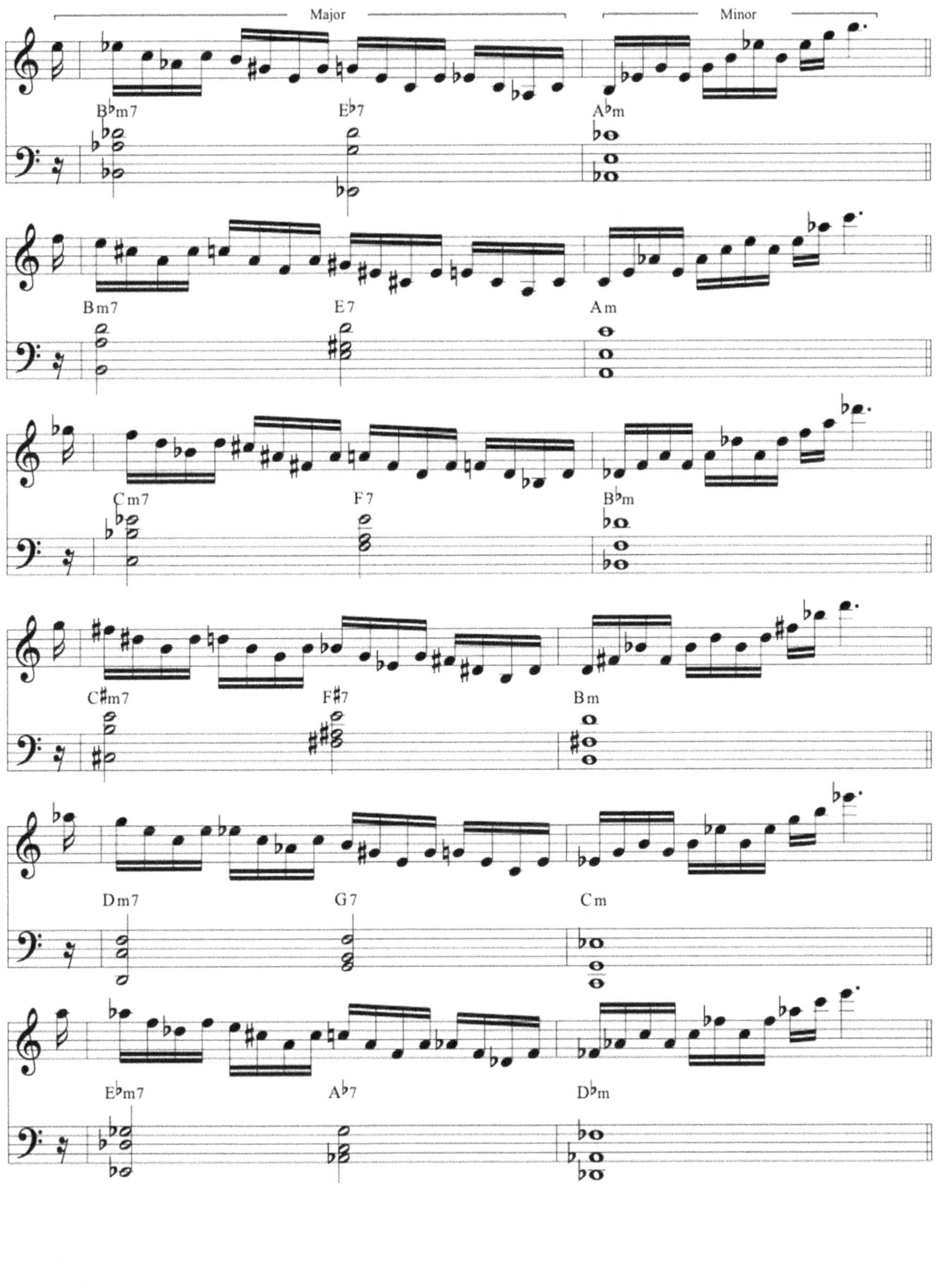

Appendix 6.1.12. Major Triple Augmented to Minor Triple Augmented

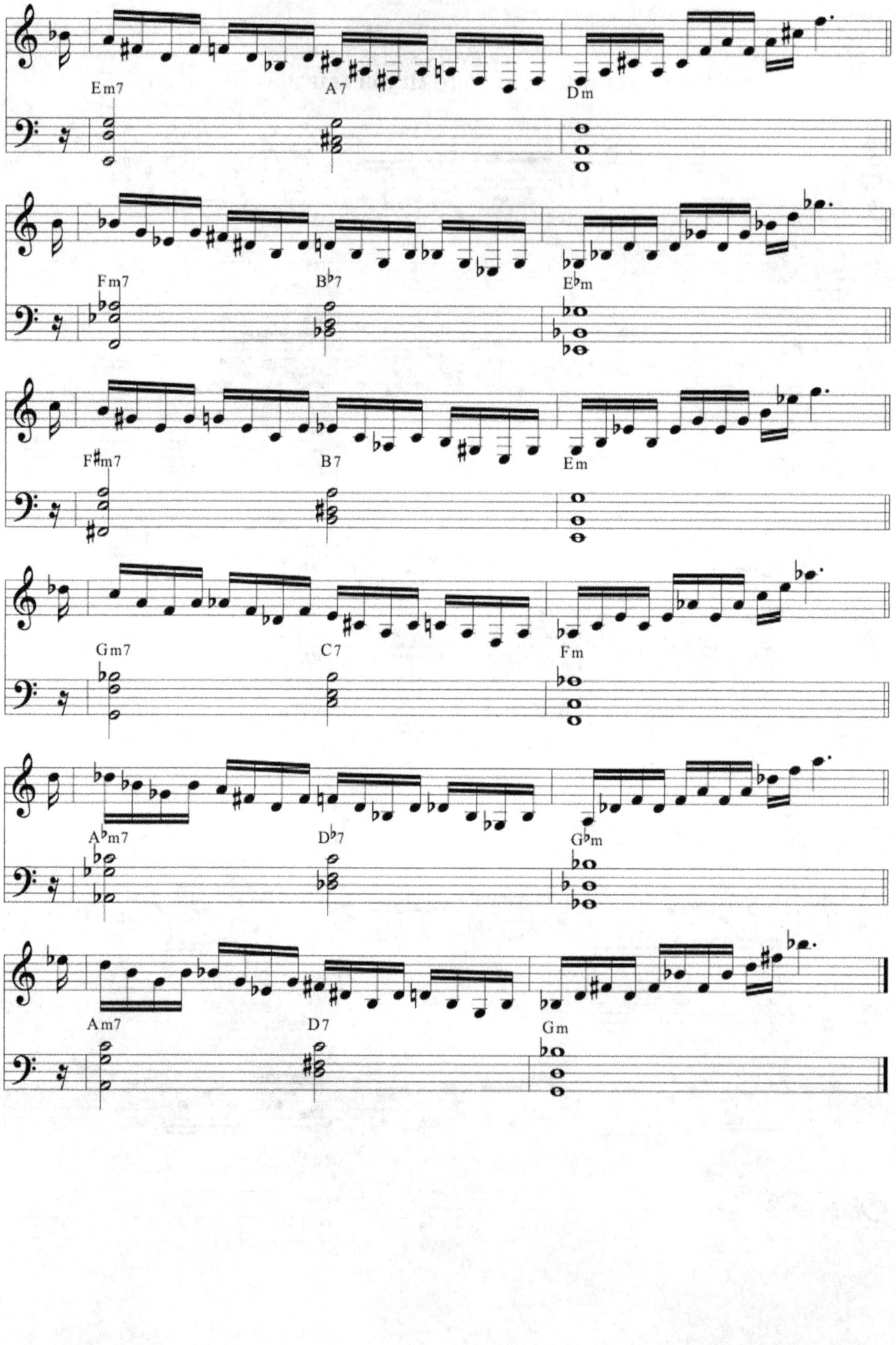

- Same as previous example but played over a m7(b5)–7(b9) progression.
- The major system played over the minor ii-V is more effective than when played over the common ii-V.

APPENDIX 6.1.13.
TRIPLE AUGMENTED THROUGH MINOR ii-V-i

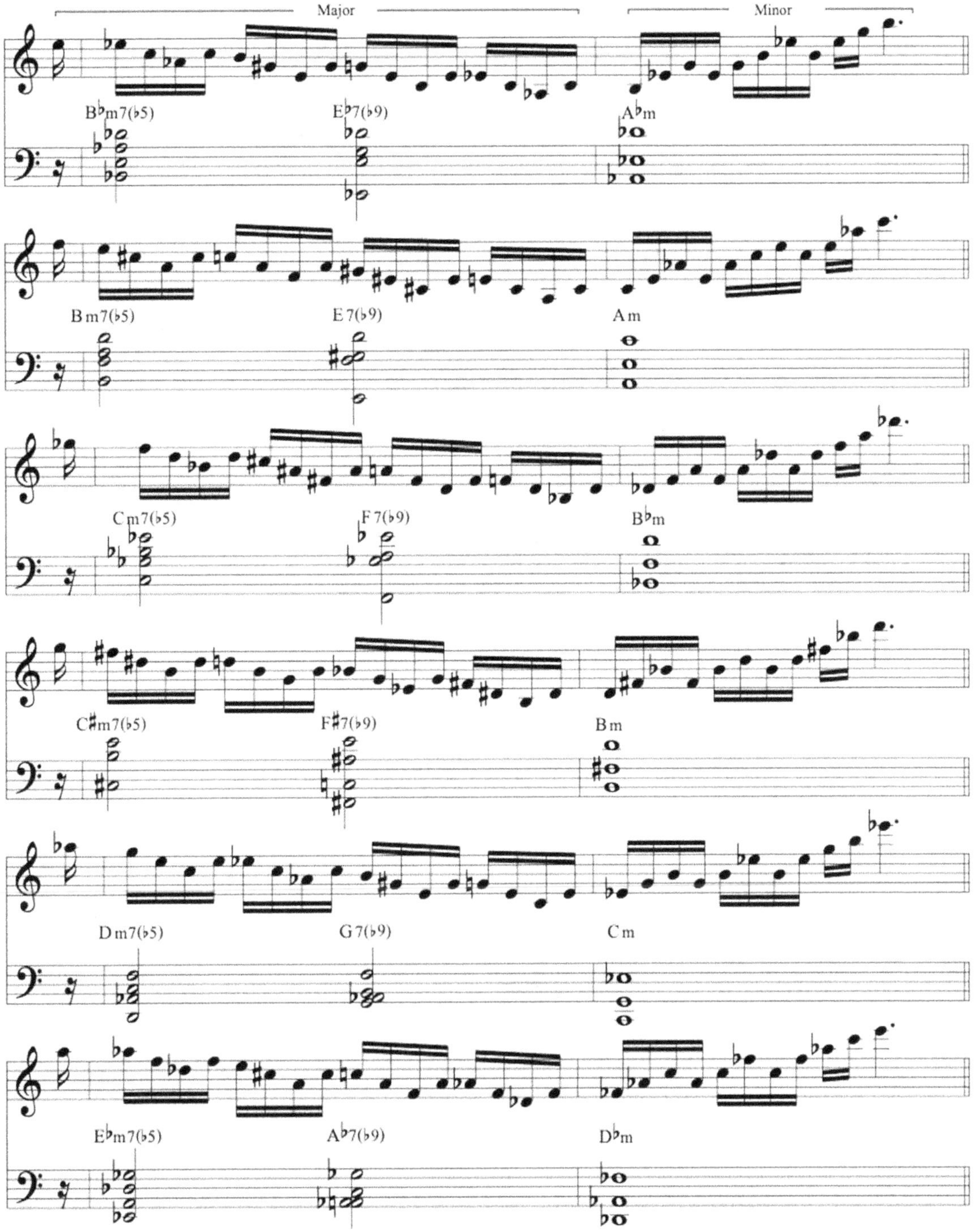

Appendix 6.1.13. Triple Augmented Through Minor ii-V-i

- This motif runs through scale steps 5-4-3-2 of each triad in the system, before going up a half step to the 5 of the next triad.

APPENDIX 6.1.14.
TRIPLE AUGMENTED THROUGH COMMON ii-V-I, ADDITIONAL MOTIF

Appendix 6.1.14. Triple Augmented Through Common ii-V-I, Additional Motif

6.1.15. Graph: Key Orbits

Description: A Combination of Substitute ii-V-I's and Triple Augmented Roots.

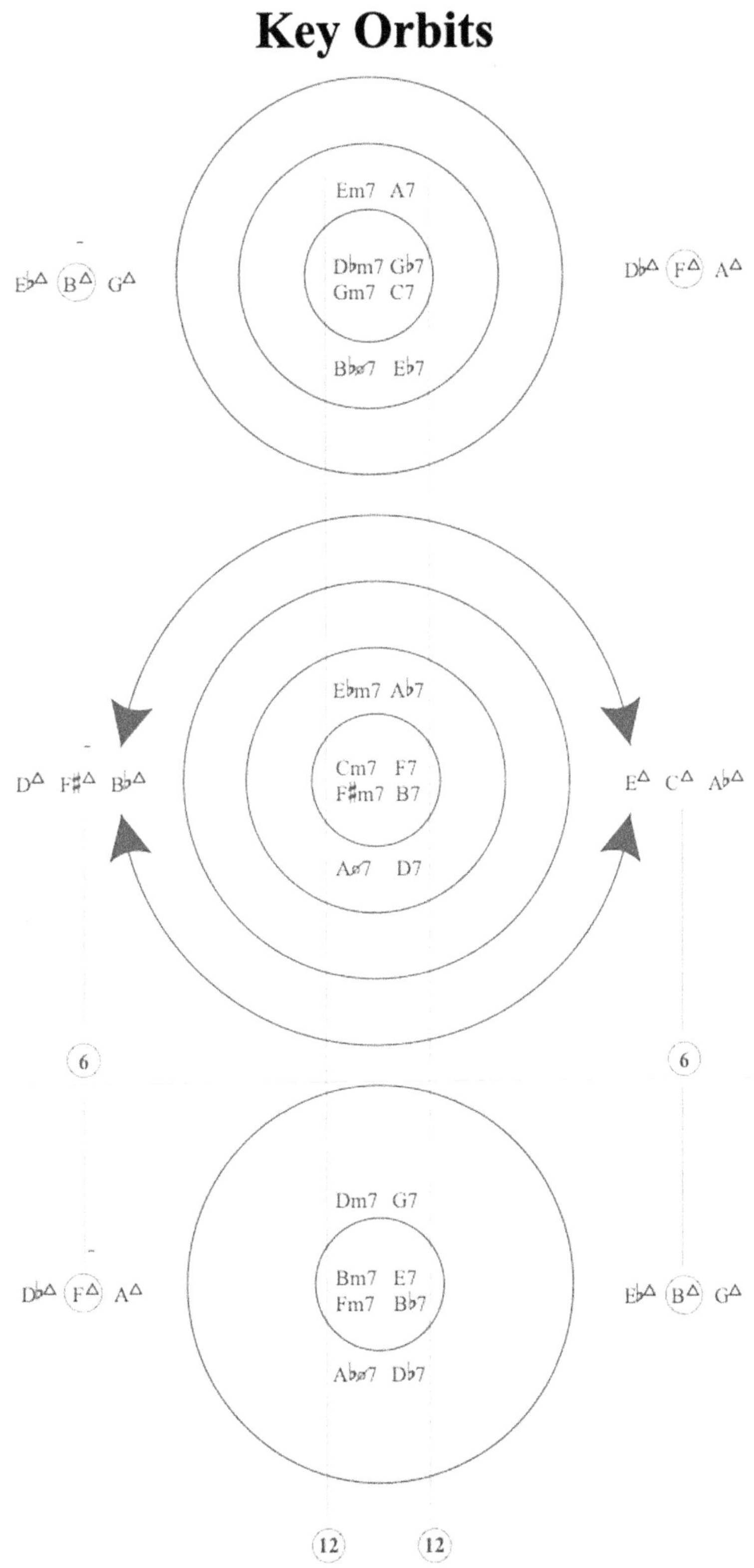

6.2. The Root Progression System (R.P.S.)

- The RPS involves learning, through repetition, specific melodic motifs through all possible intervals and/or disparities. The system works like this: One motif ascends in m2 to maximum range, descends in M2, ascends in m3, descends in M3, ascends in P4, descends in tritone, ascends in P5, descends in m6, ascends in M6, descends in m7, ascends in M7. The system will not always return to where it began because of range considerations. The system starts wherever you end. The exercise becomes shorter as the intervals expand. The alternative method for this system is to keep the system revolving by continuing the relevant interval in an accessible range.

The Root Progression System

The Root Progession System

M3 dwn.
P4 up
Tritone
m6 dwn.
M6 up
m7 dwn.
M7 up

6.2.1. "Spy Boy" (Traditional)

Spy-Boy
Traditional
Alvin Batiste
Concert Lead
B♭ma7 Am7 D7 Gm7 C7 Fm7 B♭7alt.
E♭ma7 E♭ma7 E♭m7 A♭7(♯11) E♭m7 A♭7(♯11)
B♭ma7 B♭ma7 C7 C7
Dm7 G7b9 Cm7 F7alt.
B♭ma7 Am7 D7 Gm7 C7 Fm7 B♭7alt.
E♭ma7 E♭ma7 E♭m7 A♭7(♯11) E♭m7 A♭7(♯11)
B♭ma7 B♭ma7 C7 C7
Cm7 F7alt. B♭ma7 B♭ma7
D♭m7 D7 Gma7 Bma7 Bmaj7

2

Bm7 C7alt. Fma7 Ama7 Ama7
Am7 B♭7alt. E♭ma7 Gma7 Gma7
Gm7 C7alt. Cm7 F7alt.
B♭ma7 Am7 D7 Gm7 C7 Fm7 B♭7alt.
E♭ma7 E♭ma7 E♭m7 A♭7(♯11) E♭m7 A♭7(♯11)
B♭ma7 B♭ma7 C7 C7
Cm7 F7alt. B♭ma7 B♭ma7

6.2.2. Ionian/Augmented

APPENDIX 6.2.2.
Ionian, Augmented via The R.P.S.
C Ionian
C Augmented Scale
C maj 7
D♭maj 7
D maj 7
E♭maj 7
E maj 7
F maj 7
G♭maj 7
G maj 7
A♭maj 7
A maj 7

2

APPENDIX 6.2.2.
Ionian, Augmented via The R.P.S.

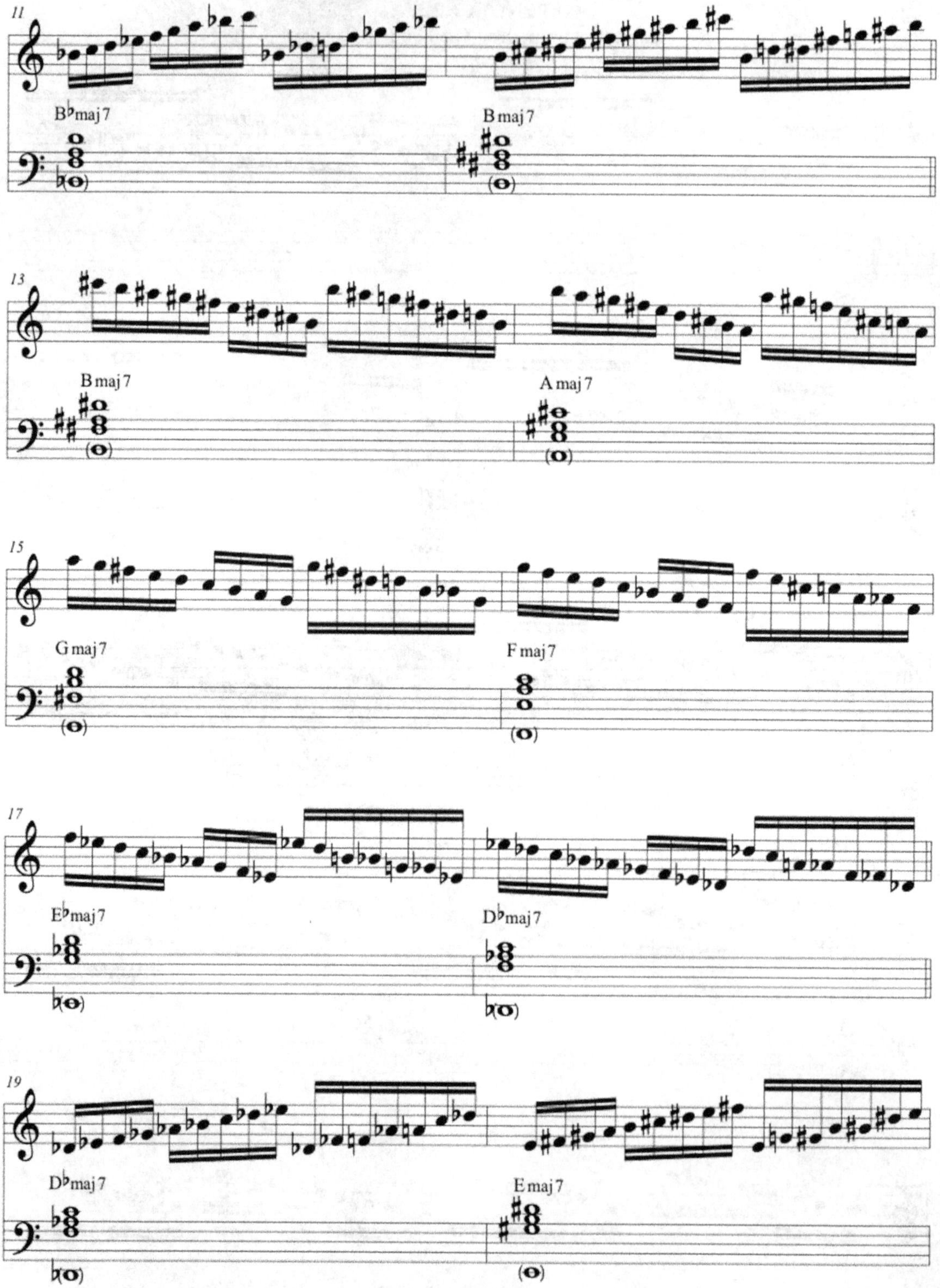
11
B♭maj7
Bmaj7
13
Bmaj7
Amaj7
15
Gmaj7
Fmaj7
17
E♭maj7
D♭maj7
19
D♭maj7
Emaj7

APPENDIX 6.2.2. 3

Ionian, Augmented via The R.P.S.

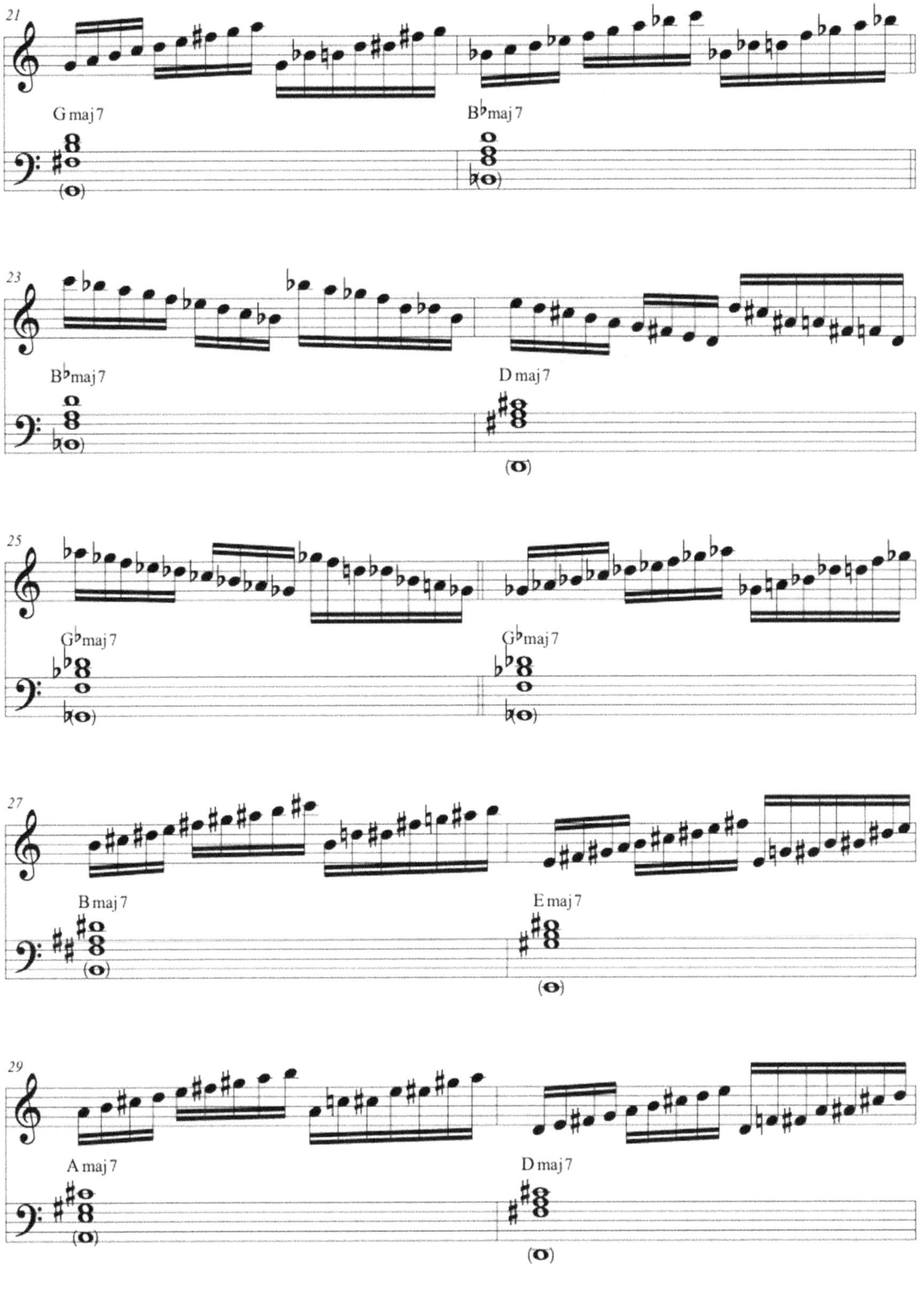
21
G maj 7
B♭maj 7
23
B♭maj 7
D maj 7
25
G♭maj 7
G♭maj 7
27
B maj 7
E maj 7
29
A maj 7
D maj 7

4

APPENDIX 6.2.2.
Ionian, Augmented via The R.P.S.

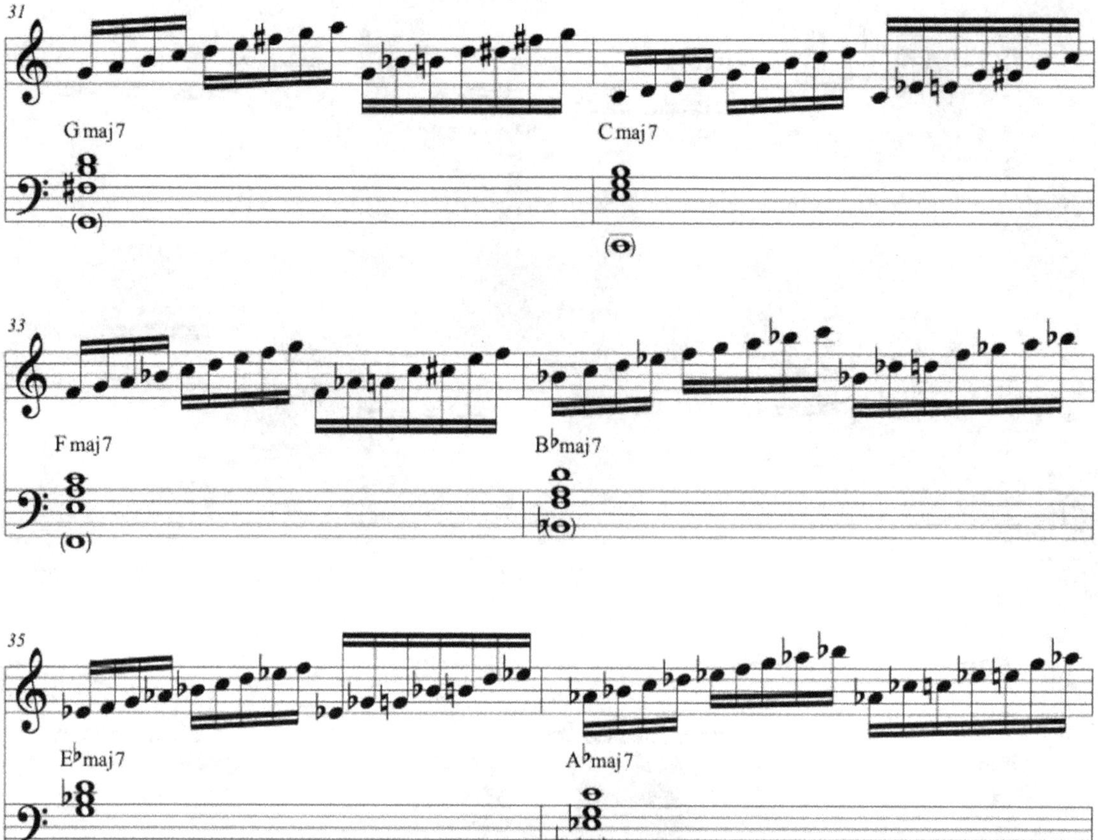
31
G maj7
C maj7
33
F maj7
B♭maj7
35
E♭maj7
A♭maj7
37
D♭maj7
D♭maj7
39
G maj7
G maj7

APPENDIX 6.2.2. 5

Ionian, Augmented via The R.P.S.

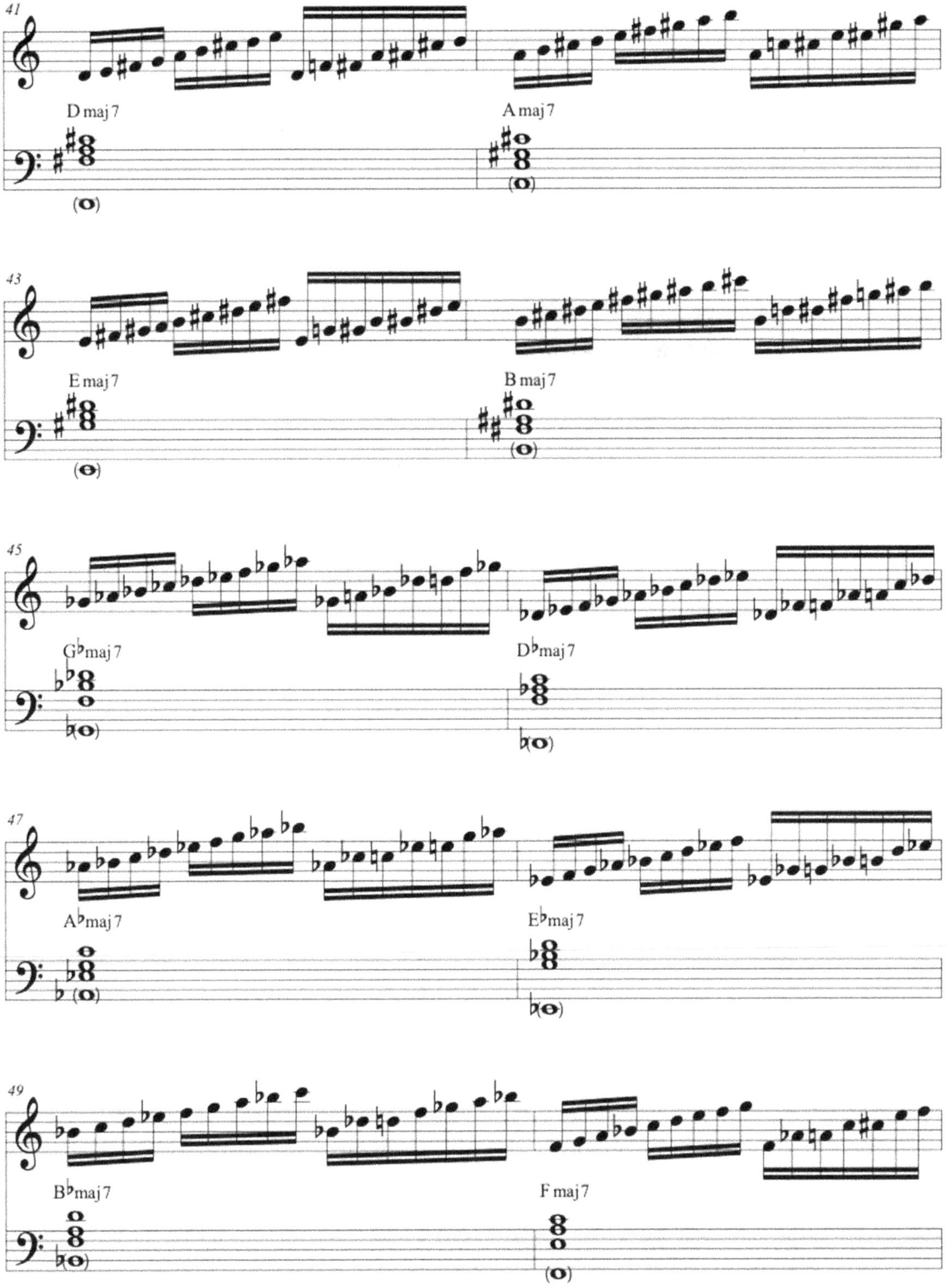
41
D maj 7
A maj 7
43
E maj 7
B maj 7
45
G♭maj 7
D♭maj 7
47
A♭maj 7
E♭maj 7
49
B♭maj 7
F maj 7

6

APPENDIX 6.2.2.
Ionian, Augmented via The R.P.S.

51
Cmaj7
Cmaj7
53
A♭maj7
Emaj7
55
Emaj7
D♭maj7
57
B♭maj7
Gmaj7
59
Gmaj7
Fmaj7

APPENDIX 6.2.2.
Ionian, Augmented via The R.P.S.

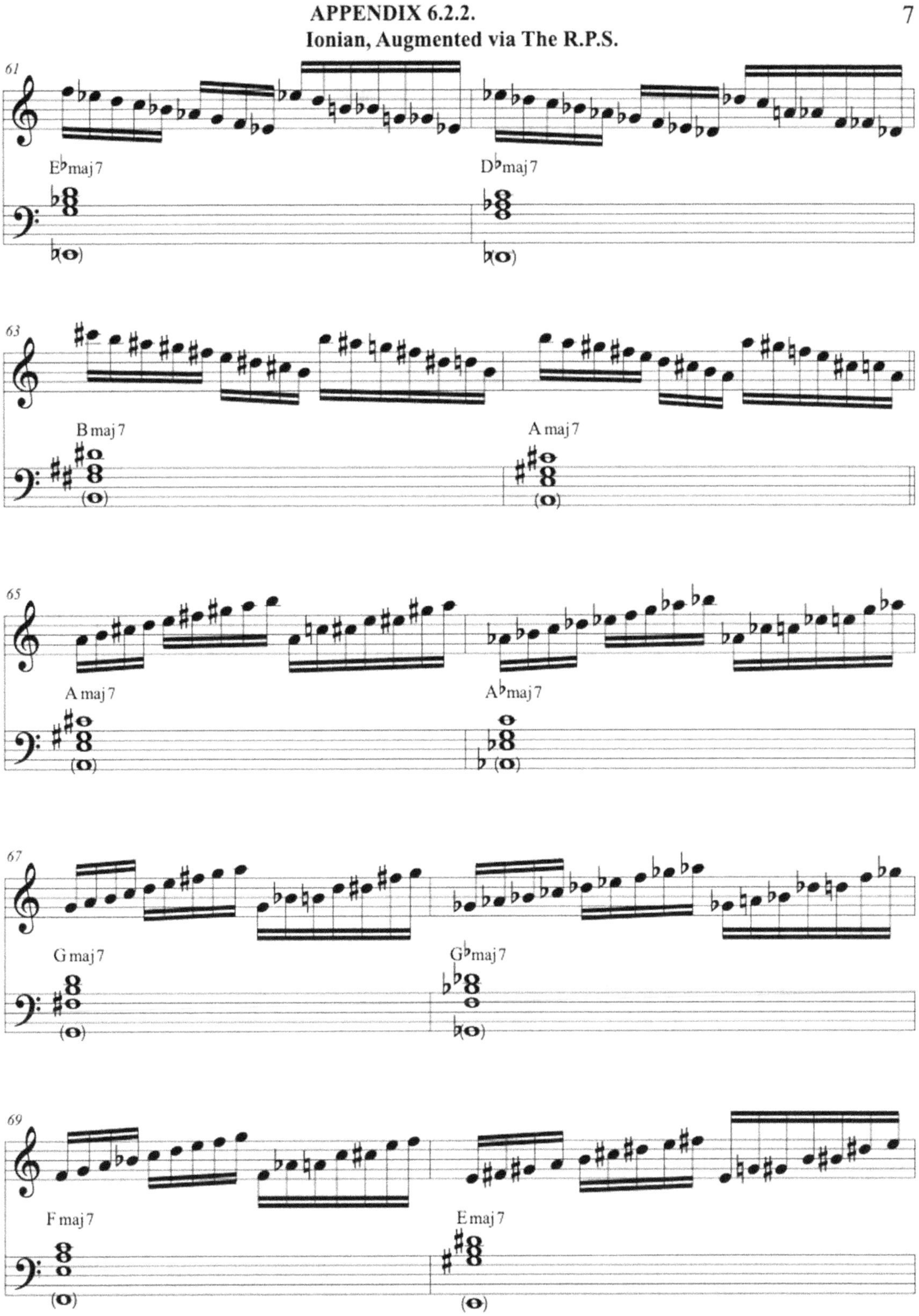
7
61
E♭maj7
D♭maj7
63
B maj7
A maj7
65
A maj7
A♭maj7
67
G maj7
G♭maj7
69
F maj7
E maj7

8

APPENDIX 6.2.2.
Ionian, Augmented via The R.P.S.

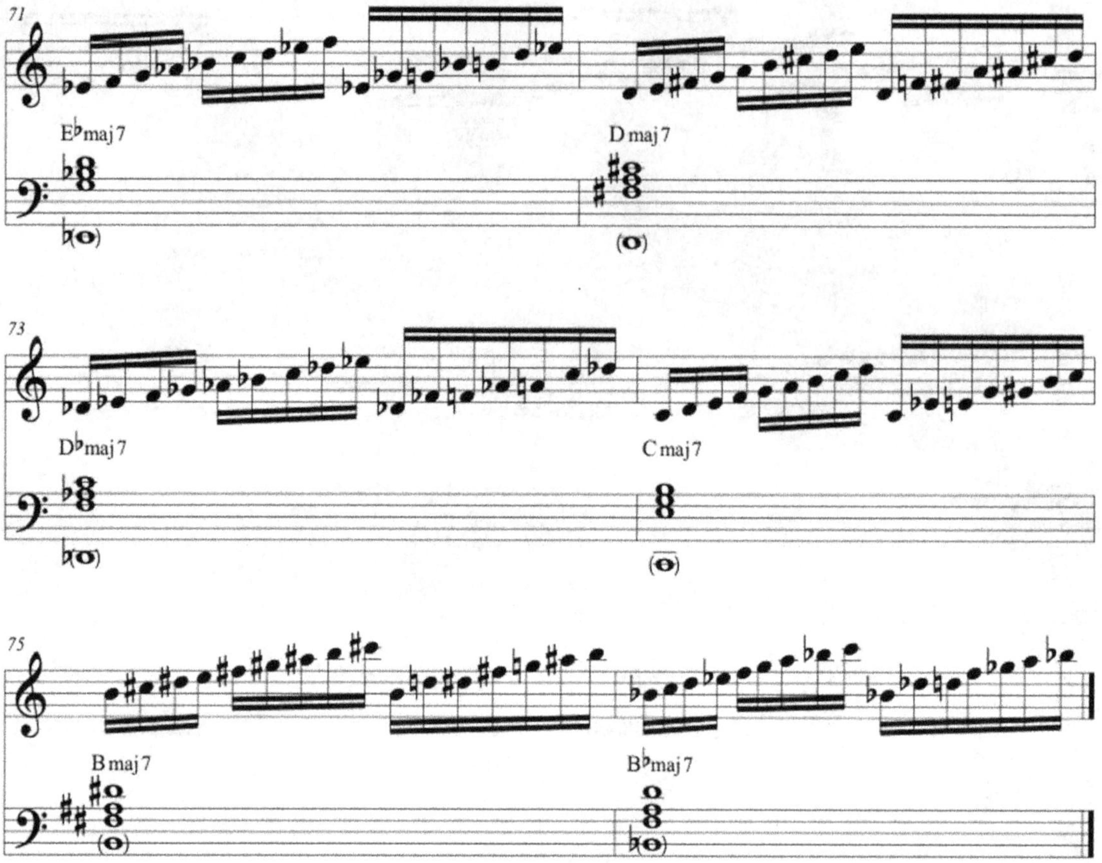

6.2.2.1 Aeolian

APPENDIX 6.2.2.1
Aeolian via The R.P.S.

C Aeolian
Cm♭6
Cm7
Cm9
Cm11
C♯m♭6
C♯m7
C♯m9
C♯m11
3
Dm♭6
Dm7
Dm9
Dm11
E♭m♭6
E♭m7
E♭m9
E♭m11
5
Em♭6
Em7
Em9
Em11
Fm♭6
Fm7
Fm9
Fm11
7
F♯m♭6
F♯m7
F♯m9
F♯m11
Gm♭6
Gm7
Gm9
Gm11
9
A♭m♭6
A♭m7
A♭m9
A♭m11
Am♭6
Am7
Am9
Am11

2

APPENDIX 6.2.2.1
Aeolian via The R.P.S.

11
B♭m♭6 B♭m7 B♭m9 B♭m11 Bm♭6 Bm7 Bm9 Bm11
13
Bm♭6 Bm7 Bm9 Bm11 Am♭6 Am7 Am9 Am11
15
Gm♭6 Gm7 Gm9 Gm11 Fm♭6 Fm7 Fm9 Fm11
17
E♭m♭6 E♭m7 E♭m9 E♭m11 C♯m♭6 C♯m7 C♯m9 C♯m11
19
C♯m♭6 C♯m7 C♯m9 C♯m11 Em♭6 Em7 Em9 Em11

APPENDIX 6.2.2.1 3
Aeolian via The R.P.S.

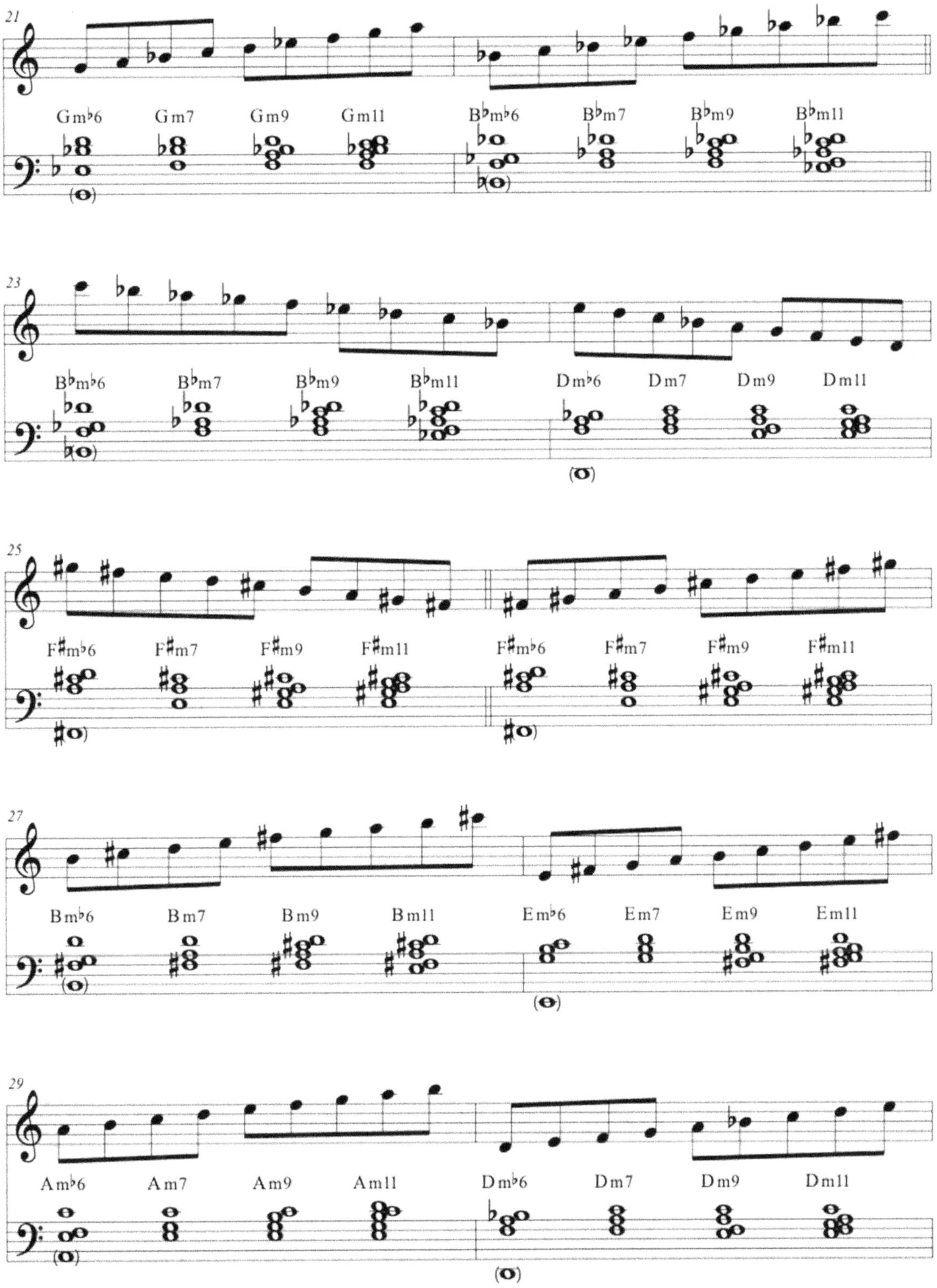
21
Gm♭6 Gm7 Gm9 Gm11 B♭m♭6 B♭m7 B♭m9 B♭m11
23
B♭m♭6 B♭m7 B♭m9 B♭m11 Dm♭6 Dm7 Dm9 Dm11
25
F♯m♭6 F♯m7 F♯m9 F♯m11 F♯m♭6 F♯m7 F♯m9 F♯m11
27
Bm♭6 Bm7 Bm9 Bm11 Em♭6 Em7 Em9 Em11
29
Am♭6 Am7 Am9 Am11 Dm♭6 Dm7 Dm9 Dm11

4

APPENDIX 6.2.2.1
Aeolian via The R.P.S.

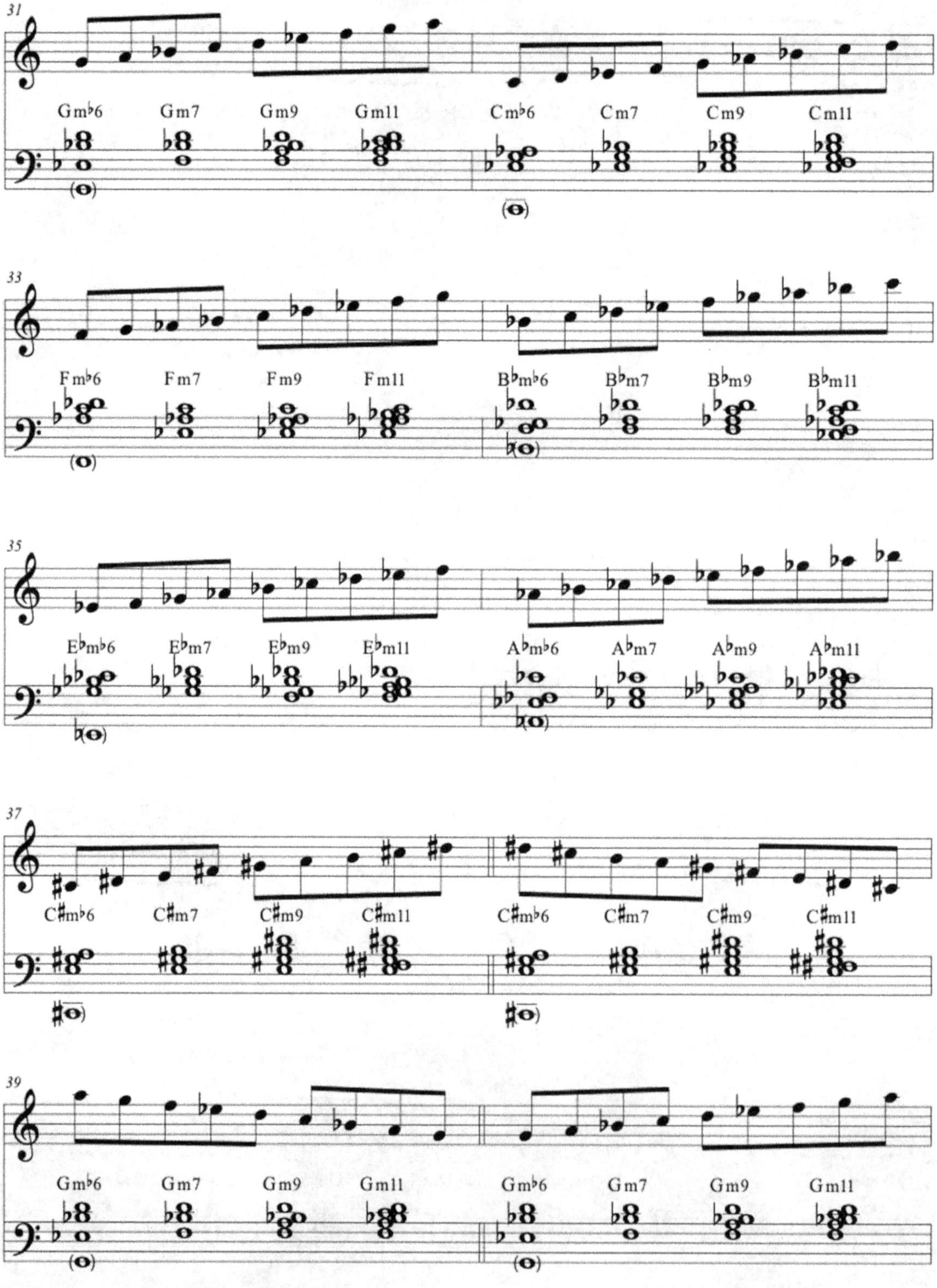
31
Gm♭6 Gm7 Gm9 Gm11
Cm♭6 Cm7 Cm9 Cm11
33
Fm♭6 Fm7 Fm9 Fm11
B♭m♭6 B♭m7 B♭m9 B♭m11
35
E♭m♭6 E♭m7 E♭m9 E♭m11
A♭m♭6 A♭m7 A♭m9 A♭m11
37
C♯m♭6 C♯m7 C♯m9 C♯m11
C♯m♭6 C♯m7 C♯m9 C♯m11
39
Gm♭6 Gm7 Gm9 Gm11
Gm♭6 Gm7 Gm9 Gm11

APPENDIX 6.2.2.1 5
Aeolian via The R.P.S.

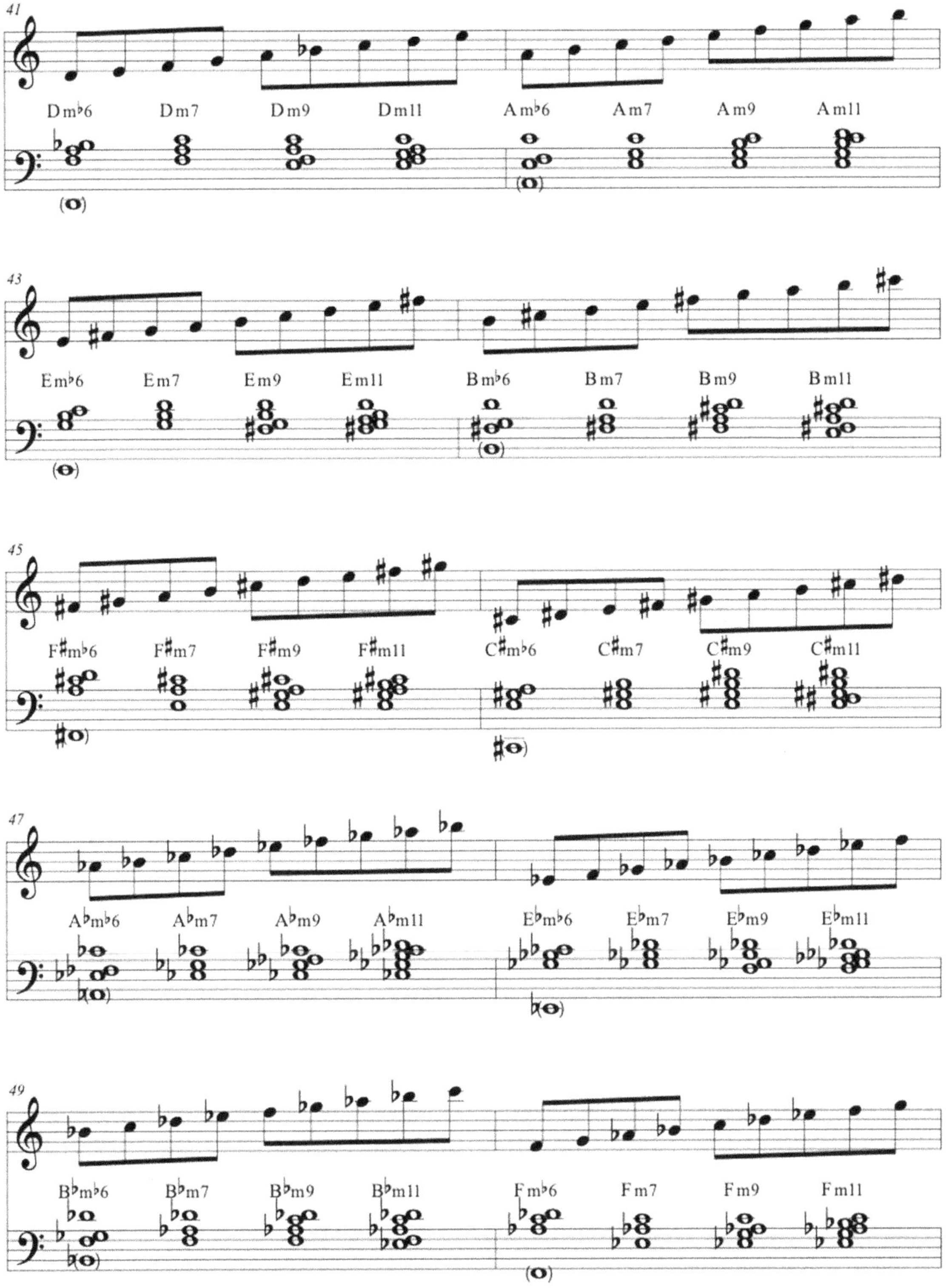
41
Dm♭6 Dm7 Dm9 Dm11 Am♭6 Am7 Am9 Am11
43
Em♭6 Em7 Em9 Em11 Bm♭6 Bm7 Bm9 Bm11
45
F♯m♭6 F♯m7 F♯m9 F♯m11 C♯m♭6 C♯m7 C♯m9 C♯m11
47
A♭m♭6 A♭m7 A♭m9 A♭m11 E♭m♭6 E♭m7 E♭m9 E♭m11
49
B♭m♭6 B♭m7 B♭m9 B♭m11 Fm♭6 Fm7 Fm9 Fm11

6

APPENDIX 6.2.2.1
Aeolian via The R.P.S.

51
Cm♭6 Cm7 Cm9 Cm11 Cm♭6 Cm7 Cm9 Cm11
53
A♭m♭6 A♭m7 A♭m9 A♭m11 Em♭6 Em7 Em9 Em11
55
Em♭6 Em7 Em9 Em11 C♯m♭6 C♯m7 C♯m9 C♯m11
57
B♭m♭6 B♭m7 B♭m9 B♭m11 Gm♭6 Gm7 Gm9 Gm11
59
Gm♭6 Gm7 Gm9 Gm11 Fm♭6 Fm7 Fm9 Fm11

APPENDIX 6.2.2.1 7

Aeolian via The R.P.S.

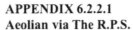

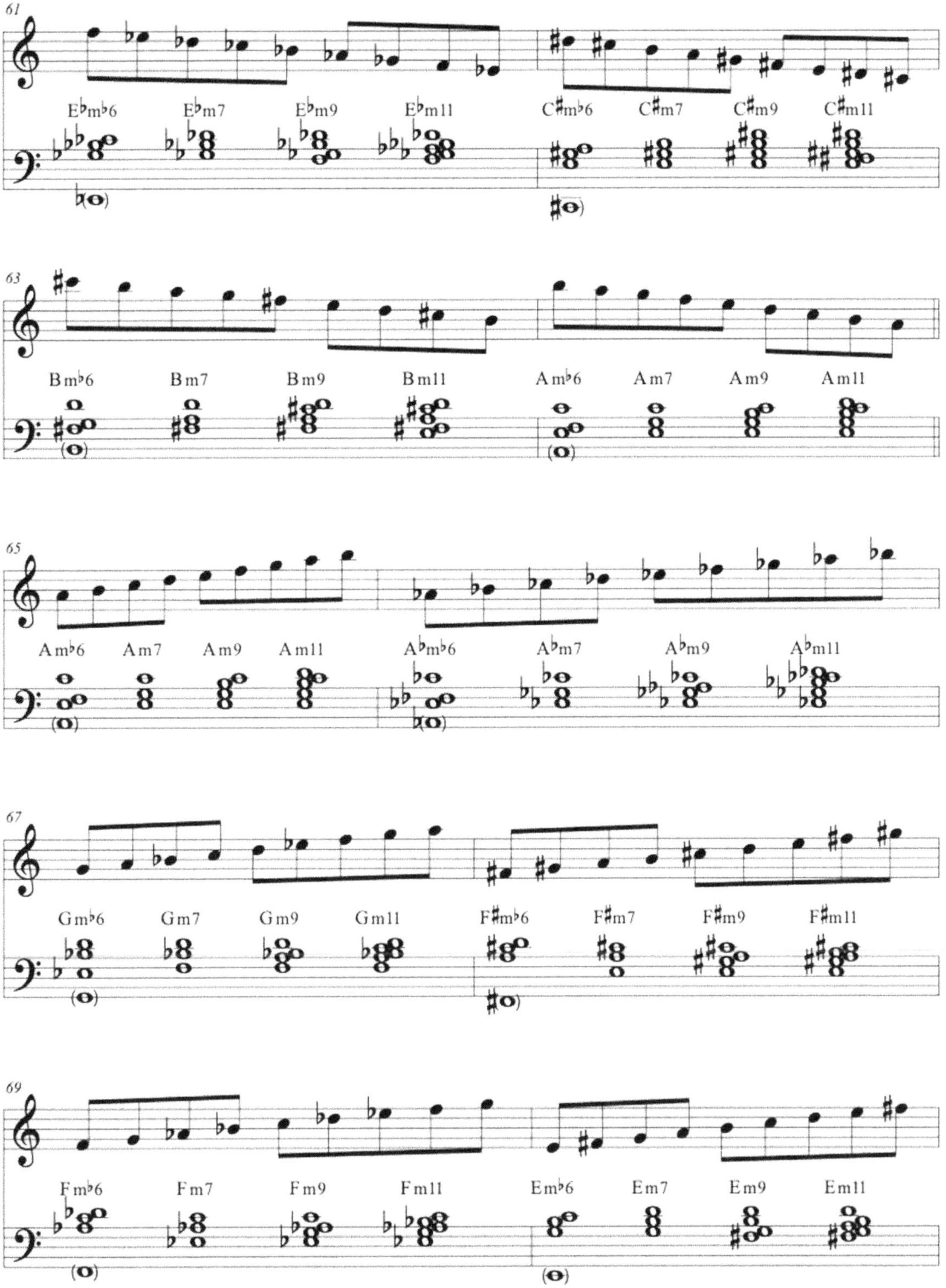
61
E♭m♭6 E♭m7 E♭m9 E♭m11 C♯m♭6 C♯m7 C♯m9 C♯m11
63
Bm♭6 Bm7 Bm9 Bm11 Am♭6 Am7 Am9 Am11
65
Am♭6 Am7 Am9 Am11 A♭m♭6 A♭m7 A♭m9 A♭m11
67
Gm♭6 Gm7 Gm9 Gm11 F♯m♭6 F♯m7 F♯m9 F♯m11
69
Fm♭6 Fm7 Fm9 Fm11 Em♭6 Em7 Em9 Em11

8

APPENDIX 6.2.2.1
Aeolian via The R.P.S.

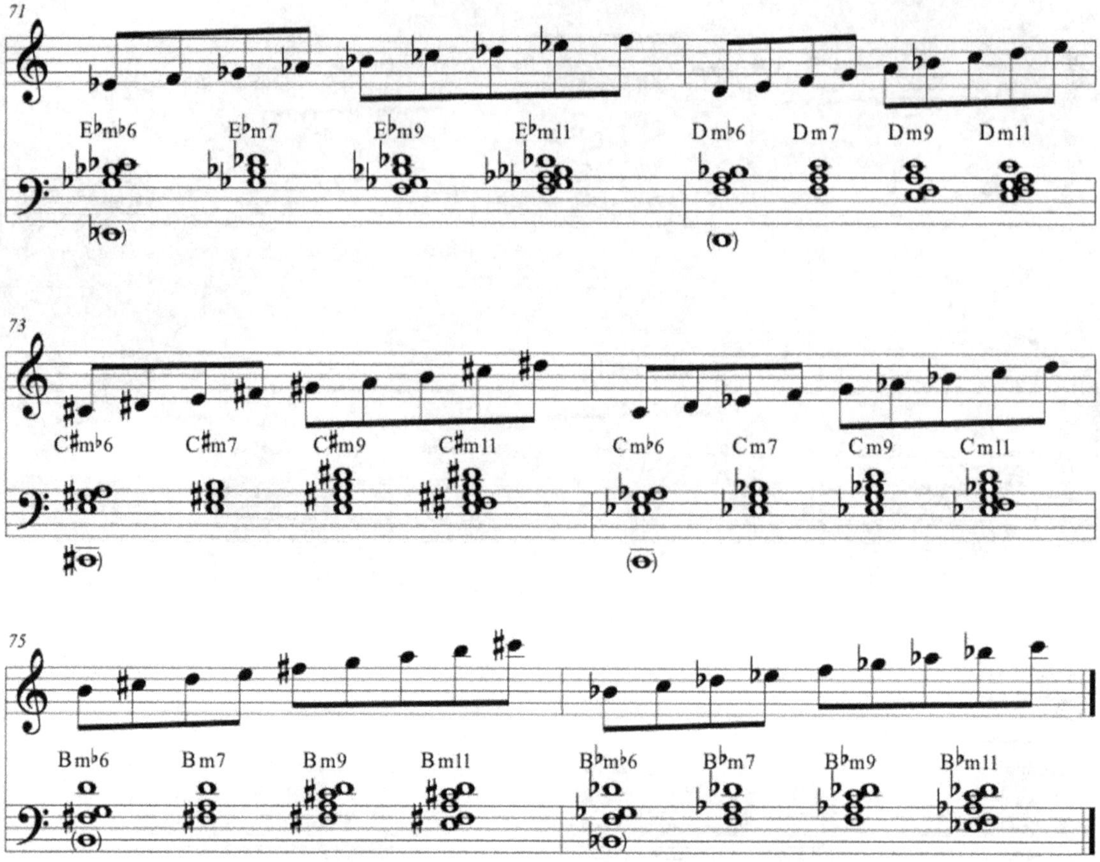
71
E♭m♭6
E♭m7
E♭m9
E♭m11
Dm♭6
Dm7
Dm9
Dm11
73
C♯m♭6
C♯m7
C♯m9
C♯m11
Cm♭6
Cm7
Cm9
Cm11
75
Bm♭6
Bm7
Bm9
Bm11
B♭m♭6
B♭m7
B♭m9
B♭m11

6.2.3. Major Augmented /Minor Equivalent

APPENDIX 6.2.3.
Major Augmented/Minor Equivalent via The R.P.S.

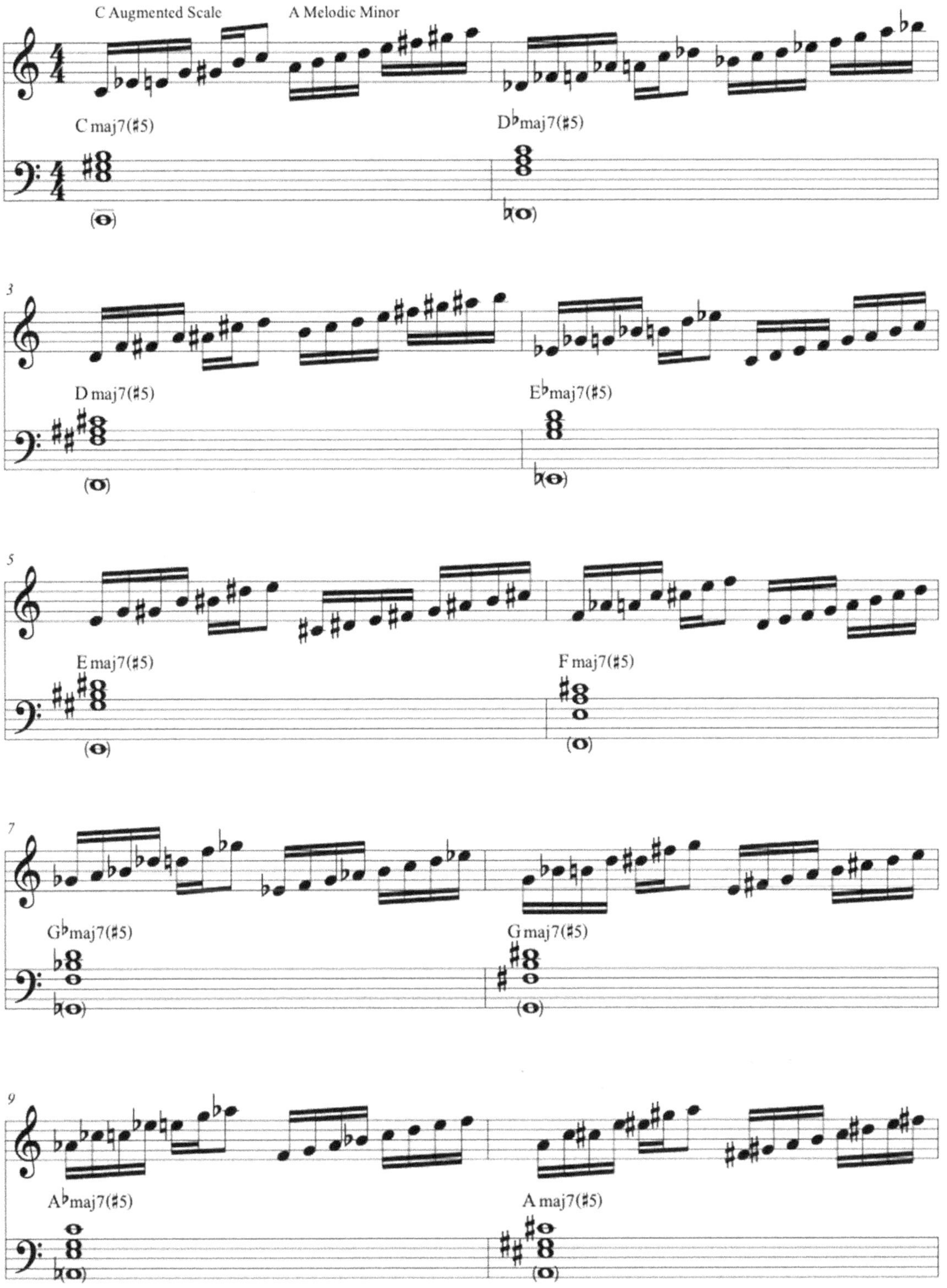

2

APPENDIX 6.2.3.
Major Augmented/Minor Equivalent via The R.P.S.

APPENDIX 6.2.3. 3

Major Augmented/Minor Equivalent via The R.P.S.

4

APPENDIX 6.2.3.
Major Augmented/Minor Equivalent via The R.P.S.

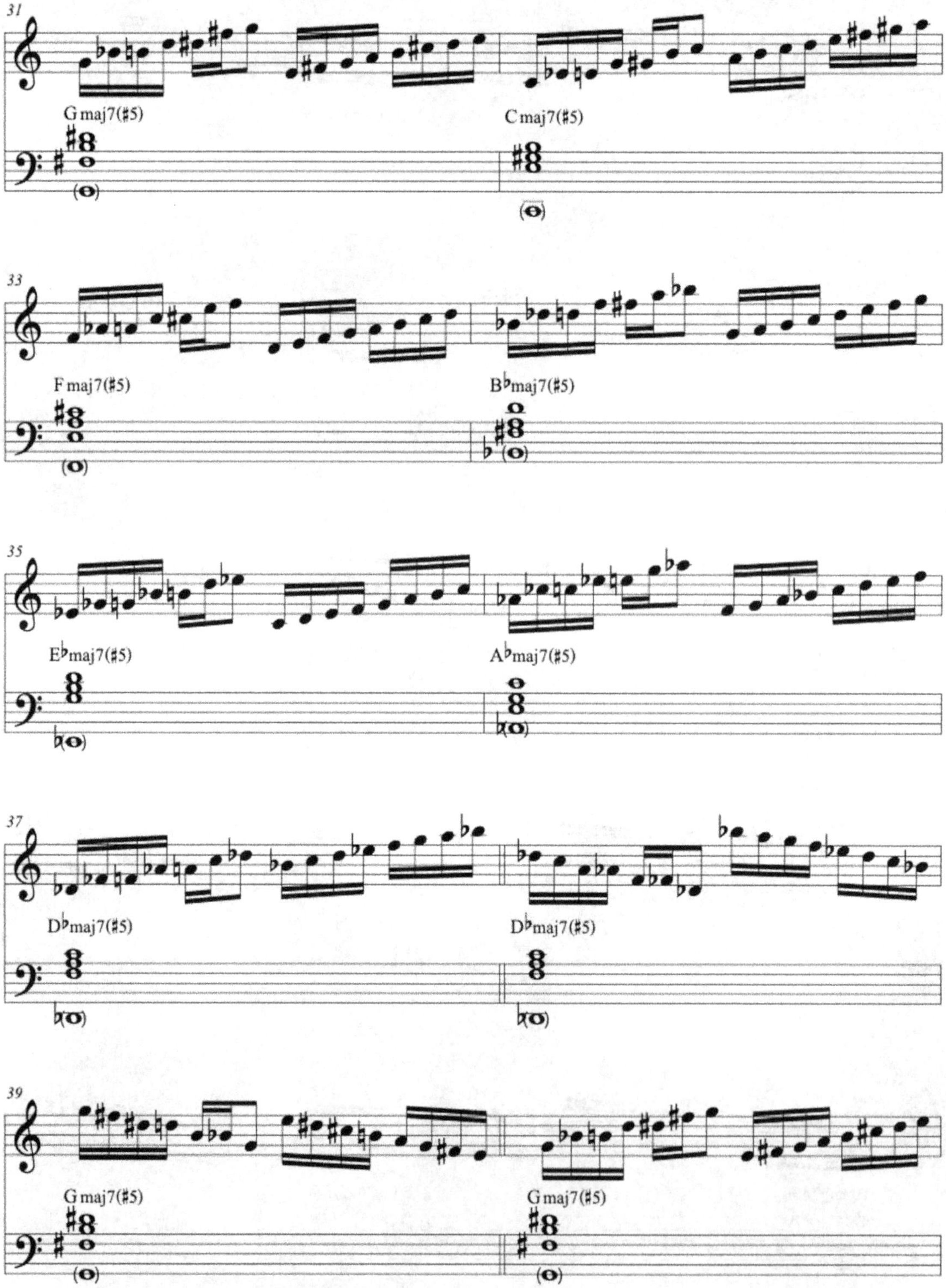

APPENDIX 6.2.3. 5

Major Augmented/Minor Equivalent via The R.P.S.

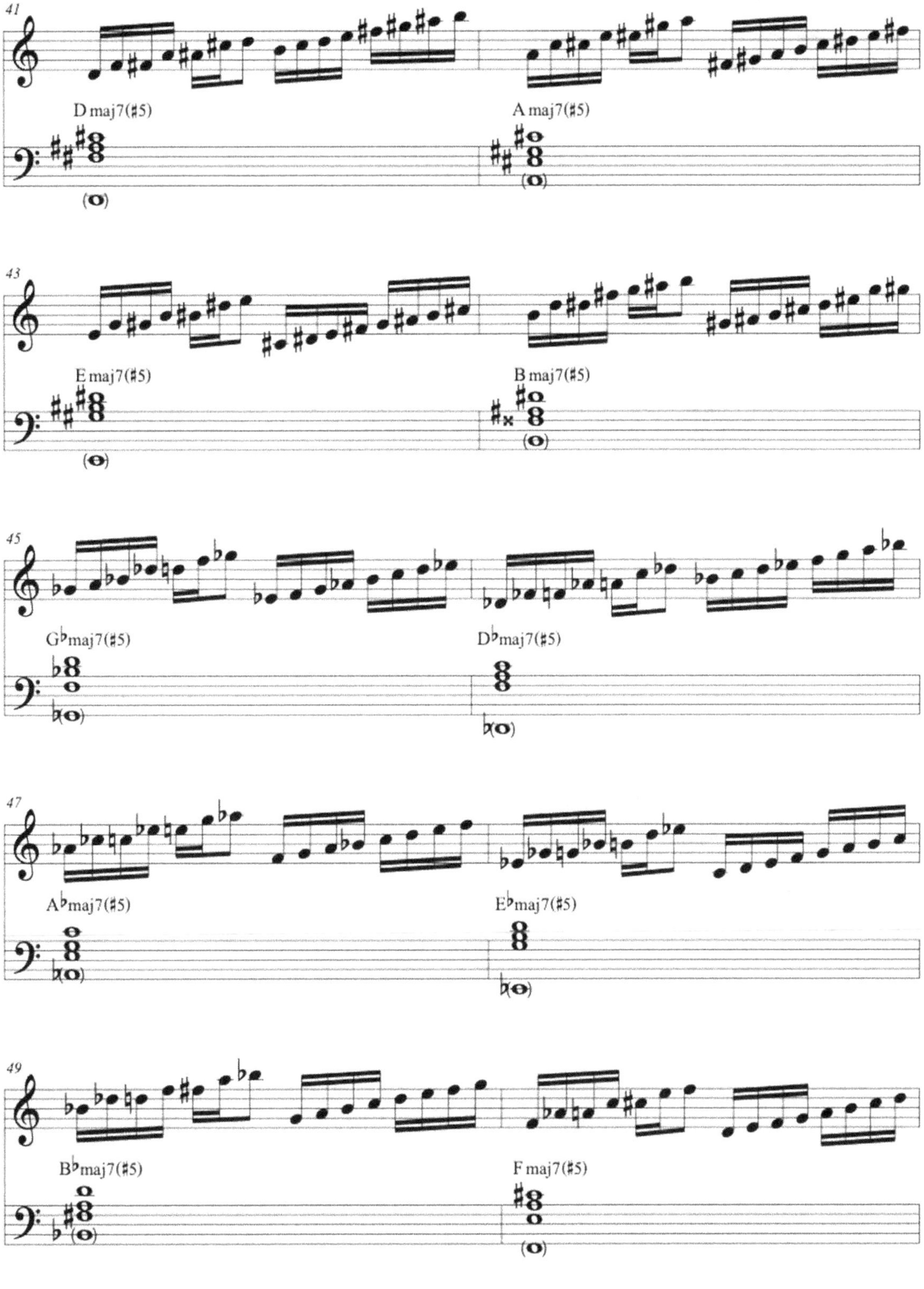

6

APPENDIX 6.2.3.
Major Augmented/Minor Equivalent via The R.P.S.

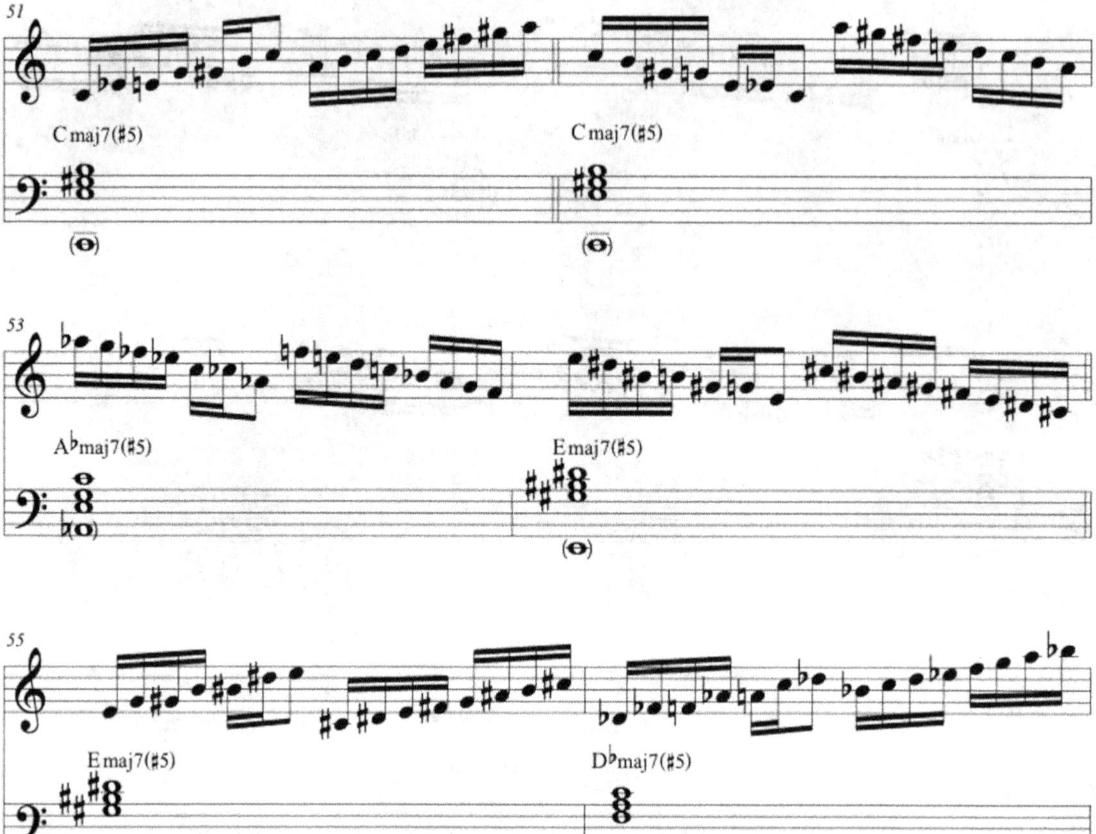

APPENDIX 6.2.3. 7

Major Augmented/Minor Equivalent via The R.P.S.

8

APPENDIX 6.2.3.
Major Augmented/Minor Equivalent via The R.P.S.

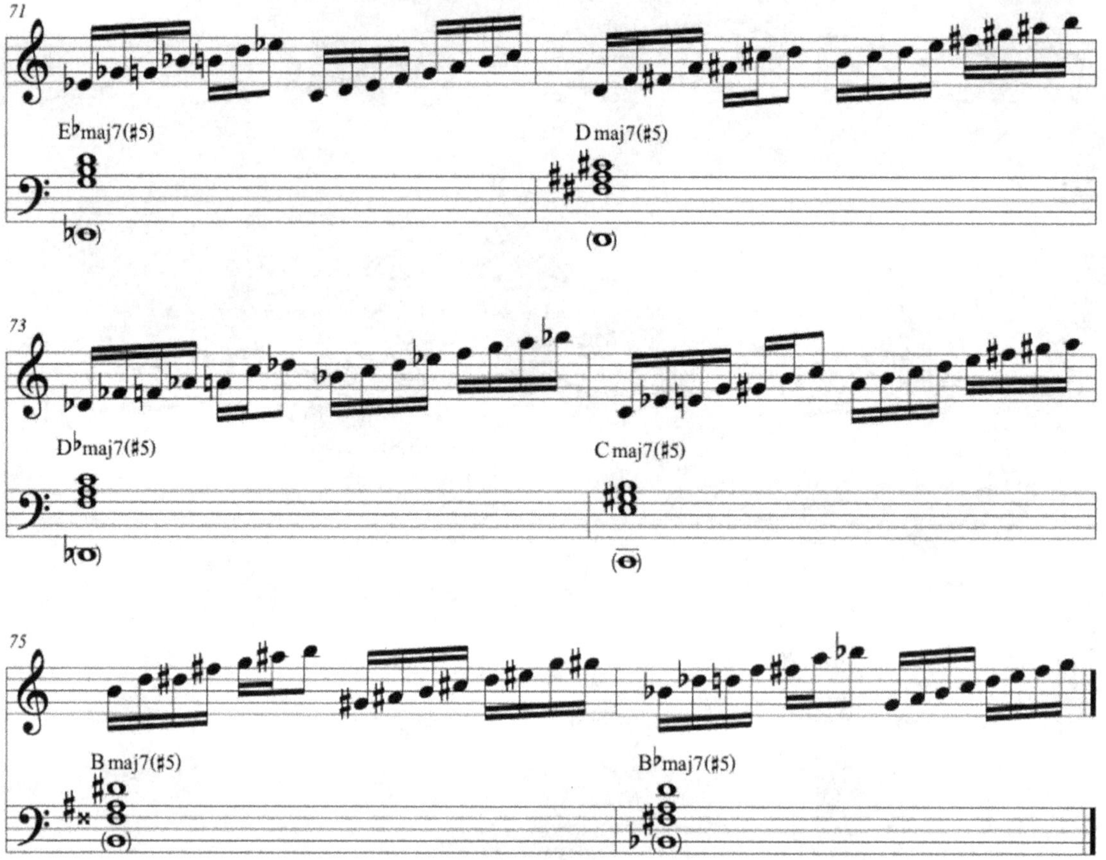

6.2.4. Dorian

Appendix 6.2.4.
Dorian via The R.P.S.

C Dorian
Cm6 Cm7 Cm9 Cm11 C♯m6 C♯m7 C♯m9 C♯m11
Dm6 Dm7 Dm9 Dm11 E♭m6 E♭m7 E♭m9 E♭m11
Em6 Em7 Em9 Em11 Fm6 Fm7 Fm9 Fm11
F♯m6 F♯m7 F♯m9 F♯m11 Gm6 Gm7 Gm9 Gm11
A♭m6 A♭m7 A♭m9 A♭m11 Am6 Am7 Am9 Am11

2

Appendix 6.2.4.
Dorian via The R.P.S.

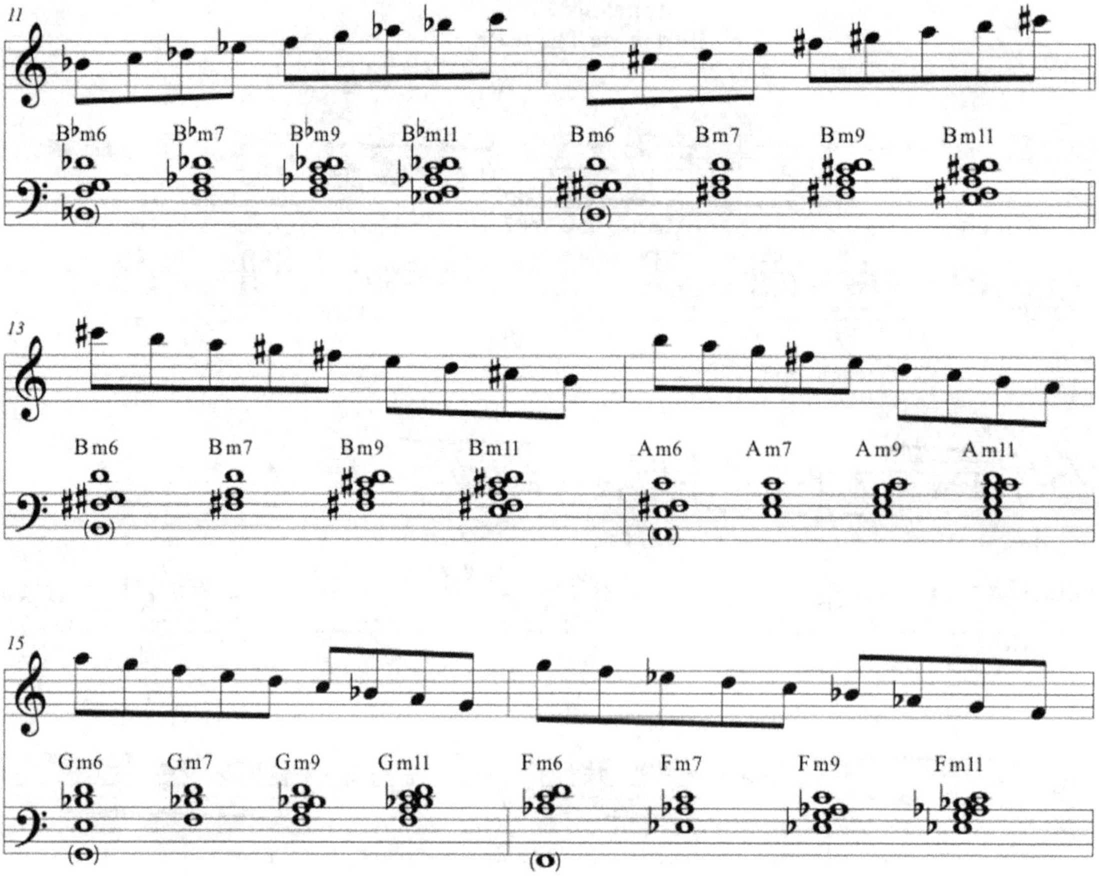
11
B♭m6 B♭m7 B♭m9 B♭m11 Bm6 Bm7 Bm9 Bm11
13
Bm6 Bm7 Bm9 Bm11 Am6 Am7 Am9 Am11
15
Gm6 Gm7 Gm9 Gm11 Fm6 Fm7 Fm9 Fm11
17
E♭m6 E♭m7 E♭m9 E♭m11 C♯m6 C♯m7 C♯m9 C♯m11
19
C♯m6 C♯m7 C♯m9 C♯m11 Em6 Em7 Em9 Em11

Appendix 6.2.4. 3

Dorian via The R.P.S.

21
Gm6 Gm7 Gm9 Gm11 B♭m6 B♭m7 B♭m9 B♭m11
23
B♭m6 B♭m7 B♭m9 B♭m11 Dm6 Dm7 Dm9 Dm11
25
F♯m6 F♯m7 F♯m9 F♯m11 F♯m6 F♯m7 F♯m9 F♯m11
27
Bm6 Bm7 Bm9 Bm11 Em6 Em7 Em9 Em11
29
Am6 Am7 Am9 Am11 Dm6 Dm7 Dm9 Dm11

4

Appendix 6.2.4.
Dorian via The R.P.S.

31
Gm6 Gm7 Gm9 Gm11
Cm6 Cm7 Cm9 Cm11
33
Fm6 Fm7 Fm9 Fm11
B♭m6 B♭m7 B♭m9 B♭m11
35
E♭m6 E♭m7 E♭m9 E♭m11
A♭m6 A♭m7 A♭m9 A♭m11
37
C♯m6 C♯m7 C♯m9 C♯m11
C♯m6 C♯m7 C♯m9 C♯m11
39
Gm6 Gm7 Gm9 Gm11
Gm6 Gm7 Gm9 Gm11

Appendix 6.2.4. 5

Dorian via The R.P.S.

41
Dm6 Dm7 Dm9 Dm11 Am6 Am7 Am9 Am11
43
Em6 Em7 Em9 Em11 Bm6 Bm7 Bm9 Bm11
45
F♯m6 F♯m7 F♯m9 F♯m11 C♯m6 C♯m7 C♯m9 C♯m11
47
A♭m6 A♭m7 A♭m9 A♭m11 E♭m6 E♭m7 E♭m9 E♭m11
49
B♭m6 B♭m7 B♭m9 B♭m11 Fm6 Fm7 Fm9 Fm11

6

Appendix 6.2.4.
Dorian via The R.P.S.

51
Cm6 Cm7 Cm9 Cm11 Cm6 Cm7 Cm9 Cm11
53
A♭m6 A♭m7 A♭m9 A♭m11 Em6 Em7 Em9 Em11
55
Em6 Em7 Em9 Em11 C♯m6 C♯m7 C♯m9 C♯m11
57
B♭m6 B♭m7 B♭m9 B♭m11 Gm6 Gm7 Gm9 Gm11
59
Gm6 Gm7 Gm9 Gm11 Fm6 Fm7 Fm9 Fm11

Appendix 6.2.4.
Dorian via The R.P.S.

7

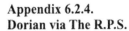

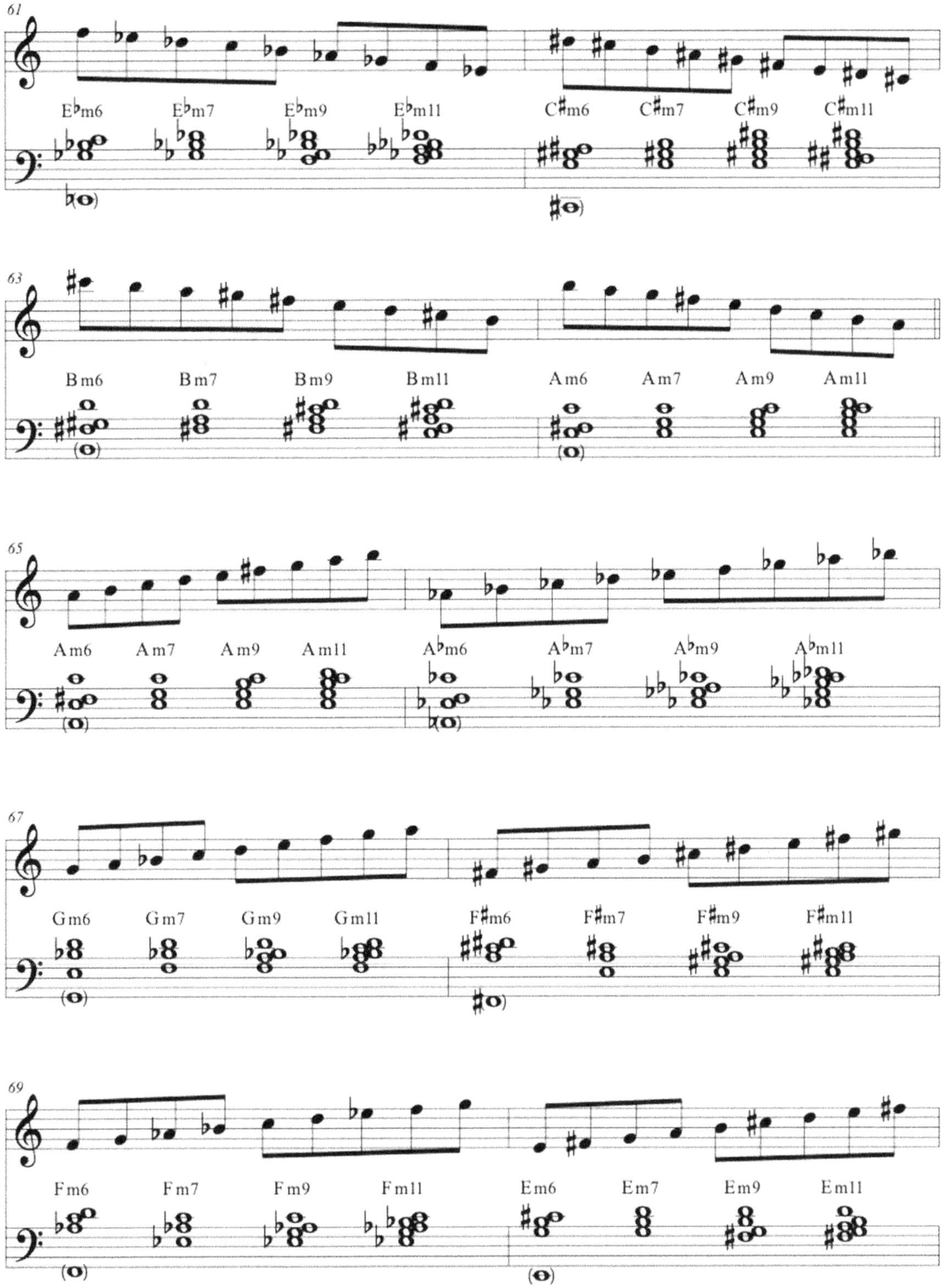
61
E♭m6 E♭m7 E♭m9 E♭m11
C♯m6 C♯m7 C♯m9 C♯m11
63
Bm6 Bm7 Bm9 Bm11
Am6 Am7 Am9 Am11
65
Am6 Am7 Am9 Am11
A♭m6 A♭m7 A♭m9 A♭m11
67
Gm6 Gm7 Gm9 Gm11
F♯m6 F♯m7 F♯m9 F♯m11
69
Fm6 Fm7 Fm9 Fm11
Em6 Em7 Em9 Em11

Appendix 6.2.4.
Dorian via The R.P.S.

71
E♭m6
E♭m7
E♭m9
E♭m11
Dm6
Dm7
Dm9
Dm11
73
C♯m6
C♯m7
C♯m9
C♯m11
Cm6
Cm7
Cm9
Cm11
75
Bm6
Bm7
Bm9
Bm11
B♭m6
B♭m7
B♭m9
B♭m11

6.2.5. Major Lydian

APPENDIX 6.2.5.
Major Lydian via The R.P.S.

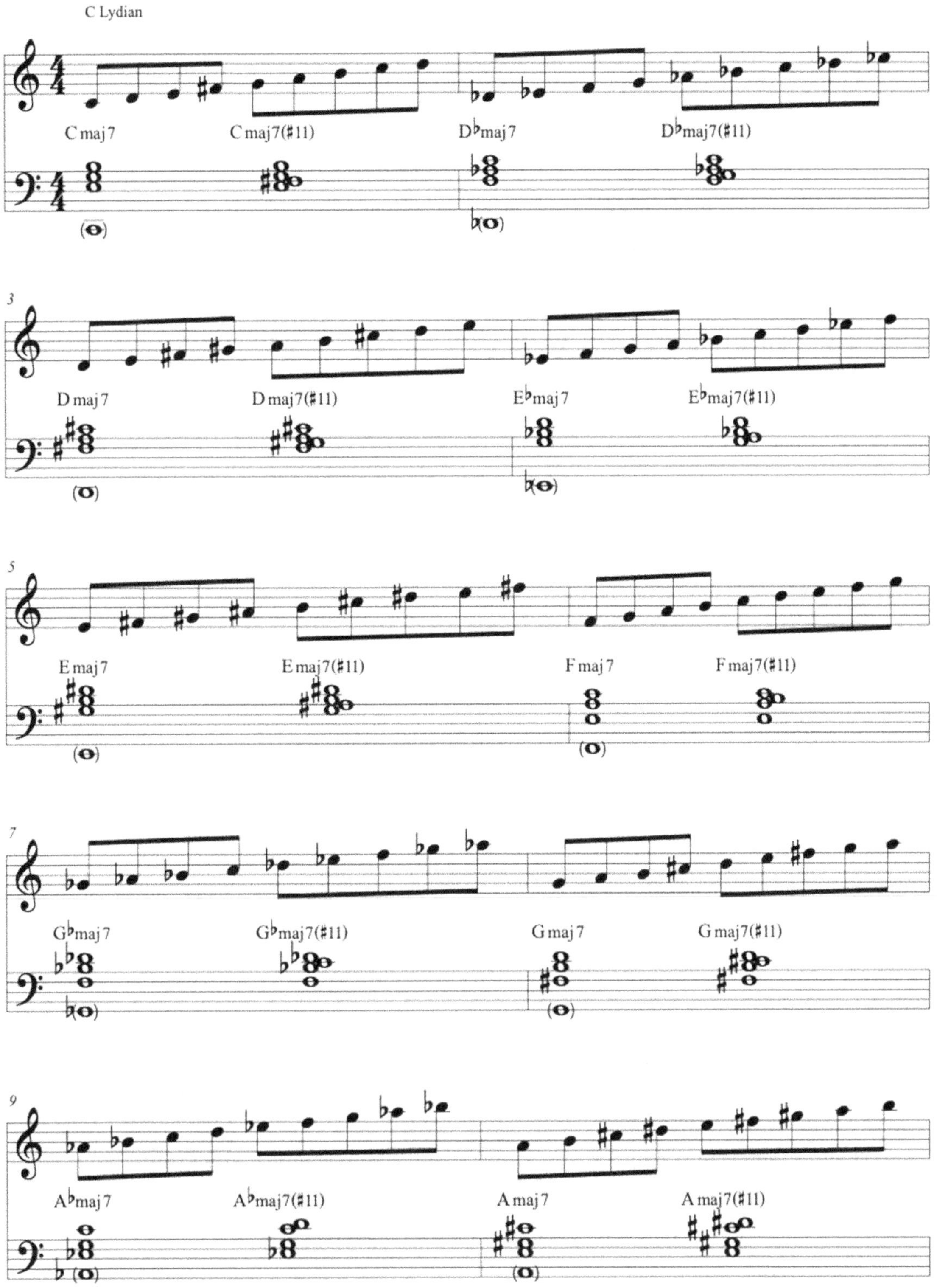

2

APPENDIX 6.2.5.
Major Lydian via The R.P.S.

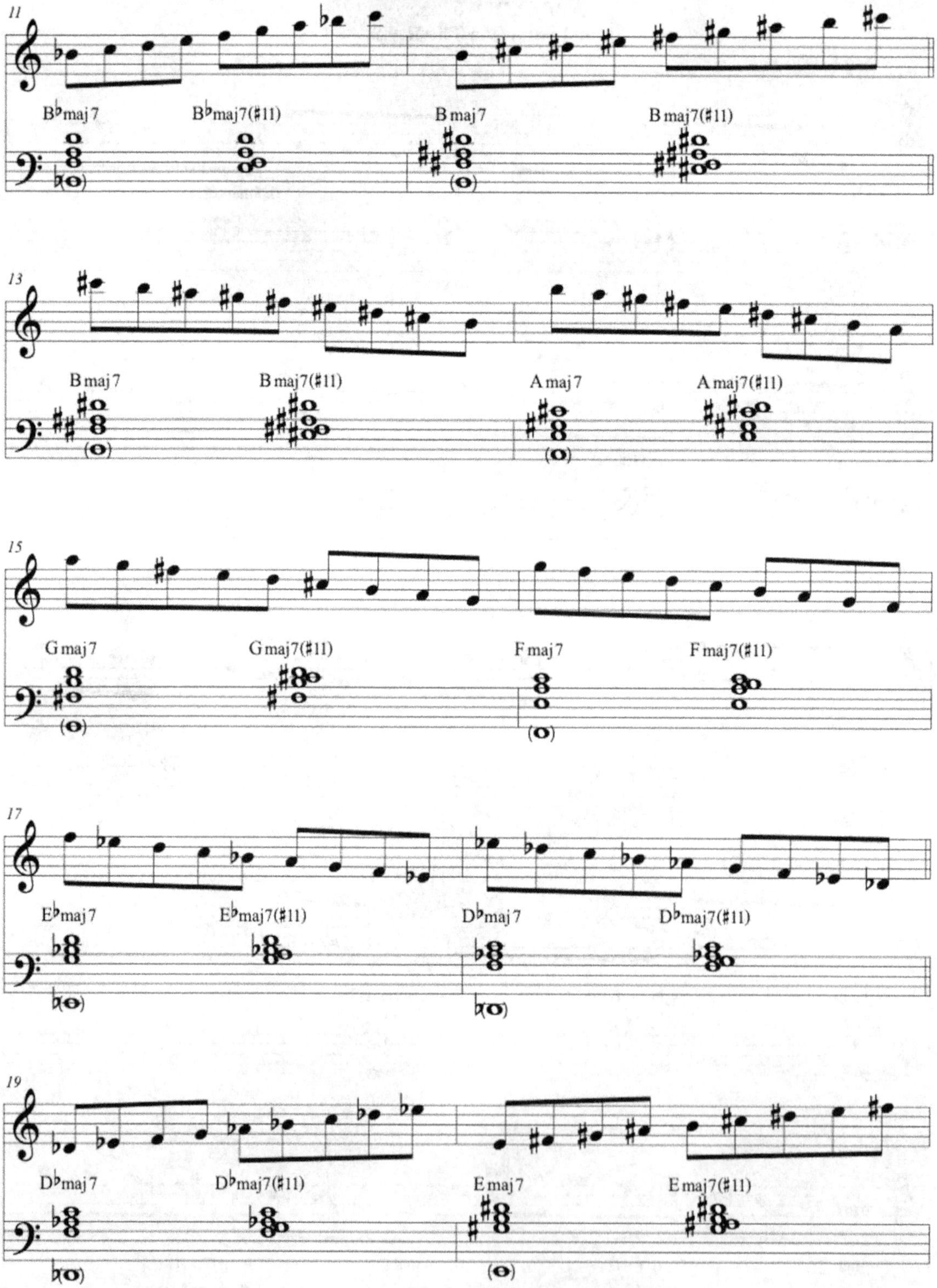
11
B♭maj7
B♭maj7(♯11)
B maj7
B maj7(♯11)
13
B maj7
B maj7(♯11)
A maj7
A maj7(♯11)
15
G maj7
G maj7(♯11)
F maj7
F maj7(♯11)
17
E♭maj7
E♭maj7(♯11)
D♭maj7
D♭maj7(♯11)
19
D♭maj7
D♭maj7(♯11)
E maj7
E maj7(♯11)

APPENDIX 6.2.5. 3

Major Lydian via The R.P.S.

21
Gmaj7
Gmaj7(♯11)
B♭maj7
B♭maj7(♯11)
23
B♭maj7
B♭maj7(♯11)
Dmaj7
Dmaj7(♯11)
25
G♭maj7
G♭maj7(♯11)
G♭maj7
G♭maj7(♯11)
27
Bmaj7
Bmaj7(♯11)
Emaj7
Emaj7(♯11)
29
Amaj7
Amaj7(♯11)
Dmaj7
Dmaj7(♯11)

4

APPENDIX 6.2.5.
Major Lydian via The R.P.S.

31
Gmaj7
Gmaj7(♯11)
Cmaj7
Cmaj7(♯11)
33
Fmaj7
Fmaj7(♯11)
B♭maj7
B♭maj7(♯11)
35
E♭maj7
E♭maj7(♯11)
A♭maj7
A♭maj7(♯11)
37
D♭maj7
D♭maj7(♯11)
D♭maj7
D♭maj7(♯11)
39
Gmaj7
Gmaj7(♯11)
Gmaj7
Gmaj7(♯11)

APPENDIX 6.2.5. 5

Major Lydian via The R.P.S.

41
D maj 7
D maj 7(♯11)
A maj 7
A maj 7(♯11)
43
E maj 7
E maj 7(♯11)
B maj 7
B maj 7(♯11)
45
G♭maj 7
G♭maj 7(♯11)
D♭maj 7
D♭maj 7(♯11)
47
A♭maj 7
A♭maj 7(♯11)
E♭maj 7
E♭maj 7(♯11)
49
B♭maj 7
B♭maj 7(♯11)
F maj 7
F maj 7(♯11)

6

APPENDIX 6.2.5.
Major Lydian via The R.P.S.

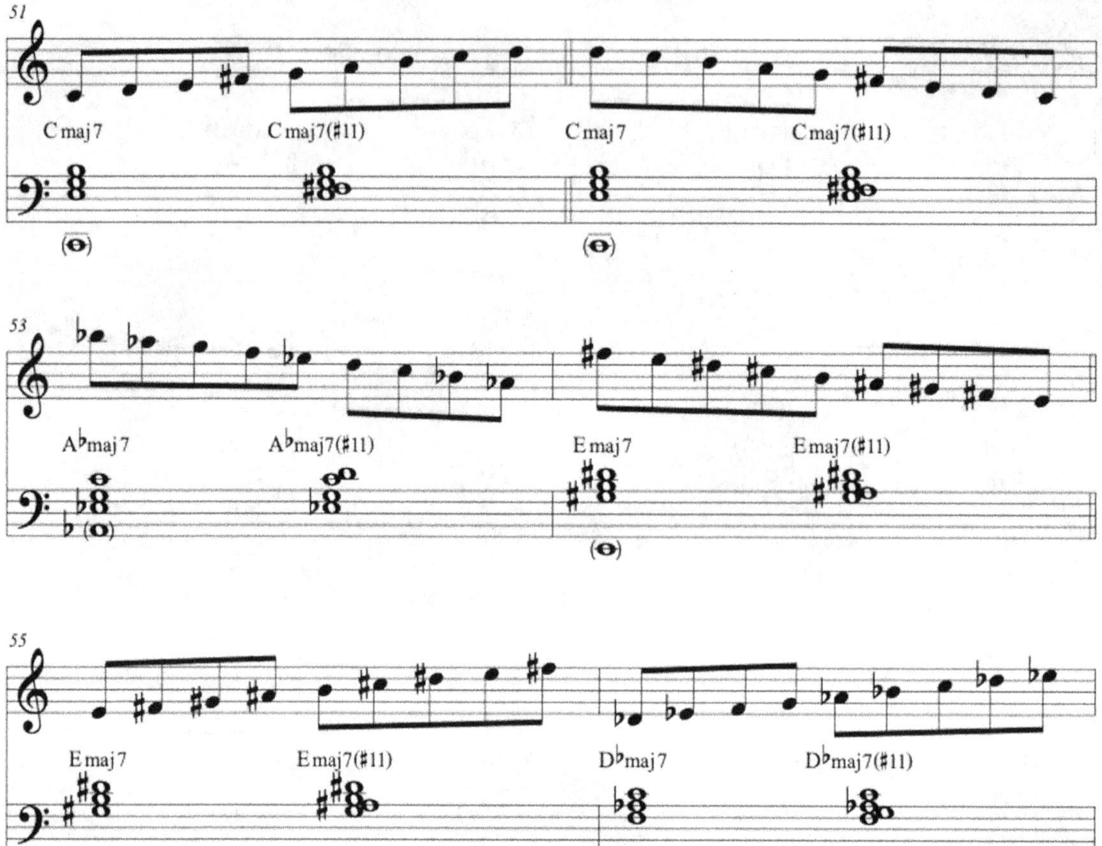
51
Cmaj7
Cmaj7(♯11)
Cmaj7
Cmaj7(♯11)
53
A♭maj7
A♭maj7(♯11)
Emaj7
Emaj7(♯11)
55
Emaj7
Emaj7(♯11)
D♭maj7
D♭maj7(♯11)
57
B♭maj7
B♭maj7(♯11)
Gmaj7
Gmaj7(♯11)
59
Gmaj7
Gmaj7(♯11)
Fmaj7
Fmaj7(♯11)

APPENDIX 6.2.5.
Major Lydian via The R.P.S.

7

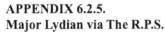

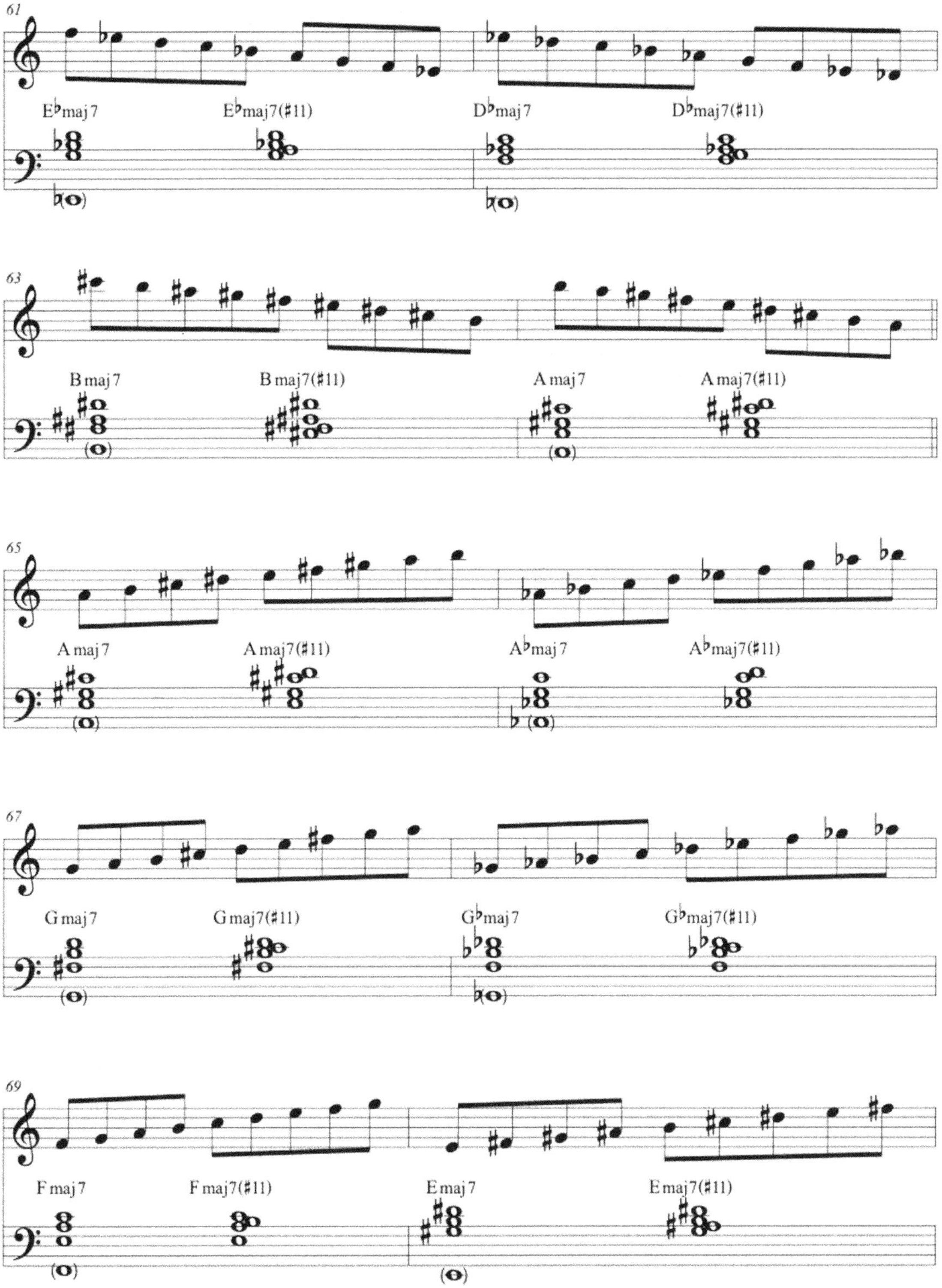
61
E♭maj7
E♭maj7(♯11)
D♭maj7
D♭maj7(♯11)
63
B maj7
B maj7(♯11)
A maj7
A maj7(♯11)
65
A maj7
A maj7(♯11)
A♭maj7
A♭maj7(♯11)
67
G maj7
G maj7(♯11)
G♭maj7
G♭maj7(♯11)
69
F maj7
F maj7(♯11)
E maj7
E maj7(♯11)

8

APPENDIX 6.2.5.
Major Lydian via The R.P.S.

71
E♭maj7
E♭maj7(♯11)
D maj7
D maj7(♯11)
73
D♭maj7
D♭maj7(♯11)
C maj7
C maj7(♯11)
75
B maj7
B maj7(♯11)
B♭maj7
B♭maj7(♯11)

6.2.6. Mixolydian

APPENDIX 6.2.6.
Mixolydian via The R.P.S.

2

APPENDIX 6.2.6.
Mixolydian via The R.P.S.

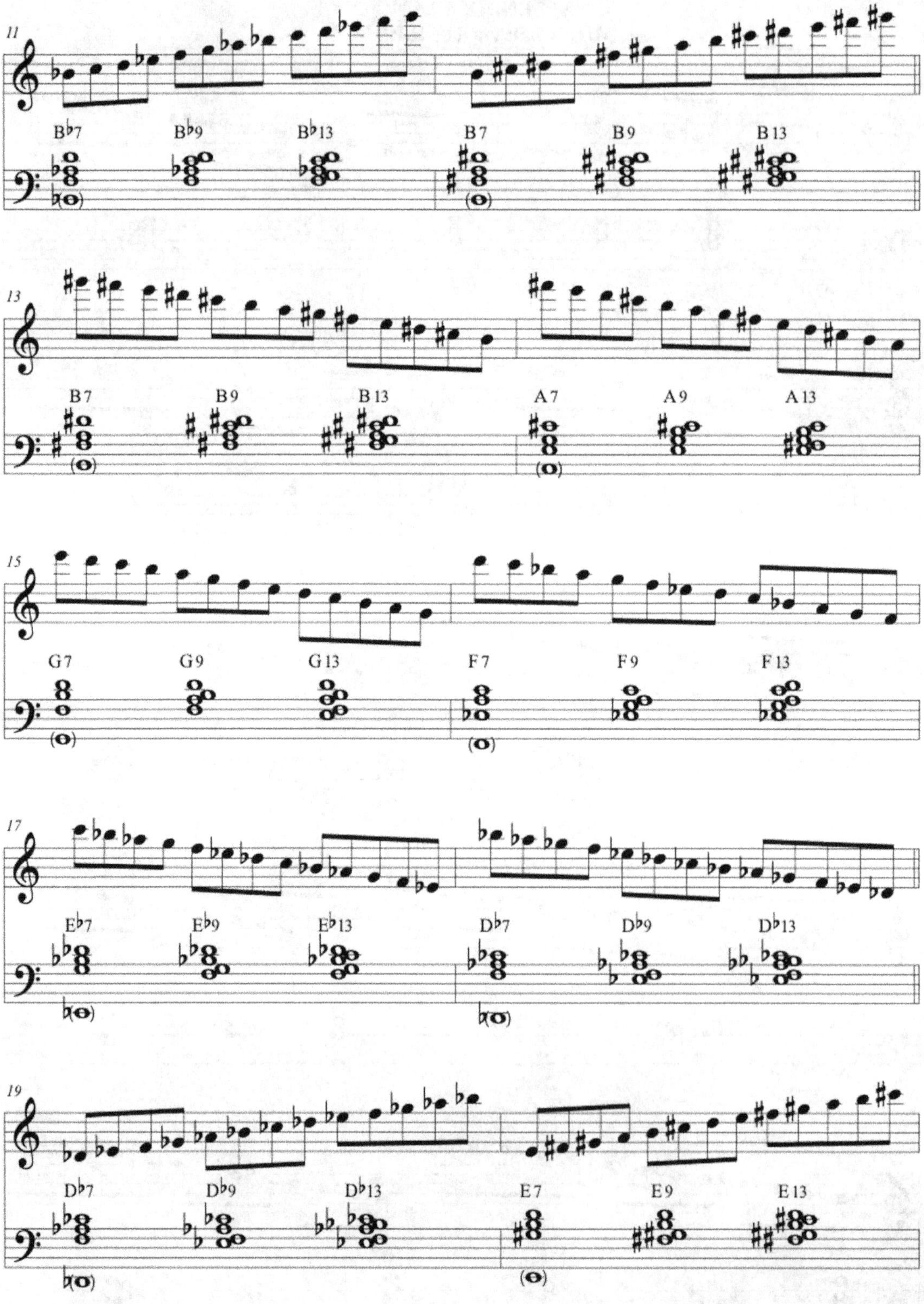
11
B♭7
B♭9
B♭13
B7
B9
B13
13
B7
B9
B13
A7
A9
A13
15
G7
G9
G13
F7
F9
F13
17
E♭7
E♭9
E♭13
D♭7
D♭9
D♭13
19
D♭7
D♭9
D♭13
E7
E9
E13

APPENDIX 6.2.6.
Mixolydian via The R.P.S.

3

21
G7 G9 G13 B♭7 B♭9 B♭13
23
B♭7 B♭9 B♭13 D7 D9 D13
25
F♯7 F♯9 F♯13 F♯7 F♯9 F♯13
27
B7 B9 B13 E7 E9 E13
29
A7 A9 A13 D7 D9 D13

APPENDIX 6.2.6.
Mixolydian via The R.P.S.

4

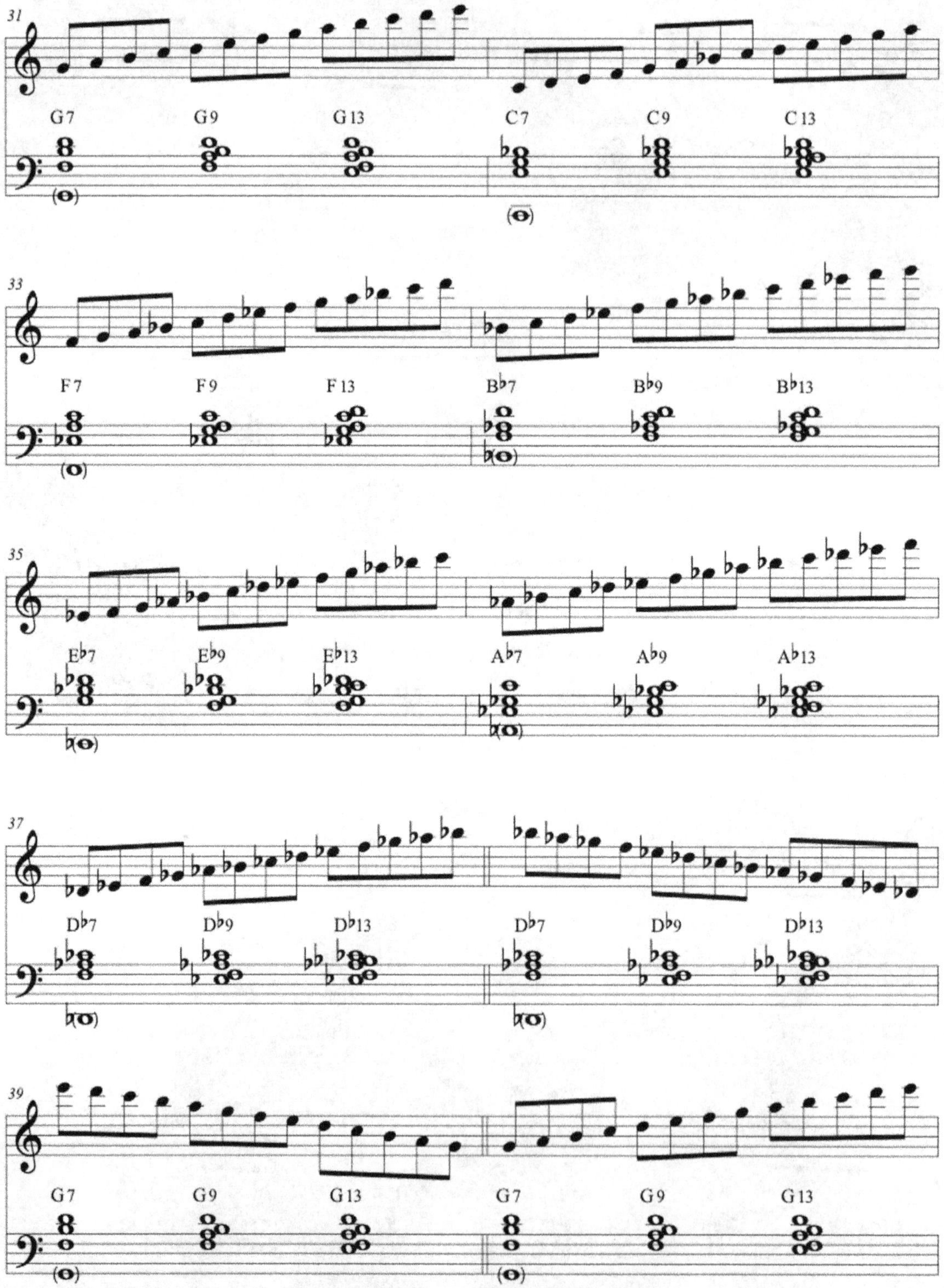
31
G7 G9 G13 C7 C9 C13
33
F7 F9 F13 B♭7 B♭9 B♭13
35
E♭7 E♭9 E♭13 A♭7 A♭9 A♭13
37
D♭7 D♭9 D♭13 D♭7 D♭9 D♭13
39
G7 G9 G13 G7 G9 G13

APPENDIX 6.2.6.
Mixolydian via The R.P.S.

5

41
D 7
D 9
D 13
A 7
A 9
A 13
43
E 7
E 9
E 13
B 7
B 9
B 13
45
F♯7
F♯9
F♯13
D♭7
D♭9
D♭13
47
A♭7
A♭9
A♭13
E♭7
E♭9
E♭13
49
B♭7
B♭9
B♭13
F 7
F 9
F 13

6

APPENDIX 6.2.6.
Mixolydian via The R.P.S.

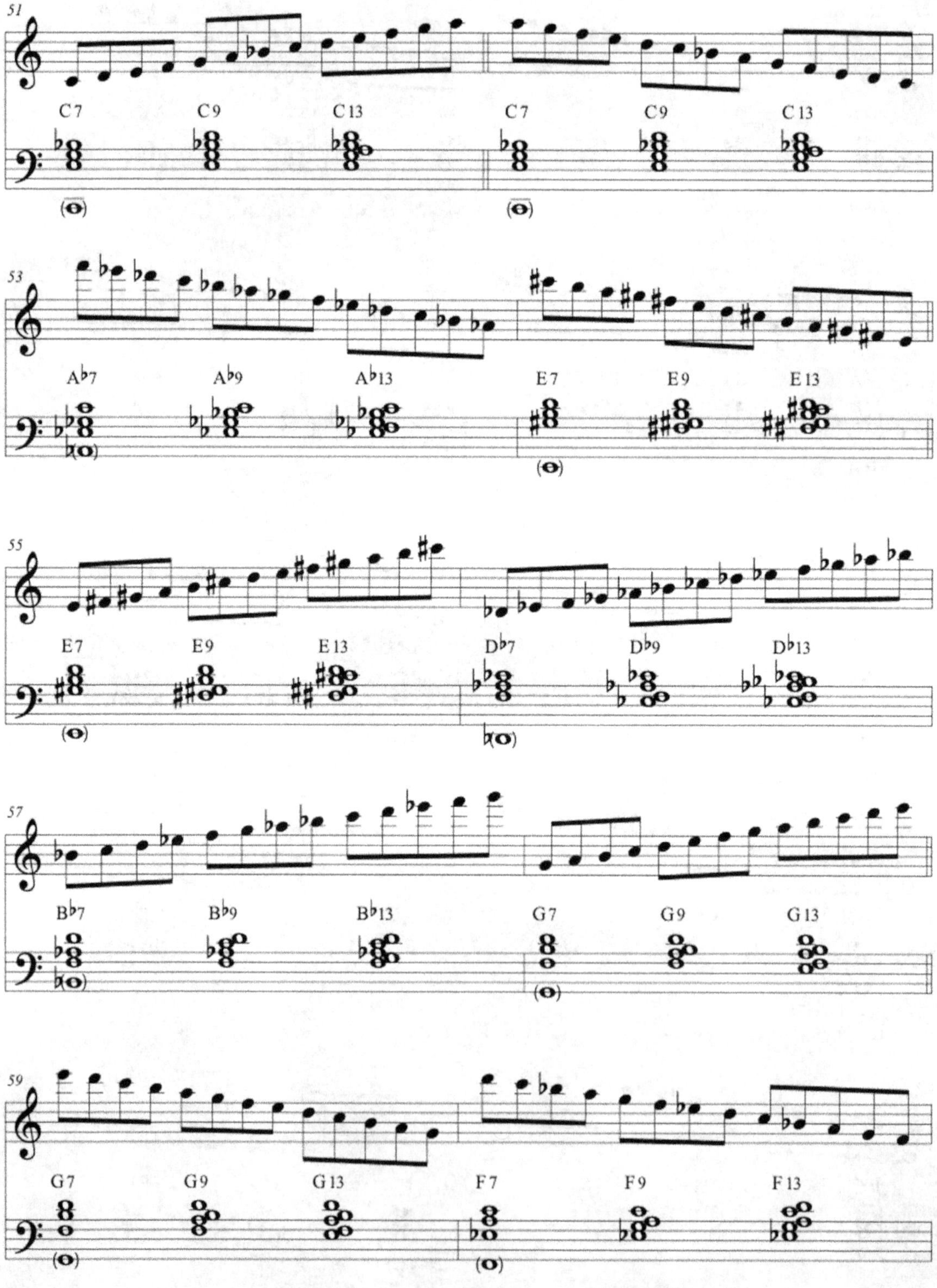
51
C7 C9 C13 C7 C9 C13
53
A♭7 A♭9 A♭13 E7 E9 E13
55
E7 E9 E13 D♭7 D♭9 D♭13
57
B♭7 B♭9 B♭13 G7 G9 G13
59
G7 G9 G13 F7 F9 F13

APPENDIX 6.2.6.
Mixolydian via The R.P.S.

7

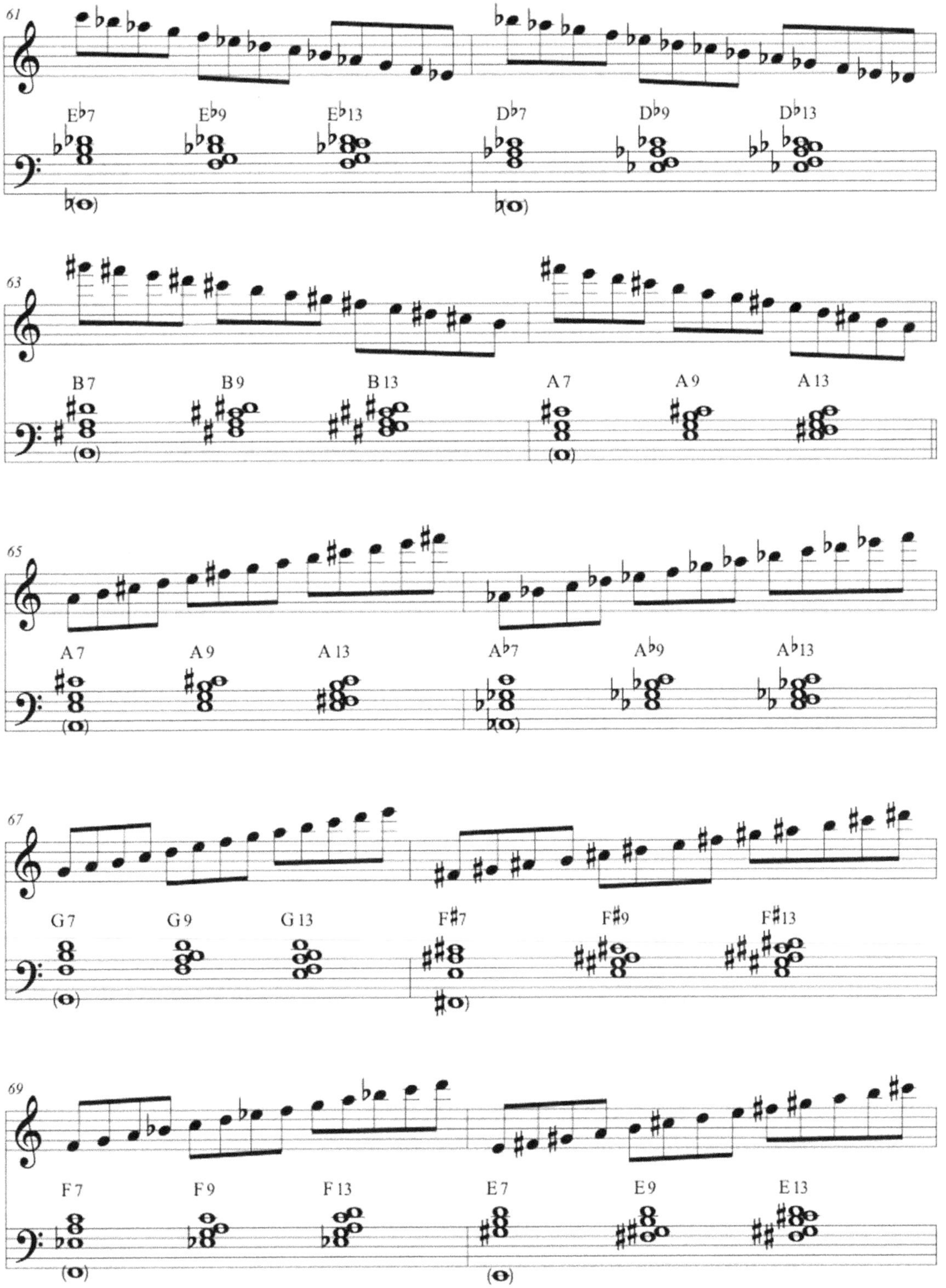
61
E♭7
E♭9
E♭13
D♭7
D♭9
D♭13
63
B7
B9
B13
A7
A9
A13
65
A7
A9
A13
A♭7
A♭9
A♭13
67
G7
G9
G13
F♯7
F♯9
F♯13
69
F7
F9
F13
E7
E9
E13

8

APPENDIX 6.2.6.
Mixolydian via The R.P.S.

71
E♭7
E♭9
E♭13
D7
D9
D13
73
D♭7
D♭9
D♭13
C7
C9
C13
75
B7
B9
B13
B♭7
B♭9
B♭13

6.2.7. Dominant Bebop

APPENDIX 6.2.7.
Dominant (V7) Bebop via The R.P.S.

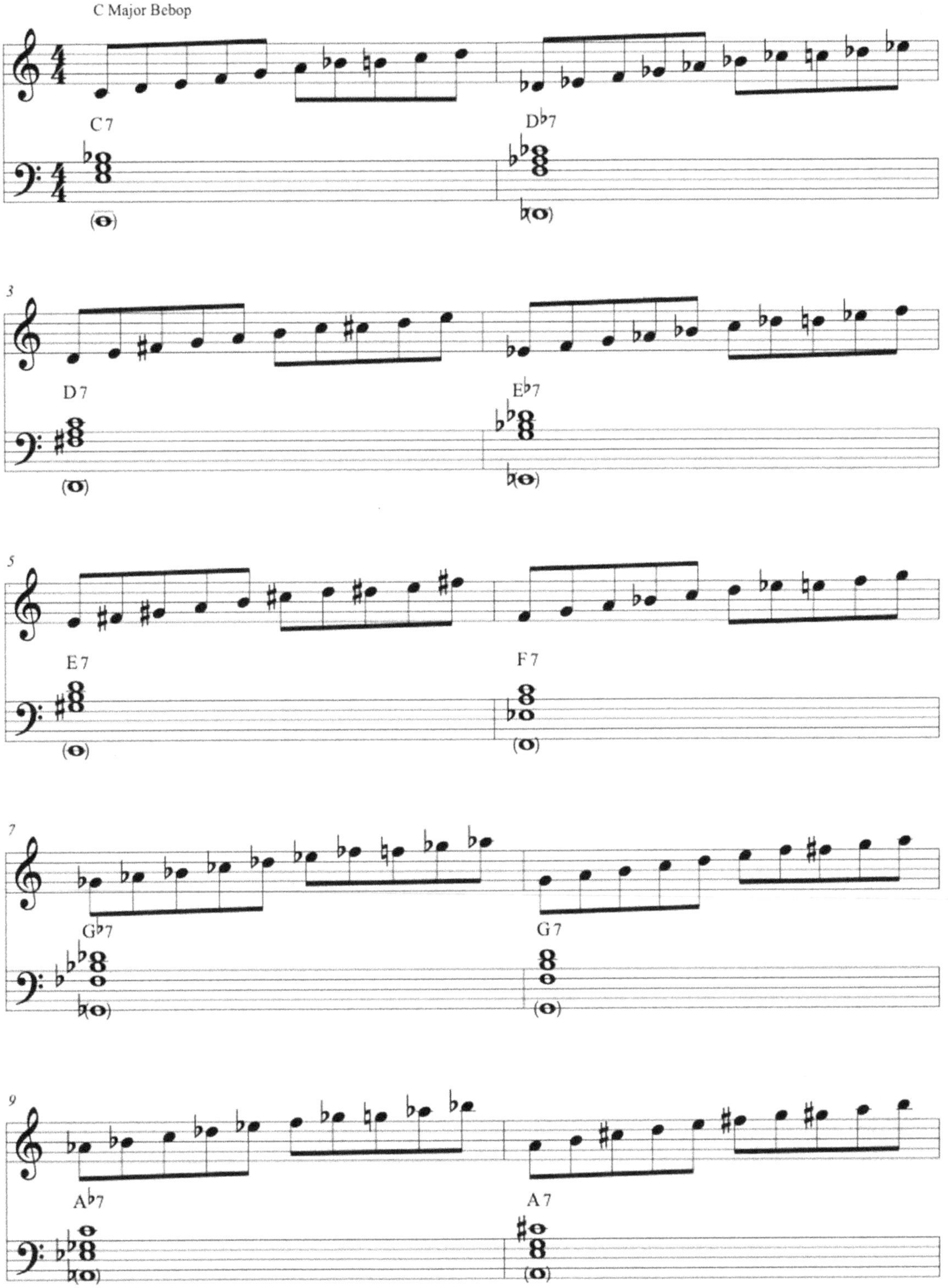

2

APPENDIX 6.2.7.
Dominant (V7) Bebop via

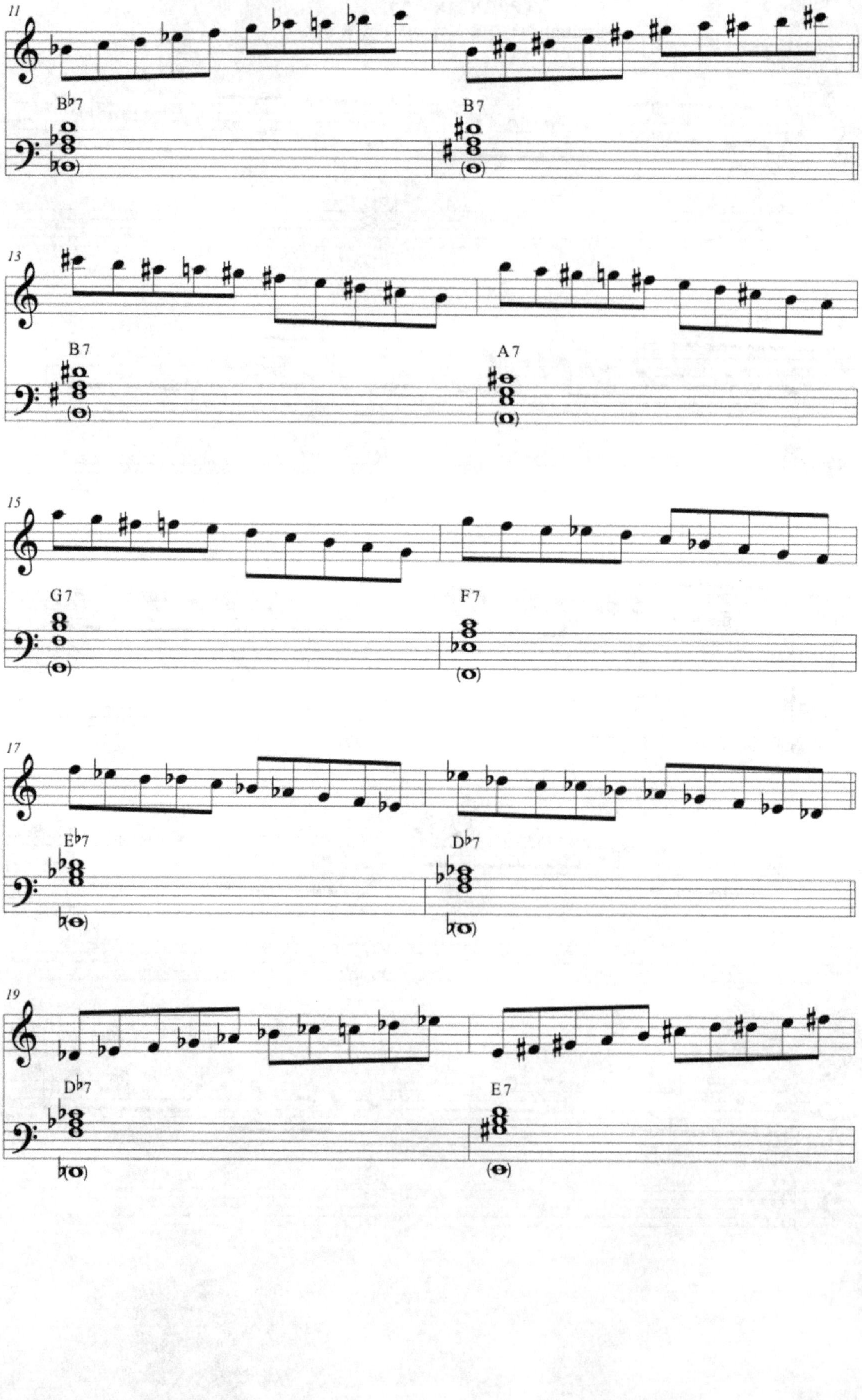

APPENDIX 6.2.7. 3

Dominant (V7) Bebop via

4

APPENDIX 6.2.7.
Dominant (V7) Bebop via

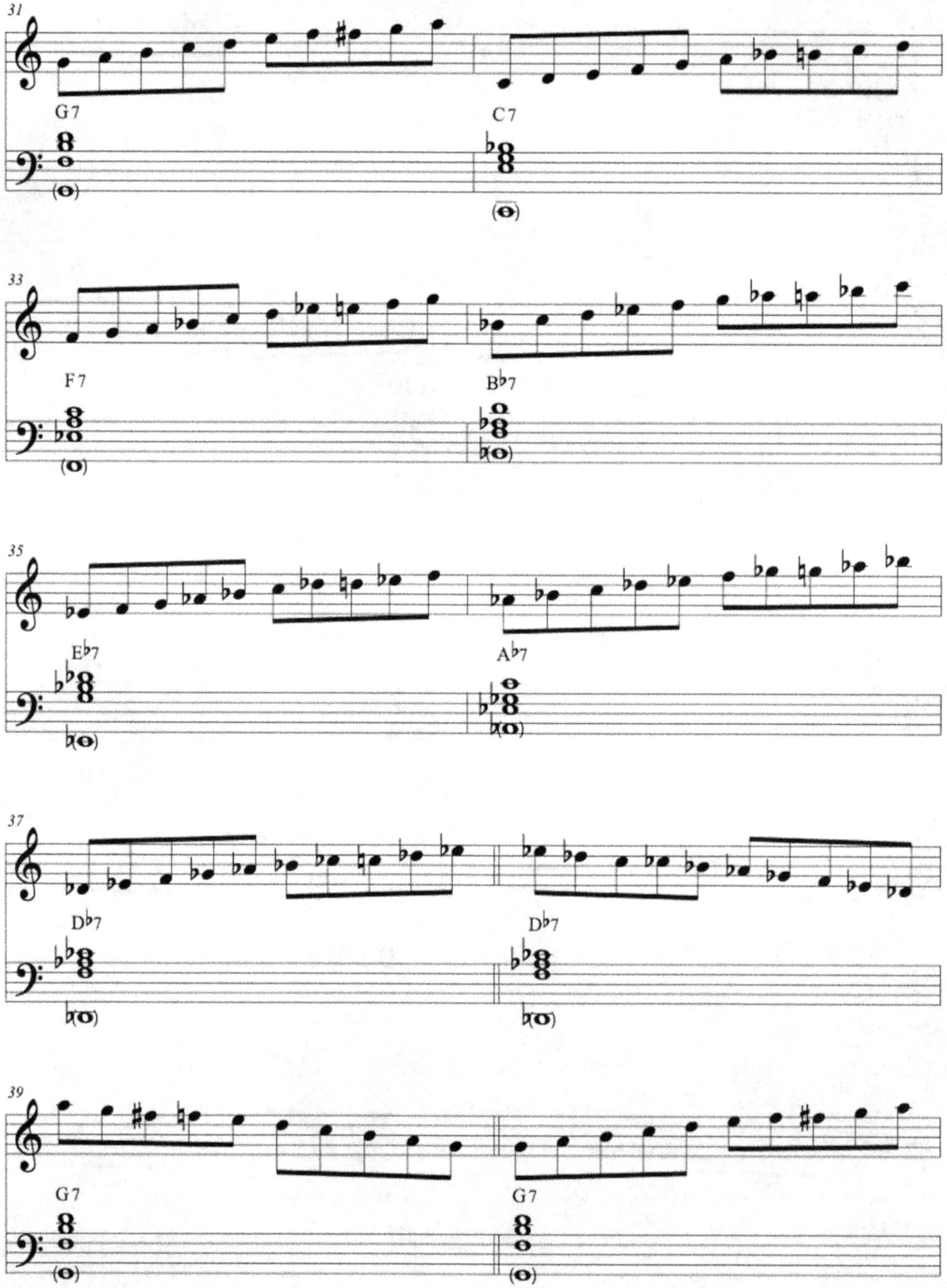

APPENDIX 6.2.7. 5

Dominant (V7) Bebop via

6

APPENDIX 6.2.7.
Dominant (V7) Bebop via

APPENDIX 6.2.7. 7

Dominant (V7) Bebop via

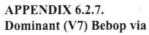

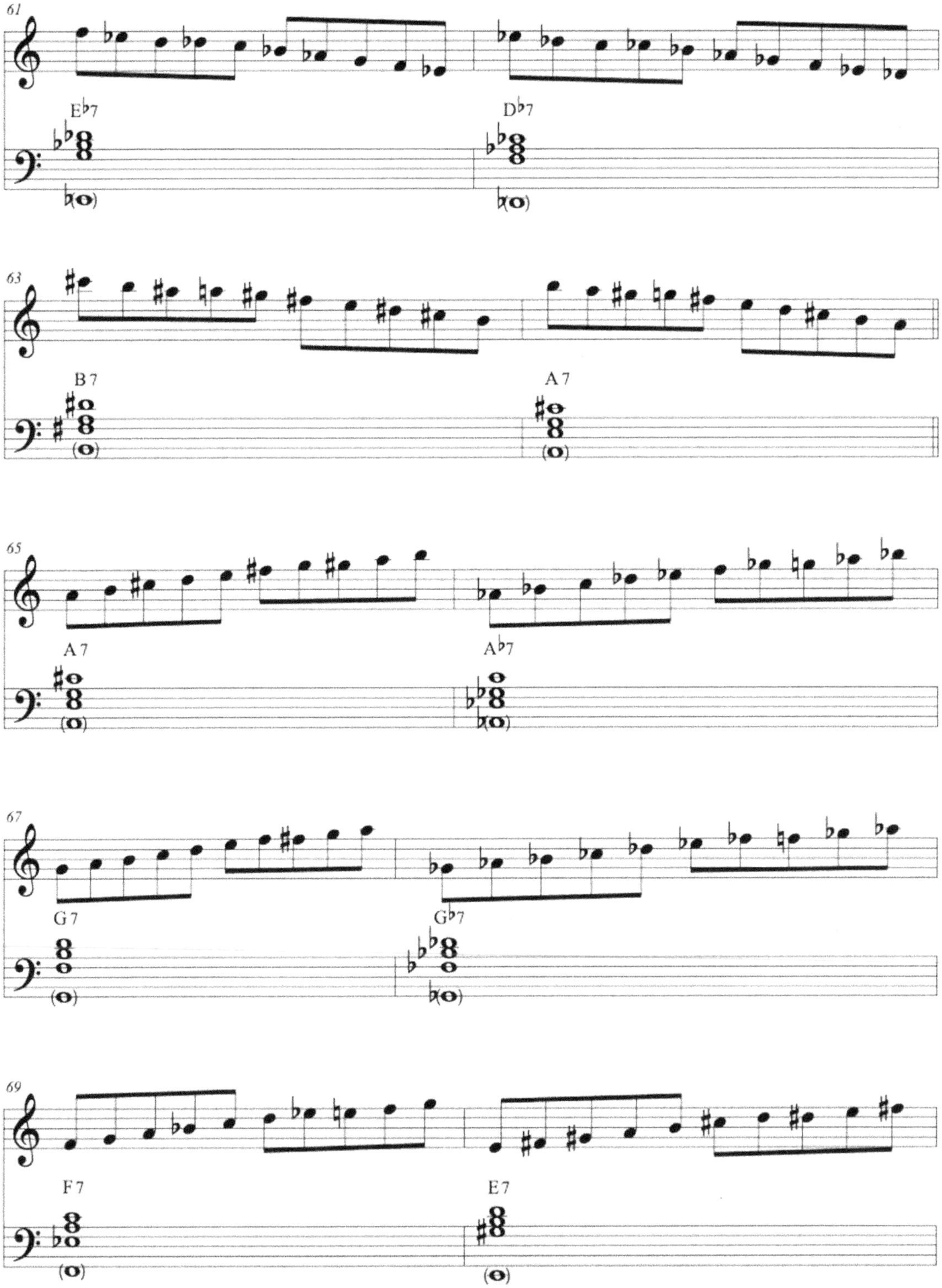

8

APPENDIX 6.2.7.
Dominant (V7) Bebop via

6.2.8. Major 6 Diminished

APPENDIX 6.2.8
Major 6 Diminished via The R.P. S.

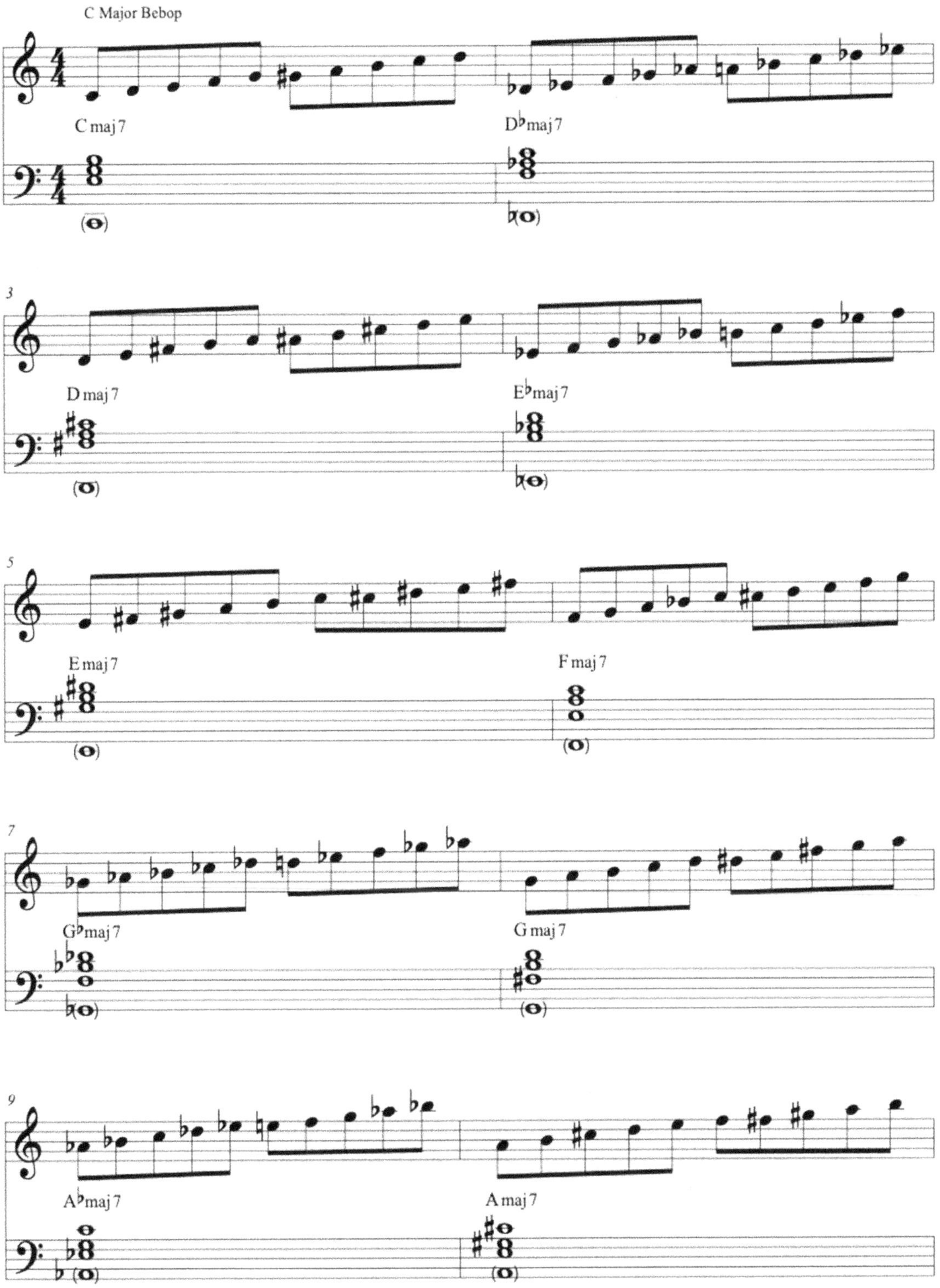

2

APPENDIX 6.2.8
Major 6 Diminished via The R.P. S.

11
B♭maj7
Bmaj7
13
Bmaj7
Amaj7
15
Gmaj7
Fmaj7
17
E♭maj7
D♭maj7
19
D♭maj7
Emaj7

APPENDIX 6.2.8 3

Major 6 Diminished via The R.P. S.

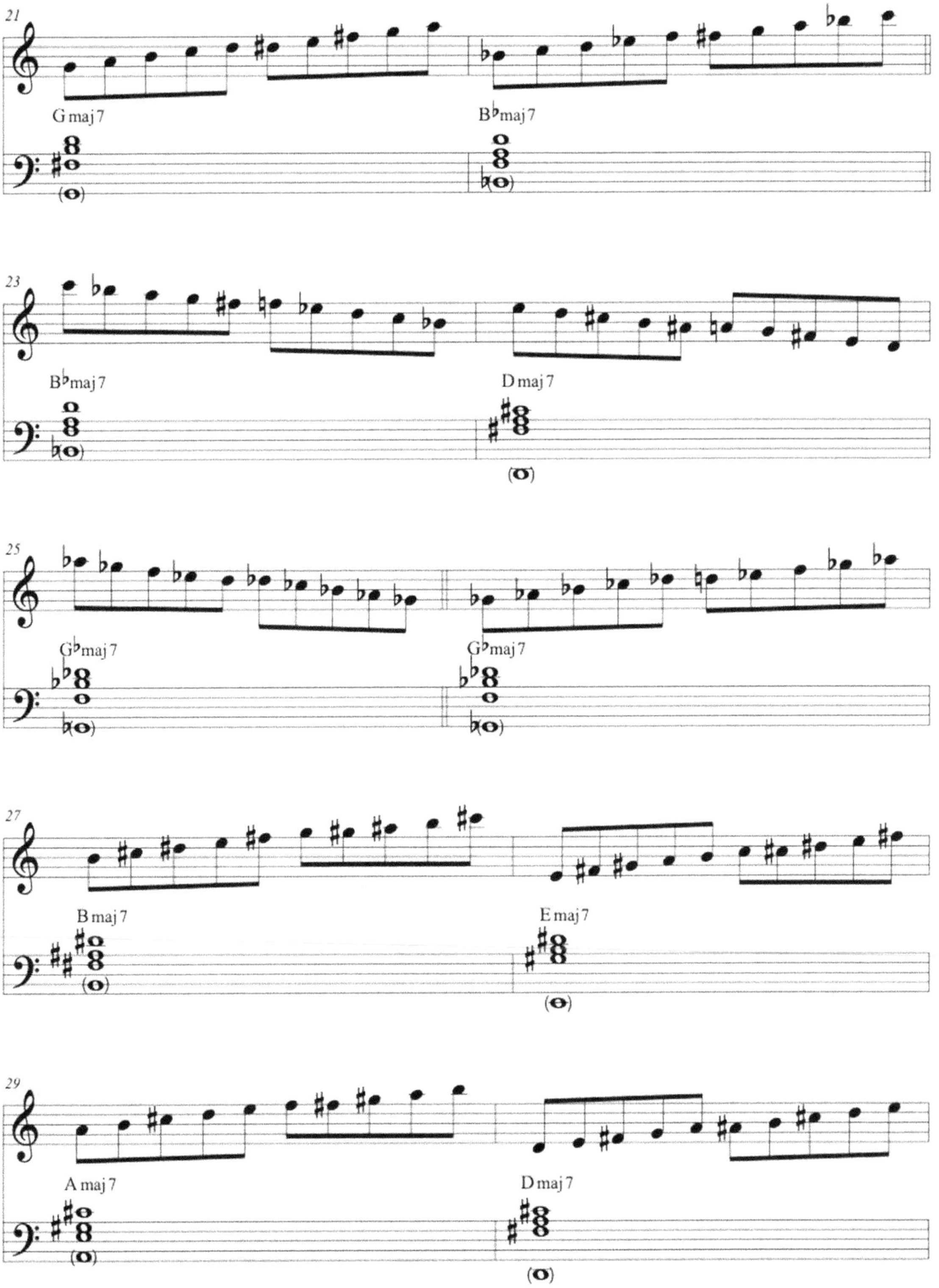
21
G maj 7
B♭maj 7
23
B♭maj 7
D maj 7
25
G♭maj 7
G♭maj 7
27
B maj 7
E maj 7
29
A maj 7
D maj 7

4

APPENDIX 6.2.8
Major 6 Diminished via The R.P. S.

31
Gmaj7
Cmaj7
33
Fmaj7
B♭maj7
35
E♭maj7
A♭maj7
37
D♭maj7
D♭maj7
39
Gmaj7
Gmaj7

APPENDIX 6.2.8
Major 6 Diminished via The R.P. S.

5

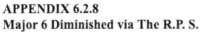

41
D maj 7
A maj 7
43
E maj 7
B maj 7
45
G♭maj 7
D♭maj 7
47
A♭maj 7
E♭maj 7
49
B♭maj 7
F maj 7

6

APPENDIX 6.2.8
Major 6 Diminished via The R.P. S.

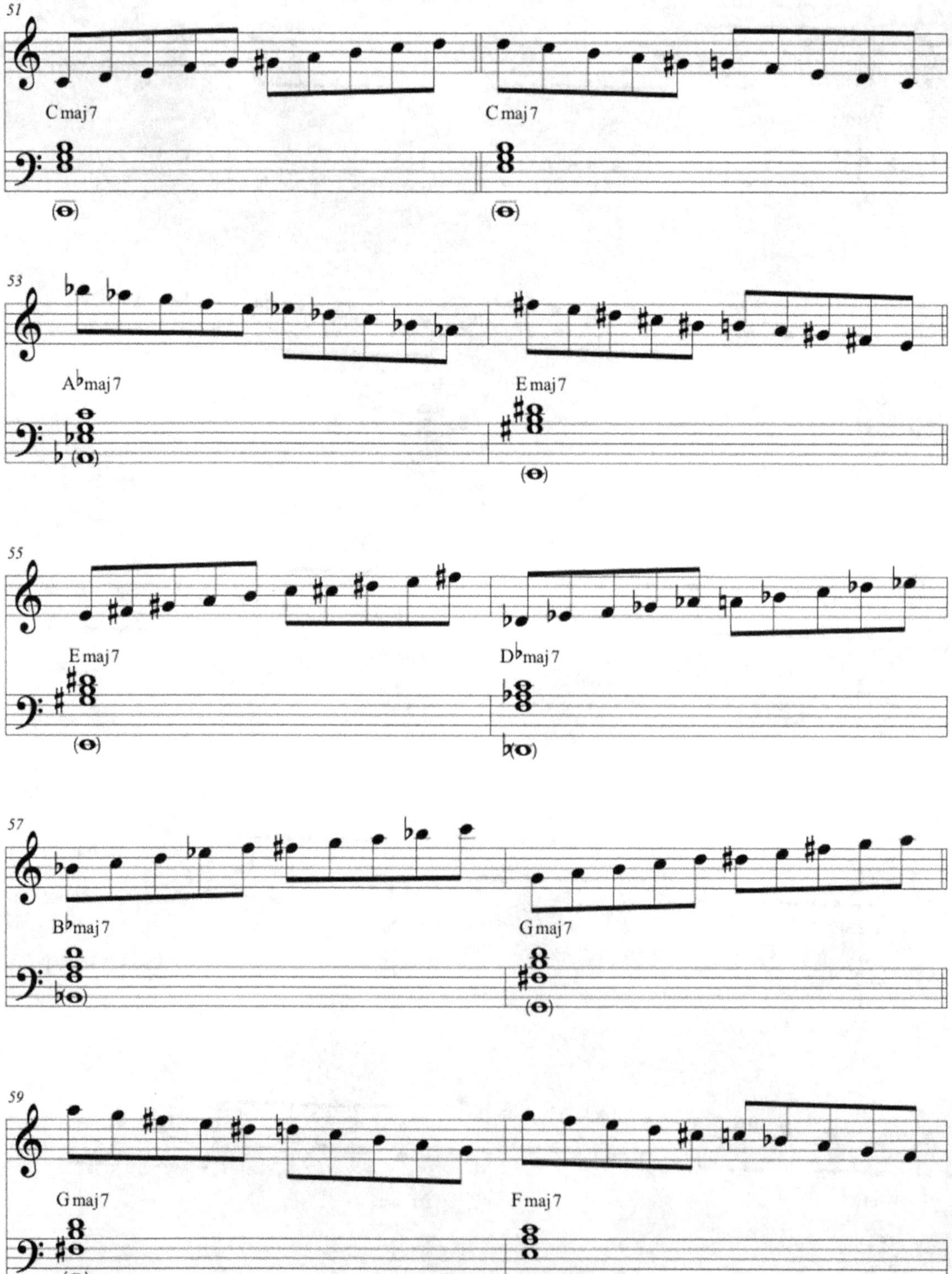
51
Cmaj7
Cmaj7
53
A♭maj7
Emaj7
55
Emaj7
D♭maj7
57
B♭maj7
Gmaj7
59
Gmaj7
Fmaj7

APPENDIX 6.2.8 7
Major 6 Diminished via The R.P. S.

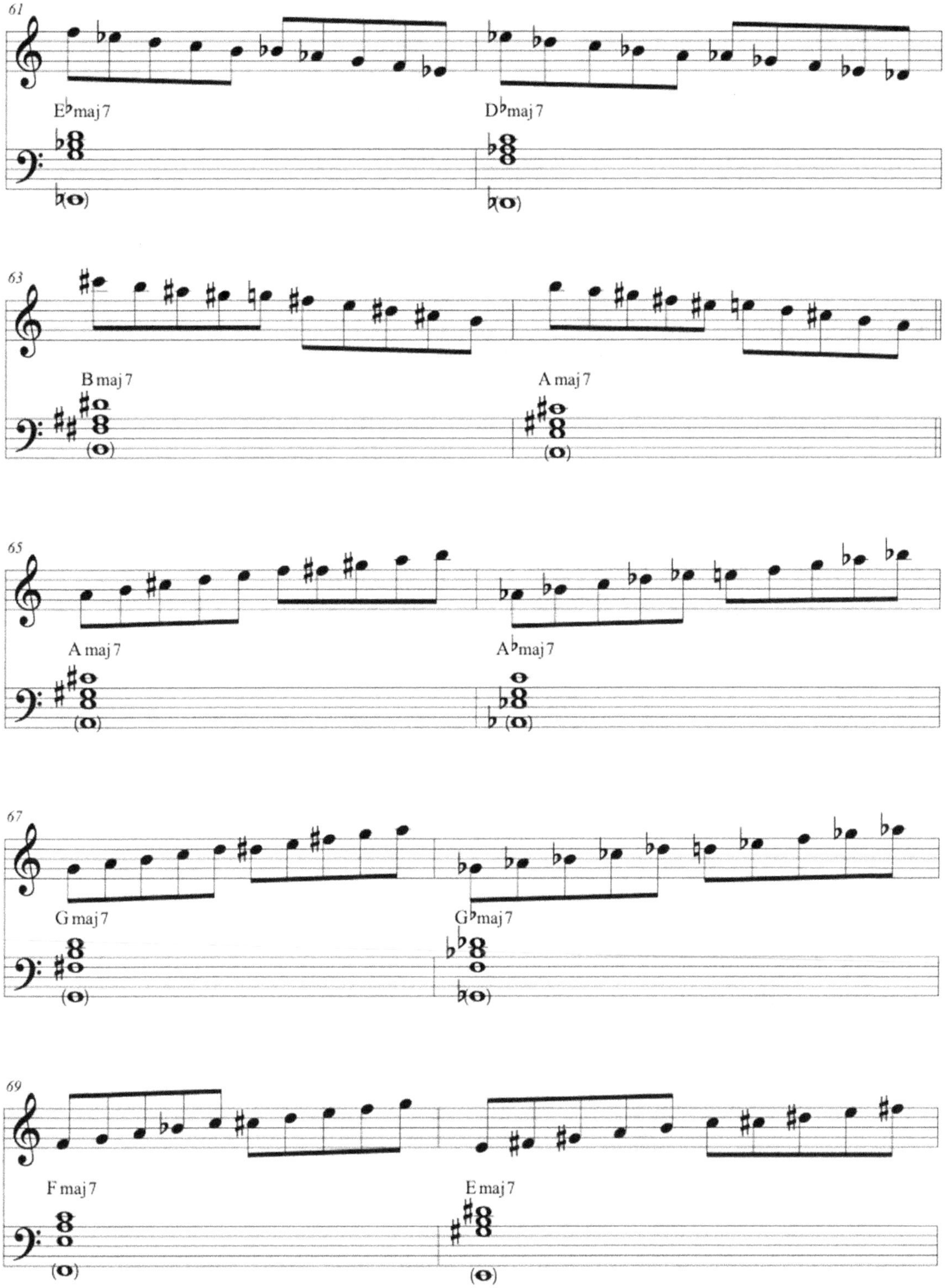
61
E♭maj 7
D♭maj 7
63
B maj 7
A maj 7
65
A maj 7
A♭maj 7
67
G maj 7
G♭maj 7
69
F maj 7
E maj 7

8

APPENDIX 6.2.8
Major 6 Diminished via The R.P. S.

6.2.9. Whole Tone

APPENDIX 6.2.9.
Whole Tone via The R.P.S.

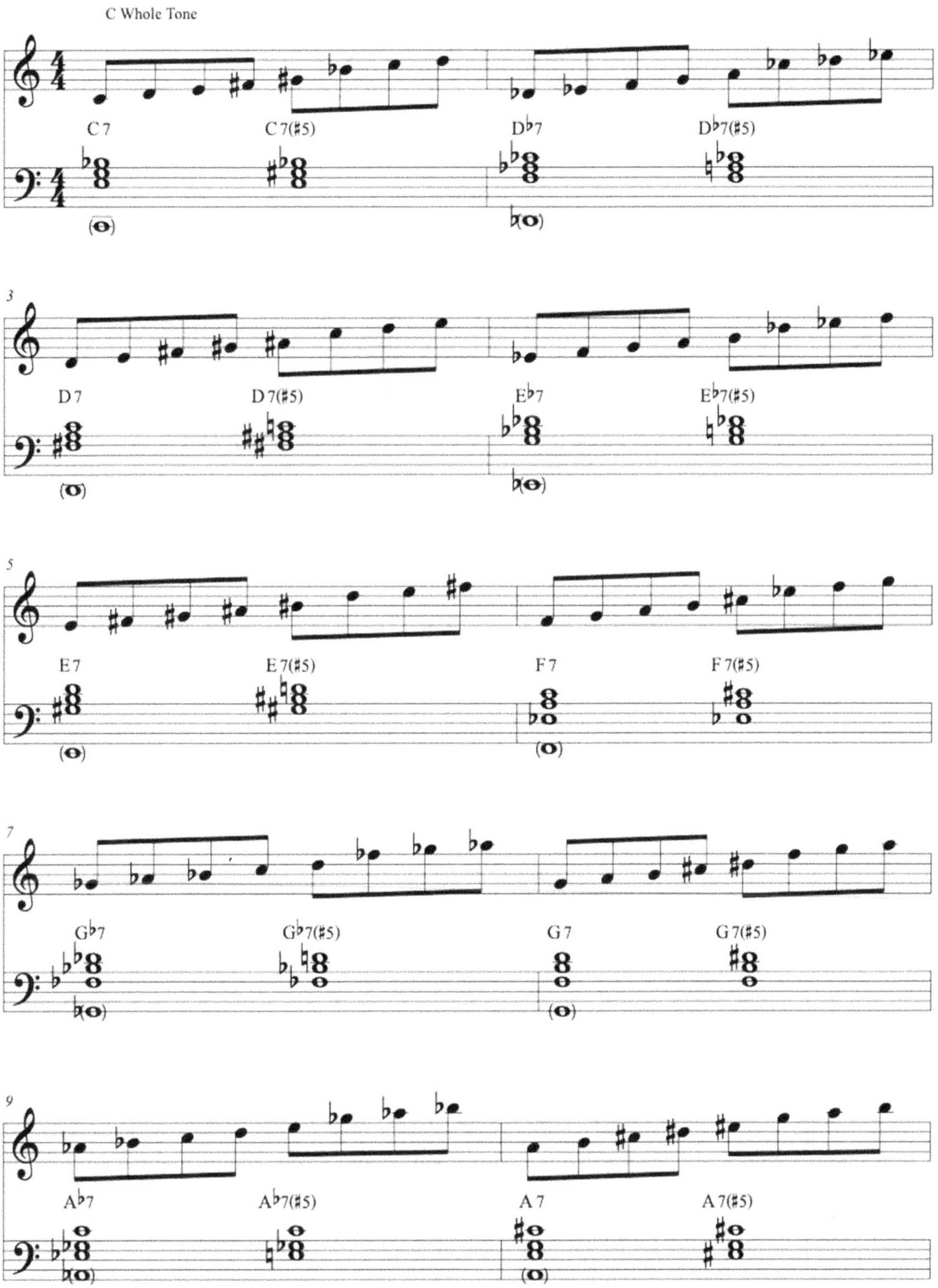

2

APPENDIX 6.2.9.
Whole Tone via The R.P.S.

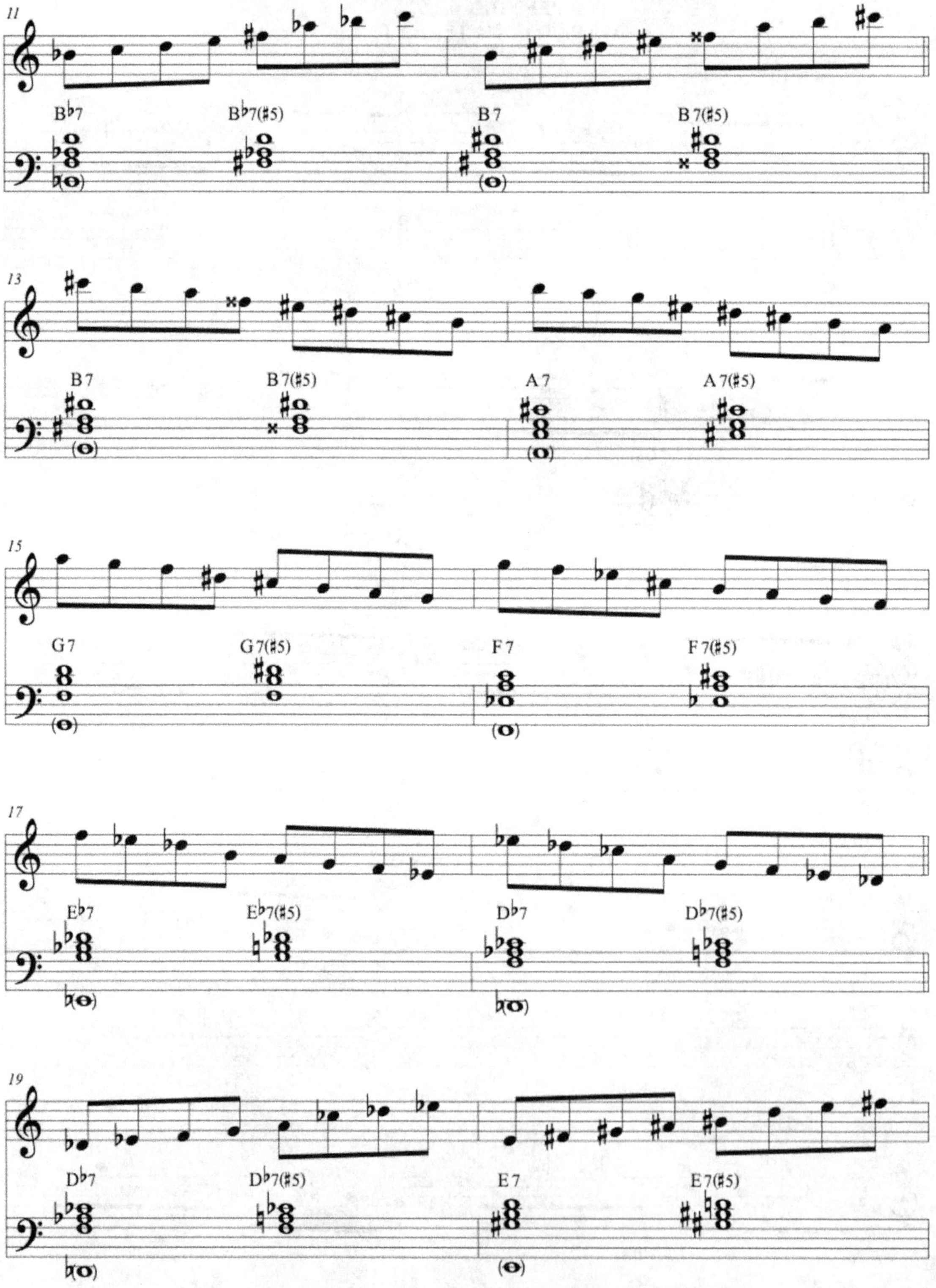
11
B♭7
B♭7(♯5)
B7
B7(♯5)
13
B7
B7(♯5)
A7
A7(♯5)
15
G7
G7(♯5)
F7
F7(♯5)
17
E♭7
E♭7(♯5)
D♭7
D♭7(♯5)
19
D♭7
D♭7(♯5)
E7
E7(♯5)

APPENDIX 6.2.9.
Whole Tone via The R.P.S. 3

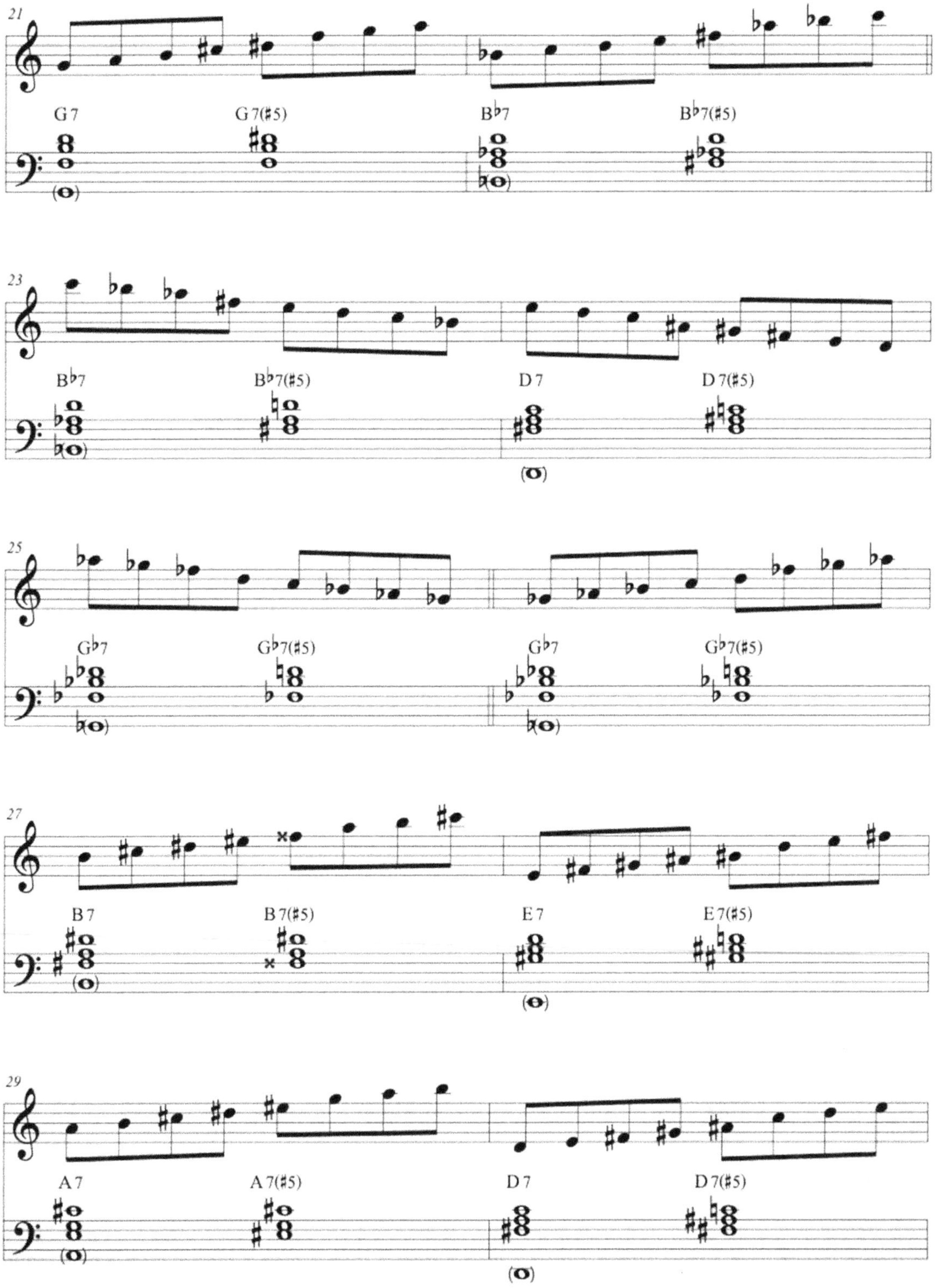
21
G 7
G 7(♯5)
B♭7
B♭7(♯5)
23
B♭7
B♭7(♯5)
D 7
D 7(♯5)
25
G♭7
G♭7(♯5)
G♭7
G♭7(♯5)
27
B 7
B 7(♯5)
E 7
E 7(♯5)
29
A 7
A 7(♯5)
D 7
D 7(♯5)

4

APPENDIX 6.2.9.
Whole Tone via The R.P.S.

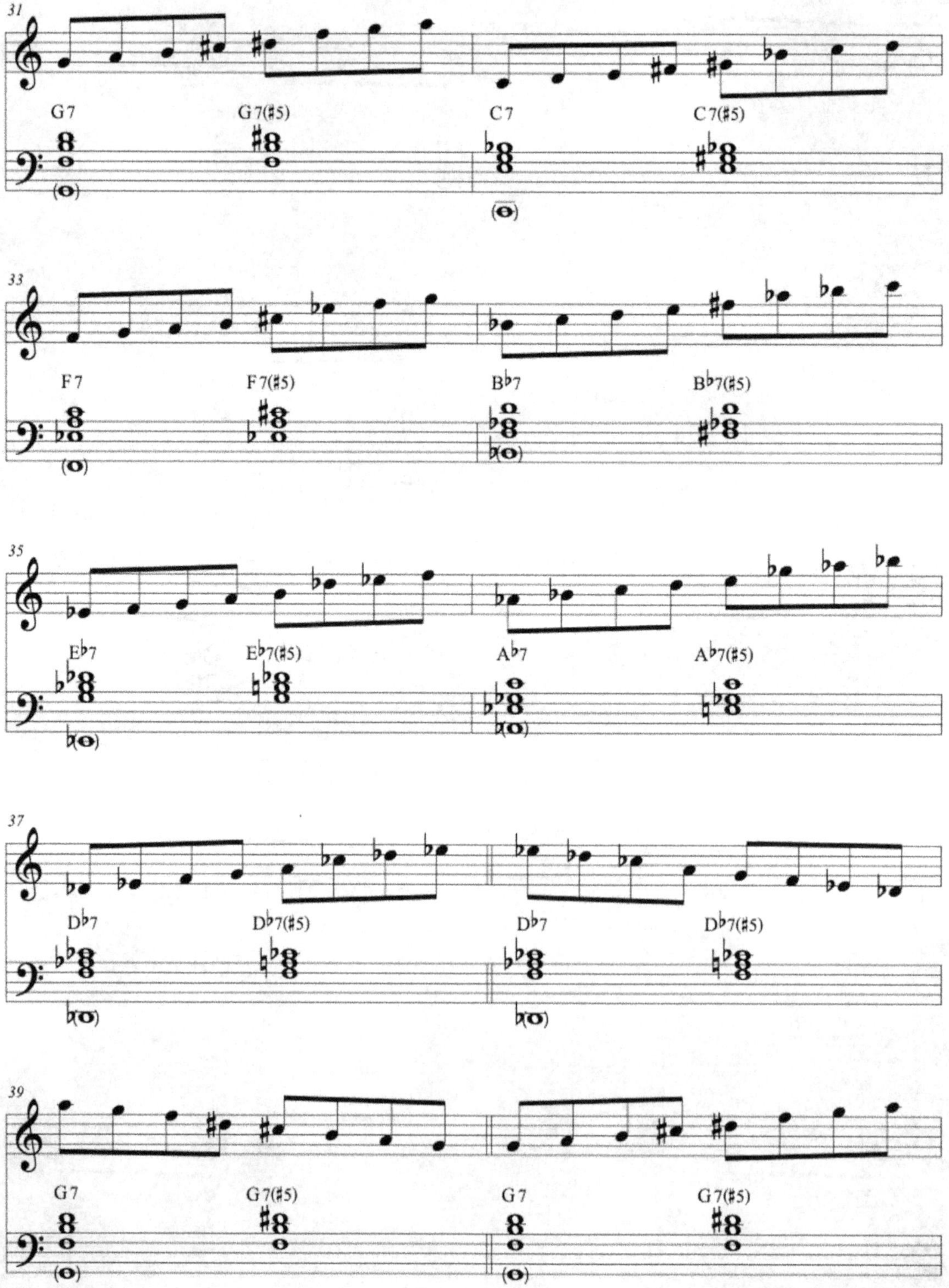
31
G7
G7(♯5)
C7
C7(♯5)
33
F7
F7(♯5)
B♭7
B♭7(♯5)
35
E♭7
E♭7(♯5)
A♭7
A♭7(♯5)
37
D♭7
D♭7(♯5)
D♭7
D♭7(♯5)
39
G7
G7(♯5)
G7
G7(♯5)

APPENDIX 6.2.9.
Whole Tone via The R.P.S.

5

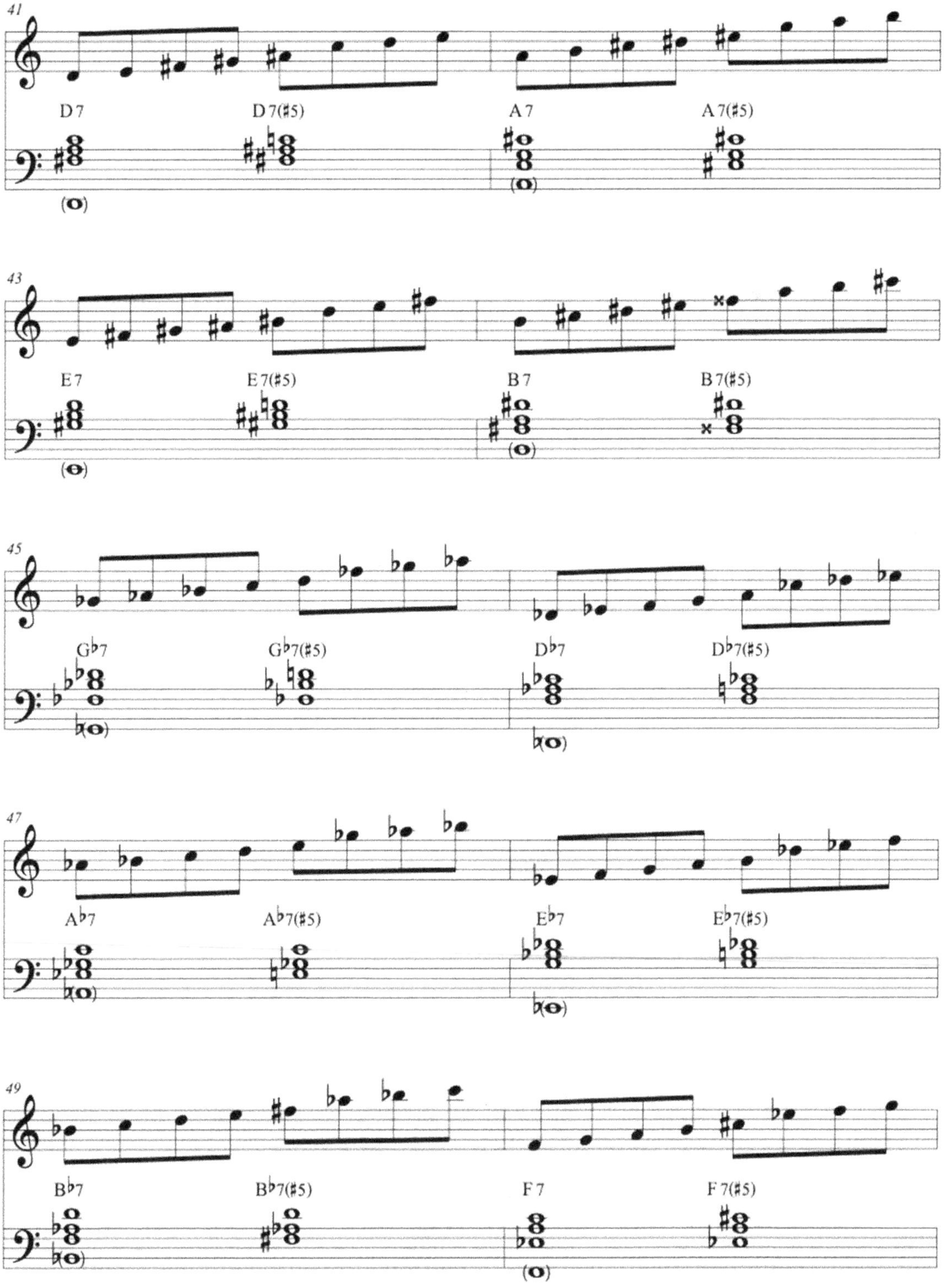
41
D 7
D 7(♯5)
A 7
A 7(♯5)
43
E 7
E 7(♯5)
B 7
B 7(♯5)
45
G♭7
G♭7(♯5)
D♭7
D♭7(♯5)
47
A♭7
A♭7(♯5)
E♭7
E♭7(♯5)
49
B♭7
B♭7(♯5)
F 7
F 7(♯5)

6

APPENDIX 6.2.9.
Whole Tone via The R.P.S.

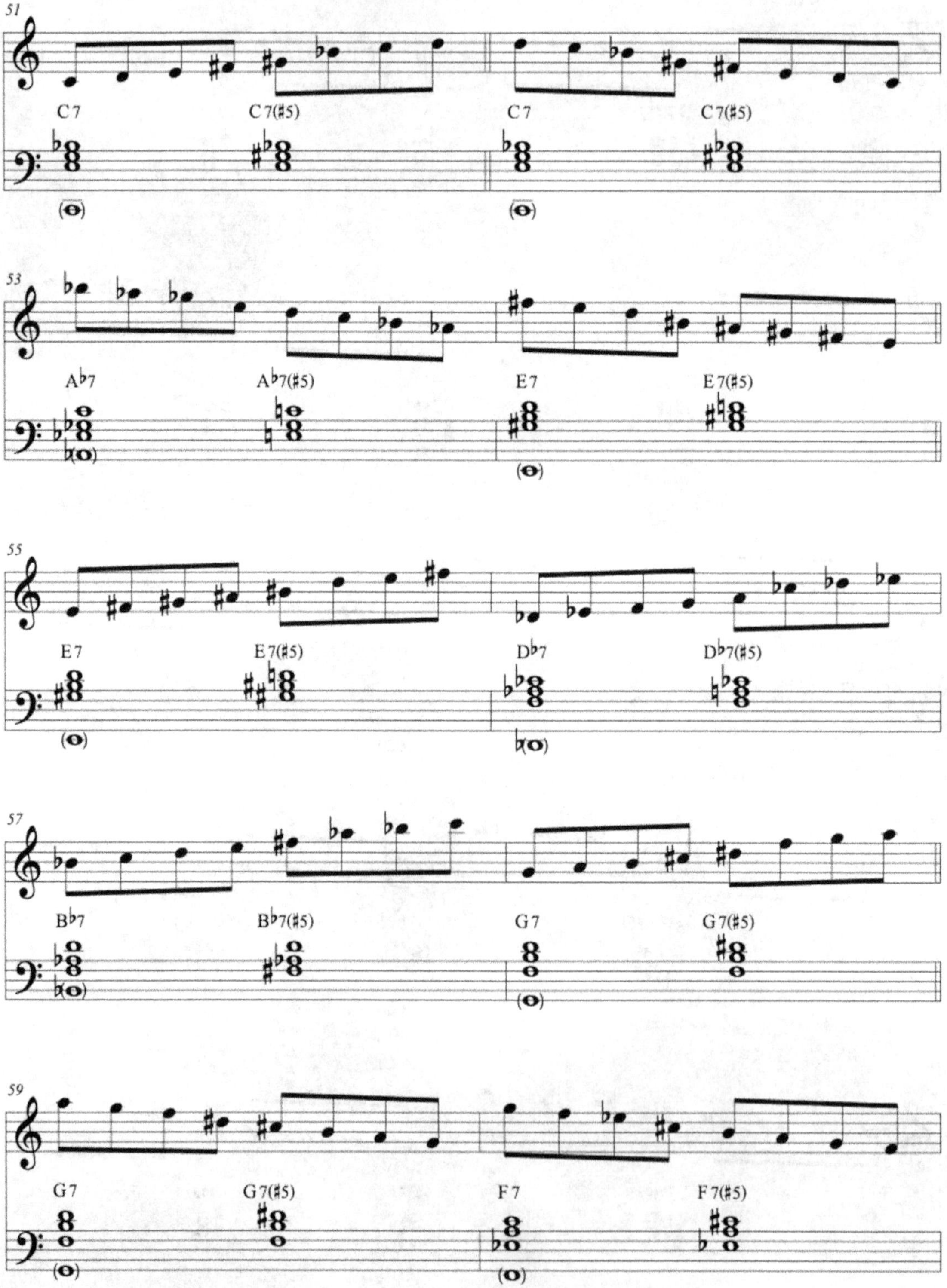
51
C7
C7(♯5)
C7
C7(♯5)
53
A♭7
A♭7(♯5)
E7
E7(♯5)
55
E7
E7(♯5)
D♭7
D♭7(♯5)
57
B♭7
B♭7(♯5)
G7
G7(♯5)
59
G7
G7(♯5)
F7
F7(♯5)

APPENDIX 6.2.9. 7
Whole Tone via The R.P.S.

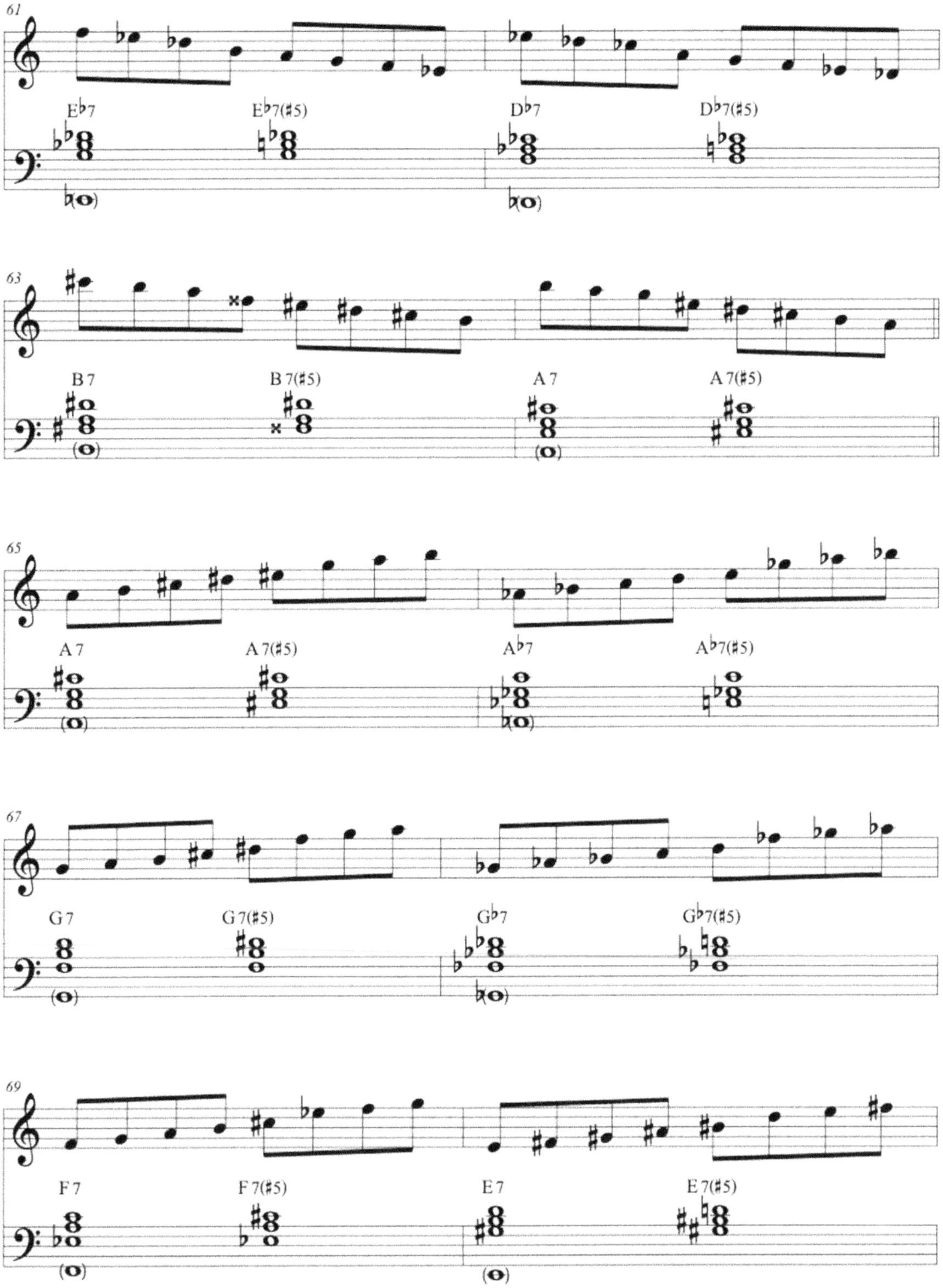
61
E♭7
E♭7(♯5)
D♭7
D♭7(♯5)
63
B 7
B 7(♯5)
A 7
A 7(♯5)
65
A 7
A 7(♯5)
A♭7
A♭7(♯5)
67
G 7
G 7(♯5)
G♭7
G♭7(♯5)
69
F 7
F 7(♯5)
E 7
E 7(♯5)

8

APPENDIX 6.2.9.
Whole Tone via The R.P.S.

71
E♭7
E♭7(♯5)
D 7
D 7(♯5)
73
D♭7
D♭7(♯5)
C 7
C 7(♯5)
75
B 7
B 7(♯5)
B♭7
B♭7(♯5)

6.2.10. Ionian/Aeolian

APPENDIX 6.2.10.
Ionia/Aeolian (Pentatonic) via The R.P.S.

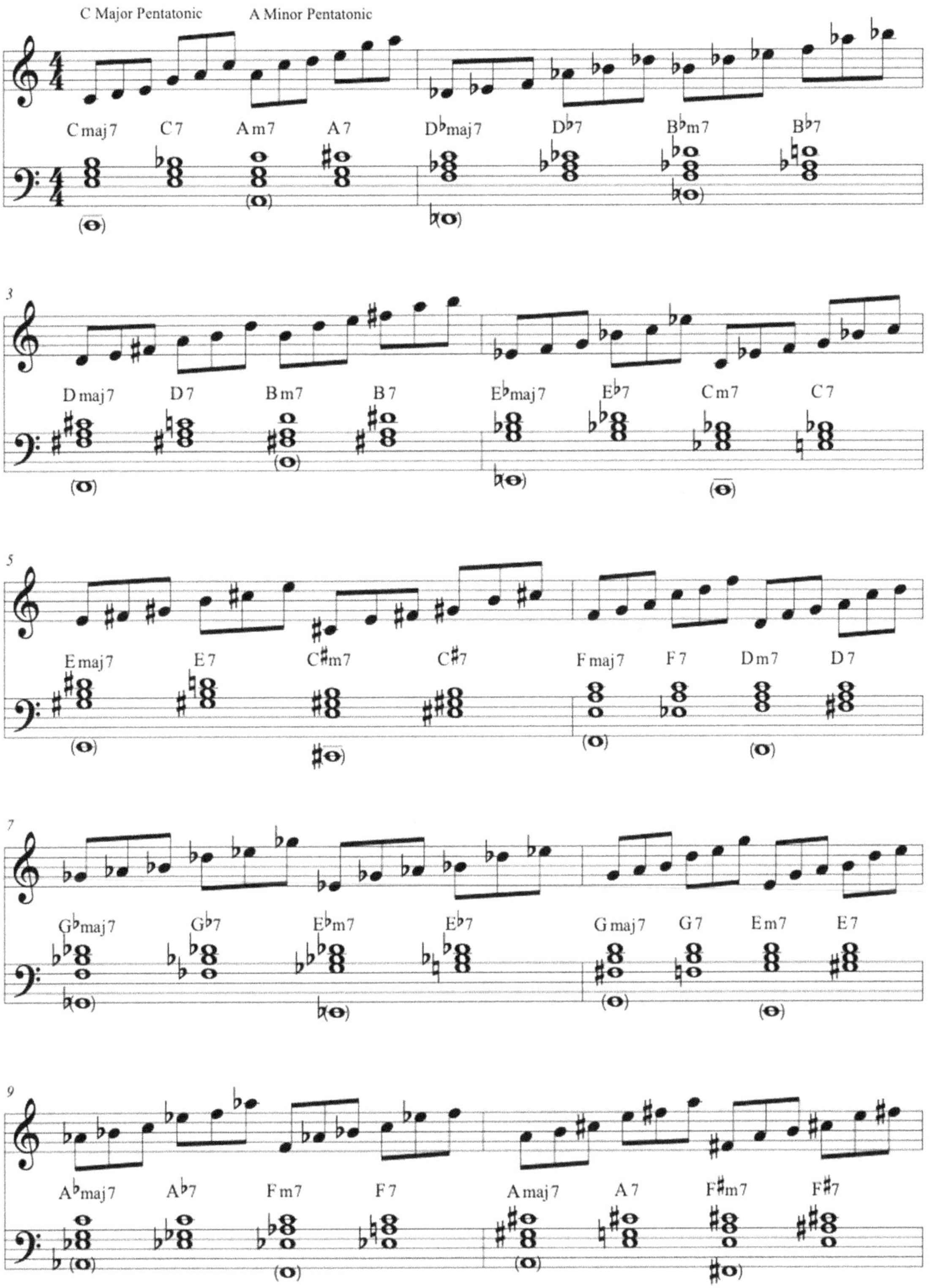

2

APPENDIX 6.2.10.
Ionia/Aeolian (Pentatonic) via The R.P.S.

APPENDIX 6.2.10.
Ionia/Aeolian (Pentatonic) via The R.P.S.

3

4

APPENDIX 6.2.10.
Ionia/Aeolian (Pentatonic) via The R.P.S.

APPENDIX 6.2.10.
Ionia/Aeolian (Pentatonic) via The R.P.S. 5

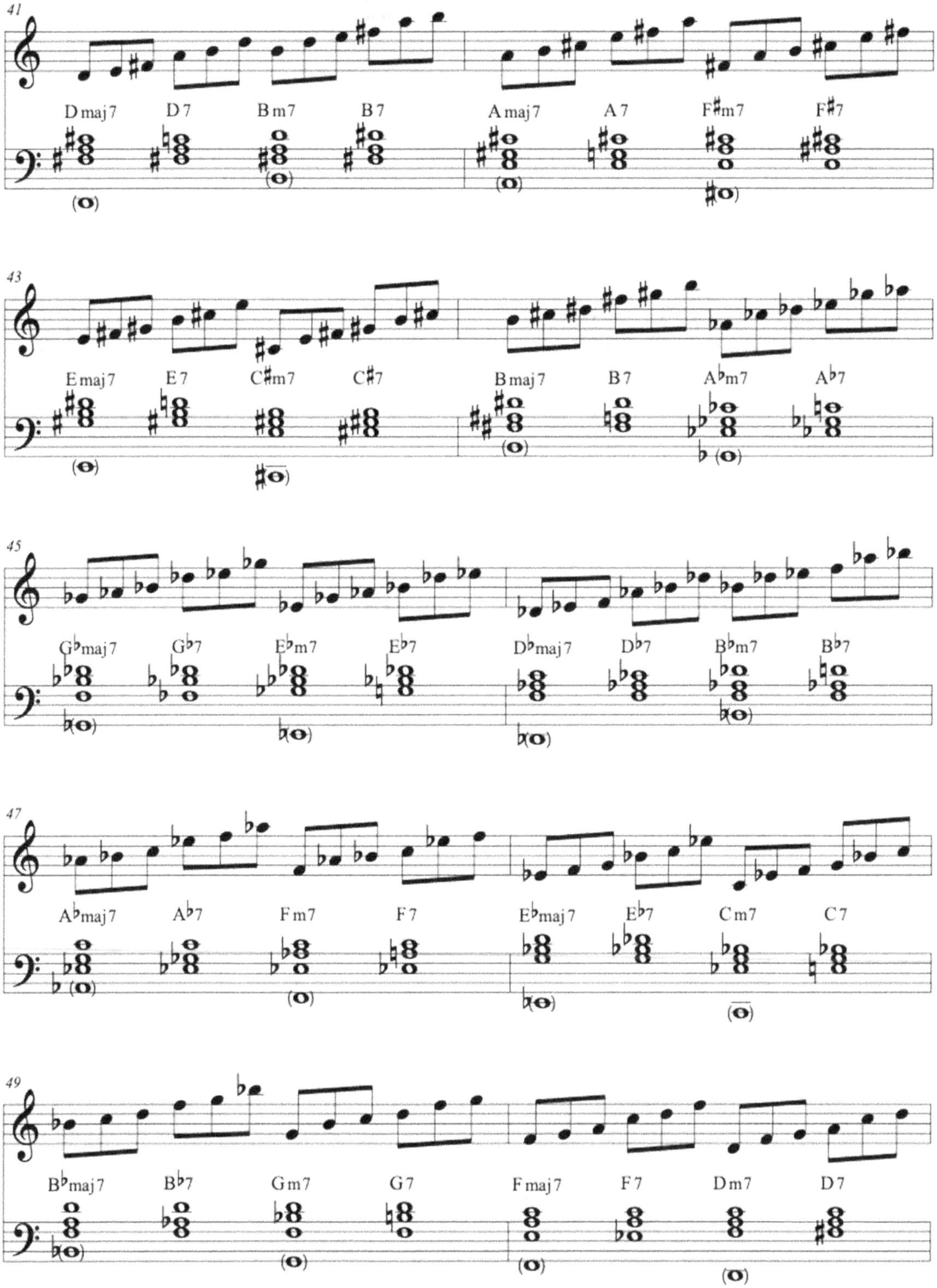

6

APPENDIX 6.2.10.
Ionia/Aeolian (Pentatonic) via The R.P.S.

APPENDIX 6.2.10. 7

Ionia/Aeolian (Pentatonic) via The R.P.S.

8

APPENDIX 6.2.10.
Ionia/Aeolian (Pentatonic) via The R.P.S.

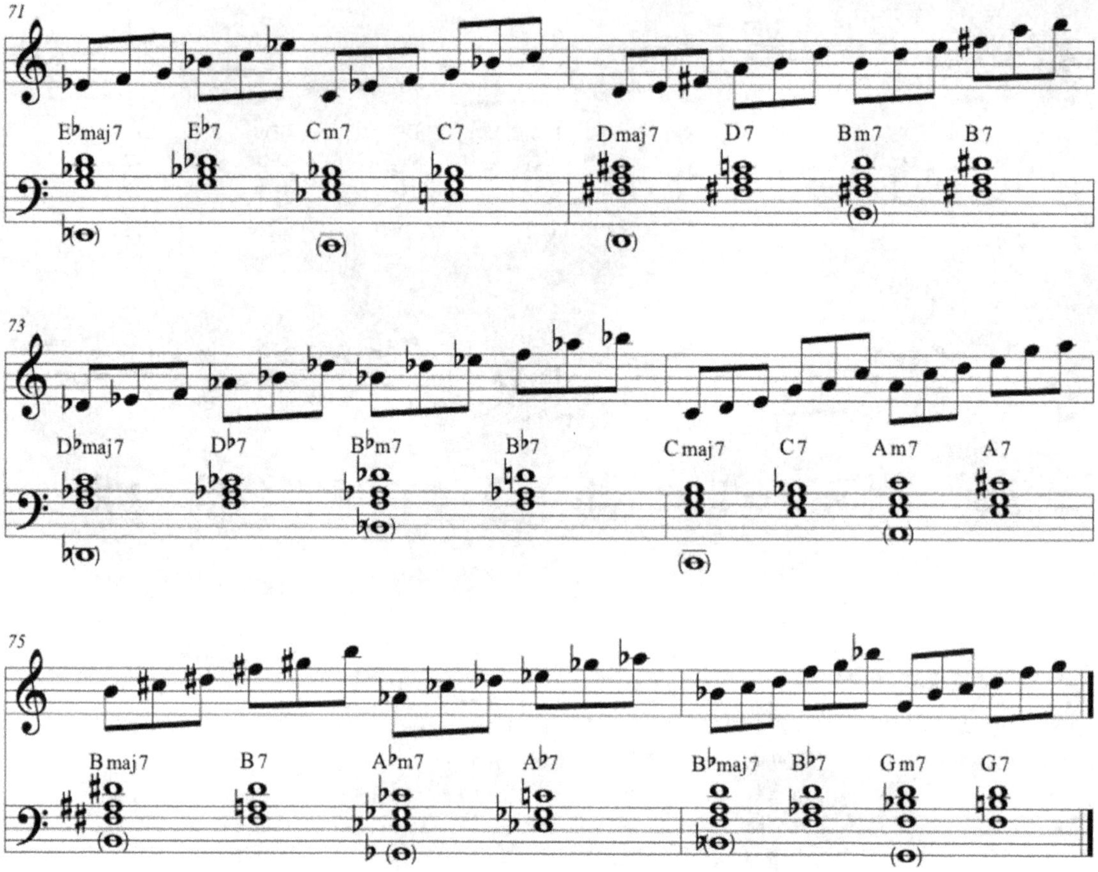

6.2.11. Harmonic Minor

APPENDIX 6.2.11.
Harmonic Minor via The R.P.S.

2

APPENDIX 6.2.11.
Harmonic Minor via The R.P.S.

11
13
Bmaj7
B7
A♭m7
A♭7
Amaj7
A7
F♯m7
F♯7
15
Gmaj7
G7
Em7
E7
Fmaj7
F7
Dm7
D7
17
E♭maj7
E♭7
Cm7
C7
D♭maj7
D♭7
B♭m7
B♭7
19
D♭maj7
D♭7
B♭m7
B♭7
Emaj7
E7
C♯m7
C♯7

APPENDIX 6.2.11. 3

Harmonic Minor via The R.P.S.

21
Gmaj7 G7 Em7 E7 B♭maj7 B♭7 Gm7 G7
23
B♭maj7 B♭7 Gm7 G7 Dmaj7 D7 Bm7 B7
25
G♭maj7 G♭7 E♭m7 E♭7 G♭maj7 G♭7 E♭m7 E♭7
27
Bmaj7 B7 A♭m7 A♭7 Emaj7 E7 C♯m7 C♯7
29
Amaj7 A7 F♯m7 F♯7 Dmaj7 D7 Bm7 B7

4

APPENDIX 6.2.11.
Harmonic Minor via The R.P.S.

31
Gmaj7 G7 Em7 E7 Cmaj7 C7 Am7 A7
33
Fmaj7 F7 Dm7 D7 B♭maj7 B♭7 Gm7 G7
35
E♭maj7 E♭7 Cm7 C7 A♭maj7 A♭7 Fm7 F7
37
D♭maj7 D♭7 B♭m7 B♭7 D♭maj7 D♭7 B♭m7 B♭7
39
Gmaj7 G7 Em7 E7 Gmaj7 G7 Em7 E7

APPENDIX 6.2.11. 5

Harmonic Minor via The R.P.S.

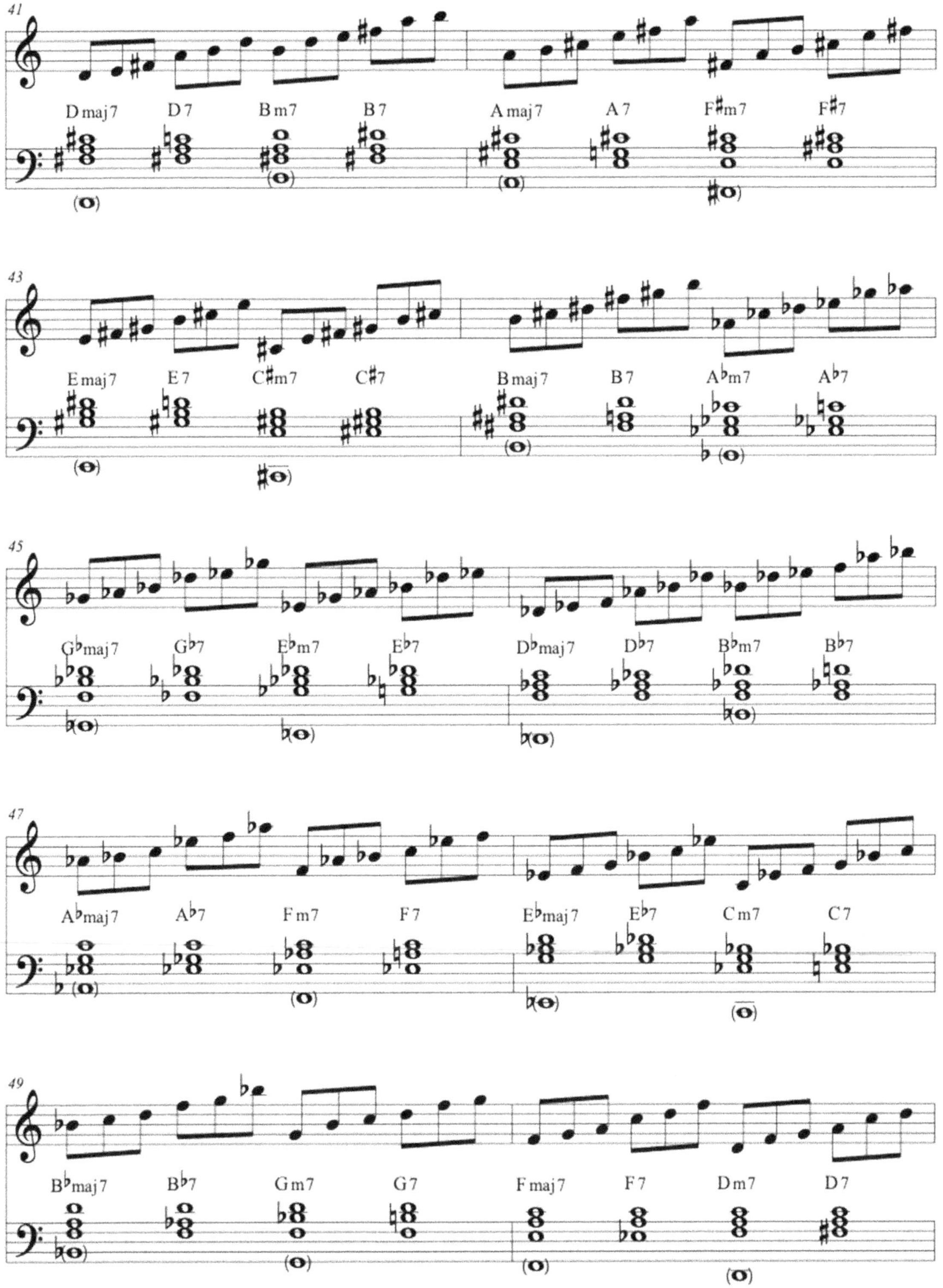
41
Dmaj7 D7 Bm7 B7 Amaj7 A7 F♯m7 F♯7
43
Emaj7 E7 C♯m7 C♯7 Bmaj7 B7 A♭m7 A♭7
45
G♭maj7 G♭7 E♭m7 E♭7 D♭maj7 D♭7 B♭m7 B♭7
47
A♭maj7 A♭7 Fm7 F7 E♭maj7 E♭7 Cm7 C7
49
B♭maj7 B♭7 Gm7 G7 Fmaj7 F7 Dm7 D7

6

APPENDIX 6.2.11.
Harmonic Minor via The R.P.S.

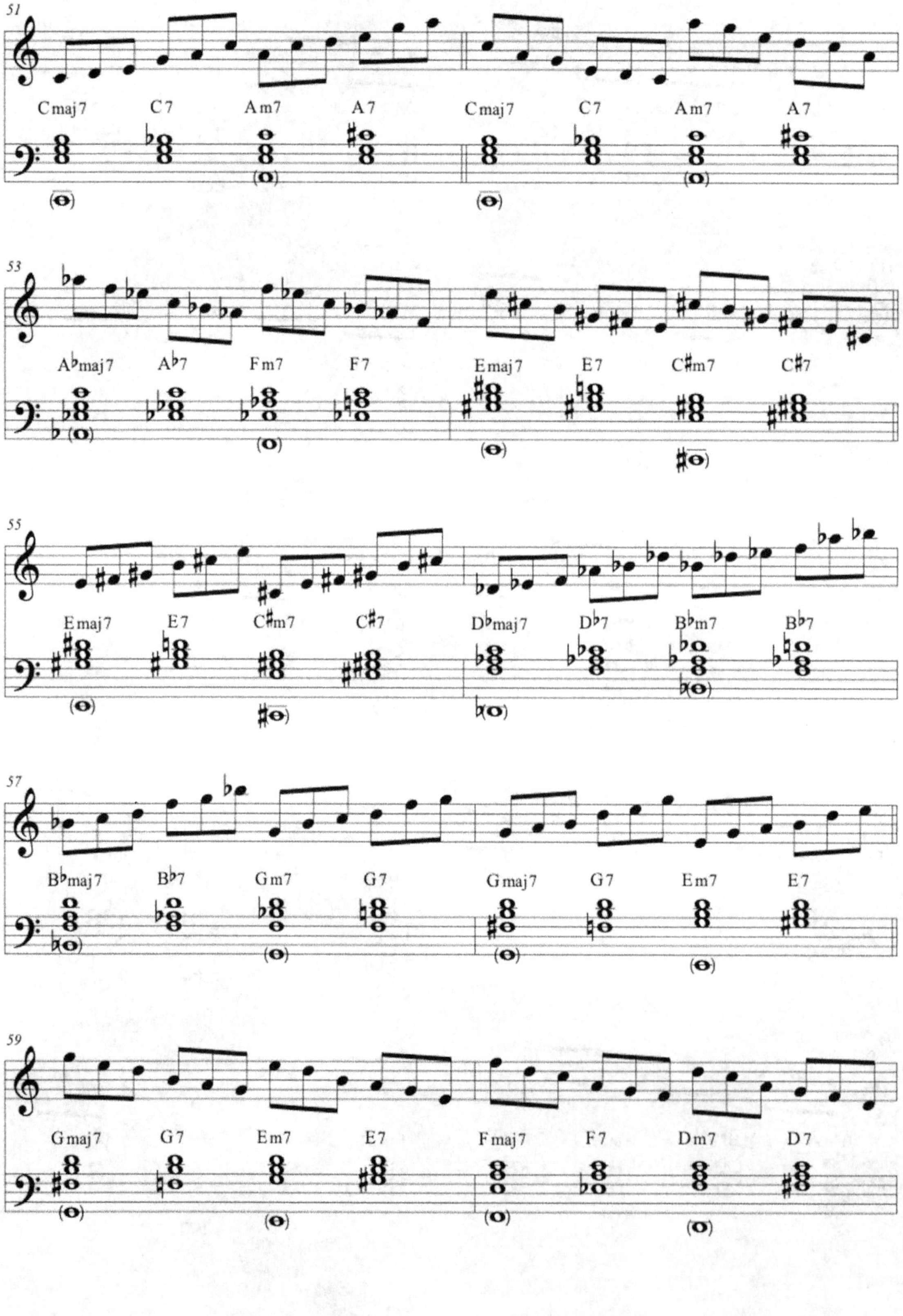
51
Cmaj7 C7 Am7 A7 Cmaj7 C7 Am7 A7
53
A♭maj7 A♭7 Fm7 F7 Emaj7 E7 C♯m7 C♯7
55
Emaj7 E7 C♯m7 C♯7 D♭maj7 D♭7 B♭m7 B♭7
57
B♭maj7 B♭7 Gm7 G7 Gmaj7 G7 Em7 E7
59
Gmaj7 G7 Em7 E7 Fmaj7 F7 Dm7 D7

APPENDIX 6.2.11. 7
Harmonic Minor via The R.P.S.

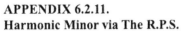

61
E♭maj7 E♭7 Cm7 C7 D♭maj7 D♭7 B♭m7 B♭7
63
Bmaj7 B7 A♭m7 A♭7 Amaj7 A7 F♯m7 F♯7
65
Amaj7 A7 F♯m7 F♯7 A♭maj7 A♭7 Fm7 F7
67
Gmaj7 G7 Em7 E7 G♭maj7 G♭7 E♭m7 E♭7
69
Fmaj7 F7 Dm7 D7 Emaj7 E7 C♯m7 C♯7

8

APPENDIX 6.2.11.
Harmonic Minor via The R.P.S.

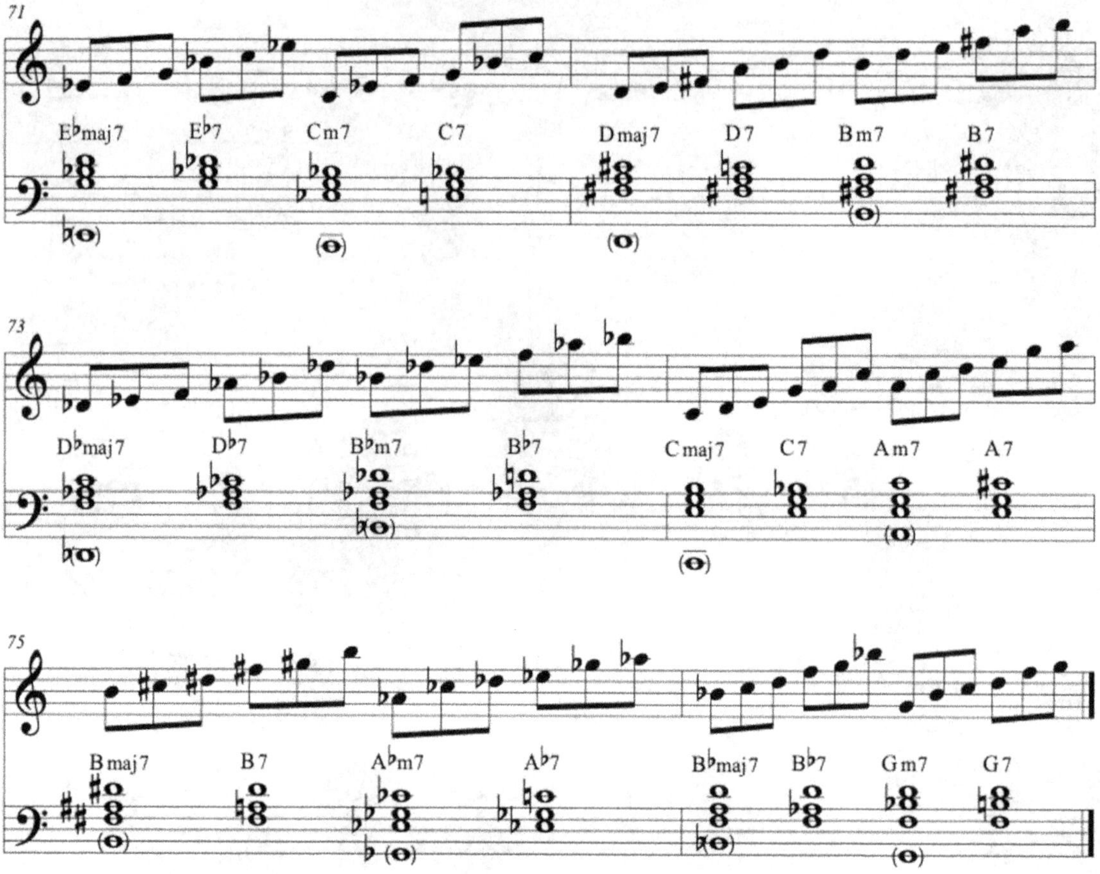
71
E♭maj7
E♭7
Cm7
C7
Dmaj7
D7
Bm7
B7
73
D♭maj7
D♭7
B♭m7
B♭7
Cmaj7
C7
Am7
A7
75
Bmaj7
B7
A♭m7
A♭7
B♭maj7
B♭7
Gm7
G7

6.2.12. Blues Scale

APPENDIX 6.2.12.
Blues Scale via R.P.S.

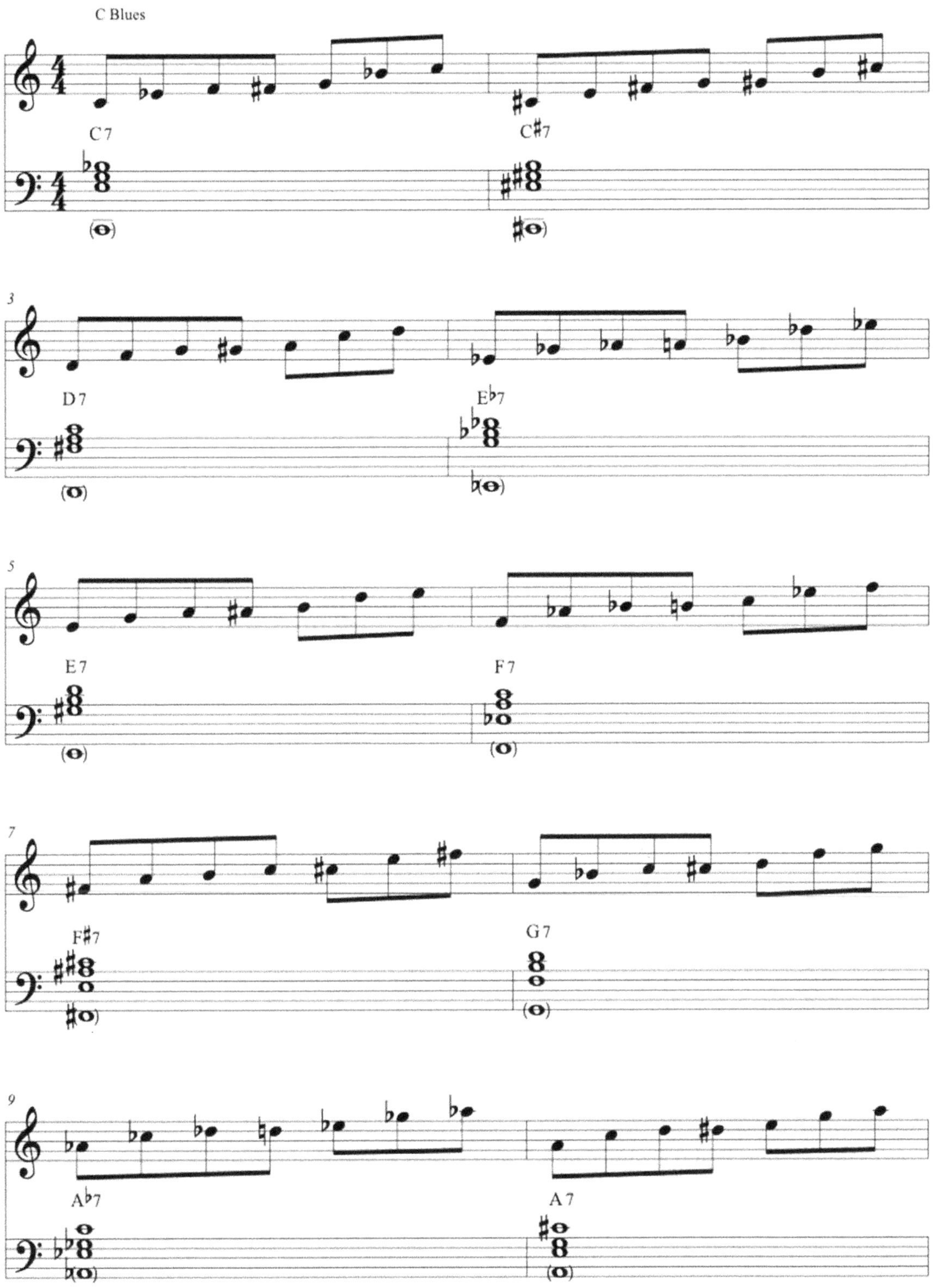

2

APPENDIX 6.2.12.
Blues Scale via R.P.S.

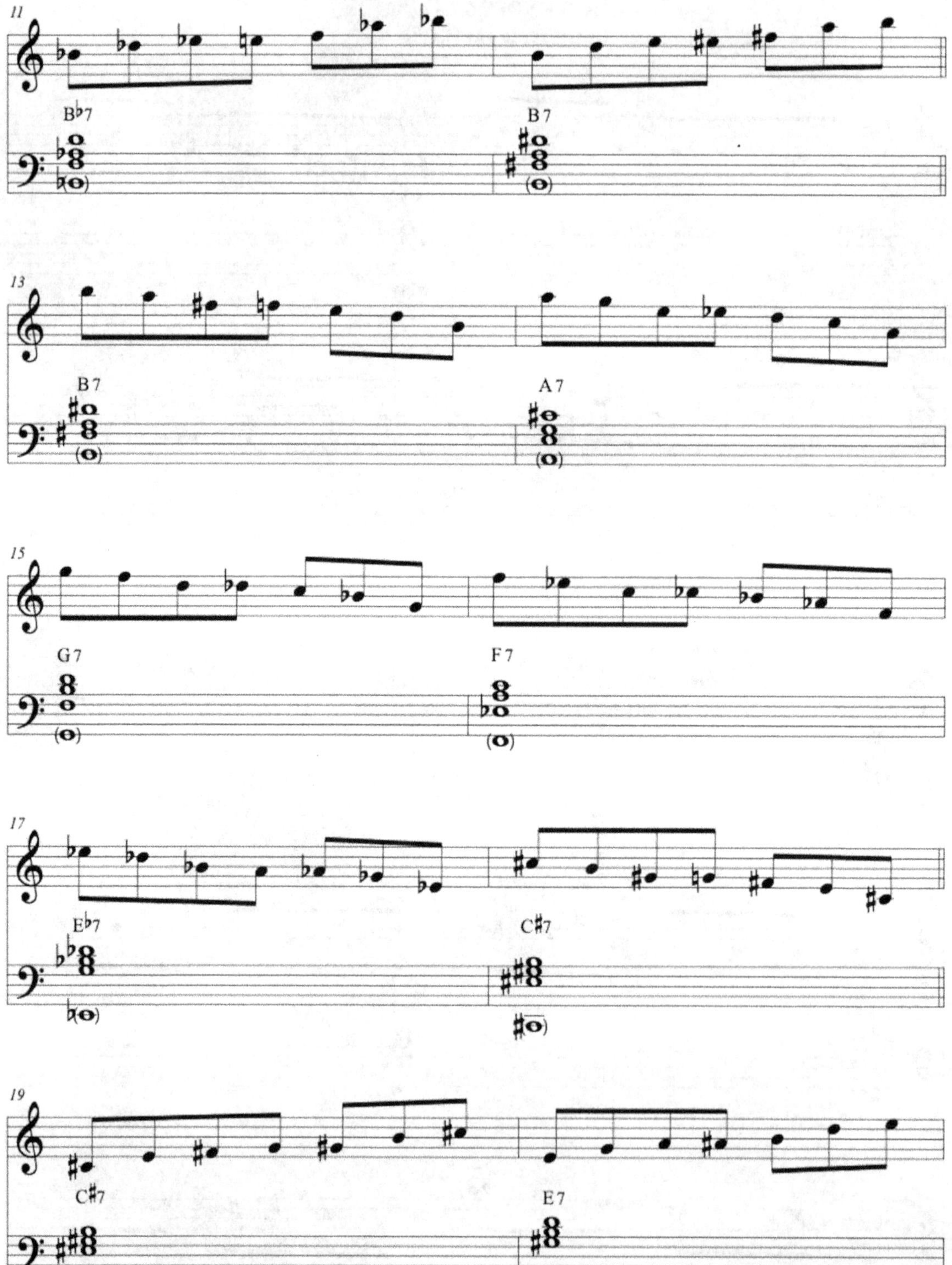
11
B♭7
B7
13
B7
A7
15
G7
F7
17
E♭7
C♯7
19
C♯7
E7

APPENDIX 6.2.12. 3

Blues Scale via R.P.S.

21
G 7
B♭7
23
B♭7
D 7
25
F♯7
F♯7
27
B 7
E 7
29
A 7
D 7

4

APPENDIX 6.2.12.
Blues Scale via R.P.S.

31
G7
C7
33
F7
B♭7
35
E♭7
A♭7
37
C♯7
C♯7
39
G7
G7

APPENDIX 6.2.12. 5

Blues Scale via R.P.S.

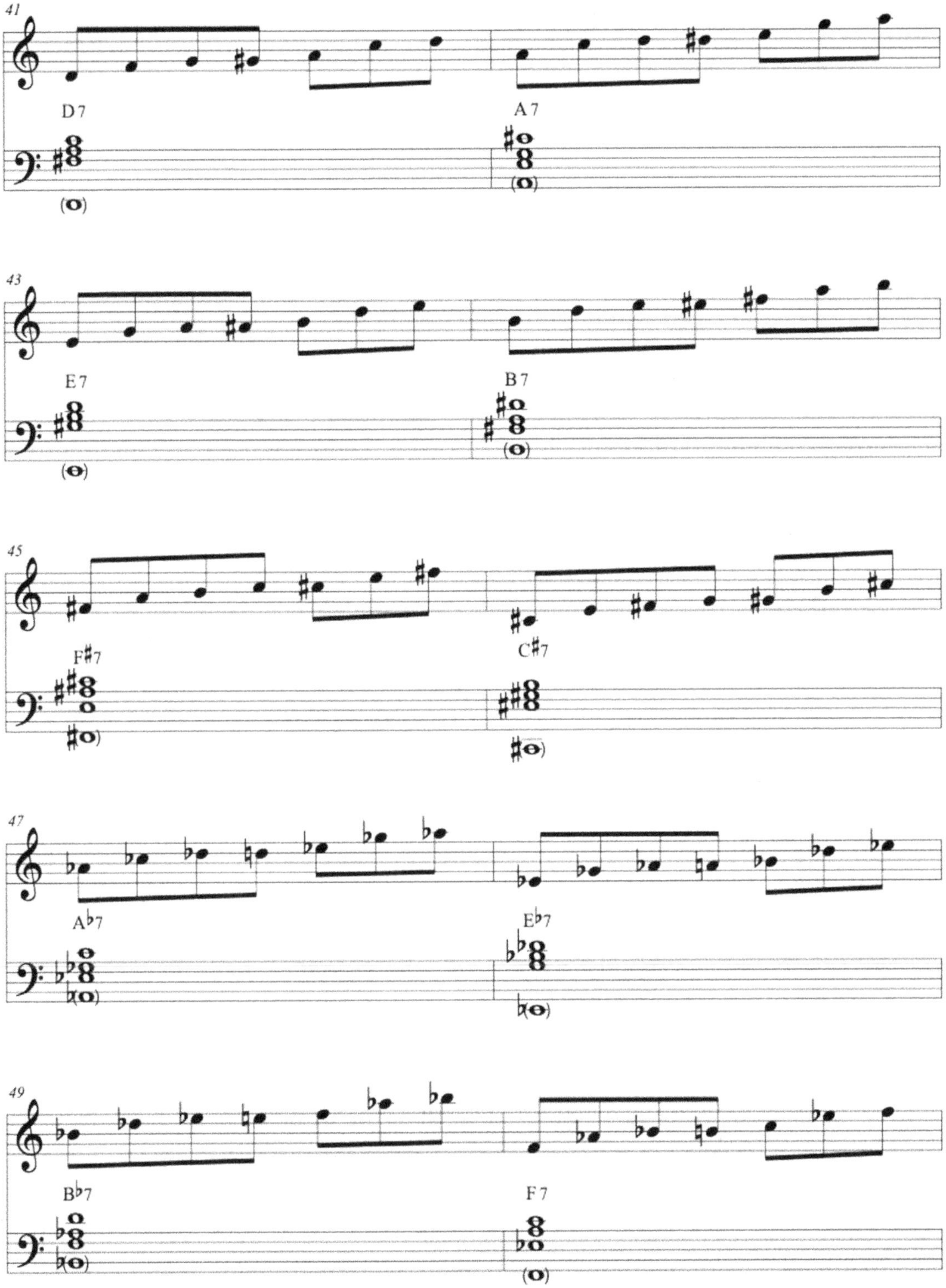
41
D 7
A 7
43
E 7
B 7
45
F♯7
C♯7
47
A♭7
E♭7
49
B♭7
F 7

6

APPENDIX 6.2.12.
Blues Scale via R.P.S.

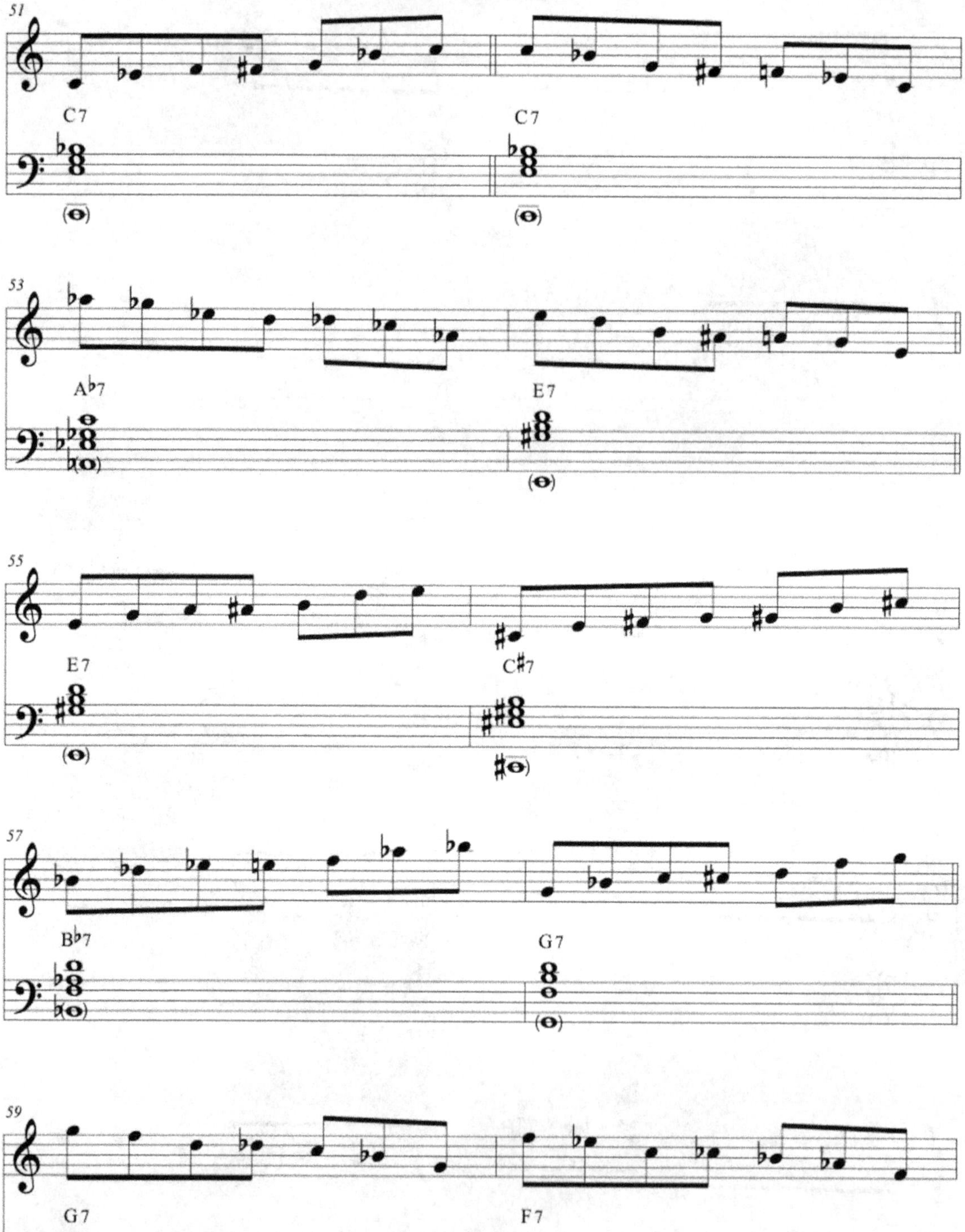
51
C7
C7
53
A♭7
E7
55
E7
C♯7
57
B♭7
G7
59
G7
F7

APPENDIX 6.2.12.
Blues Scale via R.P.S.

7

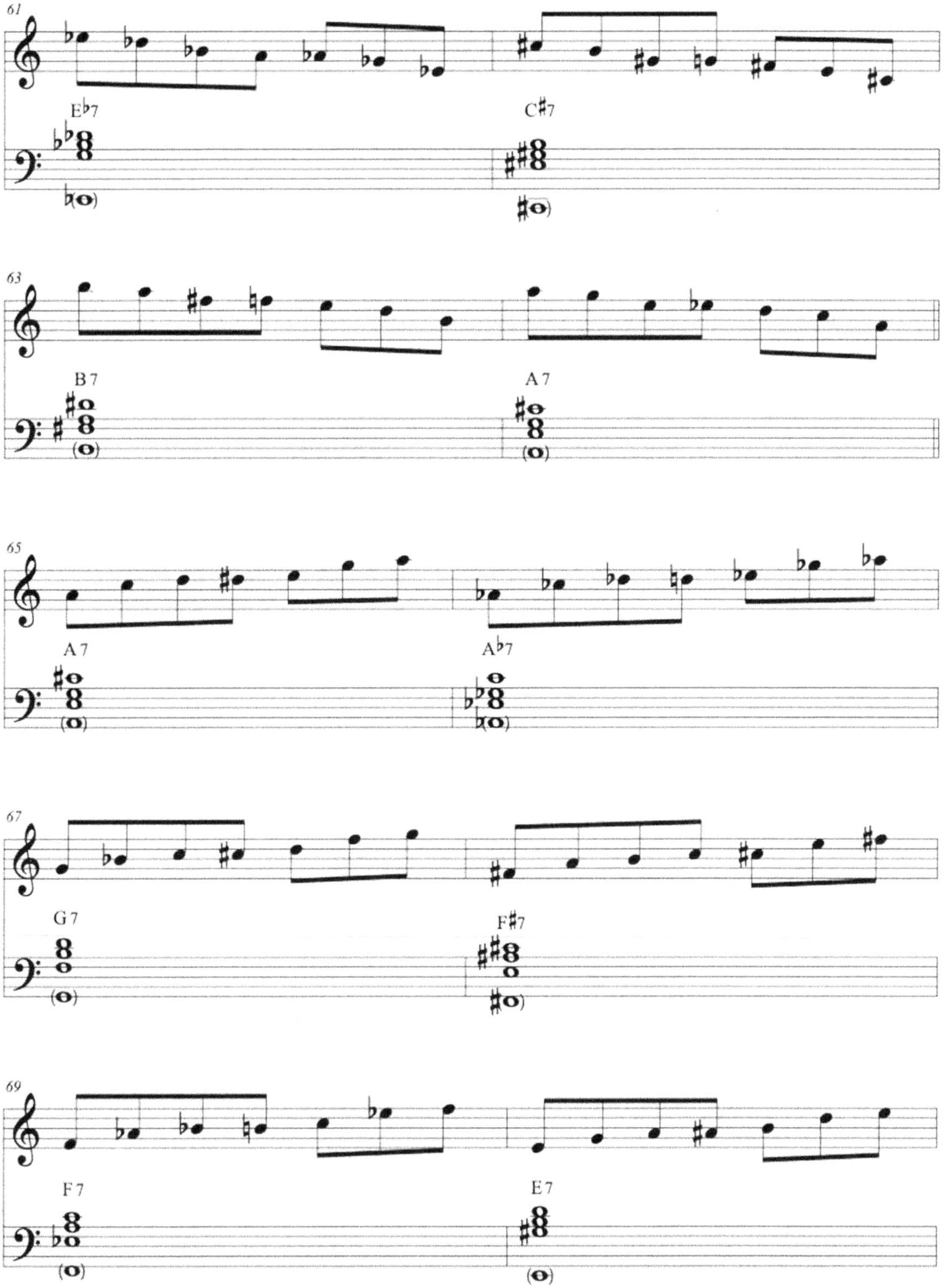
61
E♭7
C♯7
63
B7
A7
65
A7
A♭7
67
G7
F♯7
69
F7
E7

8

APPENDIX 6.2.12.
Blues Scale via R.P.S.

6.3. Modulation Grid

Modulation Grid—possibilities of Dominant and Diminished cycle
- Modulating to different keys with B Fully Diminished 7th, change one note down a step:

Ab	Ab	Ab	Ab ->	Abb
F	F	F ->	Fb	F
D	D ->	Db	D	D
B ->	Bb	B	B	B
Bo7	Bb7	Db7	E7	G7

Change one note up a step

Ab	Ab	Ab	Ab ->	A
F	F	F ->	F#	F
D	D ->	D#	D	D
B ->	C	B	B	B
Bo7	DØ7	FØ7	AbØ7	BØ7

6.3.1. One Note Down a Half Step

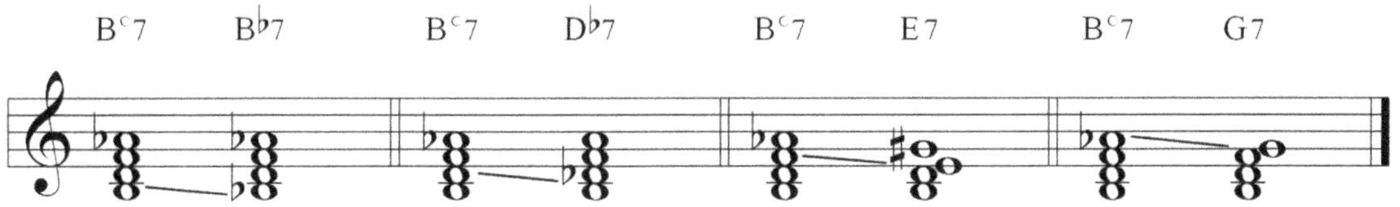

6.3.2. One Note Up a Half Step

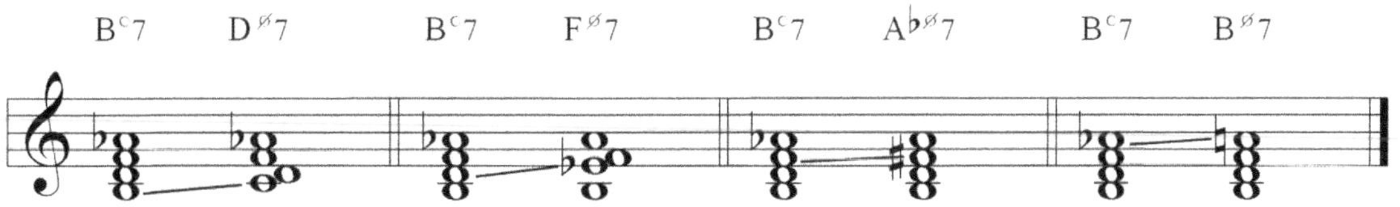

6.4. Super-Dominant (Chord)

6.4.1. Ten-Note Voicing

Description: F9 + Bmin9(maj7) = tritone away from min9maj7 chord
Creates a maj7 disparity between the notes in the first and second chord

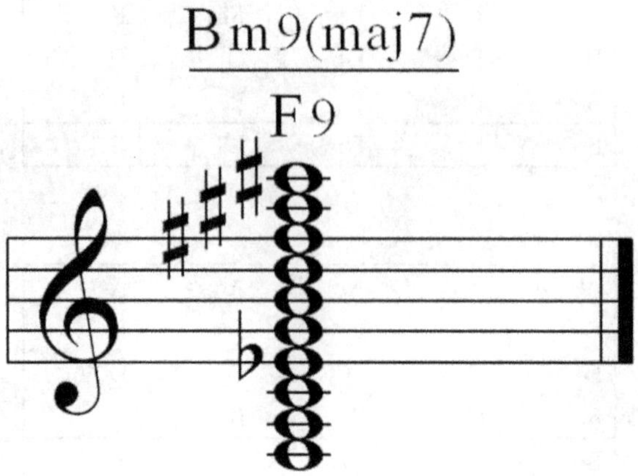

6.4.2. Eleven-Note Voicing

Description: An 11-note dominant chord, the only note missing is the major 7th of the root. It is an (almost) complete tone row vertically, in dominant. Its purpose is to be experienced as one texture, that is, the ending note to a big band chart, or a big resolution in dominant. A serial way of near justifying all twelve notes. There are no substitutes, they are already there. You must use every member of the chord. No omissions of chord tones.
A compositional element (as opposed to accompaniment).

6.4.3. Two-Base

1) 9th chord on bottom, then a Min$^{6/9}$(maj7) a tritone away.
[Major seventh becomes a suspension against the root]

- Concept originates from Miles's version of *Two Bass Hit*

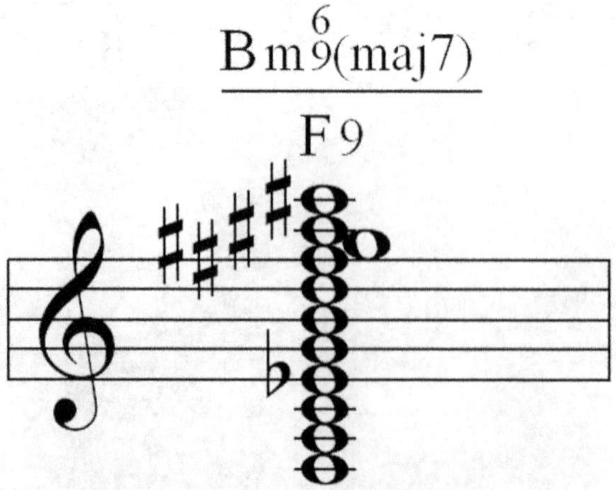

6.5. Bitonality

6.5.1. Conventional Bitonality in Major

Description:

Major and Dominant Functions

Triads	Chord Symbol	Function	Scale Solution
D C	Cmaj13(#11) C13(#11)	Major/Dominant	Lydian/Lydian Dom.
E C	Cmaj7(#5)	Major	Augmented
F# C	C7b9(#11)	Dominant	Inverted Diminished
A C	C13(b9)	Dominant	Inverted Diminished
Bb C	C9sus	Dominant	Mixolydian
B C	Cmaj7(#11#9)	Major	C-Eb-E-F#-G-B-C

6.5.2. Conventional Bitonality in Minor

Description: **See Chapter 8.2 for condensed corollary**

Minor Bitonality

Triads	Chord Symbol	Scale Solution
Bb C-	Cm9sus	Dorian
B C-	Cm(maj7b5)	C-D-Eb-Gb-G-A-B-C
D C-	Cm13(b5)	C-D-Eb-F-Gb-G-A-B-C
F C-	Cm13sus	Melodic Minor
G C-	Cm(maj9)	Melodic Minor

APPENDIX 6.5.1.
CONVENTIONAL BITONALITY IN MAJOR

Lydian
D△/C△
Cmaj13(♯11)
Lydian Dominant
D△/C△
C13(♯11)
Augmented
E△/C△
Cmaj7(♯5)
Melodic Minor Equivilent
E△/C△
Cmaj7(♯5)
Inverted Diminished (Half-Whole)
F♯△/C△
C7(♭9♯11)
Inverted Diminished (Half-Whole)
A△/C△
C13(♭9)
Mixolydian
B♭△/C△
C9sus
Synthetic Solution
B△/C△
Cmaj7(♯11♯9)
E♭△/D♭△
D♭maj13(♯11)
E♭△/D♭△
D♭13(♯11)
F△/D♭△
D♭maj7(♯5)
F△/D♭△
D♭maj7(♯5)
G△/D♭△
D♭7(♭9♯11)
B♭△/D♭△
D♭13(♭9)
B△/D♭△
D♭9sus
C△/D♭△
D♭maj7(♯11♯9)

Appendix 6.5.1. Conventional Bitonality in Major

E△/D△ Dmaj13(♯11)
E△/D△ D13(♯11)
F♯△/D△ Dmaj7(♯5)
F♯△/D△ Dmaj7(♯5)
A♭△/D△ D7(♭9♯11)
B△/D△ D13(♭9)
C△/D△ D9sus
C♯△/D△ Dmaj7(♯11♯9)
F△/E♭△ E♭maj13(♯11)
F△/E♭△ E♭13(♯11)
G△/E♭△ E♭maj7(♯5)
G△/E♭△ E♭maj7(♯5)
A△/E♭△ E♭7(♭9♯11)
C△/E♭△ E♭13(♭9)
D♭△/E♭△ E♭9sus
D△/E♭△ E♭maj7(♯11♯9)

Appendix 6.5.1. Conventional Bitonality in Major

F♯△/E△ Emaj13(♯11)
F♯△/E△ E13(♯11)
A♭△/E△ Emaj7(♯5)
A♭△/E△ Emaj7(♯5)
B♭△/E△ E7(♭9♯11)
C♯△/E△ E13(♭9)
D△/E△ E9sus
E♭△/E△ Emaj7(♯11♯9)
G△/F△ Fmaj13(♯11)
G△/F△ F13(♯11)
A△/F△ Fmaj7(♯5)
A△/F△ Fmaj7(♯5)
B△/F△ F7(♭9♯11)
D△/F△ F13(♭9)
E♭△/F△ F9sus
E△/F△ Fmaj7(♯11♯9)

Appendix 6.5.1. Conventional Bitonality in Major

A♭△/G♭△ G♭maj13(♯11)
A♭△/G♭△ G♭13(♯11)
B♭△/G♭△ G♭maj7(♯5)
B♭△/G♭△ G♭maj7(♯5)
C△/G♭△ G♭7(♭9♯11)
E♭△/G♭△ G♭13(♭9)
E△/G♭△ G♭9sus
F△/G♭△ G♭maj7(♯11♯9)
A△/G△ Gmaj13(♯11)
A△/G△ G13(♯11)
B△/G△ Gmaj7(♯5)
B△/G△ Gmaj7(♯5)
D♭△/G△ G7(♭9♯11)
E△/G△ G13(♭9)
F△/G△ G9sus
F♯△/G△ Gmaj7(♯11♯9)

Appendix 6.5.1. Conventional Bitonality in Major

B♭△/A♭△ A♭maj13(♯11)
B♭△/A♭△ A♭13(♯11)
C△/A♭△ A♭maj7(♯5)
C△/A♭△ A♭maj7(♯5)
D△/A♭△ A♭7(♭9♯11)
G△/A♭△ A♭13(♭9)
G♭△/A♭△ A♭9sus
G△/A♭△ A♭maj7(♯11♯9)
B△/A△ Amaj13(♯11)
B△/A△ A13(♯11)
C♯△/A△ Amaj7(♯5)
C♯△/A△ Amaj7(♯5)
E♭△/A△ A7(♭9♯11)
F♯△/A△ A13(♭9)
G△/A△ A9sus
A♭△/A△ Amaj7(♯11♯9)

Appendix 6.5.1. Conventional Bitonality in Major

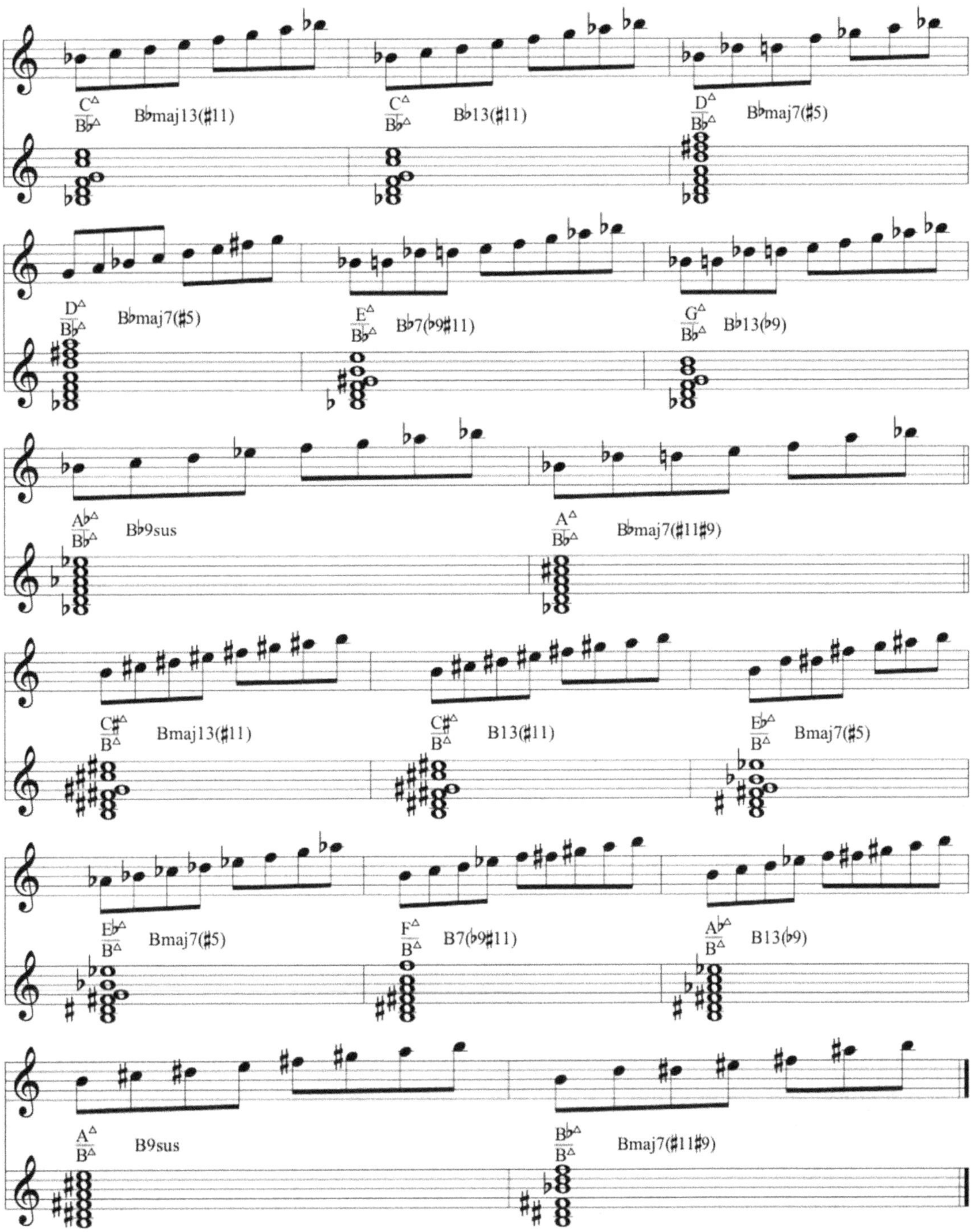
C△/B♭△ B♭maj13(♯11)
C△/B♭△ B♭13(♯11)
D△/B♭△ B♭maj7(♯5)
D△/B♭△ B♭maj7(♯5)
E△/B♭△ B♭7(♭9♯11)
G△/B♭△ B♭13(♭9)
A♭△/B♭△ B♭9sus
A△/B♭△ B♭maj7(♯11♯9)
C♯△/B△ Bmaj13(♯11)
C♯△/B△ B13(♯11)
E♭△/B△ Bmaj7(♯5)
E♭△/B△ Bmaj7(♯5)
F△/B△ B7(♭9♯11)
A♭△/B△ B13(♭9)
A△/B△ B9sus
B♭△/B△ Bmaj7(♯11♯9)

APPENDIX 6.5.2.
CONVENTIONAL BITONALITY IN MINOR

Dorian
Synthetic Solution
Synthetic Solution
B♭△ / C-
Cm9sus
B△ / C-
Cm(maj7♭5)
D△ / C-
Cm13(♭5)
Melodic Minor
Melodic Minor
F△ / C-
Cm13sus
G△ / C-
Cm(maj9)
B△ / D♭-
D♭m9sus
C△ / D♭-
D♭m(maj7♭5)
E♭△ / D♭-
D♭m13(♭5)
G♭△ / D♭-
D♭m13sus
A♭△ / D♭-
D♭m(maj9)
C△ / D-
Dm9sus
C♯△ / D-
Dm(maj7♭5)
E△ / D-
Dm13(♭5)
G△ / D-
Dm13sus
A△ / D-
Dm(maj9)

Appendix 6.5.2. Conventional Bitonality in Minor

D♭△/E♭-
E♭m9sus
D△/E♭-
E♭m(maj7♭5)
F△/E♭-
E♭m13(♭5)
A♭△/E♭-
E♭m13sus
B♭△/E♭-
E♭m(maj9)
D△/E-
Em9sus
E♭△/E-
Em(maj7♭5)
F♯△/E-
Em13(♭5)
A△/E-
Em13sus
B△/E-
Em(maj9)
E♭△/F-
Fm9sus
E△/F-
Fm(maj7♭5)
G△/F-
Fm13(♭5)
B♭△/F-
Fm13sus
C△/F-
Fm(maj9)

Appendix 6.5.2. Conventional Bitonality in Minor

E△/F♯-
F♯m9sus
F△/F♯-
F♯m(maj7♭5)
A♭△/F♯-
F♯m13(♭5)
B△/F♯-
F♯m13sus
C♯△/F♯-
F♯m(maj9)
F△/G-
Gm9sus
F♯△/G-
Gm(maj7♭5)
A△/G-
Gm13(♭5)
C△/G-
Gm13sus
D△/G-
Gm(maj9)
G♭△/A♭-
A♭m9sus
G△/A♭-
A♭m(maj7♭5)
B♭△/A♭-
A♭m13(♭5)
D♭△/A♭-
A♭m13sus
E♭△/A♭-
A♭m(maj9)

Appendix 6.5.2. Conventional Bitonality in Minor

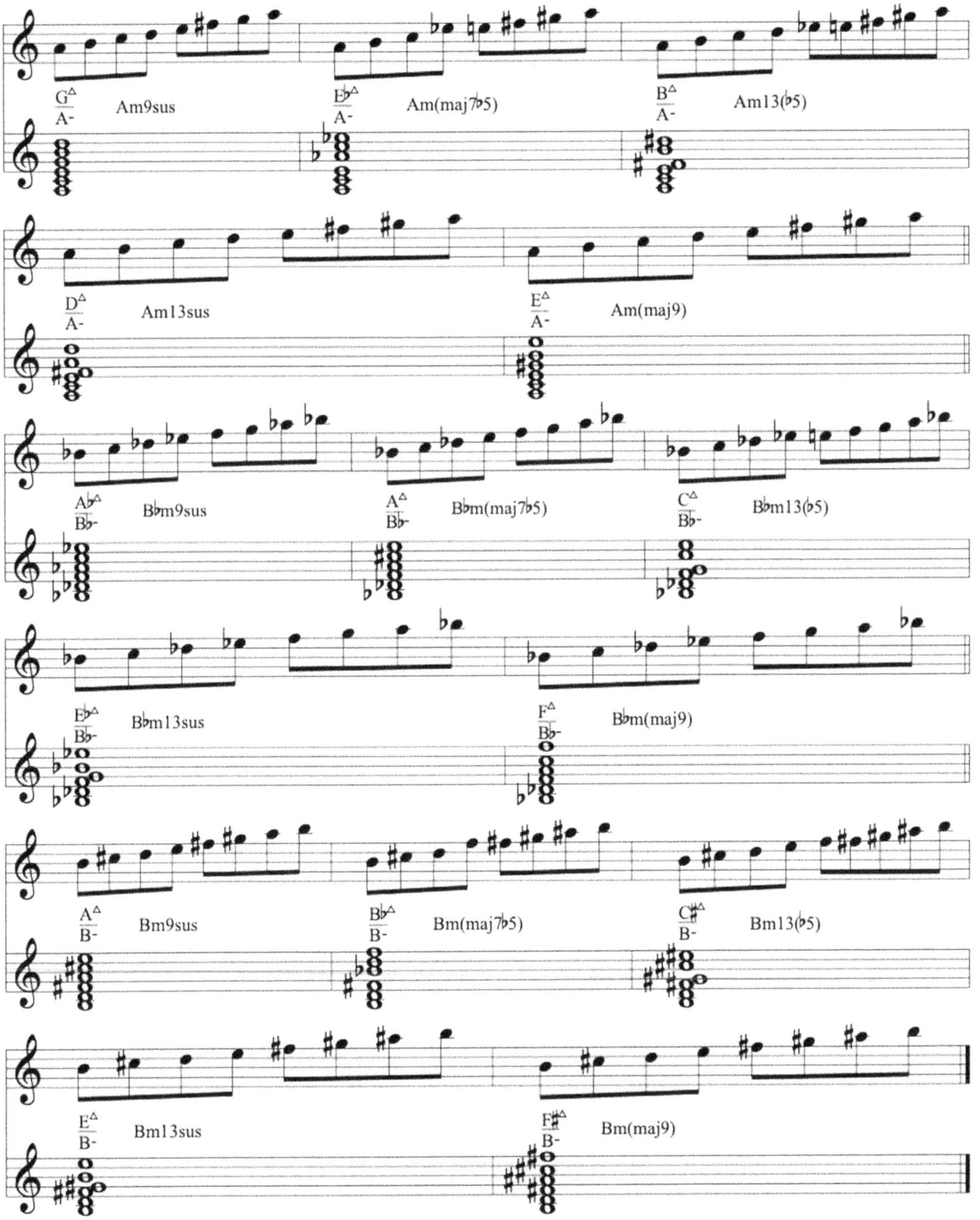
G△/A-
Am9sus
E♭△/A-
Am(maj7♭5)
B△/A-
Am13(♭5)
D△/A-
Am13sus
E△/A-
Am(maj9)
A♭△/B♭-
B♭m9sus
A△/B♭-
B♭m(maj7♭5)
C△/B♭-
B♭m13(♭5)
E♭△/B♭-
B♭m13sus
F△/B♭-
B♭m(maj9)
A△/B-
Bm9sus
B♭△/B-
Bm(maj7♭5)
C♯△/B-
Bm13(♭5)
E△/B-
Bm13sus
F♯△/B-
Bm(maj9)

Chapter 7

POLYMORPHIC ROOT SYSTEM

The PRS employs bi-chord and poly-chord symbol notation as a system of pitch class and set theory groupings (0, 3, 4, 7, 8) thereby enabling users not overly comfortable with the tradition of Western set theory or music notation (or even aware of these complex theoretical constructions) to easily embrace these compound structures.

System #1 (Prototype)

||: F	D#	C#	B	A	G	F#	E	D	C	Bb	G#	:||
Db	B	A	G	F	Eb	D	C	Bb	Ab	Gb	E	

System #2 (The Double)

||: F	D#	C#	B	A	G	F#	E	D	C	Bb	G#	:||
Db-	B-	A-	G-	F-	Eb-	D-	C-	Bb-	Ab-	Gb-	E-	

A chord from system #1 will produce the following *Exponent Chords*:

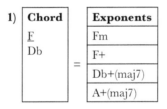

1) **Chord**		**Exponents**
F / Db	=	Fm
		F+
		Db+(maj7)
		A+(maj7)

While a chord from system #2 offers the following Exponents:

2) **Chord**		**Exponents**		**Derivative**
F / Db-	=	Fm	F+(maj7)*	E+
		Db	Db+(maj7)	C+
		A(maj7)*	A+(maj7)	G#+
		Am(maj7)*		

The exponent chords in System 2 marked with an asterisk are *Differential Chords* generated when the bottom triad is changed from a major to a minor triad. The major 7ths contained in the Exponent Chords of System #2 produce *Derivatives* which in turn form a Triple Augmented System, through the notes E, C, and G#. Branching off into System #2a, by extracting 4 alternating chords, from System 2 each a semi-tone apart, produces all 12 notes of the chromatic scale in the Derivatives of each chord without any repeated notes.

2a) F/Db-	=	Ab+, C+, E+ (Derivative 1)
D#/B-	=	F#+, A#+, D+ (Derivative 2)
F#/D-	=	A+, C#+, F+ (Derivative 3)
E/C-	=	G+, B+, D#+ (Derivative 4)

12-Tone Deduction (Derivative)

System #2b involves taking any chord from System #2, that is, F/Db- and then deducing which notes out of the chromatic scale are missing from that chord. Through that deduction the remaining six notes of the chromatic scale were found to be the Derivatives of two opposing systems, which in turn formed two augmented triads with a major 7th root disparity. Thus, in the example of F/Db-, which contains the notes Db-Fb-Ab, F-A-C, the missing notes are Eb-G-B, D, F#-A#

2b)

C A F	A# F# D	(Derivative #2)
Ab Fb Db	B G Eb	(Derivative #4)
(6)	(6)	

- *Go up a whole tone from the root of the Chord from System #2 and form an Augmented Triad based on that root;*
- Then, go up a major 7th away from the Augmented Triad and form another Augmented Triad

D+
Eb+
F
Db-

12-Tone Deduction (Singularity)

To achieve the derivative based structure from the chord in Model #2 of the Double Hexagon, the reduction formula is:

Model #1: Down a Whole Step from Root Chord

Eb B- F Db-

Model #2: Up a Whole Step from Root Chord

G Eb- F Db-

What's the Point?

Every note of "Model" #1 and #2 has the potential to support the other eleven-tones of the chromatic scale (from a "root" perspective)—a matter of [aural] perception—The PRS.

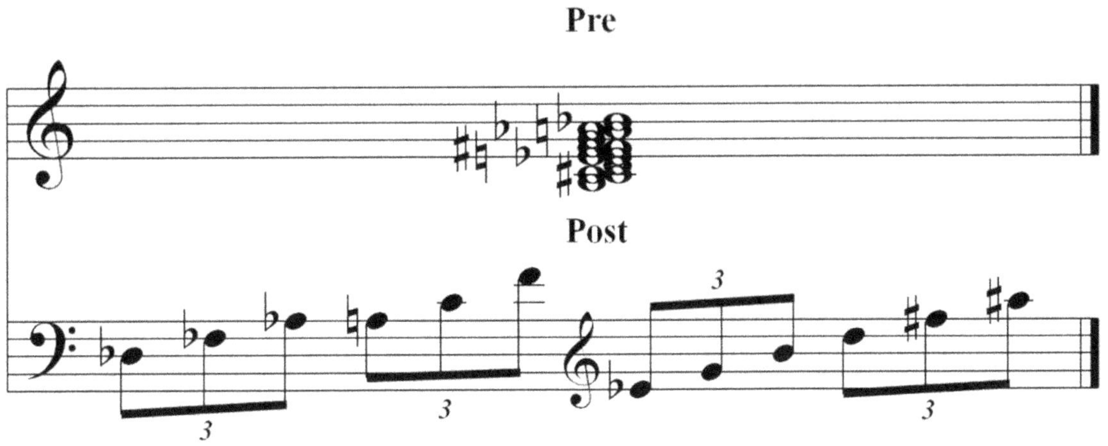

7.1. System 1 (Prototype)

F△/D♭△
D♯△/B△
C♯△/A△
B△/G△
A△/F△
G△/E♭△
F♯△/D△
E△/C△
D△/B♭△
C△/A♭△
B♭△/G♭△
G♯△/E△

7.2. System 2 (The Double)

F△/D♭-
D♯△/B-
C♯△/A-
B△/G-
A△/F-
G△/E♭-
F♯△/D-
E△/C-
D△/B♭-
C△/A♭-
B♭△/G♭-
G♯△/E-

7.3. Variation 1

F△/D♭△
B△/C△
D♯△/B△
A△/B♭△
C♯△/A△
G△/A♭△
B△/G△
F△/G♭△
A△/F△
D♯△/E△
G△/E♭△
C♯△/D△
E△/C△
A♯△/B△
D△/B♭△
G♯△/A△
C△/A♭△
F♯△/G△
B♭△/G♭△
E△/F△
G♯△/E△
D△/E♭△
F♯△/D△
C△/D♭△

7.4. Variation 2

F△/D♭-
B△/C△
D♯△/B-
A△/B♭△
C♯△/A-
G△/A♭△
B△/G-
F△/G♭△
A△/F-
D♯△/E△
G△/E♭-
C♯△/D△
E△/C-
A♯△/B△
D△/B♭-
G♯△/A△
C△/A♭-
F♯△/G△
B♭△/G♭-
E△/F△
G♯△/E-
D△/E♭△
F♯△/D-
C△/D♭△

7.5. Variation 3

F△/D♭△
F△/D♭-
E△/C△
E△/C-
D♯△/B△
D♯△/B-
D△/B♭△
D△/B♭-
C♯△/A△
C♯△/A-
C△/A♭△
C△/A♭-
B△/G△
B△/G-
B♭△/G♭△
B♭△/G♭-
A△/F△
A△/F-
G♯△/E△
G♯△/E-
G△/E♭△
G△/E♭-
F♯△/D△
F♯△/D-

7.6. Variation 4

7.7. Variation 5

Chapter 8

COMPOSITION AND ARRANGING

8.1. McGill Paper (with compositions)

Arranging Methods

Term Paper

Private Lessons in Composition

Tom McGill

York University

PhD

Graduate Program in Music

Musi5006B

Ron Westray

Fall 2018

Table of Contents

1 Introduction

This *Arranging Methods* paper discusses arranging concepts with examples to clarify the ideas. The methods target big band configurations up to full brass, sax, and trombone sections that are supported by a rhythm section of bass and drums. The concepts were extracted from weekly labs with Professor Westray, as well as the book called *The Contemporary Arranger: Definitive Addition* (Sebeski 1994). Section 2 of this document provides details of the concepts with examples that are largely from the author's arrangements. Section 3 describes seven original arrangements that identify the concepts and other influential objectives that were used to create these compositions. The supporting scores and jazz standard lead sheets are in the appendix of Original Arrangements.

2 Arranging Concepts

2.1 Balance

Tonal Balance (Sebesky 1994, 2)

- Distribute any set of instruments for best sound

Melody Balance

- Minimize number of unique melodic ideas
- Create unity through developing each melodic idea (i.e., motifs)
- Grow composition organically through motif development

Instrumentation

- Add instruments for development
- Start slow and build
- Tendency is to start to fast rather than building interest organically

Time

- Be aware of total time and develop melody to match available time

2.2 Economy

- Omit what is not absolutely necessary
- Every component must have a reason (i.e., less is more)

2.3 Focus

- Arranger's job to divert listener to primary elements
    - Primary—soloist
    - Secondary—background sax, strings
    - Tertiary—rhythm section

2.4 Variety

- Variety is important to maintain listener interest
- Change opportunities
    - tone color/timbre
    - instrument combinations
    - add more instruments strategically up to full tutti
    - muting—many combinations
    - voicing—clustered, open, semi-open, closed
    - unison vs. multi-part

- Create a list of all possibilities from opportunity categories above before starting to broaden creative process
- Write a detailed sketch or outline (Sebesky 1994, 8)
    - treble clef plus two bass clefs
    - notate instruments selected beside each theme
    - notate with chord types to define harmonic rhythm
- **Example of changing the harmony and instrumentation to create variety.**
    - Bar 5, 13, 27 show variety for the same theme in All the Things Your Are (version 2) located in the appendix, as shown in Figure 8.1

Figure 8.1 Three variations used on the same theme of the A sections of the same chorus.

2.5 Brass Combo Arranging

- Determine sound quality and select instruments
    - Potential characteristics—big, powerful, open, light, intimate, etc.
- Example of 4 trombones doubling 4 trumpets
    - Trombones double 1 octave lower (see Figure 8.2)
    - Closed voicing for brilliance and mobility
    - Example in Figure 8.2 from All the Things You Are, bar 31

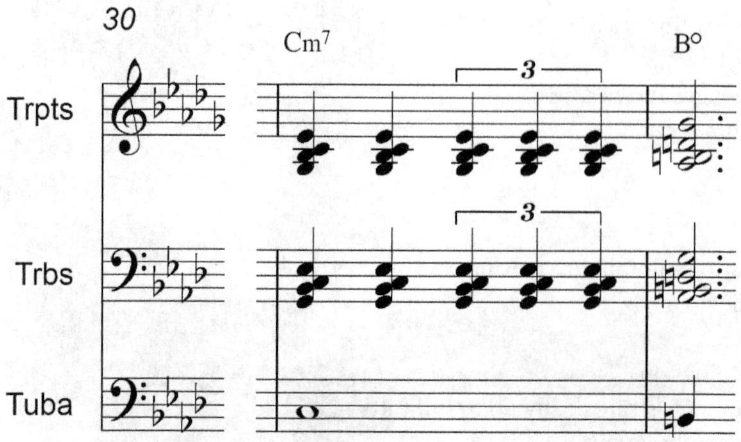

Figure 8.2 Trombones doubling trumpets with closed voicings.

- Other factors
  - Semi-open for grounded/anchored sound (Sebesky 1994, 33)
  - No doubling for intimate sound
  - Do not interrupt doubling until change of mood required
  - Octave doubling works for strong and rhythmic composition
    - Avoid for ballad since overpowering
  - Ways to make small ensembles sound bigger
    - Use octave doubling
    - Trumpet and trombone motion should be parallel not contrary
    - Omit 3rds and add 6ths, 9ths and higher order extensions
- Voicing rules
  - Melody voice must always be highest within the full set of voices
    - Lower voices must not overpower upper voices
  - Clusters effective with brass
  - Use 7ths and 3rds in lower to middle register. Altered extension in higher registers.
  - Leave out the 5th since it weakens resonance (Sebesky 1994, 4)
  - Separate octave doubling with 5 note chords to end phrase and move to a new voicing
  - Use higher number chord tones for closure chords

2.6 Brass and Woodwind Combo Arranging

- Sax sections
  - Voicing types
    - clustered, closed, semi-open and open (see Figure 8.3)
    - Semi-open uses drop 2
      - Creates mellower, less dynamic sound
    - Fully open
      - Good for ballads, slow moving, creates organ like sound
      - Cluster
      - Good for parallel closed melodic motion
      - 2^{nd-s} create "bite" in tonality

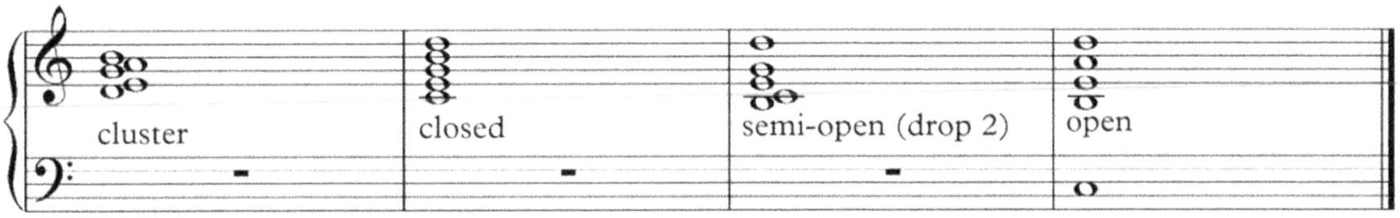

Figure 8.3 Voicing options—example Cmaj7 chord.

  - Examples of big band wind sections (Sebeski 1994,)
    - Goodman, Shaw—2 altos, one tenor, one baritone
    - Herman Herd—3 tenors, 1 baritone
    - Glen Miller—clarinet plus 2 alto, 2 tenor in closed voicing
    - Thornhill—clarinet and French horn unison over alto, 2 tenor, baritone (velvety)
    - If 5th sax added—2 altos, 2 tenors, one baritone
      - Typical in contemporary jazz
  - Examples of big band trombone sections (Westray 2018)
    - Ellington—3 trombones
    - Basie—4 trombones
    - Kenton—5 trombones (double top and bottom)

- Voicing of mixed woodwinds
  - clustered voicings not preferred for woodwinds
    - better voiced in 3rds, 4ths
  - Clarinet blends with many woodwinds
    - Voice in 3rds
- Section sound levels must be balanced through adding or subtracting instruments (i.e., no amplifiers)
- Voicing procedures vary with arrangers
  - Ellington vs. Hefti, Cohn vs. Russo
  - Basie or Herman example
    - 4 trumpets, 4 trombones, 5 saxes, bass
    - Trombones often double the trumpets.
    - Saxes overlap trumpets and trombones
- Doubling
  - Baritone sax often doubles bottom trombone
  - Trombone often doubles trumpet one octave lower
  - 2nd Tenor often doubles lead alto sax
  - 2nd alto often doubles 1st trumpet

2.7 Rhythmic Signature

- A unique rhythmic pattern created by the composer used to
  - Lead into a new section
  - Or as a background to create movement under a sustained melody note (e.g., whole note or longer)
- Create rhythmic pattern and then determines melodic and harmonic content that will use the pattern. Demonstrated by the pattern on left of Figure 8.4 becomes trombone melody on the right (i.e., see bar 13 of All the Things You Are, version 2 in appendix)
  - Used by Mingus

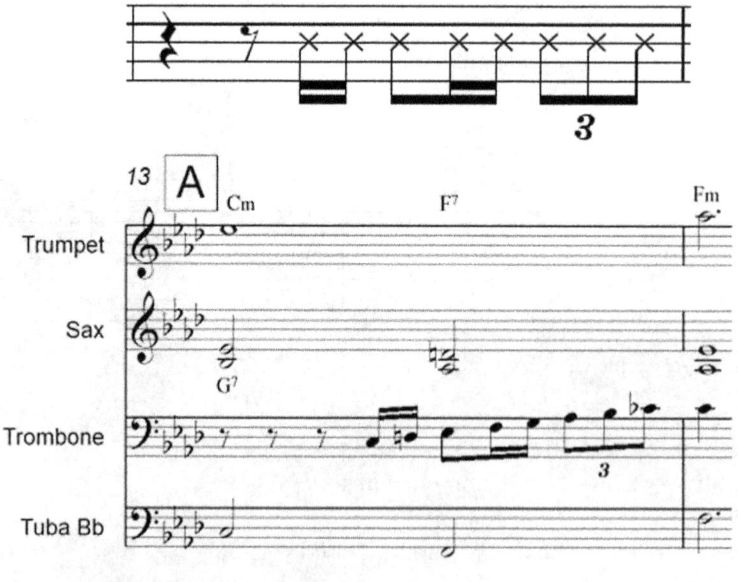

Figure 8.4 Rhythmic pattern becomes a rhythmic signature.

2.8 Root Displacement

- Takes the form of A/B (i.e., A chord over B root)
  - "A" can be any of chord over any root "B"
- Often used to simplify recognizing chord extension in a simpler format
- Example in Figure 8.5 of chord displacement

- Expected lead sheet chord progression is Bbm to Eb^7 to Ab^{maj7} (i.e., ii^{m7}-V^7-I^{maj7})
- Eb^7 substitutes are $A7^{(\#9)}$/Eb
  - $A7^{(\#9)}$ represents $^{\#}4$, $^{b}7$, $^{b}9$, 3rd ,^{13} extensions with respect to an Eb root
- then A^7 tritone substitute of Eb^7 with $Eb7^{(b9)}$/A
  - Eb^7 represents $^{\#}4$, $^{b}7$, $^{b}9$, 3rd ,5th extensions with respect to an A root

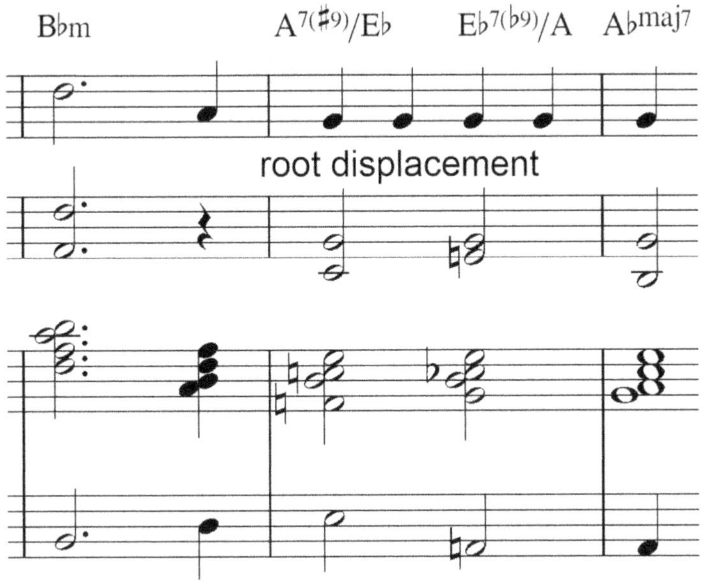

Figure 8.5 Root displacement from Bar 10,11,12 of All the Things You Are (Version 3).

2.9 Voice Leading

- 5 part harmony
  - Each part is an individual voice with voice leading
  - Organic movement objective is to limit movement between notes to a semi-tone for a single voice
  - Avoid doubling of voices
    - implies ^{9th}, ^{13th}, are required in major and minor tonality
    - implies dominant tonality can use altered accidentals (ie. $^{b}9$, $^{\#}9$, 11, $^{\#}11$, $^{b}13$)
    - fully diminished 7^{ths} can use 9th and ^{13th}
  - When harmonizing melody with large leaps
    - upper voice must deviate from closed voicing to prevent voice crossing of lower voices as shown in Figures 8.6. Lower 4 voices follow organic voice leading.

Figure 8.6 Upper voice of misty deviates from closed voicing.

- Figure 8.7 is an example of organic voice leading through suspensions from All the Things Your Are (version 3) in bars 18, 19 and 20 (i.e., see score in appendix).

Figure 8.7 Organic voicing leading with suspensions.

2.10 Fractal Displacement

- Various meanings
  - Shifting the beat or beat fraction on which a motif begins
  - Or changing the note values or rest within a motif while maintaining its recognizable shape.
  - Or using an alternative time over the time signatures value as shown in Figure 8.8.
    - Upper 3 staffs (i.e., Trumpets, Sax, Trombones) follow a 5-tuple, 6-tuple and 7-tuple feel over the 4/4 time of the lower bass clef (i.e., bass)

Figure 8.8 Rhythmic displacement example.

There are many alternative time types possible over a 4/4 signature as shown in Figure 8.9.

Figure 8.9 Example of fractal displacement options over 4/4 time.

2.11 Block Chord Harmonization of Melody

- Harmonic rhythm often provides chord changes on the 1st beat of each bar or on one and three of bar with many melodic notes filling in between these anchored chord changes.
  - Each of these melody notes can be harmonized with block chords
  - Block chords are common in the works of George Shearing
- Example in Figure 8.10 for a common ii^7–V^7 sequence
  - 3 melody notes between ii^7 – V^7 changes (i.e., Bb^{m7} to Eb^7)
  - Step 1 chose a matching set of bass note using one of these 3 methods
    1) Cycle of 5ths counting backward 3 melody notes from destination (i.e., Eb7) as shown in Figure 8.10
       - Large font chords represent the lead sheet anchor chords on beats 1 and 3
       - Smaller font chords harmonized the intervening melody notes
       - Repeating C melody notes are harmonized with C7^{b9}, F^{m7}, Bb^9 to reach the destination Eb^7 with the C (i.e., 13th) on top

Figure 8.10 Block harmonization of all melody notes using circle of 4ths.

2) Chromatic descending sequence
    - Figure 8.11 uses chromatic tritone sub (i.e., D^7 to C^7) and then a circle of fourths harmonization of C^7 to F^{m7}

Figure 8.11 Block harmonization using chromatic and circle of 4ths.

3) Chromatic rising sequence (less common approach)

2.12 Chord Progression Forms

- Following chord progression forms are useful as introductions, backgrounds or new compositions. Chords are selected to align with the tonality of the chorus and introduce the first chord of the chorus
  1) iii-VI-ii^{m7}-V^7
  2) III – VI – ^{b}III – ^{b}VI - II- V – ^{b}VI – ^{b}II – I.
     - 4 bar intro each chord receives 2 beats
     - Many chord qualities supported
       - Alternate minor 7 chords and dominant 7s
         - Example – E^{m7} A^7 Eb^{m7} Ab^7 Dm^7 G^7 Ab^{m7} Db^7 I^{maj7}
       - All Dominant 7s
         - E^7 A^7 Eb^7 Ab^7 D^7 G^7 Ab^7 Db^7 to I^{maj7}
     - Alternating "half-diminished 7s" with dominant 7s
  3) Pedal on 5th of V^7 as an intro
     - Rhythmically climb the modes belonging to the tonic key
     - Last half bar of the intro strike V^7 to introduce tonic chord on beat one of A section
     - Example
     - D pedal
       - Rhythmic 1st inversion triads of D^m, E^m, F^{maj}, G^{maj}, A^m
  4) Tadd Dameron
     - Chord changes - $^b III^7$ $^b VI^7$ $^b II^7$ I^{maj7} (see Figure 8.12)

Figure 8.12 Todd Dameron Progression in Green Dolphin (Version 2) Bar 5.

5) Down semi-tone and Up whole tone chord sequence
   - Example - Ab^{m7} G^{7} A^{m7} Ab^{7} Bb^{m7} A^{7} B^{m7} Bb^{7} C^{m7} B^{7} Db^{7} C^{maj7}
   - Going up a tone is equivalent to down a semi-tone due to minor 3rd relationship
6) Semi-tone climb to cycle of 4ths sequence
   - Example – C^{6} C#^{dim7} Dm^{7} Eb^{dim7} E^{m7} A^{7} D^{m7} G^{7} C^{maj7}
7) Semi-tone bassline descent with alternating major 7th and dominant 7th chords (Figure 8.13)
   - Example—Bb^{maj7}, A7$^{b9\#4}$, Ab^{maj7}, G7$^{b9\#4}$, Gb^{maj7}, F7$^{b9\#4}$, etc.

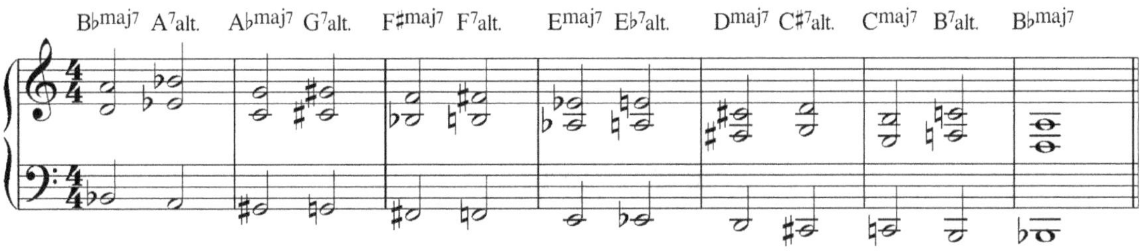

Figure 8.13 Chromatic bass line with alternating maj7s and alt7s.

8) Repeating Pitch top voice over various changes (see Figure 8.14)

Figure 8.14 Fixed melody note over various chord changes, misty (V1) bars 2 to 5.

9) Extending tonic in the style of Monk - I^{maj7}, ii^{m7}, ^{b}iii7, iii^{m7}, I^{maj7} (see Figure 8.15)

Figure 8.15 Extending tonic example from Misty (Version 1).

10) Dominant 7th substitutes related by a minor 3rd
   - Ab^{7}, F^{7}, B^{7}, D^{7} share the diminished minor 3rd axis and are interchangeable leading to Db^{7} (i.e., tritone sub) and C^{maj7}, as shown in the sax section of Figure 8.16 from bars 8,9,10 of *Green Dolphin Street* (version 2)

Figure 8.16 Dominant 7th diminished axis substitutes.

2.13 Quartal Harmony

- Common in the works of McCoy Tyner
- Chords are constructed from four stacked 4ths of diatonic tones within the mode
    - Dorian top interval is a 3rd. Other modes top interval is a 4th.
    - Dorian inversions use the tones of the first inversion but stacked such that the 3rd interval may appear within the stack rather than on the top interval
    - Ionian chords are never stacked on the root. The lowest pitch of the chord is either the 3rd or the 5th.
- Planing Chords are formed from choosing diatonic pitches from the given mode (i.e., Dorian, Mixolydian, Lydian, etc.)
- Figure 8.17 bar 12,13,14, harmonizes quartile using Dorian, Mixolydian and Ionian modes from Misty (Version 2) in the Appendix.

- The Bb^{m7} Dorian is the 2nd inversion and therefore does not have a stacked 3rd on top
- Bar 13 beats 2 to 4, planes in the Mixolydian mode for Eb^{7}
- Bar 14 beat 1, shows an Ionian quartal in the 2nd inversion built on the 5th
- Inversions are used to enable harmonizing each melody note while maintaining the anchored chords of lead sheet

- Figures 18 through 15 are derived from Professor Westray's studio sessions (Westray 2018).

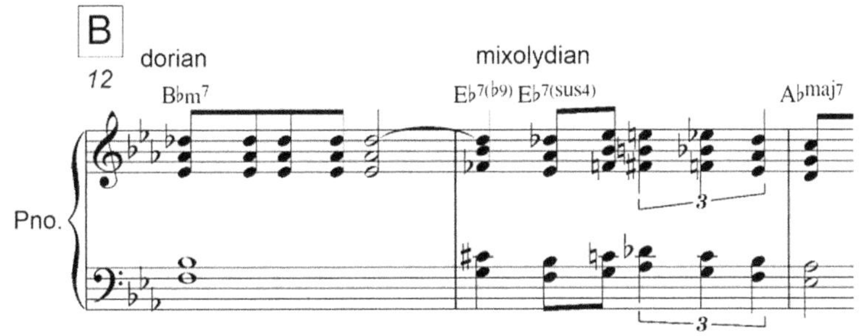

Figure 8.17 Dorian, Mixolydian, Ionian Harmonization Example from Misty(V2).

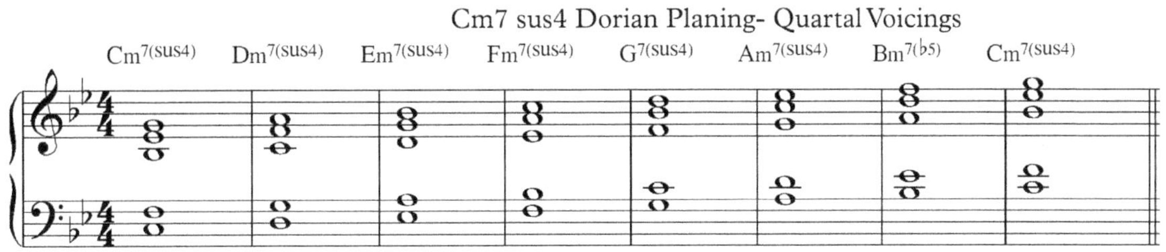

Figure 8.18 Dorian Planing.

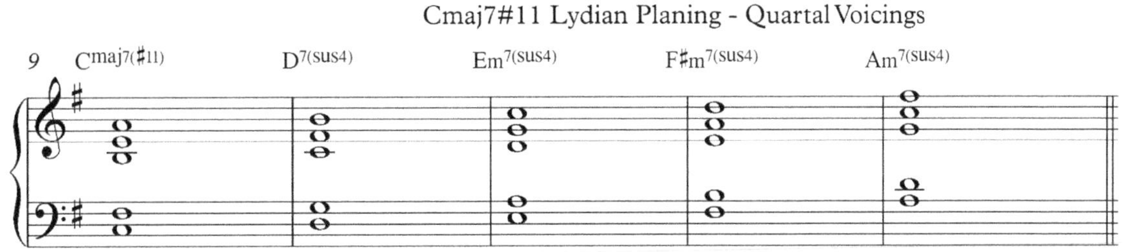

Figure 8.19 Lydian Planing.

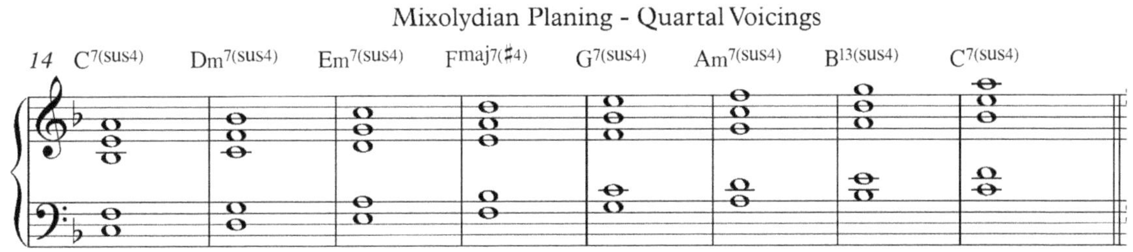

Figure 8.20 Mixolydian Planing.

Lydian Dominant Inversions - Quartal Voicings

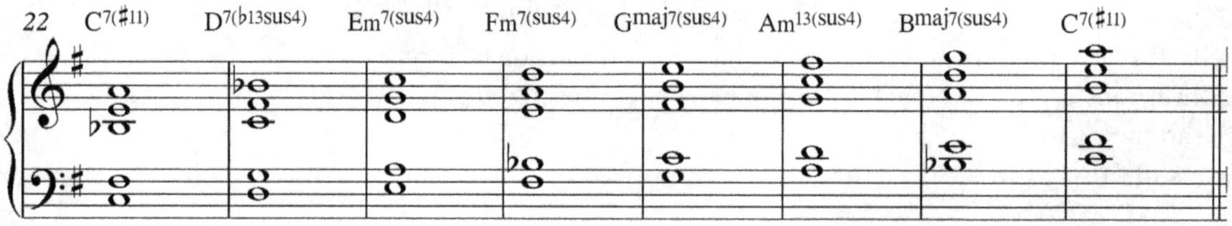

Figure 8.21 Lydian Dominant Planing.

Dorian Chromatic Planing - Quartal Voicings

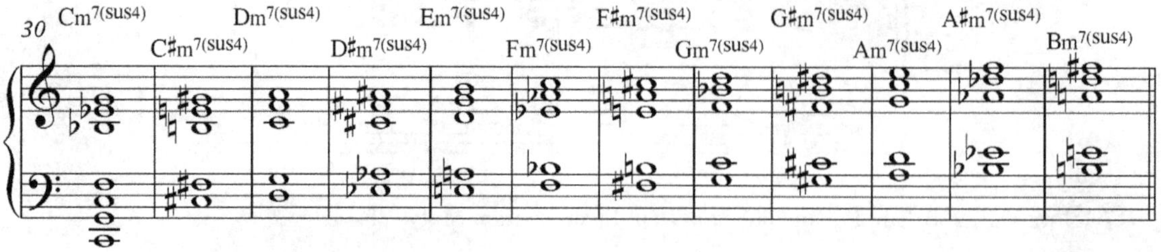

Figure 8.22 Dorian Chromatic Planing.

Example 56, below, demonstrates four cadences amid the use of inversions.

- The first cadence uses the root position chords of ii^m-V^7 with the 1st inversion of the tonic.
- The 2nd cadence uses the 1st inversion of ii^m-V^7 with the 2nd inversion of the tonic.
- The 3rd cadence uses the 2nd inversion of ii^m-V^7 with the 1st inversion of the tonic.
- The 4th cadence uses the 2nd inversion of ii^m-V^7 adding a 9th to the ii^{m7} and the 2nd inversion of the tonic.

ii-V7-I - Quartal Voicings

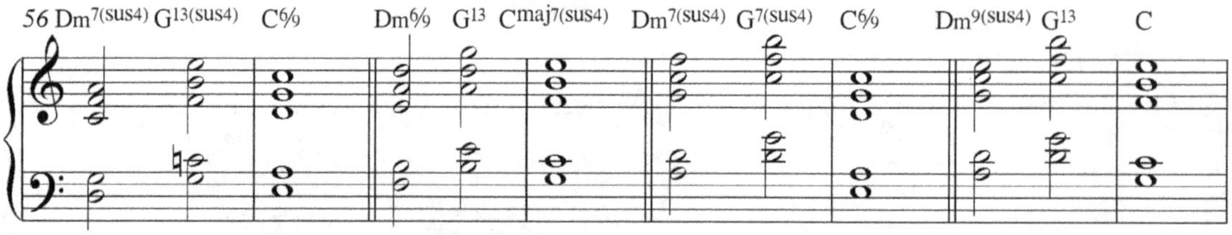

Figure 8.23 Examples of iim-V7-I voicings.

- There are only two possible whole tone scales which are separated by a semi-tone. Consequently, two systems are required to support both whole tone scales.

Whole Tone Planing Minor System 1 - Quartal Voicings

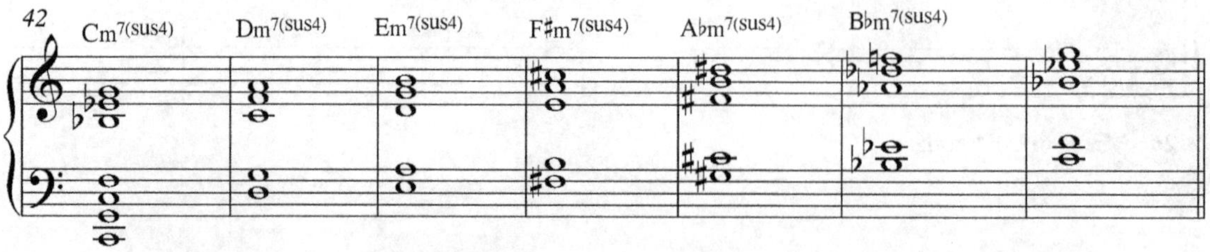

Figure 8.24 Whole Tone Planing Minor System 1.

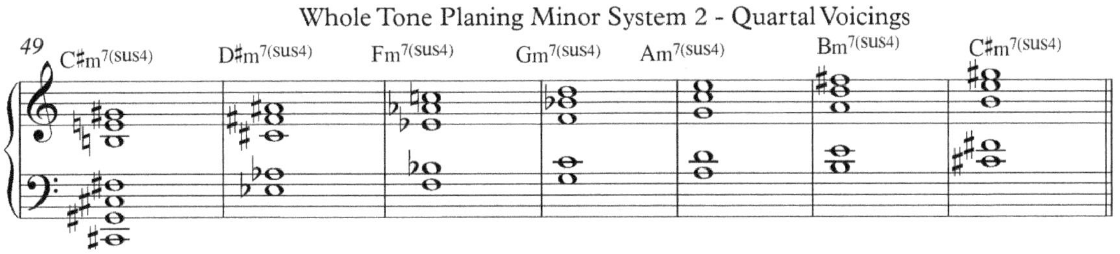

Figure 8.25 Whole Tone Planing Minor System 2.

3 Application of Arranging Concepts

- All scores and lead sheets discussed in Section 3 are located in Appendix 6

3.1 Example—*All the Things You Are* (Version 1) Investigating Sebesky's Concepts

- Arrangement created based on the appendix lead sheet of *All the Things You Are* (Aebersold 1988, 2))
- Version 1 in the appendix is an outline or sketch of 1 treble clef (i.e., trumpets) and 2 bass clefs (i.e., trombones, tuba) (Sebesky 1994, 8)
- Investigates economy, variety, timing, and voicing for a brass ensemble (Sebesky 1994, 2)
- Section A1
  - As per Sebesky's recommendation – starts slowly with only the trumpet section and creates variety and interest through changing timbre by adding trombones in bar 7
  - Bars 2,3—reharmonized using circle of 4ths
  - Bars 4, 5—reharmonized using chromatic, tritone subs
  - In bars 7and 8, trombones enter to build tension for the 2nd A section
    - Bar 7, trombones plane on Cmajor
    - Bar 8, trombones reharmonized with circle of 4ths
- Section A2
  - As per Sebesky, starts to build
    - Trombones fill in background and create a repetitive rhythm (&2, &3, 4, &4)
    - Trombones double Trumpets but one octave lower. (Sebesky 1994, 33)
  - Bar 11 and 13, reharmonized using circle of 4ths
  - Bar 16, reharmonized using chromatic, tritone subs which leads to Section B
- Section B
  - Continues rhythmic trombones in background spaces of trumpets
- Section A3
  - Change harmony of a specific melodic theme frequently (Sebesky 1994, 10)
    - Reharmonized F^{m}, Bb^{m}, Eb^{7}, Abmaj (i.e., with backdoor substitutes Ab^{m7}, Bb^{m7}, Gb^{7}, Abmaj) in bars 25-28
    - Reharmonized Db^{m}, Gb^{7}, C^{m} in bar 30 to Ab^{m}, Db^{7}, C^{m} with Tritone sub
    - Trombone support changes from a rhythmic approach to counterpoint using 3rds and 6ths.
  - Contrary motion used in bars 28, 30, 32
  - Tuba used for counterpoint in bars 32 and 36.

3.2 Example—*All the Things You Are* (Version 2) with Rhythmic Signature

- Version 2 in Appendix 6 is an expanded sketch with 2 treble clefs (i.e., trumpets, saxes) and 2 bass clefs (i.e., trombones, tuba) (Sebesky 1994, 8)
- Investigates Sebeski's rules for brass and wind ensemble by adding sax section
- Added intro that follows "jazz standard" intro chord changes for *All the Things You Are* (lead sheet) in the Appendix.
- Experimented with rhythmic signature in bar 12, 13, 14, 16, 19, 21-24, 29, 30, 33, 34, 39, 40
- Experimented with root displacement in bar 7

3.3 Example—*Green Dolphin Street* (Version 1) with Rhythmic Displacement

- Composition experiments with various length timing feels (i.e., tuplets) over a 4/4 time, called rhythmic displacement.
    - Uses chord progressions from the Real Book as shown in the Appendix, called *Green Dolphin Street* (Lead Sheet) (Kaper 1947, 147)
- Introduction
    - Time feel accelerates from 1 beat per bar, to 2, to 3 to 4 leading to the 5 tuplet feel of bar 5 (i.e., bar 1 of A)
    - Uses chromatic iim7-V7 sequence while maintaining accelerating rhythm from 2 beat per bar to 4 beats per bar. (i.e., see type 2 in previous Chord Progression Forms)
- Section A
    - Instrumentation uses 5 closed voicings for sax, with a trumpet soloist
    - Time feel continues to change in each bar, in a 4 bar sequence of 5,6,7,6 / 5,6,7,6
    - The 6 beat feel in bars 6 and 10 aligns with the original quarter note triplets of the melody.
        - The first 2 beats of theses bars are used to foreshadow the last 2 beats (i.e., statement and response) of quarter note triplets
    - Bars 5, 6 (Section A bar 1 and 2)
        - sax voices increased to 5 parts with baritone sax doubling the alto
        - without roots or doubling of the trumpet
    - Trombone contrary motion used on beats 3 and 4 of bar 6
    - Bar 7, 8
        - Rhythmic 5 voice sax part alternates between G^7 to C^{m7} to create motion
        - Sax simplified in beats 1, 2 of bar 8 to let the piece breath
    - Bars 9 and 10
        - used a 4 stacked ii^{m7}-V^7 sequence
        - trombones use contrary motion on beats 3 and 4 of bar 10
    - Bar 11
        - Chord motion alternates between C^{maj7}/C and bitonal B/C
    - Bar 12
        - Uses fractal displacement accelerating run (ie 6th apart) to return to introduce Section B
- Section B
    - Time is based on a 12/8 feel but with accents on a 6/4 feel
    - The 6/4 feel emphasizes beats 1 and 3, whereas in Section C, beats 2 and 4 are emphasized.
    - 1st Trombone doubles the melody
    - Sax, Trumpets and trombone, all align the melodic rhythm with a 6/4 emphasize over 12/8 time while the bassline keeps the 4/4 time.
    - Highest note of accompaniment never exceeds the melody register (i.e., rule)
    - Bar 28—uses fractal displacement accelerating run with 3 part harmony between trumpet, sax and trombone.
- Section C
    - Time is based on a 12/8 feel but with the accents on a 6/4 feel
        - The 6/4 feel emphasizes beats 2 and 4
    - Orchestration roles are similar to Section B except the time shifted 6/4 feel is supported.
    - Trumpets are providing shots on the "tri" of beats one and 3 (ex. one-**tri**-plet)
        - Last 4 bars—Trumpet one emphasizes melody while lower voices provide movement
        - Bars 24 and 26—add emphasizes on 2 and 4 to help identify the 4 bar phrase.
- Coda
    - Coda follows the tag sequence of $E^m/A^7/D^m/G^7$ twice with 2 bars of Cmaj to close on the tonic.
    - These final 6 bars decelerate the time feel from 12/8, to 8/8, to 6/4, to 4/4, to 2/2, to one.
    - Trombone doubles the sax.

3.4 Example—*Green Dolphin Street* (Version 2) Using Voicings Without Doubling

- Follows Real Book standard chord changes (see Appendix 6)
- Uses super Locrian mode in bars 1, 11, 28, 33
- Voicings of all chords
  - no doubling
  - Always 5 distinct voices (ie. reduced from 7 voices in previous version)
- Bar 7—changed chord sequence to start on C^{m7} and alternate ending on G^7 to resolve to C^{m7} in bar 8.
- Bars 8,9,10
  - Created counter-melody and rhythm in the sax section
  - Harmony follows sequence of related dominants through minor 3rds (ie. F^7 B^7 D^7) leading to D^7 tritone then Db^7 and resolving on C^{maj} in bar 11
- Bar 11
  - Uses chromatic 6^{ths} in C^{maj} to super Locrian 6ths in A^7 to resolve to D^m in bar 13

3.5 Example—*Misty* (Version 1) Melody Harmonized with Block Chords

- Each chord of lead sheet (Stang 2001, 243) considered an anchor that can not be moved
  - Melody harmonizing chords fit between anchor chords.
- Harmonized Each Note of the Melody with block chords
  - Harmonic rhythm often provides chord changes on the 1st beat of each bar or on one and three of bar with many melodic notes filling in between these significant chord changes
- Misty reharmonized on single treble clef with tight voicings and attention to voice leading
  - 5 voices without doubling used
  - Lower voices separated from single upper voice since a melody with leaps into upper range can lead to voice crossings in the lower voices
  - Objective to create each voice as its own melody.
    - Used Organic objective which targets voice leading of a semi-tone step for a single voice's note to note transitions
- Introduction added to explore a holding a single note in top voice with multiple chords supporting in an extended progression.
- A two bar ending was added to explore extending tonic (i.e., I^{maj7}, ii^{m7}, $^{b}iii^{7}$, iii^{m7}, I^{maj7}) in the style of Monk
- Other notes
  - Approaching I^{maj7} tonic from semi-tone below (VII^7) is equivalent to a plagal (ie. IV^7-I^{maj7}) since VII is in the minor 3 family of IV.
  - Tritone V^7 sub is not recommended before a I minor tonic
  - V^7 can be extended with inversions using the related fully diminished 7th chords
    - Based on 2 diminished chords that make up the half/whole scale.
  - Tonic extension used by Monk commonly was I^{maj7}, ii^{m7}, $^{b}iii^{7}$, and iii^{m7} in bar 24 to 26

3.6 Example—Misty with Quartal Harmony

- Uses quartal harmony
  - Includes dorian, Mixolydian, Ionian, Lydian quartal types
- Most melody notes are harmonized with quartal chords
- Quartal Planing used in bar 7, 11, and 15
- Bars 8 to 9 and 18 to 19—voice leading used to move from quartal chords to dominant with extensions.

4 Conclusions

This *Arranging Methods* paper discusses key arranging concepts with examples to clarify the ideas. The methods target big band configurations up to full brass, sax and trombone sections that are supported by a rhythm section of bass and drums. Figure 8.26 identifies the set of arranging concepts discussed in this paper in the left column and identifies the arrangements that used these concepts. These original arrangements enabled the author to explore the application and sound qualities of each concept in a meaningful way.

	All the Things (V1)	**All the Things (V2)**	**All the Things (V3)**	**Green Dolphin (V1)**	**Green Dolphin (V2)**	**Misty (V1)**	**Misty (V2)**
Balance	✓	✓	✓	✓	✓	✓	✓
Economy	✓	✓	✓	✓	✓	✓	✓
Focus	✓	✓	✓	✓	✓	✓	✓
Variety	✓	✓	✓	✓	✓	✓	✓
Brass Combo	✓						
Woodwind Combo						✓	
Brass & Woodwind Combo		✓					
Solo Piano							✓
Rhythmic Signature		✓	✓				
Root Displacement		✓	✓				
Voice Leading	✓	✓	✓	✓	✓	✓	✓
Fractal Displacement				✓	✓		
Block Chord Melody Harm.						✓	✓
Extending Tonic						✓	
Common Progression Intro			✓	✓	✓		
Diminished Axis subs					✓		
Reharmonized standard	✓	✓	✓	✓	✓	✓	✓
Quartal Harmony							✓

Figure 8.26 Summary of original composition's usage of arranging concepts.

5 Bibliography

Aebersold, Jamey. 1988. *Play-A-Long Book: Volume 43*. Albany: Aebersold.
Berg, Shelton. 1990. *Jazz Improvisation: The Goal Note Method*. Lou Fischer Pub. Carlsbad, CA.
Cook, Nicholas. 1987. *A Guide to Musical Analysis*. London: J.M. Dent and Sons.
Kaper, Bronislaw. 1947. Green Dolphin Street. in *The Real Book of Jazz: Volume 1*. Opensource.
La Rue, Jan. 1970. *Guidelines for Style Analysis*. New York and London: Norton.
Levine, Mark. 1995. *The Jazz Theory Book*. Petaluma CA: Sher Music.
Mullholland, Joe. 2013. *The Berklee Book of Jazz Harmony*. Boston: Berklee College.
Sussman, Richard. 2012. *Jazz Composition and Arranging in the Digital Age*. Oxford: Oxford Press.
Sebesky, Don.1994. *Contemporary Arranger: The Definitive Addition*. Van Nuys: Alfred Pub.
Stang, Aaron. 2001. *Just Jazz Real Book*. Burbank: Warner Bros.
Westray, Ron. 2018. *Musi5006B Studio Lectures. Private Lessons in Composition*. Toronto: York University.

6 Discography

Brubeck, Dave. 1959. *Time Out.* CL1397, NYC: Columbia.
Coltrane, John. 1958. *Blue Train.* DP7460952, NYC: Blue Note.
Coltrane, John. 1960. *Giant Steps.* UDCD605, NYC: Atlantic.
Davis, Miles. 1959. *Kind of Blue.* 88697-33552-2, NYC: Columbia.
Davis, Miles. 1949. *Birth of the Cool.* Cap 57-60005, LA: Capital.
Ellington, Duke. 1963. *Money Jungle.* CDP7463982, NYC: Blue Note.
Evans, Bill. 1961. *At the Village Vanguard.* SRCD1961–2, NYC: Riverside.
Harris, Barry. 1960. *At the Jazz Workshop.* RLP 12–326, Riverside: SanFransico.
Mingus, Charles. 1956. *Pithecanthropus Erectus.* Atlantic 1237.
Mingus, Charles. 1957c. *The Clown.* Atlantic 1260.
Mingus, Charles. 1959. *Ah Um.* Columbia CL 1370.
Mingus, Charles. 1960a. *Charles Mingus Presents Charles Mingus.* Candid CJM 8005.
Mingus, Charles.1961. *Charles Mingus Presents Charles Mingus.* London: Candid CCD 79005.
Mingus, Charles. 1963c. *The Black Saint and the Sinner Lady.* Impulse A35.
Mingus, Charles. 1972. *Let My Children Hear Music.* Columbia KC 31039.
Tyner, McCoy. 1967. *The Real McCoy.* BST84264, NYC: Blue Note.
Tyner, McCoy. 1967. *Sahara.* SP9039-A, NYC: Milestone.
Monk, Thelonious. 1987. *It's Monk Time.* 25218-6231-2, NYC: Riverside.

7 Appendix of Original Arrangements

All The Things You Are

(Version 1)

Arranged by Tom McGill

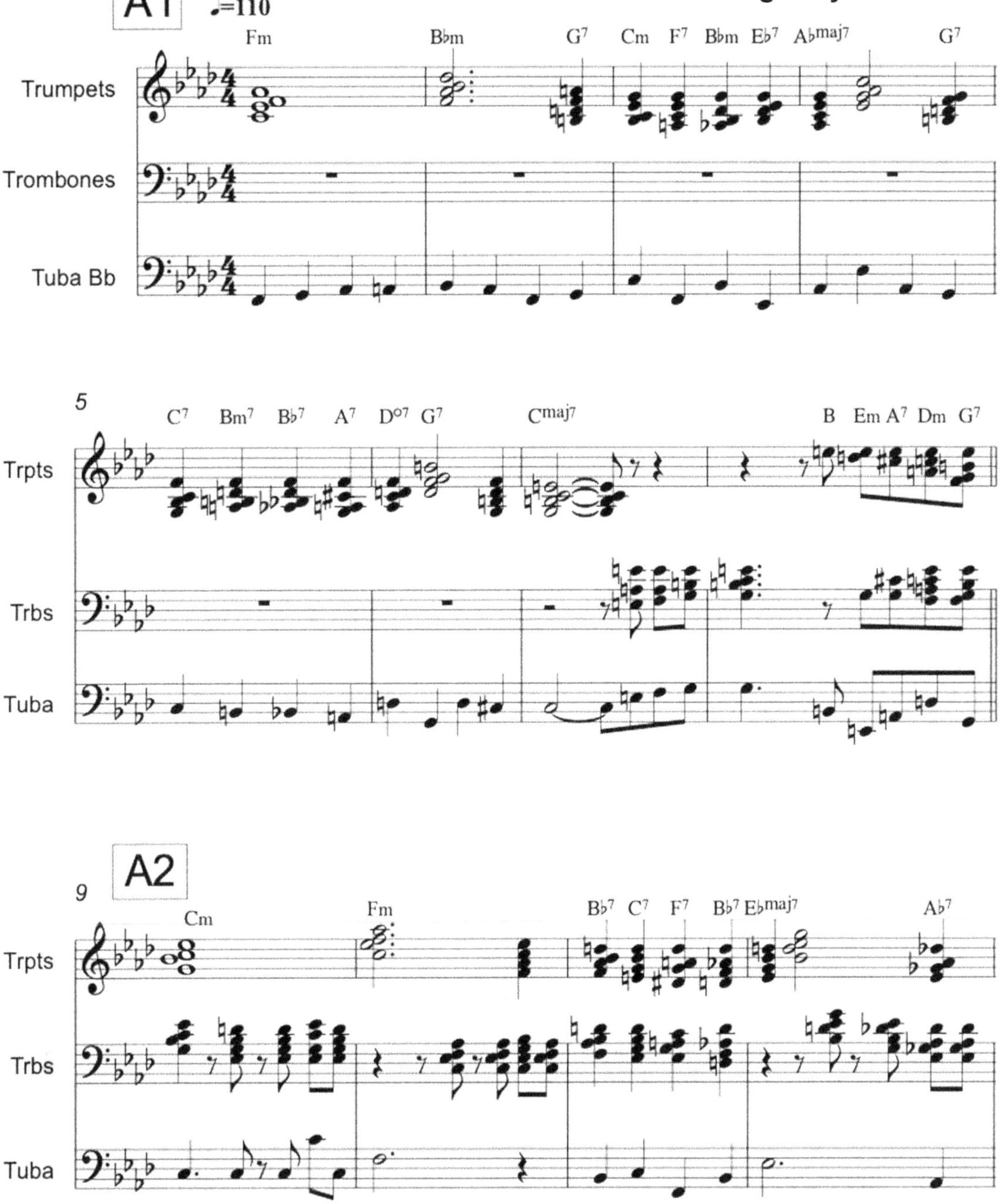

13
D♭maj7 G♭7(♯11) B7(♭9) E7 Aø7 A♭o7 Aø7 D7 Gmaj7 C7 B7 B♭7
Trpts
Trbs
Tuba
B
17
nat.
Aø7 D7 Gmaj7
Trpts
Trbs
Tuba
21
G♭ø7 B7(♯9) E7 E♭(sus4) E♭7
Trpts
Trbs
Tuba

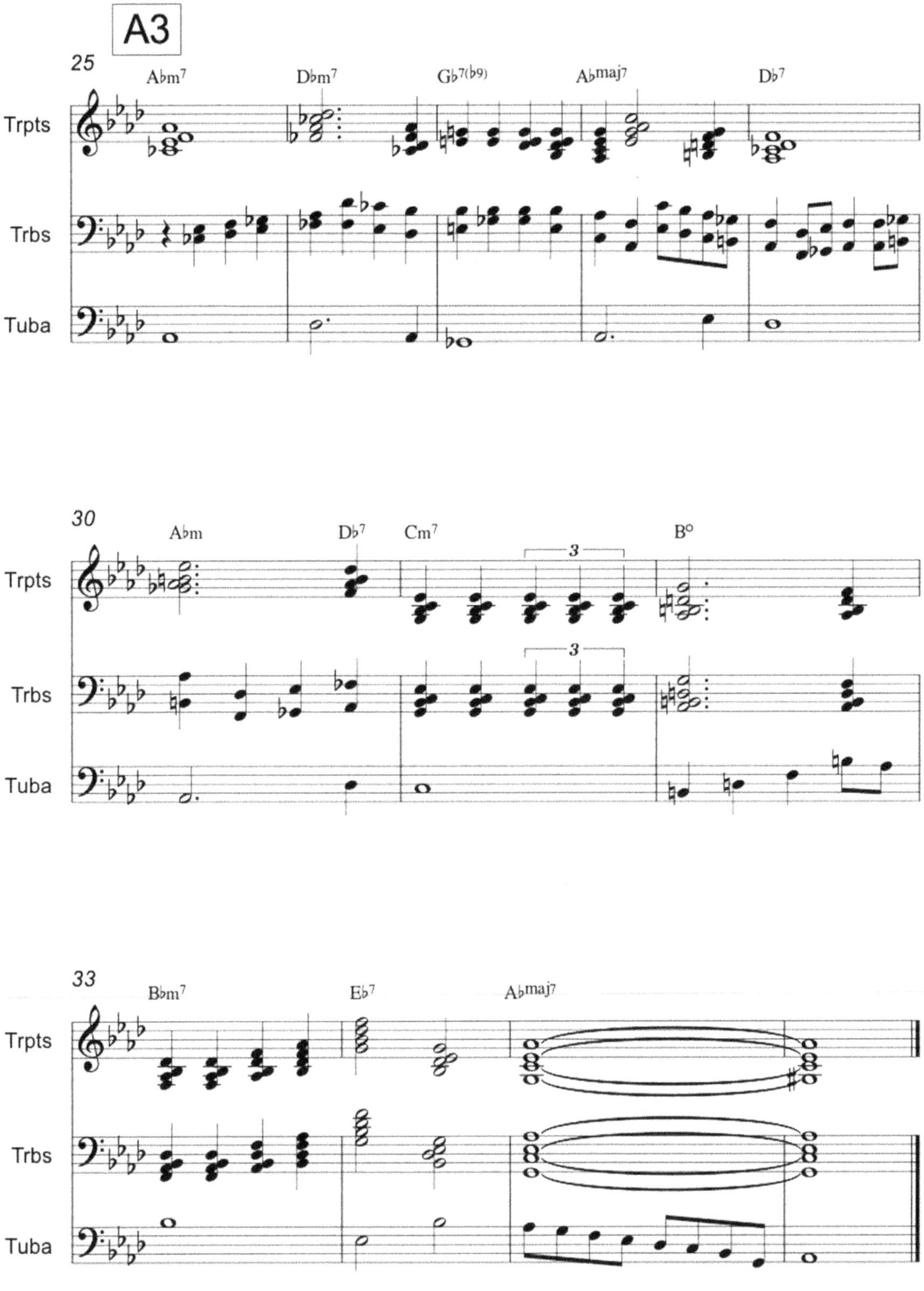
A3
25
Abm7
Dbm7
Gb7(b9)
Abmaj7
Db7
Trpts
Trbs
Tuba
30
Abm
Db7
Cm7
B°
3
33
Bbm7
Eb7
Abmaj7

28

All The Things You Are

(Version 2) **Arranged by Tom McGill**

A2
13
Cm F7 Fm B♭(sus4) B♭7 E♭maj7 A♭7
G7
Trpts
Sax
Trbs
Tuba
17
D♭maj7 G♭7(♯11) B7(♭9) E7 Aø7 A♭o7 Aø7 D7 Gmaj7 C7 B7 B♭7
21
B
nat.
Aø7 D7 Gmaj7
w/half scale in 3rds
G in 6ths

25
Gb⌀7
B7(#9)
E7
Eb(sus4)
Eb7
Trpts
Sax
Trbs
Tuba
A3
29
Abm7
Dbm7
Gb7(b9)
Abmaj7
33
Db7
Abm
Db7
Cm7
Bo
3

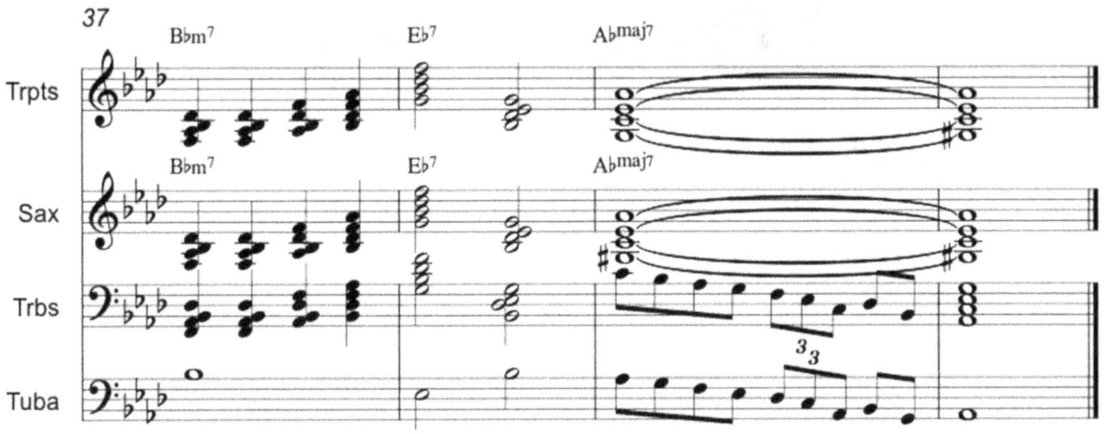
37
B♭m7
E♭7
A♭maj7
Trpts
B♭m7
E♭7
A♭maj7
Sax
Trbs
Tuba
3
3

All The Things You Are

♩=100
(Version 3)
Arranged by Tom McGill
Saxes
Trumpets
Trombones
Tuba Bb
5
D♭
C7
h/w scale
3
Sax
Trpts
Trbs
Tuba
9
A1
Fm
B♭m
A7(♯9)/E♭
E♭7(♭9)/A
A♭maj7
root displacement

13
D♭maj7
D∅7 +9+11
G7(♭9)
Cmaj7
G7
h/w scale
Sax
Trpts
Trbs
Tuba
17
A2
Cm
Cm6
Fm7
Fm6
B♭7
B♭6
E♭(sus4)
E♭7
Sax
Trpts
Trbs
Tuba
21
A♭(sus4)
A♭maj7
A♭6
Am7
D7
Gmaj7
B7(♭13)
B♭7
Sax
Trpts
Trbs
Tuba

25
B
A∅7
D7(♭9)
Gmaj7
Sax
Trpts
Trbs
Tuba
3
29
F♯∅7
B7(♭9)
E7
E(sus4)
E♭(♯11)
E♭7
3
A3
33
A♭m7
D♭m7
G♭7(♭9)
A♭maj7

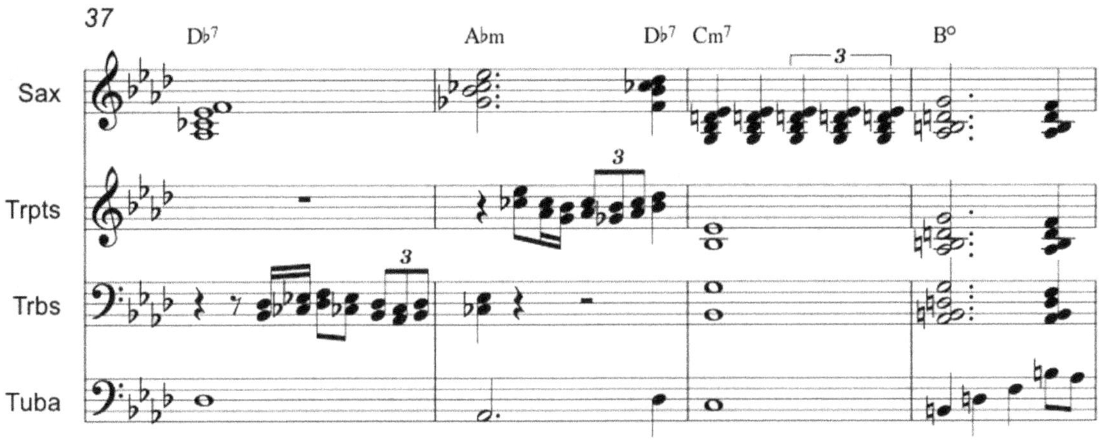
37
D♭7
A♭m
D♭7
Cm7
B°
Sax
Trpts
Trbs
Tuba

41
B♭m7
E♭9
E♭7
A♭maj7
Sax
B♭m7
E♭7
A♭maj7
Trpts
Trbs
Tuba

Green Dolphin Street

(Version 1)

Arranged by Tom McGill

9
Trumpet
Saxes
Trombone
Bass
Drum Kit
Bm7 F7 Dm7 G7 Fm7 B♭7 A♭m7 D♭7

11
Trumpet
Saxes
Trombone
Bass
Drum Kit
B/C Cmaj7 A7

B
13
1.
Dm7
G7
Trumpet
Saxes
Trombone
Bass
Drum Kit

15
Cmaj7
Trumpet
Saxes
Cmaj7
Trombone
Bass
Drum Kit

17
Fm7
B♭7
Trumpet
Saxes
Trombone
Bass
Drum Kit

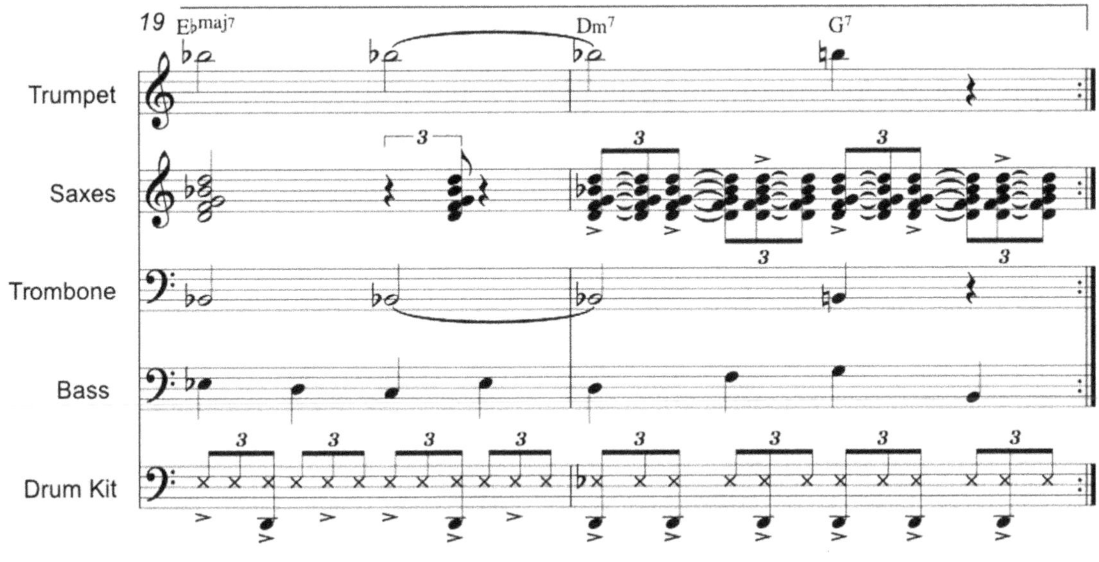
19
E♭maj7
Dm7
G7
Trumpet
Saxes
Trombone
Bass
Drum Kit

C
21
2. Dm7 Dm/C Bø7 E7 Am7 Am/G F♯ø7 B7
Trumpet
Saxes
Trombone
Bass
Drum Kit

To Coda
25
Em7 A7 Dm7 G7
Trumpet
Saxes
Trombone
Bass
Drum Kit

27
Cmaj7
D.S. al Coda
Trumpet
Saxes
Trombone
Bass
Drum Kit

29
coda
rit..
Em7
A7
Dm7
G7
Em7
A7
Dm7
G7
Cmaj7
Trumpet
Saxes
Trombone
Bass
Drum Kit

Green Dolphin Street

(Version 2)

Arranged by Tom McGill

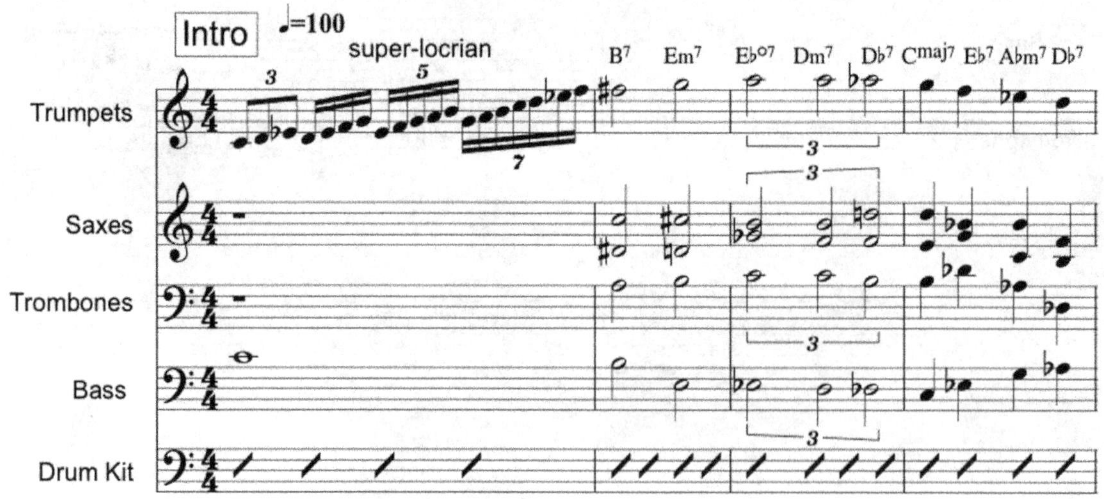

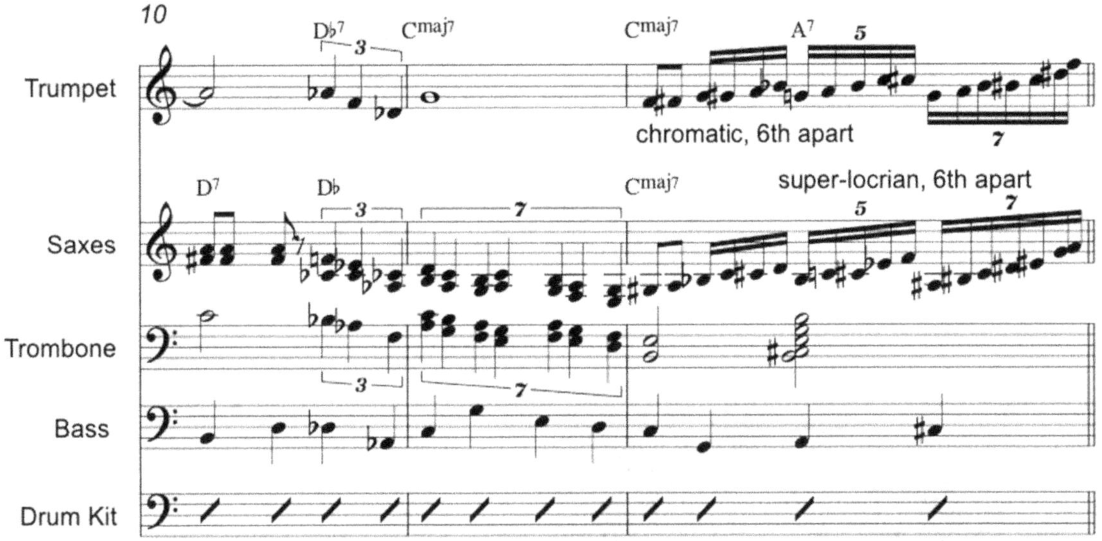
10
Trumpet
Saxes
Trombone
Bass
Drum Kit
D♭7
Cmaj7
Cmaj7
A7
chromatic, 6th apart
D7
D♭
Cmaj7
super-locrian, 6th apart

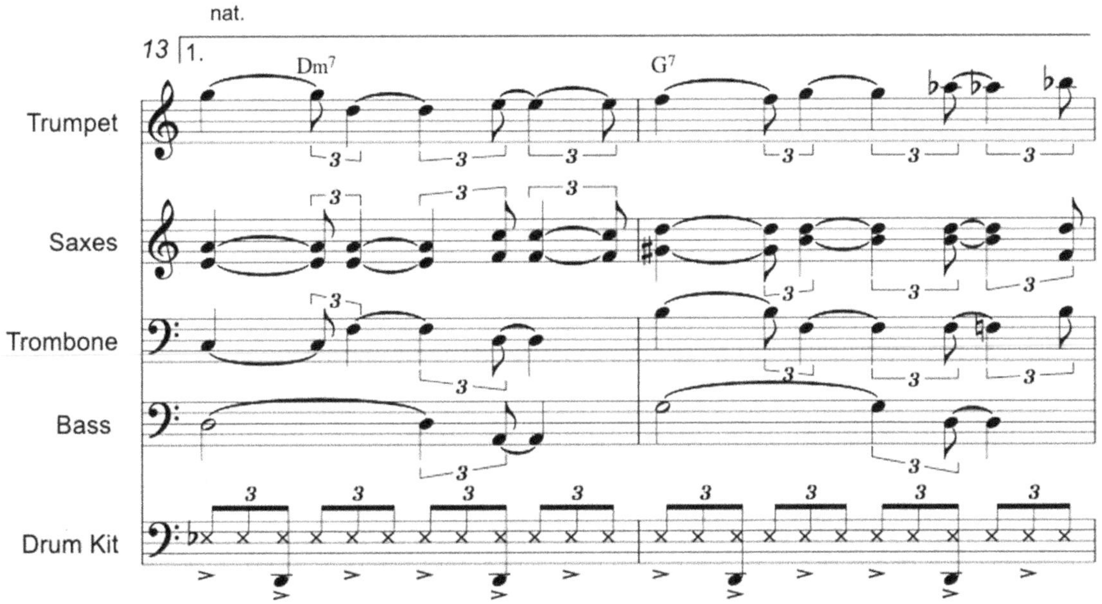
nat.
13
1.
Dm7
G7
Trumpet
Saxes
Trombone
Bass
Drum Kit

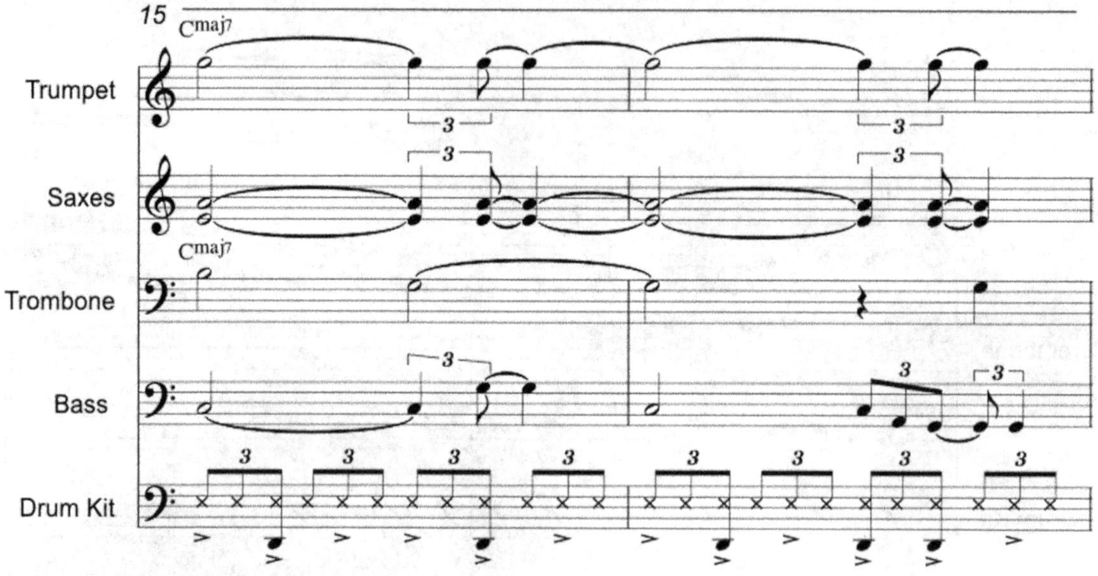
15
Cmaj7
Trumpet
Saxes
Cmaj7
Trombone
Bass
Drum Kit

17
Fm7
B♭7
Trumpet
Saxes
Trombone
Bass
Drum Kit

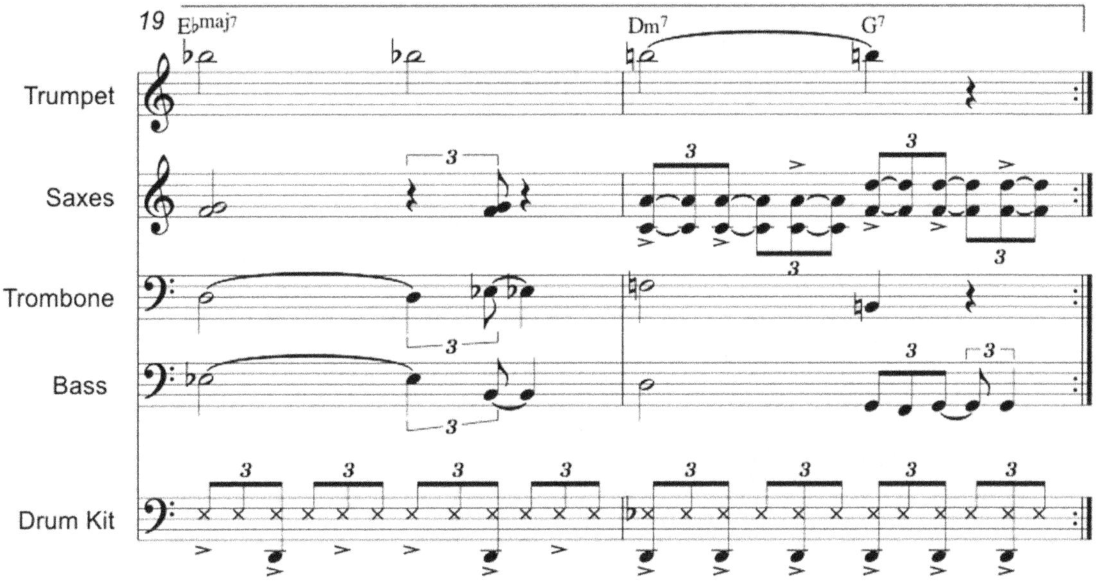
19
E♭maj7
Dm7
G7
Trumpet
Saxes
Trombone
Bass
Drum Kit

C
21
2.
nat. Dm7
Dm/C
Bø7
E7
Am7
Am/G
F♯ø7
Trumpet
Saxes
Trombone
Bass
Drum Kit

To Coda
24
B7(♭13 ♭9) B7(♭13 #9) Em7 A7 Dm7 G7
Trumpet
Saxes
Trombone
Bass
Drum Kit

27
Cmaj7 Dm7 G7alt.
D.S. al Coda
Trumpet
super-locrian 3rd apart
Saxes
Trombone
Bass
Drum Kit

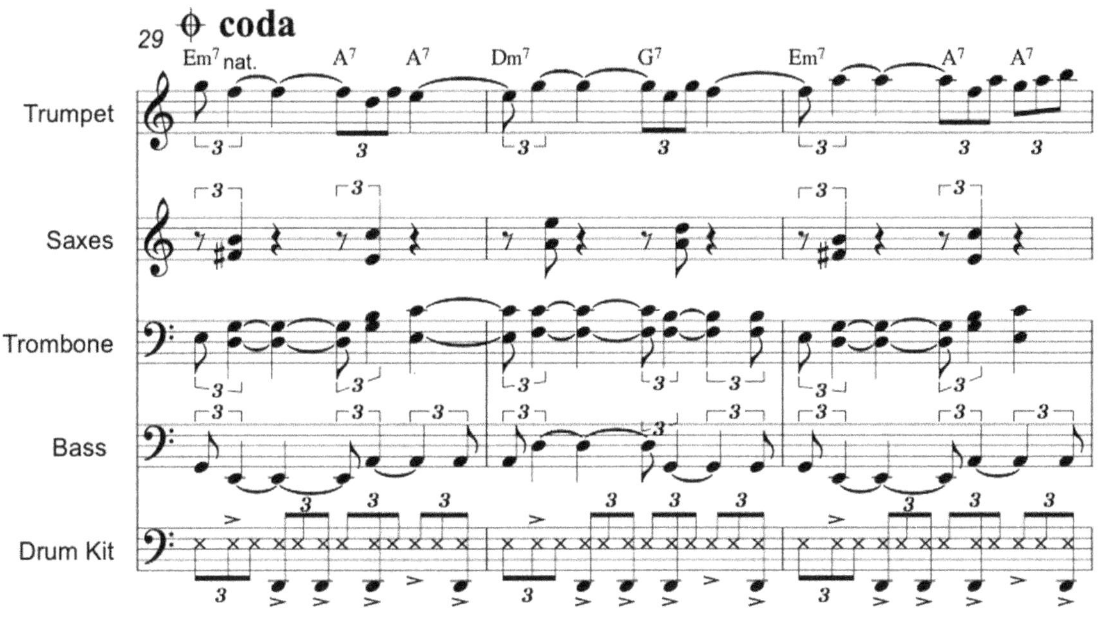
29
coda
Em7 nat.
A7
A7
Dm7
G7
Em7
A7
A7
Trumpet
Saxes
Trombone
Bass
Drum Kit

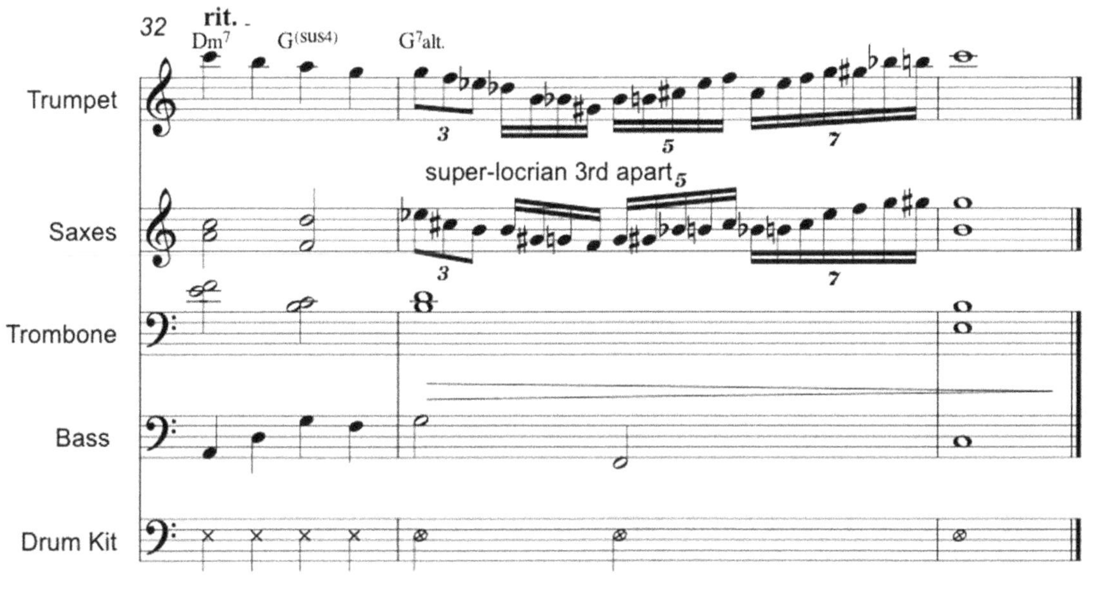
32
rit.
Dm7
G(sus4)
G7alt.
super-locrian 3rd apart
Trumpet
Saxes
Trombone
Bass
Drum Kit

Misty

(Lead Sheet)

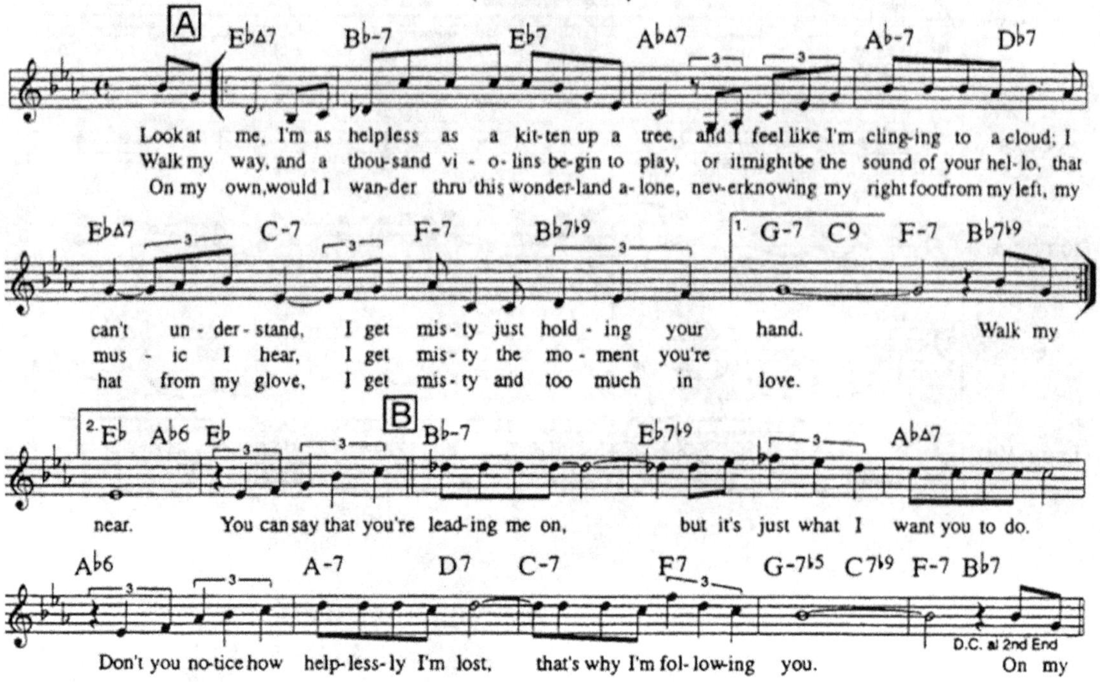
A
E♭Δ7 B♭-7 E♭7 A♭Δ7 A♭-7 D♭7
Look at me, I'm as helpless as a kit-ten up a tree, and I feel like I'm cling-ing to a cloud; I
Walk my way, and a thou-sand vi - o- lins be-gin to play, or it might be the sound of your hel- lo, that
On my own, would I wan-der thru this wonder-land a- lone, nev-er knowing my right foot from my left, my
E♭Δ7 C-7 F-7 B♭7♭9 1. G-7 C9 F-7 B♭7♭9
can't un - der - stand, I get mis - ty just hold - ing your hand. Walk my
mus - ic I hear, I get mis- ty the mo - ment you're
hat from my glove, I get mis- ty and too much in love.
2. E♭ A♭6 E♭ B B♭-7 E♭7♭9 A♭Δ7
near. You can say that you're lead-ing me on, but it's just what I want you to do.
A♭6 A-7 D7 C-7 F7 G-7♭5 C7♭9 F-7 B♭7
Don't you no-tice how help-less-ly I'm lost, that's why I'm fol- low-ing you. On my
D.C. al 2nd End

Misty

(Version 1 - block chord melody)

Arranged by Tom McGill

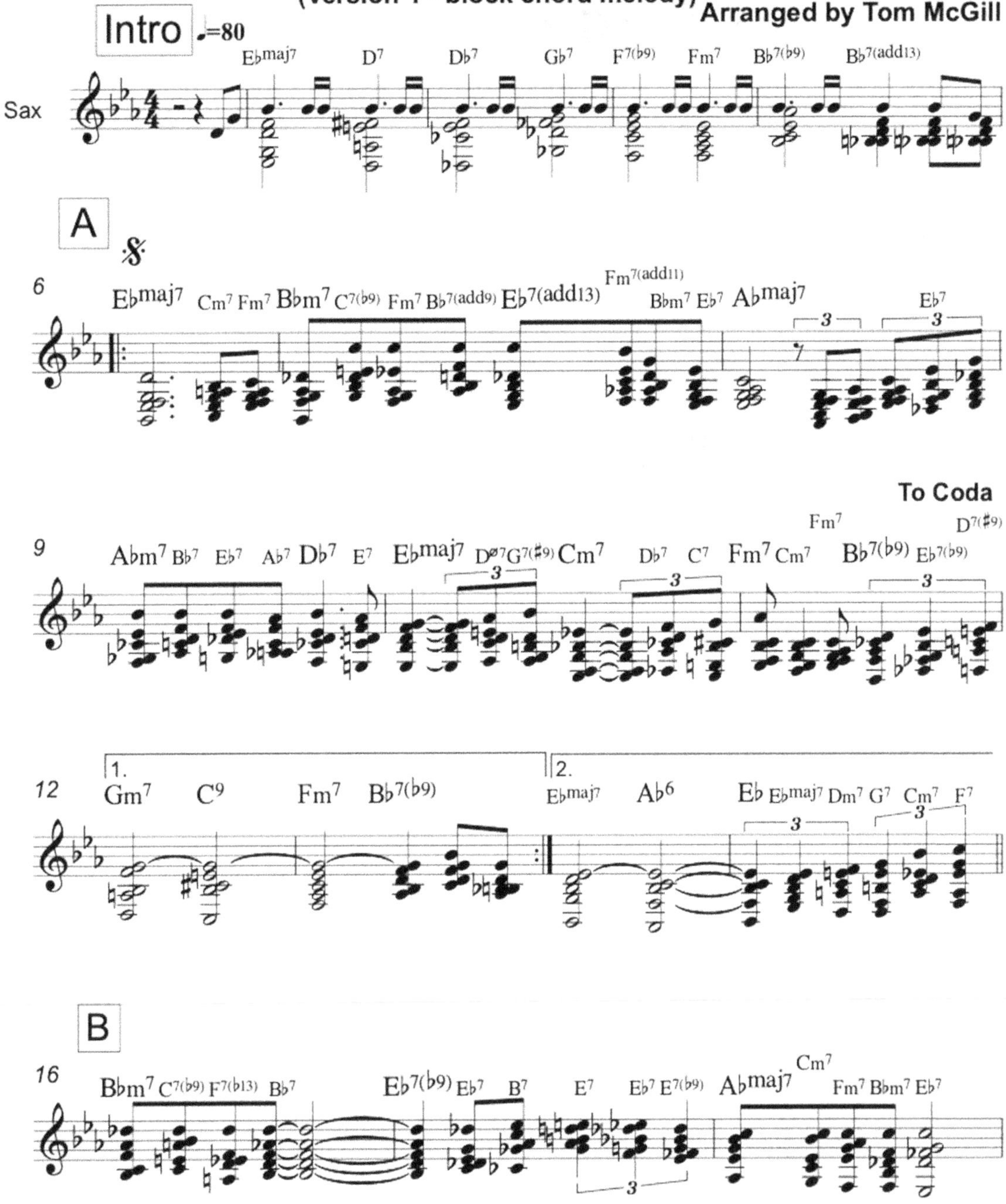

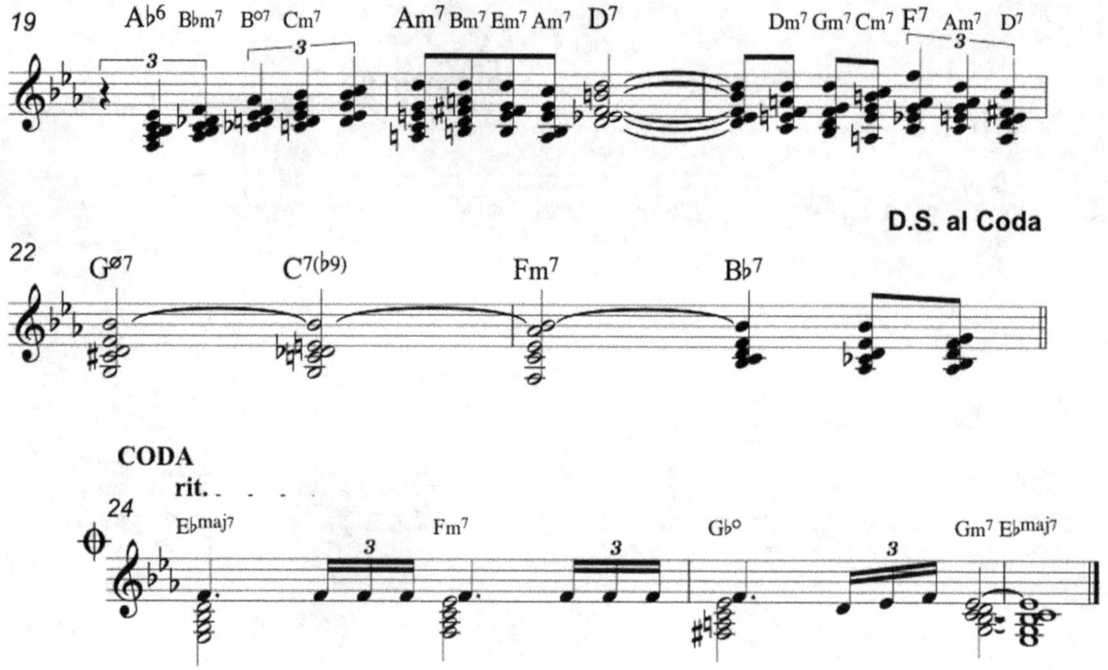
19
A♭6 B♭m7 B°7 Cm7
Am7 Bm7 Em7 Am7 D7
Dm7 Gm7 Cm7 F7 Am7 D7
3
D.S. al Coda
22
Gø7
C7(♭9)
Fm7
B♭7
CODA
rit.
24
E♭maj7
Fm7
G♭°
Gm7 E♭maj7

Misty

(Version 2 - quartals)

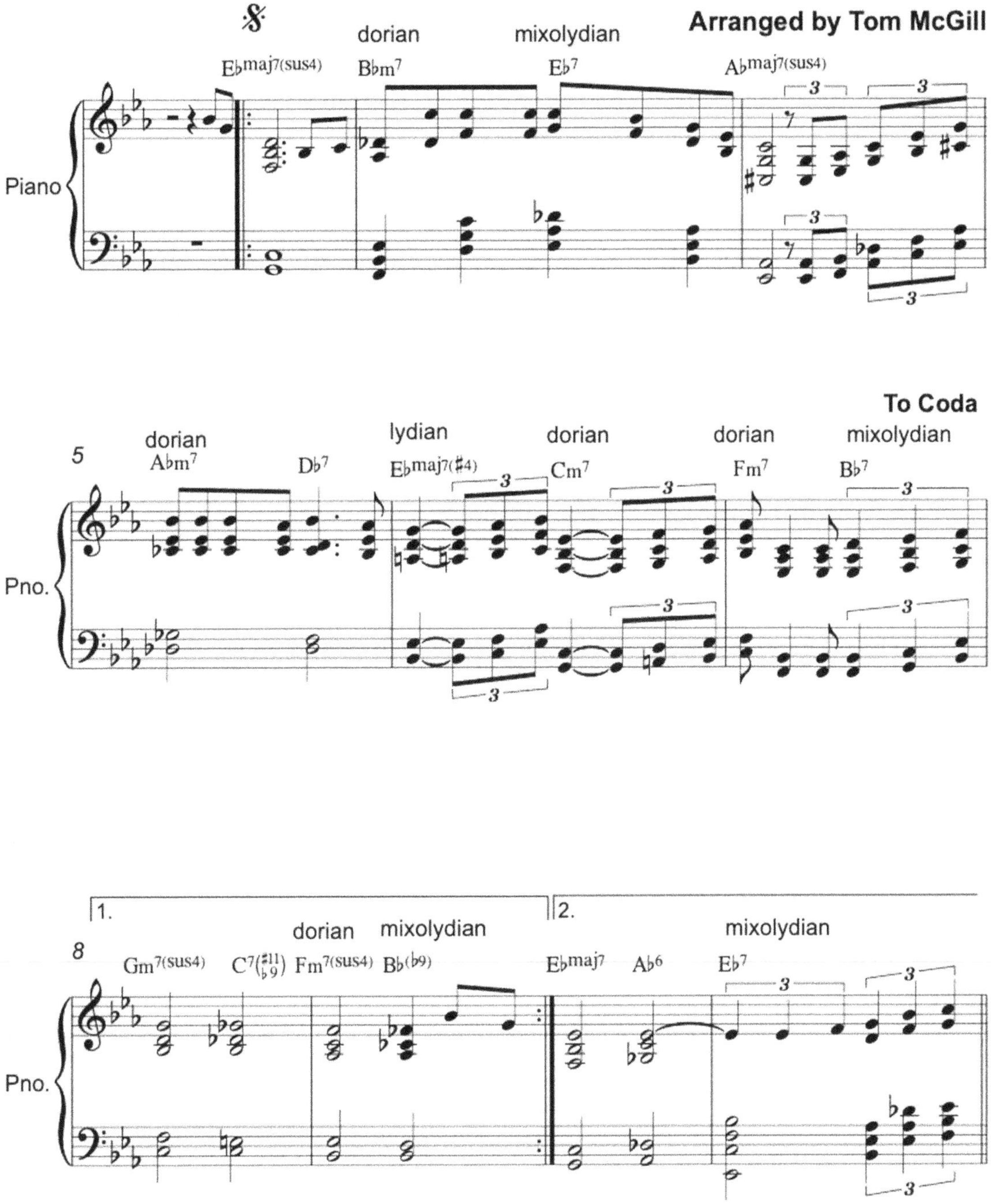
Arranged by Tom McGill
dorian
mixolydian
E♭maj7(sus4)
B♭m7
E♭7
A♭maj7(sus4)
Piano
To Coda
5
dorian
A♭m7
D♭7
lydian
E♭maj7(♯4)
dorian
Cm7
dorian
Fm7
mixolydian
B♭7
Pno.
1.
2.
8
Gm7(sus4)
C7(♯11 ♭9)
dorian
Fm7(sus4)
mixolydian
B♭(♭9)
E♭maj7
A♭6
mixolydian
E♭7
Pno.

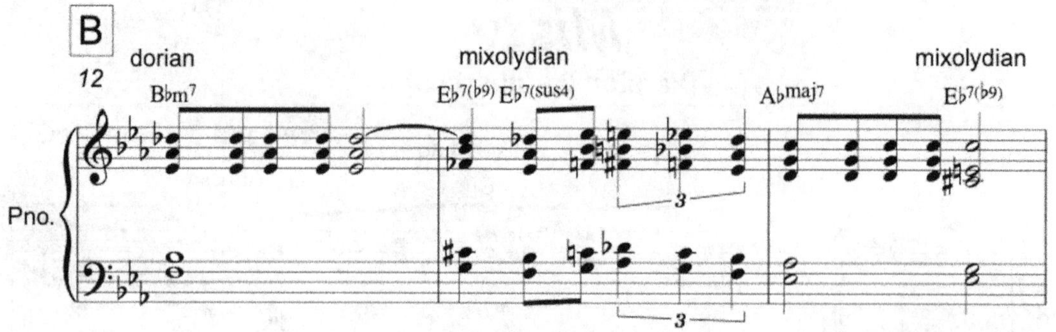
B
dorian
mixolydian
mixolydian
12
Bbm7
Eb7(b9) Eb7(sus4)
Abmaj7
Eb7(b9)
Pno.
3
3

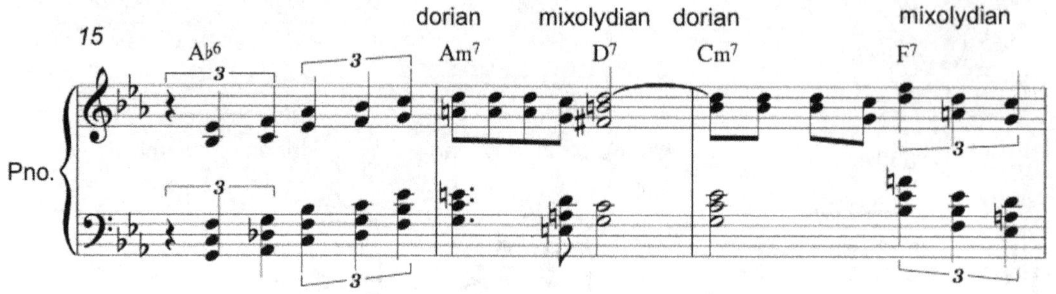
dorian
mixolydian dorian
mixolydian
15
Ab6
Am7
D7
Cm7
F7
3
3
Pno.
3
3
3
3

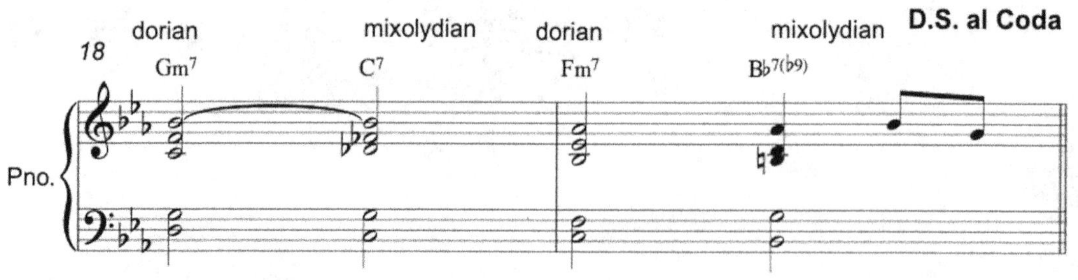
dorian
mixolydian
dorian
mixolydian
D.S. al Coda
18
Gm7
C7
Fm7
Bb7(b9)
Pno.

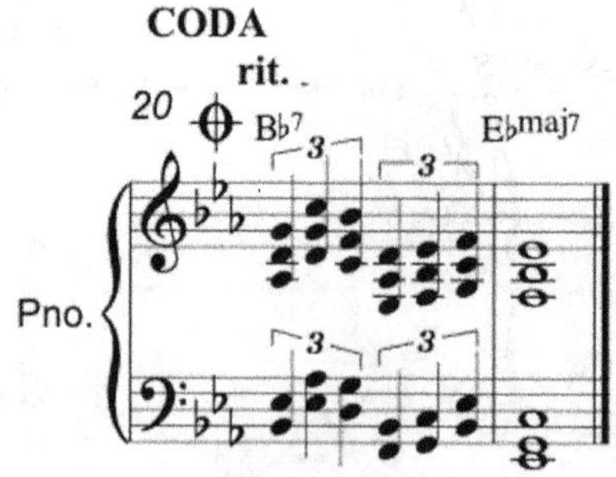
CODA
rit.
20
Bb7
Ebmaj7
3
3
Pno.
3
3

8.2. McGill Theory Report (with bibliography)

Jazz Theory Report

Tom McGill

York University
PhD
Graduate Program in Music
Advanced Jazz Theory - Musi 6520
Ron Westray

March 2018

Table of Contents

1 Introduction

- The following report summarizes a set of jazz theory techniques and presents original compositions to demonstrate these concepts.

2 Chord vs Scale Relationships

2.1 Scale Types over Dominant (V^7) Chords

1. Mixolydian ($^b7$)
2. Lydian Dominant (#4,$^b7$)
3. Whole Tone
4. Inverted Diminished also called the half/whole scale or the "two in one"[1]
    a. Stacks 2 diminished chords
    b. Chord symbol V^{7b9} (not $^b13$)
5. Super Locrian also called altered or altered whole tone
    a. Chord symbol V^{7b13}

2.2 Scale Types over Half-Diminished (ø7) Chords

1. Locrian or 7th degree of major scale (ex. Dmaj7 scale over $C^{ø7}$)
2. Dorian or 2nd degree of harmonic minor (ex. Bbm harmonic over $C^{ø7}$)
3. 6th degree of Melodic minor (ex. Eb melodic over $C^{ø7}$)
4. Diminished also called whole/half
5. Dorian or 2nd degree of harmonic major (ex. Bbm harmonic major over $C^{ø7}$)

Note melodic minor scales always use the ascending melodic scale in jazz.

2.3 Scale Type over Minor-Major

- Chord symbol - iim $^{\Delta 7}$
- Scale – lydian dominant scale on 4th degree of melodic minor
- Example – Am $^{\Delta 7}$ use D lydian dominant scale

2.4 Scale Type over Chord with #9

- Chord symbol – $V7^{\#9}$
- Scale – half/whole
- Example – $B7^{\#9}$ uses B half/whole scale
- Also known as 2 in 1

2.5 Chord Type for Phrygian Mode

- Chord – $IV^{\#11}$/III
- Scale - Phrygian
- Example –
    - F/E (Fmaj triad over E)
    - Voicing – $F^{\#11}$/E
    - Scale – 3rd scale degree of the major scale (i.e., Cmaj scale with tonic E)

---

1 Terminology from Westray's studio lectures in 2018 winter term. 2 in 1 is 2 fully diminished chords stacked

- Phyrgian Triangle[2]
  - $IV^{\#11}$/III defines the Phrygian sound and is compatible with I or V roots.

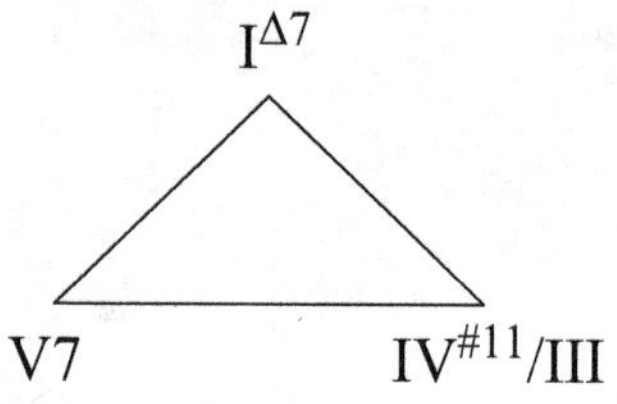

3 Systems

- Scales are covered in the sections above.
- LICs include passing tones such as bebop scales that add a $^{b}13$ to the major scale or major 7th to a Mixolydian scale.
- The following describes chord/scale system relationships.

3.1 Triple Augmented System

3.1.1 Ionian

- Chord symbol - $I^{\Delta 7+5}$
- Scale – 1, $^{\#}9$, 3, 5, $^{\#}5$, Δ7, 8
- Based on 3 key centers separate by a major 3rd
- Example
  - $F^{\Delta 7+5}$ stacks 3 triads F, Db, A
  - b6 resolution sequence – Db to A to F
- All triads work over the tonic (i.e., not 7th chords). Avoid Δ^7 over V^7
- Early adopter was Oliver Nelson. Used by Coltrane in Giant Steps

3.1.2 Minor

- Substituting minor chords possible
- Example
  - Db^{m} to F^{maj}
  - F^{m} to A^{maj}
  - A^{m} to Db^{maj}
- Each of the minor chords are also found in the triple augment scale (i.e., Dbmaj and Dbmin)
- Flat 6 triad to I triad is a cadence with similar closure to a V^7 to 1 cadence

3.1.3 Bitonality

- 2 types
  - Triad over unrelated bass note
  - Triad over unrelated triad

2 Phyrgian triangle terminology from Westray's studio lectures in 2018 winter term.

- 12 chords over 12 roots define the set of bitonal possibilities
- appropriate scale determined by extensions/alterations defined by the upper triad over the lower scale.
    - Examples
        - G#/B is $B^{b9\ 13}$ is dominant scale family use half/whole scale
        - E/C is $C^{\#5\Delta7}$ uses the major 7th and leads to the triple augmented system/scale
        - C/Bb is is $Bb^{9\ \#11\ 13}$ uses Bb lydian dominant or lydian major

3.2 Other Rules

- Extensions are alterations of greater that one octave such as #11 or #9
- Alterations are less that one octave such as b6, #5 but also b9
- $V7^{b13\#11}$ implies Super Locrian scale
- $V7^{b9\ 13}$ implies half/whole

4 Chord Progressions

4.1 The X-Configuration[3]

A common jazz chord progression is the iim^7, V^7, $I^{\Delta7}$. The tritone of each of these chords can be used as a substitute.

iim^7		V^7		$I^{\Delta7}$	
	X		X		
TT of iim^7		TT of V^7		TT of $I^{\Delta7}$	(TT means tritone which is 6 half-steps)

Example for major

Dm^7		G^7		$C^{\Delta7}$
	X		X	
Ab^{m7}		Db^7		$Gb^{\Delta7}$

- There are 3 unique chord sequence that achieve a $C^{\Delta7}$ resolution (i.e., $Dm^7/G^7/C^{\Delta7}$, $Dm^7/Db^7/C^{\Delta7}$, $Abm^7/Dbm^7/C^{\Delta7}$)
- similarly 3 to reach a $Gb^{\Delta7}$.

Example for melodic minor and super locrian scales

Dm^{maj7}		$G^{7\#4}$		$C^{\Delta7}$
	X		X	
Abm^{maj7}		$Db^{7\#4}$		$Gb^{\Delta7}$

- melodic minor scale is always the ascending version in jazz

3 X-configuration terminology from Westray's studio lectures in 2018 winter term.

4.2 Chromatic Descending vs Whole Tone Rising Bassline for Secondary Dominant Sequences

- A common secondary V7 chord sequence follows the circle of fifths in a counter-clockwise direction such as C, F, Bb, Eb, etc. However, another interesting sequence inserts the tritone sub of the adjacent V^7 on alternate chords in the sequence which results in a chromatic bass line. This is shown by the arrows in Figure 1 which link C, B, Bb, A, and Ab.

Figure 1 – Circle of Fifths with chromatic baseline

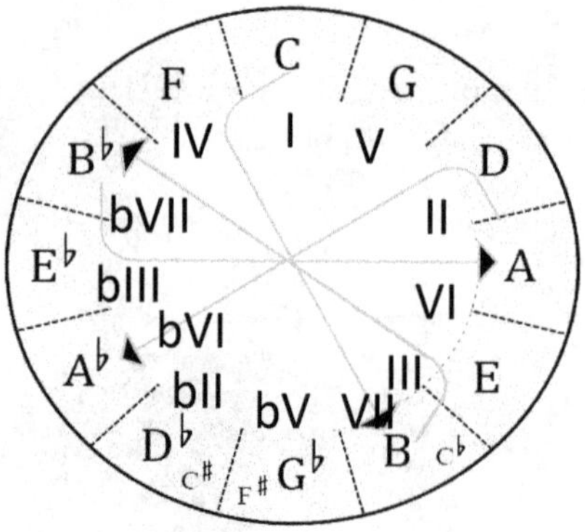

- half/whole scale sequence over V^7 chords with a chromatic descending baseline is the same as half/whole scale sequence over V^7 chords with a whole tone ascending baseline.
  - Half/whole scales are an option for V^{7b9} chord symbols (ie. also called Spanish tinge)
  - Creates a contrary motion of descending baseline with rising half/whole scales

4.3 Related Dominants

- Major key has a full diminished chord on the leading tone which defines 4 related (V7) dominants which are a semi-tone below each of the 4 notes of the diminished chord
- Example –
  - $Eb^{ø7}$ defines 4 related dominants which are B^7, D^7, F^7, Ab^7 (minor 3rd apart)
  - All 4 related dominants share the same half/whole scale
  - Each of the $V^{7's}$ can resolve to the same tonic $E^{\Delta 7}$ (i.e., $I^{\Delta 7}$)
  - Four iim7 V7 $I^{\Delta 7}$ chord sequences are:
    - Common $F\#^{m7}$ B^7 $E^{\Delta 7}$
    - Backdoor A^{m7} D^7 $E^{\Delta 7}$
    - Tritone C^{m7} F^7 $E^{\Delta 7}$
    - Other $Eb^{ø7}$ $Ab7^{b9}$ $E^{\Delta 7}$
  - Four ii 7 V7 $i^{\Delta 7}$ chord sequence using $C\#m^{\Delta 7}$ (the relative minor of E)
    - Common $F\#^{ø7}$ B^7 $C\#m^{\Delta 7}$
    - Backdoor $A^{ø7}$ D^7 $C\#m^{\Delta 7}$
    - Tritone $C^{ø7}$ F^7 $C\#m^{\Delta 7}$
    - Other $Eb^{ø7}$ $Ab7^{b9}$ $C\#m^{\Delta 7}$

5 Chord Substitutions

- Substitution through changing quality of chord
  - major to minor
  - maj^7 to $^b7$
  - $I^{\Delta 7}$ to iiim7 or vim7 (tonic subs)
  - V^7 to V^{7alt} (altered/subs.)

- Common chord changes and substitute examples
  - I VI^7 II^7 V^7
  - I vi^7 ii^7 V^7
  - iii vi^7 ii^7 V^7
  - all of above with tritone subs as per x-configuration
  - for more see (Lawn 1993, 111)

6 Whole Tone Scale

- two points of departure cover all/both types
- WRT blues
  - First degree whole tone
  - IV, V both use the other whole tone scale
- Blues progression for whole tone
  - I^7 IV^7 I^7 I^7 / IV^7 IV^7 I^7 I^7/ V^7 IV^7 I^7 I^7(V^7)
  - Only 2 triads with inversion cover all possiblities
    1) Example C^7 blues uses 2 triads
       - C^{+5}
       - D^{+5}
- Another interesting bass line sequence of V^7 ascends by a whole tone (i.e., C^7, D^7, E^7, etc.). The same set of inverted diminished scale (i.e., half/whole) can be used over a secondary dominant sequence the descends by a semi-tone or rises by a whole tone. There are only 3 possible inverted diminished scales before the sequence repeats which explains this phenomenon.

For example:

- Descending Semi-tone Sequence C^7, B^7, Bb^7 uses the C,B,Bb half/whole scales
- Ascending Whole Step Sequence C^7, D^7, E^7 uses the C,D,E half/whole scales which are the same as the C, B, Bb scales but starts from a different note in the scale.

7 Method for Harmonizing Each Note of a Melody

- Harmonic rhythm often provides chord changes on the 1st beat of each bar or on one and three of bar with many melodic notes filling in between these significant chord changes
- Example for common vi^7 – ii^7 – V^7 - $I^{\Delta 7}$ sequence
  - Assume 8 melodic notes between vi^7 – ii^7 changes
  - Step 1 chose a matching bass note using one of these methods
    1) Chromatic descending sequence (ie. 8 notes)
    2) Cycle of 5ths counting backwards from destination
    3) Chromatic rising sequence (less common approach)

8 Extending Resolution of Tonic

- Chords change every beat
- Common application is a chord sequence with 2 bars of tonic

- Example;
  - Type 1: chromatic movement

Cmaj7	**Bb7**	**Eb^{maj7}**	**A7**	**Ab^{maj7}**	**G7**	**C^{maj7}**
Imaj^7	^{b}VII^7	^{b}III^7	VI7(T.T.^{7})	^{b}VI^7	V^7	Imaj^7
	Down 5th	Down to tritone(TT7)	down chromatically to dominant			
Alternating dominant 7s and major 7s						

- Type 2: 3m_V7 alternating movement

Cmaj^7	**Eb^7**	**Ab^{maj7}**	**B^7**	**E^{maj7}**	**G^7**	**C^{maj7}**
Imaj^7	^{b}III^7	^{b}VI7maj^7	^{b}VII^7	III^7	V^7	Imaj^7
Up min. 3rd	Down 5th	Up min. 3rd	Down 5th	Up min. 3rd	Down 5th	
Alternating dominant 7s and major 7s						

- Example of Type 1 with Bitonal major triads

Maj triad / Over root	**B/ C**	**E/ B**	**F/ Eb**	**B/ A**	**Bb/ Ab**	**Db/ G7**	**B/ C**
	Imaj7	^{b}VII7	^{b}III 7	VI7(TT7)	^{b}VI7	V7	Imaj7

- Example of Type 2 with Bitonal major triads

Maj triad / Over root	**B/ C**	**F Eb**	**Bb/ Ab**	**Db/ B**	**F#/ E**	**A/ G**	**B/ C**
	I^{maj7}	^{b}III^7	^{b}VI7^{maj7}	^{b}VII^7	III^7	V^7	I^{maj7}

9 Extending ii-V7-I

- Option to double time and chain extended ii-V7-I with extending resolution of tonic
- Example – extend Em7-A7-Dmaj7

Em^7	F^7	Bb^{maj7}	C#^{7}	F#^{maj7}	A^7	D^{maj7}
iim^7	^{b}III^7	^{b}VI7maj^7	VII^{maj7}	III^{maj7}	V^7	I^{maj7}
Up min_2	Down 5th	Up min_3	Down P5	Up min_3	Down P5	
	Alternating dominant 7s and major 7s					

- Note F7/Db7/A7 are part of triple augment system (alternate chords in sequence)
- Example – extend Dm7-G7-Cmaj7

D^{m7}	Eb7	Ab^{maj7}	B7	E^{maj7}	G^7	C^{maj7}
iim^7	^{b}III^7	^{b}VI7^{maj7}	VII^{maj7}	III^{maj7}	V^7	I^{maj7}
Up min_2	Down P5	Up min_3	Down P5	Up min_3	Down P5	
	Alternating dominant 7s and major 7s					

- Note F7/Db7/A7 are part of triple augment system (alternate chords in sequence)

10 Substitutes for I - vi7 - iim7 - V7

- Common sequence in *Rhythm Changes*
- Duke Ellington sub: I - VI7^{b9} - II7 - V7
  - VI7^{b9} with scale, inverted diminished or also called half/whole
  - II7 allows dominant scale with extension or alterations
- Monk substitution
  - Uses circle of 4ths/5ths over I-VI-II-V roots
  - Example 1:

Gb^7/ Bb	**B^7/ G**	**E^7/ C**	**A^7/ F**	**D^7/ Bb**	**G^7/ G**	**C^7/ C**	**F^7/ F**
I	VI	II	V	I	VI	II	V

- Example 2: with 2nd and 3rd last changes using tritones

Gb^7/ Bb	**B^7/ G**	**E^7/ C**	**A^7/ F**	**D^7/ Bb**	**Db^7/ G**	**Gb^7/ C**	**F^7/ F**
I	VI	II	V	I	VI	II	V

- Example 3: with 2nd and 4th last changes using tritones

Gb^7/ Bb	**B^7/ G**	**E^7/ C**	**A^7/ F**	**Ab^7/ Bb**	**G^7/ G**	**Gb^7/ C**	**F7/ F**
I	VI	II	V	I	VI	II	V

11 Summary of Composition's Coverage of Jazz Theory Concepts

	Missing you	**East of Sun (reharm.)**	**Satin Doll (reharm.)**	**Phr-entranced**	**That Whole Thing**	**Road Less Travelled**	**Bail-ando**	**Gin & More Tonic**	**I Got Ning-ed**
Mix. Over V7	✓						✓		
Lyd. Dom over V7	✓						✓		
Whole T. over V7					✓				
Half/whole over V7	✓				✓	✓	✓		
Super Loc. over V7				✓			✓		
Locrian over ø7							✓		
Dori. harm. min over ø7	✓						✓		
6deg mel. min. over. ø7	✓								
Whole/half over. ø7							✓		
Dorian harm maj over. ø7							✓		
#9 scales									
Phryg. mode	✓			✓					
Triple Aug	✓								
Bitonal		✓		✓					
x-config			✓			✓			
Chrom. Desc. Bass w V7						✓			
Whole Asc. Bass w V7						✓			
Rel. Dom. To I$^{\Delta7}$ common			✓			✓			
Rel. Dom. To I$^{\Delta7}$ B. door			✓			✓			
Rel. Dom. To I$^{\Delta7}$ TriTone		✓	✓			✓			
Rel. Dom. To I$^{\Delta7}$ other						✓			
Rel. Dom. To im$^{\Delta7}$							✓		
Chord subs		✓				✓			
Whole tone scale				✓					
Planing							✓		
Extending Tonic								✓	
Extending ii-V7-I								✓	
Duke I-VI7b9-ii7-V7									✓
Monk sub I-vi-ii-V									✓

12 Bibliography

Berg, Shelton. 1990. *Jazz Improvisation: The Goal Note Method*. Lou Fischer Pub. Carlsbad, CA.
Lawn, Richard. 1993. *Jazz Theory and Practice*. Alfred Music Publishing. Van Nuys, CA.
Levine, Mark. 1995. *The Jazz Theory Book*. Petaluma CA: Sher Music.
Sussman, Richard. 2012. *Jazz Composition and Arranging in the Digital Age*. Oxford: Oxford Press.
Mullholland, Joe. 2013. *The Berklee Book of Jazz Harmony*. Boston: Berklee College.
Westray, Ron. 2017–18. *Presentations and Materials for MUSI 6250 Studio-Lectures*. Toronto: York University.

13 Discography

Brubeck, Dave. 1959. *Time Out*. CL1397, NYC, Columbia.
Coltrane, John. 1958. *Blue Train*. DP7460952, NYC, Blue Note.
Coltrane, John. 1960. *Giant Steps*. UDCD605, NYC, Atlantic.
Davis, Miles. 1959. *Kind of Blue*. 88697-33552-2, NYC, Columbia.
Ellington, Duke. 1963. *Money Jungle*. CDP7463982, NYC, Blue Note.
Evans, Bill. 1961. *At the Village Vanguard*. SRCD1961–2, NYC, Riverside.
Harris, Barry. 1960. *At the Jazz Workshop*. RLP 12–326, SanFransico: Riverside.
Tyner, McCoy. 1967. *The Real McCoy*. BST84264,NYC: Blue Note.
Tyner, McCoy. 1967. *Sahara*. SP9039-A, NYC: Milestone.
Monk, Thelonious. 1987. *It's Monk Time*. 25218-6231-2, NYC: Riverside.

14 Appendix A : Compositions Demonstrating Jazz Theory Concepts

Missing You (explores scale/chord relationships)

Missing You

Tom McGill

G maj (A dorian)
Eb melodic minor
F7 w passing tone
Am
Cm
F7
C
G maj
E harm. m. B mix
E dorian
A mix
Am
F♯ø7
B7
Em
A7
G maj
D alt.
B dorian
Bbm mel. (TT sub)
Am
D7
Bm
B♭m
G maj
Dmix
G maj
Am
D7
Gmaj7

East of the Sun (standard reharmonized)

East of the Sun
(reharmonized)
bitonal
Gmaj7 Bm7 C° Em7/D Gmaj7 Bm7/F♯ E7 E7(♯5)
bitonal
5 Am D7 Cm Bm7 Am Cm7/G F7 E7
x-config, TT-sub
9 Am D7/A A♭m7 G7 F♯ø7 B7 Em B7(♭13)
13 A7 Bm7 Em A7 F7 E7 D(sus4) D7
bitonal
17 Gmaj7 Bm7 C° Em7/D Gmaj7 Bm7/F♯ E7 E7(♯5)
bitonal
21 Am D7 Cm Bm7 Am Cm7/G F7 E7
25 Am Am/G F♯ø7 B7(♯9) A7 Bm7 Em7 A7
29 Am E♭7(♯5) D7 D7/C Bm B♭m
33 Am Am/B Am/C Am/D D7 Gmaj7 Am (D7)

Satin Doll (standard reharmonized)

Satin Doll

(reharmonized)

Duke

19
Dm7
G7
Fm7
B♭7
Em7
A7
Gm7
C7
Pno.

23
Am7
D7
Bm7
E7
Cmaj7
Pno.

Phr-entranced (uses Phrygian mode)

Phr-entranced

Tom McGill

21 Dm7
G7alt.
Cmaj7
F(sus4)/E
f
p
A
25 F♯11/E
Cmaj7
mp
29 F♯11/E
Cmaj7
f

Road Less Travelled (V7s, chromatic descending is like a whole tone rising bassline)

The Road Less Travelled

Tom McGill

Bailando en La Oscuridad (Latin feel using minor harmony)

Bailando en la Oscuridad

(Dancing in the Dark)

Tom McGill

Gin and More Tonic (extending tonic and ii-V-1 with chord sequence)

I Got Ninged (uses Duke and Monk substitutions for I-vi-ii-V)

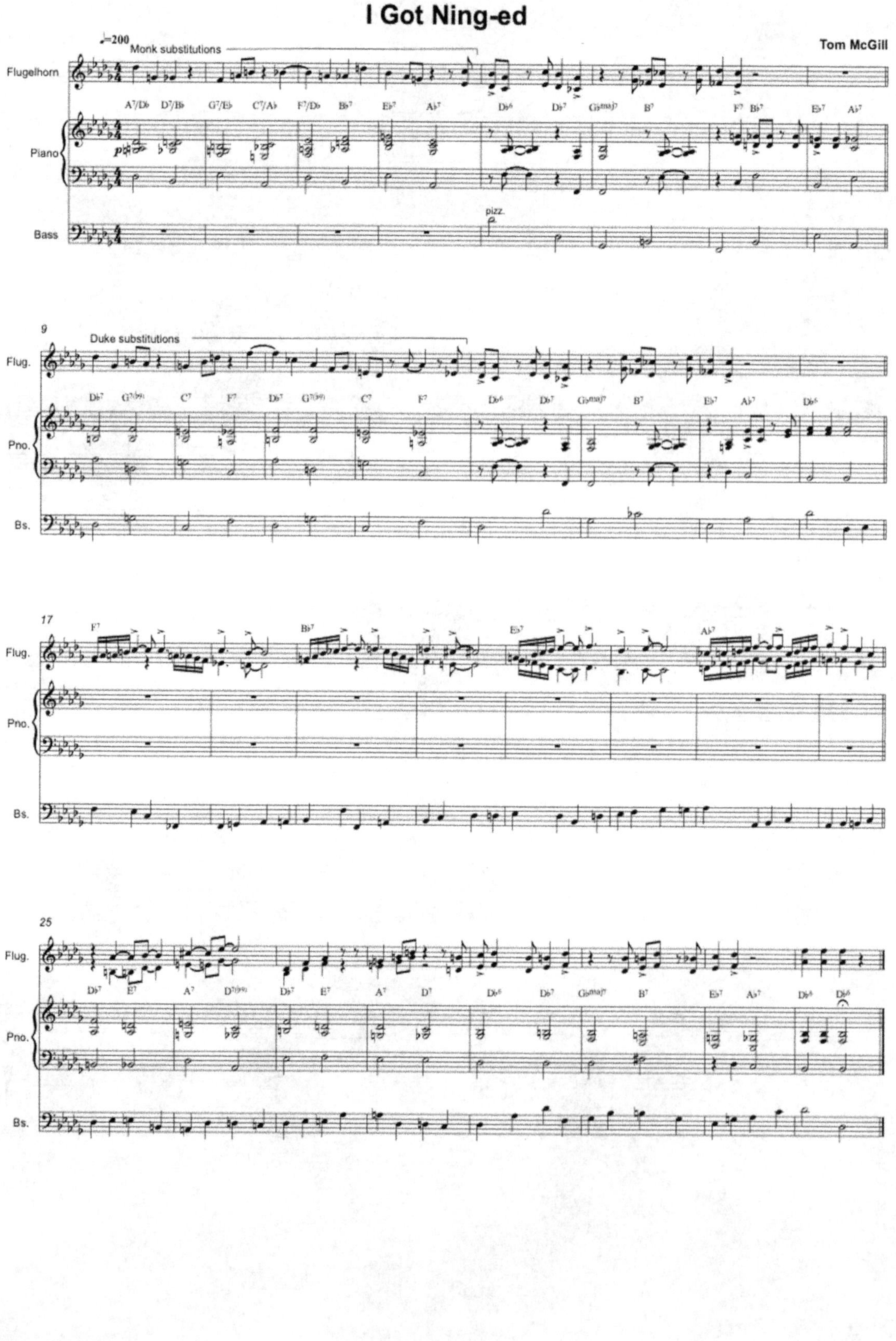

Please Don't Talk (uses circle of 4ths to harmonize each melody note)

Please Don't Talk About Me

(reharmonized: circle of 4ths, chord per melody note)

Sam Stept

Note: Chords symbols in large font are targets, small font are fillers.

Please Don't Talk (uses chromatic bassline with tritones to harmonize each melody note)

Note: Chords symbols in large font are targets, small font are fillers.

8.3 **Profs. Miscellaneous Tips (The In Between)**

These tips are a collection of advice for musicians, particularly those in jazz or contemporary music contexts. Let's break down and expand on each tip:

1. When dealing with modes, the root of the chord is the key center: this tip emphasizes the importance of understanding the root note of a chord when working with musical modes. The root defines the key or tonal center of the music.
2. Phrygian and iiim7 chord are separate entities: Phrygian is a musical mode, and a iiim7 chord typically refers to a minor 7th chord based on the third degree of a major scale. These two concepts should not be confused or treated as the same thing.
3. Median Substitution: This refers to substituting the tonic (I) chord with the Median (iii) chord in a chord progression, adding a different perspective to inverse functions.
4. Use Dorian on min7 chords unless they are a part of a larger progression where a different mode may be more appropriate.
5. Melodic Minor is frequently used/substituted for other forms of minor in jazz improvisation: It's a versatile choice for creating interesting melodic lines.
6. Vertically, Cm6/9 and min./maj.7 are savvier choices at resolution than Dorian (m7)—providing smoother harmonic effects compared to using Dorian mode in [minor] resolutions to tonic.
7. Dorian mode is well-suited for use with minor 7th chords, particularly as the ii-7 chord in a ii-V-I progression.
8. The addition of a flat-9 in a V7 chord (7b9) can introduce a distinctive and colorful "tinge" to the chord quality.
9. Include the perfect 5th (P5) when constructing chord voicings that also utilize the augmented 4th (#4) or augmented 5th (#5) to create more tension in the harmony. Conversely, include (P4) Suspension (Sus) against Maj3 (ala T. Monk, ala Maiden Voyage [D7 Sus]).
10. **Distribution**—have Baritone play above tenor voicing (Ellington) or baritone doubles tenor: this tip relates to arranging for a horn section, indicating that the baritone saxophone should play above the tenor saxophone voicing or double the tenor saxophone part, as was often done in the music of Duke Ellington.
11. **Five-Note Voicing**: Finding five distinct functions for a rootless voicing can be challenging. Doubling one note of the chord is a practical solution.
12. **Hits**: Assign functions to the rhythmic spaces between the melody and the countermelody.
13. **Brainstorm**: Don't think in terms of instrumentation; think of concepts first, then disperse among instrumentation; function first, designation second: focus on the musical concepts and functions before assigning specific instruments. In other words, consider the musical roles and interactions first, and then decide which instruments will fulfill those roles. Write philosophical ideas down; then decide and select the instruments that best suit those metaphors.
14. **Three Staff Manipulation** (Condensed Scoring): **The first staff** is for the melody, **the second staff** is for punches and padding, and **the third staff** serves the bass function. Stems can be directed up or down for each staff, and the middle 'zones' fill in the functions (harmonic/rhythmic) between registers.
15. **Orchestration** is just the multiplying of the number of (chord) voices and assigning them to various instruments: simply put, increasing the number of voices in a chord, distributing them among different instruments.
16. **Intervallic Diversity**: creating more complexity by utilizing diverse interval combinations to create "tension and release" (and interest) in chord voicings; higher intervals imply lower intervals. If you have a 13th in the chord, it means that the 7th and 9th are already included (otherwise, it would [just] be a Maj6 chord). And, so on....

    Examples:

    - Minor 3rd vs. M9 (m2)
    - Major 7th vs. root (m2)
    - V7 vs. root (P2)
    - Major 7th vs. Maj6 (P2)
    - 13th vs. V7 (Maj7 or m2)

8.4 Appendix: B^{b} Transpositions (Select Transcriptions)

Clifford Brown: Trumpet
Sonny Rollins: Tenor Saxophone
Ritchie Powell: Piano
George Morrow: Bass
Max Roach: Drums

Untitled Blues

Clifford Brown - *At The Cotton Club 1956*
Rare Live Recordings - RLR 88624
Recorded May 29, 1956

Transcribed by Giovanni Ceccatell
Edited by Ron Westray

2

Untitled Blues

Dm7 G7 C7 Dm7 G7
33
D
C7 Gm7 C7
F7 C7 Em7 A7
41
Dm7 G7 C7 Dm7 G7
45
E
C7 Gm7 C7
F7 C7 Em7 A7
53
Dm7 G7 C7 Dm7 G7
57
F
C7 Gm7 C7

Untitled Blues

3

F7 C7 Em7 A7
65
Dm7 G7 C7 Dm7 G7
69
G
C7 Gm7 C7
F7 C7 Em7 A7
77
Dm7 G7 C7 Dm7 G7
81
H
C7 Gm7 C7
F7 C7 Em7 A7
89
Dm7 G7 C7 Dm7 G7
93

4

Untitled Blues

I C7 Gm7 C7
101 F7 C7 Em7 A7
105 Dm7 G7 C7 Dm7 G7
J C7 Gm7 C7
113 F7 C7 Em7 A7
117 Dm7 G7 C7 Dm7 G7
K C7 Gm7 C7
125 F7 C7 Em7 A7

Untitled Blues 5

Dm7 G7 C7 Dm7 G7
L C7 Gm7 C7
F7 C7 Em7 A7
Dm7 G7 C7 Dm7 G7
M C7 Gm7 C7
F7 C7 Em7 A7
Dm7 G7 C7 Dm7 G7
N C7 Gm7 C7

6

Untitled Blues

F7 C7 Em7 A7
161
Dm7 G7
165
C7 Dm7 G7
167
O
C7
Gm7 C7
171
F7 C7
173
Em7 A7 Dm7 G7 C7 Dm7 G7
176
P
C7 Gm7 C7

Untitled Blues 7

F7 C7 Em7 A7
185
3
Dm7 G7 C7 Dm7 G7
189
Q
C7 Gm7 C7
F7 C7 Em7 A7
197
Dm7 G7 C7 Dm7 G7
201
R
C7 Gm7 C7
F7 C7 Em7 A7
209
Dm7 G7 C7 Dm7 G7
213

8

Untitled Blues

S
C7
Gm7
C7
221
F7
C7
Em7
A7
225
Dm7
G7
C7
Dm7
G7
T
C7
Gm7
C7
233
F7
C7
Em7
A7
237
Dm7
G7
C7
Dm7
G7
U
C7
Gm7
C7
245
F7
C7
Em7
A7

Untitled Blues

9

249
Dm7 G7 C7 Dm7 G7
V
C7 Gm7 C7
257
F7 C7 Em7 A7
261
Dm7 G7 C7 Dm7 G7
W
C7 Gm7 C7
269
F7 C7 Em7 A7
273
Dm7 G7 C7 Dm7 G7
X
C7 Gm7 C7
3
3

10 **Untitled Blues**

281
F7
C7
Em7
A7
285
Dm7
G7
C7
Dm7
G7
Y
C7
Gm7
C7
293
F7
C7
Em7
A7
297
Dm7
G7
C7
Dm7
G7
Z
C7
Gm7
C7
305
F7
C7
Em7
A7
309
Dm7
G7
C7
Dm7
G7
AA
C7

John Coltrane: Tenor Saxophone
Thelonious Monk: Piano
Ahmed Abdul-Malik: Bass
Shadow Wilson: Drums

Evidence

John Coltrane Solo

Thelonious Monk Quartet with John Coltrane at Carnegie Hall
Blue Note - 35173
Recorded November 29, 1957

Thelonious Monk
Transcribed by Ron Westray
Edited and Nomenclated by Kamil Qui

2

Evidence

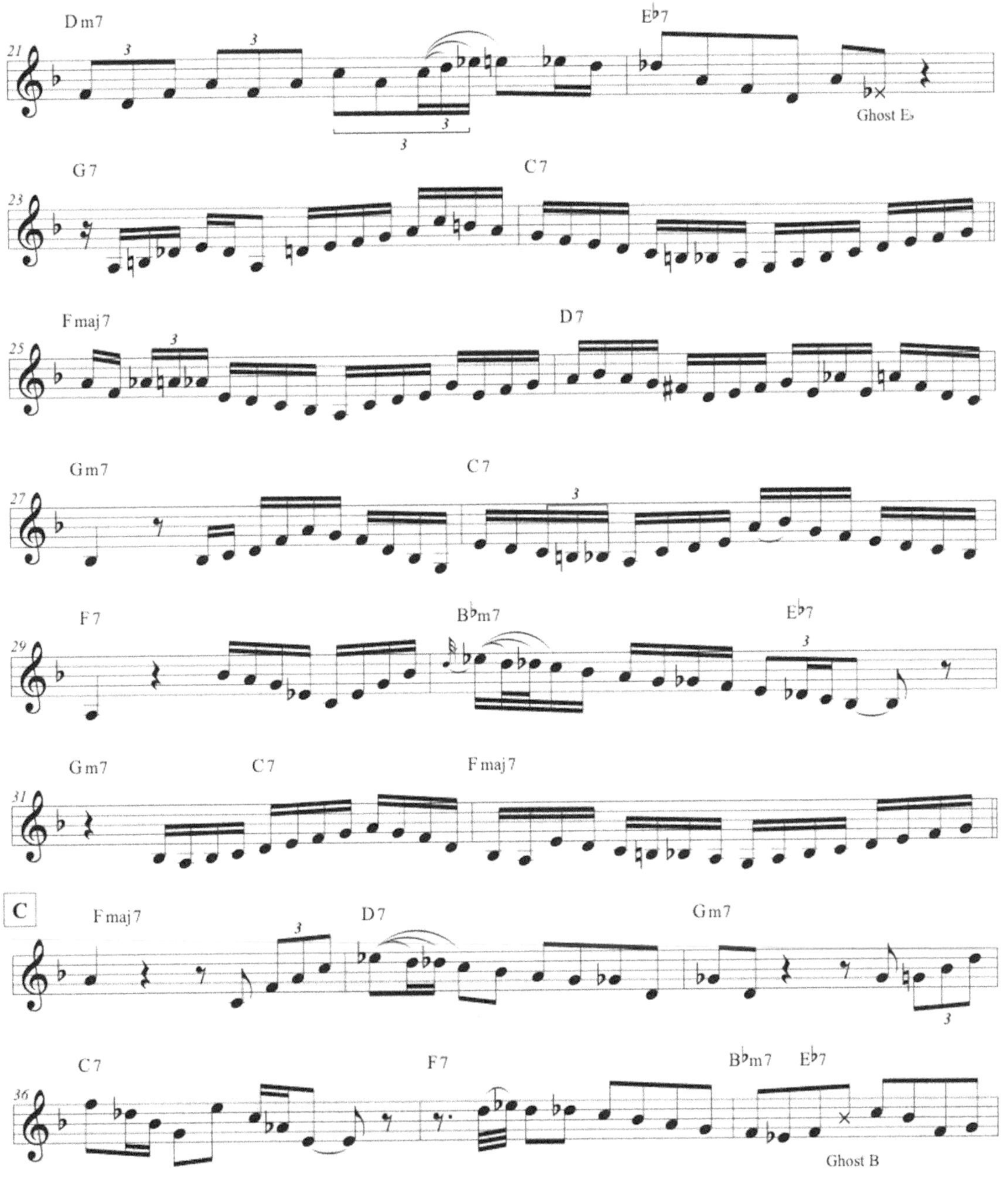
Dm7
E♭7
Ghost E♭
G7
C7
Fmaj7
D7
Gm7
C7
F7
B♭m7
E♭7
Gm7
C7
Fmaj7
C
Fmaj7
D7
Gm7
C7
F7
B♭m7
E♭7
Ghost B

Evidence

3

Gm7
C7
Fmaj7
Fmaj7
D7
Gm7
C7
F7
B♭m7
E♭7
Gm7
C7
Fmaj7
Cm7
F7
B♭maj7
E♭7
Dm7
Ghost G
E♭7
G7
C7
Fmaj7
D7
Gm7
C7
Ghost G, A

4

Evidence

F7 B♭m7 E♭7 Gm7 C7 Fmaj7
61
D
Fmaj7 D7 Gm7
C7 F7 B♭m7 E♭7
68
Gm7 C7 Fmaj7
71
Fmaj7 D7
73
Gm7 C7
75
F7 B♭m7 E♭7
77
Gm7 C7 Fmaj7
79

Evidence 5

Cm7
F7
B♭maj7
E♭7
Dm7
6
E♭7
G7
C7
Fmaj7
D7
Gm7
C7
F7
B♭m7
E♭7
Gm7
C7
Fmaj7
E

John Coltrane: Tenor Saxophone
Thelonious Monk: Piano
Ahmed Abdul-Malik: Bass
Shadow Wilson: Drums

Nutty

John Coltrane Solo

Thelonious Monk Quartet with John Coltrane at Carnegie Hall
Blue Note - 35173
Recorded November 29, 1957

Thelonious Monk
Transcribed by Ron Westray
Edited and Nomenclated by Kamil Qui

2 **Nutty**

Gm7 C7 Fmaj7
A3
Dm7 G7 Cmaj7 A7
Dm7 G7 Cmaj7 A7
Dm7 G7 G7 G7 A7
Dm7 G7 Cmaj7 A7 Dm7
A4
Cmaj7 A7 Dm7 G7
Cmaj7 A7 Dm7 G7
Cmaj7 A7 Dm7 G7

Nutty 3

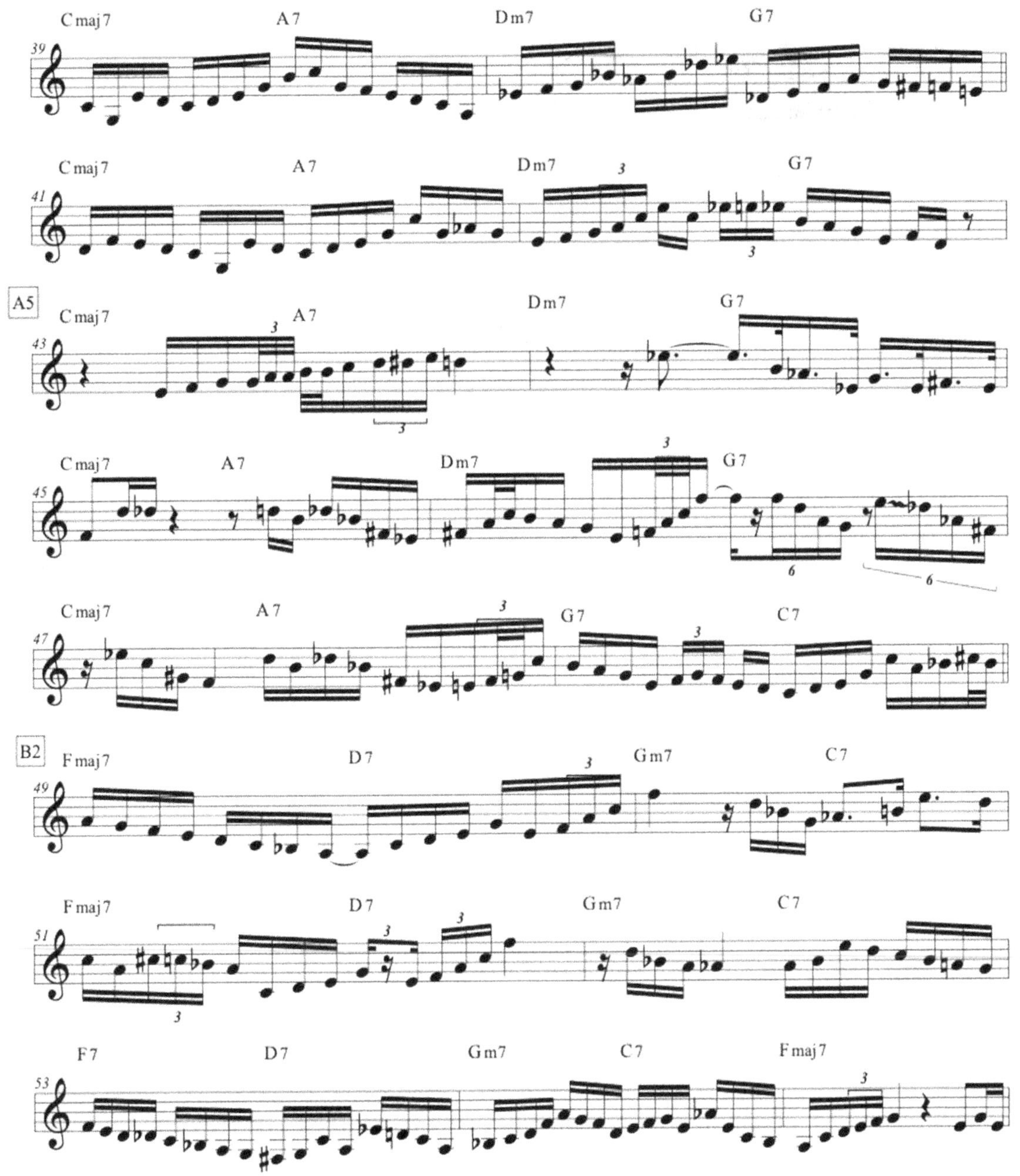
Cmaj7
A7
Dm7
G7
A5
B2
Fmaj7
D7
Gm7
C7
F7

4 **Nutty**

A6
Dm7 G7 Cmaj7 A7 Dm7 G7 Cmaj7 A7
56
Dm7 G7 Cmaj7 A7 Dm7 G7
60
Tag
Cmaj7 A7 Dm7 G7 Cmaj7 Am7
63

John Coltrane: Tenor Saxophone
Red Garland: Piano
Donald Byrd: Trumpet
George Joyner: Bass
Art Taylor: Drums

Billie's Bounce

John Coltrane Solo

The Red Garland Quintet with John Coltrane - *Dig It!*
Prestige - PRLP 7229
Recorded December 13, 1957

Charlie Parker
Transcribed by Ron Westray

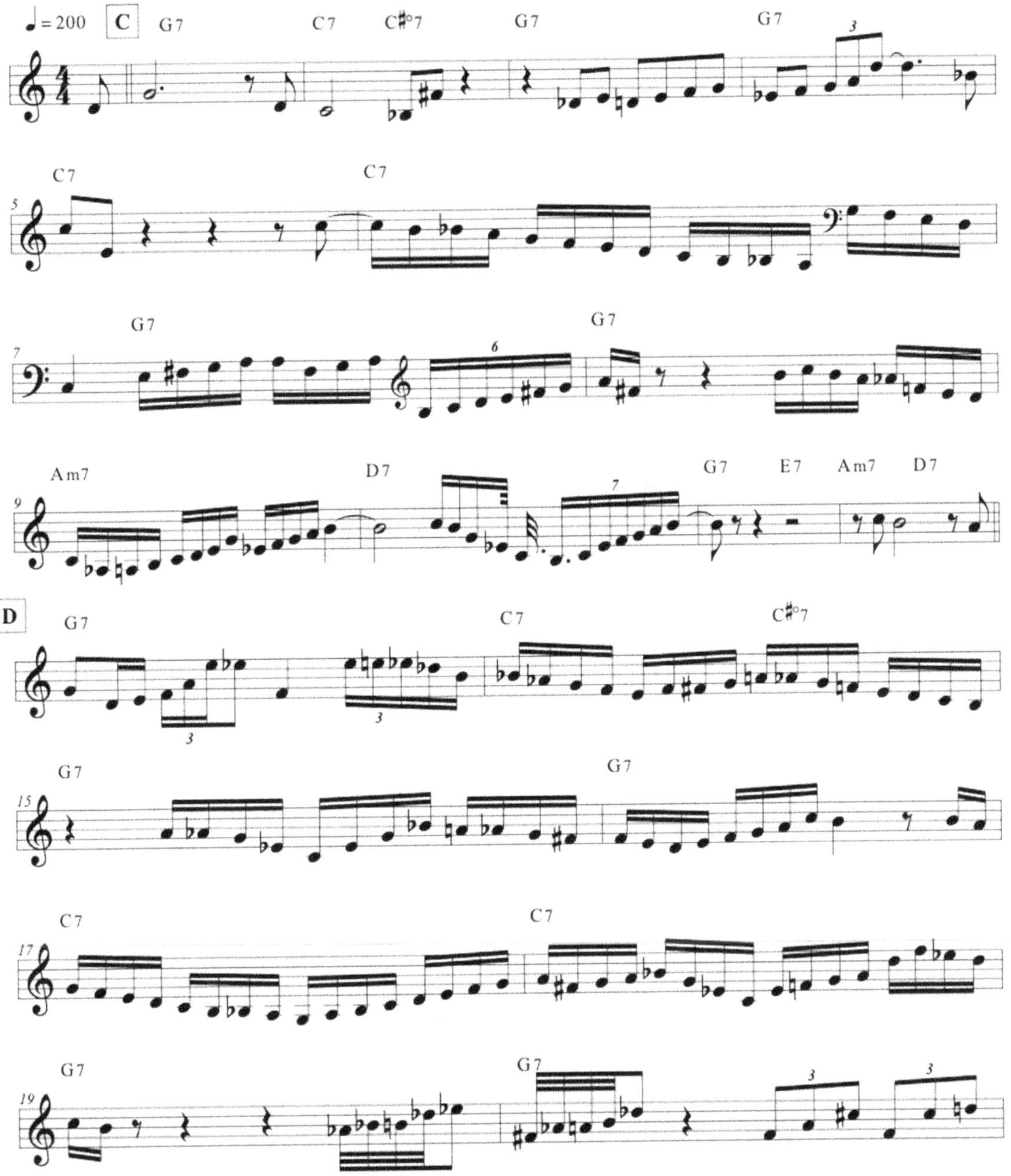

2 **Billie's Bounce**

Am7 D7
G7 E7 Am7 D7
E G7 C7 C♯°7
G7 G7
C7 C7
G7 G7
A min7 D7
G7 E7 A min7 D7

Billie's Bounce 3

F
G7
C7
C#°7
G7
G7
C7
C7
G7
G7
Am7
D7
G7
E7
Am7
D7
G
G7
C7
C#°7
G7
G7
C7

4 **Billie's Bounce**

C7 G7 G7
54
Am7 D7
57
G7 E7 Am7 D7
59
H
G7 C7 C#°7 G7
64
G7 C7 C7
67
G7 G7 Am7
3
70
D7 G7 E7 Am7 D7
I
G7 C7 C#°7 G7

Billie's Bounce 5

G7
C7
C7
6
G7
G7
Am7
3
3
D7
G7
E7
Am7
D7
J
76
78
80
82
84

John Coltrane: Tenor Saxophone
Donald Byrd: Trumpet
Red Garland: Piano
Paul Chambers: Bass
Art Taylor: Drums

Black Pearls

John Coltrane Solo
Black Pearls
Prestige - PRLP 7316
Recorded May 23, 1958

John Coltrane
Transcribed by Ron Westray
Edited and Nomenclated by Kamil Qui

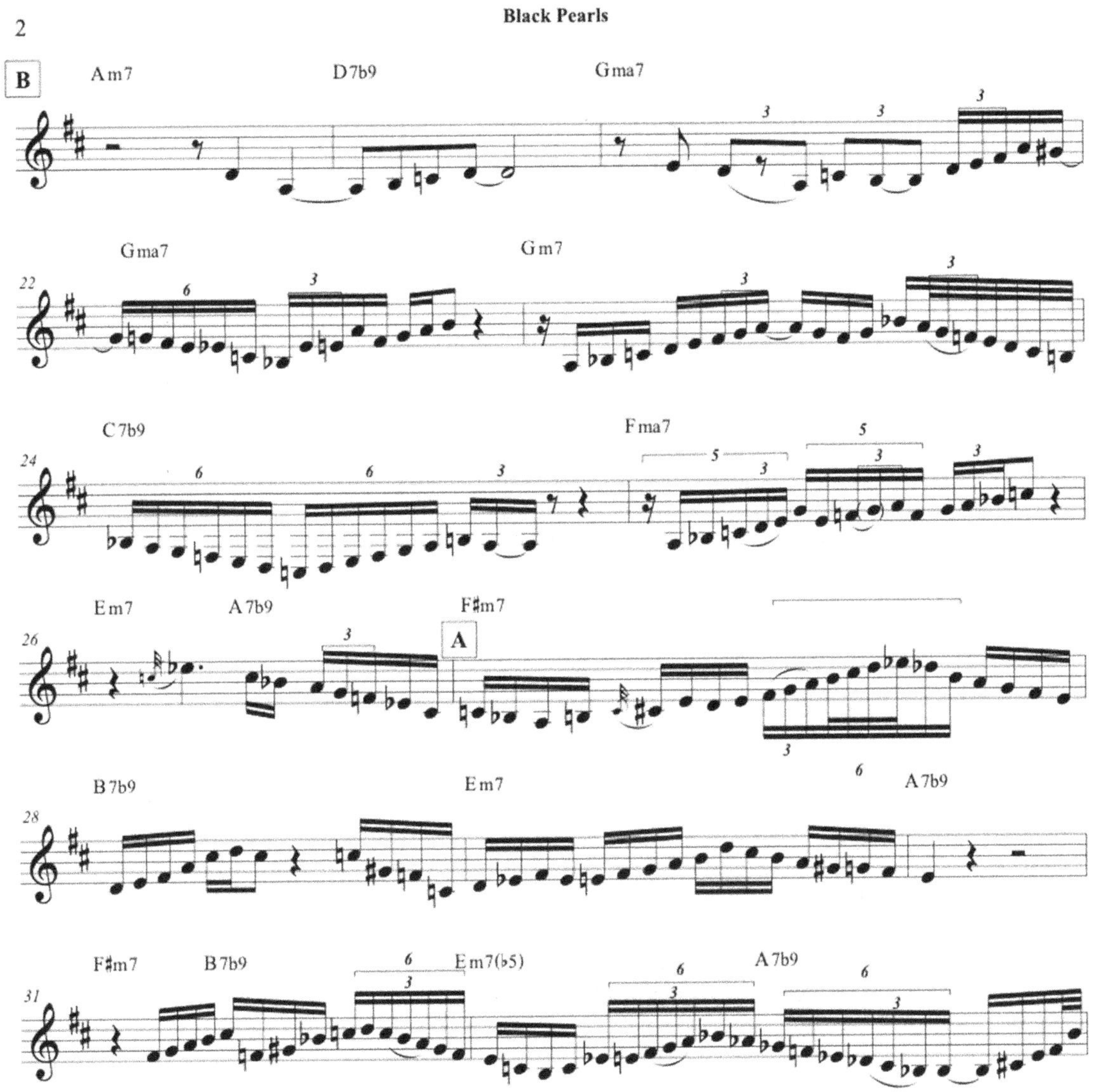
2
Black Pearls
B
Am7
D7b9
Gma7
Gma7
Gm7
C7b9
Fma7
Em7
A7b9
F♯m7
A
B7b9
Em7
A7b9
F♯m7
B7b9
Em7(♭5)
A7b9
Dma7
Dmaj7
A 2nd Chorus
F♯m7
B7b9

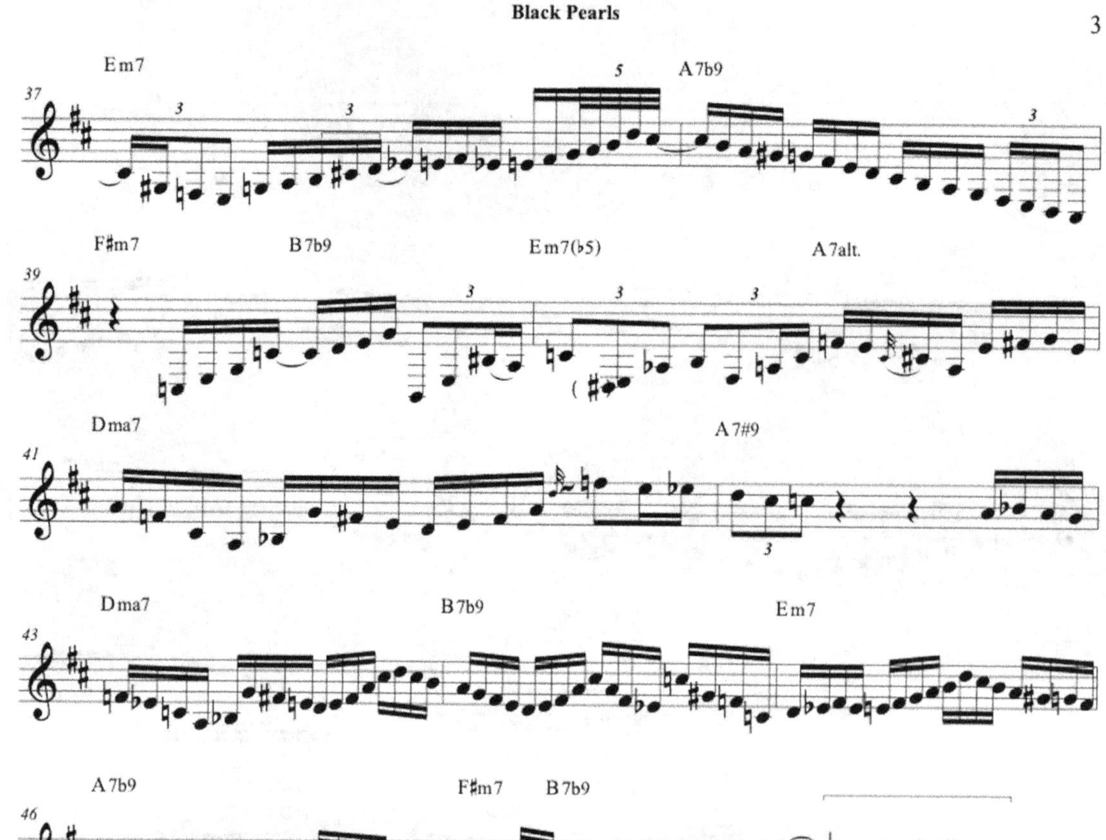
Black Pearls
3
Em7
A7b9
F♯m7
B7b9
Em7(♭5)
A7alt.
Dma7
A7♯9
Dma7
B7b9
Em7
A7b9
F♯m7
B7b9
Ghost Tone G
Em7(♭5)
A7b9
Dma7
Dmaj7
Ghost G
B
Am7
D7b9

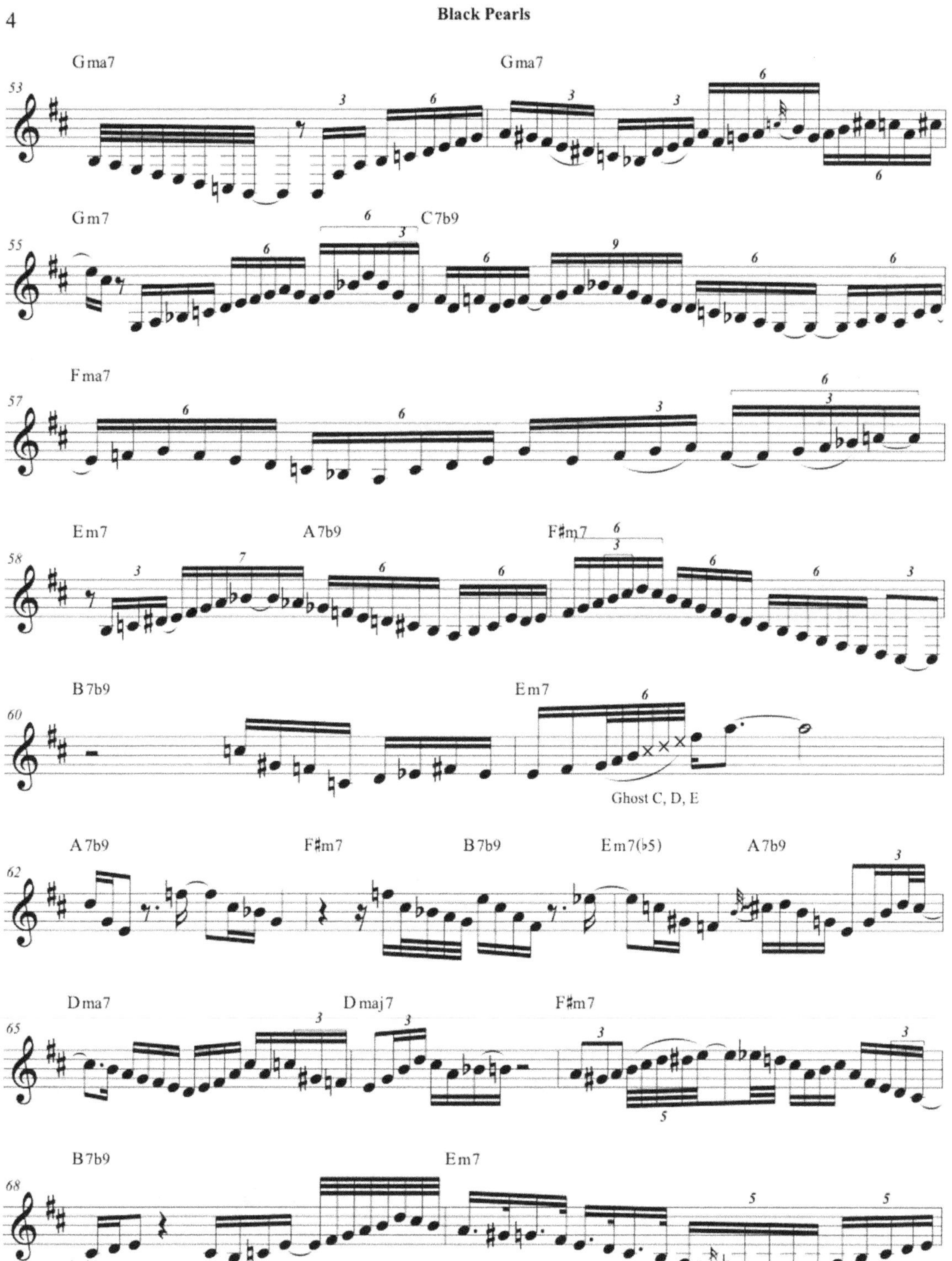
4
Black Pearls
Gma7
Gma7
Gm7
C7b9
Fma7
Em7
A7b9
F♯m7
B7b9
Em7
Ghost C, D, E
A7b9
F♯m7
B7b9
Em7(♭5)
A7b9
Dma7
Dmaj7
F♯m7
B7b9
Em7

Black Pearls
5
A7b9
F♯m7
B7b9
Em7(♭5)
A7alt.
Dma7
A7#9
Ghost D
Dma7
B7b9
Em7
A7b9
F♯m7
B7b9
Em7(♭5)
A7b9
Dma7
Dmaj7
C
Am7
D7b9
Gma7
Gma7

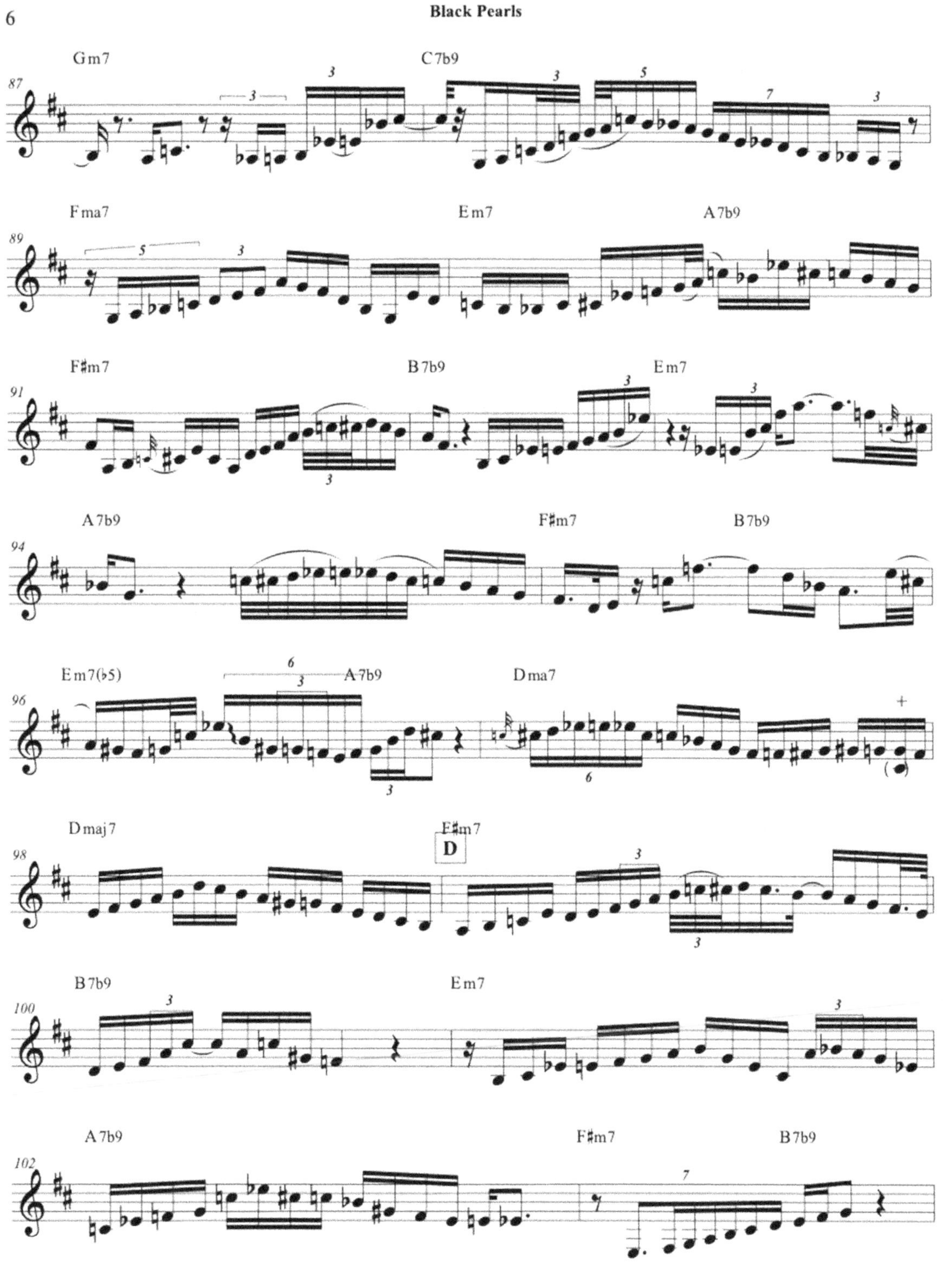
6
Black Pearls
Gm7
C7b9
Fma7
Em7
A7b9
F♯m7
B7b9
Em7
A7b9
F♯m7
B7b9
Em7(♭5)
A7b9
Dma7
Dmaj7
D
F♯m7
B7b9
Em7
A7b9
F♯m7
B7b9

Black Pearls
7
Em7(♭5)
A7alt.
Dma7
A7#9
Dma7
B7b9
Em7
A7b9
F♯m7
B7b9
Em7(♭5)
A7b9
Dma7
Dmaj7
Ghost C, B
E
Am7
D7b9

8

Black Pearls

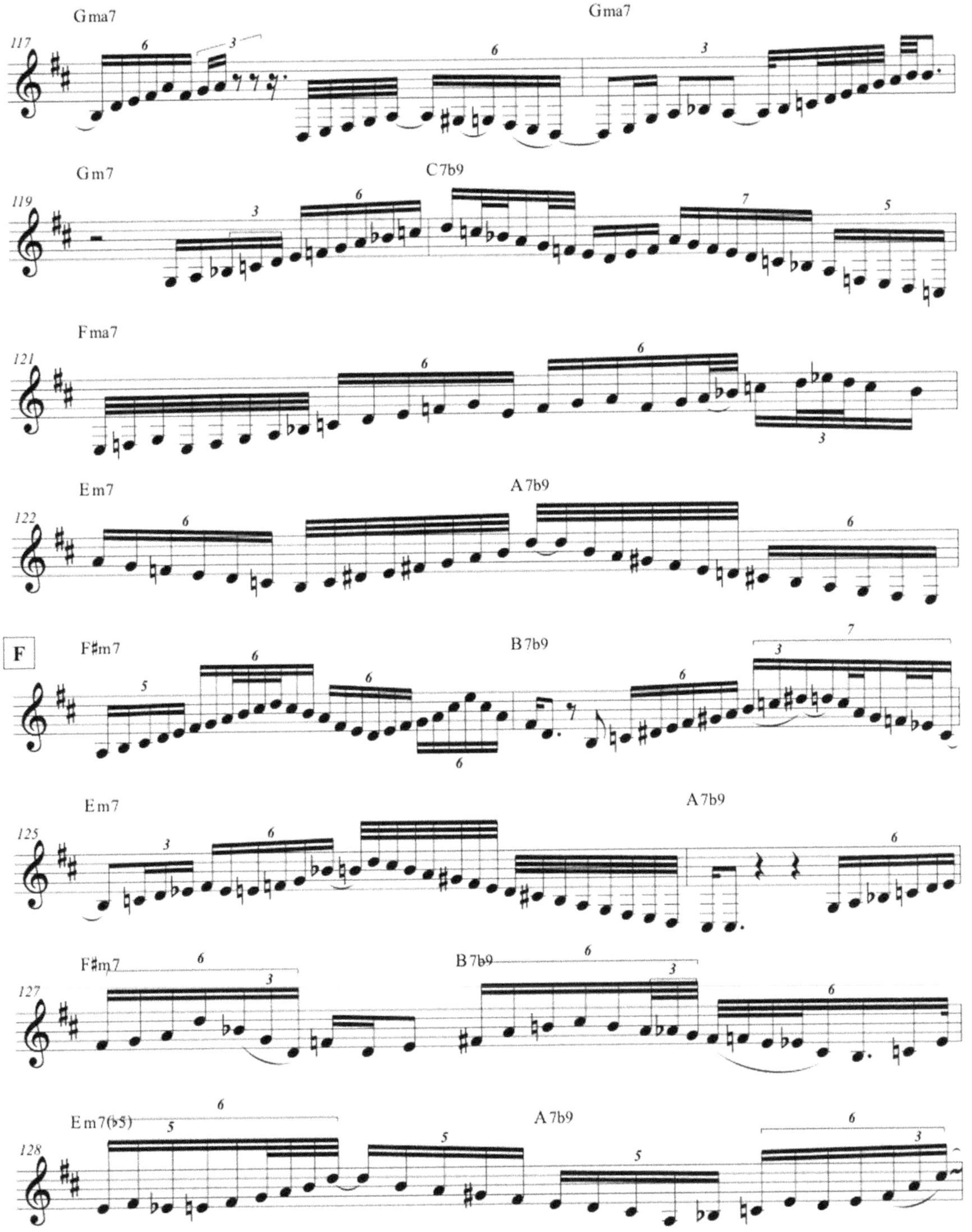

117
Gma7
Gma7
119
Gm7
C7b9
121
Fma7
122
Em7
A7b9
F
F♯m7
B7b9
125
Em7
A7b9
127
F♯m7
B7b9
128
Em7(♭5)
A7b9

Black Pearls

John Coltrane: Tenor Saxophone
Donald Byrd: Trumpet
Red Garland: Piano
Paul Chambers: Bass
Art Taylor: Drums

Sweet Sapphire Blues

John Coltrane Solo

Black Pearls
Prestige - PRLP 7316
Recorded May 23, 1958

Bob Weinstock
Transcribed by Ron Westray
Edited and Nomenclated by Kamil Qui

2

Sweet Sapphire Blues

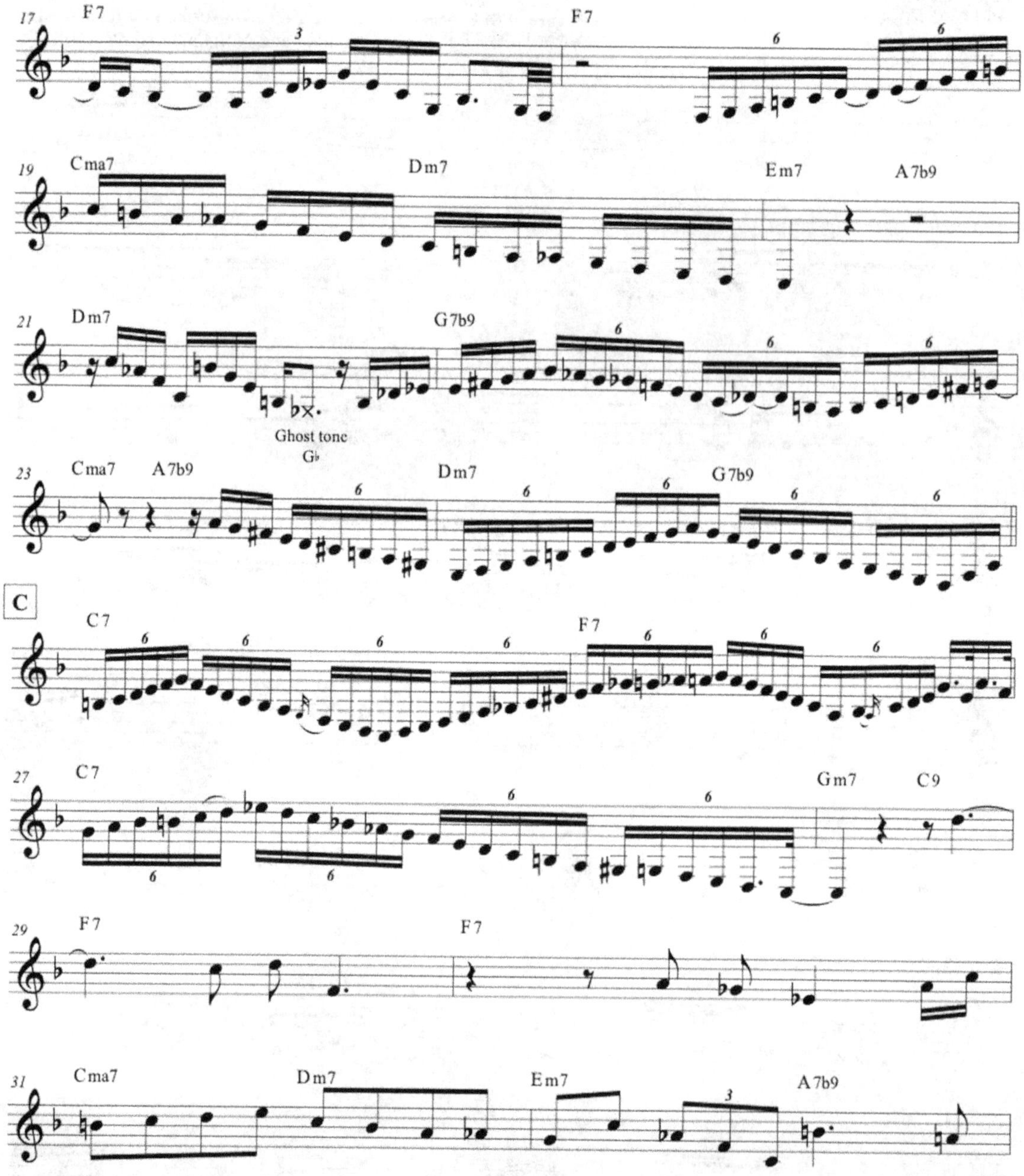
17
F7
F7
19
Cma7
Dm7
Em7
A7b9
21
Dm7
G7b9
Ghost tone
G♭
23
Cma7
A7b9
Dm7
G7b9
C
C7
F7
27
C7
Gm7
C9
29
F7
F7
31
Cma7
Dm7
Em7
A7b9

Sweet Sapphire Blues

3

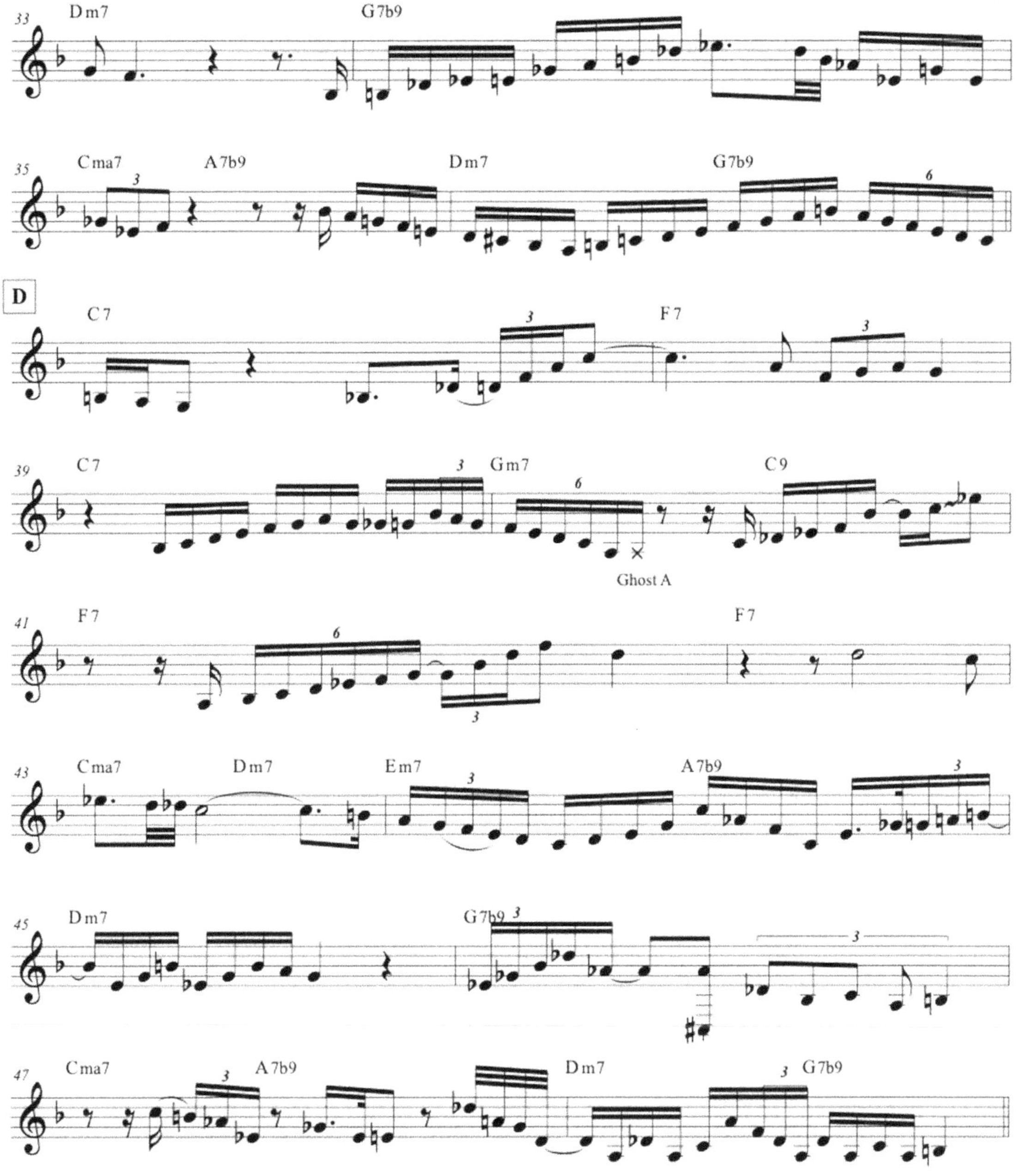
33 Dm7 G7b9
35 Cma7 A7b9 Dm7 G7b9
D
C7 F7
39 C7 Gm7 C9
Ghost A
41 F7 F7
43 Cma7 Dm7 Em7 A7b9
45 Dm7 G7b9
47 Cma7 A7b9 Dm7 G7b9

Sweet Sapphire Blues

4
E
C7
F7
51
C7
Gm7
C9
53
F7
F7
55
Cma7
Dm7
Em7
A7b9
Ghost A
57
Dm7
G7b9
59
Cma7
A7b9
Dm7
G7b9
F
C7
F7
63
C7
Gm7
C9

Sweet Sapphire Blues

5

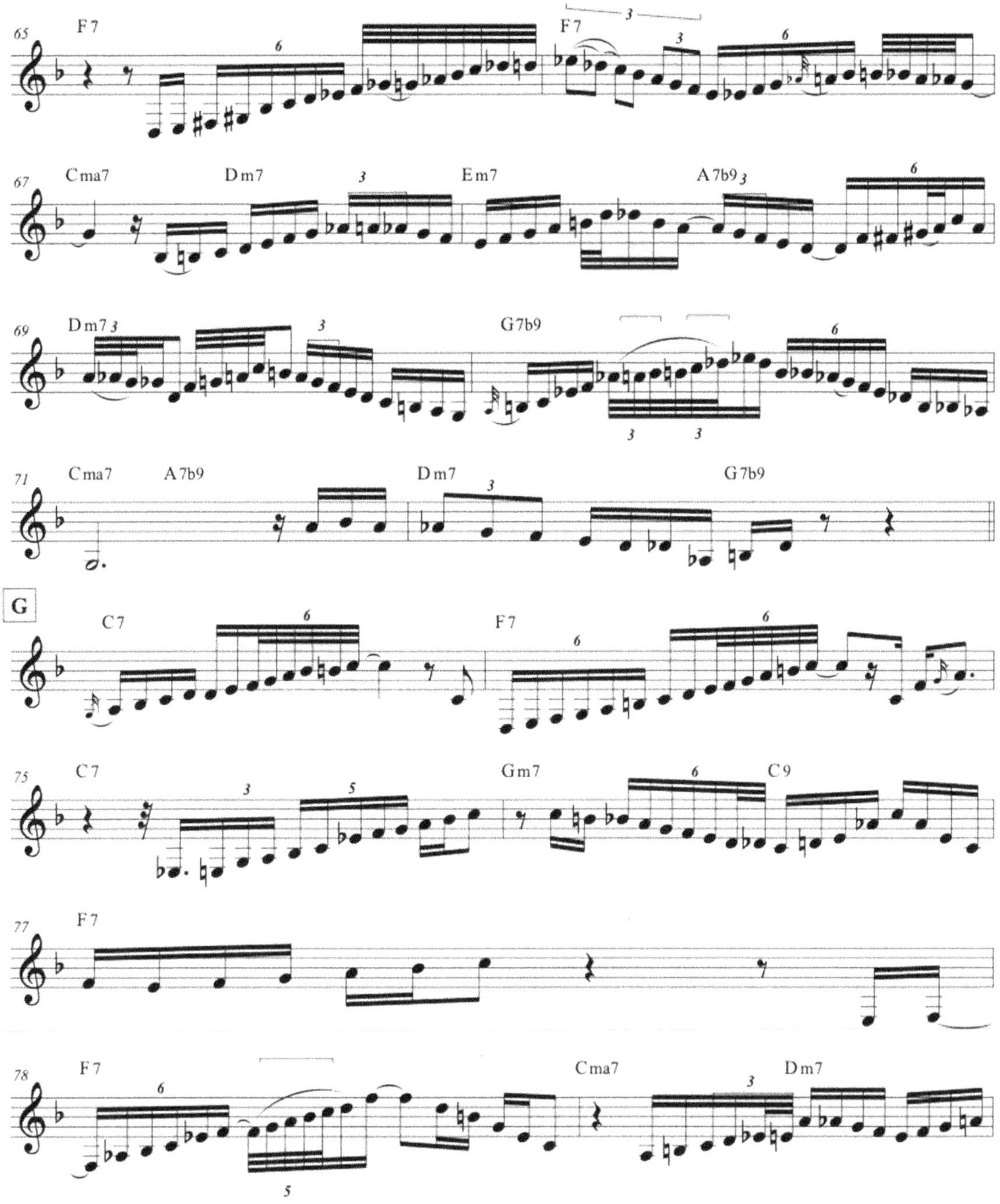
65
F7
F7
67
Cma7
Dm7
Em7
A7b9
69
Dm7
G7b9
71
Cma7
A7b9
Dm7
G7b9
G
C7
F7
75
C7
Gm7
C9
77
F7
78
F7
Cma7
Dm7

6

Sweet Sapphire Blues

Em7
A7b9
Dm7
G7b9
Cma7
A7b9
Dm7
G7b9
H
C7
F7
C7
Gm7
C9
Ghost E♭
F7
F7
Cma7
Dm7
Em7
A7b9
Dm7
G7b9
Cma7
A7b9
Dm7 G7b9

Sweet Sapphire Blues

7

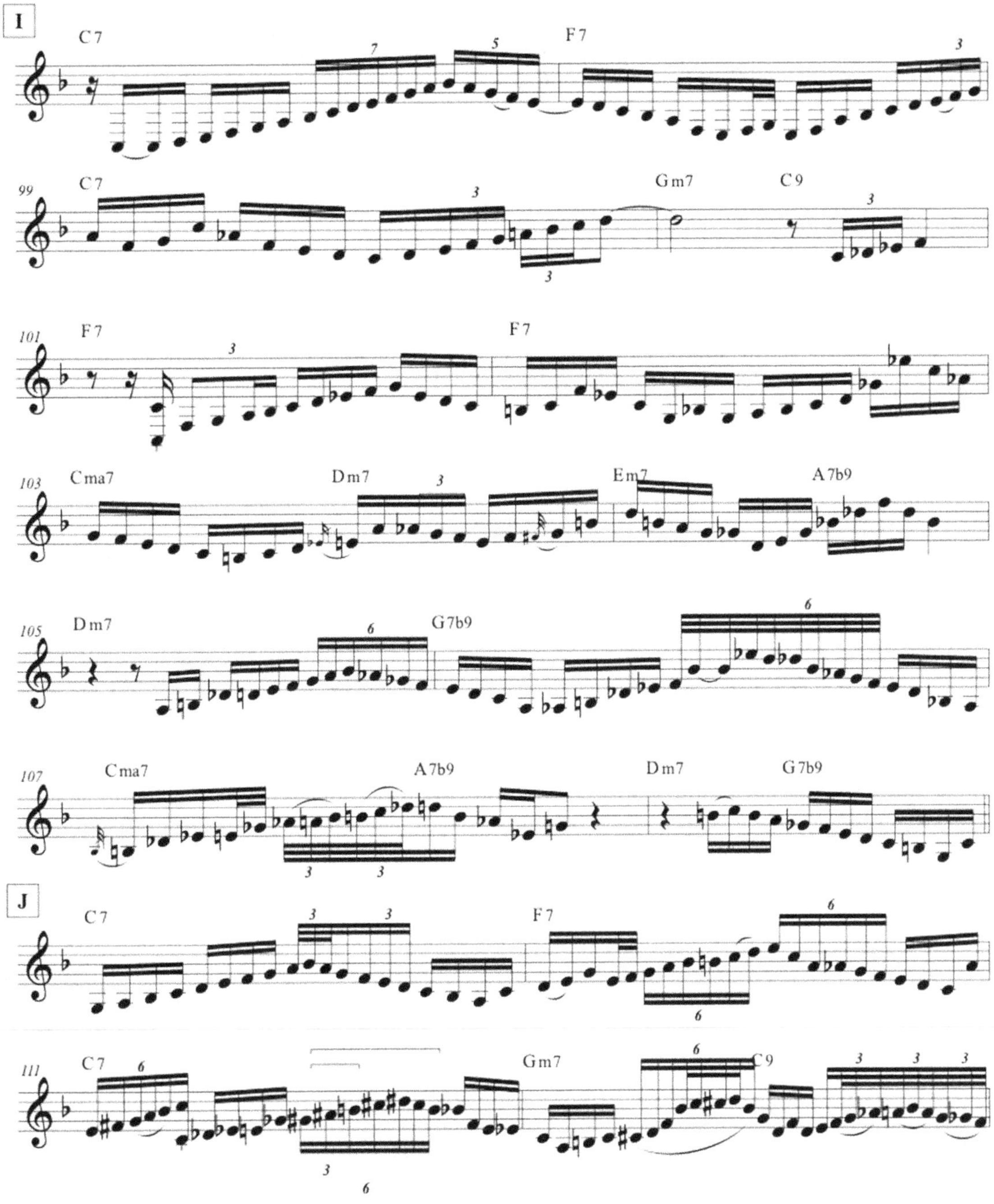
I
C7
F7
99
C7
Gm7
C9
101
F7
F7
103
Cma7
Dm7
Em7
A7b9
105
Dm7
G7b9
107
Cma7
A7b9
Dm7
G7b9
J
C7
F7
111
C7
Gm7
C9

8

Sweet Sapphire Blues

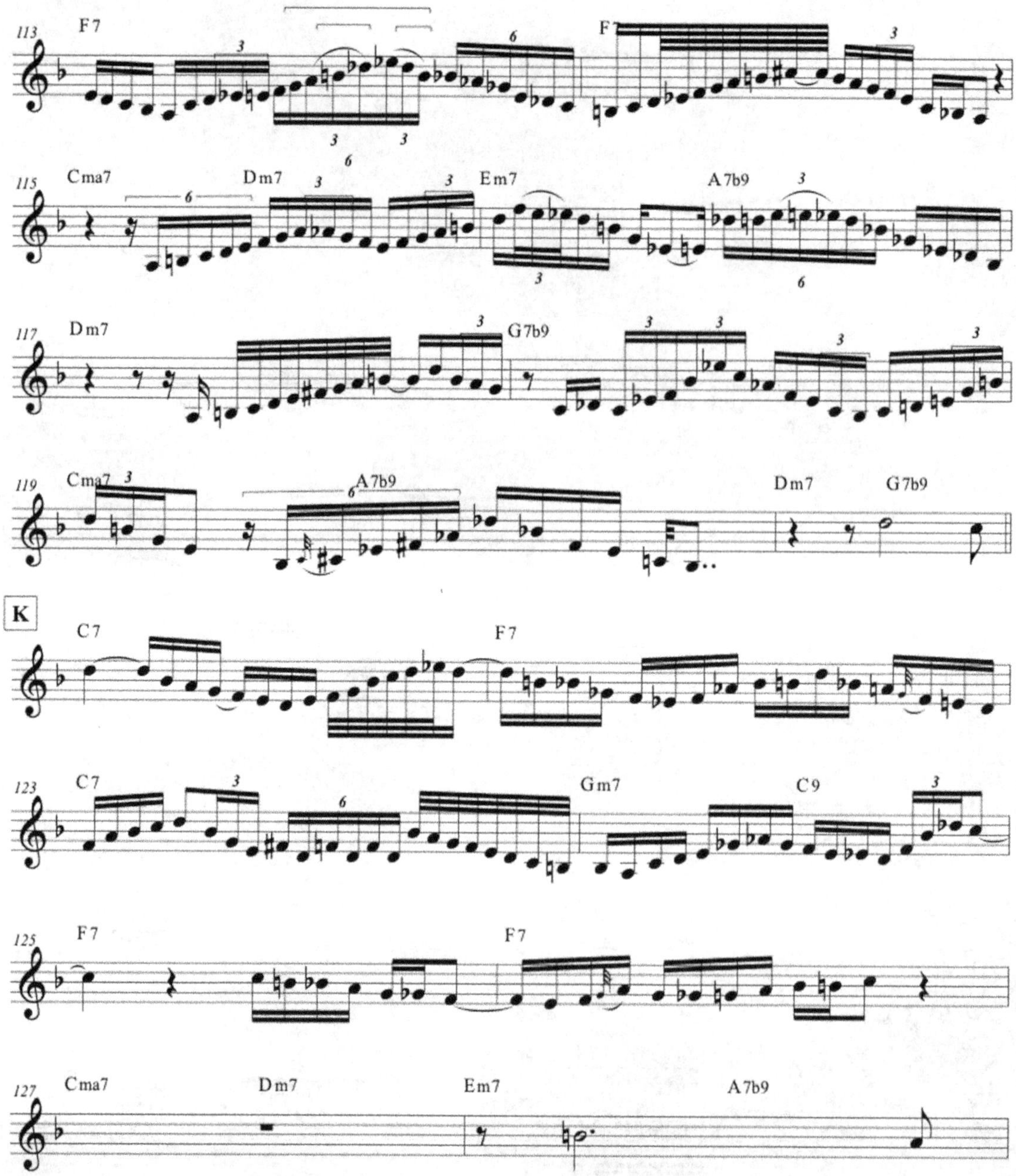
113
F7
F7
115
Cma7
Dm7
Em7
A7b9
117
Dm7
G7b9
119
Cma7
A7b9
Dm7
G7b9
K
C7
F7
123
C7
Gm7
C9
125
F7
F7
127
Cma7
Dm7
Em7
A7b9

Sweet Sapphire Blues

9

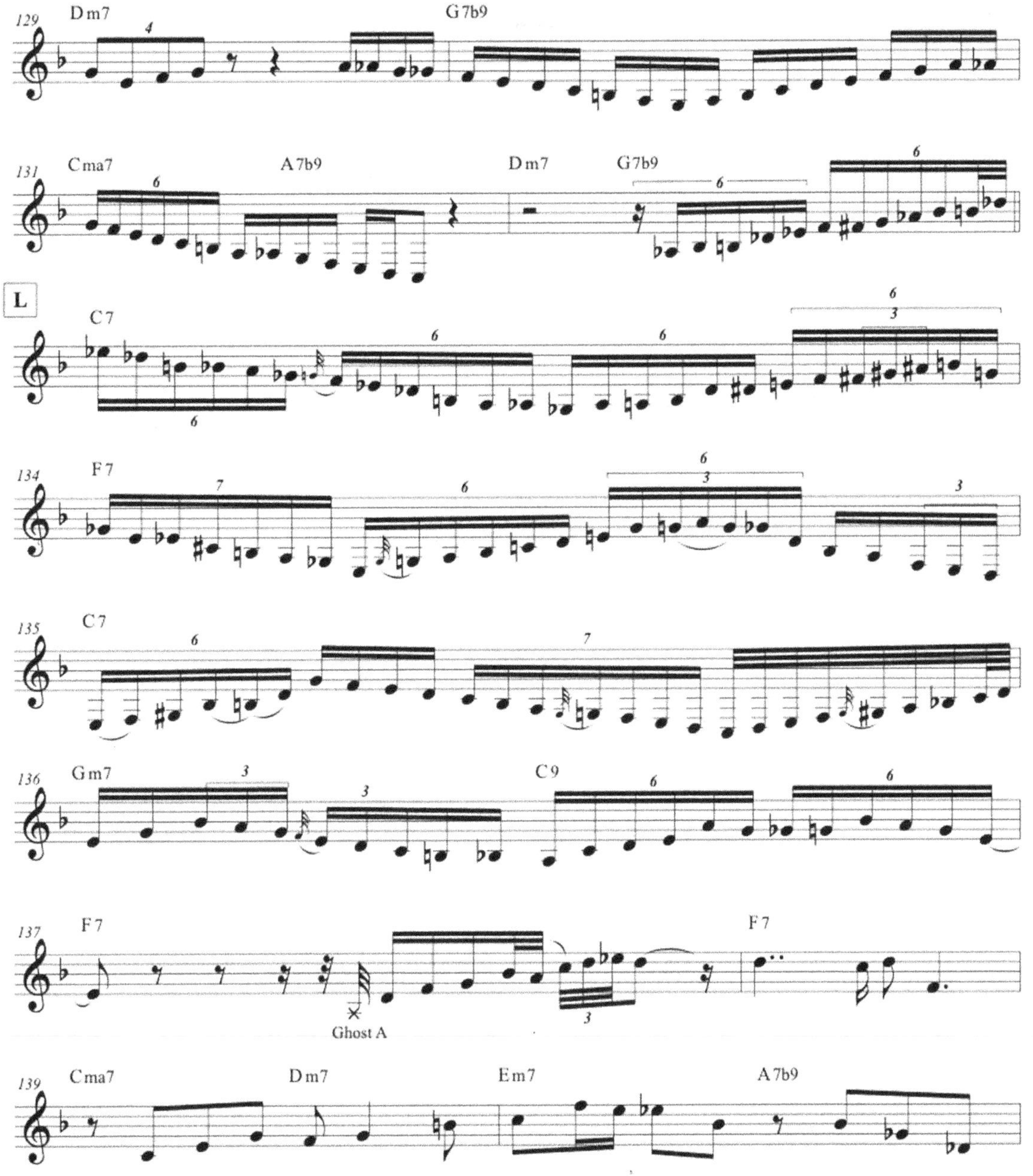
129
Dm7
G7b9
131
Cma7
A7b9
Dm7
G7b9
L
C7
134
F7
135
C7
136
Gm7
C9
137
F7
Ghost A
F7
139
Cma7
Dm7
Em7
A7b9

10

Sweet Sapphire Blues

141
Dm7
G7b9
143
Cma7
A7b9
Dm7
G7b9
M
C7
F7
147
C7
Gm7
C9
149
F7
F7
151
Cma7
Dm7
Em7
A7b9
153
Dm7
G7b9
155
Cma7
A7b9
Dm7
G7b9

Sweet Sapphire Blues

11

N
C7
F7
159
C7
Gm7
C9
161
F7
F7
163
Cma7
Dm7
Em7
A7b9
165
Dm7
G7b9
167
Cma7
A7b9
Dm7
G7b9
O
C7
F7
171
C7
Gm7
C9

12

Sweet Sapphire Blues

173
F7
F7
175
Cma7
Dm7
Em7
A7b9
177
Dm7
G7b9
179
Cma7
A7b9
Dm7
G7b9
P
C7
F7
183
C7
Gm7
C9
185
F7
F7
Cma7
Dm7
Em7
A7b9
189
Dm7
G7b9
191
Cma7
A7b9
Dm7
G7b9
Q

John Coltrane: Tenor Saxophone
Miles Davis: Trumpet
Cannonball Adderley: Alto Saxophone
Bill Evans: Piano
Paul Chambers: Bass
Jimmy Cobb: Drums

If I Were A Bell

John Coltrane Solo

Jazz At The Plaza, Vol. 1: Miles Davis Sextet
Columbia - C 32470
Recorded September 9, 1958

Frank Loesser
Transcribed by Ron Westray
Edited and Nomenclated by Kamil Qui

2 **If I Were A Bell**

Gmaj7 G7 Cmaj7 C♯°7
Gmaj7 C7 Bm7(♭5) E7
Am7 D7
Gmaj7 Bm7 E7
B
A9 D7 Gmaj7 Cm7 F7
Bm7(♭5) E7 A7 Am7 D7
Gmaj7 G7 Cmaj7 D7 Gmaj7 F♯m7(♭5) B7
Em7 C♯m7(♭5) F♯7 Bm7 E°7 Am7 D7
Ghost Tone
G or A♭

If I Were A Bell 3

4

If I Were A Bell

Gmaj7 Gmaj7
Bm7(♭5) E7 A7 Am7 D7
Gmaj7 G7 Cmaj7 D7 Gmaj7 F♯m7(♭5) B7
Em7 C♯m7(♭5) F♯7 Bm7 E°7 Am7 D7
A7 D7 Gmaj7 Cm7 F7
Bm7(♭5) E7(♭9) A7
Am7 D7 Gmaj7 G7 Cmaj7 C♯°7
Gmaj7 C7 Bm7(♭5) E7 Am7

If I Were A Bell 5

D7 Gmaj7 Bm7 E7
D
A9 D7 Gmaj7 Cm7 F7
Bm7(♭5) E7 A7
Ghost F♯
Am7 D7 Gmaj7 G7
Cmaj7 D7 Gmaj7
F♯m7(♭5) B7 Em7
C♯m7(♭5) F♯7 Bm7 E°7
Am7 D7 A7
Ghost B

6

If I Were A Bell

D7
Gmaj7
Bm7(♭5)
E7(♭9)
Ghost E
A7
Am7
D7
Gmaj7
G7
Cmaj7
C♯o7
Gmaj7
C7
Bm7(♭5)
E7
Am7
D7
Gmaj7
Bm7
E7
E
Vamp
A-7
D7
B-7
E7
A-7
D7
B-7
E7
A-7
D7
B-7
B7

If I Were A Bell 7

140
E7
A-7
D7
143
Bm7
E7
145
A-7
D7
B-7b5
148
E7b9
A-7
D7
151
B-7
E7
Am7
D7
154
D7
Bm7
E7
157
Am7
D7
Gmaj7

John Coltrane: Tenor Saxophone
Miles Davis: Trumpet
Wynton Kelly: Piano
Paul Chambers: Bass
Jimmy Cobb: Drums

On Green Dolphin Street

John Coltrane Solo

Miles Davis & John Coltrane: Live In Stockholm, 1960
Dragon Records - DRLP 90/91
Recorded March 22, 1960

Bronislau Kaper
Ned Washington
Transcribed by Ron Westray
Edited and Nomenclated by Kamil Qui

2

On Green Dolphin Street

B
Fmaj7 Fmaj7 Fm7 Fm7
Ghost Tone G
37
G9 F#9 Fmaj7 Am7 D7
41
Gm7 C7 Fmaj7 F7
Ghost A
Ghost A
45
B♭m7 E♭7 A♭maj7 Gm7 C7
49
Fmaj7 Fmaj7 Fm7 Fm7
53
G9 F#9 Fmaj7 Am7 D7
57
Gm7 Em7(♭5) A7 Dm7 G7 G#°7
Ghost B♮
61
Am7 D7 Gm7 C7 Fmaj7 D7 Gm7 C7

On Green Dolphin Street 3

C
Fmaj7
Fmaj7
Fm7
Fm7
G9
F♯9
71
Fmaj7
Am7
D7
Gm7
Throat
(Ghost Tongue)
C7
75
Fmaj7
F7
B♭m7
E♭7
79
A♭maj7
80
Gm7
C7
81
Fmaj7
Over tone
Fmaj7
Fm7
Fm7
85
G9
F♯9
Ghost F♮
87
Fmaj7
Am7
D7
Ghost F♮

4

On Green Dolphin Street

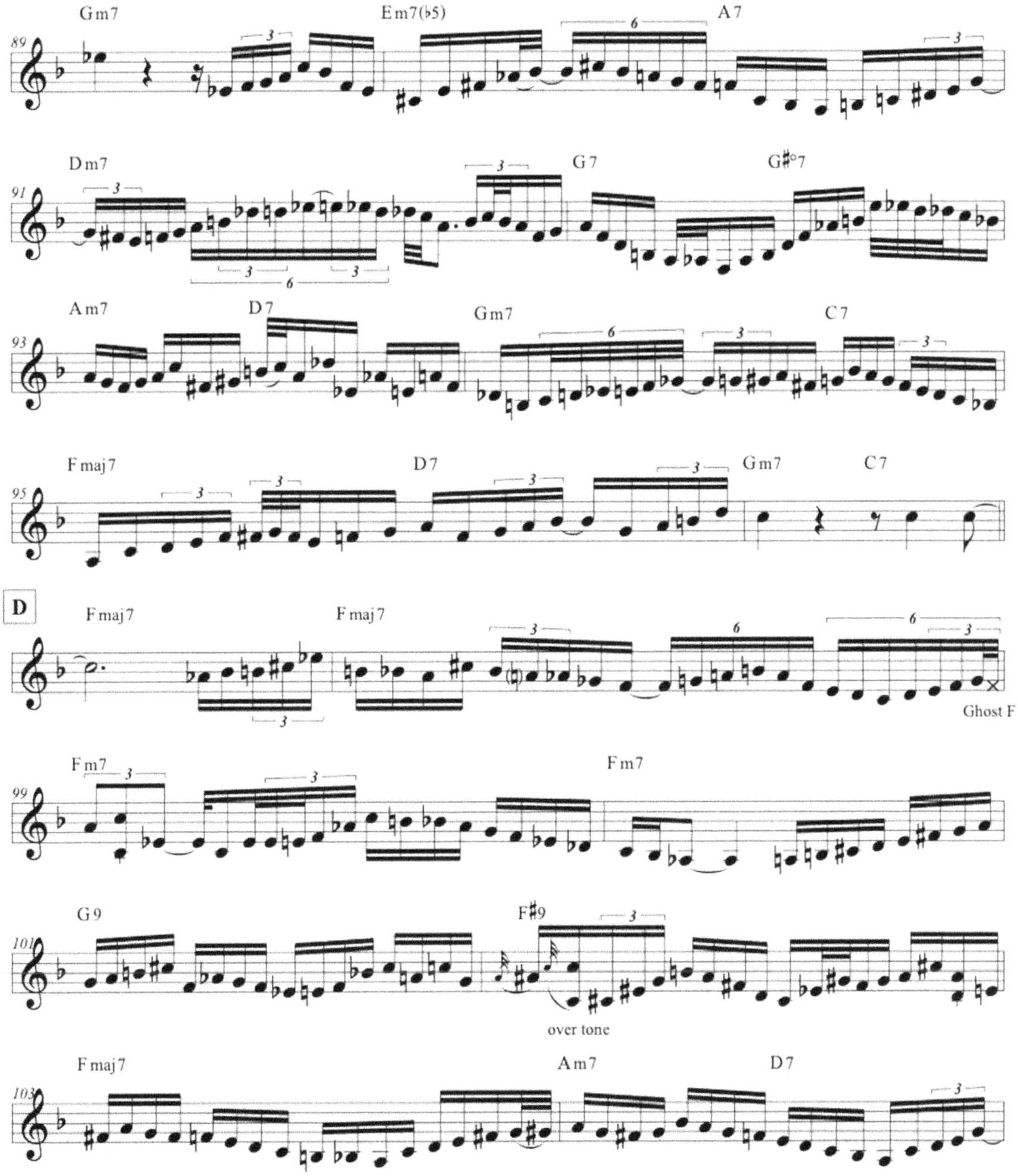
Gm7
Em7(♭5)
A7
Dm7
G7
G♯°7
Am7
D7
Gm7
C7
Fmaj7
D7
Gm7
C7
D
Fmaj7
Fmaj7
Ghost F
Fm7
Fm7
G9
F♯9
over tone
Fmaj7
Am7
D7

On Green Dolphin Street

5

Gm7
C7
Fmaj7
F7
B♭m7
E♭7
A♭maj7
Gm7
C7
Ghost C
Fmaj7
Fmaj7
Fm7
Fm7
G9
F♯9
Fmaj7
Am7
D7
Gm7

6

On Green Dolphin Street

Em7(♭5) A7 Dm7 G7 G♯°7 Am7 D7
Gm7 C7 Fmaj7 D7 Gm7 C7
E
Fmaj7 Fmaj7
Fm7 Fm7
G9 F♯9
Fmaj7 Am7 D7
Gm7 C7
Fmaj7 F7

On Green Dolphin Street 7

B♭m7
E♭7
A♭maj7
Gm7
C7
Fmaj7
Fmaj7
Fm7
Fm7
G9
F♯9
Fmaj7
Am7
D7
Gm7
Em7(♭5)
A7
Dm7
G7
G♯°7
Am7
D7

8

On Green Dolphin Street

158
Gm7 C7 Fmaj7 D7 Gm7 C7
F
Fmaj7 Fmaj7 Fm7 Fm7
165
G9 F#9 Fmaj7 Am7 D7
169
Gm7 C7 Fmaj7 F7
173
B♭m7 E♭7 A♭maj7 Gm7 C7
Ghost
Ab and C
177
Fmaj7 Fmaj7 Fm7 Fm7
181
G9 F#9 Fmaj7 Am7 D7
185
Gm7 Em7(♭5) A7 Dm7 G7 G#°7

On Green Dolphin Street

9

189
Am7
D7
Fork F
Gm7
C7
Fmaj7
D7
Gm7
C7
G
Fmaj7
Fmaj7
Fm7
Fm7
Ghost G
197
G9
F♯9
Fmaj7
Am7
D7
201
Gm7
C7
Fmaj7
F7
205
B♭m7
E♭7
207
A♭maj7
Gm7
C7
209
Fmaj7
Fmaj7
Front F/
Fork F
211
Fm7
Fm7
Ghost G

10

On Green Dolphin Street

G9 F#9 Fmaj7 Am7 D7
213
Gm7 Em7(♭5) A7 Dm7 G7 G#°7
217
Am7 D7 Gm7 C7 Fmaj7 D7 Gm7 C7
221
H
Fmaj7 Fmaj7 Fm7 Fm7

John Coltrane: Tenor Saxophone
Miles Davis: Trumpet
Wynton Kelly: Piano
Paul Chambers: Bass
Jimmy Cobb: Drums

Walkin'

John Coltrane Solo

Miles Davis & John Coltrane: Live In Stockholm, 1960
Dragon Record - DRLP 90/91
Recorded March 22, 1960

Richard Carpenter
Transcribed by Ron Westray
Edited and Nomenclated by Kamil Qui

2

Walkin'

Am7 D7 G7 Am7 D7
33
D
G7 C7 G7 G7
C7 C7 G7 G7
41
Am7 D7 G7 Am7 D7
45
Scoop
E
G7 C7 G7 G7
C7 C7 G7 G7
53
Am7 D7 G7 Am7 D7
57
F
G7 C7 G7 G7

Walkin' 3

C7 C7 G7 G7
65
Am7 D7 G7 Am7 D7
69
G
G7 C7 G7 G7
C7 C7 G7 G7
77
Am7 D7 G7 Am7 D7
81
H
G7 C7 G7 G7
C7 C7 G7 G7
89
Am7 D7 G7 Am7 D7
93
Palm D
Ghost C

4

Walkin'

I
G7 C7 G7 G7
101
C7 C7 G7 G7
105
Am7 D7 G7 Am7 D7
J
G7 C7 G7 G7
113
C7 C7 G7 G7
117
Am7 D7 G7 Am7 D7
K
G7 C7 G7
124
G7 C7 C7

Walkin' 5

G7 Ghost Tongue G.T G7 Am7
127
D7 G7 Am7 D7
130
L
G7 C7 G7
G7 C7 C7
136
G7 G7 Am7
139
D7 G7 Am7 D7
142
M
G7 C7 G7
G7 C7
148

6 **Walkin'**

C7
G7
G7
150
Am7
D7
153
C7
Am7
D7
155
N
G7
C7
G7
G7
C7
160
C7
G7
162
G7
Am7
D7
164
G7
Am7
D7
167
Ghost F A

Walkin' 7

O
G7 C7 G7 G7 C7
174
C7 G7 G7 Am7
178
D7 G7 Am7 D7
P
G7 C7 G7 G7
Ghost G
185
C7 C7 G7 G7
189
Am7 Ghost G D7 G7 Am7 D7
Q
G7 C7 G7 G7
Ghost D
197
C7 C7

8 **Walkin'**

G7 G7
199
Am7 D7
201
G7 Am7 D7
203
R
G7 C7
G7 G7
207
C7 C7
209
G7 G7
211
Am7 D7
213

Walkin' 9

G7 Am7 D7
215
S G7 C7
G7 G7
219
C7 C7
221
G7 G7 Am7 (throat)
223
D7 G7 Am7 D7
226
T G7 C7 G7 G7
C7 C7 G7 G7
233

10 **Walkin'**

Am7 D7 G7 Am7 D7
237
Ghost G
U
G7 C7 G7 G7 C7
C7 G7 G7
246
Am7 D7 G7 Am7 D7
249
V
G7 C7 G7
G7 C7 C7
256
G7 G7 Am7
259
D7 G7 Am7 D7
262

Walkin' 11

W
G7
C7
G7
G7
269
C7
C7
G7
G7
273
Am7
D7
G7
Am7
D7
3
3
X
G7
C7
G7
G7
281
C7
C7
G7
G7
285
Am7
D7
G7
Am7
D7
Y
G7
C7
G7
G7

John Coltrane: Tenor Saxophone
Duke Ellington: Piano
Jimmy Garrison: Bass
Elvin Jones: Drums

Take The Coltrane

John Coltrane Solo

Duke Ellington & John Coltrane
Impulse! - A-30
Recorded September 26, 1962

Duke Ellington
Transcribed by Ron Westray
Edited and Nomenclated by Kamil Qui

2

Take The Coltrane

D7
C7
G7
33
Palm key
D
G7
C7
(B7)
Ghost
C7
G7
41
Ghost
Ghost
D7
C7
G7
45
Ghost
Ghost
E
G7
C7
G7
C7
G7
53
D7
C7
G7
57
F
G7
C7
G7
Ghost
Ghost

Take The Coltrane 3

65
C7
G7
Ghost
Ghost
69
D7
C7
G7
Ghost
G
G7
C7
(F♯m7)
(B7)
Fake Fingering
77
C7
G7
Ghost
Ghost
81
D7
C7
G7
Ghost
H
G7
C7
G7
(B7)
89
C7
G7
93
D7
C7
G7
Ghost

4

Take The Coltrane

I
G7
C7
G7
101
C7
G7
Ghost
105
D7
C7
G7
J
G7
C7
G7
Ghost
113
C7
G7
117
D7
C7
Ghost
G7
K
G7
C7
G7
(B7)
8vb
125
C7
G7
(8vb)

Take The Coltrane 5

D7
C7
G7
129
Ghost
L
G7
Duke Ellington's Solo
M
G7
C7
137
G7
C7
141
G7
D7
C7
145
G7
G7
N
C7
Ghost
149
G7
(B7)
C7
153
G7
A7
D7
Ghost
Ghost
Ghost
Ghost
157
G7
G7
O
C7
Ghost
Ghost

6 **Take The Coltrane**

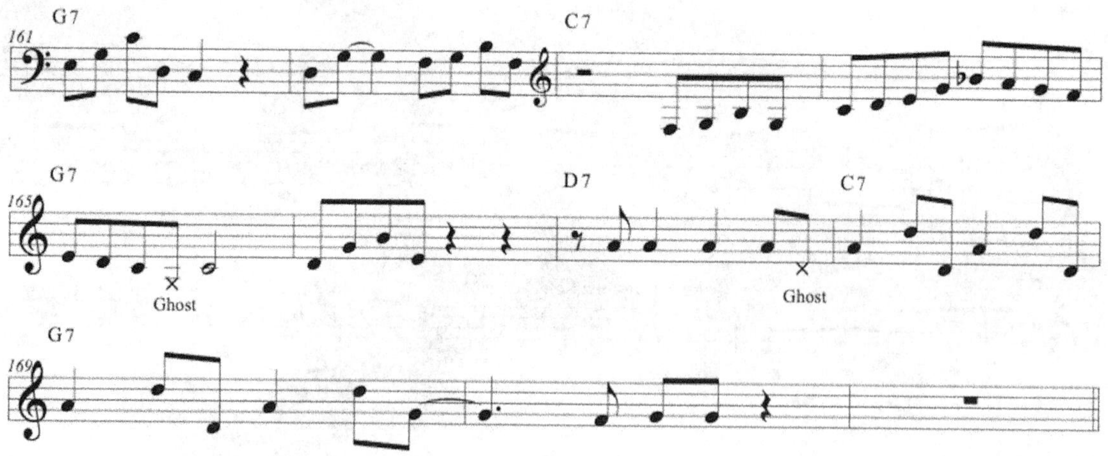
G7
161
C7
G7
165
Ghost
D7
Ghost
C7
G7
169

John Coltrane: Soprano Saxophone
McCoy Tyner: Piano
Jimmy Garrison: Bass
Elvin Jones: Drums

Autumn Leaves

John Coltrane Solo

'The Graz Concert, 1962
In Crowd Records - 996693
Recorded November 28, 1962

Transcribed by Ron Westray
Edited and Nomenclated by Kamil Qui

2
Autumn Leaves
B
Dm7 G7(b9) Cma7 Fma7
37
Bm7(b5) E7(b9) Am6 A7(b9)
41
Dm7 G7(b9) Cma7 Fma7
45
Bm7(b5) E7(b9) Am6 Am6
49
Bm7(b5) E7(b9) Am6 Am6 (G7b9)
53
Dm7 G7(b9) Cma7 Cma7
57
Bm7(b5) E7(b9) Am7 D7(b9) Gm7C7(b9)
61
Fma7 Bm7(b5) E7(b9) Am6 Am6 (G7b9)

Autumn Leaves
3
C
Dm7 G7(♭9) Cma7 Fma7
69
Bm7(♭5) E7(♭9) Am6 A7(♭9)
73
Dm7 G7(♭9) Cma7 Fma7
77
Bm7(♭5) E7(♭9) Am6 Am6
81
Bm7(♭5) E7(♭9) Am6 Am6 (G7b9)
85
Dm7 G7(♭9) Cma7 Cma7
89
Bm7(♭5) E7(♭9) Am7 D7(♭9) Gm7 C7(♭9)
93
Fma7 Bm7(♭5) E7(♭9) Am6 Am6 (G7b9)

4

Autumn Leaves

D
Dm7 G7(♭9) Cma7 Fma7
101
Bm7(♭5) E7(♭9) Am6 A7(♭9)
105
Dm7 G7(♭9) Cma7 Fma7
109
Bm7(♭5) E7(♭9) Am6 Am6
113
Bm7(♭5) E7(♭9) Am6 Am6 (G7b9)
117
Dm7 G7(♭9) Cma7 Cma7
121
Bm7(♭5) E7(♭9) Am7 D7(♭9) Gm7 C7(♭9)
125
Fma7 Bm7(♭5) E7(♭9) Am6 Am6 (G7b9)

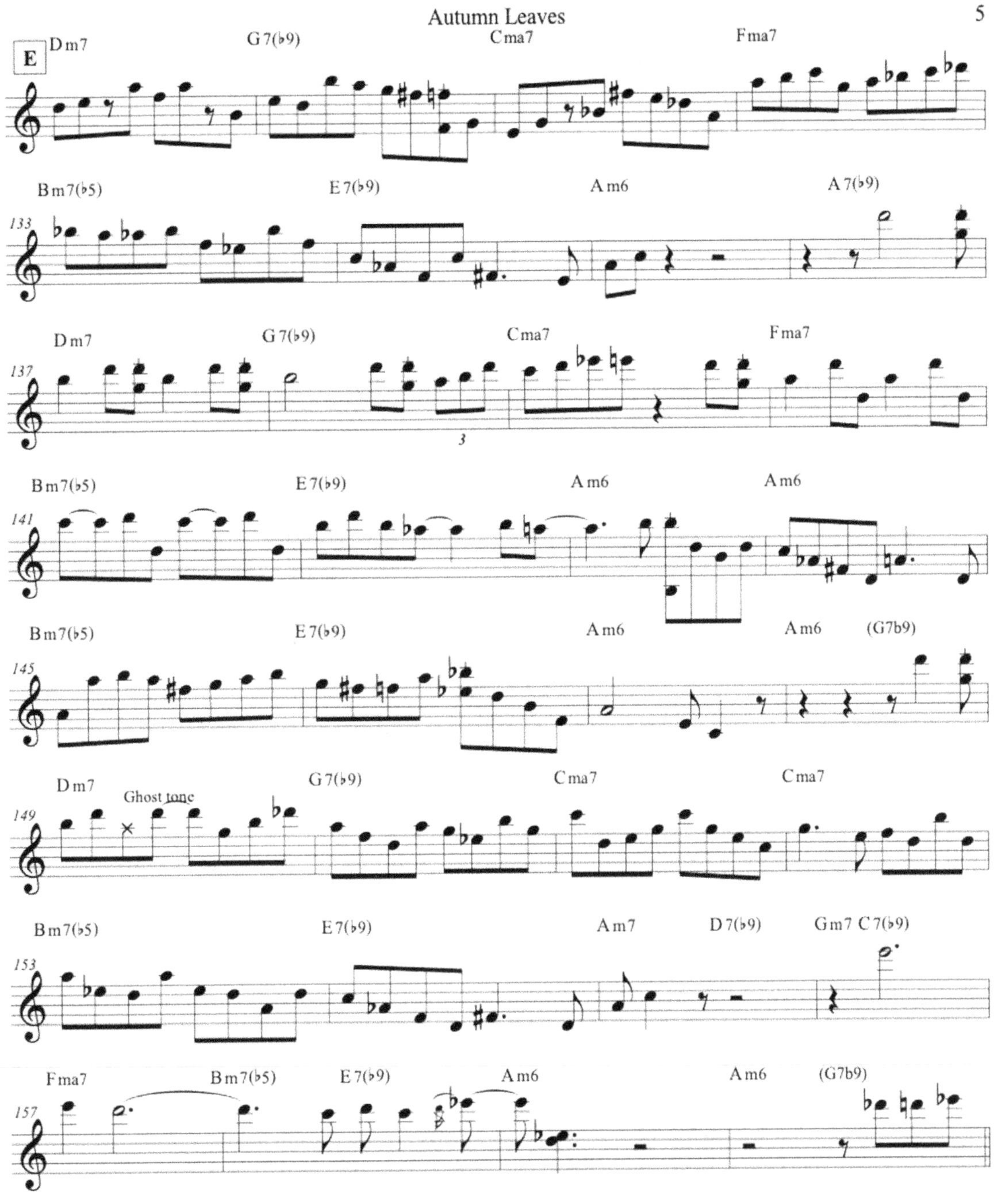
Autumn Leaves
5
E
Dm7 G7(♭9) Cma7 Fma7
133 Bm7(♭5) E7(♭9) Am6 A7(♭9)
137 Dm7 G7(♭9) Cma7 Fma7
3
141 Bm7(♭5) E7(♭9) Am6 Am6
145 Bm7(♭5) E7(♭9) Am6 Am6 (G7b9)
149 Dm7 G7(♭9) Cma7 Cma7
Ghost tone
153 Bm7(♭5) E7(♭9) Am7 D7(♭9) Gm7 C7(♭9)
157 Fma7 Bm7(♭5) E7(♭9) Am6 Am6 (G7b9)

6

Autumn Leaves

F
Dm7
G7(♭9)
Cma7
Fma7
Bm7(♭5)
E7(♭9)
Am6
A7(♭9)
165
169
173
Am6
177
(G7b9)
181
Cma7
185
Am7
D7(♭9)
Gm7 C7(♭9)
Ghost
189

Autumn Leaves
7
G
Dm7
G7(b9)
Cma7
Fma7
197
Bm7(b5)
E7(b9)
Am6
A7(b9)
201
Dm7
G7(b9)
Cma7
Fma7
205
Bm7(b5)
E7(b9)
Ghost
Am6
Am6
209
Bm7(b5)
E7(b9)
Am6
Am6
(G7b9)
213
Dm7
G7(b9)
Cma7
Cma7
217
Bm7(b5)
E7(b9)
Am7
D7(b9)
GmC7(b9)
221
Fma7
Bm7(b5)
E7(b9)
Am6
Am6
(G7b9)

8

Autumn Leaves

Dm7
G7(♭9)
Cma7
Fma7
225
Bm7(♭5)
E7(♭9)
Am6
A7(♭9)
229
Dm7
G7(♭9)
Cma7
Fma7
233
Bm7(♭5)
E7(♭9)
Am6
Am6
237
Bm7(♭5)
E7(♭9)
Am6
Am6
(G7b9)
241
Dm7
G7(♭9)
Cma7
Cma7
245
Bm7(♭5)
E7(♭9)
Am7
D7(♭9)
Gm7
C7(♭9)
249
Fma7
Bm7(♭5)
E7(♭9)
Am6
Am6
(G7b9)
253

Autumn Leaves
9
Dm7 G7(b9) Cma7 Fma7
257
Bm7(b5) E7(b9) Am6 A7(b9)
261
Dm7 G7(b9) Cma7 Fma7
265
Bm7(b5) E7(b9) Am6 Am6
269
Bm7(b5) E7(b9) Am6 Am6 (G7b9)
273
Dm7 G7(b9) Cma7 Cma7
277
Bm7(b5) E7(b9) Am7 D7(b9) Gm7 C7(b9)
281
3
Fma7 Bm7(b5) E7(b9) Am6 Am6 (G7b9)
285

10 Autumn Leaves

Dm7 G7(♭9) Cma7 Fma7
289
Bm7(♭5) E7(♭9) Am6 A7(♭9)
293
Dm7 G7(♭9) Cma7 Fma7
297
Bm7(♭5) E7(♭9) Am6 Am6
301
3
Bm7(♭5) E7(♭9) Am6 Am6 (G7b9)
305
3
Dm7 G7(♭9) Cma7 Cma7
309
Bm7(♭5) E7(♭9) Am7 D7(♭9) Gm7 C7(♭9)
313
Fma7 Bm7(♭5) E7(♭9) Am6 Am6 (G7b9)
317
3

I Want To Talk About You

John Coltrane: Tenor Saxophone
McCoy Tyner: Piano
Jimmy Garrison: Bass
Elvin Jones: Drums

John Coltrane Solo
(Sans Cadenza)
℗ 1963 The Verve Music Group
Live at Birdland Jazzclub
Recorded, January 1, 1963

Billy Eckstine
Transcribed by Ron Westray

TWF 2019

I Want To Talk About You

2

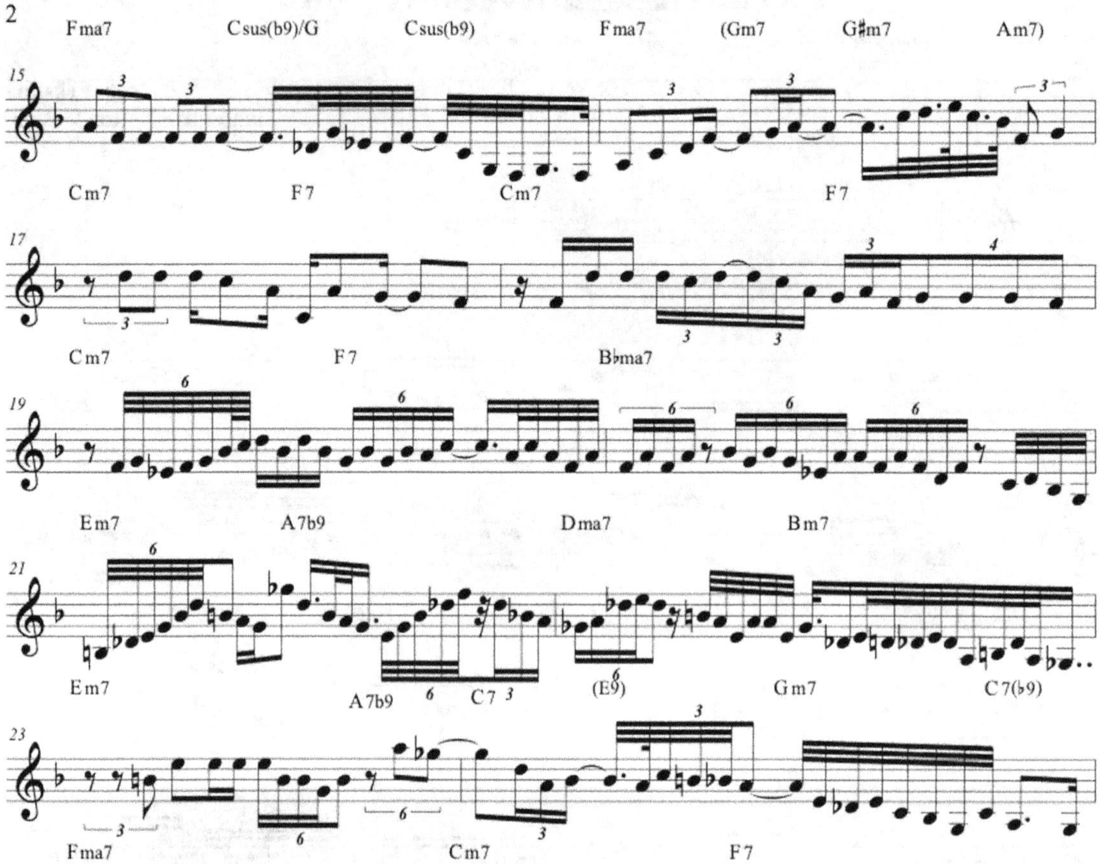
Fmaj7 Csus(b9)/G Csus(b9) Fma7 (Gm7 G♯m7 Am7)
15
Cm7 F7 Cm7 F7
17
Cm7 F7 B♭ma7
19
Em7 A7b9 Dma7 Bm7
21
Em7 A7b9 C7 (E9) Gm7 C7(b9)
23
Fma7 Cm7 F7
25
B♭ma7 B♭m7 E♭7
27
Am7 (Db7) D7b9 (E7) Gm7 C7alt.
29
Am7 D7alt. Gm7 C7alt.
31

I Want To Talk About You

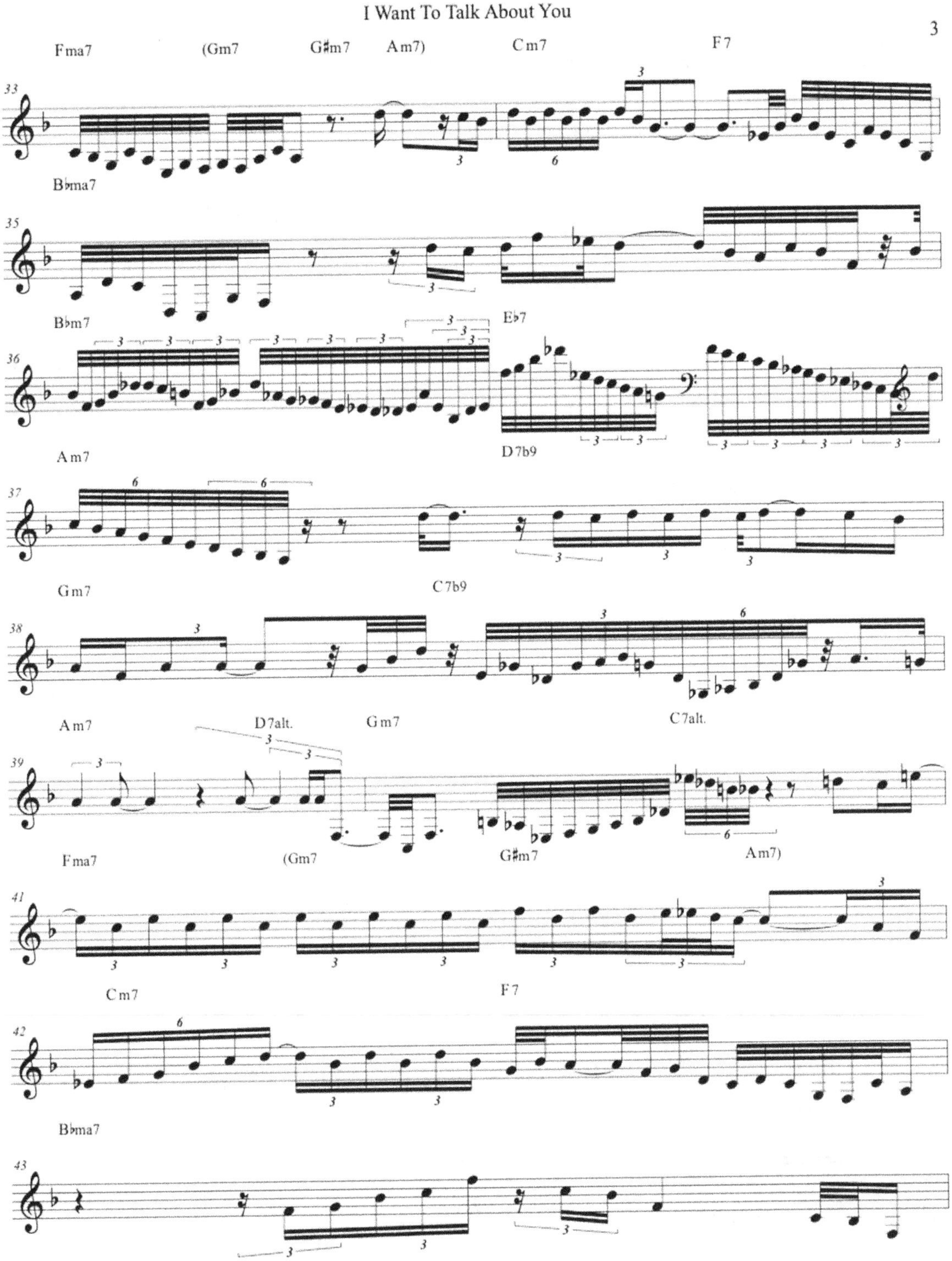

I Want To Talk About You

4
44
B♭m7
E♭7
45
Am7
D7b9
46
Gm7
C7b9
47
Fma7
Csus(b9)/G
Csus(b9)
48
Fma7
(Gm7
G♯m7
Am7)
49
Cm7
F7
50
Cm7
F7
51
Cm7
F7
52
B♭ma7
Em7
A7b9

I Want To Talk About You

5
Dma7
Bm7
Em7
A7b9
C7
(E9)
Gm7
C7(♭9)
Fma7
Cm7
F7
B♭ma7
B♭m7
E♭7
Am7
(Db7)
D7b9
(E7)
Gm7
C7alt.
Am7
D7alt.
Gm7
C7alt.
Cm7
F7
Cm7
F7
Cm7
F7

I Want To Talk About You

6

B♭ma7
Em7
A7b9
Dma7
Bm7
Em7
A7b9
C7
(E9)
Gm7
C7(♭9)
Fma7
(Gm7 G♯m7 Am7)
Cm7
F7
B♭ma7
B♭m7
E♭7
Am7(Db7)
D7b9
(E7)
Gm7
Am7
B♭m(M7)
F♯7
Am7
D7
Gm7
Am7
B♭m(M7)
F♯7
C13(♭9)

John Coltrane: Tenor Saxophone
Johnny Hartman: Vocals
McCoy Tyner: Piano
Jimmy Garrison: Bass
Elvin Jones: Drums

Autumn Serenade

John Coltrane Solo

John Coltrane and Johnny Hartman
Impulse! - A-40
Recorded March 7, 1963

Peter De Rose, Sammy Galop
Transcribed by Ron Westray
Edited and Nomenclated by Kamil Qui

2 **Autumn Serenade**

B♭7
Gm7
C7
Fmaj7
Dm7/A
Am7(♭5)
D7alt
Gm7
C7
B
Fm(maj7)
Ghost tongue
C7
Fm(maj7)
Ghost/
Subtone-ish
B♭7
Gm7
Tongue
C7
Am7
D7
Dm7
G7

Autumn Serenade 3

46
D♭7
C7
Fmaj7
C7
Ghost
Vamp
Fmaj7
C7
Fmaj7
52
C7
7
Fmaj7
3
54
C7
Fmaj7
6
C7
57
Fmaj7
C7
Fmaj7
C7
Subtone
Head Out
Fm(maj7)
10
G♭13(♯11)
softly
Vamp
Fmaj7
G♭13
Fmaj7
G♭13
Fmaj7
soft
Subtone
78
G♭13
Fmaj7
G♭13
Fmaj7

John Coltrane: Tenor Saxophone
Johnny Hartman: Vocals
McCoy Tyner: Piano
Jimmy Garrison: Bass
Elvin Jones: Drums

Lush Life

John Coltrane Solo

John Coltrane and Johnny Hartman
Impulse! - A-40
Recorded March 7, 1963

Billy Strayhorn
Transcribed by Ron Westray
Edited and Nomenclated by Kamil Qui

2

Lush Life

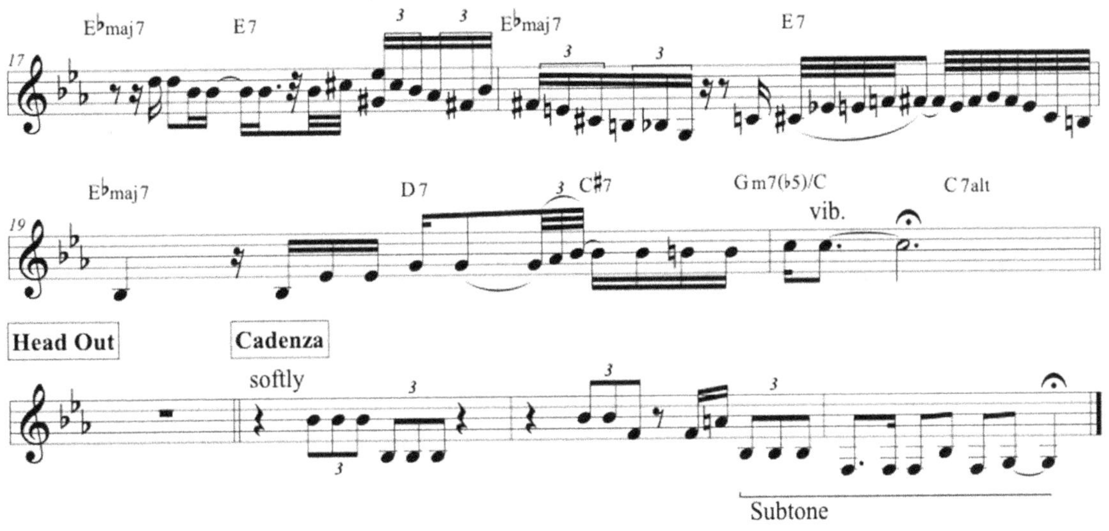
E♭maj7
E7
E♭maj7
E7
E♭maj7
D7
C♯7
Gm7(♭5)/C
C7alt
vib.
Head Out
Cadenza
softly
Subtone

John Coltrane: Tenor Saxophone
Johnny Hartman: Vocals
McCoy Tyner: Piano
Jimmy Garrison: Bass
Elvin Jones: Drums

They Say It's Wonderful

John Coltrane Solo

John Coltrane and Johnny Hartman
Impulse! - A-40
Recorded March 7, 1963

Irving Berlin
Transcribed by Ron Westray
Edited and Nomenclated by Kamil Qui

2

They Say It's Wonderful

Gm7
Gm7(♭5)
C7(♭9)
Vib.
Palm D
Subtone
Fmaj7
Palm D
Am7
D7
Gm7
pull back
Palm D
Scoop
st.
Palm D
Gm7(♭5)
C7(♭9)
Fmaj7
Am7
A♭°7
Palm D
Gm7
Gm7(♭5)
C7(♭9)
Vib.
mf
Cm7
Vib.
f
F7
B♭maj7
E♭7(♭9)
Palm D
Dm7
Am7
Vib.
Bm7
(D7)

They Say It's Wonderful

3

Am7
Bm7(♭5)
E7(♭9)
Am7
A♭m7
Palm D#
Gm7
Gm7(♭5)
C7(♭9)
Am7
D7(♭9)
Gm7
C7
Scoop
Vib.
Fmaj7

John Coltrane: Tenor Saxophone
McCoy Tyner: Piano
Jimmy Garrison: Bass
Roy Haynes: Drums

Dear Old Stockholm

John Coltrane Solo

John Coltrane - *Dear Old Stockholm*
Impulse! - GRD-120
Recorded April 23, 1963

Varmeland

Transcribed by Ron Westray
Edited and Nomenclated by Kamil Qui

2

Dear Old Stockholm

Dm7
33
Dm7
A
C♯13
C♯13
41
C♯13
45
C♯13
49
C♯13
53
C♯13
57
C♯13
61

Dear Old Stockholm 3

C♯13
65
C♯13
69
Ghost Tone
C♯13
73
Ghost
Ghost
C♯13
77
C♯13
81
C♯13
85
3
C♯13
89
C♯13
93
Ghost

4

Dear Old Stockholm

C♯13
97
Ghost
C♯13
101
C♯13
105
C♯13
109
C♯13
113
C♯13
117
C♯13
121
C♯13
125

Dear Old Stockholm 5

C♯13
129
C♯13
133
C♯13
137
Ghost
Ghost
B
Dm6/C♯
Ghost
Dm6/C♯
145
Ghost
Dm6/C♯
149
Fork F
Fork
Dm6/C♯
153
Fork
Fork
Dm6/C♯
157
6

6 Dear Old Stockholm

Dm6/C♯
161
C
Dm6/C♯
Dm6
Dm6
169
Fork
Dm6
173
Fork E
Fork
Dm6
177
Dm6
181
Dm6
185
Fork
Fork
Dm6
189
Ghost

Dear Old Stockholm 7

Dm6
193
Dm6
197
Dm6
201
3
Dm6
205
Palm
Dm6
209

I Want To Talk About You

John Coltrane: Tenor Saxophone
McCoy Tyner: Piano
Jimmy Garrison: Bass
Elvin Jones: Drums

John Coltrane Solo
(Sans Cadenza)
℗ 1980 Pablo Records
Live in Stockholm, Sweden
Recorded, October 22, 1963

Billy Eckstine
Transcribed by Ron Westray
Edited and Nomenclated by Kamil Qui

2

I Want To Talk About You

Fma7 Csus(b9)/G Csus(b9) Fma7 (Gm7 G♯m7 Am7)
Cm7 F7 Cm7 F7
Cm7 F7 B♭ma7
Em7 A7b9 Dma7 Bm7
Em7 A7b9 C7 (E9) Gm7 C7(♭9)
Fma7 Cm7 F7
B♭ma7 B♭m7 E♭7
Am7 (Db7) D7b9 (E7) Gm7 C7alt.

I Want To Talk About You
3
Am7
D7alt.
Gm7
C7alt.
Fma7
(Gm7
G♯m7
Am7)
Cm7
F7
B♭ma7
B♭m7
E♭7
Am7
D7♭9
Gm7
C7♭9
Am7
D7alt.
Gm7
C7alt.
Fma7
(Gm7
G♯m7
Am7)

4

I Want To Talk About You

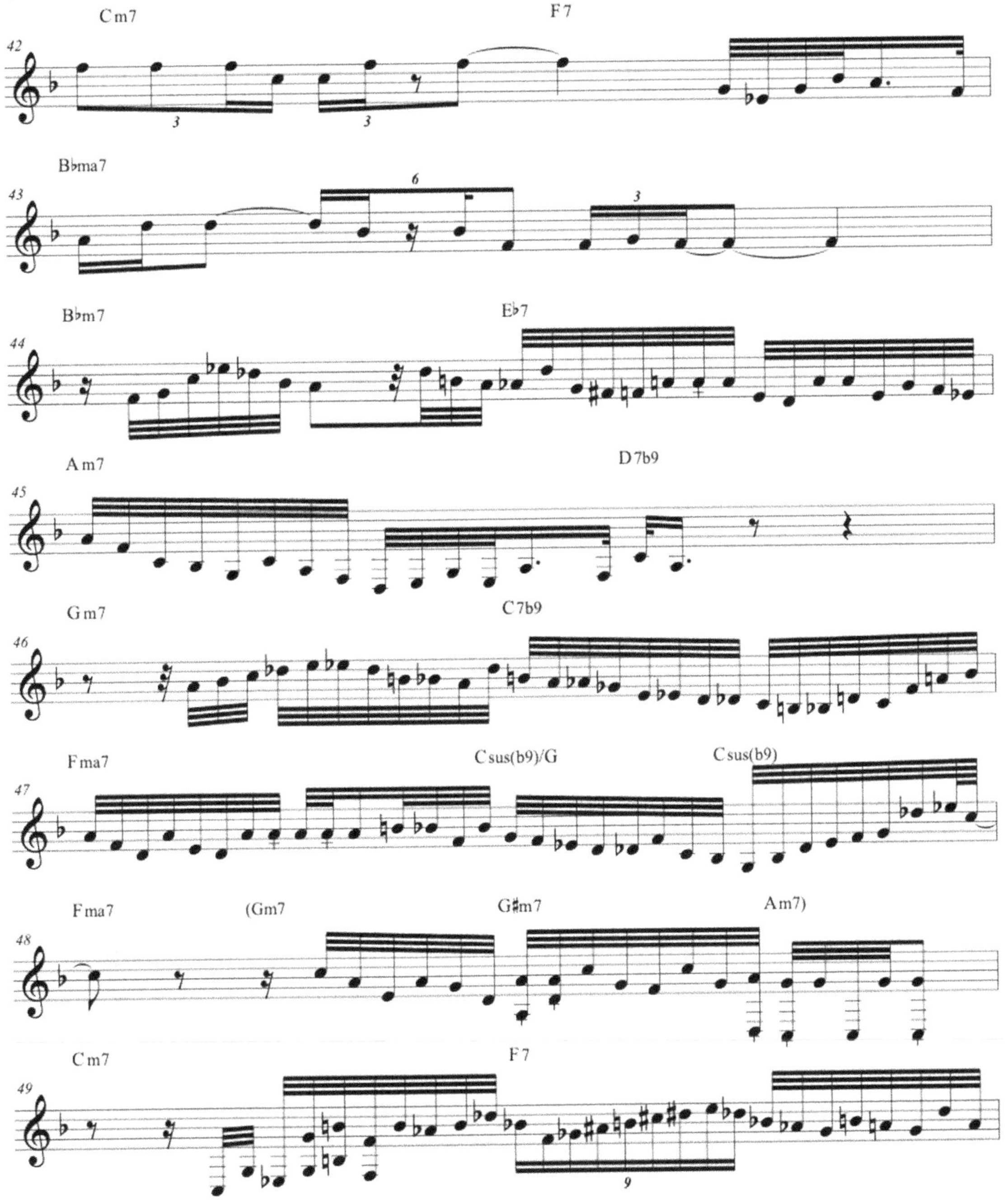
Cm7
F7
42
B♭ma7
43
6
3
B♭m7
E♭7
44
Am7
D7b9
45
Gm7
C7b9
46
Fma7
Csus(b9)/G
Csus(b9)
47
Fma7
(Gm7
G♯m7
Am7)
48
Cm7
F7
49
9

I Want To Talk About You
5
50 Cm7 F7
51 Cm7 F7 B♭ma7
Ghost
53 Em7 A7b9 Dma7 Bm7
55 Em7 A7b9
56 C7 (E9) Gm7 C7(♭9)
57 Fma7 Cm7 F7
59 B♭ma7 B♭m7 E♭7
61 Am7 (Db7) D7b9 (E7) Gm7 C7alt.
vib

6 I Want To Talk About You

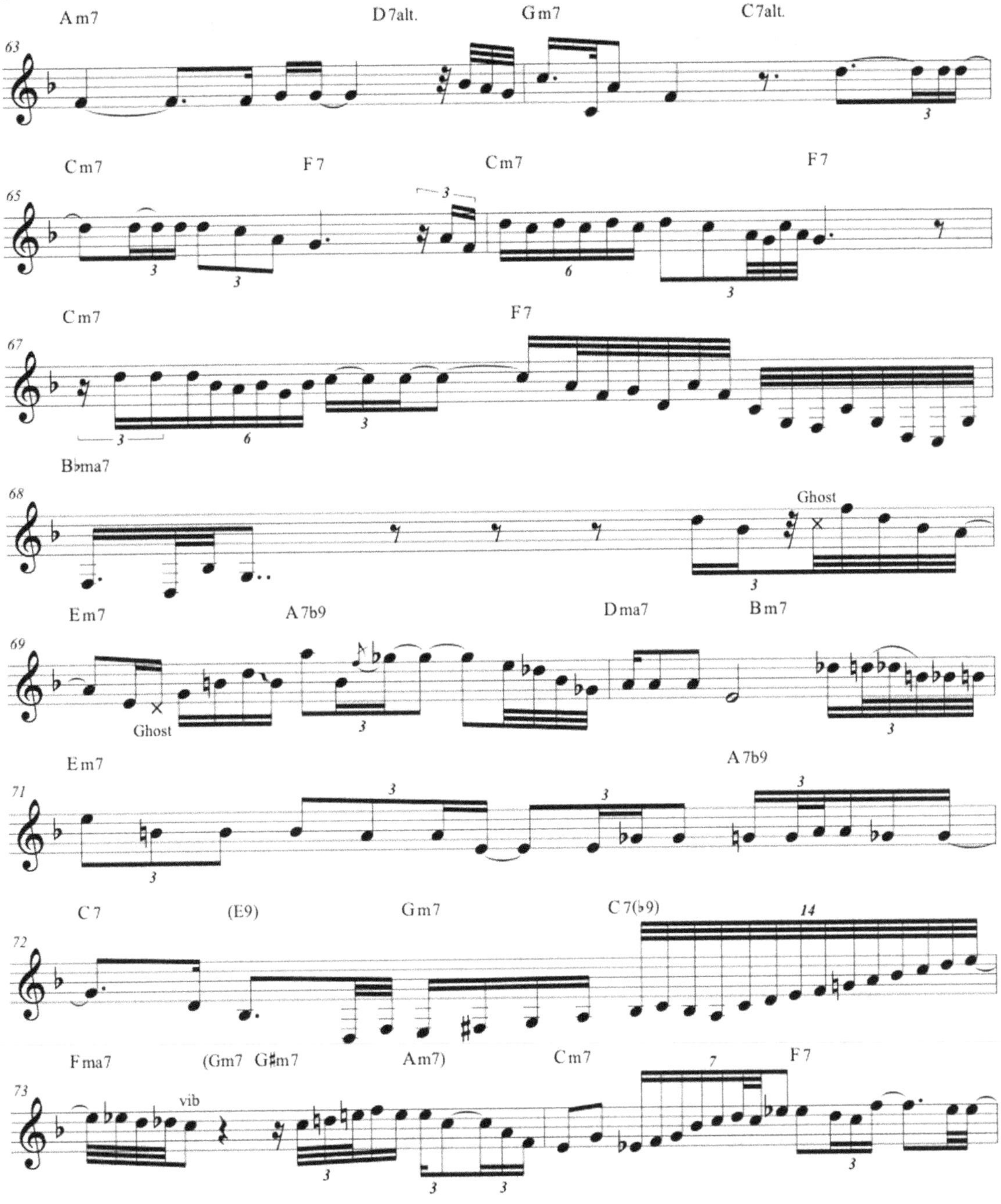
Am7 D7alt. Gm7 C7alt.
63
Cm7 F7 Cm7 F7
65
Cm7 F7
67
B♭ma7
68
Ghost
Em7 A7b9 Dma7 Bm7
69
Ghost
Em7 A7b9
71
C7 (E9) Gm7 C7(♭9)
72
14
Fma7 (Gm7 G♯m7 Am7) Cm7 F7
73
vib
7

I Want To Talk About You 7

B♭ma7
B♭m7
E♭7
Am7
(D♭7)
D7♭9
(E7)
Gm7
Am7
B♭m(M7)
F♯7
Am7
D7
Gm7
Am7
B♭m(M7)
F♯7
C13(♭9)

John Coltrane: Tenor Saxophone
McCoy Tyner: Piano
Jimmy Garrison: Bass
Elvin Jones: Drums

Crescent

John Coltrane Solo

John Coltrane - *Crescent*
Impulse! - A-66
Recorded June 1, 1964

John Coltrane
Cross-Transcribed & Edited by Ron Westray
Edited & Nomenclated by Kamil Qui

2 **Crescent**

C+7
Fm7
B7
Em$^{6}_{9}$
A7(♭9)
Dm$^{6}_{9}$
C
C7
Fm7
Fm7
B+7
Em7
A7
Dm$^{6}_{9}$
Ghost tone
C or A

Crescent 3

D
C 7alt
Fm6/9
82
B+7
84
Em7
87
A 7alt
89
Dm6/9
E
C 7alt
93
Fm6/9
95
B 7
B 13(♭9)
Em6/9

4 **Crescent**

Em9 6
A7
Dm9 6
Vibrato
F
C7
Fm9 6
B7
Em9 6
A7
Dm9 6
G
C+7
Fm9 6
B7
Em(maj7)
A7alt

Crescent 5

124
A 7alt
Dm6/9
H
C+7
Fm6/9
130
B 7
132
Em6/9
135
A 7
Dm6/9
138
I
C+7
141
F m7
143
B 13

6 **Crescent**

Em(maj7)
A7
Dm6/9
J
C7
C+7
Fm6/9
B+13(♯11)
B+7
Em6/9
A+9
Dm6/9
K
C7alt
C7alt

Crescent 7

Fm6/9
B7
Em6/9
vib.
A9
Em7
Head Out Rubato
B♭maj7(♯11)/A
Fmaj7(♯11)/E
In Time F♯m7(♭5)
B7
Em6
A7sus
A7

8 Crescent

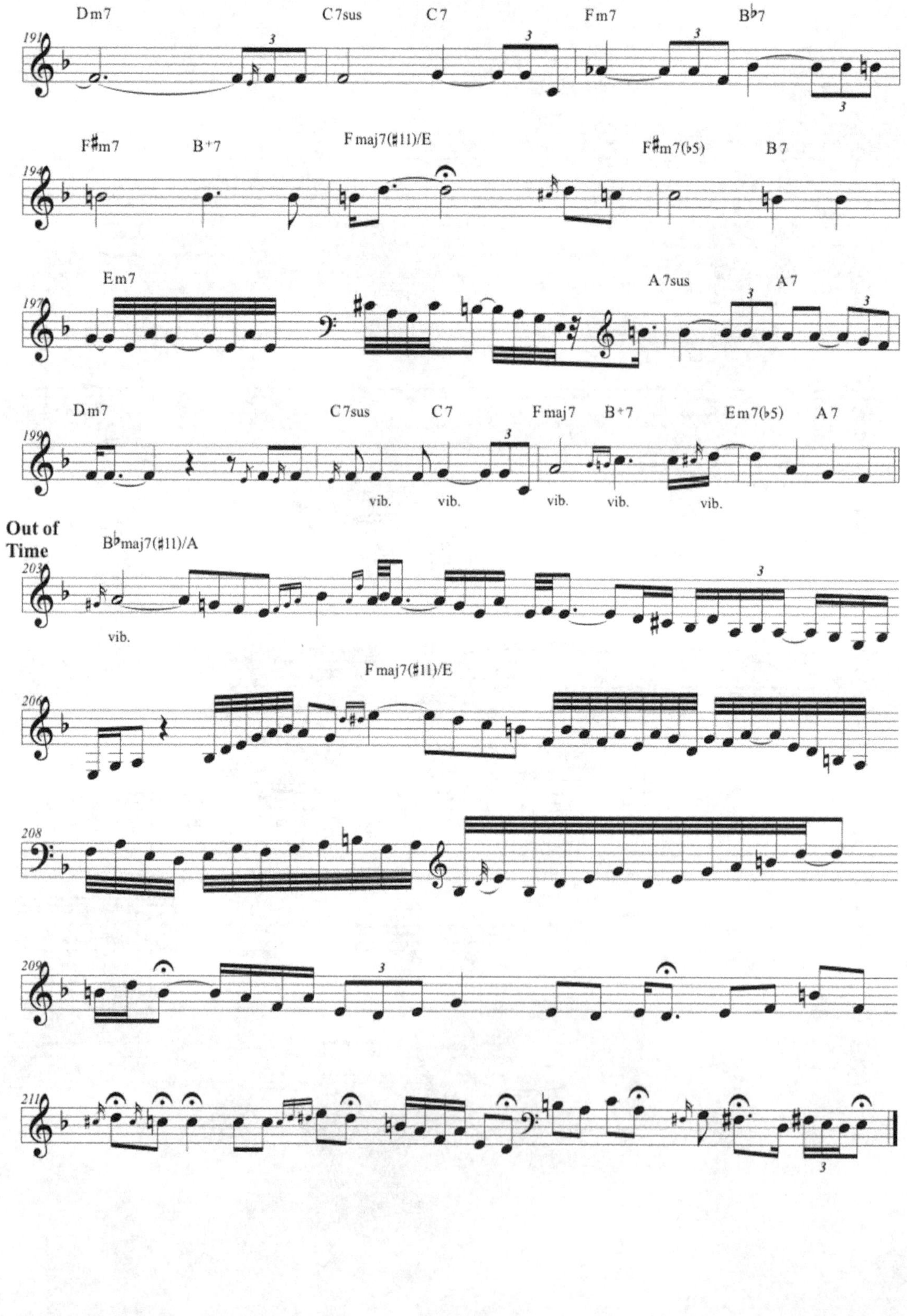
Dm7
C7sus
C7
Fm7
B♭7
191
F♯m7
B+7
Fmaj7(♯11)/E
F♯m7(♭5)
B7
194
Em7
A7sus
A7
197
Dm7
C7sus
C7
Fmaj7
B+7
Em7(♭5)
A7
199
vib.
Out of Time
B♭maj7(♯11)/A
203
vib.
Fmaj7(♯11)/E
206
208
209
211

Wynton Marsalis: Trumpet, Composer
Herlin Riley: Drums
Marcus Roberts: Piano
Reginald Veal: Bass
Wes Anderson: Alto Saxophone
Todd Williams: Tenor Saxophone
Trombone: Wycliffe Gordon

Blue Interlude

Wynton Marsalis - Blue Interlude
Sony BMG Music Entertainment
Released May 5, 1992

Wynton Marsalis
Transcribed by Ron Westray

Blue Interlude

2
F7
B♭7
E♭7
E♭7
E♭7
Am7(♭5)
D7♭9
Gm6
Gm6
Band In
B
Dm13
Dm13
Am13/D
Am13/D
D13
D13
G13
G13
B♭m7/E♭
B♭m7/E♭
B2
Dm13
lay back
Dm13
Am13/D
1/2 valve----->
Am13/D
1/2 valve----->
D13
D13
G13
G13
B♭m7/E♭
B♭m7/E♭

Blue Interlude

B3
Dm13
Dm13
Am13/D
Am13/D
D13
D13
G13
G13
B♭m7/E♭
B♭m7/E♭
(cue)
Dm13
Dm13
Am13/D
Am13/D
D13
D13
G13
G13
B♭m7/E♭
lay back
B♭m7/E♭

AFTERWORD

Emphasizing the necessity of a structured teaching approach, my research goals delineate the challenges and misconceptions within jazz pedagogy. They underscore the significance of historical and contemporary knowledge, seek to demystify theoretical aspects, and advocate for a balanced presentation of material tailored to diverse learning styles. The integration of various tools and methodologies, such as transcription and chord/scale analysis, demonstrates a commitment to both historical understanding and practical application—allowing students to accelerate their learning and gain a comprehensive understanding of the subject matter. In discussing my research focus and goals related to the theoretical and practical aspects of music, specifically within the context of what is commonly referred to as jazz, my work aims to demystify the underlying constants that influence aural response and musical expression.

Tentanda via.
—*Ron Westray*

Printed in the USA
CPSIA information can be obtained
at www.ICGtesting.com
JSHW061530260124
55806JS00002B/4

9 781839 989711